THIS BOOK ON LOAN
PROPERTY OF
DUNBARTON HIGH SCHOOL

DATE SEPT	STUDENT'S NAME	HOME ROOM NO.	ISSUED BY	CONDITION

0 7 0 - 0 2

THIS BOOK ON LOAN
PROPERTY OF
DUNBARTON HIGH SCHOOL

DATE SEPT	STUDENT'S NAME	HOME ROOM NO.	ISSUED BY	CONDITION

College and Apprenticeship Mathematics

12

Addison-Wesley Secondary Mathematics Authors

Robert Alexander
Elizabeth Ainslie
Paul Atkinson
Maurice Barry
Cam Bennet
Barbara J. Canton
Ron Coleborn
Fred Crouse
Garry Davis
Jane Forbes
George Gadanidis
Liliane Gauthier
Florence Glanfield
Katie Pallos-Haden
Peter J. Harrison
Carol Besteck Hope
Terry Kaminski
Brendan Kelly
Stephen Khan
Ron Lancaster
Duncan LeBlanc
Antonietta Lenjosek
Kevin Maguire
Rob McLeish
Jim Nakamoto
Nick Nielsen
Linda Rajotte
Brent Richards
David Sufrin
Peter Taylor
Paul Williams
Elizabeth Wood
Rick Wunderlich
Paul Zolis
Leanne Zorn

Mary Doucette
Bonnie Edwards
Paul Pogue
Margaret Sinclair
Kevin Spry

Addison Wesley

Developmental Editors
Sue Lishman
Ingrid D'Silva

Senior Consulting Mathematics Editor
Lesley Haynes

Coordinating Editor
Mei Lin Cheung

Production Coordinator
Stephanie Cox

Editorial Contributors
Marg Bukta
Kelly Davis
Janine LeBlanc
Gay McKellar
Alison Rieger

Product Manager
Susan Cox

Managing Editor
Enid Haley

Publisher
Claire Burnett

Design/Production
Pronk&Associates

Art Direction
Pronk&Associates

Electronic Assembly/Technical Art
Pronk&Associates

The publisher has taken every care to meet or exceed industry
specifications for the manufacturing of textbooks. The spine and the
endpapers of this sewn book have been reinforced with special fabric
for extra binding strength. The cover is a premium, polymer-reinforced
material designed to provide long life and withstand rugged use. Mylar
gloss lamination has been applied for further durability.

ISBN: 0-201-77112-8

This book contains recycled product and is acid free.

Printed and bound in Canada

2 3 4 5 GG 06 05 04 03 02

Program Consultants and Reviewers

Nancy Anstett
Iroquois Ridge High School
Halton District School Board
Oakville

Frank Dalla Corte
St. Elizabeth Catholic High School
York Catholic District School Board
Thornhill

Duncan LeBlanc
Head of Mathematics
Sir Robert L. Borden Business and
Technical Institute
Toronto

Antonietta Lenjosek
Head of Mathematics and Business
St. Mark High School
Ottawa Carleton Catholic School Board
Manotick

Sandra G. McCarthy
Head of Mathematics
South Carleton High School
Ottawa Carleton District School Board
Richmond

Gizele M. Price
Holy Name of Mary Secondary School
Mississauga

Jamie Pyper
ESSO Centre for Mathematics Education
University of Western Ontario

Anthony Ribeiro
Department of Mathematics
Centennial College
Toronto

Assessment Consultant

Lynda E.C. Colgan
Professor
Department of Education
Queen's University
Kingston

CONTENTS

3 Measurement in Design

4 Geometry in Design

5 Sampling

6   Data Analysis

7   Analysis of Graphical Models

College and Apprenticeship Mathematics 12

This book prepares you for your path beyond grade 12, whether you choose a two-year college program or an apprenticeship option. It combines new content you have not seen in previous grades, with some content you need to revisit for success at college. Working with this content now will help prepare you for any college entrance examinations you may need to take.

Your Book Organization

Mathematics is about more than individual skills and concepts. It's about thinking through a problem, creating solutions in specific applications, and communicating ideas. It's about working independently, and collaborating with others.

In this book, chapters develop specific areas of content and, where appropriate, provide structured Project suggestions. **Explore/Research/Report** sections highlight mathematics as it relates to your world beyond grade 12.

> **Chapter 1: Trigonometry**
> **Chapter 2: Algebra**

These chapters relate to content of previous grades. Each chapter has a **Pre-Test**, to help you and your teacher identify topics on which you need to focus attention. These chapters appear early because they include some review, and because the college entrance examinations emphasize trigonometry and algebra skills.

> **Explore/Research/Report: Preparing for Community College**

Investigate some of the programs that colleges offer in your areas of interest. Find out about the requirements of various colleges, and start to shape your plans for next year.

> **Chapter 3: Measurement in Design**
> **Chapter 4: Geometry in Design**

Fashion, construction, landscaping, and home décor all involve design. In Chapters 3 and 4, you will learn to work with metric and imperial units to create solutions for specific design problems. These chapters may be especially important if you follow an apprenticeship option.

> **Explore/Research/Report: Planning an Apartment**

Use your design talents to plan your own space, while investigating some of the real options you might have once you're on your own.

> **Chapter 5: Sampling**
> **Chapter 6: Data Analysis**
> **Chapter 7: Analysis of Graphical Models**

Pick up almost any newspaper today and it is likely to report survey results or an analysis of data. Chapters 5, 6, and 7 help you develop the critical skills of an informed consumer. They emphasize content related to college business programs.

> **Explore/Research/Report: Data Analysis**

Explore the stock market in an extended project.

Chapter Organization

Most chapters in *Addison-Wesley College and Apprenticeship Mathematics 12* follow the same structure.

Chapter Project

A chapter starts with a short introduction to a specific application, such as landscaping. The content you develop in the chapter will help you work with this application near the end of the chapter. The **Chapter Project** provides specific exercises to support your research and problem solving.

Chapter Projects give you opportunities to:
- Apply your mathematics knowledge in a specific area.
- Collaborate with other students to solve a problem.
- Develop your research skills.
- Develop your problem-solving skills.

After each Chapter Project, the **Career Profile** highlights a profession in which people use mathematics regularly. Mathematics-related careers cover a wide variety of possible interests, and our examples range from paramedics to marketing specialists. Each **Career Profile** provides background information on relevant college programs for each career area.

Necessary Skills

Necessary Skills gives a refresher in the prerequisite skills you need for the chapter. Your teacher will probably assign **Necessary Skills** before you work with the numbered sections in the chapter.

Occasionally, a "New" skill comes up in **Necessary Skills**. You didn't cover this skill in previous grades, usually because it wasn't in the curriculum. We teach it in **Necessary Skills** because you have all the related concepts you need to develop an understanding quickly.

Numbered Sections

These develop the new content of the course. **Investigations** are included regularly, to help you build understanding. Numbered sections consolidate results through **Examples**.

Watch for **Take Note** boxes: they highlight important results or definitions.

Exercises are organized into A, B, and C categories according to their level of difficulty.

✓ You'll see that some exercises have a check mark beside them; try these exercises to be sure you have covered all core curriculum requirements.

Each exercise set identifies one exercise for each of the four categories of the provincial **Achievement Chart**.

- Knowledge/Understanding
- Thinking/Inquiry/Problem Solving
- Communication
- Application

These show you what to expect when you are being assessed on any of the four categories. Our selection provides examples only. Each exercise set has many exercises that relate to each of the categories of achievement. Exercises that are labelled are not limited to one category, but the focus helps to simplify assessment.

Ongoing Review

Self-Checks are one-page reviews that occur mid-chapter. They allow you to check your knowledge and understanding of the content of preceding sections. They include **Performance Assessment** exercises.

Each chapter review starts with a **Mathematics Toolkit** that summarizes important chapter results. The Toolkit, together with the **Review Exercises**, helps you study the contents of a chapter.

The **Self-Test** at the end of each chapter helps you prepare for a class test. The **Self-Test** concludes with a **Performance Assessment**, an exercise that allows you to demonstrate your level of achievement.

Cumulative Reviews after Chapters 2, 4, and 7 cover material covered from Chapter 1 forward.

Technology

Scientific calculators, spreadsheets, dynamic geometry software, and graphing calculators are tools that can help you solve applied problems. Technology tools are especially powerful for solving problems with large or unwieldy numbers—for example the authentic applications you'll study in this course. This book establishes a few standard technology tools—for calculator and computer applications—and provides explicit instruction for their use.

The **Utilities** at the end of this book provide additional support for working with calculators and computer software.

This book also contains some investigations where we suggest research on the Internet to obtain current figures, or to follow specific activities. You may start your search on the Pearson Education Canada web site, where you'll find suggested search words to help focus your research.

Communication

Communication is a key part of all learning. It is also a critical part of how you demonstrate your mathematical ability, in class assessments or in college entrance examinations. This book provides many ways for you to improve your mathematical communication.

Presentations of **Solutions** to **Examples** model clear, concise mathematical communication. Following a **Solution** to an **Example** will help you develop clear communication skills.

Discuss questions prompt you to think about solutions or the implications of new concepts, and to share your thinking. The more you "talk through" the math, the more likely you will understand the concepts.

Selected exercises ask you to explain your reasoning, or describe your findings. Each numbered section also contains an exercise highlighted with a "Communication" emphasis.

Assessment

Several features in this book relate to a balanced assessment approach.

- **Achievement Chart Categories** are highlighted in each exercise set.
- **Communication** opportunities appear in **Examples**, *Discuss* suggestions, and exercises.
- **Self-Checks** support your knowledge and understanding.
- **Chapter Projects** present applied problems for you to solve.
- **Self-Tests** provide a sample of the type of chapter test your teacher might use.
- **Performance Assessment** suggestions appear in every Self-Test and in every Self-Check, providing opportunities for you to demonstrate a level-4 performance.
- **Explore/Research/Report** sections give opportunities to work on open-ended problems.

1 Trigonometry

Chapter Project

The Ambiguous Case

Suppose you are given a set of measurements for a triangle.
Can you draw just one triangle to fit the specifications?
You will investigate this question, and study its implications.

Curriculum Expectations

By the end of this chapter, you will:

> Solve problems involving trigonometry in right triangles.

> Demonstrate an understanding of the signs of the sine, cosine, and tangent of obtuse angles.

> Demonstrate accuracy and precision in working with metric measures.

> Determine side lengths and angle measures in oblique triangles, using the Cosine Law and the Sine Law, and solve related problems.

> Identify applications of trigonometry in occupations and in post-secondary programs related to the occupations.

1 Pre-Test

In Grade 10, you studied trigonometry in right triangles. Use this pre-test to check the skills that we will review in Sections 1.1 and 1.2.

1. Use a scientific calculator to determine the sine, cosine, and tangent of each angle to 4 decimal places.

    a) 47°   **b)** 23°   **c)** 65°   **d)** 88°

2. Use a scientific calculator to determine the measure of $\angle M$ to the nearest degree.

    a) $\sin M = 0.7070$ **b)** $\cos M = 0.4312$ **c)** $\tan M = 1.5762$

    d) $\cos M = 0.9983$ **e)** $\sin M = 0.1003$ **f)** $\tan M = 0.2242$

3. Copy this right triangle.

    a) Mark the sides of the triangle in relation to the angle θ. Label them "adjacent," "opposite," and "hypotenuse."

    b) State the ratio formulas for $\sin \theta$, $\cos \theta$, and $\tan \theta$ in a right triangle.

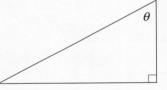

4. Calculate length b in each triangle.

    a)

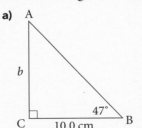

    b)

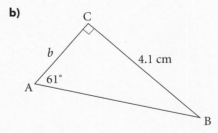

5. Calculate the measure of $\angle A$ in each triangle.

    a)

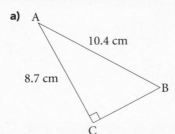

    b)

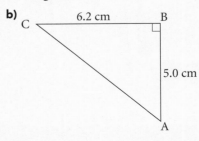

6. Calculate each value of x to 1 decimal place.

a)

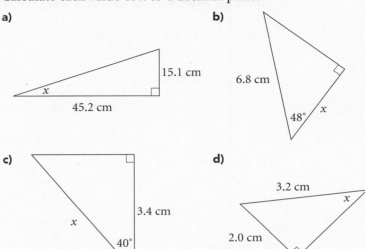

b)

c)

d)

7. A contractor will build a wheelchair ramp to access a doorway that is 0.7 m above ground level (below left). According to the local building code, the angle of inclination of the ramp must be 8°. How long will the ramp be?

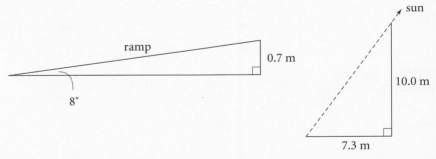

8. A 10-m flagpole casts a shadow 7.3 m long (above right). Calculate the angle of elevation of the sun.

2 Review: Ratio and Proportion

Recall that a ratio is the comparison of two or more quantities expressed in the same units.

Example 1

Triangle ABC is shown. Write the ratio of the lengths of each pair of sides.

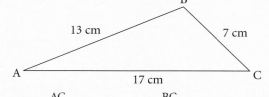

a) $\dfrac{AB}{AC}$ **b)** $\dfrac{AC}{BC}$ **c)** $\dfrac{BC}{AB}$ **d)** $\dfrac{BC}{AC}$

Solution

a) $\dfrac{AB}{AC} = \dfrac{13}{17}$ **b)** $\dfrac{AC}{BC} = \dfrac{17}{7}$ **c)** $\dfrac{BC}{AB} = \dfrac{7}{13}$ **d)** $\dfrac{BC}{AC} = \dfrac{7}{17}$

A proportion is a statement that two ratios are equal. We may use a proportion to solve a problem. In many situations, we know three terms in a proportion and we need to determine the fourth term.

Example 2

Determine the value of x in each proportion.

a) $\dfrac{x}{7} = \dfrac{5}{8}$ **b)** $\dfrac{12.3}{19.2} = \dfrac{x}{9.6}$ **c)** $\dfrac{9.4}{6.5} = \dfrac{30.4}{x}$

Solution

To determine the value of x in each proportion, we must isolate x.

a) $\dfrac{x}{7} = \dfrac{5}{8}$ Multiply each side by 7.

$$\dfrac{7 \times x}{7} = \dfrac{7 \times 5}{8}$$

$$x = \dfrac{7 \times 5}{8}$$

$$= \dfrac{35}{8}$$

$$= 4.375$$

b) $\dfrac{12.3}{19.2} = \dfrac{x}{9.6}$ Multiply each side by 9.6.

$$\dfrac{9.6 \times 12.3}{19.2} = \dfrac{x \times 9.6}{9.6}$$

$$\dfrac{118.08}{19.2} = x$$

$$x = 6.15$$

c) $\dfrac{9.4}{6.5} = \dfrac{30.4}{x}$ Invert the fractions so x is in the numerator.

$$\dfrac{6.5}{9.4} = \dfrac{x}{30.4}$$ Multiply each side by 30.4.

$$\dfrac{30.4 \times 6.5}{9.4} = \dfrac{30.4 \times x}{30.4}$$

$$x = \dfrac{197.6}{9.4}$$

$$\doteq 21.0$$

Discuss

Why did we round x to 1 decimal place?

Exercises

Round answers to 1 decimal place when necessary.

1. A rectangle is 36 cm by 24 cm. Write the ratio of the length to the width.

2. Determine the value of b in each proportion.

    a) $\dfrac{b}{8} = \dfrac{5}{12}$ **b)** $\dfrac{b}{5.4} = \dfrac{7.2}{4.5}$

    c) $\dfrac{9}{b} = \dfrac{15}{25}$ **d)** $\dfrac{8}{b} = \dfrac{28}{54}$

3. Determine the value of t in each proportion.

    a) $\dfrac{9}{25} = \dfrac{t}{12.5}$ **b)** $\dfrac{4.2}{9.8} = \dfrac{t}{4.5}$

    c) $\dfrac{9.5}{24} = \dfrac{35}{t}$ **d)** $\dfrac{49}{26} = \dfrac{21}{t}$

4. Determine the value of a in each proportion.

    a) $\dfrac{9}{14} = \dfrac{a}{21}$ **b)** $\dfrac{2.7}{8.4} = \dfrac{6.6}{a}$

    c) $\dfrac{35}{a} = \dfrac{9.5}{24}$ **d)** $\dfrac{a}{106} = \dfrac{27}{164}$

3 Review: The Pythagorean Theorem

The Pythagorean Theorem states that in any right triangle, the area of the square on the hypotenuse is equal to the sum of the areas of the squares on the other two sides.

Recall that the hypotenuse is the side opposite the right angle.

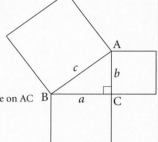

Area of square on AB = Area of square on BC + Area of square on AC

$$c^2 \quad = \quad a^2 \quad + \quad b^2$$

When we know the lengths of two sides of a right triangle, we can use the Pythagorean Theorem to calculate the length of the third side.

Note: The keystrokes in this text are for a TI-83 Plus or a TI-30X IIS. The screens are those you will see if you use a TI-83 Plus. If your calculator is different, check your manual.

Example 1

Calculate the length of the hypotenuse of this triangle.

Solution

Use the Pythagorean Theorem.

$$h^2 = 7^2 + 24^2$$
$$h^2 = 625$$
$$h = \sqrt{625}$$
$$ = 25$$

The hypotenuse is 25 cm long.

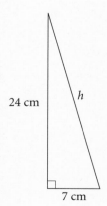

Example 2 Determine length x in this triangle.

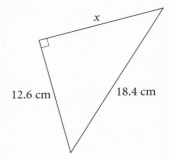

Solution

Use the Pythagorean Theorem.
$$18.4^2 = x^2 + 12.6^2$$
$$18.4^2 - 12.6^2 = x^2$$
$$x^2 = 18.4^2 - 12.6^2$$
$$x = \sqrt{18.4^2 - 12.6^2}$$

Use a calculator.

Press: [2nd] [x^2] 18.4 [x^2] [−]
12.6 [x^2] [ )] [ENTER]

The length of x is approximately 13.4 cm.

Exercises

1. In each triangle, determine the length of the hypotenuse.

a)

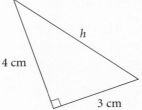

b)

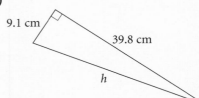

2. Determine each length.

a)

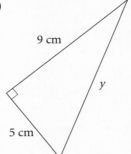

b)

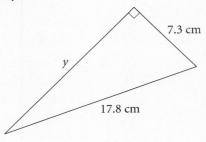

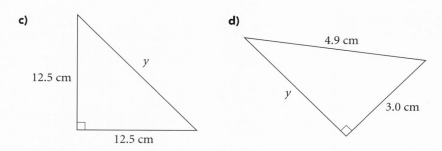

c) 12.5 cm, 12.5 cm, y

d) 4.9 cm, 3.0 cm, y

3. The hypotenuse of a right triangle is 5 m long. One leg of the triangle is 1.3 m. Calculate the length of the other leg.

4 New: Approximate Numbers and Significant Digits

We should always consider the accuracy of numbers used in calculations, since the final result should not be written with any more accuracy than is appropriate.

You can count to determine the number of people in your classroom at this moment. This number is *exact*. Since, by definition 60 min = 1 h, the 60 and 1 are also exact numbers.

All numbers obtained by measurement are *approximate*. For example, if you measure the length of the line below, you will find that it is approximately 4.6 cm.

This means that the length is closer to 4.6 cm than to either 4.5 cm or 4.7 cm. We say that the length is 4.6 cm to the nearest tenth of a centimetre. This means that the length is between 4.55 cm and 4.65 cm. In the number 4.6, the digits 4 and 6 are called *significant digits*.

An approximate number may include some zeros to locate the decimal point. Such zeros are not significant digits. For example, the length of the line above, expressed in metres, is 0.046 m. The zeros on the left are placeholders and are not significant. Similarly, in a measurement of 2700 m, the zeros on the right do not contribute to the value of the number. We cannot omit them, since they hold the 2 and the 7 in the thousands column and the hundreds column, respectively. These zeros are placeholders and not significant digits.

TAKE NOTE

Rules for Determining Significant Digits of an Approximate Number

- All non-zero digits are significant.
- Zero is significant only when:
  – It appears between two significant digits.
  – It appears on the right of a number after the decimal point.

Example

Determine the number of significant digits in each approximate number.

a) 57.32 cm **b)** 30.057 kg **c)** 0.0067 mm

d) 27 000 000 cm **e)** 107.90 g

Solution

a) 57.32 cm
All the digits are non-zero, so they are significant.
57.32 cm has 4 significant digits.

b) 30.057 kg
The zeros are between significant digits. All the digits are significant.
30.057 kg has 5 significant digits.

c) 0.0067 mm
The leading zeros are holding the decimal point in place, so they are not significant. The digits 6 and 7 are significant.
0.0067 mm has 2 significant digits.

d) 27 000 000 cm
The zeros are placeholders, showing the position of the decimal point, so they are not significant. The digits 2 and 7 are significant.
27 000 000 cm has 2 significant digits.

e) 107.90 g

The zero between the digits 1 and 7 is significant. The zero on the right of the number is after the decimal point, and so is significant. All the digits are significant.

107.90 g has 5 significant digits.

Discuss

Where is the decimal point in the number in part d?

In calculations with approximate numbers, the *accuracy* of a number refers to the significant digits it has. When we work with approximate numbers, we should always consider their accuracy. Calculation cannot increase the accuracy of numbers. So, the final result should not be reported with greater accuracy than the least accurate number used.

Exercises

1. Identify each number as approximate or exact.

a) A carton contains 12 eggs.

b) The speed of a car is 55 km/h.

c) A car has 6 cylinders.

d) A calculator has 50 keys and its battery lasts for 50 h.

2. Determine the number of significant digits in each approximate number.

a) 27.2	**b)** 6027	**c)** 30.5
d) 0.124	**e)** 0.008	**f)** 28.03
g) 200	**h)** 0.004 05	**i)** 28 050
j) 25.080	**k)** 300.1	**l)** 0.0205
m) 10	**n)** 136.900	**o)** 10 100

The word *trigonometry* means "triangle measurement." We can use trigonometry to calculate the lengths of sides and the measures of angles in any triangle. In this section, we will use the trigonometric ratios (sine, cosine, and tangent) to calculate the lengths of sides of right triangles.

To label a triangle, we use capital letters for the vertices and the corresponding small letters for the lengths of the sides opposite the vertices. So, $\triangle ABC$ is labelled as shown.

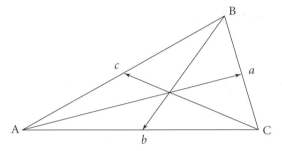

Recall that the sides of a right triangle are described by their positions relative to angles in the triangle. The hypotenuse is the longest side. It is opposite the right angle. The two shorter sides are the *legs* of the right triangle. In right $\triangle ABC$, below left, a is the length of the side *opposite* angle A, and c is the length of the side *adjacent* to angle A.

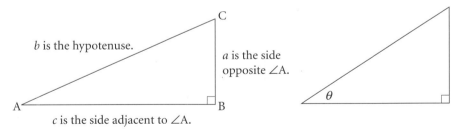

Sometimes, we use a Greek letter, such as θ, to indicate the measure of an angle (above right).

We can form ratios using the lengths of these sides taken two at a time. Three of these trigonometric ratios are the sine, cosine, and tangent of $\angle A$, abbreviated to sin A, cos A, and tan A.

If $\angle A$ is an acute angle in a right triangle, then:

$$\sin A = \frac{\text{Length of side opposite } \angle A}{\text{Length of hypotenuse}}$$

$$\cos A = \frac{\text{Length of side adjacent to } \angle A}{\text{Length of hypotenuse}}$$

$$\tan A = \frac{\text{Length of side opposite } \angle A}{\text{Length of side adjacent to } \angle A}$$

We can use a scientific calculator to determine these ratios, in decimal form, for any angle. A graphing calculator is a scientific calculator. The keystrokes presented in this text are for a Texas Instruments scientific calculator, such as a TI-83 Plus or a TI-30X IIS. These calculators are direct entry calculators. That is, operations and numbers are entered as you read them, from left to right. If you use a different calculator, try the keystrokes listed. If your calculator does not show the correct answer, refer to the manual that came with your calculator.

In this course, we measure an angle in degrees, but other units can be used to measure an angle and these are programmed into many scientific calculators. If necessary, change the units to degrees as follows.

TI-30X IIS calculator:

If "DEG" appears on your calculator screen, your calculator is in Degree mode. If "RAD" or "GRAD" appears, you must change the mode to degrees. Press (DRG), then the right or left arrow key until DEG is underlined. Press (ENTER =).

TI-83 Plus calculator:

Press [MODE]. If Radian is highlighted, use the arrow keys to move the cursor to Degrees, then press [ENTER].

Example 1

Determine the value of a. Round your answer to 1 decimal place.

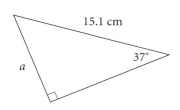

Solution

Label the triangle. Identify the opposite and adjacent sides to $\angle A$ and the hypotenuse.

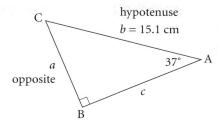

We are asked to find the length of a, which is opposite $\angle A$.

We know the measures of $\angle A$ and the hypotenuse. Form a trigonometric ratio that involves length a and the hypotenuse.

$$\frac{\text{Length of side opposite } \angle A}{\text{Length of hypotenuse}} = \frac{a}{15.1}$$ This ratio is $\sin 37°$.

$$\sin 37° = \frac{a}{15.1}$$ Multiply both sides by 15.1.

$$15.1 \times \sin 37° = a$$

Check that the calculator is in degree mode.

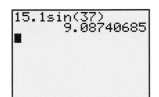

Press: 15.1 [SIN] 37 [ )] [ENTER]

To 1 decimal place, $a \doteq 9.1$
Length a is approximately 9.1 cm.

In *Example 1*, we wrote $15.1 \times \sin 37°$; usually, we omit the $\times$ sign and write $15.1 \sin 37°$.

In many cases, when we are given information about a triangle we need to draw a diagram before we can solve the problem.

Example 2

In $\triangle XYZ$, $\angle X = 16°$, $\angle Y = 90°$, and $z = 7.6$ cm. Calculate length y.

Solution

Draw and label $\triangle XYZ$.

We know the measure of $\angle X$ and the length of the side adjacent to $\angle X$. We need to find the length of the hypotenuse. Write a trigonometric ratio that uses these lengths.

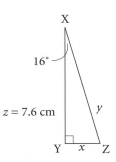

$$\frac{\text{Length of side adjacent to } \angle X}{\text{Length of hypotenuse}} = \frac{7.6}{y}$$

This is cos 16°.

$$\cos 16° = \frac{7.6}{y}$$

Multiply each side by y.

$$y \cos 16° = 7.6$$

Divide both sides by cos 16°.

$$y = \frac{7.6}{\cos 16°}$$

Use a calculator.

Press: 7.6 [÷] [cos] 16 [ )] [ENTER]

$y \doteq 7.9$

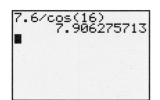

7.6/cos(16)
        7.906275713

Length y is approximately 7.9 cm.

Trigonometry can be used to determine distances that cannot be measured directly. Recall that the angle of depression is the angle between the horizontal and the line of sight from the observer's eye to a point below eye level (below left). The angle of elevation is the angle between the horizontal and the line of sight from the observer's eye to a point above eye level (below right).

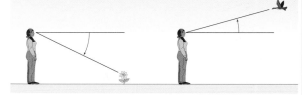

Example 3

From the top of a vertical cliff that overlooks the ocean, a person measures the angle of depression of a boat at sea as 9°. The height of the cliff is 142 m. How far is the boat from the base of the cliff? Give the distance to the nearest metre.

Solution

Draw a diagram. Let c represent the distance of the boat from the foot of the cliff, and θ the measure of the angle between the line of sight and the cliff.

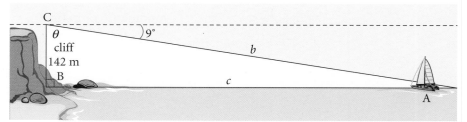

The angle between the horizontal and the line of sight is 9°. So the angle, θ, between the line of sight and the cliff is 90° − 9°, or 81°.

We now know the measure of θ and the length of the side adjacent to this angle. We need to determine the length of the side opposite θ. Write a trigonometric ratio.

$$\frac{\text{Length of side opposite } \theta}{\text{Length of side adjacent to } \theta} = \frac{c}{142}$$

This is tan 81°.

$$\tan 81° = \frac{c}{142}$$

Multiply each side by 142.

$$142 \tan 81° = c$$

Use a calculator.

Press: 142 [TAN] 81 [ )] [ENTER]

$c \doteq 897$

The boat is approximately 897 m from the base of the cliff.

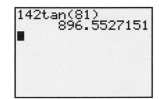

Discuss

We could have calculated a different angle and a different trigonometric ratio to solve this problem. Which method is easier? Why?

1.1 **Exercises**

A

1. For △ABC below left, write the ratio of sides for each trigonometric ratio.

a) sin A **b)** cos A **c)** tan B **d)** cos B

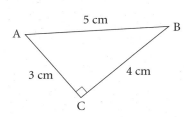

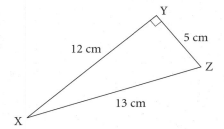

 2. For ∠X in △XYZ above right, identify the trigonometric ratio equal to each fraction.

a) $\frac{5}{12}$ **b)** $\frac{5}{13}$ **c)** $\frac{12}{13}$

3. Determine each trigonometric ratio to 4 decimal places.

a) cos 49° **b)** tan 81° **c)** sin 52° **d)** tan 22°

e) sin 17° **f)** cos 63° **g)** tan 9° **h)** sin 66°

B

4. Determine length x in each triangle. Give the length to 1 decimal place.

a)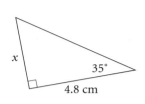

35°
4.8 cm
x

b)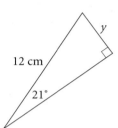

x
44°
7.9 mm

c)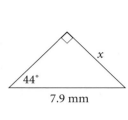

18.3 mm
58°
x

5. Determine length y in each triangle. Give the length to the nearest unit.

a)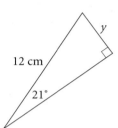

y
12 cm
21°

b)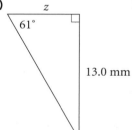

y
49°
35.0 mm

c)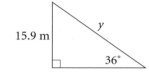

y
15.9 m
36°

6. Determine length z in each triangle. Give the length to the nearest tenth of a unit.

a)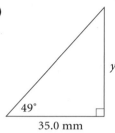

z
61°
13.0 mm

b)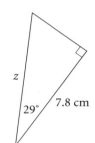

z
29°
7.8 cm

c)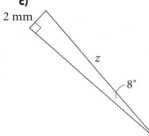

2 mm
z
8°

7. A ramp has an incline of 7.5°. The horizontal length of the ramp is 200 m.

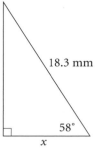

ramp
7.5°
200 m
26.3

a) To the nearest metre, what is the vertical height of the ramp?

b) Calculate the length of the ramp. Give the length to the nearest metre.

8. **Knowledge/Understanding** For each triangle, determine the length indicated. Answer to the nearest unit.
   a) △ABC: ∠C = 47°, ∠B = 90°, and a = 8 cm; calculate c.
   b) △XYZ: ∠Y = 90°, ∠Z = 32°, and y = 15 m; calculate x.
   c) △LMN: ∠M = 90°, ∠N = 64°, and m = 12 mm; calculate n.

9. For each triangle, determine the length indicated, to the nearest tenth.
   a) △XYZ: ∠X = 41°, ∠Y = 90°, and x = 11.3 m; calculate y.
   b) △ABC: ∠A = 90°, ∠C = 38°, and b = 9.4 cm; calculate c.
   c) △DEF: ∠E = 90°, ∠F = 63°, and d = 4.5 m; calculate e.

10. **Application** A guy wire is attached to the top of a vertical tower and to an anchor point on horizontal ground 20 m from the base of a tower (below left). The guy wire makes an angle of 75° with the ground. Determine the height of the tower to the nearest metre.

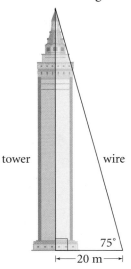

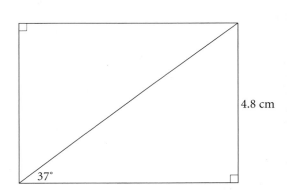

11. A rectangle is 4.8 cm wide (above right). A diagonal of the rectangle makes an angle of 37° with the longer side of the rectangle.
   a) Determine the length of the diagonal to the nearest millimetre.
   b) Determine the length of the rectangle to the nearest millimetre.

12. A ladder is 3.0 m long. It is leaning against a wall. The foot of the ladder makes an angle of 76° with the ground. How far up the wall is the top of the ladder? Give the length to the nearest tenth of a metre.

13. Sam is flying a kite. She has let out the string to a length of 210 m. The string makes an angle of 48° with the horizontal. The string is taut and Sam's hand is 1.45 m above the ground.

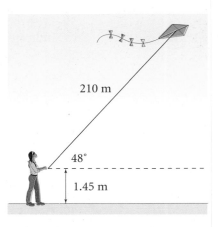

210 m

48°

1.45 m

a) What is the vertical distance between Sam's hand and the kite?

b) How high is the kite above the ground?

14. Triangle ABC has these measurements: $\angle B = 90°$, $\angle A = 34°$, and $b = 14$ cm.

a) Sketch $\triangle ABC$.

b) Which of the two legs do you think is longer? Explain your answer.

c) Determine the lengths a and c to verify your answer in part b.

15. Communication In $\triangle XYZ$, $\angle Y = 90°$, $\angle Z = 45°$, and $y = 8.6$ cm.

a) What should be true about the lengths of the two legs? Explain.

b) Calculate to verify your answer in part a.

c) What statement can you make about sin 45° and cos 45°? Explain.

16. Thinking/Inquiry/Problem Solving Mario and Keely are on a hiking trip. It will be dark in 1.5 h. They have to decide whether to stop for the night or to hike to a campsite at the base of a tower they can see in the distance. They know the height of the tower is 312 m. They use a clinometer to determine that the angle of elevation to the top of the tower is 3°.

Mario and Keely have been walking at 3 km/h. Should they stop for the night or continue to the tower? Justify your answer with a diagram and calculations. Include any assumptions you make.

There are situations in which we need to know the measure of an angle, but we cannot use a protractor. For example, a machinist uses a sine bar and precision slip gauges to measure an angle. This device uses the lengths of two sides of a right triangle, and a trigonometric ratio to calculate the measure of the angle.

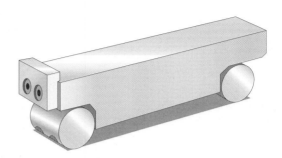

Determining the measure of an acute angle from a trigonometric ratio

Use the SIN^{-1}, COS^{-1}, or TAN^{-1} function on a scientific calculator to determine the measure of an angle when its trigonometric ratio is known. For example, given tan A = 0.6, to calculate ∠A, press [2nd] [TAN] 0.6 [ )] [ENTER] to display 30.96375653. So, ∠A ≐ 31°.

Example 1

Determine the measure of ∠A to the nearest degree.

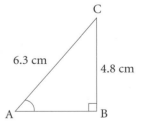

Solution

The side with length 4.8 cm is opposite ∠A, and the side with length 6.3 cm is the hypotenuse of the right triangle. Use these lengths to write a trigonometric ratio.

$$\frac{\text{Length of side opposite } \angle A}{\text{Length of hypotenuse}} = \frac{4.8}{6.3} \qquad \text{This is sin A.}$$

$$\sin A = \frac{4.8}{6.3} \qquad \text{Use a calculator.}$$

Press: [2nd] [SIN] 4.8 [÷] 6.3 [)] [ENTER]

∠A ≐ 50°

```
sin⁻¹(4.8/6.3)
          49.63240646
```

Discuss

Some calculators require the user to insert brackets. Why do we always include the right bracket [ )] in a key sequence when the calculator automatically provides the left bracket?

Example 2 Hussain and Mike conducted an experiment to determine the angle of elevation of the sun. Hussain held a 100-cm stick vertical on level ground. Mike measured the length of its shadow as 52 cm. Calculate the angle of elevation of the sun to the nearest degree.

Solution

Draw and label a sketch.

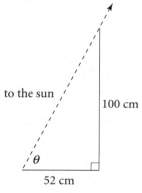

to the sun

100 cm

θ

52 cm

To determine θ, the angle of elevation of the sun, use the known lengths to write a trigonometric ratio. The leg that is 100 cm long is opposite θ, and the leg that is 52 cm long is adjacent to θ.

$$\frac{\text{Length of side opposite } \theta}{\text{Length of side adjacent to } \theta} = \frac{100}{52}$$ This is tan θ.

$$\tan \theta = \frac{100}{52}$$ Use a calculator.

Press: [2nd] [TAN] 100 [÷] 52 [)] [ENTER]

$\theta \doteq 63°$

```
tan⁻¹(100/52)
          62.52556837
```

The angle of elevation of the sun is approximately 63°.

Discuss

Describe how the angle of elevation of the sun changes during the day.

To *solve a triangle* means to determine the measures of all the sides and angles of the triangle.

Example 3 Solve △XYZ, given that ∠X = 90°, x = 8.2 cm, and z = 6.0 cm. Round all angle measures to the nearest degree and all lengths to the nearest tenth of a centimetre.

Solution

Sketch and label △XYZ.

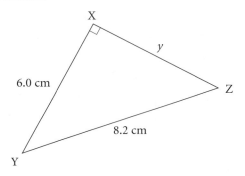

Since △XYZ is a right triangle, we can use the Pythagorean Theorem to calculate y.

$$8.2^2 = 6.0^2 + y^2 \qquad \text{Subtract } 6.0^2 \text{ from both sides.}$$
$$8.2^2 - 6.0^2 = y^2$$
$$y = \sqrt{8.2^2 - 6.0^2} \qquad \text{Use a calculator.}$$

Press: [2nd] [x²] 8.2 [x²] [−] 6.0 [x²] [ENTER]

To the nearest tenth of a centimetre, y = 5.6 cm.

To determine the measure of ∠Y, use the given lengths of sides to write a trigonometric ratio. The side of length 6.0 cm is adjacent to ∠Y, and the side of length 8.2 cm is the hypotenuse.

$$\frac{\text{Length of side adjacent to } \angle Y}{\text{Length of hypotenuse}} = \frac{6.0}{8.2} \qquad \text{This is cos Y.}$$

$$\cos Y = \frac{6.0}{8.2} \qquad \text{Use a calculator.}$$

Press: [2nd] [COS] 6.0 [÷] 8.2 [ )] [ENTER]

∠Y ≐ 43°

Recall that the sum of the angles in a triangle is 180°.

```
cos⁻¹(6.0/8.2)
            42.97028393
■
```

To determine ∠Z, use this property.

∠Z ≐ 180° − 90° − 43°

    ≐ 47°

The side XZ, or y, is approximately 5.6 cm, ∠Y is approximately 43°, and ∠Z is approximately 47°.

Discuss

Describe another method to calculate the measure of ∠Z.

1.2 Exercises

A

1. For △ABC, write the ratio of sides for each trigonometric ratio.

    a) sin C

    b) cos C

    c) tan C

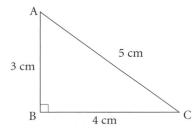

2. Determine the measure of each angle to the nearest degree.

    a) sin X = 0.6735   **b)** tan B = 1.674   **c)** cos Z = 0.3176

    d) sin K = 0.7419   **e)** cos A = 0.5490   **f)** tan G = 0.6203

 3. Determine the measure of each angle to the nearest degree.

    a) $\sin Y = \frac{5}{8}$ **b)** $\cos A = \frac{11}{15}$ **c)** $\sin C = \frac{5.2}{6.7}$

    d) $\tan K = \frac{4.3}{8.7}$ **e)** $\cos Z = \frac{3.6}{12.0}$ **f)** $\tan B = \frac{14.2}{9.6}$

 4. Determine the measure of each ∠A to the nearest degree.

    a)

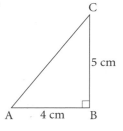

    b)

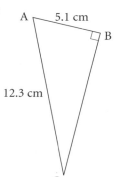

    c)

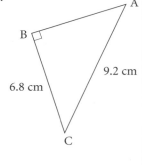

B

5. Determine the measures of the acute angles in each triangle to the nearest tenth of a degree.

a)

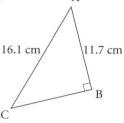

16.1 cm, 11.7 cm

b)

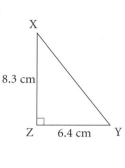

8.3 cm, 6.4 cm

c)

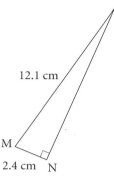

12.1 cm, 2.4 cm

✓ **6.** Determine the measure of the indicated side or angle. Give each measure to the nearest degree or tenth of a centimetre.

a)

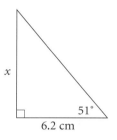

x, 51°, 6.2 cm

b)

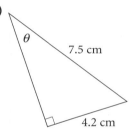

θ, 7.5 cm, 4.2 cm

c)

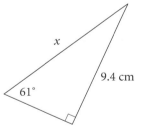

x, 61°, 9.4 cm

d)

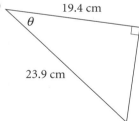

19.4 cm, θ, 23.9 cm

✓ **7.** Solve each triangle. Give each measure to the nearest degree and/or the nearest unit.

a)

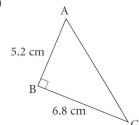

5.2 cm, 6.8 cm

b)

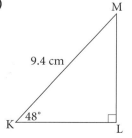

9.4 cm, 48°

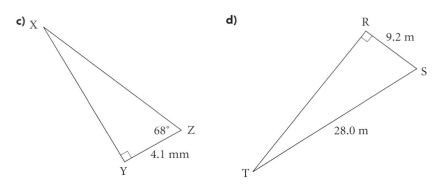

c) X

68° Z

4.1 mm

Y

d) R

9.2 m

S

28.0 m

T

8. Calculate each indicated angle to the nearest degree, and each indicated side to the nearest tenth of a unit.

a) Given $\triangle ABC$: $\angle B = 90°$, $a = 4.9$ m, and $c = 6.5$ m; calculate $\angle A$.

b) Given $\triangle XYZ$: $\angle Y = 90°$, $y = 9.2$ cm, and $z = 4.7$ cm; calculate $\angle X$.

c) Given $\triangle RST$: $\angle T = 90°$, $\angle S = 65°$, and $s = 7.4$ cm; calculate t.

d) Given $\triangle JKL$: $\angle K = 90°$, $k = 25.2$ mm, and $j = 11.3$ mm; calculate $\angle L$.

✓ **9. Knowledge/Understanding** Solve each triangle. Round each angle to the nearest degree, and each length to the nearest tenth of a unit.

a) $\triangle ABC$: $\angle B = 90°$, $b = 34$ cm, and $a = 27$ cm

b) $\triangle JKL$: $\angle K = 90°$, $j = 37.8$ m, and $k = 41.5$ m

c) $\triangle PQR$: $\angle Q = 90°$, $r = 4.0$ cm, and $q = 5.0$ cm

d) $\triangle XYZ$: $\angle Y = 90°$, $z = 8.0$ cm, and $x = 4.0$ cm

10. Solve each triangle.

a) $\triangle RST$: $\angle T = 90°$, $\angle S = 54°$, and $r = 9.1$ mm

b) $\triangle LMN$: $\angle M = 90°$, $\angle L = 37°$, and $m = 15.6$ cm

c) $\triangle ABC$: $\angle C = 90°$, $\angle B = 78°$, and $b = 4.9$ m

d) $\triangle DEF$: $\angle E = 90°$, $\angle F = 41°$, and $d = 4$ cm

11. A ladder 3.5 m long is leaning against a wall. The foot of the ladder is 1.0 m from the wall. To the nearest degree, what angle does the ladder make with the ground?

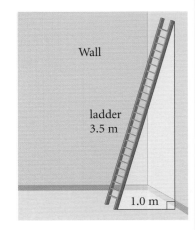

Wall

ladder
3.5 m

1.0 m

12. Application A bracket that holds a hanging plant is attached to a wall. The vertical and horizontal legs are 13.0 cm and 19.5 cm, respectively. What is the measure of angle A?

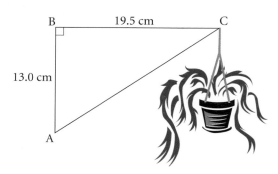

13. A ramp rises 1 m for every 10 m of horizontal distance. The ramp is inclined at an angle, θ, to the horizontal. Determine the measure of θ to the nearest degree.

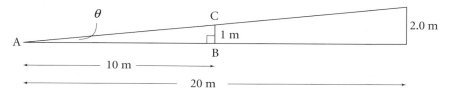

14. A staircase has 3 main parts: the stringer, the riser, and the tread. A carpenter must obey local building codes when she constructs a staircase.

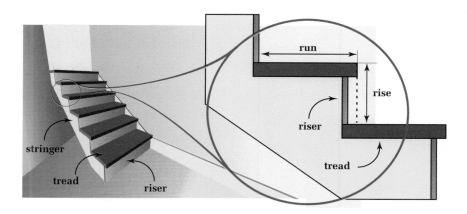

The code of one community requires that the sum of the riser and the tread must not exceed 449 mm. Calculate the angle of a staircase whose riser is 175 mm. Assume the measures are at the maximum allowed by the code.

✓ **15. Communication** A helicopter is hovering 6000 m above the ground. A searchlight on the ground is a horizontal distance of 1700 m from the helicopter.

a) Draw a sketch of this situation.

b) The searchlight is aimed so its beam shines on the helicopter. Calculate the measure of the angle of elevation of the helicopter from the searchlight.

16. A cable car rises 150 m for every 50 m it travels horizontally. What angle does the cable make with level ground?

✓ **17. Thinking/Inquiry/Problem Solving**

a) Use a ruler and grid paper. Draw a right △ABC for each ratio.

i) $\tan A = \frac{1}{2}$ ii) $\tan A = \frac{3}{4}$ iii) $\tan A = 1$

b) Calculate the measure of ∠A for each triangle in part a.

c) Describe what happens to the measure of ∠A and to the shape of △ABC as tan A increases.

d) Predict the shape of △ABC and the measure of ∠A when $\tan A = \frac{4}{3}$. Draw the triangle and calculate the measure of ∠A to verify your prediction.

e) What is the greatest possible value of tan A in a right triangle? Explain.

✓ **18. Communication** When you solve a triangle, you calculate the measures of all the sides and angles. Why is it better to calculate using the given measures rather than previously calculated measures?

C

19. Determine the measure of each indicated side or angle.

a)

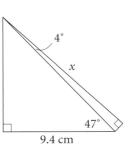

b)

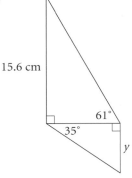

c)

The length of one piece of roof truss is 8.5 m. This piece of the truss is set at an angle of 37° to the horizontal and the other piece is set at an angle of 58°. This truss can be represented by an acute triangle. Suppose we want to calculate the lengths of the pieces of the truss. Since this triangle does not contain a right angle, we cannot use the methods of earlier sections to solve the triangle.

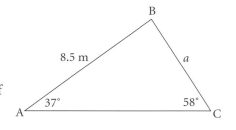

In this section, we will determine unknown measures in acute triangles. Recall from *Necessary Skills 4* that any measurement is approximate, and its accuracy is indicated by the number of significant digits. This table shows the measurement of an angle and corresponding accuracy of its trigonometric function.

Measure of Angle to Nearest:	Accuracy of Trigonometric Ratios
1°	2 significant digits
0.1°	3 significant digits
0.01°	4 significant digits

When calculating with approximate numbers, we write the final answer with the same number of significant digits as the least accurate number used in the calculation. To avoid rounding errors, carry as many digits as possible until an approximate answer is required.

We can find the length of the second non-horizontal piece of the roof truss described above.

We want to calculate the length of BC, or a.
Triangle ABC is not a right triangle. Divide △ABC into two right triangles by constructing an altitude from B to AC at D. BD is perpendicular to AC.

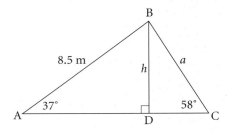

There are now two right triangles, △ABD and △CBD. They have a common side BD, whose length is represented by h.

In right △ABD, we know one length and one acute angle, so we can calculate h.

$$\frac{h}{8.5} = \sin 37°$$
$$h = 8.5 \sin 37° \qquad ①$$

In right △CBD, we now know one side and one angle, so we can calculate a.

$$\frac{h}{a} = \sin 58°$$
$$h = a \sin 58° \qquad ②$$

Use equations ① and ②. The left sides are equal, so the right sides are also equal.

$a \sin 58° = 8.5 \sin 37°$ Divide each side by $\sin 58°$.

$$a = \frac{8.5 \sin 37°}{\sin 58°} \qquad \text{Use a calculator.}$$

Press: 8.5 [SIN] 37 [)] [÷] [SIN] 58 [)] [ENTER]

Each given measurement had 2 significant digits, so round the value of a to 2 significant digits.

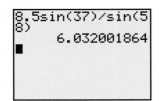

$$a \doteq 6.0$$

The length of side BC is approximately 6.0 cm.

We can use this method to develop a formula for determining the length of a side in any triangle.

Draw △ABC and altitude BD. Label a, c, and the altitude, h.

In △ABD,

$$\frac{h}{c} = \sin A$$

$$h = c \sin A \qquad ①$$

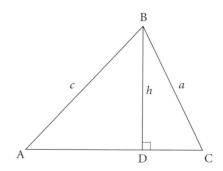

In △CBD,

$$\frac{h}{a} = \sin C$$

$$h = a \sin C \qquad ②$$

From equations ① and ②:

$a \sin C = c \sin A$ Divide both sides by sin C.

$a = \dfrac{c \sin A}{\sin C}$ Divide both sides by sin A.

$\dfrac{a}{\sin A} = \dfrac{c}{\sin C}$

To show $\dfrac{b}{\sin B} = \dfrac{c}{\sin C}$, draw AE perpendicular to BC in △ABC.

Since $\dfrac{a}{\sin A} = \dfrac{c}{\sin C}$ and $\dfrac{b}{\sin B} = \dfrac{c}{\sin C}$,

then $\dfrac{a}{\sin A} = \dfrac{b}{\sin B} = \dfrac{c}{\sin C}$.

This important result is the Sine Law.

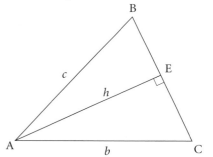

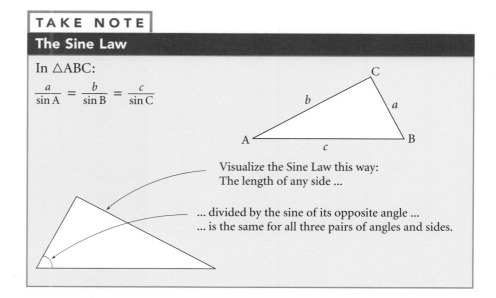

TAKE NOTE

The Sine Law

In △ABC:

$$\frac{a}{\sin A} = \frac{b}{\sin B} = \frac{c}{\sin C}$$

Visualize the Sine Law this way:
The length of any side ...

... divided by the sine of its opposite angle ...
... is the same for all three pairs of angles and sides.

Example 1 Determine the length a.

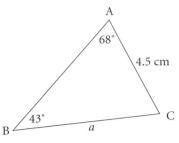

Solution

We know $\angle B$ and length b, its opposite side. We also know $\angle A$, and we wish to determine length a. Use the Sine Law:

$$\frac{a}{\sin A} = \frac{b}{\sin B}$$

Substitute the values.

$$\frac{a}{\sin 68°} = \frac{4.5}{\sin 43°}$$

Multiply each side by $\sin 68°$.

$$a = \frac{4.5 \sin 68°}{\sin 43°}$$

Use a calculator.

Press: 4.5 [SIN] 68 [ )] [÷] [SIN] 43
[ )] [ENTER]

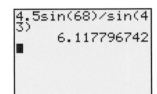

The length of side a is approximately 6.1 cm.

Discuss

Describe how to find length a given the measures $\angle B = 43°$, $\angle C = 69°$, and $b = 4.5$ cm.

Recall, to solve a triangle means to find the measures of all the sides and angles. A diagram will help you visualize the information given and decide on a strategy to solve the triangle.

Example 2 Solve acute $\triangle ABC$, when $\angle C = 75°$, $b = 8.2$ cm, and $c = 10.1$ cm.

Solution

Draw a diagram.

We must determine the measures of $\angle A$, $\angle B$, and the length of side a.

We know the measures of $\angle C$ and c. We also know b, so we can use the Sine Law to find the measure of $\angle B$.

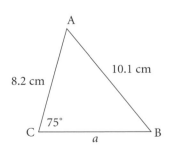

$$\frac{b}{\sin B} = \frac{c}{\sin C}$$ Substitute the values.

$$\frac{8.2}{\sin B} = \frac{10.1}{\sin 75°}$$ Invert the fraction.

$$\frac{\sin B}{8.2} = \frac{\sin 75°}{10.1}$$ Multiply both sides by 8.2.

$$\sin B = \frac{8.2 \; \sin 75°}{10.1}$$ Use a calculator.

Press: 8.2 [SIN] 75 [)] [÷] 10.1 [ENTER]

Do not clear the screen.

Press: [2nd] [SIN] [2nd] [(-)] [)] [ENTER]

∠B ≐ 52°

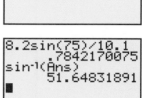

Use the angle sum property to find the measure of ∠A.

$$75° + 52° + ∠A ≐ 180°$$
$$127° + ∠A ≐ 180°$$
$$∠A ≐ 180° - 127°$$
$$≐ 53°$$

Use the Sine Law to determine a.

$$\frac{a}{\sin A} = \frac{c}{\sin C}$$ Substitute the values.

$$\frac{a}{\sin 53°} = \frac{10.1}{\sin 75°}$$ Multiply each side by sin 53°.

$$a = \frac{10.1 \sin 53°}{\sin 75°}$$ Use a calculator.

Press: 10.1 [SIN] 53 [)] [÷] [SIN]

75 [)] [ENTER]

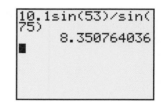

$a ≐ 8.4$

The length of side a is approximately 8.4 cm, and the measures of ∠A and ∠B are approximately 53° and 52°, respectively.

Discuss

An alternative key sequence to determine the measure of ∠B is [2nd] [SIN] 8.2 [SIN] 75 [)] [÷] 10.1 [)] [ENTER]. Which sequence do you prefer, and why?

When calculating the measure of a side in some triangles, we may not be able to immediately use the Sine Law.

Example 3

Laphong and Stephanie stand approximately 50 m apart on level ground. Laphong measures the angle of elevation of a hot-air balloon to be 58°. The angle of elevation for Stephanie is 41°. How far is Laphong from the hot-air balloon?

Solution

Draw △SLB to represent the situation. Label the triangle with the measures given.

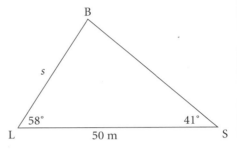

We know the measure of ∠S and the length, b. We are asked to find the length, s, but we do not know the measure of ∠B. We cannot use the Sine Law directly because we do not know one side and its opposite angle. We know two angles in the triangle, so we can use the angle sum property to calculate the third angle.

$$58° + 41° + ∠B = 180°$$
$$99° + ∠B = 180°$$
$$∠B = 81°$$

Now use the Sine Law.

$$\frac{s}{\sin S} = \frac{b}{\sin B}$$ Substitute the values.

$$\frac{s}{\sin 41°} = \frac{50}{\sin 81°}$$ Multiply each side by sin 41°.

$$s = \frac{50 \sin 41°}{\sin 81°}$$ Use a calculator.

Press: 50 [SIN] 41 [ )] [÷] [SIN]
81 [ )] [ENTER]

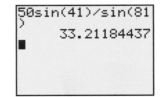

The original measure of 50 m has only 1 significant digit, so round the value of s to 1 significant digit also.

$$s \doteq 30$$

Laphong is approximately 30 m away from the hot-air balloon.

A

1. Given each expression for side a, calculate its measure. Give your answers to 1 decimal place.

   a) $a = \dfrac{27 \sin 62°}{\sin 34°}$

   b) $a = \dfrac{3 \sin 70°}{\sin 60°}$

   c) $a = \dfrac{13.4 \sin 55°}{\sin 48°}$

2. Given each value of sin P, calculate the measure of acute $\angle P$ to the nearest degree.

   a) $\sin P = 0.79$

   b) $\sin P = 0.65$

   c) $\sin P = \dfrac{3}{4}$

3. Given each expression for sin B, calculate the measure of acute $\angle B$.

   a) $\sin B = \dfrac{3 \sin 50°}{5}$

   b) $\sin B = \dfrac{87 \sin 43°}{74}$

   c) $\sin B = \dfrac{1.2 \sin 12°}{3.1}$

B

4. Determine the length of each indicated side. Round your answers to the nearest 0.1 cm.

   a)
   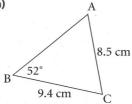

   b)
   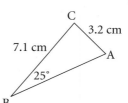

   c)
   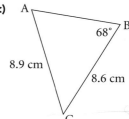

5. In each acute $\triangle ABC$, determine the measure of acute $\angle A$ to the nearest degree.

   a)
   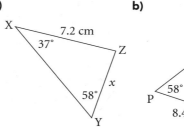

   b)

   c)
   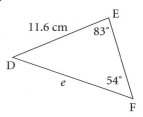

6. Determine the length of each indicated side. Answer to the nearest tenth of a unit.

   a)
   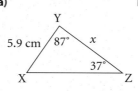

   b)
   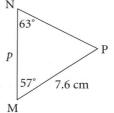

   c)
   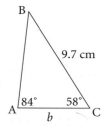

7. Determine the measure of each indicated side or acute angle. Give the lengths to one decimal place, and the angles to the nearest degree.

a)
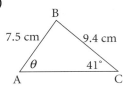

b)
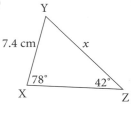

c)
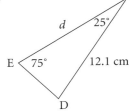

d)
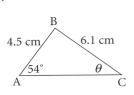

e)
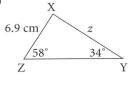

f)
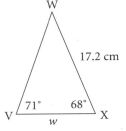

✓ **8. Knowledge/Understanding** Solve each acute triangle.

a)
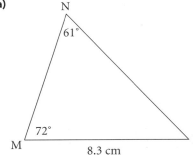

b)
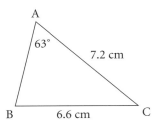

✓ **9.** Solve each acute triangle.

a) △ABC given ∠B = 63°, ∠C = 47°, and b = 9.2 cm

b) △PQR given ∠P = 42°, ∠Q = 53°, and r = 7.7 cm

c) △KMN given ∠K = 55°, ∠N = 55°, and k = 6.2 cm

✓ **10. Application** An A-frame building has a roof as shown. The angle at the vertex of the A-frame is 55°. The distance from the vertex of the roof to the endpoints of the crossbeam is 10 m. Calculate the length of the crossbeam.

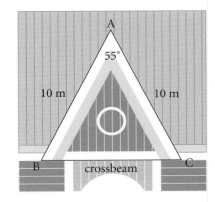

11. Ships A and B at sea are 15.6 km apart. A port, C, can be seen from the deck of each ship. The angles between the line joining the ships and the lines of sight to the port are 58° and 72°, respectively. How far is each ship from the port?

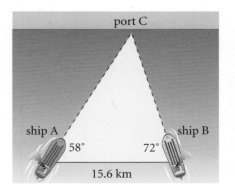

12. Thinking/Inquiry/Problem Solving
A landscape designer is making a triangular garden (below left). The garden is to be enclosed by a fence costing $1.50/m. What will be the cost of the fence?

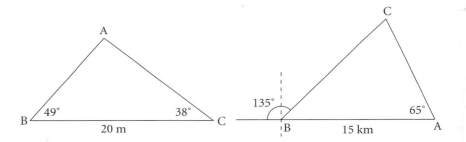

13. A boat leaves a dock at point A on a lake and travels 15 km due west to point B on the lake. The boat then makes a 135° turn and travels to a dock at point C (above right). Line AC makes an angle of 65° with AB. What is the shortest distance between the dock at C and the dock at A?

14. Three straight roads join three towns, A, B, and C. The road between towns A and B is 35 km long. The road between towns A and C makes an angle of 70° with the road between towns A and B, and an angle of 60° with the road between towns C and B. A person drives from A to B to C. Determine the total distance driven.

15. Communication Look at the exercises you have completed. Assume you know three measures in a triangle. Explain the conditions under which the Sine Law may be used to calculate the length of a side and the measure of an angle.

1. Determine the measure of each indicated side or angle.

   a) $\triangle ABC$ with $\angle C = 90°$, $\angle B = 41°$, $BC = 9.0$ cm; find b.

   b) $\triangle ABC$ with $\angle B = 90°$, $BC = 1.8$ cm, $AC = 4.2$ cm, ; find $\angle C$.

2. From the top of a cliff 95 m high, the angle of depression of a boat at sea is 11°. How far is the boat from the base of the cliff?

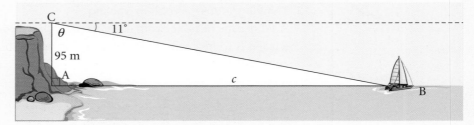

3. In each acute $\triangle ABC$, determine the length of side a.

   a)

   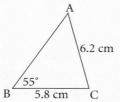

   b)

   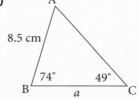

4. Determine the measure of each acute $\angle A$.

   a)

   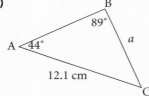

   b)

   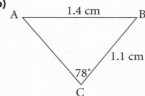

Performance Assessment

5. To reach the top of the mountain at a ski resort, skiers must take two lifts. The first lift takes skiers from the base of the mountain to the transfer point. It travels 2200 m at an angle of inclination of 41°. The second lift takes skiers from the transfer point to the mountaintop. It travels 1500 m at an angle of inclination of 48°. How high is the top of the mountain? Explain your strategy and the steps you used to solve this problem. Which trigonometric definitions and laws did you use? Why?

We have used trigonometry to solve problems that involve right triangles and acute triangles. Triangles can also contain obtuse angles.

When you input (SIN) 150 ( )) (ENTER) on a scientific calculator, the result is 0.5. So, the sine of an obtuse angle does exist. We can obtain the value of the sine, cosine, and tangent of an obtuse angle from a calculator. You will investigate the relationship between the trigonometric ratios of acute and obtuse angles.

Investigation **1** **Trigonometric Ratios of Related Angles**

1. Copy this table.

Angle A	sin A	cos A	tan A
2°			
5°			
20°			
67°			
79°			
83°			
97°			
101°			
113°			
160°			
175°			
178°			

2. Use a calculator. Complete the second column. Write each ratio to 4 decimal places.

3. Write down pairs of ∠A that have the same value for sin A. How are the angles related?

4. Complete the third column. What do you notice about the values of cos A for the pairs of angles you identified in exercise 3?

5. Complete the fourth column. What do you notice about the values of tan A for the pairs of angles you identified in exercise 3?

6. For each of sine, cosine, and tangent, describe the relationship between the trigonometric ratios of the related angles. Verify your results using several different pairs of angles.

Recall that two angles are supplementary if their sum is 180°. In *Investigation 1*, you discovered the relationship between a trigonometric ratio of any acute angle and the same trigonometric ratio of its supplement. Here is a summary of the results.

TAKE NOTE

Trigonometric Ratios of Obtuse Angles

Given an acute angle, A, and its supplementary obtuse angle, $(180° - A)$:

$\sin A = \sin(180° - A)$ The sine of an obtuse angle is positive.
$\cos A = -\cos(180° - A)$ The cosine of an obtuse angle is negative.
$\tan A = -\tan(180° - A)$ The tangent of an obtuse angle is negative.

That is, the sine of an obtuse angle equals the sine of its supplementary acute angle, but the cosine or tangent of an obtuse angle is the opposite of the cosine or tangent of its supplementary acute angle.

We can apply these results to any obtuse angle.
For example, $\sin 150° = \sin 30°$
$\cos 150° = -\cos 30°$
$\tan 150° = -\tan 30°$

This means that when the sine of an angle is positive, the angle could be acute or obtuse.

Example

Angle A is between 0° and 180°. In each case, state whether $\angle A$ is acute or obtuse, or whether two possible angles exist. Then determine the measure(s) of $\angle A$ to the nearest degree.

a) $\cos A = -\dfrac{5}{8}$ **b)** $\sin A = \dfrac{3}{4}$

Solution

a) $\cos A = -\dfrac{5}{8}$

The cosine of $\angle A$ is negative, so $\angle A$ is obtuse.

Press: [2nd] [COS] [(-)] 5 [÷] 8 [ )] [ENTER]

```
cos⁻¹( -5/8)
         128.6821875
■
```

Angle A is approximately 129°.

b) $\sin A = \frac{3}{4}$

The sine of $\angle A$ is positive. There are two measures of $\angle A$ for which $\sin A = \frac{3}{4}$, one acute, the other obtuse.

Press: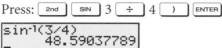

```
sin⁻¹(3/4)
         48.59037789
■
```

$A \doteq 49°$

Recall, $\sin A = \sin (180° - A)$

$\angle A \doteq 49°$ or $\angle A \doteq 180° - 49°$
$\doteq 131°$

Angle A is approximately 49° or 131°.

TAKE NOTE

The Sine of an Obtuse Angle

When A is between 0° and 180°, there are two measures of $\angle A$ for every value of sin A.

To determine these values:

- Use ⟨2nd⟩ ⟨SIN⟩ to find the measure of acute $\angle A$.
- Subtract the measure of acute $\angle A$ from 180° to find the measure of obtuse $\angle A$.

A

1. Calculate the sine, cosine, and tangent of each angle to 4 decimal places.

  a) 6°   **b)** 9°   **c)** 81°

  d) 24°   **e)** 53°   **f)** 47°

  g) 174°   **h)** 151°   **i)** 99°

  j) 156°   **k)** 127°   **l)** 133°

2. Predict whether each value will be positive or negative. Use a scientific calculator to verify your prediction.

  a) $\cos 45°$ **b)** $\tan 115°$ **c)** $\sin 93°$

  d) $\tan 64°$ **e)** $\sin 175°$ **f)** $\cos 122°$

  g) $\sin 89°$ **h)** $\tan 98°$ **i)** $\cos 143°$

3. Refer to exercise 2. Explain how you can predict which values will be negative.

B

4. Knowledge/Understanding

  a) Calculate the sine of each $\angle A$ to 4 decimal places.

  i) $\angle A = 49°$ **ii)** $\angle A = 27°$ **iii)** $\angle A = 53°$

  iv) $\angle A = 88°$ **v)** $\angle A = 144°$ **vi)** $\angle A = 98°$

  b) For each $\angle A$ from part a, determine the measure of $\angle B$ so that $\sin B = \sin A$.

5. Angle B is between 0° and 180°, and $\cos B = -\frac{3}{8}$.

  a) How many values of $\angle B$ are there?

  b) Is $\angle B$ acute or obtuse? Explain.

  c) Calculate the measure of $\angle B$.

6. Angle Z is between 0° and 180°, and $\cos Z = \frac{4}{7}$.

  a) How many values of $\angle Z$ are there?

  b) Is $\angle Z$ acute or obtuse? Explain.

  c) Calculate the measure of $\angle Z$.

7. Angle A is between 0° and 180°, and $\sin A = \frac{4}{9}$.

  a) How many values of $\angle A$ are there?

  b) Determine the measure(s) of $\angle A$ to the nearest degree.

8. Each $\angle A$ is between $0°$ and $180°$. Find the possible values of $\angle A$.

   a) $\sin A = \frac{1}{2}$ **b)** $\cos A = \frac{4}{5}$ **c)** $\cos A = -\frac{2}{3}$

   d) $\sin A = 0.4770$ **e)** $\cos A = -0.5843$ **f)** $\sin A = 0.0021$

9. Communication Refer to exercise 8. Explain why some trigonometric ratios give two values for $\angle A$ while others give only one value for $\angle A$.

10. Angle C is between $0°$ and $180°$. Determine all possible values of $\angle C$ when:

   a) $\tan C = \frac{1}{3}$ **b)** $\cos C = -0.5$ **c)** $\sin C = \frac{2}{3}$

11. Application Angle A is obtuse.

   a) $\sin A = \frac{5}{13}$; calculate $\cos A$ to 3 decimal places.

   b) $\cos A = -0.825$; calculate $\sin A$ to 3 decimal places.

12. Thinking/Inquiry/Problem Solving

   a) Determine the sine and cosine of each angle to 4 decimal places.

        i) $40°$ **ii)** $22°$ **iii)** $39°$

        iv) $68°$ **v)** $50°$ **vi)** $1°$

        vii) $51°$ **viii)** $89°$

   b) Identify pairs of angles such that the sine of one is equal to the cosine of the other. How are the angles related?

   c) Use part b to make a conjecture about trigonometric ratios of angles. Verify your conjecture for some different angles.

A radar station is tracking two ships. At noon, the ships are 5 km and 8 km away from the radar station. The angle between the lines of sight to the ships is 70°. How far apart are the ships at noon?

We draw a diagram
to represent the
situation.

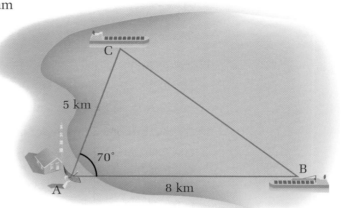

We are given the measures of two sides, AB and AC, and ∠A, their *included angle.* When we substitute values into the Sine Law to calculate *a*, we get these ratios:

$$\frac{a}{\sin 70°} = \frac{5}{\sin B} = \frac{8}{\sin C}$$

No matter which pair of ratios we choose to work with, there are always two unknown measures. So, the Sine Law cannot be used to solve this problem.

There is another law, called the Cosine Law, that we can use to calculate measures in triangles.

TAKE NOTE

The Cosine Law

In any △ABC:

$$a^2 = b^2 + c^2 - 2bc \cos A$$
$$b^2 = a^2 + c^2 - 2ac \cos B$$
$$c^2 = a^2 + b^2 - 2ab \cos C$$

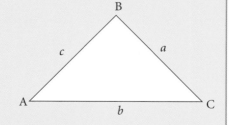

To use the Cosine Law, we must know:

- the measures of two sides and their included angle, or
- the measures of all three sides.

Discuss

Describe the patterns you can see in the equations of the Cosine Law.
How can you use these patterns to help remember the formulas?

Return to the opening situation.

In $\triangle ABC$, we know the measures of sides b and c, and $\angle A$. To calculate a, use the Cosine Law.

$a^2 = b^2 + c^2 - 2bc \cos A$ Substitute the values.

$a^2 = 5^2 + 8^2 - 2(5)(8) \cos 70°$ Use a calculator.

Press: 5 $\boxed{x^2}$ $\boxed{+}$ 8 $\boxed{x^2}$ $\boxed{-}$ 2 $\boxed{\times}$ 5 $\boxed{\times}$ 8 $\boxed{\cos}$ 70 $\boxed{)}$ $\boxed{\text{ENTER}}$

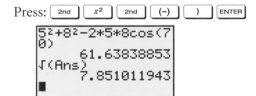

$a^2 \doteq 61.638\ 388\ 53$ Do not clear the screen.

$a \doteq \sqrt{61.638\ 388\ 53}$

Press: $\boxed{\text{2nd}}$ $\boxed{x^2}$ $\boxed{\text{2nd}}$ $\boxed{(-)}$ $\boxed{)}$ $\boxed{\text{ENTER}}$

```
5²+8²-2*5*8cos(7
0)
        61.63838853
√(Ans)
        7.851011943
■
```

The given measures have 1 significant digit, so round to 1 significant digit.

$a \doteq 8$

The ships are approximately 8 km apart at noon.

Discuss

An alternative key sequence to determine the measure of a is $\boxed{\text{2nd}}$ $\boxed{x^2}$ $\boxed{(}$
5 $\boxed{x^2}$ $\boxed{+}$ 8 $\boxed{x^2}$ $\boxed{-}$ 2 $\boxed{\times}$ 8 $\boxed{\times}$ 5 $\boxed{\cos}$ 70 $\boxed{)}$ $\boxed{)}$ $\boxed{\text{ENTER}}$. Which sequence do you prefer? Explain.

Sometimes we know the lengths of all three sides of a triangle, and we need to determine the measure of an angle.

Recall, the cosine of an acute angle is positive, and the cosine of an obtuse angle is negative.

Example

In △ABC, $a = 7.2$ cm, $b = 3.6$ cm, and $c = 5.0$ cm. Determine the measure of ∠A to the nearest degree.

Solution

Draw a diagram.

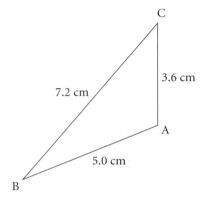

Use the Cosine Law. Choose the formula that uses cos A.

$$a^2 = b^2 + c^2 - 2bc \cos A \qquad \text{Substitute the values.}$$
$$7.2^2 = 3.6^2 + 5.0^2 - 2(3.6)(5.0)\cos A \qquad \text{Evaluate the powers.}$$
$$51.84 = 12.96 + 25 - 36 \cos A$$
$$51.84 = 37.96 - 36 \cos A \qquad \text{Subtract 37.96 from}$$
$$51.84 - 37.96 = -36 \cos A \qquad \text{each side.}$$
$$13.88 = -36 \cos A \qquad \text{Divide each side by } -36.$$
$$\frac{13.88}{-36} = \cos A \qquad \text{Use a calculator.}$$

Press: [2nd] [COS] 13.88 [÷] [(-)] 36 [)] [ENTER]

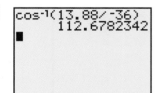

The measure of ∠A is approximately 113°.

Discuss

How could you solve the equation obtained by substituting the values more efficiently?

Discuss

Describe how to decide which equation of the Cosine Law to use.

A

1. Given each expression for side b, calculate its measure.

a) $b^2 = 9^2 + 3^2 - 2(9)(3)\cos 23°$

b) $b^2 = 62^2 + 56^2 - 2(62)(56)\cos 37°$

c) $b^2 = 16.1^2 + 20.3^2 - 2(16.1)(20.3)\cos 42°$

d) $b^2 = 5.6^2 + 7.2^2 - 2(5.6)(7.2)\cos 113°$

2. Given each value of cos A, calculate the measure of $\angle A$.

a) $\cos A = \dfrac{4}{5}$ **b)** $\cos A = 0.5796$

c) $\cos A = -0.3824$ **d)** $\cos A = -0.4313$

e) $\cos A = 0.1144$ **f)** $\cos A = -0.9899$

3. Given each expression for cos C, calculate the measure of $\angle C$.

a) $\cos C = \dfrac{62^2 + 53^2 - 38^2}{2(62)(53)}$ **b)** $\cos C = \dfrac{45^2 + 32^2 - 50^2}{2(45)(32)}$

c) $\cos C = \dfrac{5^2 + 3^2 - 7^2}{2(5)(3)}$ **d)** $\cos C = \dfrac{4.1^2 + 2.6^2 - 5.5^2}{2(4.1)(2.6)}$

B

 4. Calculate the length of each side b.

a)   **b)**   **c)**

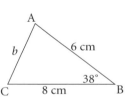 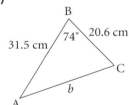 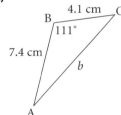

 5. Determine the measure of $\angle A$ in each triangle.

a)   **b)**   **c)**

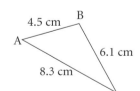 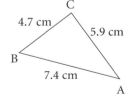 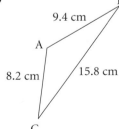

6. Knowledge/Understanding Solve each △ABC.

a)

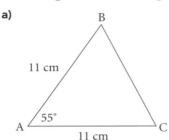

b)

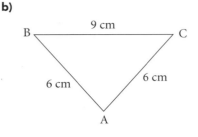

c)

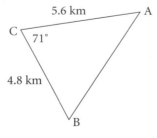

d)

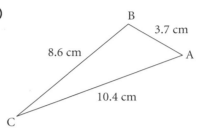

7. Solve each triangle.

a) △ABC given ∠B = 68°, c = 15.7 cm, and a = 18.4 cm

b) △DEF given ∠D = 130°, e = 9.8 cm, and f = 9.4 cm

c) △RST given ∠S = 118°, r = 8.5 cm, and t = 5.4 cm

8. Solve each triangle.

a) △KMN given k = 5.2 cm, m = 2.7 cm, and n = 6.5 cm

b) △PQR given q = 3.1 cm, r = 1.9 cm, and p = 4.7 cm

c) △XYZ given x = 9.6 cm, y = 8.2 cm, and z = 4.8 cm

9. From a point, C, on shore, an observer sees two ships at sea. Ship A is 5.6 km from the observer and ship B is 4.8 km from the observer. The angle between the sight lines to the ships is 71° (below left). Determine the distance between the ships.

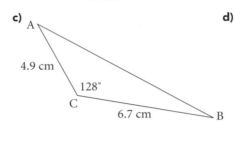

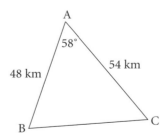

10. Two straight roads intersect in town A at an angle of 58°. The distance from town A to town B is 48 km. The distance from town A to town C is 54 km (above right). A straight road, connecting town B to town C, is under construction. Determine the length of the new road.

11. Application To determine the length of a small lake, a surveyor takes measurements. From a point, C, the distances to points A and B at the ends of the lake are 854 m and 788 m. The angle between the lines of sight to the two points is 107°. Determine the length of the lake.

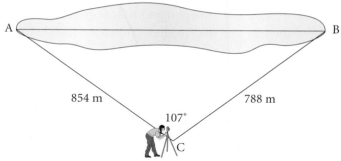

12. A hockey net is 1.8 m wide. A player is 6.0 m from one goalpost and 6.7 m from the other. Within what angle must she keep her shot in order to score a goal?

13. A lighthouse is located at point A. A ship travels from point B to point C. At point B, the distance between the ship and the lighthouse is 7.5 km. At point C, the distance between the ship and the lighthouse is 8.6 km. Angle BAC is 58°. Determine the distance between B and C.

14. Communication Do the Sine Law and the Cosine Law apply to right triangles? Include examples in your explanation.

15. In the Canadian Football League, the distance from one upright to the other upright on the goalposts is 6.16 yards. A field goal kicker kicks from a point 41 yd. from one upright and 41.5 yd. from the other. Within what angle must he kick the football in order to make the field goal?

16. Thinking/Inquiry/Problem Solving
In quadrilateral ABCD, AB = 2.96 cm, BC = 3.75 cm, CD = 3.49 cm, AD = 3.06 cm, and ∠B = 121.1°. Calculate the measure of ∠D.

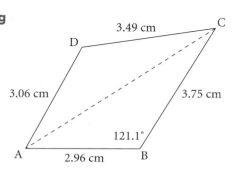

In an earlier grade, you learned how to solve a right triangle using the Pythagorean Theorem and trigonometric ratios. Now you may also use the Sine Law and the Cosine Law in any triangle to calculate the lengths of sides and the measures of angles. You must look at the information given, then choose the appropriate method.

Example 1 Calculate the length AC in each triangle.

a)

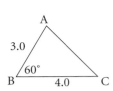

b)

c)

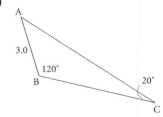

Solution

a) △ABC is not a right triangle. We have information about the lengths, a and c, and the measure of included ∠B. Use the Cosine Law in △ABC to calculate the length b.

Use the formula $b^2 = a^2 + c^2 - 2ac \cos B$.   Substitute the values.
$$b^2 = 4^2 + 3^2 - 2(4)(3) \cos 60°$$ Use a calculator.
$$b^2 = 13$$
$$b = \sqrt{13}$$
$$\doteq 3.6$$

AC is approximately 3.6 cm.

b) △ABC is a right triangle. We have information about the length of c, and the measure of ∠C and ∠B. Use the sine ratio to calculate the length b.

$$\sin 30° = \frac{3}{b}$$

$$b \sin 30° = 3$$ Multiply each side by b.

$$b = \frac{3}{\sin 30°}$$ Divide each side by $\sin 30°$.

$$= 6$$ Use a calculator.

AC is 6 cm.

c) $\triangle ABC$ is not a right triangle. We have information about the length, c, and the measures of $\angle B$ and $\angle C$. Since we know the length of one side and the measure of its opposite angle, we can use the Sine Law to determine b.

Choose the proportion that uses the information given and the length of the unknown side.

$$\frac{b}{\sin B} = \frac{c}{\sin C}$$

Substitute the values.

$$\frac{b}{\sin 120°} = \frac{3.0}{\sin 20°}$$

Multiply each side by sin 120°.

$$b = \frac{3.0 \sin 120°}{\sin 20°}$$

Use a calculator.

$$\doteq 7.6$$

AC is approximately 7.6 cm.

In navigation, direction is often represented using a bearing. This is the angle between the north line and the direction, measured in a clockwise direction and expressed using 3 digits. The bearings 215° and 025° are shown below.

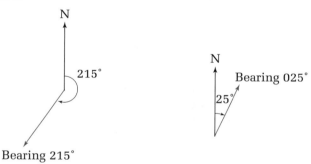

Bearing 215°

Bearing 025°

Sailors can use trigonometry to calculate distances at sea.

Example 2

A boat is proceeding on a bearing of 045° at 12 kn (nautical miles per hour). At 3:00 p.m. the captain sights a navigation buoy at 020°. He sights the same buoy at 230° at 4:15 p.m. How far (in nautical miles) is the boat from the buoy at 4:15 p.m.?

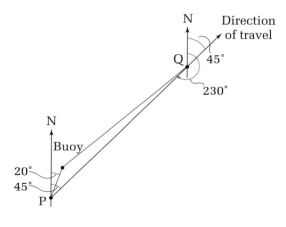

Solution

Draw $\triangle PBQ$ to represent the boat at P at 3:00 p.m., at Q at 4:15 p.m., and the buoy at B.

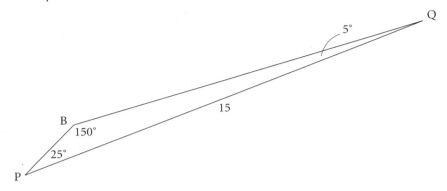

From the information given, $\angle P = 45° - 20°$, or $25°$.

The boat takes 1 h 15 min, or 1.25 h, to travel from P to Q.

So, $PQ = 1.25 \times 12$, or 15

The direction of travel of the boat makes an angle of 45° with the north-south direction, so $\angle Q = 230° - 180° - 45°$, or $5°$.

Using the angle sum property, $\angle B = 180° - 25° - 5°$, or $150°$.
We also know length b, so we know one angle and the length of its opposite side. Use the Sine Law to calculate length p.

$$\frac{b}{\sin B} = \frac{p}{\sin P}$$ Substitute the values.

$$\frac{15}{\sin 150°} = \frac{p}{\sin 25°}$$ Multiply each side by $\sin 25°$.

$$\frac{15 \sin 25°}{\sin 150°} = p$$ Use a calculator.

$$p \doteq 12.678\ 547\ 85$$

The original data have 2 significant digits, so round p to 2 significant digits.

$$p \doteq 13$$

The boat is approximately 13 nautical miles from the buoy at 4:15 p.m.

Discuss

Describe how you would calculate the distance between the boat and the buoy at 3:00 p.m.

A

✓ **1.** Calculate length c in each triangle.

a)

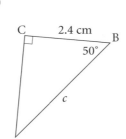

b)

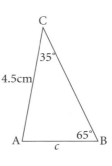

c)

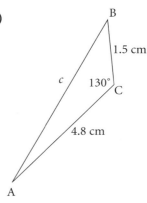

B

✓ **2.** Calculate the measure of $\angle C$ in each triangle.

a)

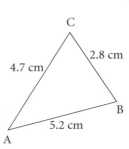

b)

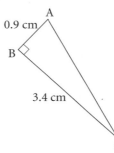

c)

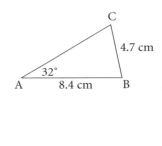

✓ **3. Knowledge/Understanding** Solve each triangle.

    a) $\triangle ABC$ given $\angle A = 42°$, $\angle C = 34°$, and $c = 12.0$ cm

    b) $\triangle PQR$ given $\angle R = 112°$, $p = 31.2$ cm, and $r = 45.0$ cm

    c) $\triangle ABC$ given $\angle A = 78°$, $\angle B = 90°$, and $a = 5.9$ cm

✓ **4. Communication** Choose one part of exercise 3. Describe your strategy for solving the triangle.

✓ **5.** Two ships leave port at the same time. One sails at 17 km/h on a bearing of 25°. The other ship sails at 21 km/h on a bearing of 43°. How far apart are the ships after 2 h?

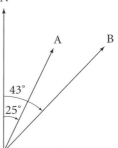

6. The longer sides of a triangular park measure 251.0 m and 208.2 m, respectively. The angle between the longest and shortest side is 56.0°.

   a) What is the angle between the shorter two sides of the park?

   b) How long is the shortest side?

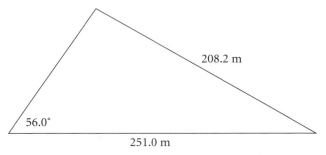

7. A surveyor's assistant stands on horizontal ground 34 m from the base of a building. She measures the angle of elevation to the top of the building to be 37°. Her eye level is 1.5 m. Calculate the height of the building.

8. **Application** A tower is supported by two guy wires, both attached to the ground on the same side of the tower. The angle of inclination of the first guy wire is 42° and the angle of inclination of the second guy wire, 1.5 m away, is 28° (below left).

   a) What is the measure of ∠ABC?

   b) Determine the length of each guy wire.

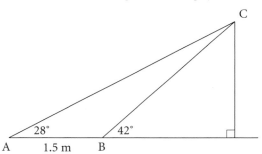

9. Three towns, A, B, and C, are joined by three straight roads. The road between towns A and C is 140 km long and makes an angle of 30° with the road between towns A and B, and an angle of 18° with the road between towns C and B.

   a) Without doing any calculations, predict which pair of towns is closest together.

   b) Verify your prediction by calculation.

10. Thinking/Inquiry/Problem Solving Angle parking allows more cars to park along a street than does parallel parking. However, the cars use more of the street width when angle parked.

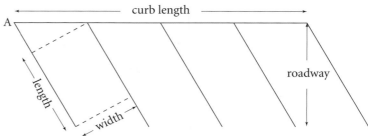

a) Each car requires a space 2.7 m wide. Determine the curb length required to park 20 cars when $\angle A = 50°$.

b) Suppose 20 cars had to be parked in 60 m of curb length. Determine the measure of $\angle A$.

c) Each car requires a space 6.5 m long. Determine the width of roadway used for parking when $\angle A = 50°$.

C

11. The pilot of an airplane encounters a group of thundershowers. To detour around these, she turns at an angle of 21° to the original path, then flies for a while. She turns the airplane again to intercept her original path at an angle of 35°, 70 km from where she left it. How much further did she travel because of the detour?

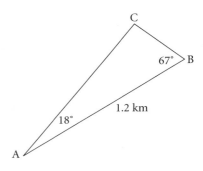

12. Two cabins, A and B, are located 1.2 km apart on the same side of a river. A boat launch is located across the river at C. Angles A and B are 18° and 67° respectively.

a) Determine the distance of each cabin from the boat launch.

b) Calculate the width of the river.

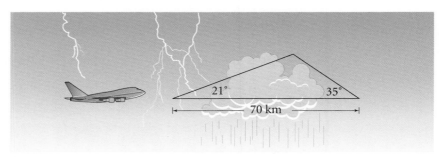

1.7 — Selecting a Strategy

To solve some problems, you may have to use a combination of the Sine Law, the Cosine Law, and right triangle trigonometry.

Example 1

Solve $\triangle MNP$ given $\angle N = 82°$, $p = 6.4$ cm, and $m = 7.9$ cm.

Solution

We need to determine $\angle M$, $\angle P$, and n.
Draw a diagram.

We know the lengths of two sides and the measure of the included angle.
Use the Cosine Law to determine n.

$n^2 = m^2 + p^2 - 2mp \cos N$ Substitute the values.
$n^2 = 7.9^2 + 6.4^2 - 2(7.9)(6.4) \cos 82°$ Use a calculator.
$n \doteq 9.449\ 699\ 256$

The length of side n is approximately 9.4 cm.

Use the Sine Law to calculate $\angle P$.

$\dfrac{\sin P}{p} = \dfrac{\sin N}{n}$ Substitute the values.

$\dfrac{\sin P}{6.4} = \dfrac{\sin 82°}{9.4}$ Multiply both sides by 6.4.

$\sin P = \dfrac{6.4 \sin 82°}{9.4}$ Use a calculator.

$\doteq 0.674\ 225\ 068$ Press: 2nd SIN 2nd (–)) ENTER

$\angle P \doteq 42.394\ 001\ 17°$
$\angle P$ is approximately 42°.

Use the sum of the angles of a triangle to determine $\angle M$.
$82° + 42° + \angle M \doteq 180°$
$124° + \angle M \doteq 180°$
$\angle M \doteq 180° - 124°$
$\doteq 56°$

Example 2

To determine the height of a cliff, a surveyor took some measurements. From a point, C, on the shore, directly across the river from point B, the angle of elevation of the top of the cliff is 41°. From a point, D, 25 m down the river from C, ∠CDB = 70°. How high is the cliff?

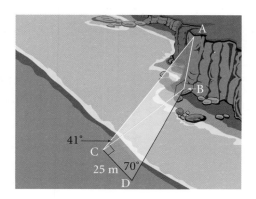

Solution

Triangles ABC and BCD are at right angles to one another.

The height of the cliff is AB. To determine this height, we need to know the length of one side of △ABC.

BC is a side of both triangles. Use right △BCD to determine the length of BC. Sketch △BCD.

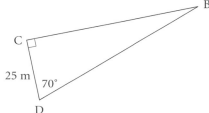

Use the tangent ratio.

$\frac{BC}{25} = \tan 70°$ Multiply both sides by 25.

$BC = 25 \tan 70°$ Use a calculator.

    $\doteq 68.686\ 935\ 49$ Do not clear the screen.

Sketch right △ABC. We know BC and ∠C.

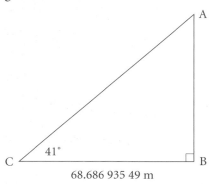

Use the tangent ratio.

$$\frac{AB}{68.686\ 935\ 49} \doteq \tan 41°$$ Multiply both sides by 68.686 935 49.

$$AB \doteq 68.686\ 935\ 49 \tan 41°$$ Press: (×) (TAN) 41 ( )) (ENTER =)

$$\doteq 59.708\ 642\ 08$$

The cliff is approximately 60 m high.

Discuss

Why is it appropriate to round the answer to 60 m?

In an earlier grade, you determined an inaccessible height. *Example 3* shows an alternate method to obtain such a height.

Example 3

Kim and Oren used a tape and a clinometer to determine the height of a tall building standing on level ground. From point A, they measured the angle of elevation of the top of the building as 31°. They walked 40 m closer to the building to point B, then measured the angle of elevation as 37°. How tall is the building?

Solution

Draw a diagram.

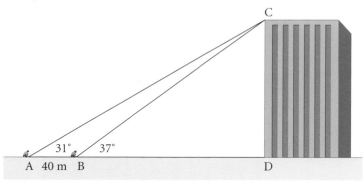

We can determine the height, CD, of the building using right △ACD or right △BCD. First, we need to determine the length AC or BC.

In obtuse △ABC, the obtuse angle at B is the supplement of 37°, so ∠B = 143°. Use the angle sum property to determine the measure of ∠C.

$$31° + 143° + ∠C = 180°$$
$$174° + ∠C = 180°$$
$$∠C = 180° - 174°$$
$$= 6°$$

Use the Sine Law to determine the length of BC in △ABC.

$$\frac{a}{\sin A} = \frac{c}{\sin C}$$ Substitute the values.

$$\frac{BC}{\sin 31°} = \frac{40}{\sin 6°}$$ Multiply both sides by $\sin 31°$.

$$BC = \frac{40 \sin 31°}{\sin 6°}$$ Use a calculator.

$$\doteq 197.090\ 078\ 2$$ Do not round.

Use the sine ratio to determine CD in right △BCD.

$$\frac{CD}{197.090\ 078\ 2} \doteq \sin 37°$$ Multiply both sides by 197.090 078 2.

$$CD \doteq 197.090\ 078\ 2 \sin 37°$$

$$\doteq 118.611\ 77$$

The building is approximately 120 m tall.

B

1. Two trees are 150 m apart. From a point halfway between the trees, Arturo measures the angles of elevation of their tops as 9° and 11°. How tall are the trees?

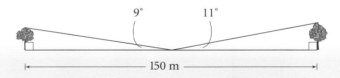

2. **Knowledge/Understanding** Two buildings are 38 m apart. From the top of the shorter building, the angle of elevation of the top of the taller building is 27° and the angle of depression of the base is 35°. Determine the height of each building.

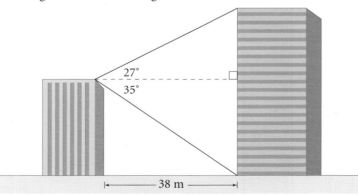

3. The area of a triangle is given by $A = \frac{1}{2} \times$ Base $\times$ Height. Determine the area of each triangle.

a)

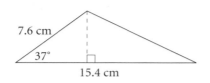

7.6 cm
37°
15.4 cm

b)

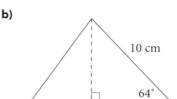

10 cm
64°
12 cm

4. Application From an observation tower that overlooks a small lake, the angles of depression of point A, on one side of the lake, and point B, on the opposite side of the lake, are 6° and 11°, respectively. The points and the tower are in the same vertical plane and the distance from A to B is 1 km. Determine the height of the tower.

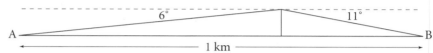

A ⟶ 6° ⟶ 11° ⟶ B
1 km

5. Two chains support a weight at the same point. The chains are attached to the ceiling and are 7.0 m and 5.6 m in length. The angle between the chains is 110°. How far apart are the chains at the ceiling?

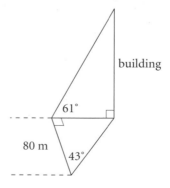

7.0 m   5.6 m
110°

6. Calculate the height of the building in the diagram below.

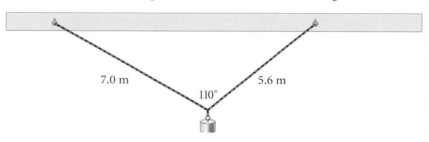

building
61°
80 m
43°

7. To calculate the height of the clouds one night, Amir and Suraya stood 3050 m apart. Amir shone a light on the clouds and Suraya measured the angle of elevation of the light reflecting from the clouds as 16°. The angle of inclination of the beam of light was 77°. What was the height of the clouds?

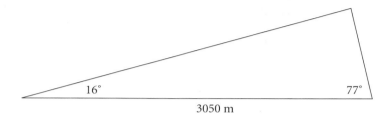

3050 m

8. David and Susan want to calculate the distance between their cottages. The cottages are on opposite sides of a lake. They mark a point, A, 100 m along the shore from Susan's cottage. They measure ∠DSA as 82° and ∠SAD as 77°. Determine the distance between their cottages.

9. The edges of a saw tooth are 1.1 cm and 0.8 cm long. The base of the tooth is 0.6 cm long. Determine the angle at which the edges meet.

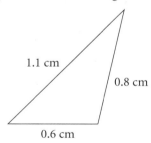

10. Communication From a certain point, the angle of elevation of the top of a tower is 31°. Another point, in the same vertical plane as the original point and the tower, is 130 m closer to the tower. From this point, the angle of elevation of the top of the tower is 38°.

a) Draw a diagram.

b) Describe how to calculate the height of the tower.

11. From the top of a lighthouse on a cliff, the angles of depression of two boats in the same vertical plane are measured as 5.4° and 3.6°. The boats are 1000 m apart. Determine the height of the top of the lighthouse above water level.

12. A children's playground is triangular. The sides of the playground measure 200 m, 250 m, and 300 m. Calculate the area of the playground.

✓ **13.** A baseball diamond is a square with sides 27.4 m. The pitcher's mound is 18.4 m from home plate on the line joining home plate and second base. How far is the pitcher's mound from first base?

✓ **14. Thinking/Inquiry/Problem Solving** A tunnel is to be constructed to join two towns at opposite sides of a mountain. To determine the cost of the project, the exact distance through the mountain must be found. Explain how to use trigonometry to calculate this distance.

C

15. Determine the area of △ABC in terms of b, c, and sin A.

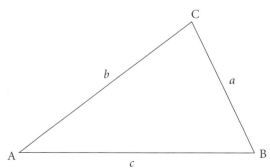

Self-Check 1.4–1.7

1. Angle A is between 0° and 180° and sin A = 0.9544. Determine the measure(s) of ∠A.

2. Determine the length of side *d* in each triangle.

   a)

   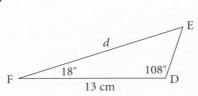

   b)

   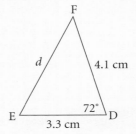

3. Determine the measure of ∠A in each triangle.

   a)

   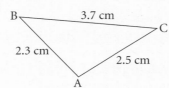

   b)

   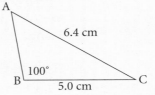

4. A wire runs from the top of a post, P, to the ground where it passes through an anchor. Then it is attached to the top of another post, Q. The angles of inclination of the wires are 39° and 28°. The length of the wire from post P to the anchor is 4.8 m, and from the anchor to post Q is 6.4 m. Calculate the distance between the posts.

   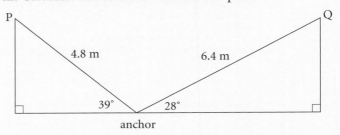

5. An oil pipeline is constructed around an obstacle. Two straight sections of pipeline, one 4.28 km long and the other 3.44 km long, are joined so the angle between them is 159°. How much more pipe will be used as a result of the obstacle?

In this chapter, you've solved many problems starting with just three measurements for a specific triangle. Do three specific triangle measurements always give you enough information to construct a single triangle? Or is it possible to construct different triangles with the same three measures?

In *Investigation 1*, you will examine the number of different triangles you can construct for given sets of information. Then, you will relate the results to your chapter work with the Sine Law.

Investigation 1 Determining the Number of Possible Triangles

Work with a partner. You will each need a protractor, compasses, and a metric ruler.

For each part of the *Investigation*, complete exercise 1 independently. Compare your results with your partner before proceeding to exercise 2.

Part A: Given the Lengths of Three Sides

1. Construct △ABC given AB = 4.5 cm, BC = 5.0 cm, and AC = 4.0 cm.

• Draw a line segment 4.5 cm long. Label its endpoints A and B.

• Set the compass to a width of 5.0 cm. Put the compass point on B and draw an arc.

• Set your compass to a width of 4.0 cm. Put the compass point on A and draw an arc that intersects the first arc. Label the point of intersection C.

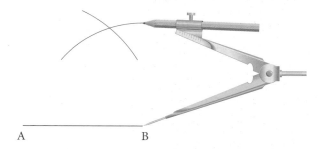

• Draw line segments BC and AC.

2. Compare your result for exercise 1 with your partner. You may find your triangles are identical in orientation, as well as size and shape. However, even if you constructed your triangles on opposite sides of line segment AB, you haven't really drawn "different" triangles. Discuss with your partner, and record what you think it means for two triangles to be different.

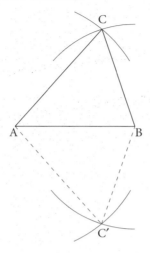

3. Repeat the process of exercise 1 to construct each triangle. Then repeat exercise 2.

a) △XYZ given XY = 2.5 cm, YZ = 4.5 cm, and XZ = 6.5 cm

b) △KLM given KL = 5.0 cm, LM = 3.0 cm, and KM = 3.0 cm

4. Is it possible to construct △DEF given DE = 2.0 cm, EF = 4.0 cm, and DF = 8.0 cm? Explain.

5. Write a statement about the number of triangles you can construct if you know the lengths of all three sides.

Part B: Given Two Sides and the Angle Between Them

1. Construct △RST given RS = 3.0 cm, ∠S = 48°, and ST = 4.0 cm.

- Draw a line segment 3.0 cm long. Label its endpoints R and S.
- Use your protractor to measure a 48° angle with vertex at S. Make the arm of the angle quite long. Label the endpoint of the arm Q.
- Set the compass to a width of 4.0 cm. Put the compass point on S and draw an arc that intersects SQ. Label the point of intersection T.
- Draw line segment TR.

2. In exercise 1, how many different triangles was it possible to construct? Explain.

3. Repeat the process of exercise 1 to construct each triangle. Then repeat exercise 2.
   a) △LMN given LM = 3.5 cm, ∠M = 105°, and MN = 4.5 cm
   b) △DEF given EF = 4.0 cm, ∠F = 25°, and DF = 6.0 cm

4. Write a statement about the number of triangles possible if you know the lengths of two sides and the measure of the angle between them.

Part C: Given One Side and Two Angles

1. Construct △ABC given ∠B = 68°, BC = 4.0 cm, and ∠C = 49°.
   - Draw line segment BC 4.0 cm long.
   - Use your protractor to draw a 68° angle with vertex at B.
   - Use your protractor to draw a 49° angle with vertex at C.
   - Label the point of intersection of the arms of the 68° and 49° angles A.
   - Draw line segments BA and CA.

2. In exercise 1, how many different triangles was it possible to construct? Explain.

3. Repeat the process in exercise 1 to construct each triangle. Then repeat exercise 2.
   a) △KLM given ∠L = 130°, LM = 6.0 cm, and ∠M = 20°
   b) △XYZ given ∠Y = 25°, YZ = 4.5 cm, and ∠Z = 112°

4. Is it possible to construct △PQR given ∠Q = 110°, QR = 5.0 cm, and ∠R = 95°? Explain.

5. Write a statement about the number of triangles that are possible if you know the length of one side and the measure of two angles.

Part D: Given Two Sides and One Angle not Formed by Those Two Sides

1. Construct △ABC given ∠B = 51°, AB = 5.5 cm, and AC = 4.5 cm.
- Draw line segment AB 5.5 cm long.
- Use your protractor to draw a 51° angle with vertex at B. Make the arm of the angle quite long. Label the endpoint of the arm Q.
- Set the compass to a width of 4.5 cm. Put the compass point on A. Draw an arc that intersects BQ. How many points of intersection are possible? Label the point(s) of intersection C.
- Draw the line segment(s) AC.

2. In exercise 1, how many different triangles was it possible to construct? Explain.

3. Repeat the process in exercise 1 to construct each triangle, then repeat exercise 2.
a) △PQR given ∠Q = 35°, QP = 6.0 cm, and PR = 3.6 cm
b) △RST given ∠S = 48°, SR = 4.0 cm, and RT = 5.5 cm

4. In exercise 1, you should have found that two triangles were possible. Use your protractor to measure ∠C in each triangle. Determine the sum of these angles.

5. In exercise 3a, two triangles were possible. Use your protractor to measure ∠R in each triangle. Determine the sum of these angles. How does this answer compare to your answer to exercise 4?

6. Is it possible to construct △XYZ given ∠Y = 47°, XY = 5.0 cm, and XZ = 3.3 cm? Explain.

7. Write a statement about the number of possible triangles if you know the lengths of two sides and the measure of one angle not formed by those two sides.

The Ambiguous Case and The Sine Law

The word "ambiguous" means "more than one meaning." In *Part D* of *Investigation 1*, △ABC is ambiguous because we can draw two different triangles with the given measurements.

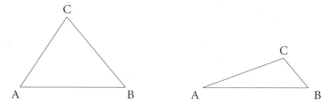

In both triangles, ∠B = 51°, AB = 5.5 cm, and AC = 4.5 cm

When we know the lengths of two sides and the measure of a non-included angle of a triangle and we are asked to solve the triangle, we must check for the ambiguous case. If two triangles are possible, we must solve both of them.

Example 1 Solve △ABC in which ∠B = 40°, b = 4 cm, and c = 6 cm.

Solution

Draw a sketch.

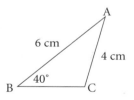   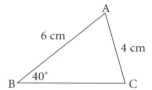

Use the Sine Law to determine the measure of $\angle C$:

$\dfrac{\sin C}{6} = \dfrac{\sin 40°}{4}$ Multiply both sides by 6.

$\sin C = \dfrac{6\sin 40°}{4}$ Use a calculator; do not clear the screen.

$\sin C \doteq 0.964\ 181\ 415$ Press: [2nd] [SIN] [2nd] [(–)] [ )] [ENTER =]

$\angle C \doteq 74.6°$

The sines of supplementary angles are equal, so $\angle C$ could also be $180° - 74.6° \doteq 105.4°$.

We must solve the triangle for both measures of $\angle C$.

For acute $\triangle ABC$ with $\angle C \doteq 74.6°$:	**For obtuse $\triangle ABC$ with $\angle C \doteq 105.4°$:**
Use the angle sum property to determine the measure of $\angle A$.	Use the angle sum property to determine the measure of $\angle A$.
$40° + 74.6° + \angle A \doteq 180°$	$40° + 105.4° + \angle A \doteq 180°$
$114.6° + \angle A \doteq 180°$	$145.4° + \angle A \doteq 180°$
$\angle A \doteq 180° - 114.6°$	$\angle A \doteq 180° - 145.4°$
$\doteq 65.4°$	$\doteq 34.6°$
Use the Sine Law to determine the measure of side a.	Use the Sine Law to determine the measure of side a.
$\dfrac{a}{\sin 65.4°} = \dfrac{4}{\sin 40°}$	$\dfrac{a}{\sin 34.6°} = \dfrac{4}{\sin 40°}$
$a = \dfrac{4\sin 65.4°}{\sin 40°}$	$a = \dfrac{4\sin 34.6°}{\sin 40°}$
$\doteq 5.658\ 081\ 116$	$\doteq 3.533\ 632\ 176$

In acute $\triangle ABC$, $\angle C$ and $\angle A$ are approximately 74.6° and 65.4° and a is approximately 5.7 cm. In obtuse $\triangle ABC$, $\angle C$ and $\angle A$ are approximately 105.4° and 34.6° respectively and a is approximately 3.5 cm.

1. In $\triangle KLM$, $\angle M = 33°$, $k = 7$ cm, and $m = 5$ cm.
Draw two different triangles, then calculate the measure of $\angle K$.

2. In $\triangle ABC$, $\angle A = 38°$, $a = 6.4$ cm, and $c = 7.8$ cm.
Determine two possible measures for $\angle C$ and side b.

3. Solve $\triangle KMN$ given $\angle K = 28°$, $n = 3.2$ cm, and $k = 2.4$ cm.

Trigonometry and the Ambiguous Case

In *Part D* of *Investigation 1*, you should have found that when you are given information about the lengths of two sides and the measure of one non-included angle (SSA) there may be one triangle, two triangles, or no triangle. We can use trigonometry to determine the conditions for each case.

 Investigation 2 | ### Determining the Conditions for the Ambiguous Case

Suppose we wish to determine the length(s) of AC in △ABC, AB = 5 cm, and ∠B = 30°, in each case.

    i) One triangle exists

    ii) No triangle exists

    iii) Two triangles exist

1. If ∠C = 90°, one triangle will result. Use the sine ratio to determine the value of AC if △ABC is right angled at C. Draw the triangle.

2. For what lengths of AC will there be no possible triangle? Explain with the aid of a diagram.

3. Use the cosine ratio to determine the length of BC in right △ABC.

4. For what lengths of AC will two triangles result? Explain with the aid of a diagram.

5. For what lengths of AC will one non-right triangle result? Explain with the aid of a diagram.

6. Repeat exercises 1 to 5, using △XYZ with ∠Y = 45° and XY = 6 cm.

7. Write a report to explain the conditions that are necessary for each case — one triangle, two triangles, and no triangle — when given information about the lengths of two sides and one non-included angle for a triangle.

Survey Technician

Anna has always been interested in geography. She enjoys the outdoors, but also likes the challenge of precision work. She decided to train as a survey technician at a community college.

Job Description

Survey technicians perform some or all of these duties:

- Assist surveyors by conducting a general or comprehensive study of the land.
- Use a variety of tools to measure features of Earth such as longitude, latitude, angles, and contours.
- Accurately record measurements and enter data into computers.
- Assist in the preparation of drawings, charts, and reports based on surveys.

Working Conditions

- Regular work hours
- Work in both the field and the office
- Physically demanding work
- Jobs with government agencies, mining companies, construction and engineering firms

Qualifications and Training

- High school diploma
- Successful completion of a survey technician program at community college
- Computer skills a must
- Ability to do precise measurements
- Good communication skills

Where's the Math?

Survey technicians use trigonometry to measure and analyse features of Earth's surface, such as angles and contours. They may also measure and map underwater and underground areas, plot collected data to scale, and carry out calculations using measurements made with surveying instruments.

Review Exercises

MATHEMATICS TOOLKIT

Trigonometry Tools

Trigonometric Ratios of Acute Angles

$$\sin A = \frac{\text{Length of side opposite } \angle A}{\text{Length of hypotenuse}}$$

$$\cos A = \frac{\text{Length of side adjacent to } \angle A}{\text{Length of hypotenuse}}$$

$$\tan A = \frac{\text{Length of side opposite } \angle A}{\text{Length of side adjacent to } \angle A}$$

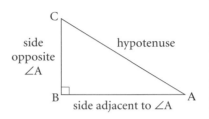

Trigonometric Ratios of Angles between 0° and 180°

> For any acute angle A:

$$\sin A = \sin (180° - A)$$
$$\cos A = -\cos (180° - A)$$
$$\tan A = -\tan (180° - A)$$

The Sine Law

> In any $\triangle ABC$:

$$\frac{a}{\sin A} = \frac{b}{\sin B} = \frac{c}{\sin C}$$

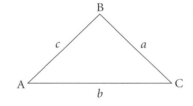

The Cosine Law

> In any $\triangle ABC$:

$$a^2 = b^2 + c^2 - 2bc \cos A$$
$$b^2 = a^2 + c^2 - 2ac \cos B$$
$$c^2 = a^2 + b^2 - 2ab \cos C$$

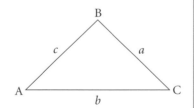

1.1   **1.** Determine length of each side x.

a)

b)

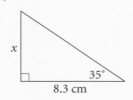

c)

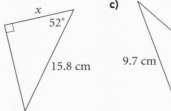

2. A guy wire is anchored to the ground 18 m from the base of a tower. The guy wire makes an angle of 71° with the ground. How high up the tower is the guy wire attached?

1.2 **3.** Determine the measure of each ∠C to the nearest degree.

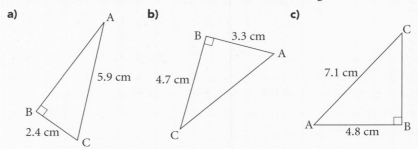

a)

b)

c)

4. A ramp rises vertically 1.5 m for every 10.0 m of horizontal distance. Determine the angle of inclination of the ramp.

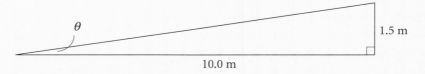

1.3 **5.** Determine the length of each side *x*.

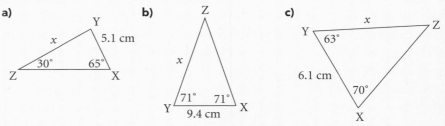

a)

b)

c)

6. Determine the measure of each ∠Z to the nearest degree.

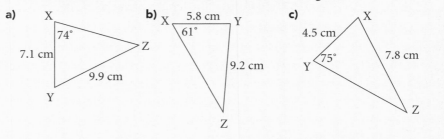

a)

b)

c)

7. At a certain time, the angles of elevation of an airplane, measured from two tracking stations, A and B, 5.8 km apart, are 47° and 53°. Determine the distance between the airplane and tracking station B. (Assume the tracking stations and the airplane are in the same vertical plane.)

1.4 **8. a)** Determine the sine, cosine, and tangent of each ∠A.

    i) ∠A = 55°   **ii)** ∠A = 133°   **iii)** ∠A = 79°

    b) For each ∠A from part a, determine the measure of ∠B so that sin B = sin A.

9. Angle M is between 0° and 180° and sin M = 0.4432. Determine the measures of ∠M.

1.5 **10.** Determine each indicated measure.

a)   **b)**   **c)**

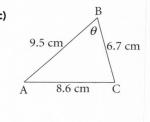

11. Solve each triangle.

    a) △ABC given ∠B = 61°, ∠C = 47°, and b = 7.2 cm

    b) △PQR given ∠Q = 108°, p = 4.7 cm, and r = 6.8 cm

    c) △XYZ given x = 7.3 cm, y = 9.4 cm, and z = 5.1 cm

    d) △RST given ∠T = 29°, r = 6.2 cm, and t = 4.8 cm

12. From a point on shore, an observer sees two ships at sea. Ship A is 4.9 km from the observer and ship B is 7.3 km from the observer. The angle between the lines of sight to the ships is 67°. Determine the distance between the ships.

1.6 **13.** Determine the length of each side a.

a)   **b)**   **c)**

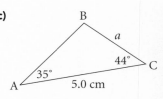

14. A farmer has a triangular field. From one corner of the field, it is 435 m to the second corner and 656 m to the third corner. The angle between the lines of sight to the second and third corners is 49°. Calculate the perimeter of the field to the nearest metre.

15. From the top of a building 70 m high, the angle of depression of a car on a road is 27°. How far is the car from the foot of the building?

16. A sailboat leaves a port on a bearing of 025°. After sailing for 1.5 km, the boat turns and sails on a bearing of 165° for 1.7 km. How far is the boat from port?

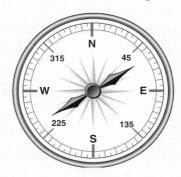

1.7 **17.** Two cabins are in the same vertical plane as a tower, and on opposite sides of the tower. The tower is 118 m high. The angles of depression of the cabins are 10° and 6°. Determine the distance between the cabins.

18. Determine the area of △DEF given ∠E = 48°, d = 15.1 cm, and f = 7.9 cm.

19. From one point, the angle of elevation of the top of a tall building is 5°. From another point, in the same vertical plane 150 m closer to the building, the angle of elevation is 15°. Determine the height of the building.

20. Two trees are 100 m apart. From the midpoint between the trees, Bozena measures the angles of elevation of their tops as 7° and 10°. How tall are the trees?

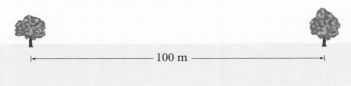

100 m

1. Determine the value of x to 1 decimal place.

a)

b) 8.1 cm

c)

x

62°

14.0 cm

x

7.1 cm

9.1 cm

x

37° 122°

9.6 cm

2. Communication Explain how to decide whether to use the Sine Law or the Cosine Law to calculate a measure in a non-right triangle.

3. Knowledge/Understanding Solve each triangle.

a) $\triangle$KMN given $\angle$M = 90°, n = 7.5 cm, and k = 4.8 cm

b) $\triangle$ABC given $\angle$B = 63°, $\angle$C = 31°, and b = 7.5 cm

c) $\triangle$XYZ given $\angle$Y = 54°, x = 7.1 cm, and z = 4.9 cm

4. Halima is flying a kite and has let out 150 m of string. The angle of inclination of the string is 58°. How high is the kite above the ground?

5. Application A bridge is to be built to join points A and B on opposite sides of a river. To determine the distance across the river, a point, C is marked on the same side of the river as A. The distance from A to C is 87 m, $\angle$BAC = 45°, and $\angle$BCA = 64°. Determine the length of the bridge.

6. Two points, A and B, are on the same side of a tower in the same vertical plane as the tower. The angle of elevation of the top of the tower from point A is 28°. Point B is closer to the tower, 140 m from point A. The angle of elevation of the top of the tower from point B is 37°. Determine the height of the tower.

7. Thinking/Inquiry/Problem Solving Determine the area of a triangle that has sides measuring 5 cm, 9 cm, and 12 cm.

8. A tool and die maker is to construct two plates.

The first is to be a 3.5 by 5.5-cm rectangular plate with pre-drilled holes at three of the four vertices. The holes are 0.5 cm in diameter and their centres are located 0.8 cm from the edge of the plate.

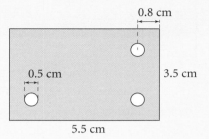

The second is to be a circular boilerplate with radius 1.3 m. It will have ten pre-drilled holes evenly spaced around the plate. Each hole will be 5 cm in diameter and its centre will be 10 cm from the outer rim of the plate.

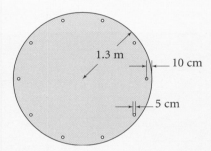

a) Describe how to determine the angles between the centres of the holes in the rectangular plate. Calculate the angles.

b) Describe how to determine the distance between the centres of two adjacent holes in the circular boilerplate. Calculate this distance.

2 Algebra

This chapter reviews algebra skills that are prerequisite for college admission. Assess your mastery of these skills on page 80 of Necessary Skills. Look for "Maintaining Your Mastery" sections throughout later chapters of this book.

Curriculum Expectations

By the end of this chapter, you will:

> Rearrange a formula to isolate any variable in it.

> Demonstrate mastery of key algebraic skills, including the ability to solve linear equations, to solve systems of linear equations, to graph a linear function from its equation, and to determine the slope and intercepts of a linear function from its equation.

> Factor expressions of the form $ax^2 + bx + c$.

> Solve quadratic equations by factoring.

> Evaluate any variable in a given formula drawn from an application by substituting into the formula and using the appropriate order of operations on a scientific calculator.

1 Review: Assessing Your Mastery

Refresh your algebra skills.

1. Solve each equation.

   a) $2(x + 4) = 6$

   b) $3(x - 3) + 4x + 7 = 5x - 3$

2. Determine the slope and y-intercept of each line.

   a) $y = -2x + 6$

   b) $-3x + y = 10$

   c) $x - 2y = -8$

3. Graph each line in exercise 2.

4. Solve each linear system by graphing.

   a) $y = -x + 5$
   $y = -3x + 3$

   b) $x - y = 2$
   $3x + y = -14$

   c) $5x + y = 16$
   $2x - 3y = 3$

5. Solve each linear system by substitution.

   a) $y = -3x - 9$
   $2x + 3y = -6$

   b) $3x + y = 18$
   $x + 2y = 11$

   c) $2x + 8y = 8$
   $y - 10 = 2x$

6. Solve each linear system by elimination.

   a) $x + y = 10$
   $x - y = 6$

   b) $5x + 2y = 5$
   $3x - 4y = -23$

   c) $2x + 3y = 18$
   $6x - 5y = -2$

7. Simplify each polynomial.

   a) $4x^2 - 3x + 4 - 2x^2 - x - 11$

   b) $(2x + 5) + (16x - 3)$

   c) $(a - 5) - (5a + 2)$

8. Expand and simplify.

   a) $(x + 4)(x + 3)$

   b) $(a + 4)(a - 6)$

   c) $2(y - 1)(y - 2)$

   d) $-6(m + 2)(m - 3)$

9. Factor.

   a) $x^2 + 3x + 2$

   b) $a^2 - 5a + 6$

   c) $m^2 - 3m - 10$

10. Factor.

    a) $2x^2 + 11x + 12$

    b) $6w^2 - 7w - 3$

    c) $8x^2 - 10x + 3$

11. Solve each quadratic equation.

    a) $x^2 + 7x + 12 = 0$

    b) $3y^2 - 12y - 36 = 0$

    c) $3x^2 - 10x + 8 = 0$

    d) $8y^2 + 18y - 5 = 0$

2 Review: Exponent Laws

Here is a summary of the exponent laws.

Multiplying Powers $x^m \times x^n = x^{m+n}$
To multiply powers with the same base, keep the base and add the exponents.

Dividing Powers $x^m \div x^n = x^{m-n}$
To divide powers with the same base, keep the base and subtract the exponents.

Power of a Power $(x^m)^n = x^{mn}$
To raise a power to a power, keep the base and multiply the exponents.

Power of a Product $(xy)^m = x^m y^m$
To raise a product to a power, raise each factor to the power.

Power of a Quotient $\left(\frac{x}{y}\right)^m = \frac{x^m}{y^m}, y \neq 0$
To raise a quotient to a power, raise each factor to the power.

Zero Exponent $x^0 = 1, \; x \neq 0$
A power with a zero exponent is equal to 1.

Negative Exponent $x^{-m} = \frac{1}{x^m}$ or $x^m = \frac{1}{x^{-m}}$
A power with a negative exponent is the reciprocal of a power with the same base raised to the corresponding positive exponent.

Example 1

Write as a single power.

a) $3^2 \times 3^5$ **b)** $\frac{7^6}{7^2}$ **c)** $(4^8)^3$ **d)** $\frac{5^3}{4^3}$

Solution

a) $3^2 \times 3^5 = 3^{2+5}$ **b)** $\frac{7^6}{7^2} = 7^{6-2}$ **c)** $(4^8)^3 = 4^{8 \times 3}$ **d)** $\frac{5^3}{4^3} = \left(\frac{5}{4}\right)^3$
$\quad\quad\quad\quad\quad = 3^7$ $\quad\quad\quad\quad = 7^4$ $\quad\quad\quad\quad\quad\quad = 4^{24}$

Example 2 Evaluate. Use exponent laws.

a) $\left(\frac{1}{2} + \frac{2}{3}\right)^0$ **b)** 8^{-2} **c)** $\left(3\left(\frac{1}{2}\right)^{-1}\right)^4$ **d)** $\frac{12^3}{4^3}$

Solution

a) $\left(\frac{1}{2} + \frac{2}{3}\right)^0 = 1$ **b)** $8^{-2} = \frac{1}{8^2}$

$= \frac{1}{64}$

c) $\left(3\left(\frac{1}{2}\right)^{-1}\right)^4 = 3^4\left(\frac{1}{2}\right)^{-4}$ **d)** $\frac{12^3}{4^3} = \left(\frac{12}{4}\right)^3$

$= 81(16)$ $= (3)^3$

$= 1296$ $= 27$

Exercises

1. Write as a single power.

a) $3^2 \times 3^{-1}$ **b)** $\frac{5^7}{5^4}$ **c)** $\frac{7^2}{7^{-5}}$

d) $(8^2)^4$ **e)** $2^9 \times 2$ **f)** $4^3 \times 4^2 \times 4^5$

2. Write as a power with a positive exponent.

a) $x^2 \times x^{-5}$ **b)** $\frac{b^3}{b^5}$ **c)** $(x^{-3})^2$

3. Write as a single power, then evaluate.

a) $3^{-2} \times 3^3 \times 3$ **b)** $\frac{6^7}{6^5}$ **c)** $\left(\frac{2}{5}\right)^2$

4. Evaluate.

a) x^0 **b)** x^{-3} **c)** $(a \times a^{13} \times a^{-9})^0$

3 Review: Collecting Like Terms

In mathematics, a term is a number, a variable, or a combination of a number and variables.

$3x$, $-7y^2$, $9xyz$, -3, a, and $-4xy$ are examples of terms.

Recall that terms that have the same variables are *like terms* and may be combined.

$6x$ and $-2x$ are like terms.

$5y$ and $3y^2$ are not like terms.

Example

Simplify by collecting like terms.

a) $2x + 7 + 3x$ **b)** $4a + 2b + 5a + 6b$

Solution

a) $2x + 7 + 3x = 2x + 3x + 7$

$\qquad\qquad\quad = 5x + 7$

b) $4a + 2b + 5a + 6b = 4a + 5a + 2b + 6b$

$\qquad\qquad\qquad\qquad = 9a + 8b$

Discuss

In part a, why can we not combine 5x and 7? In part b, why can we not combine 9a and 8b?

Exercises

1. Simplify by collecting like terms.

a) $5x + 2 + 5x$ **b)** $4y - 7y + 8$ **c)** $-3m - 9 + 8m$

d) $4x^2 - 3x + 3x^2$ **e)** $-5ab + 4a + 3ab$ **f)** $6y^3 - 10y - 9y^3$

2. Simplify.

a) $4x + 2y - 3x + 5y$ **b)** $-4y - 7y + 8x + 6x$ **c)** $6x^2 - 3x - 8x^2 - 7x$

d) $10a - 4b - 7b + 4a$ **e)** $-8a + 4b + 3b - 5a$ **f)** $8x + 5y - 7x - 12y$

4 Review: The Distributive Law

Recall that to expand the product $4(3x - 1)$, we use the distributive law. Each term inside the brackets is multiplied by 4.

$4(3x - 1) = 4(3x) + 4(-1)$

$\qquad\qquad = 12x - 4$

Example

Expand and simplify.

a) $5(3x + 2)$ **b)** $4a(3a^2 - 7a + 5)$ **c)** $-4a(3a^2 - 7a + 5)$

Solution

a) $5(3x + 2) = 5(3x) + 5(2)$
$$= 15x + 10$$

b) $4a(3a^2 - 7a + 5) = 4a(3a^2) + 4a(-7a) + 4a(5)$
$$= 12a^3 - 28a^2 + 20a$$

c) $-4a(3a^2 - 7a + 5) = -4a(3a^2) - 4a(-7a) - 4a(5)$
$$= -12a^3 + 28a^2 - 20a$$

Discuss

Compare the results of parts b and c. What do you notice?

Exercises

1. Expand.

a) $2(4x + 5)$ **b)** $3(3a - 7)$ **c)** $-5(2x - 8)$ **d)** $3y(y - 2)$

e) $4x(2x + 5)$ **f)** $7m(-3m + 4)$ **g)** $9(3x - 8)$ **h)** $-6x(5 - 4x)$

2. Expand.

a) $3(4x^2 + 2x + 7)$ **b)** $-2(3a^2 - 5a + 2)$ **c)** $3x(2x^2 + 3x - 7)$

d) $4y(5y^2 + 6y - 3)$ **e)** $-4x(3x^2 - 2x + 5)$ **f)** $5m(5m^2 + 4m - 1)$

g) $-2x(3 + 5x - 8x^2)$ **h)** $-z(9z^2 - 2z - 4)$ **i)** $7x(5x^2 - 4x + 9)$

5 Review: Common Factoring

In the previous section, we expanded a product and wrote it as a sum. Recall that we may reverse the process. We factor an expression by writing it as a product of factors.

In the expression $2x + 8$, 2 is a factor of each term. It is a common factor. To factor $2x + 8$, we factor each term: $2(x) + 2(4)$.

Identify the common factor, 2.

Use the distributive law to write the sum as a product.

$2x + 8 = 2(x + 4)$

Factor.

a) $6x - 9$ **b)** $3x^2 + 5x$ **c)** $8y^2 - 12y$

Solution

a) $6x - 9 = 3(2x) - 3(3)$ 3 is the common factor.

$= 3(2x - 3)$

b) $3x^2 + 5x = x(3x) + x(5)$ x is the common factor.

$= x(3x + 5)$

c) $8y^2 - 12y = 4y(2y) - 4y(3)$ $4y$ is the common factor.

$= 4y(2y - 3)$

Exercises

1. Factor.

   a) $5x - 10$ **b)** $6y + 8$ **c)** $7a - 14b$

   d) $12a + 36$ **e)** $9j - 6k$ **f)** $2h - 2$

   g) $4x^2 - 8$ **h)** $6x + 9$ **i)** $10w^2 - 15$

2. Factor.

   a) $3 + 18x$ **b)** $5xy - 7x$ **c)** $12m + 5m^2$

   d) $5y^2 - y$ **e)** $4x + 6x^2 - 9x^3$ **f)** $2xy + 5xz$

   g) $12a - 5ac - 2ab$ **h)** $mn + 2n - 5np$ **i)** $a - 4ac - 7ad$

3. Factor.

   a) $9x^2 + 18x$ **b)** $6a^2 - 15a$ **c)** $18x + 27xy$

   d) $8x^3 - 4x$ **e)** $6mn + 9n$ **f)** $24x^2 + 16x$

   g) $14ab - 21a$ **h)** $3x^2 + 12x$ **i)** $5y^3 - 15y$

6 Review: Slope of a Line

Recall that the slope of a line segment is $\frac{\text{rise}}{\text{run}}$.

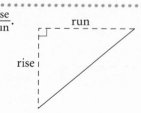

When the line segment rises to the right, it has a positive slope.

When the line segment falls to the right, it has a negative slope.

When the line segment is horizontal, it has a zero slope.

When the line segment is vertical, it has an undefined slope.

Example 1 Determine the slope of line segment AB.

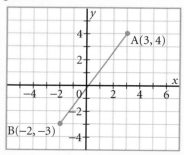

A(3, 4)

B(−2, −3)

Solution

From the diagram,
slope of AB = $\frac{\text{rise}}{\text{run}}$
$= \frac{7}{5}$

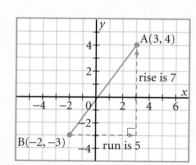

A(3, 4)

rise is 7

B(−2, −3)   run is 5

Recall that the slope of a line through two points is the same as the slope of the line segment that joins the two points.

Example **2**

Determine the slope of the line through each pair of points.
  a) D(−3, 5) and E(2, −5)   **b)** A(−2, −4) and B(2, 5)

Solution

a) D(−3, 5) and E(2, −5)

Slope of DE = $\frac{\text{rise}}{\text{run}}$

$= \frac{-10}{5}$

$= -2$

The slope of the line is −2.

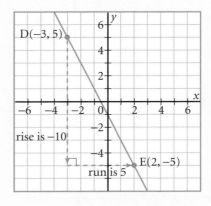

b) A(−2, −4) and B(2, 5)

Slope of AB = $\frac{\text{rise}}{\text{run}}$

$= \frac{9}{4}$

The slope of the line is $\frac{9}{4}$.

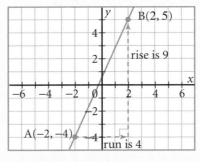

Exercises

1. Determine the slope of each line segment.

a)
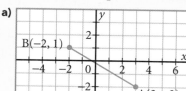

b)
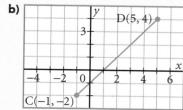

c)
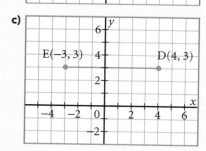

d)
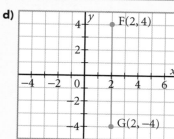

e)
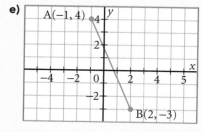

f)
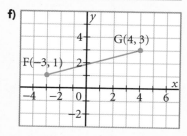

2. Use the direction of each line segment in exercise 1 to describe its slope.

3. Determine the slope of the line through each pair of points.

a) A(4, 3) and B(6, 7)

b) C(−3, 1) and D(6, 2)

c) J(−2, −3) and K(4, −5)

d) M(5, 1) and N(5, −3)

e) L(4, 2) and N(1, −5)

f) R(−2, 5) and S(3, −2)

g) D(−2, 3) and E(3, 3)

h) B(−1, −3) and C(3, 5)

To solve an equation means to find the value of the variable that makes the right side of the equation equal to the left side.

When solving an equation, you can:
- Add the same term to each side of the equation.
- Subtract the same term from each side of the equation.
- Multiply or divide each side of the equation by the same non-zero number.

Many equations have variable terms on both sides of the equation. The first step is to collect the variable terms on one side.

Example 1   Solve and check.

a) $5x + 2 = 3x - 8$ b) $-3x + 7 = 2x - 3$

Solution

a)
$$5x + 2 = 3x - 8$$
$$5x + 2 - 3x = 3x - 8 - 3x \qquad \text{Subtract } 3x \text{ from each side.}$$
$$2x + 2 = -8$$
$$2x + 2 - 2 = -8 - 2 \qquad \text{Subtract 2 from each side.}$$
$$2x = -10$$
$$\frac{2x}{2} = \frac{-10}{2} \qquad \text{Divide each side by 2.}$$
$$x = -5$$

Check.

To check that the solution is correct, use substitution.

If $x = -5$,   Left side $= 5x + 2$ Right side $= 3x - 8$

$$\begin{aligned}
&= 5(-5) + 2 &&= 3(-5) - 8 \\
&= -25 + 2 &&= -15 - 8 \\
&= -23 &&= -23
\end{aligned}$$

Since the left side and right side are equal, $x = -5$ is correct.

b)
$$-3x + 7 = 2x - 3$$
$$-3x + 7 + 3x = 2x - 3 + 3x \qquad \text{Add } 3x \text{ to each side.}$$
$$7 = 5x - 3$$
$$7 + 3 = 5x - 3 + 3 \qquad \text{Add 3 to each side.}$$
$$10 = 5x$$
$$\frac{10}{5} = \frac{5x}{5} \qquad \text{Divide each side by 5.}$$
$$2 = x$$

Check.

If $x = 2$,   Left side $= -3x + 7$ Right side $= 2x - 3$

$$= -3(2) + 7 \qquad\qquad\qquad = 2(2) - 3$$
$$= -6 + 7 \qquad\qquad\qquad\quad = 4 - 3$$
$$= 1 \qquad\qquad\qquad\qquad\quad = 1$$

Since the left side and right side are equal, $x = 2$ is correct.

Some equations need to be simplified before we can solve them.

Example 2   Solve.

$$3(2x - 5) - 4(x + 3) = 2x - (3x - 1) + 2$$

Solution

$$
\begin{aligned}
3(2x - 5) - 4(x + 3) &= 2x - (3x - 1) + 2 \\
6x - 15 - 4x - 12 &= 2x - 3x + 1 + 2 && \text{Use the distributive law.} \\
2x - 27 &= -x + 3 && \text{Simplify each side.} \\
2x - 27 + x &= -x + 3 + x && \text{Add } x \text{ to each side.} \\
3x - 27 &= 3 \\
3x - 27 + 27 &= 3 + 27 && \text{Add 27 to each side.} \\
3x &= 30 \\
\frac{3x}{3} &= \frac{30}{3} && \text{Divide each side by 3.} \\
x &= 10
\end{aligned}
$$

Check.

If $x = 10$,

Left side $= 3(2x - 5) - 4(x + 3)$ Right side $= 2x - (3x - 1) + 2$

$$= 3(2(10) - 5) - 4((10) + 3) \qquad\qquad = 2(10) - (3(10) - 1) + 2$$
$$= 3(15) - 4(13) \qquad\qquad\qquad\quad = 2(10) - (30 - 1) + 2$$
$$= 45 - 52 \qquad\qquad\qquad\qquad\quad = 20 - 29 + 2$$
$$= -7 \qquad\qquad\qquad\qquad\qquad\quad = -7$$

Since the left side and right side are equal, $x = 10$ is correct.

Discuss

Why should you always check your solution? Why should you always check your solution in the given equation?

To solve an equation that involves fractions, we first eliminate the fractions by multiplying each side by the common denominator.

Example 3 Solve.

$$\frac{1}{3}x - \frac{1}{2} = \frac{1}{4}x + 2$$

Solution

$$\frac{1}{3}x - \frac{1}{2} = \frac{1}{4}x + 2$$

The common denominator is 12.

Multiply each side of the equation by 12.

$$12\left(\frac{1}{3}x - \frac{1}{2}\right) = 12\left(\frac{1}{4}x + 2\right)$$

$$12\left(\frac{1}{3}x\right) - 12\left(\frac{1}{2}\right) = 12\left(\frac{1}{4}x\right) + 12(2) \qquad \text{Use the distributive law.}$$

$$4x - 6 = 3x + 24 \qquad \text{Simplify.}$$
$$x - 6 = 24 \qquad \text{Collect like terms.}$$
$$x = 30$$

Check.

If $x = 30$, Left side $= \frac{1}{3}x - \frac{1}{2}$ Right side $= \frac{1}{4}x + 2$

$$= \frac{1}{3}(30) - \frac{1}{2} \qquad\qquad = \frac{1}{4}(30) + 2$$

$$= 9\frac{1}{2} \qquad\qquad\qquad = 9\frac{1}{2}$$

Since the left side and right side are equal, $x = 30$ is correct.

Notice, in *Example 3,* that multiplying each side of an equation by a number is the same as multiplying each term by that number.

TAKE NOTE

To Solve a Linear Equation with Fractions

1. Eliminate fractions by multiplying each term of the equation by the common denominator of the fractions.

2. Simplify each side of the equation, if possible.

3. Collect the variable terms on one side of the equation, and the numbers on the other side.

4. Divide each side of the equation by the coefficient of the variable term.

Example 4 Solve. Check the solution.

$$\frac{x+1}{2} - \frac{x-3}{3} = \frac{x+5}{3}$$

Solution

$$\frac{x+1}{2} - \frac{x-3}{3} = \frac{x+5}{3}$$

$$6\left(\frac{x+1}{2}\right) - 6\left(\frac{x-3}{3}\right) = 6\left(\frac{x+5}{3}\right) \quad \text{Multiply each term by the common denominator, 6.}$$

$$3(x+1) - 2(x-3) = 2(x+5)$$

$$3x + 3 - 2x + 6 = 2x + 10$$

$$x + 9 = 2x + 10$$

$$9 = x + 10$$

$$-1 = x$$

Check.

If $x = -1$,　　Left side $= \dfrac{x+1}{2} - \dfrac{x-3}{3}$　　　　　Right side $= \dfrac{x+5}{3}$

$$= \frac{-1+1}{2} - \frac{-1-3}{3} \qquad\qquad\qquad = \frac{-1+5}{3}$$

$$= 0 - \frac{-4}{3} \qquad\qquad\qquad\qquad\qquad = \frac{4}{3}$$

$$= \frac{4}{3}$$

Since the left side and right side are equal, $x = -1$ is correct.

2.1 Exercises

A

 1. Solve.

　a) $x + 2 = 6$　　　　**b)** $3x = 9$　　　　**c)** $x - 4 = 2$

　d) $n + 3 = -5$　　　**e)** $4x = -12$　　　**f)** $x + 6 = 14$

　g) $-3y = -15$　　　**h)** $4x = 20$　　　**i)** $z - 4 = -9$

2. Solve.

　a) $\frac{1}{4}y = -3$　　　　**b)** $\frac{x}{3} = 4$　　　　**c)** $-\frac{1}{3}y = -2$

　d) $5 = \frac{m}{2}$　　　　**e)** $-1 = \frac{1}{2}w$　　　**f)** $11 = \frac{w}{2}$

 3. Solve.

　a) $2x + 6 = 16$　　　**b)** $5b - 3 = 12$　　　**c)** $3y + 5 = -7$

　d) $6a - 1 = 11$　　　**e)** $3x + 6 = 15$　　　**f)** $7y - 5 = 58$

4. Solve.

　a) $3x - 4 = 10$　　　**b)** $4b + 2 = 7$　　　**c)** $-3y + 4 = -4$

d) $2a - 1 = 6$ **e)** $2x + 3 = 8$ **f)** $5y - 7 = 12$

g) $3b - 2 = 13$ **h)** $4 = 2x + 5$ **i)** $6 = 7 - 3x$

✓ **5.** Solve.

     a) $5 = \frac{4}{3}m$ **b)** $-\frac{2}{5}n = 4$ **c)** $\frac{1}{4}x - 1 = 3$

     d) $\frac{1}{2}y + 2 = 10$ **e)** $\frac{x}{4} - 1 = -2$ **f)** $-\frac{1}{2}y - 3 = -7$

B

✓ **6.** Solve. Check the solutions.

     a) $3x + 2 = 2x + 5$ **b)** $2x + 1 = 3x - 2$ **c)** $4y - 2 = 2y - 4$

     d) $2a + 3 = -2a - 5$ **e)** $-3x + 3 = 2x - 7$ **f)** $-5y - 3 = -7y - 5$

     g) $4b - 3 = b - 6$ **h)** $-3x - 10 = 2x + 5$ **i)** $2x - 8 = 10 - 4x$

7. Solve.

     a) $5x - 4 = -x + 3$ **b)** $-2x + 8 = 3x - 7$ **c)** $2y - 6 = 4y - 8$

     d) $5a + 7 = 2a + 5$ **e)** $3x - 11 = -2x - 7$ **f)** $-9y + 5 = -7y + 10$

     g) $b - 9 = 7b - 6$ **h)** $4x - 15 = -3x - 12$ **i)** $8x + 9 = 10x - 4$

✓ **8. Knowledge/Understanding** Solve. Check the solutions.

     a) $3x - 4 + 5x + 7 = 4x + 2 - 5x + 10$

     b) $4a + 2a - 6 - 3a = a + 7 - 5 - 2a$

     c) $2x - 8 - 4x + 5 = 5x + 7 - 3x - 10$

     d) $3(2x - 1) + 2(x + 5) = -1$

9. Solve. Check the solutions.

     a) $4(x - 1) - (x + 3) = 2x + 2$

     b) $3y - 2(y - 7) = 3(y - 4) + 8$

     c) $2(x - 4) - 3(x - 1) = 4x - (-4 + 2x)$

     d) $-3(y - 4) + 5(y - 2) = 3(y - 1) + 2y$

✓ **10.** Solve.

     a) $3x - 2(2x + 3) - 4 = 5(x - 3) - 8$

     b) $3x + 5 + 4x - 7 = -4x + 2 - x - 5$

     c) $5y - 9(y - 2) + 6 = 4 - (8 - 7y) + 9$

     d) $4(3x - 2) + 3(3x + 4) = 2(5x - 3) + 3(2x + 2)$

11. Solve.

     a) $-2(x - 4) - 3(2x + 1) = 2(x - 4) - 3$

     b) $-3(2x + 4) - 5(2 - x) = 4(x - 2) - (5 - x)$

     c) $6y + 2(3y - 1) - 9 = -(4 - 3y) + 5$

     d) $5(3x - 2) - 4x + 7 = 4(x - 6) - 2(8 - 3x) - 5$

✓ **12.** Solve. Check the solutions.

a) $\frac{1}{2}x + \frac{2}{5} = \frac{1}{5}x - \frac{1}{2}$

b) $\frac{1}{3}x - \frac{1}{2} = \frac{1}{2}x + \frac{1}{3}$

c) $x + \frac{1}{2} = \frac{1}{3}x + \frac{1}{2}$

d) $\frac{y}{4} + \frac{1}{5} = \frac{y}{20} + \frac{4}{5}$

13. Solve.

a) $\frac{1}{3}x - \frac{1}{4} = \frac{1}{12}x - \frac{1}{2}$

b) $\frac{3}{5}x - \frac{1}{2} = \frac{1}{2}x + \frac{4}{5}$

c) $x - \frac{3}{4} = \frac{3}{2}x + \frac{1}{2}$

d) $\frac{1}{8}y + \frac{3}{2} = \frac{1}{2}y + \frac{7}{8}$

✓ **14. Communication** Examine this solution to the equation $\frac{x}{3} - 2 = \frac{5}{18}$.

$$\frac{x}{3} - 2 = \frac{5}{18}$$

$$54\left(\frac{x}{3}\right) - 54(2) = 54\left(\frac{5}{18}\right)$$

$$18x - 108 = 15$$

$$18x = 123$$

$$\frac{18x}{18} = \frac{123}{18}$$

$$x = \frac{123}{18}$$

$$= \frac{41}{6}$$

Explain how a change in the second line of the solution could have made the solution more efficient.

15. Solve.

a) $\frac{x-1}{2} + \frac{x+2}{3} = \frac{x+1}{6}$

b) $\frac{x-5}{4} + \frac{x+1}{3} = \frac{x-2}{6}$

c) $\frac{x-1}{2} - \frac{x-2}{5} = \frac{x+3}{10}$

d) $\frac{x+3}{2} = \frac{x-1}{7} + \frac{x+5}{2}$

16. Solve.

a) $\frac{2x-3}{5} - \frac{x+5}{2} = \frac{x-1}{5} + \frac{x+2}{2}$

b) $\frac{3y+1}{3} + \frac{y+2}{4} = \frac{2y-1}{2} + \frac{4y-1}{3}$

c) $\frac{3-x}{2} - \frac{5+x}{3} = \frac{x+2}{9}$

d) $\frac{-2x+1}{5} - \frac{x+2}{4} = \frac{x+1}{2} - \frac{3x-2}{10}$

17. Solve.

a) $\frac{1}{2}(x-2) + \frac{1}{3}(x-4) = \frac{1}{6}(x+1) - \frac{3}{2}$

b) $\frac{4}{5}(x+3) - \frac{1}{2}(x+2) = \frac{1}{2}(3x-2) + \frac{3}{5}$

c) $\frac{2}{3}(x+2) + \frac{1}{4}(3x-1) = \frac{1}{6}(4x+1) - \frac{1}{2}(x+3)$

d) $\frac{5}{6}(x-1) + \frac{1}{5}(2x+3) = \frac{1}{2}(x+2) + \frac{2}{5}(x-3)$

e) $\frac{3}{4}(2x+7) - \frac{1}{3}(4-x) = \frac{3}{8}(4x+5) - \frac{5}{6}(x+4)$

f) $\frac{1}{4}(4-y) - \frac{3}{5}(2y+5) = -\frac{1}{2}(4y+5) - \frac{3}{4}(2y+7)$

2.2 Working with Formulas

Until now, we have had only one variable in each equation. When we work with a formula, we may have an equation with several variables.
For example, the formula for area, A, of a rectangle with length l and width w is $A = lw$.

Also, the simple interest, I dollars, on a principal, P dollars, invested at an annual interest rate r for t years is $I = Prt$.

When we work with formulas, we must evaluate the formula for given values of the variables.

Example 1

Use a calculator to evaluate the given formula for the indicated values.

a) $SA = 4\pi r^2$, $r = 9.5$ b) $A = P(1 + i)^n$, $P = \$1200$, $i = 0.03$, $n = 4$

Solution

a) $SA = 4\pi r^2$
Substitute 9.5 for r.
$SA = 4\pi(9.5)^2$
$\doteq 1134.1$

b) $A = P(1 + i)^n$
Substitute 1200 for P, 0.03 for i, and 4 for n.
$A = 1200(1 + 0.03)^4$
$\doteq 1350.61$

We can use the method for solving an equation to solve a formula for any variable.

Example 2

The density D of an object with mass M and volume V is $D = \frac{M}{V}$.

a) Solve the formula for M.

b) Calculate the mass of an object with density 19.3 g/cm³ and volume 12.3 cm³.

Solution

a) $D = \frac{M}{V}$

$DV = \frac{MV}{V}$ Isolate M. Eliminate fractions. Multiply each side by a common denominator.

$DV = M$ Simplify.

b) Use $M = DV$

Substitute $D = 19.3$ and $V = 12.3$.

$M = DV$

$M = (19.3)(12.3)$

$ = 237.39$

The mass of the object is 237.39 g.

Example 3

The perimeter P of a rectangle with length l and width w is $P = 2(l + w)$.

a) Solve the formula for l.

b) Calculate the length of a rectangle with perimeter 30 cm and width 3 cm.

Solution

a)
$$P = 2(l + w)$$
$$P = 2l + 2w \qquad \text{Use the distributive law.}$$
$$P - 2w = 2l + 2w - 2w \qquad \text{Isolate the term that contains } l. \text{ Subtract } 2w$$
$$P - 2w = 2l \qquad\qquad\qquad \text{from each side.}$$
$$\frac{P - 2w}{2} = \frac{2l}{2} \qquad\qquad \text{Divide each side by 2.}$$
$$\frac{P - 2w}{2} = l$$

b) Use $l = \dfrac{P - 2w}{2}$.

Substitute $P = 30$ and $w = 3$.

$$l = \frac{30 - 2(3)}{2}$$
$$ = \frac{30 - 6}{2}$$
$$ = \frac{24}{2}$$
$$ = 12$$

The length of the rectangle is 12 cm.

Discuss

Describe another method you could have used to find l in part b. Which method do you think is easier? Why?

A

✓ **1.** Evaluate each given formula for the indicated values.

    a) $A = lw$, $l = 8.4$ m, $w = 3.1$ m   **b)** $A = \pi r^2$, $r = 11$ cm

    c) $P = 2l + 2w$, $l = 1.3$ km, $w = 0.8$ km

✓ **2. Knowledge/Understanding** Evaluate each given formula for the indicated values.

    a) $D = \frac{M}{V}$, $M = 18$ kg, $V = 7.2$ L

    b) $A = \frac{1}{2}bh$, $b = 5.0$ cm, $h = 2.2$ cm

    c) $S = \dfrac{a\left(1 - \left(\frac{1}{r}\right)^n\right)}{r - 1}$, $r = 1.035$, $a = \$79$, $n = 11$

B

3. The area, A, of a rectangle with length l and width w is $A = lw$.

    a) Solve the formula for w.

    b) Calculate the width of a rectangle with area 16 m² and length 10 m.

✓ **4.** The speed, S, of an object, travelling a distance d, over time t, is $S = \frac{d}{t}$.

    a) Solve the formula for d.

    b) Calculate the distance an object travels in 17 s at a speed of 5 m/s.

5. The formula for the area, A, of a triangle with base b and height h is $A = \frac{1}{2}bh$.

    a) Solve the formula for b.

    b) Calculate the base of a triangle with area 24 cm² and height 6 cm.

✓ **6. Application** The formula for the circumference C of a circle, with radius r, is $C = 2\pi r$. Calculate the diameter of a circle with circumference 24.0 cm.

✓ **7.** The simple interest, I dollars, on a principal, P dollars, invested at a monthly interest rate r, for t months is $I = Prt$. (Recall that r is expressed as a decimal.)

    a) Solve the formula for r.

    b) A principal of \$850 is invested for 2 months. The simple interest earned is \$17. Calculate the monthly interest rate.

8. When a principal, P dollars, is invested for n compounding periods, at an interest rate i per period, the amount A is $A = P(1 + i)^n$. (Recall that i is expressed as a decimal.)

    a) Solve the formula for P.

b) Calculate the principal that amounts to $1900 with an interest rate of 5% per year for 7 compounding years.

9. The equation of a line with slope m and y-intercept b in slope-intercept form is $y = mx + b$.

   a) Solve the formula for m.

   b) Calculate the slope of a line passing through $(2, 5)$ with y-intercept 3.

10. The formula for the volume, V, of a cylinder with radius r and height h is $V = \pi r^2 h$. A cylinder has volume 706.9 cm^3 and height 9.0 cm. Calculate its radius.

11. **Thinking/Inquiry/Problem Solving** The formula $F = \frac{9}{5}C + 32$ is used to convert temperature in degrees Celsius, C, to degrees Fahrenheit, F.

   a) Write a formula to convert degrees Fahrenheit to degrees Celsius. That is, solve the formula for C.

   b) The highest recorded temperature in North America is 134.0°F on July 10, 1913. What is the equivalent temperature in degrees Celsius?

   c) At what temperature in degrees Fahrenheit does water freeze?

12. **Communication** The cosine law for $\triangle$ABC is $a^2 = b^2 + c^2 - 2bc \cos A$, where a, b, and c are sides of the triangle and A is the measure of $\angle$A in degrees.

   a) Solve the formula for $\cos A$.

   b) Why do we not solve the formula for A?

   c) Determine the measure of $\angle$A given $a = 23$ cm, $b = 54$ cm, and $c = 32$ cm.

13. The area of a trapezoid, A, with side lengths a and b, and height h, is $A = \frac{h(a + b)}{2}$.

   a) Solve the formula for b.

   b) Calculate the length of one side of a trapezoid with area 66 mm^2, one side length 7 mm, and the height 12 mm.

14. The sum of a geometric series, S_n, with n terms is $S_n = \frac{a(r^n - 1)}{r - 1}$, where a is the first term and r is the common ratio.

   a) Solve the formula for a.

   b) Determine the value of the first term in a series with common ratio 3, sum 1093, and number of terms 7.

Derek has a job in sales. He earns a monthly salary of $1500, plus a commission of 10% of the value of his sales.

The table shows Derek's commission for different amounts of sales. The graph illustrates how his commission relates to his sales.

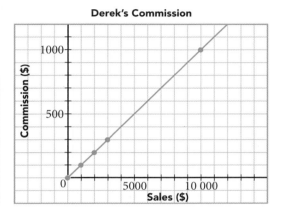

Derek's Commission

Sales ($)	Commission ($)
0	0
1000	$0.1(1000) = 100$
2000	$0.1(2000) = 200$
3000	$0.1(3000) = 300$
10 000	$0.1(10\ 000) = 1000$

The graph is a straight line through the origin. Because it goes through the origin, it illustrates direct variation linear growth. The commission is a function of the sales. This relationship can be written as $c = 0.1s$, where c is the commission in dollars and s is the value of the sales in dollars. This is a linear function.

The relationship between Derek's monthly earnings, e dollars, may also be expressed as a linear function of s.

Then $e = 0.1s + 1500$ or $e = \frac{1}{10}s + 1500$

earnings   commission   salary

This graph illustrates Derek's monthly earnings as a function of his sales.

The graph is a straight line that does not go through the origin. It illustrates partial variation linear growth.

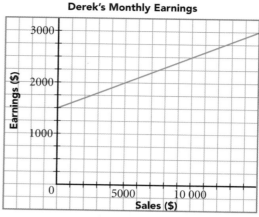

Derek's Monthly Earnings

For every change of 10 units horizontally, there is a change of 1 unit vertically. The slope of the graph is $\frac{1}{10}$ or 0.1. In each case, Derek's earnings increase by $0.10 for each dollar in sales. The rate of change of earnings is 0.10. This rate of change is the slope of the line.

Recall that, in general, any relation that can be written in the form $y = mx + b$ is a linear function and its graph is a straight line with slope m and y-intercept b.

For example, the graph of $y = \frac{1}{2}x + 3$ is a straight line with slope $\frac{1}{2}$. The line intersects the y-axis where $x = 0$ and $y = 3$. This value for y is the y-intercept.

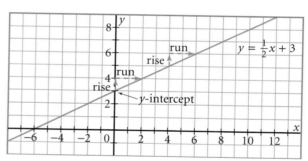

Example 1 Determine the slope and y-intercept of the graph of each equation.

a) The value y of a rare dime appreciates with time, x.

$y = 0.85x + 0.10$

b) The number of litres of gas, y, remaining in a courier's gas tank depends on x, the kilometres driven.

$y = -0.089x + 45$

c) The water level, y metres, in an unattended pool decreases with time, x.

$3x + 4y = 17$

Solution

a) Compare $y = 0.85x + 0.10$ to $y = mx + b$.
$m = 0.85$ and $b = 0.10$
The slope is 0.85 and the y-intercept is 0.10.

b) Compare $y = -0.089x + 45$ to $y = mx + b$.
$m = -0.089$ and $b = 45$
The slope is –0.089 and the y-intercept is 45.

c) $3x + 4y = 17$
Rearrange the equation to the form $y = mx + b$.
$4y = -3x + 17$ $\qquad$ Subtract $3x$ from each side.
$\frac{4y}{4} = \frac{-3x}{4} + \frac{17}{4}$ $\qquad$ Divide each term by 4.
$y = -\frac{3}{4}x + \frac{17}{4}$
Compare $y = -\frac{3}{4}x + \frac{17}{4}$ to $y = mx + b$.
$m = -\frac{3}{4}$ and $b = \frac{17}{4}$
The slope is $-\frac{3}{4}$ and the y-intercept is $\frac{17}{4}$.

Recall that there are different methods to sketch the graph of a linear function.

Example 2 Sketch the graph of each equation.

a) A rubber-stamp manufacturer charges for stamps according to the equation $y = 2x + 10$, where y is the total cost in dollars and x is the number of letters.

b) A lab technician prepares patient medication vials using the equation $y = \frac{1}{3}x + 1$, where y is the volume of the medication in millilitres, and x, the mass of the patient in kilograms.

c) A toy parachute's height, y metres, relative to a window it is dropped from, decreases with time, x seconds.
$2x + 3y - 6 = 0$

Solution

a) $y = 2x + 10$ Create a table of values.

Choose 3 values of x, then calculate the corresponding values of y.

Substitute $x = -2$.   Substitute $x = 0$.   Substitute $x = 1$.

$y = 2(-2) + 10$ $y = 2(0) + 10$ $y = 2(1) + 10$
$\quad = -4 + 10$ $\quad = 0 + 10$ $\quad = 2 + 10$
$\quad = 6$ $\quad = 10$ $\quad = 12$

x	y
−2	6
0	10
1	12

Plot the points on a grid, then join them with a straight line.

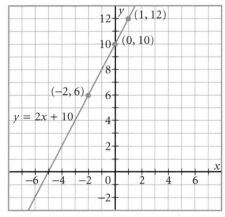

Discuss

Why do we plot 3 points, and not 2 points or 10 points?

b) $y = \frac{1}{3}x + 1$

Since the equation is written in $y = mx + b$ form, the graph is a line.

Use the slope and y-intercept to graph the line. The slope is $\frac{1}{3}$ and the y-intercept is 1.

On a grid, mark the point at $(0, 1)$. Use the slope to locate two other points on the line. Begin at $(0, 1)$. Move up 1 and 3 right. Repeat to obtain a third point on the line. Draw a line through the points.

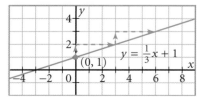

c) $2x + 3y - 6 = 0$

Calculate the intercepts.

For the y-intercept, substitute $x = 0$, then solve for y.

$2(0) + 3y - 6 = 0$

$$3y = 6$$
$$y = 2$$

The y-intercept is 2.

For the x-intercept, substitute $y = 0$, then solve for x.

$2x + 3(0) - 6 = 0$

$$2x = 6$$
$$x = 3$$

The x-intercept is 3.

Plot the points $(0, 2)$ and $(3, 0)$. To obtain a third point, choose another value for x.

Let $x = -3$. Substitute $x = -3$ in the equation, then solve for y.

$$2x + 3y - 6 = 0$$
$$2(-3) + 3y - 6 = 0$$
$$-6 + 3y - 6 = 0$$
$$3y - 12 = 0$$
$$3y = 12$$
$$y = 4$$

Plot the point $(-3, 4)$. Draw the line.

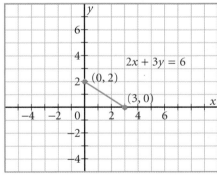

Discuss:

Why does the graph only exist between (0, 2) and (3, 0)?

When an equation has the form $y = mx + b$, we can use a graphing calculator to graph it.

Example 3 Graph the equation $y = \frac{2}{3}x + 1$.

Solution

Press MODE. Make sure that items are highlighted as shown in the screen below left. If any one item is not highlighted, use the arrow keys and ENTER to highlight it.

Press 2nd ZOOM for FORMAT. Make sure the items are highlighted as shown in the screen below right. If any one item is not highlighted, use the arrow keys and ENTER to highlight it.

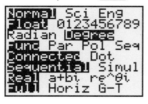
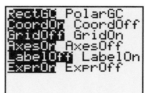

Press Y=. Use CLEAR and the arrow keys to clear all equations.

If any of Plot 1, Plot 2, or Plot 3 at the top of the screen is highlighted, use the arrow keys and ENTER to remove the highlighting.

Make sure the cursor is beside Y1=. Press 2 ÷ 3 X,T,θ,n + 1 to enter the equation $y = \frac{2}{3}x + 1$. Note that X,T,θ,n is a variable key. You always use this key to enter the variable in an equation. Your screen should look like the screen below left.

Press ZOOM 6 to change the settings to the standard window. A graph of the function $y = \frac{2}{3}x + 1$ appears as shown in the screen below right.

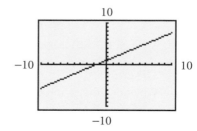

Exercises

A

✓ **1.** State the slope and y-intercept of each equation.

   a) $y = 2x + 3$
   b) $y = \frac{1}{2}x - 2$
   c) $y = -4x + 1$

✓ **2.** Determine the slope and vertical intercept of each linear equation.

   a) A helicopter is travelling at maximum speed toward a boat in distress. The equation that relates its distance, D, in nautical miles, away from the boat to the time travelled, t minutes, is $D = -0.5t + 23$.

   b) The cost, C, of an order of supplies from a hardware company is dependent upon the mass, m, of the shipment. The cost equation is $C = 24 + 2.50m$.

   c) The distance, d, a vehicle is from its destination is related to the time travelled, t hours, by the equation $d = -90t + 450$.

3. Use 3 points to graph each equation.

   a) $3x + y = 1$
   b) $x + y = 2$
   c) $x - y = 4$

4. Use the slope and y-intercept to graph each equation.

   a) $y = 2x - 1$
   b) $y = \frac{1}{3}x + 2$
   c) $y = \frac{3}{2}x + 1$

B

✓ **5.** Use the intercepts to graph each equation.

   a) $2x + 5y = 10$
   b) $3x - 2y = 6$
   c) $4x + 3y = 12$

6. Graph each line.

   a) $y = 2$
   b) $x = 3$
   c) $y = -1$
   d) $x = 5$

7. Determine the slope and y-intercept of each equation.

   a) $2x + 3y = 9$
   b) $3x - y = 1$
   c) $-2x + 5y - 10 = 0$
   d) $x + 2y = 6$
   e) $x - 3y = 3$
   f) $4x - 5y + 15 = 0$

✓ **8. a)** Use 3 points to graph each equation.

   i) $y = -2x$
   ii) $3x - 5y = 0$

   b) Explain why you cannot use the intercepts to graph the lines in part a.

9. Determine the slope and y-intercept of each equation.

   a) $3x - 3y - 9 = 0$
   b) $7x - 4y = 5$
   c) $2y - 3x - 4 = 0$
   d) $-x + 5y = -8$
   e) $y - 3x = 4$
   f) $5x + 4y = 10$

10. The equation for the circumference, C, of a circle with diameter, d, is given by the equation $C = \pi d$.

a) What are the slope and vertical intercept?

b) What does the slope represent? Is there a unit for the slope?

c) What does the vertical intercept represent?

d) Graph the equation.

e) What happens to C if d is doubled? What happens if it is tripled?

11. Graph each equation.

a) Mei telemarkets for a computer company and earns commission on the number of responses she generates. Her weekly salary, S, is determined by the equation $S = \frac{5}{2}x + 200$, where x is the number of callbacks received.

b) A car is travelling west toward Huntsville. The distance, d kilometres, is related to the time travelled, t hours, by the equation $d = -80t + 240$. The driver starts her stop-watch at 0 when she is 240 km east of Huntsville.

c) A local promoter is organizing an outdoor summer music concert in the park. The profit, P dollars, is a function of the number of tickets, t, sold. The equation is $P - 25t - 12\,000 = 0$.

12. Graph each equation.

a) The boiling point, $T°C$, of water depends upon the height, H metres, above sea level. A formula that relates these two variables is $T + 0.0034H = 100$.

b) A tanker truck drives onto a weigh scale and is then filled with crude oil. The mass, M kilograms, of the truck and the volume, V barrels, of crude oil are related by the equation $M - 180V - 14\,000 = 0$.

 13. Graph each equation.

a) $4x + 3y - 12 = 0$ **b)** $2x - 4y + 8 = 0$ **c)** $-x + 5y - 5 = 0$

14. Knowledge/Understanding Graph each equation.

a) $y = 3x + 2$ **b)** $7x - 14y = 21$ **c)** $2y + 3x - 6 = 0$

15. Graph each equation.

a) $3x - 4y - 8 = 0$ **b)** $3x + y = 4$ **c)** $y - 3x = 2$

d) $4x - 5y = -20$ **e)** $3y - 4x = -12$ **f)** $2x - 4y = -6$

 16. Communication You know three methods to graph a line. When you are given the equation of a line, how do you know which method to use? Is one method better than the other two? Explain, with examples of equations.

17. Frances has a job in sales. She earns a salary of $2000 per month, plus a commission of 8% of her sales. Her monthly salary, *m* dollars, is determined by $m = 2000 + 0.08s$, where *s* dollars is her monthly sales. Draw a graph to represent her monthly earnings on sales up to $10 000.

18. Application Alexia is a plumber. Her rates are $50 per service call and $40 per hour.

  a) Write an equation to represent Alexia's total charges.

  b) Draw a graph to represent the amount Alexia would charge for any call up to 8 h.

19. Thinking/Inquiry/Problem Solving Rocco's computer needs repair. The repair company charges a $25 flat rate plus $40 for every 30 min of repair. Rocco's bill is $145 before taxes. How long did the repair person spend fixing his computer?

Linh has a cellular phone. She investigates two payment plans.
The monthly cost at Cellular A is $25, plus 10¢ per minute.
The monthly cost at Talk to Me is $5, plus 20¢ per minute.
To help her decide which plan to use, she drew this graph.

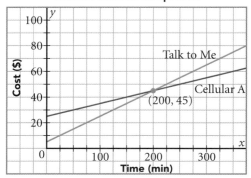

Cost vs. Time for cell phones

The coordinates of the point of intersection are (200, 45). This means that
the cost is the same, $45, when 200 min are used.

Discuss

If fewer than 200 min are needed, it is cheaper to buy a plan from Talk to Me. If
more than 200 min are needed, it is cheaper to buy a plan from Cellular A. How
do we know this from the graph?

We can write an equation for the cost of each payment plan.

Let n represent the number of minutes and C, the cost in dollars.

At Cellular A: $C = 25 + 0.1n$
At Talk to Me: $C = 5 + 0.2n$

Each equation is linear. Recall that these equations together form a linear
system. To solve a linear system means to determine the coordinates of the
point of intersection of the lines.
The solution of this linear system is $(200, 45)$.

Example 1

A lunchtime pizza business has start-up costs of $200. The cost of making a slice of pizza is $1.50. So cost, C dollars, is $C = 1.50n + 200$, where n is the number of slices made. A slice of pizza sells for $2. The revenue, R dollars, earned on sales of n pizza slices is $R = 2.00n$. Determine the number of slices that must be sold for the business to break even.

Solution

Graph each linear equation.

$C = 1.50n + 200$

Choose 3 values of n, then calculate the corresponding C value.

Substitute $n = 0$.   Substitute $n = 200$.   Substitute $n = 500$.
$C = 1.50(0) + 200$ $C = 1.50(200) + 200$ $C = 1.50(500) + 200$
$= 200$ $= 500$ $= 950$

The coordinates of the ordered pairs are $(0, 200)$, $(200, 500)$, and $(500, 950)$. Plot the points, then join them with a straight line.

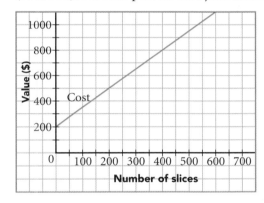

$R = 2n$

Choose 3 values of n, then calculate the corresponding R value.

Substitute $n = 0$.   Substitute $n = 200$.   Substitute $n = 500$.
$R = 2(0)$ $R = 2(200)$ $R = 2(500)$
$= 0$ $= 400$ $= 1000$

The coordinates of the ordered pairs are $(0, 0)$, $(200, 400)$, and $(500, 1000)$.

Plot the points on the same grid and join them with a straight line.

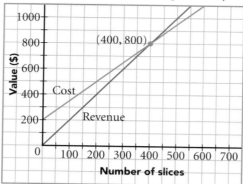

Determine the coordinates of the point of intersection of the lines.
From the graph, the point of intersection is (400, 800).

When 400 slices of pizza are made and sold, the production cost and sales revenue are both $800. Thus, the business will break even when it makes and sells 400 slices of pizza.

Example 2 Use a graphing calculator to solve this linear system.

$x + y = 2$
$x + 4y = -4$

Rearrange each equation to the form $y = mx + b$.

$x + y = 2$ $\qquad\qquad$ $x + 4y = -4$
$\quad y = -x + 2$ $\qquad\qquad$ $4y = -x - 4$
$\qquad\qquad\qquad\qquad\qquad y = -\dfrac{x}{4} - 1$

We input these equations in the graphing calculator.

$y = -x + 2$ $\qquad$ ①
$y = -\dfrac{x}{4} - 1$ $\qquad$ ② $\qquad$ The equations are numbered for reference.

Press $\boxed{\text{Y=}}$. Use $\boxed{\text{CLEAR}}$ and the arrow keys to clear all equations.
Press $\boxed{\text{ZOOM}}$ **6** to select the standard window, below left.

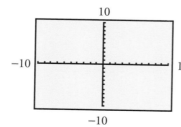
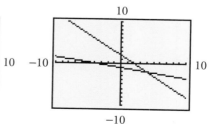

If any of Plot 1, Plot 2, or Plot 3 at the top of the screen is highlighted, use the arrow keys and ENTER to remove the highlighting.

Make sure the cursor is beside Y1=. Press (-) X,T,θ,n + 2 to enter equation ①: $y = -x + 2$.

- Use ▼ to move the cursor next to Y2=. Press (-) X,T,θ,n ÷ 4 - 1. You have entered equation ②: $y = -\frac{x}{4} - 1$.
- Press GRAPH to see the screen, bottom right previous page.

To determine the coordinates of the point of intersection, press 2nd TRACE for CALC. Then press **5** to select **intersect**.

Use ◄ or ► to move the cursor close to the point of intersection, and to the left of the point. Press ENTER to see a screen similar to that below left.

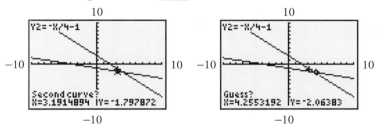

Use ► to move the cursor to the right of the point of intersection and close to the point. Press ENTER to see a screen similar to that above right.

Press ENTER again. The calculator displays the screen below, with the coordinates of the point of intersection.

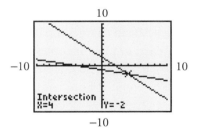

The solution of the system is (4, –2).

A

✓ **1.** Solve each system graphically.

a) $y = x + 1$
   $y = 2$

b) $y = 2x - 1$
   $y = 4$

c) $y = -3x - 2$
   $y = 1$

✓ **2.** Solve each system graphically.

a) $y = -3$
   $y = \frac{3}{2}x$

b) $x = 4$
   $y = \frac{1}{2}x + 2$

c) $y = \frac{4}{3}x - 4$
   $y = 0$

B

3. Solve each system graphically.

a) $y = x$
   $y = 3x - 2$

b) $y = -x + 1$
   $y = 2x + 4$

c) $y = \frac{3}{4}x + 2$
   $y = \frac{1}{2}x + 3$

✓ **4.** Solve each system graphically.

a) $y = \frac{2}{3}x - 1$
   $y = -\frac{2}{3}x + 3$

b) $y = 2x - 1$
   $y = -2x - 5$

c) $y = -x + 1$
   $y = -\frac{1}{2}x + 2$

5. **Knowledge/Understanding** Solve each system graphically.

a) $2x - 3y = -1$
   $4x + 7y = 37$

b) $3x - 4y = 12$
   $x - 2y = 4$

c) $x - 3y = -15$
   $x + 3y = 9$

6. A manufacturer of weight-training machines must choose a company to print a promotional brochure. Quick and Clear charges $900 for set up and $0.50 per copy. Miles Ahead charges a flat fee of $1500 and $0.38 per copy. The cost, C dollars, to print n copies at each company is: $C = 0.50n + 900$ and $C = 0.38n + 1500$. How many brochures must be printed for the prices to be equal at both companies?

✓ **7.** **Communication** Attempt to solve this system graphically.

$6x - 3y = 2$
$8x - 4y = 13$

Explain why this system cannot be solved graphically.

8. A certain air conditioning unit costs $1800 to buy and $60 per month to operate. Cost, C dollars, for n months is $C = 60n + 1800$. A more expensive unit costs $2600 to buy but only $50 to operate. Cost, C dollars, for n months is $C = 50n + 2600$. After how many months would the total cost of the two systems be the same?

9. Regular light bulbs cost $0.55 and use electricity costing $6 for 1000 h ($0.006/h). An energy-saving light bulb costs $1.15 and uses $4 worth of electricity for every 1000h ($0.004/h). The cost, C dollars, of using a regular bulb for h hours is $C = 0.006h + 0.55$. The cost for the energy-saver bulb is $C = 0.004h + 1.15$.

a) Graph the linear system.

b) After how many hours is it cheaper to use the energy-saver bulb? What is the cost of using the energy-saver bulb at this point?

c) Suppose you use the energy-saver bulb. How much do you save after 1000 h of use?

10. Solve each system graphically.

a) $y = x - 6$
   $x + 4y = -4$

b) $x - 5y = -15$
   $3x + y = 3$

c) $x - 4y = 9$
   $x + 3y = -12$

11. Kelvin is planning to rent a car for one week. Two local rental companies have different payment plans.
Company A charges $200 per week for an economy car, with no charge for the distance driven. The cost, C dollars, is given by the equation $C = 200$. Company B charges a $25 administration fee plus 35¢ per kilometre for an economy car. The cost, C dollars, for x kilometres driven is $C = 25 + 0.35x$. Determine the distance driven that will result in equal costs at the two companies.

12. Application The amount charged to cater a luncheon by Tina's Catering is $100 plus $15 per meal. Norman's Catering charges $25 plus $20 per meal. Determine the number of meals that will result in equal costs at the two companies.

13. A particular brand of car with a normal engine costs $16 500 to purchase, and approximately $0.22/km to operate. The same car with a fuel-injection engine costs $17 200 but only $0.20/km to operate. After how many kilometres does the total cost to buy and operate the car with the fuel-injection engine equal that of the normal engine?

14. Market research for a new product indicates that the product can be sold at $50 per unit. The fixed costs to run the company are $8640. The product costs $30 per unit. Determine the break-even point for the company, where the cost and revenue are equal.

15. Thinking/Inquiry/Problem Solving

a) Determine a linear system that has the solution $(2, -5)$.

b) Is the system in part a the only possible system? Explain.

2.5 Solving Linear Systems Algebraically

In Section 2.4, we solved linear systems graphically. The graphical solution requires grid paper or a graphing calculator. In this section, we will review two algebraic methods of solution. The two methods are *substitution* and *elimination*.

At the point of intersection of two lines, the x- and y-values are the same on each line. We use this fact when we solve by substitution.

Example 1

The cost, C dollars, to send a fax with number of pages, p, at a local telecom store is $C - 0.25p = 5.00$. At a business supply store, the cost is $C = 0.75p$. How many pages would Zaina have to send for the cost to be equal at each store? What is the equivalent cost?

Solution

We must solve the linear system.

$C - 0.25p = 5.00$ ①
$C = 0.75p$ ②

From equation ②, substitute $C = 0.75p$ in equation ①.

$0.75p - 0.25p = 5.00$ This is an equation in one variable.
        $0.5p = 5.00$ Solve the equation.
           $p = 10$

Substitute $p = 10$ in equation ② to obtain the corresponding value for C.
$C = 0.75p$
  $= 0.75(10)$
  $= 7.50$
The solution to the system is $(10, 7.50)$.

It would cost $7.50 at either company if 10 pages need to be faxed.

Discuss

Could we have substituted $p = 10$ in equation ①?
Why did we choose equation ②?

We use this method when one of the variables has a coefficient 1, so we can rearrange the equation to isolate that variable easily.

Example 2

Solve this system. Check the solution.

$2x + y = 4$
$3x - 2y = 13$

Solution

$2x + y = 4$ ①
$3x - 2y = 13$ ②

The variable y has a coefficient 1 in equation ①.
Rearrange equation ① to isolate y.

$y = 4 - 2x$

Substitute for y in equation ②.

$$3x - 2y = 13$$
$$3x - 2(4 - 2x) = 13$$
$$3x - 8 + 4x = 13$$
$$7x - 8 = 13$$
$$7x = 21$$
$$x = 3$$

Substitute $x = 3$ in equation ①.

$$2x + y = 4$$
$$2(3) + y = 4$$
$$6 + y = 4$$
$$y = -2$$

The solution of the system is $(3, -2)$.

Check.

Substitute $x = 3$ and $y = -2$ in equation ①: $2x + y = 4$.

Left side $= 2x + y$ Right side $= 4$
            $= 2(3) + (-2)$
            $= 6 - 2$
            $= 4$

Since the left side and right side are equal, $(3, -2)$ satisfies equation ①.

Substitute $x = 3$ and $y = -2$ in equation ②: $3x - 2y = 13$.

$$\begin{aligned}\text{Left side} &= 3x - 2y && \text{Right side} = 13\\ &= 3(3) - 2(-2)\\ &= 9 + 4\\ &= 13\end{aligned}$$

Since the left side and right side are equal, $(3, -2)$ satisfies equation ②.

Since the solution satisfies both equations, the solution is correct.

Discuss

Why would it be considerably harder to rearrange equation ① to isolate x rather than y?

Elimination

When none of the coefficients of the variables in a linear system is 1, we can use the method of elimination to solve the system. This method uses the fact that if we add left sides and right sides of the equations in a linear system, the resulting equation is also true.

Consider this system:

$$\begin{aligned}4x - 2y &= 10 && ①\\ 2x + 2y &= 8 && ②\end{aligned}$$

Since $-2y$ and $2y$ are opposites, their sum is zero. So, by adding equations ① and ② we eliminate the y-terms.

$$\begin{array}{rl}
& 4x - 2y = 10\\
\text{Add.} & \underline{2x + 2y = 8}\\
& 6x = 18\\
& x = 3
\end{array}$$

Substitute $x = 3$ in equation ①.

$$\begin{aligned}4(3) - 2y &= 10\\ 12 - 2y &= 10\\ 2y &= 2\\ y &= 1\end{aligned}$$

The solution of the system is $(3, 1)$.

Sometimes we need to multiply an equation by a constant to obtain two opposite terms. This is illustrated in *Example 3*.

We use the property that an equation can be multiplied by a constant without changing the equality.

Example 3

A company sold 5 standard air conditioning units and 4 deluxe units for $39 000. The next month, the company sold 4 standard and 2 deluxe units for $24 000. How much does each unit sell for?

Solution

Let x dollars represent the cost of one standard unit.
Let y dollars represent the cost of one deluxe unit.

The cost of 5 standard units is $5x$ dollars.
The cost of 4 deluxe units is $4y$ dollars.

So, the revenue in the first month is $5x + 4y = 39\ 000$.
The revenue in the second month is $4x + 2y = 24\ 000$.

The linear system is:
$$5x + 4y = 39\ 000 \qquad ①$$
$$4x + 2y = 24\ 000 \qquad ②$$

No two terms are opposites. Make the second terms opposite.
Multiply equation ② by –2 to get $-4y$.
Then $4y$ and $-4y$ are opposites.

Copy ①	$5x + 4y = \quad 39\ 000$
Multiply ② by –2.	$-8x - 4y = -48\ 000$ ③ Label the new equation ③.
Add.	$\overline{-3x \qquad\quad = -9\ 000}$
	$x = \quad 3\ 000$

Substitute $x = 3000$ in equation ① to determine y.
$$5x + 4y = 39\ 000$$
$$5(3000) + 4y = 39\ 000$$
$$15\ 000 + 4y = 39\ 000$$
$$4y = 24\ 000$$
$$y = 6000$$

The solution of the system is $(3000,\ 6000)$.

The standard units sell for $3000 and the deluxe units sell for $6000.

Discuss
Could we have substituted $x = 3000$ in equation ①? Explain.

We may need to multiply both equations by constants to obtain two opposite terms.

Example 4

A company bought 2 model A electrical components and 3 model B electrical components for $1500. In the next order, the company bought 3 model A and 4 model B components for $2075. How much did the company pay for each model type?

Solution

Let a dollars represent the cost of model A components.
Let b dollars represent the cost of model B components.

$2a + 3b = 1500$ ①
$3a + 4b = 2075$ ②

No two terms are opposite. Make the first terms opposite.

Multiply ① by 3. $6a + 9b = 4500$ ③
Multiply ② by –2. $\underline{-6a - 8b = -4150}$ ④
Add. $b = 350$

Substitute $b = 350$ in equation ① to determine a.
$2a + 3(350) = 1500$
$2a + 1050 = 1500$
$2a = 450$
$a = 225$

The solution of the system is (225, 350).

The company paid $225 for each model A component and $350 for each model B component.

Discuss

How did we know to multiply equation ① by 3 and equation ② by –2? Could we have multiplied by different numbers to solve the system? Explain.

A

✓ **1.** Solve by substitution.

a) $y = x + 1$
$y = -x + 6$

b) $y = -2x$
$y = x + 3$

c) $y = 2x + 4$
$y = x + 4$

d) $y = x + 3$
$y = -2x - 3$

e) $y = 2x + 10$
$y = x + 7$

f) $y = -x - 1$
$y = -2x + 1$

2. Solve by substitution.

a) $x = y$
$2x + 3y = 5$

b) $x + y = 1$
$y = 2x - 5$

c) $x = y - 1$
$x + 3y = 11$

d) $y = x + 1$
$2x + y = 4$

e) $x = y + 2$
$x + 3y = 6$

f) $x + 2y = 3$
$y = x + 3$

✓ **3.** Solve by elimination.

a) $x + y = 4$
$x - y = -2$

b) $x + y = 1$
$x - y = 5$

c) $2x + 3y = 5$
$-2x + 3y = 1$

d) $3x - y = -10$
$3x + y = -8$

e) $x - y = 2$
$x + y = 0$

f) $2x + y = 3$
$2x - y = 5$

4. Solve by elimination.

a) $x + 2y = -1$
$3x - 2y = -11$

b) $2x - y = 1$
$2x + y = 11$

c) $3x + 5y = 8$
$2x - 5y = -3$

d) $3x + 4y = -10$
$2x - 4y = -5$

e) $5x - 3y = -6$
$-5x - y = 2$

f) $-2x + 6y = 22$
$2x - 3y = -10$

B

5. An airplane cruises at a constant velocity of 840 km/h during the 5430-km trip from Montreal to London, England. The equation that describes its motion is $d = -840t + 5430$, where d is its distance from London in kilometres, and t is the time in hours since the airplane reached its cruising velocity. The plane must start its descent when it is 90 km from London, so $d = 90$ when it starts its descent. How long has the plane been cruising when it starts its descent?

6. Pyramid Stables charges $20/h (including insurance) for trail rides. Sara's Stables charges $16/h, with a separate insurance fee of $12. The cost, C dollars, for h hours of riding is $C = 20h$ and $C = 16h + 12$.

a) How many hours of riding would result in the same cost at either stable?

b) If you wish to ride for 2 h, which stable would you choose? Explain.

✓ **7.** Green Thumb Garden Products produces wheelbarrows and carts. A wheelbarrow has one front wheel and a garden cart has two wheels. The company has 500 wheels to make a total of 300 wheelbarrows and carts. An equation that shows there is a total of 300 items is $w + c = 300$, where w represents the number of wheelbarrows and c represents the number of carts. An equation that shows there is a total of 500 wheels is $w + 2c = 500$. How many wheelbarrows and how many carts can be made?

✓ **8.** The fuel consumption of a Mercedes-Benz is 11 L/100 km (0.11 L/km) for city driving, and 8 L/100 km (0.08 L/km) for highway driving. During one week, the car used 62 L of fuel to travel a total of 600 km both in the city and on the highway. If the car travelled c kilometres in the city and h kilometres on the highway during that week, the equations are $c + h = 600$ and $0.11c + 0.08h = 62$. Solve the system to determine the distances driven in the city and on the highway.

✓ **9. Knowledge/Understanding** Solve.

a) $2x + y = -1$
$3x - 2y = 16$

b) $y = 2x + 11$
$2x + y = -5$

c) $2x - 3y = 1$
$x + 2y = -7$

d) $5x + 3y = 2$
$4x + 2y = 0$

e) $3y + x = 14$
$2x + y = 3$

f) $2x + 3y = 0$
$4x + 2y = 8$

✓ **10. Communication** Explain when it is better to solve a system algebraically rather than graphically. Include examples in your explanation.

11. An airplane can travel at 800 km/h with a tailwind, and 730 km/h against the wind. Let s represent the airplane's speed in still air in km/h and w the wind speed in km/h. A system of equations that represents the situation is $s + w = 800$ and $s - w = 730$. Solve the system to determine the wind speed and the speed of the plane in still air.

12. A coffee shop uses two different types of coffee to make a house blend. A dark French roast costing $4.95 per pound is mixed with a lighter Kenyan roast costing $3.75 per pound. The two types of coffee must be mixed together to make 50 pounds of the house blend. The house blend will cost $4.35 per pound.

a) State the unknown quantities and define suitable variables for each.

b) Write equations to represent the mass of coffee and the cost of coffee.

c) Solve the linear system to determine the mass of each kind of coffee that should be used.

13. A carpenter buys lumber from a local supplier. Cedar costs $430 a bundle and pine $265 a bundle. The accounts book indicates that last month he bought 10 bundles and paid $3145. How many bundles of each type of wood were purchased?

14. Application The outside of Sarah's house needs painting. She has to decide between two companies. One company charges $100 for materials plus $30/h. The second company charges $135 for materials plus $25/h.

   a) How many hours of painting would result in the same cost at both companies?

   b) Sarah's house will likely require about 15 h of painting. Which company should she choose? Explain.

15. Original's manufactures silk-screen T-shirts featuring local graphic designers. The company produces two types of T-shirts: a multi-colour shirt, and a standard one-colour shirt. One deluxe shirt costs $8 for materials and $30 for labour. One standard shirt costs $5 for materials and $12 for labour. Original's budget is $1700 for materials and $5700 for labour for one month. How many of each type of shirt can be produced in one month?

16. A pension fund seeks to invest $1 million. To satisfy its current and future obligations, the fund must earn $54 000 per year. The fund has two sorts of investments open to it: stocks paying 4% per year and corporate bonds paying 6% per year. How much should the pension fund invest in each investment in order to earn exactly the desired income?

17. Thinking/Inquiry/Problem Solving Two sales employees earn different salaries. Mo earns a weekly base salary of $250 plus 10% of his sales. His salary, y dollars, is determined by the equation $y = 250 + 0.1x$, where x dollars represents his weekly sales. Sylvia earns a weekly base salary plus 40% of her weekly sales. Both employees earned the same weekly salary when they had $500 of weekly sales. Determine Sylvia's base salary.

C

18. Solve.

a) $\dfrac{x}{5} + \dfrac{y}{2} = \dfrac{19}{10}$

$\dfrac{x}{4} - \dfrac{y}{9} = \dfrac{1}{6}$

b) $\dfrac{x}{5} + \dfrac{y}{5} = 1$

$\dfrac{x}{4} + \dfrac{y}{8} = 1$

c) $\dfrac{x}{3} - \dfrac{y}{4} = \dfrac{5}{12}$

$\dfrac{x}{5} + \dfrac{y}{4} = \dfrac{13}{20}$

d) $\dfrac{x}{2} - \dfrac{y}{2} = 2$

$\dfrac{x}{4} - \dfrac{y}{8} = \dfrac{9}{8}$

e) $\dfrac{x}{3} + \dfrac{y}{2} = \dfrac{1}{6}$

$\dfrac{x}{4} - \dfrac{y}{3} = -\dfrac{11}{12}$

f) $\dfrac{x}{8} + \dfrac{y}{4} = 1$

$\dfrac{x}{9} - \dfrac{y}{3} = \dfrac{1}{3}$

1. Solve.
   a) $5x - 7 = 18$ b) $4y + 3 = -2y - 6$ c) $7 - 4x = 2x - 5$

2. Solve.
   a) $3x + 5 - 6x + 7 = 5x - 4 + x - 1$
   b) $2y - 3(y - 4) = 2(y - 5) - 11$
   c) $4(x + 3) - 2(x - 4) = x - (-4 + 3x)$
   d) $3(x - 5) + 2(x + 3) = 2(4x - 5) + 4(x + 7)$

3. Solve each formula for the indicated variable.
   a) The area of a triangle: $A = \frac{1}{2}bh$, for h
   b) The equation of a line: $y = mx + b$, for x
   c) The area of a trapezoid: $A = \frac{h(a + b)}{2}$, for b
   d) The general term of an arithmetic sequence: $t_n = a + (n - 1)d$, for n

4. Determine the slope and y-intercept of each line.
   a) $y = 3x - 7$ b) $y - 4x = 9$
   c) $2x + 2y = -1$ d) $8x - 4y - 4 = 0$

5. Graph each line.
   a) $y = 3x - 5$ b) $4x + 3y = 12$ c) $y = \frac{1}{2}x + 3$

6. Solve each system graphically.
   a) $-x - 2y = -7$ b) $3x + y = -5$ c) $3x + y = 3$
      $3x - 2y = 5$ $3x + 2y = -12$ $x + y = 5$

7. Solve each system by substitution.
   a) $y = -3x + 3$ b) $x + y = 1$ c) $4x - 3y = 9$
      $7x - 2y = 20$ $2x + 3y = 11$ $2x - y = 5$

8. Solve each system by elimination.
   a) $3x - 5y = -9$ b) $x - 2y = 7$ c) $7x + 6y = 2$
      $4x + 5y = 23$ $3x + 4y = 1$ $x + 8y = -4$

Performance Assessment

9. Nadia works part-time in computer sales. She can choose the plan by
   which she is paid.
   Plan A: 9% of the value of her monthly sales
   Plan B: $375 plus 3% of her sales
   What advice would you give to Nadia regarding the payment plan she
   should choose? Explain your reasoning and justify your answer with
   mathematics.

Simplifying Polynomials

A polynomial is a mathematical expression of variables and/or numbers connected by addition and subtraction signs. In previous courses you worked with polynomials. This work will be consolidated and extended in this section and the rest of the chapter.

Recall that a polynomial with one term is a monomial; for example, $3y$.

A polynomial with two terms is a binomial; for example, $2x - 4$.

A polynomial with three terms is a trinomial; for example, $4x^2 + 5x - 2$.

The following examples review adding, subtracting, multiplying, and dividing polynomials.

Example 1 Simplify.

a) $(2x^2 - 5x + 7) + (4x^2 + 2x - 9)$ **b)** $(4x^2 - 5x + 2) - (2x^2 - 2x - 4)$

Solution

a) $(2x^2 - 5x + 7) + (4x^2 + 2x - 9)$

$\quad = 2x^2 - 5x + 7 + 4x^2 + 2x - 9$ Remove brackets.

$\quad = 2x^2 + 4x^2 - 5x + 2x + 7 - 9$ Collect like terms.

$\quad = 6x^2 - 3x - 2$ Combine like terms.

Recall that to subtract a polynomial, add the opposite.

b) $(4x^2 - 5x + 2) - (2x^2 - 2x - 4)$

$\quad = 4x^2 - 5x + 2 - 2x^2 + 2x + 4$ Add the opposite.

$\quad = 4x^2 - 2x^2 - 5x + 2x + 2 + 4$ Collect like terms.

$\quad = 2x^2 - 3x + 6$ Combine like terms.

Example 2 Expand then simplify.

a) $(2x - 3)(x + 5)$ **b)** $(y + 2)(3y^2 - 4y + 2)$ **c)** $3(x - 2)^2$

Solution

Multiply each term of one polynomial by each term of the other polynomial.

a) $(2x - 3)(x + 5) = 2x^2 + 10x - 3x - 15$

$$= 2x^2 + 7x - 15 \qquad \text{Combine like terms.}$$

b) $(y + 2)(3y^2 - 4y + 2) = 3y^3 - 4y^2 + 2y + 6y^2 - 8y + 4$

$$= 3y^3 + 2y^2 - 6y + 4$$

c) Square the binomial first, then multiply by 3.

$$3(x - 2)^2 = 3(x - 2)(x - 2)$$
$$= 3(x^2 - 2x - 2x + 4)$$
$$= 3(x^2 - 4x + 4)$$
$$= 3x^2 - 12x + 12$$

Example 3 reviews dividing monomials.

Example 3 Simplify.

a) $\dfrac{24xy}{3}$ **b)** $\dfrac{36m^2n}{-6m}$ **c)** $\dfrac{-27b}{9b}$

Solution

To divide two monomials, divide the coefficients, then divide the variables.

a) $\dfrac{24xy}{3} = 8xy$ Divide the coefficients: $\dfrac{24}{3} = 8$

b) $\dfrac{36m^2n}{-6m} = -6mn$ Divide the coefficients: $\dfrac{36}{-6} = -6$

                                  Divide the variables: $\dfrac{m^2n}{m} = mn$

c) $\dfrac{-27b}{9b} = -3$ Divide the coefficients: $\dfrac{-27}{9} = -3$

                                    Divide the variables: $\dfrac{b}{b} = 1$

To simplify certain expressions, we add, subtract, and multiply. Remember the order of operations: multiply before adding or subtracting.

Example 4 Simplify.

a) $3(x + 3)(x - 2) + 4(x - 1)(x - 2)$ b) $4(a + 2)(a - 2) - 3(a - 3)(a + 1)$

Solution

a) $3(x + 3)(x - 2) + 4(x - 1)(x - 2)$
$= 3(x^2 - 2x + 3x - 6) + 4(x^2 - 2x - x + 2)$ Expand each set of
$= 3(x^2 + x - 6) + 4(x^2 - 3x + 2)$ binomials.
$= 3x^2 + 3x - 18 + 4x^2 - 12x + 8$
$= 7x^2 - 9x - 10$

b) $4(a + 2)(a - 2) - 3(a - 3)(a + 1)$
$= 4(a^2 - 4) - 3(a^2 - 2a - 3)$
$= 4a^2 - 16 - 3a^2 + 6a + 9$
$= a^2 + 6a - 7$

2.6 Exercises

A

✓ **1.** Simplify.

a) $(7x + 2) + (4x + 3)$ b) $(-4x - 5) + (5x - 2)$
c) $(3x - 4) + (5x - 2)$ d) $(-2x + 1) + (4x - 1)$
e) $(x + 1) + (2x - 5)$ f) $(4x - 4) + (x - 6)$

✓ **2.** Simplify.

a) $(2x + 1) - (4x + 3)$ b) $(-4z - 6) - (5z - 2)$
c) $(3x + 2) - (2x - 1)$ d) $(4a - 2) - (3a + 5)$
e) $(2x - 2) - (4x - 2)$ f) $(5w - 2) - (w - 1)$

✓ **3.** Expand then simplify.

a) $(x + 3)(x + 2)$ b) $(x + 4)(x - 3)$ c) $(x - 1)(x + 5)$
d) $(x - 2)(x - 4)$ e) $(y - 6)(y + 4)$ f) $(a + 7)(a - 1)$
g) $(z - 5)(z - 4)$ h) $(x + 8)(x - 3)$ i) $(x - 4)(x + 5)$

B

4. Simplify.
   a) $(3x^2 + 2x + 5) + (x^2 + 3x + 1)$
   b) $(2x^2 - 4x - 3) + (3x^2 - 4x + 5)$
   c) $(-4x^2 - 6x + 7) + (-5x^2 + 8x - 9)$
   d) $(3y^2 + 4y - 6) + (2y^2 - 6y + 2)$
   e) $(5x^2 - 2x + 9) + (6x^2 - 3x - 10)$
   f) $(-2y^2 + 3y - 7) + (2y^2 - 5y - 4)$

5. Simplify.
   a) $(3x^2 + 5x + 4) - (2x^2 - 4x + 6)$
   b) $(3x^2 + 2x - 4) - (-2x^2 + 7x - 5)$
   c) $(-5x^2 + 8x + 5) - (5x^2 + 6x - 3)$
   d) $(2y^2 + 3y + 9) - (-3y^2 + 2y + 7)$
   e) $(-8x^2 + x - 6) - (-4x^2 + 3x - 6)$
   f) $(-2y^2 + 5y - 8) - (12y^2 - 5y + 3)$

6. Expand then simplify.
   a) $(2x + 1)(3x + 4)$ b) $-(3x + 2)(x - 1)$ c) $(4x - 1)(2x + 1)$
   d) $(3x - 2)(2x - 3)$ e) $(4y - 5)(3y + 4)$ f) $-(2a + 7)(3a - 4)$
   g) $-(5z - 2)(3z - 4)$ h) $(2x + 5)(4x - 5)$ i) $(3x - 4)(6x + 5)$

✓ 7. a) Expand then simplify.
   i) $(x + 1)(x - 1)$ ii) $(x - 2)(x + 2)$ iii) $(x - 3)(x + 3)$
   iv) $(x - 4)(x + 4)$ v) $(2y - 5)(2y + 5)$ vi) $(a + 7)(a - 7)$
   vii) $(3z - 2)(3z + 2)$ viii) $(2x + 9)(2x - 9)$ ix) $(5x - 8)(5x + 8)$

   b) Describe the pattern in the products in part a. Use the pattern to
      simplify $(4a + 3)(4a - 3)$.

8. a) Expand then simplify.
   i) $(x + 2)^2$ ii) $(y + 5)^2$ iii) $(x + 7)^2$
   iv) $(x - 3)^2$ v) $(y - 4)^2$ vi) $(x - 8)^2$
   vii) $(2x + 5)^2$ viii) $(3y - 1)^2$ ix) $(4x + 3)^2$

   b) **Communication** Examine the pattern in the products in part a.
      Describe a short cut to square a binomial.

9. Expand then simplify.

   a) $(x + 2)(x^2 + 3x + 1)$ **b)** $-(x - 3)(x^2 + 4x + 5)$

   c) $(x - 1)(x^2 - 5x - 3)$ **d)** $(3x + 2)(2x^2 + 3x + 4)$

   e) $(3y - 1)(2y^2 + 5y + 4)$ **f)** $-(2a - 5)(3a^2 - 2a - 3)$

   g) $(5z + 2)(3z^2 + z - 4)$ **h)** $-(2x - 7)(3x^2 - 2x - 5)$

   i) $(4x + 3)(5x^2 - x + 5)$

10. Expand then simplify.

   a) $3(x + 1)(x + 5)$ **b)** $2(x + 2)(x - 3)$ **c)** $4(x - 2)(x - 5)$

   d) $5(x - 2)(2x + 1)$ **e)** $-2(4y + 3)(2y - 5)$ **f)** $-3(2a - 3)(3a - 4)$

   g) $6(5z + 3)(3z - 4)$ **h)** $3(2x + 5)(2x - 5)$ **i)** $4(x - 3)^2$

✓ 11. Simplify.

   a) $\dfrac{15a^2}{5a}$ **b)** $\dfrac{18mn}{2n}$ **c)** $\dfrac{64x^2y}{-8xy}$

   d) $\dfrac{16pq}{4pq}$ **e)** $\dfrac{-21a^2b^2}{7a^2b}$ **f)** $\dfrac{-18z^5}{-6z^3}$

✓ **12. Application** Determine the area of the shaded region.

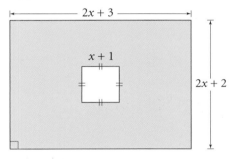

13. Simplify.

   a) $3x^2 + 2x - 5 - (2x^2 + 4x + 3)$ **b)** $4y^2 - 3y + 7 - (6y^2 - 5y - 2)$

   c) $(x + 3)(x + 2) + (x + 1)(x + 4)$ **d)** $-(x - 1)(x + 3) + (x + 1)(x - 4)$

14. Simplify.

   a) $-(x + 3)(x + 2) - (x + 1)(x + 4)$

   b) $(x - 1)(x + 3) - (x + 1)(x - 4)$

   c) $-(2a + 1)(3a - 2) + (4a - 5)(a - 3)$

   d) $(3x - 1)(2x + 4) - (3x + 1)(2x - 4)$

15. Simplify.

    a) $2(x + 1)(x + 2) + 3(x + 2)(x + 3)$

    b) $-3(x - 1)(x + 2) + 5(x + 3)(x - 4)$

    c) $2(x + 3)(x + 2) - 4(x + 1)(x + 4)$

    d) $-5(x + 1)(x - 3) - 2(x + 5)(x - 7)$

16. Knowledge/Understanding Simplify.

    a) $-3(2a + 3)(2a - 1) + 4(a - 5)(a - 3)$

    b) $-4(3x - 1)(2x + 4) - 3(3x + 1)(2x - 4)$

    c) $2(3x - 1)(2x + 3) + 3(2x + 1)^2$

    d) $-(2x - 1)^2 - (3x + 2)^2$

17. Simplify.

    a) $(5x - 2)(2x + 3) - (3x - 4)(3x + 4)$

    b) $-(2x - 1)(2x + 1) - (3x + 2)(3x - 2)$

    c) $3(4y + 3)^2 + 2(5y + 2)^2$

    d) $-2(7z - 3)^2 - 4(3z - 2)^2$

18. Expand then simplify.

    a) $(x + 1)^3$ **b)** $(x + y)^3$

    c) $(2x + y)^3$ **d)** $(3x - 2y)^3$

19. Expand then simplify.

    a) $(x^2 + x + 1)(x^2 + 2x + 3)$ **b)** $(y^2 - y - 1)(y^2 - 2y - 3)$

    c) $(2a^2 + 3a - 5)(3a^2 - 2a - 3)$ **d)** $-(4z^2 - z + 3)(5z^2 + 3z + 2)$

    e) $(x^2 + x + 1)^2$ **f)** $-(y^2 - y - 1)^2$

20. Expand then simplify.

    a) $(3x^2 - x + 2)(x - 4) + 5(2x^2 - x + 1)$

    b) $(2w^2 + 3w + 4)(w^2 - 3) - 2(w - 7)(w + 2)$

    c) $-(v^2 - 3v - 4)(v^2 + 5v + 9) - (2v^2 + 9)(v - 8)$

    d) $-(5z^2 + 2z + 9)(4z^2 + z + 1) - (2z^2 + z - 8)^2$

In Necessary Skills, page 84, we recalled that to factor an expression means to write it as a product. Factoring is the reverse of expanding.

Since $(x + 2)(x + 3)$ expands to $x^2 + 5x + 6$,
then $x^2 + 5x + 6$ factors as $(x + 2)(x + 3)$.

Consider the expansion.

$$x^2 + 5x + 6 = (x + 2)(x + 3)$$

5 is the sum of 2 and 3.
6 is the product of 2 and 3.

This information is used to factor trinomials of the form $x^2 + bx + c$.

To factor $x^2 + 6x + 8$, we find two numbers whose product is 8 and whose sum is 6.

List pairs of numbers whose product is 8, then find each sum.

Product is 8.	Sum
1, 8	$1 + 8 = 9$
$-1, -8$	$-1 - 8 = -9$
2, 4	$2 + 4 = 6$
$-2, -4$	$-2 - 4 = -6$

The numbers that have a sum of 6 are 2 and 4.

Write these numbers as the second terms in the binomials.
$x^2 + 6x + 8 = (x + 2)(x + 4)$

Example 1 Factor.

a) $x^2 - 3x - 10$ **b)** $x^2 - 7x + 12$

Solution

a) $x^2 - 3x - 10$
Find two numbers whose product is -10 and whose sum is -3.
Since the product is -10, the numbers have opposite signs.
List pairs of numbers whose product is -10, then find each sum.

Product is −10.	Sum
−1, 10	−1 + 10 = 9
1, −10	1 − 10 = −9
−2, 5	−2 + 5 = 3
2, −5	2 − 5 = −3

The numbers that have a sum of −3 are 2 and −5.
Write these numbers as the second terms in the binomials.
$x^2 − 3x − 10 = (x + 2)(x − 5)$

b) $x^2 − 7x + 12$

Find two numbers whose product is 12 and whose sum is −7.
Since the product is positive, the numbers have the same sign.
Since the sum is negative, both numbers are negative.
List pairs of negative numbers whose product is 12, then find each sum.

Product is 12.	Sum
−1, −12	−1 − 12 = −13
−2, −6	−2 − 6 = −8
−3, −4	−3 − 4 = −7

$x^2 − 7x + 12 = (x − 3)(x − 4)$

Discuss

In part b, why did we list only 3 pairs of numbers?

Recall from 2.6 Exercises, exercise 7, that when binomials such as
$(x − 3)(x + 3)$ and $(2x + 5)(2x − 5)$ are expanded, the product is always a
binomial. This binomial is special because its terms are perfect squares.

Consider $(x − 3)(x + 3) = x^2 + 3x − 3x − 9$
$$= x^2 − 9$$
and $(2x + 5)(2x − 5) = 4x^2 − 10x + 10x − 25$
$$= 4x^2 − 25$$

An expression of the form $x^2 − 9$ or $4x^2 − 25$ is a difference of squares.

Example 2 Factor each difference of squares.

a) $y^2 − 16$ **b)** $9x^2 − 49$

Solution

a) Write each term as a square.
$$y^2 - 16 = y^2 - 4^2$$
$$= (y + 4)(y - 4)$$

b) Write each term as a square.
$$9x^2 - 49 = (3x)^2 - 7^2$$
$$= (3x - 7)(3x + 7)$$

Discuss

How can you recognize whether a binomial is a difference of squares?

Sometimes a trinomial may be factored after removing a common factor. Similarly a binomial may be factored as a difference of squares after removing a common factor.

Example 3 contains polynomials that require a combination of the types of factoring.

Example 3 Factor fully.

a) $3x^2 - 48$ **b)** $2x^2 + 18x + 40$ **c)** $x^4 - 1$

Solution

a) $3x^2 - 48 = 3(x^2 - 16)$ 3 is a common factor.
$\qquad\qquad\quad = 3(x - 4)(x + 4)$ $x^2 - 16$ is a difference of squares.

b) $2x^2 + 18x + 40 = 2(x^2 + 9x + 20)$ 2 is a common factor.
$\qquad\qquad\qquad\quad = 2(x + 4)(x + 5)$ $x^2 + 9x + 20$ is a trinomial that factors.

c) $x^4 - 1 = (x^2 + 1)(x^2 - 1)$ $x^4 - 1$ is a difference of squares.
$\qquad\quad = (x^2 + 1)(x + 1)(x - 1)$ $x^2 - 1$ is another difference of squares.

Here are the steps to follow when factoring a polynomial.
1. Always remove a common factor first, if possible.
2. Determine whether the resulting expression is a trinomial, a difference of squares, or neither.

A

✓ **1.** Copy and complete the table.
Determine two numbers that have each product and sum.

	Product	Sum	Numbers
a)	6	5	
b)	6	−5	
c)	16	8	
d)	16	−8	
e)	16	−10	
f)	16	10	
g)	−12	−1	
h)	−12	4	

✓ **2.** Factor.

a) $x^2 + 3x + 2$ **b)** $x^2 + 12x + 11$ **c)** $x^2 + 4x + 3$

d) $x^2 + 14x + 13$ **e)** $x^2 + 8x + 7$ **f)** $x^2 + 6x + 5$

g) $x^2 + 18x + 17$ **h)** $x^2 + 20x + 19$ **i)** $x^2 + 24x + 23$

✓ **3.** Describe the pattern in the trinomials in exercise 2. How does this pattern relate to the binomial factors?

✓ **4.** Which binomials are a difference of squares? Explain.

a) $x^2 - 9$ **b)** $3y^2 - 25$ **c)** $36b^2 + 4$

d) $4a^2 - 64$ **e)** $a^2 - b^2$ **f)** $x^3 - y^3$

✓ **5.** Factor.

a) $x^2 - 4$ **b)** $x^2 - 9$ **c)** $a^2 - 1$

d) $y^2 - 25$ **e)** $x^2 - 16$ **f)** $x^2 - 81$

g) $x^2 - 36$ **h)** $z^2 - 49$ **i)** $x^2 - 64$

B

6. Factor.

a) $x^2 + 8x + 12$ **b)** $x^2 + 11x + 18$ **c)** $a^2 + 8a + 15$

d) $y^2 + 12y + 27$ **e)** $x^2 + 9x + 14$ **f)** $x^2 + 10x + 16$

g) $x^2 + 12x + 35$ **h)** $z^2 + 9z + 18$ **i)** $x^2 + 10x + 21$

7. Factor.

a) $x^2 - x - 20$ **b)** $x^2 - 5x - 24$ **c)** $a^2 - 2a - 15$

d) $y^2 - 2y - 8$ **e)** $x^2 - 3x - 28$ **f)** $x^2 - 3x - 18$

g) $x^2 - 5x - 14$ **h)** $z^2 - z - 30$ **i)** $x^2 - 5x - 36$

✓ **8.** Factor.

a) $x^2 + 2x - 15$ **b)** $x^2 + 3x - 18$ **c)** $a^2 + 2a - 63$

d) $y^2 + 5y - 24$ **e)** $x^2 + 2x - 48$ **f)** $x^2 + 9x - 36$

g) $x^2 + 8x - 20$ **h)** $z^2 + z - 12$ **i)** $x^2 + 6x - 16$

✓ **9.** Factor.

a) $x^2 - 4x + 3$ **b)** $x^2 - 5x + 6$ **c)** $a^2 - 7a + 10$

d) $y^2 - 9y + 18$ **e)** $x^2 - 11x + 30$ **f)** $x^2 - 8x + 15$

g) $x^2 - 11x + 24$ **h)** $z^2 - 15z + 56$ **i)** $x^2 - 16x + 48$

10. Factor.

a) $9x^2 - 25$ **b)** $4x^2 - 16y^2$ **c)** $36a^2 - 1$

d) $64y^2 - 25a^2$ **e)** $4x^2 - 81$ **f)** $49x^2 - 81z^2$

g) $25x^2 - 36$ **h)** $64z^2 - 121$ **i)** $144x^2 - 49$

11. Knowledge/Understanding Factor.

a) $x^2 - 7x - 60$ **b)** $81x^2 - 25$ **c)** $a^2 + 7a + 10$

d) $y^2 + 4y - 77$ **e)** $x^2 - 4x - 21$ **f)** $9x^4 - 25y^2$

g) $x^2 - 16x + 60$ **h)** $z^2 - 19z + 84$ **i)** $x^2 + 14x + 45$

12. Factor.

a) $x^2 + 2x + 1$ **b)** $x^2 + 6x + 9$ **c)** $a^2 + 10a + 25$

d) $y^2 - 4y + 4$ **e)** $x^2 - 12x + 36$ **f)** $x^2 - 14x + 49$

g) $x^2 + 8x + 16$ **h)** $z^2 - 16z + 64$ **i)** $x^2 - 6x + 9$

13. Communication Describe a pattern in the trinomials in exercise 12. Explain how this pattern relates to the binomial factors.

✓ **14. Application** A trinomial, such as $x^2 + 6x + 9$, can be factored as a binomial square; that is, $x^2 + 6x + 9 = (x + 3)^2$. This type of trinomial is a perfect square.

a) Without multiplying two binomials, write a trinomial that is a perfect square. (Do not use the trinomials from exercise 12.)

b) Use the same method to write 2 more trinomials that are perfect squares. Describe the method you used.

c) Explain how you can recognize whether a trinomial is a perfect square.

15. Factor fully.

a) $2x^2 + 12x + 16$ **b)** $5x^2 - 45$

c) $3a^2 + 3a - 36$ **d)** $5y^2 - 15y + 10$

e) $x^3 - 5x^2 - 24x$ **f)** $x^4 - 16$

16. Factor fully.

a) $2x^4 - 6x^3 - 20x^2$ **b)** $-3z^2 + 15z + 72$

c) $x^3 + 6x^2 + 9x$ **d)** $2x^3 - 18x$

e) $4z^3 + 20z^2 - 56z$ **f)** $50x^3 - 72x$

17. Thinking/Inquiry/Problem Solving Write three trinomials that will not factor. Explain how you determined the trinomials. Explain how you know they will not factor.

18. a) Replace each ☐ with an integer so the trinomial can be factored.

     i) $x^2 + 3x + \square$ **ii)** $x^2 + \square x + 2$

     iii) $a^2 + \square a - 8$ **iv)** $m^2 + 6m + \square$

     v) $w^2 - 2w - \square$ **vi)** $b^2 - 5b - \square$

b) Is there only one answer for each trinomial in part a? Explain.

19. What conditions must exist for a trinomial of the form $x^2 + bx + c$ to be factorable?

20. Consider the polynomial $x^2 + x + \frac{1}{4}$.

a) Determine a number that when multiplied by itself results in $\frac{1}{4}$.

b) Add the number you found in part a to itself.

c) Factor $x^2 + x + \frac{1}{4}$.

d) Factor $x^2 - x + \frac{1}{4}$.

e) Explain how parts a and b relate to parts c and d.

In Section 2.7, you factored trinomials of the form $x^2 + bx + c$, where the coefficient of the squared term is 1. In this section, we will factor trinomials of the form $ax^2 + bx + c$, where $a \neq 1$.

Consider the product of the binomials $(3x + 2)$ and $(2x + 1)$.

$$(3x + 2)(2x + 1) = 6x^2 + 3x + 4x + 2$$
$$= 6x^2 + 7x + 2$$

Suppose the terms of the binomials are written one above the other as shown below. Notice how the terms in the factors are related to the terms in the product.

| $3x$ | $+2$ |
| $2x$ | $+1$ |

$(3x \times +2)$ ⟶ One factor
$(2x \times +1)$ ⟶ Other factor

| First term in product is $6x^2$. | Last term in product is 2. | Middle term in product is $3x + 4x = 7x$. |

These relationships among the terms may be used to factor a polynomial such as $2x^2 + 5x + 3$.

First, list the possibilities for the first and last terms.

| $2x$ | x | 1 | -1 |
| x | $2x$ | 3 | -3 |

| First term in product is $2x^2$. | Last term in product is 3. |

Then, list all the possibilities for the middle term. Since there are 2 possibilities for each of the first and last terms, there are 2×2, or 4 possibilities for the middle term.

$(2x \times 1)$
$(x \times 3)$

$(2x \times -1)$
$(x \times -3)$

$(x \times 1)$
$(2x \times 3)$

$(x \times -1)$
$(2x \times -3)$

| Middle term is $6x + x = 7x$. | Middle term is $-6x - x = -7x$. | Middle term is $3x + 2x = 5x$. | Middle term is $-3x - 2x = -5x$. |

There is only one correct middle term, $5x$.
So, $2x^2 + 5x + 3 = (x + 1)(2x + 3)$

Example 1 Factor $3x^2 + 11x + 6$.

Solution

$3x^2 + 11x + 6$

List the possibilities for the first and last terms, then look for a combination that gives a middle term of $11x$.

$3x$	x		1	-1	2	-2
x	$3x$		6	-6	3	-3

First term in product is $3x^2$.   Last term in product is 6.

List all the possibilities for the middle term. Since there are 2 possibilities for the first term and 4 possibilities for the last term, there are 2×4, or 8 possibilities for the middle term.

Middle term is $18x + x = 19x$.   Middle term is $-18x - x = -19x$.   Middle term is $9x + 2x = 11x$.   Middle term is $-9x - 2x = -11x$.

Middle term is $6x + 3x = 9x$.   Middle term is $-6x - 3x = -9x$.   Middle term is $3x + 6x = 9x$.   Middle term is $-3x - 6x = -9x$.

There is only one correct middle term, $11x$.
So, $3x^2 + 11x + 6 = (3x + 2)(x + 3)$

Discuss
How could you check that the factors are correct?

Example 1 illustrates that it may be tedious to list all the possibilities for the middle term. So, we consider them mentally.

Example 2 Factor $8y^2 - 10y - 3$.

Solution

$8y^2 - 10y - 3$

List the possibilities for the first and last terms, then look for a combination that gives a middle term of $-10y$.

y	$8y$	$2y$	$4y$		-1	1
$8y$	y	$4y$	$2y$		3	-3

$-12y + 2y = -10y$

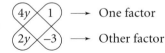

There is only one correct middle term, $-10y$.
So, $8y^2 - 10y - 3 = (4y + 1)(2y - 3)$

Example 3 Factor $6x^2 - 23x + 20$.

Solution

$6x^2 - 23x + 20$

List the possibilities for the first and last terms, then look for a combination that gives a middle term of $-23x$.

$6x$	x	$2x$	$3x$		1	-1	2	-2	4	-4
x	$6x$	$3x$	$2x$		20	-20	10	-10	5	-5

$-15x - 8x = -23x$

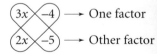

There is only one correct middle term, $-23x$.
So, $6x^2 - 23x + 20 = (3x - 4)(2x - 5)$

2.8 Exercises

A

 1. Factor.

a) $2x^2 + 7x + 3$ b) $2x^2 + 5x + 2$ c) $2a^2 + 11a + 5$

d) $2y^2 + 15y + 7$ e) $3x^2 + 7x + 2$ f) $5x^2 + 6x + 1$

B

 2. Factor.

a) $2x^2 + 3x - 2$ b) $2x^2 - 4x - 6$ c) $2a^2 + 5a - 3$

d) $2y^2 - 11y + 5$ e) $2x^2 - 7x + 5$ f) $2m^2 - 9m - 5$

3. Factor.
  a) $3y^2 - y - 2$ **b)** $3w^2 + 2w - 5$ **c)** $3a^2 - 7a + 2$
  d) $3x^2 + x - 2$ **e)** $3x^2 - 7x + 2$ **f)** $3z^2 + 5z - 2$

✓ **4.** Factor.
  a) $6n^2 + 7n + 2$ **b)** $6x^2 + 11x + 3$ **c)** $6a^2 + 17a + 5$
  d) $6y^2 + 13y + 7$ **e)** $6x^2 + 17x + 7$ **f)** $6x^2 + 23x + 7$

✓ **5.** Factor.
  a) $6b^2 - 7b + 2$ **b)** $6x^2 - 11x + 3$ **c)** $6a^2 - 17a + 5$
  d) $6y^2 - 13y + 7$ **e)** $6x^2 - 17x + 7$ **f)** $6m^2 - 23m + 7$

✓ **6.** Look at the trinomials and their factors in exercises 4 and 5.
  a) Identify the pairs of trinomials that are related.
  b) Choose one pair. Explain how you can write down the factors of one trinomial when you know the factors of the other trinomial.

Use the results of exercise 6 to factor the trinomials in exercises 7 to 10.

✓ **7.** Factor.
  a) $6x^2 + x - 2$ **b)** $6x^2 - x - 2$ **c)** $6a^2 + 7a - 3$
  d) $6a^2 - 7a - 3$ **e)** $6x^2 + 7x - 5$ **f)** $6x^2 - 7x - 5$

8. Factor.
  a) $8x^2 + 22x + 15$ **b)** $8x^2 - 22x + 15$ **c)** $8x^2 - 14x - 15$
  d) $8x^2 + 14x - 15$ **e)** $8x^2 + 2x - 15$ **f)** $8x^2 - 2x - 15$

9. Factor.
  a) $12y^2 + 26y + 10$ **b)** $12a^2 + 7a - 10$ **c)** $12a^2 - 7a - 10$
  d) $12y^2 + 11y - 15$ **e)** $12y^2 - 11y - 15$ **f)** $12x^2 - 26x + 10$

10. Factor.
  a) $15x^2 - 14x - 8$ **b)** $15x^2 - 22x + 8$ **c)** $15x^2 + 22x + 8$
  d) $15m^2 + 2m - 8$ **e)** $15x^2 + 14x - 8$ **f)** $15m^2 - 2m - 8$

✓ **11. Knowledge/Understanding** Factor.
  a) $2x^2 + 5x + 2$ **b)** $10x^2 - 17x + 3$ **c)** $7a^2 + 9a + 2$
  d) $5y^2 + 9y + 4$ **e)** $6x^2 - 2x - 8$ **f)** $4m^2 - 4m - 3$

12. Factor.
  a) $10t^2 + 19t - 15$ **b)** $4x^2 - 14x + 12$ **c)** $5c^2 - 7c - 6$
  d) $4y^2 - 17y + 4$ **e)** $7x^2 + 11x - 6$ **f)** $9x^2 - 28x + 3$

13. Factor.
  a) $4x^2 + 4x + 1$ **b)** $4x^2 + 12x + 9$ **c)** $4a^2 + 20a + 25$
  d) $4y^2 + 28y + 49$ **e)** $4x^2 + 36x + 81$ **f)** $4x^2 + 44x + 121$

14. Factor.

   a) $9x^2 - 6x + 1$ **b)** $9x^2 - 12x + 4$ **c)** $9x^2 - 24x + 16$

   d) $9x^2 - 30x + 25$ **e)** $9x^2 - 42x + 49$ **f)** $9x^2 - 48x + 64$

15. Communication

   a) Describe a pattern in the trinomials and their factors in exercises 13 and 14.

   b) Write a trinomial that has the same pattern as the trinomials in exercise 13.

   c) Repeat part b for exercise 14.

   d) Recall that a trinomial that factors as a binomial square is a perfect square. Explain how to determine whether a trinomial with a leading coefficient other than 1 is a perfect square.

16. a) Factor the trinomials in each list.

   i) $3x^2 + 4x + 1$ **ii)** $3x^2 + 4x + 1$ **iii)** $3x^2 + 4x + 1$

        $3x^2 + 7x + 2$ $3x^2 + 5x + 2$ $4x^2 + 5x + 1$

        $3x^2 + 10x + 3$ $3x^2 + 6x + 3$ $5x^2 + 6x + 1$

   b) Describe any patterns in the trinomials and their factors in part a.

   c) Extend each list in part a for three more trinomials.

   d) Make up a list of trinomials similar to these, in which there is a pattern in the trinomials and a pattern in their factors.

✓ **17. Application** Replace each □ with an integer so each trinomial factors as a perfect square.

   a) $4x^2 + \square x + 25$ **b)** $4x^2 - \square x + 16$ **c)** $25x^2 + \square x + 9$

   d) $36x^2 - \square x + 49$ **e)** $25x^2 - \square x + 36$ **f)** $16x^2 + \square x + 9$

18. Thinking/Inquiry/Problem Solving

   a) Factor each trinomial in the two lists.

   i) $3x^2 + 10x + 8$ **ii)** $3x^2 - 10x + 8$

        $3x^2 + 11x + 8$ $3x^2 - 11x + 8$

        $3x^2 + 14x + 8$ $3x^2 - 14x + 8$

   b) Are there any other trinomials that begin with $3x^2$, end with $+8$, and factor? Explain.

19. Factor fully.

   a) $12x^2 + 14x + 4$ **b)** $18x^2 - 33x + 9$ **c)** $12a^2 + 36a + 27$

   d) $40y^2 - 10y - 15$ **e)** $24x^2 - 4x - 60$ **f)** $45x^2 - 120x + 80$

The height, h metres, of a golf ball at any time, t seconds, after it is hit may be approximated by the formula $h = -5t^2 + 30t$. We can calculate the time it takes the ball to hit the ground. The ball hits the ground when its height is 0 m. We substitute $h = 0$, then solve the resulting equation.

The equation $-5t^2 + 30t = 0$ is a *quadratic equation*.

To solve quadratic equations of this type, we factor the left side, then use the zero-product property. Recall that if the product of two numbers is zero, then either one or both numbers must equal zero.

To solve the equation $-5t^2 + 30t = 0$, factor then use the zero-product property.

$$-5t^2 + 30t = 0$$
$$5t(-t + 6) = 0 \qquad 5t \text{ is a common factor.}$$

Either $\quad 5t = 0$ or $-t + 6 = 0$
$$\qquad\qquad t = 0 \qquad\qquad t = 6$$

At time $t = 0$, the ball was on the ground and the golfer was preparing to hit it. At time $t = 6$, the ball has returned to the ground. So, the ball will hit the ground 6 s after it has been struck.

Example 1

Solve.

a) $x^2 - 2x - 3 = 0$ 　　　 **b)** $x^2 - 16 = 0$ 　　　 **c)** $2y^2 + 10y - 28 = 0$

Solution

a) $\quad x^2 - 2x - 3 = 0$
$\quad (x - 3)(x + 1) = 0 \qquad$ Factor the trinomial.
$\quad$ Either $x - 3 = 0$ or $x + 1 = 0 \qquad$ Use the zero-product property.
$\qquad\qquad x = 3 \qquad\quad x = -1$
$\quad$ The solution is $x = 3$ or $x = -1$.

b) $\qquad x^2 - 16 = 0$
$\quad (x - 4)(x + 4) = 0 \qquad$ Factor the difference of squares.
$\quad$ Either $x - 4 = 0$ or $x + 4 = 0 \qquad$ Use the zero-product property.
$\qquad\qquad x = 4 \qquad\quad x = -4$
$\quad$ The solution is $x = \pm 4$.

c) $2y^2 + 10y - 28 = 0$

$\quad 2(y^2 + 5y - 14) = 0 \qquad$ 2 is a common factor.

$\quad 2(y + 7)(y - 2) = 0 \qquad$ Factor the trinomial.

Since $2 \neq 0$, apply the zero-product property to the binomials.

Either $y + 7 = 0 \quad$ or $y - 2 = 0 \qquad$ Use the zero-product property.

$\qquad y = -7 \qquad\qquad y = 2$

The solution is $y = -7$ or $y = 2$.

Some quadratic equations need to be rearranged before they are solved. We collect all terms on one side before factoring.

Example 2 Solve.

    a) $x^2 - 12 = 4x$ **b)** $9x^2 = 25$ **c)** $x(x + 6) = -9$

Solution

a) $\qquad x^2 - 12 = 4x$

$\quad\quad x^2 - 4x - 12 = 0 \qquad$ Rearrange the equation to collect all terms on one side.

$\quad (x - 6)(x + 2) = 0 \qquad$ Factor.

Either $x - 6 = 0$ or $x + 2 = 0 \qquad$ Use the zero-product property.

$\qquad x = 6 \qquad\quad x = -2$

The solution is $x = 6$ or $x = -2$.

b) $\qquad\qquad 9x^2 = 25$

$\qquad\quad 9x^2 - 25 = 0 \qquad$ Rearrange the equation.

$\quad (3x - 5)(3x + 5) = 0 \qquad$ Factor.

Either $3x - 5 = 0$ or $3x + 5 = 0 \quad$ Use the zero-product property.

$\qquad 3x = 5 \qquad\quad 3x = -5$

$\qquad x = \dfrac{5}{3} \qquad\quad x = -\dfrac{5}{3}$

The solution is $x = \pm\dfrac{5}{3}$.

c) $\qquad x(x + 6) = -9$

$\qquad\quad x^2 + 6x = -9 \qquad$ Expand.

$\quad\quad x^2 + 6x + 9 = 0 \qquad$ Rearrange.

$\quad (x + 3)(x + 3) = 0 \qquad$ Factor.

Either $x + 3 = 0 \quad$ or $x + 3 = 0 \qquad$ Use the zero-product property.

$\qquad x = -3 \qquad\quad x = -3$

The solution is $x = -3$.

In *Example 2c*, the quadratic equation has 2 equal roots.

Some quadratic equations involve trinomials of the form $ax^2 + bx + c$. Recall, from Section 2.8, how we factor this type of trinomial.

Example 3 Solve. Check the solution.

    a) $15y^2 + y - 2 = 0$ **b)** $9x^2 - 12x + 4 = 0$

Solution

a) $15y^2 + y - 2 = 0$
$$(3y - 1)(5y + 2) = 0$$
Either $3y - 1 = 0$ or $5y + 2 = 0$
$$3y = 1 \qquad\qquad 5y = -2$$
$$y = \frac{1}{3} \qquad\qquad y = -\frac{2}{5}$$

Check.

Substitute each solution in the given equation.

Substitute $y = \frac{1}{3}$.

Left side $= 15y^2 + y - 2$

$\qquad\qquad = 15\left(\frac{1}{3}\right)^2 + \frac{1}{3} - 2$ Press: 15 (1 ÷ 3) x^2 +

$\qquad\qquad = 0$ 1 ÷ 3 − 2 ENTER

$\qquad\qquad$ = Right side

Substitute $y = -\frac{2}{5}$.

Left side $= 15y^2 + y - 2$

$\qquad\qquad = 15\left(-\frac{2}{5}\right)^2 - \frac{2}{5} - 2$

$\qquad\qquad = 0$

$\qquad\qquad$ = Right side

Both solutions are correct.

b) $9x^2 - 12x + 4 = 0$
$$(3x - 2)(3x - 2) = 0$$
$$3x - 2 = 0$$
$$3x = 2$$
$$x = \frac{2}{3}$$

Check.

Substitute $x = \frac{2}{3}$.

Left side $= 9x^2 - 12x + 4$

$$= 9\left(\tfrac{2}{3}\right)^2 - 12\left(\tfrac{2}{3}\right) + 4$$
$$= 9\left(\tfrac{4}{9}\right) - 8 + 4$$
$$= 4 - 8 + 4$$
$$= 0$$
$$= \text{Right side}$$

The solution is correct.

Discuss

Why did we use a calculator to check part a, but not to check part b?

Example 4 Solve.

a) $5 + 8x - 2x^2 = 4x^2 - 3x + 9$ b) $3x(x - 1) - 5 = 2x + 7$

Solution

a) $5 + 8x - 2x^2 = 4x^2 - 3x + 9$

$\qquad\qquad 0 = 6x^2 - 11x + 4$ Collect all terms on one side.

$\qquad\qquad 0 = (2x - 1)(3x - 4)$

Either $2x - 1 = 0$ or $3x - 4 = 0$

$\qquad\qquad 2x = 1 \qquad\quad 3x = 4$

$\qquad\qquad x = \dfrac{1}{2} \qquad\quad x = \dfrac{4}{3}$

The solution is $x = \dfrac{1}{2}$ or $x = \dfrac{3}{4}$.

b) $\quad 3x(x - 1) - 5 = 2x + 7$

$\quad 3x^2 - 3x - 5 = 2x + 7$ Use the distributive law.

$\quad 3x^2 - 5x - 12 = 0$ Collect all terms on one side.

$\quad (3x + 4)(x - 3) = 0$

Either $3x + 4 = 0$ or $x - 3 = 0$

$\qquad\qquad 3x = -4 \qquad\quad x = 3$

$\qquad\qquad x = -\dfrac{4}{3}$

The solution is $x = -\dfrac{4}{3}$ or $x = 3$.

A

✓ **1.** Solve.

a) $y(y - 3) = 0$ b) $3x(x + 4) = 0$ c) $5a(3a - 2) = 0$

d) $(x + 5)x = 0$ e) $-2n(3n + 2) = 0$ f) $5q(2 - 3q) = 0$

✓ **2.** Solve.

a) $(y + 2)(y + 5) = 0$ b) $(x - 4)(x + 4) = 0$

c) $(2a - 3)(3a - 2) = 0$ d) $(x + 5)(x - 1) = 0$

e) $(2x + 7)(x + 2) = 0$ f) $(5m - 3)(2m + 3) = 0$

✓ **3.** Solve.

a) $4x^2 + 8x = 0$ b) $6y^2 - 9y = 0$ c) $7a^2 - 35a = 0$

d) $x^2 + 18x = 0$ e) $5x^2 - 7x = 0$ f) $12m + 6m^2 = 0$

B

4. Solve.

a) $x^2 + 3x + 2 = 0$ b) $n^2 + 7n + 12 = 0$ c) $y^2 + 4y - 21 = 0$

d) $x^2 - 2x - 15 = 0$ e) $a^2 - 8a + 7 = 0$ f) $x^2 + 6x + 9 = 0$

✓ **5.** Solve.

a) $x^2 - 4 = 0$ b) $y^2 - 9 = 0$ c) $a^2 - 2a + 1 = 0$

d) $p^2 - 10p + 16 = 0$ e) $x^2 - 36 = 0$ f) $3x^2 - 81x = 0$

✓ **6.** Solve.

a) $x^2 - 2x - 35 = 0$ b) $n^2 + 7n - 30 = 0$ c) $y^2 - 12y + 36 = 0$

d) $x^2 + 3x - 40 = 0$ e) $a^2 - 7a - 60 = 0$ f) $x^2 + 7x - 18 = 0$

7. Solve.

a) $x^2 = 6x$ b) $n^2 + 4n = 5$ c) $y^2 + 8 = 6y$

d) $11x + 24 = -x^2$ e) $48 - a^2 = 2a$ f) $32 - x^2 = 4x$

8. Solve.

a) $3y^2 = 5y$ b) $n^2 = 25$ c) $-y^2 = -36$

d) $11x = -7x^2$ e) $49 - a^2 = 0$ f) $-x^2 = 11x + 28$

✓ **9.** Solve.

a) $25x^2 - 9 = 0$ b) $4x^2 - 49 = 0$ c) $36a^2 - 25 = 0$

d) $64 - 25c^2 = 0$ e) $4b^2 - 9 = 0$ f) $49x^2 - 81 = 0$

10. Solve.

a) $25x^2 = 36$ b) $-64z^2 = -121$ c) $144m^2 - 49 = 0$

d) $2x^2 + 2x - 24 = 0$ e) $3a^2 - 6a - 24 = 0$ f) $2n^2 - 18 = 0$

11. Solve.

a) $98 - 2y^2 = 0$ b) $5x^2 + 30x + 45 = 0$ c) $4y^2 - 44y + 120 = 0$

d) $44z^2 - 99 = 0$ e) $150 - 54t^2 = 0$ f) $5n^2 - 10n - 240 = 0$

12. Knowledge/Understanding Solve.

a) $5x^2 + 14x - 3 = 0$ b) $2a^2 + 5a + 3 = 0$ c) $3n^2 + 4n - 4 = 0$

d) $2a^2 - a - 15 = 0$ e) $9x^2 + 12x - 21 = 0$ f) $4m^2 - 7m - 15 = 0$

13. Solve.

a) $7z^2 + 23z + 6 = 0$ b) $2x^2 + 3x - 35 = 0$ c) $3n^2 + n - 10 = 0$

d) $4x^2 - 35x + 24 = 0$ e) $8a^2 + 29a - 12 = 0$ f) $12n^2 + 31n + 7 = 0$

14. Solve.

a) $15a^2 + 19a - 8 = 0$ b) $9x^2 - 49x + 20 = 0$ c) $7m^2 - 39m - 18 = 0$

d) $14z^2 + 61z - 9 = 0$ e) $9x^2 - 12x - 32 = 0$ f) $20n^2 + 13n - 15 = 0$

15. Communication Is it possible for different quadratic equations to have the same solution? Explain. Give examples in your explanation.

16. Solve.

a) $x(6x + 1) = 2$ b) $2y(4y + 1) = 15$

c) $3a(4a + 9) = 4a - 10$ d) $5x(3x + 4) = -2(3x + 4)$

e) $(m + 4)(m - 3) = 8$ f) $(2x - 1)(3x + 5) = -6x$

17. Solve.

a) $3x(x + 3) - 2 = -x^2 - 3x + 5$ b) $2(m^2 - m + 1) = -3m^2 + 7m - 2$

c) $7(y^2 - 2y + 3) = -3(y^2 - 5y)$ d) $5(x^2 - 2x + 1) = -x^2 + 7x - 5$

e) $(2x + 5)(x - 3) = (x - 3)(x + 4)$

f) $(2a - 3)(2a + 3) = (2a + 3)(a - 4)$

18. Application When a soccer ball is kicked with a vertical speed of 19.6 m/s, its height, h metres, after t seconds is given by the formula $h = -4.9t^2 + 19.6t$. When will the soccer ball return to the ground?

19. The distance an object falls when dropped from rest is given by the formula $d = 4.9t^2$, where d is in metres and t is in seconds. An object is dropped from a height of 122.5 m. How long will it take to hit the ground?

20. Thinking/Inquiry/Problem Solving

a) Solve.

i) $x^2 - 6x + 5 = 0$ ii) $x^2 - 6x + 8 = 0$

b) Each equation in part a has the form $x^2 - 6x + c = 0$.

i) Are there other values of c for which the equation $x^2 - 6x + c = 0$ may be solved by factoring?

ii) If your answer to part i is no, explain how you know. If your answer to part i is yes, list the equations and state their solutions.

1. Simplify.

    a) $(3x^2 - 2x + 4) + (2x^2 + x - 1)$ **b)** $(x^2 - 4x + 2) - (3x^2 - 5)$

2. Expand and simplify.

    a) $(m - 4)(3m^2 - 6)$ **b)** $3(m + 1)^2$

    c) $(3w + 1)(w + 5) - 2(w - 4)$ **d)** $2(x - 1)^2 + (x - 1)$

3. Simplify.

    a) $\dfrac{4x^2}{2x}$ **b)** $\dfrac{144wz}{12z}$ **c)** $\dfrac{36m^2n}{9m}$

4. Factor.

    a) $4x - 12$ **b)** $a^2 - 9$

    c) $5w - 10wy + wyz$ **d)** $x^2 - 4$

5. Factor fully.

    a) $a^2 + 8a + 12$ **b)** $x^2 - 4x - 21$

    c) $2x^2 + 6x + 4$ **d)** $3x^2 - 75$

6. Factor.

    a) $2x^2 - x - 3$ **b)** $5x^2 + 16x + 3$

    c) $3x^2 + 5x - 2$ **d)** $25x^2 + 10x + 1$

7. Solve.

    a) $x^2 - 3x = 0$ **b)** $x^2 - 1 = 0$

    c) $14x^2 - 15x + 4 = 0$ **d)** $9x^2 - 24x + 16 = 0$

Performance Assessment

8. a) Explain why it is not correct to solve $(x - 3)(x + 4) = 8$, by setting each factor equal to 8.

    b) Determine the correct solution to $(x - 3)(x + 4) = 8$.

Career Profile

Paramedic

Janice always had an interest in health care. She decided to train at a community college for a career as a paramedic.

Job Description

- Drive an emergency response vehicle.
- Make quick and accurate diagnoses of medical problems, with support from hospital staff.
- Obtain information about patients' injuries and previous health history in order to make good treatment decisions.
- Deliver emergency care at trauma scenes and care for patients being transported to hospital.

Working Conditions

- Evening, weekend and holiday work required
- Work under pressure and at a fast pace; 8- to 12-hour shifts
- Interaction with fire, police, and hospital personnel

Qualifications and Training

- Successful completion of paramedic training at community college
- Ability to stay calm in difficult situations
- Good communication skills and an ability to listen to people

Where's the Math?

Paramedics must be able to apply the principles of equations and formulas to the calculation of problems associated with medication dosages. When administering I.V. solutions, paramedics use formulas to determine the correct drops per minute, as ordered by a physician. Paramedics also use formulas to calculate the volume of a drug to administer based on physicians' orders. When dealing with victims of poison or overdose, paramedics calculate the antidotes based on the amount of poison or medication they think the patient has ingested. The most experienced paramedics may interpret electrocardiograms and other medical tests.

MATHEMATICS TOOLKIT

Algebra Tools

> Multiplying a monomial by a polynomial

$3y(4y^2 - 3y + 4) = 12y^3 - 9y^2 + 12y$

> Multiplying two binomials

$$(2x - 3)(5x + 3) = 10x^2 + 6x - 15x - 9$$
$$= 10x^2 - 9x - 9$$

> Multiplying a binomial and a trinomial

$$(3x - 4)(2x^2 + 3x - 6) = 6x^3 + 9x^2 - 18x - 8x^2 - 12x + 24$$
$$= 6x^3 + x^2 - 30x + 24$$

> Common factoring

$5y^3 - 15y^2 - 10y = 5y(y^2 - 3y - 2)$

> Factoring a difference of squares

$9a^2 - 25b^2 = (3a + 5b)(3a - 5b)$

> Factoring trinomials

$x^2 - 3x - 10 = (x - 5)(x + 2)$

$6x^2 - 7x - 5 = (2x + 1)(3x - 5)$

> Linear functions

The equation of a line can be written in the form $y = mx + b$, where m is the slope and b is the y-intercept.

2.1   **1.** Solve.

a) $2x - 7 = 5$ b) $5y - 4 = -2y + 3$ c) $-3x - 4 = 2x + 6$

2. Solve.

a) $3x + 5 - 4x + 2 = 7x - 4 + 5x - 1$

b) $4(y + 3) - (3y - 4) = 5 - (2y + 4)$

c) $5(2x + 1) + 3(3x - 2) = 7 + 2(3x - 5)$

d) $-2(3x + 5) - 4(3 - x) = 2(x - 5) - (4 - x)$

3. Solve.

a) $\dfrac{x}{4} - \dfrac{2}{3} = \dfrac{2x}{3} - \dfrac{1}{4}$ b) $\dfrac{x + 3}{5} - \dfrac{x - 2}{2} = 1$ c) $\dfrac{1}{2}x - \dfrac{2}{3} = \dfrac{1}{3}x + \dfrac{1}{2}$

2.2 **4.** The formula for the curved area, A, of a cylinder with height h and radius r is $A = 2\pi rh$.

a) Solve the formula for r.

b) Determine the radius of a cylinder with curved area 24.0 cm^2 and height 2.0 cm.

2.3 **5.** Determine the slope and y-intercept of each line.

a) $y = 3x + 4$ b) $y = \dfrac{2}{5}x + 1$ c) $y = -\dfrac{3}{2}x - 3$

d) $y = -2$ e) $2x + 3y = 6$ f) $5x - 2y = 7$

6. Graph each line in exercise 5.

7. Graph each line.

a) $x + 2y - 4 = 0$ b) $5x - 10y = 20$ c) $3y + 2x - 6 = 0$

d) $4x - 5y = 20$ e) $4y + 3x = 12$ f) $2x - y = 2$

2.4 **8.** Solve graphically.

a) $y = x + 4$ b) $2x + y = -1$ c) $2x + 3y = 6$

   $y = -2x + 1$ $y - x = 2$ $x - y = -2$

2.5 **9.** Solve by substitution.

a) $y = -2x - 3$ b) $2x + y = 6$ c) $x + 3y = 3$

   $y = 3x - 11$ $-3x + 2y = 5$ $2x - y = -8$

10. Solve by elimination.

a) $x + y = 11$ b) $x - 2y = 8$ c) $3x + 5y = 27$

   $x - y = -3$ $3x + 4y = -6$ $4x + 2y = 8$

11. Solve.

a) $x + 2y = 5$ b) $-2x + y = 4$

   $y = -2x + 1$ $3x - 2y = -6$

c) $3x + 4y = 2$ d) $7x + 3y = 26$

   $6x + 5y = -2$ $2x - 5y = 25$

e) $x - 2y = 3$ f) $7x - 4y = 21$

   $4x - y = -2$ $3x - 5y = 9$

2.6 **12.** Expand and simplify.

a) $2(3x - 5) + 3(x + 6)$ b) $3x(2x - 1) - 4(x - 3)$

c) $(x - 5)(x + 4)$ d) $(3x + 2)(4x - 5)$

e) $(2y - 7)(2y + 7)$ f) $(2a + 3)(3a^2 - 2a - 1)$

13. Expand and simplify.

a) $2(x - 3)(x + 4)$ b) $-4(3m + 1)(m + 3)$ c) $(2y - 5)^2$

14. Expand and simplify.

a) $4x^2 - 2x + 3 - (5x^2 + 2x + 7)$

b) $2y^2 - 5y + 8 - (4y^2 - 3y - 5)$

c) $(x + 1)(x + 4) + (x + 5)(x + 3)$

d) $(n - 2)(n + 5) - (n + 3)(n - 4)$

15. Expand and simplify.

a) $3(y + 2)(y + 5) + 4(y + 1)(y + 3)$

b) $4(x - 2)(x + 3) - 5(x + 2)(x - 3)$

c) $2(x + 3)(x - 3) - 4(x + 1)(x - 1)$

d) $5(2x + 1)^2 - 2(3x + 4)^2$

2.7 **16.** Factor.

a) $x^2 + 6x + 8$ b) $x^2 - 3x - 18$

c) $a^2 - 64$ d) $y^2 + 5y - 14$

e) $25 - x^2$ f) $x^2 - 9x + 20$

17. Factor.

a) $16x^2 - 9$ b) $25x^2 - 49y^2$

c) $a^2 - 6a + 9$ d) $y^2 + 16y + 64$

e) $n^2 - 11n + 28$ f) $81x^2 - 144$

18. Factor fully.

a) $2x^2 + 16x + 30$ b) $3x^2 - 27$

c) $3a^2 - 3a - 36$ d) $5y^2 - 30y + 45$

e) $-4x^2 - 8x + 60$ f) $98 - 2x^2$

19. Factor fully.

a) $2x^3 + 10x^2 + 8x$ b) $12n^3 - 75n$

c) $4a^3 - 4a^2 - 48a$ d) $-3y^3 - 21y^2 + 54y$

e) $2x^5 - 6x^4 - 36x^3$ f) $x^4 - 81$

2.8 **20.** Factor.

a) $2y^2 + 5y + 2$ b) $3x^2 - 14x - 5$ c) $4m^2 - 13m + 3$

21. Factor.

a) $6y^2 + 7y + 2$ b) $6x^2 + 7x - 5$ c) $10m^2 - 37m + 7$

22. Factor.

a) $6x^2 + 17x + 12$ b) $15a^2 + 14a - 8$ c) $12n^2 - 41n + 35$

23. Factor fully.

a) $4y^2 - 10y - 6$ b) $18x^2 - 3x - 45$ c) $40m^2 - 110m + 75$

2.9 **24.** Solve.

a) $3x(2x - 1) = 0$ b) $(y - 3)(y + 5) = 0$ c) $2x^2 + 7x = 0$

25. Solve.

a) $m^2 + 2m - 8 = 0$ b) $x^2 + 11x + 24 = 0$
c) $y^2 - y - 6 = 0$ d) $x^2 + 10x + 25 = 0$
e) $x^2 - 25 = 0$ f) $y^2 - 7y + 12 = 0$

26. Solve.

a) $2x^2 = 5x$ b) $x^2 - 7x = -6$
c) $25n^2 - 64 = 0$ d) $2x^2 - 4x - 30 = 0$
e) $3y^2 + 15y + 18 = 0$ f) $18w^2 - 98 = 0$

27. Solve.

a) $6m^2 - m - 2 = 0$ b) $4x^2 - 35x + 24 = 0$
c) $7y^2 + 23y + 6 = 0$ d) $2x^2 + 28x + 98 = 0$
e) $3x(6x + 5) = 7$ f) $4y^2 - 42y + 54 = 0$

28. A football is thrown with a vertical speed of 14.7 m/s. Its height, h metres, after t seconds, is given by the equation $h = -4.9t^2 + 14.7t$. How long is the football in the air?

1. Solve.

   a) $3(x + 2) - 1 = 5(x - 1) + 3$

   b) $2(y + 5) - 4(2y - 5) = 3(y - 1) - 2(y - 3)$

2. **Application** The sum, S_n, of an arithmetic series is given by the formula $S_n = \frac{n}{2}(a + t_n)$, where n is the number of terms, a is the first term, and t_n is the last term.

   a) Solve the formula for n.

   b) A series has sum 1080, first term 2, and last term 70. Determine the number of terms in the series.

3. Graph each line.

   a) $y = -2x - 1$ b) $2x + 5y = 10$ c) $3x - 4y - 6 = 0$

4. Solve each system.

   a) $y = 2x - 3$ b) $x + y = 5$ c) $y = -3x + 5$

      $y = 3$ $x - y = -1$ $x + 3y = -1$

5. **Communication** Did you solve each system in exercise 4 graphically or algebraically? Explain your choice(s).

6. Expand then simplify.

   a) $(y + 4)(2y - 5)$ b) $(2x - 1)(4x^2 - 3x + 4)$

   c) $2(3x - 2)(2x - 3)$ d) $-(2a + 3)(3a - 2) + (a - 4)(2a - 3)$

7. Factor.

   a) $4x + 8xy - 6y$ b) $y^2 - y - 30$ c) $a^2 - 49$

   d) $3y^2 + y - 2$ e) $x^2 - 10x + 24$ f) $25x^2 - 64$

8. Factor fully.

   a) $2x^2 + 6x - 36$ b) $27m^2 - 75n^2$ c) $18a^2 + 21a - 15$

9. **Knowledge/Understanding** Solve.

   a) $3y^2 + 7y = 0$ b) $x^2 + 12x + 36 = 0$

   c) $6x^2 - 11x - 10 = 0$

10. **Thinking/Inquiry/Problem Solving**

    a) Write down all the factorable polynomials that have the form $2x^2 + ax - 8$.

    b) How many different polynomials did you find; that is, how many different values of a?

    c) Explain how you know that you have listed all possible polynomials of this type.

11. Check that when you factor $6x^2 + 13x + 6$, the result is $(2x + 3)(3x + 2)$. The coefficients in the original trinomial form a symmetrical pattern: 6, 13, 6.

Also, the coefficients are reversed in the two binomial factors: 2, 3 in the first factor and 3, 2 in the second factor.

Find out if this always happens. That is, when a trinomial whose coefficients form a symmetrical pattern is factored, will the coefficients always be reversed in the two binomial factors?

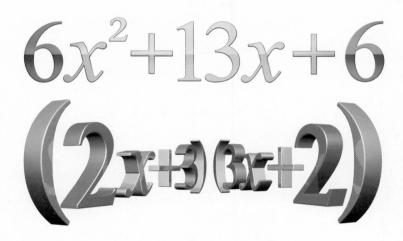

1. An 8-m ladder rests 3 m away from a wall. How high up the wall does the ladder reach?

2. A school needs to build a wheelchair ramp. The ramp must cover the 4 steps in front of the school. Each step has a height of 0.68 m. How long must the ramp be if the angle of inclination cannot exceed 8°?

3. Determine the measure of each angle to the nearest degree.
   a) $\sin \theta = 0.555$ b) $\tan A = 1.374$ c) $\cos B = 0.798$ d) $\tan C = \frac{8}{3}$

4. Solve each triangle.
   Round each angle to the nearest degree and each length to the nearest tenth.
   a) $\triangle ABC; \angle A = 18°, \angle C = 90°, a = 15.0$ cm
   b) $\triangle DEF; \angle E = 36°, \angle F = 54°, d = 3.6$ mm
   c) $\triangle XYZ; x = 10$ m, $y = 8$ m, $z = 6$ m
   d) $\triangle PQR; \angle Q = 110°, p = 124$ mm, $q = 33$ mm

5. An 18-m support wire is attached to a point on a pole 8 m from the ground.
   a) Draw a sketch of this situation.
   b) What is the angle between the wire and the ground?

6. From the top of a 120-m tower, a forest ranger observes smoke in two locations, both with angles of depression of 4°. The ranger notes the horizontal angle between the fires is 75°.
   a) Draw a sketch of this situation.
   b) How far is the tower from each fire?

7. Determine the possible values for each angle between 0° and 180°.
   a) $\sin A = \frac{2}{3}$ b) $\tan C = \frac{4}{3}$ c) $\cos E = 0.2745$ d) $\sin F = 0.9876$

8. A soccer net for a kids indoor league is 5 m wide. A player is 8 m from one goal post and 6.3 m from the other. Within what angle must a shot be taken in order to score a goal?

9. A surveyor needs to determine the width of a river. Pole A is on one bank of the river, and pole B is directly across pole A on the other bank. From where he is standing, the surveyor measures a distance of 2.7 km to pole A, 4.8 km to pole B, and an angle of 48° between the poles. How wide is the river?

10. Solve and check.

a) $9a - 10 = 2a + 11$ **b)** $2(b + 4) - 3(b + 1) = 5(b + 4) - 3b$

c) $-7x - 16 = 2x + 4$

d) $\frac{2}{3}(x + 1) + \frac{1}{4}(3x - 3) = \frac{5}{6}(x - 2) - \frac{1}{2}(x + 3) - \frac{1}{4}$

11. The distance an object travels, d, for a specific time, t, with initial velocity, v, and acceleration, a, is given by the formula $d = vt + \frac{1}{2}at^2$.

a) Solve the formula for v.

b) Determine the initial velocity if the distance travelled was 187.5 m in 15 s with an acceleration of -5.0 m/s^2.

12. Determine the slope and y-intercept of each equation.

a) $y = 3x - 2$ **b)** $4x + 3y = -15$ **c)** $-2x + 7y = 21$

13. Solve each system.

a) $7x + y = 9$ **b)** $y = -3x + 7$
  $2x + y = -1$ $5x + 2y = 13$

14. Sean's animal boarding house charges $100 plus $5 a day to look after your pet dog while you are on holidays. Kadeisha, your neighbour, offers to look after your dog for $15 a day.

a) Write an equation for each situation.

b) If you plan to be away for one week, who would you have look after your dog? Explain.

15. Simplify.

a) $(4x^2 - 5x + 7) + (3x^2 + 5x - 3)$ **b)** $(x + 3)(x - 2)$

c) $-2(x + 3)(x - 1) + 4(x - 4)(x + 1)$

d) $2(x + 3)^2 + 4(3x + 4)^2$

16. Factor.

a) $y^2 + 4y - 21$ **b)** $a^2 - 9a + 20$ **c)** $b^2 - 6b - 16$

d) $121 - x^2$ **e)** $36x^2 - 25y^2$ **f)** $5g^3 + 15g^2 - 50g$

17. Factor.

a) $3x^2 - 5x - 2$ **b)** $6y^2 + 29y + 28$ **c)** $10a^2 + 9a + 2$

d) $4g^2 - 18g + 20$ **e)** $12x^2 + 14x + 4$ **f)** $72d^2 + 6d - 36$

18. Solve.

a) $a(a - 2) = 0$ **b)** $x^2 - 6x + 5 = 0$ **c)** $2y^2 - 6y - 36 = 0$

Preparing for Community College

Work individually.

Suggested Materials:

Internet access, community college calendars

Background

Community colleges offer a variety of interesting and challenging post-secondary programs. Law enforcement, medical and computer technology, business, hospitality, tourism, childcare, and the arts are some of the many courses available at community college.

This project will help you investigate college programs that suit your interests and aptitudes, and are financially viable.

- In both the grade 10 Careers course and grade 11 Math, you evaluated your skills, interests, and aptitudes in terms of which careers would be appropriate for you. Which areas still interest you?
- Which colleges are in the area in which you live?
- Would you prefer to go to a local college or one away from home?
- How can you get information about community colleges?
- What is the tuition? What financial help is available?
- What apprenticeship programs are available?
- What types of mathematics placement tests are typically given by community colleges? How can you prepare for them?
- What are the pre-requisite courses for the programs you are interested in?

Curriculum Expectations

By the end of *Explore, Research, Report* you will:

> Retrieve information from various sources. (For example, graphs, charts, spreadsheets, and schedules)

> Make informed decisions using data provided in chart, spreadsheet, or schedule format, taking into account personal needs and preferences.

> Communicate the results of an analysis orally, in a written report, and graphically.

> Identify applications of trigonometry in occupations and in post-secondary programs related to the occupations.

Explore

How Is Mathematics Used in Careers and at Community Colleges?

Mathematics is very important to many careers and college programs, such as engineering, computer technology, or business. What other programs depend on mathematics? Consider the subject of trigonometry that you have recently studied. We might guess that angles and measurement are important components of surveying, a course offered at college. However, trigonometry is also used in careers related to design, construction, and landscaping. Make a list of careers in these areas that might use trigonometry.

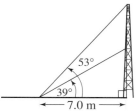

What Are Mathematics Placement Tests?

Many community colleges require students to take a test in mathematics for program placement. For example, if you want to take courses in accounting, the college may require you to write a test. The test identifies your level of mathematics and may help you choose an appropriate program. Some colleges require a basic mathematics test for admission for mature students who have been out of high school for some time. Each college has its own system of testing.

Calculators are usually not allowed for the tests, and most tests are multiple choice. Basic topics for most college tests include numeracy, algebra, and percent. Placement tests for certain technical programs may include geometry and trigonometry. For some apprenticeship programs you may need a knowledge of geometry as well as metric and imperial measures.

Areas included in the college mathematics test:

- Numeracy – addition, subtraction, multiplication, and division of fractions and decimals
- Algebra – simplifying expressions, evaluating formulas, and solving linear equations in one and two variables
- Percent – converting percents to decimals and fractions, and solving percent problems
- Geometry – calculating area and perimeter of rectangles, circles, and triangles

- Trigonometry – solving right triangles when the values of the trigonometric functions are given
- Measurement – using metric and imperial measures

Mathematics Placement Test

Now that you have reviewed the areas that the college placement test covers, complete the sample placement test on pages 162–163. Ensure you have complete solutions. You should include this test in your end-of-project report.

Research

1. **Choosing a College Program to Investigate**

   You may know of an area of study that interests you. If you are unsure about programs to investigate, there are many resources that can help you. There is a self-assessment activity on the Addison-Wesley website for the grade 11 Personal Finance course, www.awl.com/canada/school/connections. An interest assessment tool is also available on *Career Cruising*, a CD-ROM for Windows, licensed by the Ontario government for all schools. If your school does not have computer access, you can order copies of the Canada Prospects career publication from the federal government. This guide has a variety of self-assessment activities and can be ordered through the website www.careerccc.org, or through the Canada Career Consortium, 66 Slater St., Ottawa, ON, K1P 5H1.

2. **Getting Information**

   The Student Services department in your school and your local public library will have printed calendars for the colleges in your area. General publications, summarizing information about all the community colleges in your province, are also available. In Ontario, one of these guides is called "CommuniCAAT" and is available through the Ontario College Application Service, OCAS. The toll free number is 1-888-892-2228.

   The Internet is an excellent source of information on colleges. Through www.ocas.on.ca, you can access the websites of all Ontario community colleges and get the on-line version of "CommuniCAAT" and other publications about college. You can also read about the employment experiences of college graduates and apply to college on-line.

   Choose a college to investigate in depth. Ensure the college you choose offers the program in which you are interested.

3. Basic Information

For the college you have chosen, answer each question.

a) Where is the college?

b) How many full- and part-time students attend the college?

c) How many faculty members teach at the college?

d) How do you apply to the college?

e) When should you apply to the college? Is there an application deadline?

f) What employment statistics does the college have for its graduates?

g) Is it possible to transfer credits from this college to a university?

h) Are Internet, correspondence, or other forms of distance learning available?

4. Financial Information

a) What is the tuition for the program you have chosen?

b) What additional fees will you have to pay?

c) What grants, bursaries, and scholarships are available at this college?

d) What other financial aid is available for college students?

e) How can you apply for financial aid to cover the costs of college?

f) What are the college default rates for Ontario Student Assistance Program (OSAP) repayment?

5. On-Campus Services

a) What services does the Student Centre at the college provide?

b) What learning resources are available?

c) Is there a bookstore at the college?

d) What activities are available?

e) What athletic facilities and programs are provided?

f) Is childcare or babysitting available?

g) What health-care services are provided?

h) Is there on-campus housing?

i) What services are available for students with disabilities?

6. Counselling and Career Services

a) What career services are available?

b) Does the college help recent graduates find employment?

c) What kind of personal counselling is available?

d) What free workshops on topics such as time management, study skills, and essay and résumé writing are available?

7. Available Programs

a) What programs does the college offer?

b) Which programs are oversubscribed?

c) Are there any specialty programs available? Describe them.

d) What co-op programs are available?

e) What apprenticeship programs are available?

8. Information about the Program You Have Chosen to Research

a) What are the admission requirements for the program?

b) How long is the program?

c) What courses are offered in the program?

d) Can the program be studied part-time?

9. Contact with the College

a) Describe opportunities available for you to visit the college?

b) Describe in detail one or more ways in which you have made contact with the college:
- by telephoning the college and asking questions
- by asking questions through the college website
- by visiting the college
- by talking with students who have attended the college

Report

1. Prepare a written report. Include:

a) the mathematics placement test you have written

b) a list of the resources you have used

c) the name of the program and college you have investigated

d) all answers from your research

e) a conclusion that reflects what you have learned from this project
Points to consider:
- If you had a particular college program in mind before you began the project, are you still planning to pursue it?
- If you did not have a college course in mind before the project, have you discovered a program you would like to pursue?
- How has this project influenced your plans for education after high school?
- What is the most important thing you have learned from this project?

Preparing for Community College

2. Present your findings on the college and program you researched. Use tables, charts, and other visual aids where possible.

Mathematics Placement Test

1. **a)** Reduce each fraction to lowest terms.

   i) $\dfrac{7}{28}$ **ii)** $\dfrac{45}{135}$

   b) Convert each fraction in part a to a decimal correct to 2 places.

2. Evaluate.

   a) $5 \times 8 - 3(2 + 5) \div 3$ **b)** 4^2 **c)** $\dfrac{20}{3} \div 30 \times 27$ **d)** $\dfrac{35}{60 \times \frac{21}{24}}$

3. Evaluate.

   a) $1.821 - 0.2 + 3.64$ **b)** $-3.8 - 7.1$ **c)** $3.9 \times (-1.5)$

   d) $48.6 \div 6$ **e)** $(-0.02) \times (-0.06)$ **f)** $29.8 \div 100$

   g) $0.02 \div 0.005$ **h)** $(3.5 + 4.1) \times 7.1$

4. Convert to a percent.

   a) 0.35 **b)** 5.0 **c)** 0.056

5. **a)** Convert to a decimal.

   i) 15% **ii)** 140% **iii)** 0.2%

   b) Convert each value in part a to a fraction.

6. Calculate.

   a) 30% of 200 **b)** What percent of 200 is 44?

   c) 5% of what number is 25?

7. A jacket sells for $44.00.

   a) If the price is reduced by 25%, what is the selling price?

   b) What is the total cost if 15% tax is added to the sale price?

8. Solve.

   a) $7x - 2 = 3x + 22$ **b)** $3(4x - 1) = 7(x + 1)$

   c) $7 - x = 15 + x$

9. Solve.

    a) $x + 4y = 14$
        $x + 2y = 10$

    b) $3x - y = 11$
        $x + 2y = 6$

10. Evaluate each formula for the given values.

    a) $A = 2(l + w)$; $l = 5$ cm and $w = 2.1$ cm

    b) $M = (1 + p)^2 - 1$; $p = 5$

    c) $K = (40 - 3m) \div (2t)$; $m = 4$ kg and $t = 5$

11. Calculate the area and perimeter of each figure.

    a) a rectangle with length 7 cm and width 12 cm

    b) a circle with radius 10 m (use $\pi = 3.14$)

    c) an equilateral triangle with sides 2 mm and height 1.7 mm

12. In $\triangle ABC$, $\angle B = 35°$, $\angle C = 90°$, $\sin 35° \doteq 0.57$, $\cos 35° \doteq 0.82$, $\tan 35° \doteq 0.70$, and $c = 12$. Determine each value.

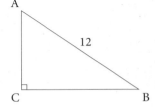

    a) $\angle A$

    b) a, correct to two decimal places

    c) b, correct to two decimal places

13. Determine each measure.

    a) A room is 3 m high. What is its approximate height in feet and inches? (1 foot = 12 inches; 1 inch $\doteq$ 2.54 cm)

    b) What is the total length if 21.655 m, 38 mm, and 2310 cm are added together?

    c) A container holds 10 gallons of oil. Approximately how many litres is this? (1 gallon = 4 quarts; 1 quart $\doteq$ 0.95 L)

3 Measurement in Design

Landscaping

Landscapers usually determine areas and volumes of irregular figures to design and sod golf greens, and build flowerbeds. You will investigate several of these methods.

Curriculum Expectations

By the end of this chapter, you will:

> Solve problems related to the perimeter and area of plane figures, and the surface area and volume of prisms, pyramids, cylinders, spheres, and cones, including problems involving combinations of these objects.

> Demonstrate accuracy and precision in working with metric measures.

> Demonstrate an understanding of the use of the imperial system in a variety of applications.

> Demonstrate a working knowledge of the measurement of length and area in the

imperial system, in relation to applications.

> Perform required conversions between the imperial system and the metric system, as necessary within projects and applications.

> Use calculators effectively in solving problems involving measurement, and judge the reasonableness of the answers produced.

> Construct (e.g., combine or modify) formulas to solve multi-step problems in particular situations.

1 Review: Operations with Fractions

Skills with fractions are essential when working with imperial units.

To reduce fractions, divide both the numerator and denominator by the largest common factor.

Example 1 Reduce.

a) $\frac{2}{4}$ **b)** $\frac{9}{12}$ **c)** $1\frac{8}{24}$

Solution

a) $\frac{2}{4} = \frac{1}{2}$ Divide the numerator and denominator by the largest common factor, 2.

b) $\frac{9}{12} = \frac{3}{4}$ Divide the numerator and denominator by the largest common factor, 3.

c) $1\frac{8}{24} = 1\frac{1}{3}$ Simplify the fractional part of the mixed number. Divide the numerator and denominator by 8.

To convert a fraction to a decimal, divide the numerator by the denominator.

Example 2 Convert to a decimal.

a) $\frac{2}{5}$ **b)** $\frac{3}{8}$ **c)** $2\frac{3}{4}$

Solution

a) $\frac{2}{5} = 0.4$ Press: 2 ÷ 5 ENTER

b) $\frac{3}{8} = 0.375$ Press: 3 ÷ 8 ENTER

c) $2\frac{3}{4} = 2.75$ Write the whole number before the decimal. Press: 3 ÷ 4 ENTER

Example 3 Evaluate.

a) $\dfrac{1}{3} \times \dfrac{2}{5}$ **b)** $\dfrac{-2}{3} \div \dfrac{3}{7}$ **c)** $\dfrac{1}{5} + \dfrac{3}{4}$ **d)** $\dfrac{1}{2} - \dfrac{2}{3}$

Solution

a) $\dfrac{1}{3} \times \dfrac{2}{5} = \dfrac{2}{15}$ Multiply numerators and multiply denominators.

Or, use a calculator.

For the TI-30X IIS, press: 1 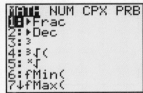 3 ⊗ 2 5

For the TI-83, press: (1 ÷ 3) × (2 ÷ 5)

MATH to obtain the screen below left.

Press ENTER to select fractions and obtain the screen below middle, then press ENTER to obtain the answer, below right.

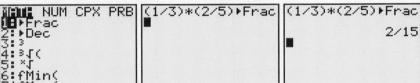

b) $\dfrac{-2}{3} \div \dfrac{3}{7} = \dfrac{-2}{3} \times \dfrac{7}{3}$ Invert the second fraction and multiply.

$$= \dfrac{-14}{9}$$

$$= -1\dfrac{5}{9}$$

Or, use a calculator.

For the TI-30X IIS, press: (−) 2 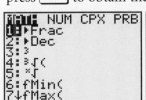 3 ÷ 3 7

For the TI-83, press: ((−) 2 ÷ 3) ÷ (3 ÷ 7)

) MATH to obtain the screen below left.

Press ENTER to select fractions and obtain the screen below middle, then press ENTER to obtain the answer, below right.

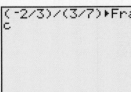

c) $\frac{1}{5} + \frac{3}{4} = \frac{1}{5} \times \frac{4}{4} + \frac{3}{4} \times \frac{5}{5}$ Determine the lowest common denominator, 20. Then write equivalent fractions with 20 as the denominator.

$= \frac{4}{20} + \frac{15}{20}$ Add only the numerators. Keep denominators the same.

$= \frac{19}{20}$

Or, use a calculator.

For the TI-30X IIS, press : 1 [A%] 5 [+] 3 [A%] 4 [ENTER =]

For the TI-83, press: [( ] 1 [÷] 5 [ )] [+] [( ] 3 [÷] 4 [ )]
[MATH] to obtain the screen below left.

Press [ENTER] to select fractions and obtain the screen below middle, then press [ENTER] to obtain the answer, below right.

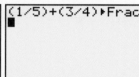

d) $\frac{1}{2} - \frac{2}{3} = \frac{1}{2} \times \frac{3}{3} - \frac{2}{3} \times \frac{2}{2}$ Determine the lowest common denominator, 6.

Write equivalent fractions.

$= \frac{3}{6} - \frac{4}{6}$ Subtract the numerators. Keep denominators the same.

$= \frac{-1}{6}$

Or, use a calculator.

For the TI-30X IIS, press: 1 [A%] 2 [−] 2 [A%] 3 [ENTER =]

For the TI-83, press: [( ] 1 [÷] 2 [ )] [−] [( ] 2 [÷] 3 [ )]
[MATH] to obtain the screen below left.

Press [ENTER] to select fractions and obtain the screen below middle, then press [ENTER] to obtain the answer, below right.

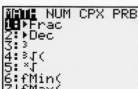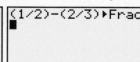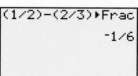

1. Reduce.

   a) $\frac{8}{10}$ b) $\frac{45}{20}$ c) $2\frac{9}{12}$ d) $\frac{-24}{16}$

2. Convert each fraction in exercise 1 to a decimal.

3. Evaluate.

   a) $\frac{2}{7} \times \frac{1}{4}$ b) $\frac{4}{3} \div \frac{5}{11}$ c) $-\frac{3}{8} + \frac{5}{6}$ d) $\frac{9}{10} - \frac{-4}{5}$

4. Evaluate.

   a) $-\frac{3}{7} \div \left(-\frac{9}{28}\right)$ b) $-\frac{5}{12} + \left(-\frac{2}{5}\right)$ c) $-\frac{63}{72} - \frac{9}{8}$ d) $-\frac{1}{3} \times \frac{9}{10}$

2 Review: Metric Units

Recall that the metric system is based on 10s. For example, 10 decimetres (dm) = 1 metre (m)

For units smaller than 1 metre, Latin prefixes are used:
deci means 10; 10 decimetres = 1 metre
centi means 100; 100 centimetres = 1 metre
milli means 1000; 1000 millimetres = 1 metre

For units larger than 1 metre, Greek prefixes are used:
deca means 10; 1 decametre = 10 metres
hecto means 100; 1 hectometre = 100 metres
kilo means 1000; 1 kilometre = 1000 metres

The metre is the standard unit of length. Prefixes are added to it for larger and smaller units. The same prefixes are used for mass and capacity.

The gram is the standard unit of mass.

The litre is the standard unit for volume.

Length	
Unit	Equivalent
kilometre (km)	1000 m
hectometre (hm)	100 m
decametre (dam)	10 m
metre (m)	1 m
decimetre (dm)	0.1 m
centimetre (cm)	0.01 m
millimetre (mm)	0.001 m

Mass	
Unit	Equivalent
kilogram (kg)	1000 g
hectogram (hg)	100 g
decagram (dag)	10 g
gram (g)	1 g
decigram (dg)	0.1 g
centigram (cg)	0.01 g
milligram (mg)	0.001 g

Capacity/Volume	
Unit	Equivalent
kilolitre (kL)	1000 L
hectolitre (hL)	100 L
decalitre (daL)	10 L
litre (L)	1 L
decilitre (dL)	0.1 L
centilitre (cL)	0.01 L
millilitre (mL)	0.001 L

Convert each measure.

a) 50 m to decimetres **b)** 100 g to milligrams

c) 1000 mL to litres **d)** 400 mm to centimetres

Solution

a) 50 m to decimetres

$1\,m = 10\,dm$, so

$50\,m = 50 \times 10\,dm$

$\qquad = 500\,dm$

b) 100 g to milligrams

$1\,g = 1000\,mg$, so

$100\,g = 100 \times 1000\,mg$

$\qquad = 100\,000\,mg$

c) 1000 mL to litres

$1\,mL = 0.001\,L$, so

$1000\,mL = 1000 \times 0.001\,L$

$\qquad = 1\,L$

d) 400 mm to centimetres

$1\,mm = 0.001\,m$

$\qquad = 0.1\,cm$, so

$400\,mm = 400 \times 0.1\,cm$

$\qquad = 40\,cm$

Exercises

1. Convert each measure.

   a) 20 kg to grams **b)** 5.0 dm to millimetres

   c) 3 kL to millilitres **d)** 8 g to milligrams

2. Convert each measure.

   a) 400 mL to litres **b)** 20 dg to kilograms

   c) 100 000 dm to kilometres **d)** 50 mm to metres

3 New: Precision and Rounding

The precision of a measure is based on the subdivision of the scale on the instrument used to take the measure. So, the smaller the subdivision of the measuring tool, the greater the precision of the measurement.

Using a ruler with centimetre increments, Jim measured the line segment below as 8 cm.

_____

Linda's ruler had 1-mm subdivisions. Her ruler had a precision of 1 mm or 0.1 cm. She measured the same segment as 8.2 cm. So, the actual measurement is 8.2 cm, to within 0.05 cm. The actual length lies between 8.15 and 8.25 cm. Linda's measurement is more precise because the number of decimal places in the measurement is greater.

Recall, when solving practical problems with real measurements, the final result should not be written with greater accuracy than is appropriate (see Chapter 1, Necessary Skills, page 10).

When we have to add or subtract approximate numbers with different precision, we round the answer to the same place as the *least precise number*, that is, the number with the least number of decimal places.

Example 1

Evaluate each approximate number. Round appropriately.

a) $4.23 + 3.256 + 1.4$ 　　　　　　b) $17.3145 - 3.12$

Solution

a) $4.23 + 3.256 + 1.4 = 8.886$　　　Use your calculator.
The least precise number, 1.4, indicates our final answer should have 1 decimal place. So, the sum is 8.9.

b) $17.3145 - 3.12 = 14.1945$　　　Use your calculator.
The least precise number, 3.12, indicates our final answer should have 2 decimal places. So, the difference is 14.19.

When we multiply, divide, or take the root of approximate numbers, we use significant digits to determine the final presentation of the answer. We round the answer to the same number of significant digits as are in the number with the *least significant digits*, used in the calculation.

Example 2

Evaluate each approximate number. Round appropriately.

a) 14.35×2.5 **b)** $\sqrt{1.50}$ **c)** $2348.4 \div 5.7$

Solution

a) $14.35 \times 2.5 = 35.875$

The number with the least number of significant digits is 2.5. Since 2.5 has 2 significant digits, we round our final answer to have 2 significant digits. So, the product is 36.

b) $\sqrt{1.50}$

There is only one number in the calculation. It has 3 significant digits (recall, 0s to the right of a decimal place and a significant number are significant). Round the final answer to 3 significant digits. So, the square root is 1.22

```
√(1.50)
        1.224744871
```

c) $2348.4 \div 5.7 = 412$

The number with the least number of significant digits is 5.7. Since it has 2 significant digits, the final answer should have 2 significant digits. Recall that 0s at the end of a number to the left of the decimal place are non-significant. So, the quotient is 410.

Exercises

1. Evaluate each approximate number. Round appropriately.

   a) 3.45×2.1 **b)** $5.3126 - 2.34$

   c) $7.1 + 2$ **d)** $4638.4 \div 5.2$

   e) $\sqrt{5.2678}$ **f)** $6.3 \times 2.45 \times 4.0$

2. Evaluate each approximate number. Round appropriately.

   a) $8.357 + 9.145 - 6.23$ **b)** $36\ 760 \div 40$

   c) 8567×800 **d)** $\dfrac{\sqrt{528.35}}{71.5} \times 4.2$

   e) $57\ 120 \div 1428$ **f)** $85.1263 \times 0.093 \times 1$

Canada adopted the metric system of measurement in 1971, but construction and manufacturing industries continue to use the *imperial system* of measurement. Many Canadians still remember their height and weight in imperial units. Your ruler may be marked in centimetres and millimetres along one edge, and inches and fractions of an inch along the other. In this chapter you will learn to work with both systems.

Length

In the imperial system, one basic unit of length is the inch, as shown on the ruler below. Each inch is divided into 16 equal parts. So, 1 part is $\frac{1}{16}$ of an inch, 2 parts are $\frac{2}{16}$ or $\frac{1}{8}$ inch, 4 parts are $\frac{4}{16}$ or $\frac{1}{4}$ inch and eight parts are $\frac{8}{16}$ or $\frac{1}{2}$ inch. The length of the division lines changes as the measurement goes from sixteenths to eighths to quarters to halves.

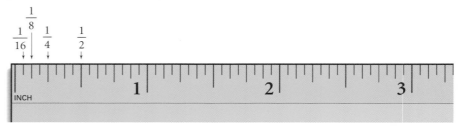

In mathematics, we often assume the numbers we work with are exact. However, when taking a measurement, there is always some degree of error. Look at the screw below. Its length is more than 8.2 cm but less than 8.3 cm. Since its length is closer to 8.3 cm than to 8.2 cm, its length would be recorded as 8.3 cm.

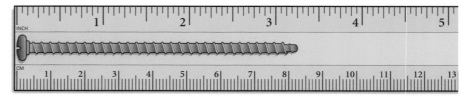

In imperial units, the screw is $3\frac{1}{4}$ inches long.

The term *accuracy* indicates how close a measurement is to its true value. If we get the same measurement each time we use a ruler, we have *precision* in our measurements.

The precision of the ruler above is 0.1 cm in metric, or $\frac{1}{16}^{\text{th}}$ inch in imperial. To take a more accurate measurement you would need a ruler with greater precision. Though not commonly used, some imperial rulers are calibrated to $\frac{1}{32}^{\text{nd}}$ of an inch.

The most commonly used measures of length in the imperial system are the inch (in. or "), foot (ft. or '), yard (yd.), and mile (mi.). These lists show the relationships between the units for the imperial and metric systems.

Metric System	Imperial System
10 mm = 1 cm	12 inches = 1 foot
100 cm = 1 m	3 feet = 1 yard
1000 m = 1 km	1760 yards = 1 mile

To estimate measures using imperial units, we use the idea that a yard is close to a metre stick in length, one foot is close to a 30-cm ruler in length, and an inch is approximately the length of a small paperclip, so about 2.5 cm.

Example 1

Estimate each length in metric and imperial units, then measure to verify your answer.

a) the dimensions of the cover of this text book

b) the dimensions of your desk

c) the height of the doorway to your classroom

Solution

a) Use centimetres or inches for the textbook.
I estimate my textbook to be 20 cm by 15 cm, or 8" by 6". The actual dimensions are approximately 24.8 cm by 19.5 cm, or $9\frac{3}{4}$" by $7\frac{3}{4}$".

b) Use centimetres or feet.
I estimate my desk to be 60 cm by 40 cm, or $1\frac{1}{2}$' by 1'. The actual dimensions are approximately 72 cm by 53 cm, or $2\frac{1}{3}$' by $1\frac{3}{4}$'.

c) Use metres or yards.
I estimate the doorway to my classroom to be 2 m by 1 m, or 2 yards by 1 yard. The actual dimensions are approximately 2.1 m by 0.92 m, or $2\frac{1}{3}$ yards by 1 yard.

Example 2
Convert each measure.

a) 8 feet to inches　　　　　　　　　**b)** 5000 m to kilometres

Solution

a) 8 feet to inches

Since 1 foot = 12 inches,

$$8 \text{ feet} = (8 \times 12) \text{ inches}$$
$$= 96 \text{ inches}$$

b) 5000 m to kilometres

Since 1000 m = 1 km,

$$5000 \text{ m} = \frac{5000}{1000} \text{ km}$$
$$= 5 \text{ km}$$

Unlike metric measurements, imperial measurements are not conventionally expressed using decimals. When presenting imperial measures, it is customary to express them as fractions, or using a smaller unit.

Sometimes we need to convert imperial units to metric units or vice versa. Usually we do all calculations in one system of units, then convert. Here is a list of conversion factors:

$$1 \text{ inch} \doteq 25.4 \text{ mm}$$
$$1 \text{ foot} \doteq 30.48 \text{ cm}$$
$$1 \text{ yard} \doteq 0.9144 \text{ m}$$
$$1 \text{ mile} \doteq 1.609 \text{ km}$$

Example 3
Convert each length.
Round your answers to the nearest tenth where appropriate.

a) 3 inches to millimetres
b) 8.9 km to miles

Solution

a) 3 inches to millimetres

Let x represent the length in millimetres.

3 inches $\doteq x$

1 inch $\doteq$ 25.4 mm

Write equal ratios.

$$\frac{3}{1} = \frac{x}{25.4}$$

$(25.4)(3) \doteq x$ Multiply each side by 25.4.

$x \doteq 76.2$

So, 3 inches is approximately 76.2 mm.

b) 8.9 km to miles

Let x represent the length in miles.

x miles $\doteq$ 8.9 kilometres

1 mile $\doteq$ 1.609 km

Write equal ratios.

$$\frac{x}{1} \doteq \frac{8.9}{1.609}$$

$x \doteq 5.531$

Recall that imperial measures are not conventionally expressed with decimals. We must express 5.5 as a fraction.

So, 8.9 km is approximately $5\frac{1}{2}$ miles.

Volume

For mass and fluid volume, imperial units used in the United States are different than those used in the United Kingdom. We will use the United States' imperial units in this text unless otherwise specified.

Imperial system units of volume are the fluid ounce (fl. oz.), pint (pt.), quart (qt.), and gallon (gal.). These tables list the relationship between commonly used units for each system.

Metric System	Imperial System
	16 fluid ounces = 1 pint
	2 pints = 1 quart
1000 mL = 1 L	8 pints = 1 gallon

Conversions for these imperial measures to their approximate metric equivalents are:

1 fluid ounce $\doteq$ 29.574 mL

1 pint $\doteq$ 0.473 L

1 gallon $\doteq$ 3.785 L

Mass

Imperial units of mass are the ounce (oz.), pound (lb.), and ton. These tables list the relationship between commonly used units for each system.

Metric System	Imperial System
$1000\,g = 1\,kg$	$16\,ounces = 1\,pound$
$1000\,kg = 1\,t$	$2000\,pounds = 1\,ton\,(US)$

Conversions for these imperial measures to their approximate metric equivalents are:

$$1\ ounce \doteq 28.35\,g$$
$$1\ pound \doteq 0.454\,kg$$
$$1\ ton \doteq 0.907\,t$$

Example 4

Convert each measure. Round your answers to the nearest tenth where appropriate.

a) 5 gallons of paint to litres

b) 15 ounces of chocolate to kilograms

c) 4 kg of cement to pounds and ounces

Solution

a) 5 gallons of paint to litres

Let x represent the volume in litres.

5 gallons = x litres

1 gallon $\doteq$ 3.785 L

Write equal ratios.

$$\frac{5}{1} \doteq \frac{x}{3.785} \qquad \text{Multiply each side by 3.785.}$$

$18.9 \doteq x$

So, 5 gallons is approximately 18.9 L.

b) 15 ounces of chocolate to kilograms

Convert ounces to grams, then convert grams to kilograms.

Let x represent the mass in kilograms.

15 ounces = x grams

1 ounce $\doteq$ 28.35 g

Write equal ratios.

$$\frac{15}{1} \doteq \frac{x}{28.35} \qquad \text{Multiply each side by 28.35.}$$

$425.25 \doteq x$

To convert grams to kilograms, recall that 1000 g = 1 kg.

$$\frac{425.25}{1000} \doteq 0.4255 \qquad \text{Divide the number of grams by 1000.}$$

So, 15 ounces is approximately 0.4 kg.

c) 4 kg of cement to pounds and ounces

Let x represent the mass in pounds.

$4 \, \text{kg} = x$ pounds

$0.454 \, \text{kg} \doteq 1$ pound

Write equal ratios.

$$\frac{4}{0.454} \doteq \frac{x}{1} \qquad \text{Multiply each side by 0.454.}$$

$$4 \doteq 0.454x$$

$$x \doteq 8.8$$

Recall that imperial units are not conventionally expressed using decimals.

Convert 0.8 pounds to ounces.

1 pound = 16 ounces

0.8 pounds = (0.8 × 16) ounces

= 12.8

So, 4 kg is approximately 8 pounds 13 ounces.

We will continue to work with the imperial system of measure throughout the rest of the chapter.

3.1 Exercises

A

1. Convert each measure.

    a) Michael is 1.6 m tall; convert to centimetres.

    b) A basketball rim is $1\frac{1}{2}$ feet in diameter; convert to inches.

    c) Dana ran a 3.4-km race; convert to metres.

    d) Troy ran a 2-mile race; convert to yards.

2. Convert each measure.

    a) Hakeem Olajuwon's height is 84 inches; convert to feet.

    b) Mount Logan's elevation is 5959 m; convert to kilometres.

    c) A hallway is 707 cm long; convert to metres.

    d) A ribbon is 15 feet long; convert to yards.

B

✓ **3.** State which imperial unit you would use to measure each length.

    a) your best friend's mass   **b)** the length of a small insect

    c) the length of a football field   **d)** the volume of gas in a car

    e) the width of a pencil

    f) the distance from Windsor to Kingston

    g) the mass of cement needed to build a bridge

4. a) Measure each line segment in centimetres.

      i) A_____B

      ii) C_____D

      iii) E_____F

    b) Convert each measure in part a to inches.

    c) Check your answers in part b by measuring each line segment in inches.

✓ **5.** Convert each length.

Round your answers to the nearest tenth where appropriate.

    a) A wood screw is 3 inches long; convert to millimetres.

    b) A cedar plank is 6 feet long; convert to centimetres.

    c) The Shahs live 8 miles out of town; convert to kilometres.

    d) A lawn is 20 yards wide; convert to metres.

6. Convert each mass.

Round your answers to the nearest tenth where appropriate.

    a) A postal letter is 20 g; convert to ounces.

    b) A bag of cement is 5 kg; convert to pounds.

    c) A recipe calls for 1 kg of chicken; convert to pounds.

    d) A truck has a load weighing 2 t; convert to tons.

✓ **7.** Convert each volume.

Round your answer to the nearest tenth where appropriate.

    a) A punch bowl holds 7 pints; convert to litres.

    b) A customer pumps 4 gallons of gas; convert to litres.

    c) A sample of lotion contains 6 fluid ounces; convert to millilitres.

    d) A herbicide is sold in $\frac{1}{2}$-gallon bottles; convert to millilitres.

✓ **8. Communication** To determine the thickness of wood that a circular saw can cut, divide the blade diameter by 2. So, if a blade is 20" in diameter, it can cut wood up to 10" thick. Is an $8\frac{1}{4}$" saw sufficient to cut a piece of wood 10 cm thick? Explain your reasoning.

9. Estimate each measure in appropriate imperial units. Compare your answers with a peer.

    a) the length of your classroom

    b) the height of your desk or table

    c) the volume of water added to drink crystals to make juice

    d) the length and width of the chalkboard

    e) the mass of a regular-size loaf of sandwich bread

    f) the volume of liquid in a pop can

    g) the outside dimensions of your school

10. Verify 2 parts from exercise 9 by taking measurements.

11. Convert each measure.

    a) $3\frac{1}{2}$ feet to inches   b) $2\frac{1}{4}$ miles to yards

    c) $2\frac{1}{2}$ yards to inches   d) 13 200 feet to miles

    e) 56 inches to feet   f) 2200 yards to miles

12. Convert each measure.

    a) 25 mL to fluid ounces   b) 3 t to pounds

    c) 5 L to gallons   d) 10 t to tons

13. **Knowledge/Understanding** Convert each measure. Round your answers to the nearest tenth where appropriate.

    a) 43 feet to centimetres   b) 2 pints to litres

    c) 1760 yards to kilometres   d) 7 yards to metres

    e) 30 gallons to litres   f) 5 pounds to kilograms

14. A certain type of screw requires at least $\frac{1}{2}$" of penetration into wood to be secure. A $\frac{1}{8}$" thick washer is needed between the screw and wood. The screw must go through a 1" board, the washer, and penetrate the wood. Determine the minimum length of screw required if the screw type is sold in $\frac{1}{4}$" increments.

15. A bolt is required to attach a metal bed frame. The total thickness of the metal is $\frac{5}{6}$". A $\frac{1}{4}$" thick nut is needed to secure the bolt. For safety reasons there should be $\frac{1}{8}$" after the nut, in case the nut loosens. What is the minimum bolt length required?

16. The speed limit on some Interstate highways in Michigan is 65 miles per hour. Determine the equivalent speed in kilometres per hour.

17. Lida's car has a 55-L tank. How many gallons of gas can she fill into the tank if it is completely empty?

18. Application In a construction project, $\frac{3}{4}$" pine boards will be attached with screws. What screw size should be used? Explain the reason for your choice.

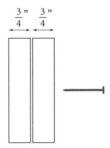

19. The speed limit on most two-lane highways in Ontario is 80 kilometres per hour. In the United States, the speed limit on two-lane highways is 50 miles per hour. Assume you drive the speed limit. Are you allowed to drive faster in Ontario or the United States? Justify your answer.

20. The marathon received much attention at the 1908 Olympic games in London, England. The International Olympic Committee added 385 yards to the distance. This was so that spectators and the royal family would have a better view of the finish line. This particular marathon set the present official marathon distance of 26 miles 385 yards. Determine this distance in kilometres.

21. Andy is following a recipe for jam that requires 5 pounds of sugar. Sugar is sold in 2-kg bags. How many bags of sugar will Andy need to purchase?

22. A bridge has a load restriction of 2 tons. Can a 1750-kg truck safely drive on the bridge? Justify your answer.

23. Thinking/Inquiry/Problem Solving In quilting, all pattern measures of blocks and seams are given in inches. Material in fabric stores is sold by the metre. How many 4" blocks can be cut from a 1-metre piece of remnant fabric that is 115 cm wide?

A group of students in a college urban planning course have completed a plan for a park. There is a path around the park. The length of the path is the sum of the lengths of the segments on the plan.

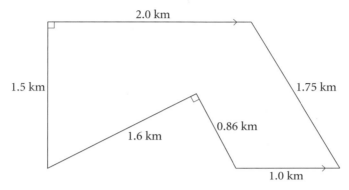

2.0 km

1.5 km

1.75 km

0.86 km

1.6 km

1.0 km

Length of path = 2.0 + 1.75 + 1.0 + 0.86 + 1.6 + 1.5
= 8.71

Since the least precise value has one decimal place, the total length of the path is 8.7 km.

Recall that the distance around a closed figure is its perimeter. The perimeter of a polygon is calculated by adding the lengths of the sides of the polygon.

For a circle, perimeter is called circumference.
Recall that the formula for the circumference, C, of a circle with diameter d is $C = \pi d$.
When the radius is known, the formula is $C = 2\pi r$.

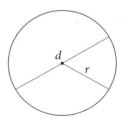

Example 1 Determine the perimeter of each figure. Round to the nearest tenth where appropriate.

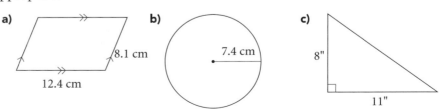

a)

8.1 cm

12.4 cm

b)

7.4 cm

c)

8"

11"

Solution

a) Recall that the opposite sides of a parallelogram are equal in length.

Perimeter = 12.4 + 8.1 + 12.4 + 8.1   or   Perimeter = 2(12.4 + 8.1)

= 41.0   = 41.0

The perimeter of the parallelogram is 41.0 cm.

b) Use the formula $C = 2\pi r$.

$C = (2)(\pi)(7.4)$ Use a calculator.

$\doteq 46.5$ Press: 2 ⬡π 7.4 ⬡ENTER=

The circumference of the circle is approximately 46.5 cm.

c) Use the Pythagorean Theorem to determine the length of the hypotenuse.

Let d represent the length of the hypotenuse.

$d^2 = 8^2 + 11^2$

$d = \sqrt{8^2 + 11^2}$ Use a calculator.

$\doteq 14$ Press: ⬡2nd ⬡x^2 8 ⬡x^2 ⬡+ 11 ⬡x^2 ⬡) ⬡ENTER=

Perimeter = 11 + 8 + 14

= 33

The perimeter of the triangle is approximately 33 inches.

Discuss

Why did we round the answers in parts a and b to the nearest tenth and part c to the nearest whole number?

Example 2

Eric measured the floor of his room as 5.0 m by 3.0 m. He needs to buy quarter-round trim for the room. He will ignore the width of the door when he decides how much trim to buy. At the store, he is told that quarter-round is sold in 8-foot strips. How many strips will he need for the room?

Solution

Draw a diagram.

5.0 m

3.0 m

The room was measured in metres and the quarter-round is sold in feet. So, the measurements must be converted.

Calculate the perimeter of the room in metres.
Perimeter = 5.0 + 3.0 + 5.0 + 3.0
$\qquad\qquad$ = 16.0
The perimeter of the room is 16.0 m.
Convert the perimeter to feet.
Let x represent the length in feet.
16 m = x feet
30.48 cm or 0.3048 m $\doteq$ 1 foot
Write equal ratios.

$$\frac{16}{0.3048} \doteq \frac{x}{1}$$

$\qquad$ 16 $\doteq$ 0.3048x $\qquad\qquad$ Multiply each side by 0.3048.

$\qquad\quad$ $x \doteq 52.5$

The perimeter of the room is approximately 52.5 feet. Since we are only calculating with imperial-unit dimensions, we need not convert to fraction form. The quarter-round is sold in 8-foot strips. To determine the number of strips needed, divide 52.5 feet by 8 feet.

$$\frac{52.5}{8} \doteq 6.56$$

Since it is not possible to buy part of a strip, Eric will need 7 strips.

Discuss

Will you get the same answer if you first convert each room dimension to feet? Explain.

Recall, a polygon is *regular* if all sides and angles are equal.

Example 3

A plan for a pool house consists of a square, semicircle, and regular semi-octagon as shown on the next page.

a) The owner would like to install large windows around the semicircle and semi-octagon. Calculate the perimeter of the window region.

b) The owner would like to plant small rose bushes around the entire house. She would like to plant 1 bush every 2 feet. How many bushes will she need?

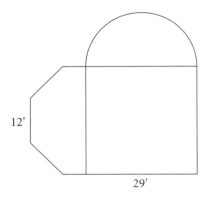

12'

29'

Solution

a) A regular octagon has 8 equal sides.

Perimeter of semi-octagon, $P_{\text{semi-octagon}} = \dfrac{12 \times 8}{2}$

$$= \dfrac{96}{2}$$

$$= 48$$

Perimeter of semicircle, $P_{\text{semicircle}} = \dfrac{\pi d}{2}$

$$= \dfrac{\pi(29)}{2}$$

$$\doteq 46$$

Total windowed perimeter = 48 + 46

$$= 94$$

The total windowed perimeter is approximately 94 feet.

b) Total house perimeter

$$= P_{\text{semi-octagon}} + P_{\text{semicircle}} + \text{side of square} + \text{side of square}$$

$$= 48 + 46 + 29 + 29$$

$$= 152$$

Number of rose bushes $= \dfrac{152}{2}$

$$= 76$$

The owner will need 76 rose bushes.

A

✓ **1.** Calculate the perimeter of each figure.

a)

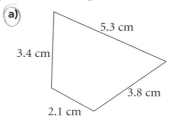
5.3 cm
3.4 cm
3.8 cm
2.1 cm

b)

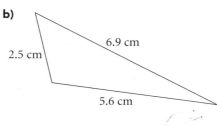
6.9 cm
2.5 cm
5.6 cm

c)

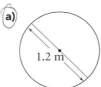
4.8 cm
5.4 cm
4.4 cm
4.8 cm
5.8 cm

d)

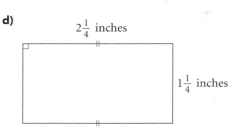
$2\frac{1}{4}$ inches
$1\frac{1}{4}$ inches

2. Calculate the perimeter of your desk or table in metric and imperial units.

B

✓ **3. Knowledge/Understanding** Calculate the perimeter of each figure.

a) a rectangle with sides 12 feet and 7 feet

b) a triangle with sides 32.4 m, 18.6 m, and 21.5 m

c) a regular hexagon with sides $6\frac{1}{2}$ inches

d) a trapezoid with sides 7.5 cm, 5.1 cm, 4.4 cm, and 4.8 cm

✓ **4.** Calculate the circumference of each circle.

a)

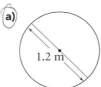
1.2 m

b)

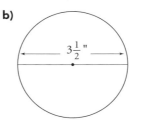
$3\frac{1}{2}$ "

c)

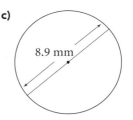
8.9 mm

5. Calculate the circumference of each circle.

    a) radius 25 mm   **b)** diameter 7"   **c)** radius 15 cm

    d) diameter 3.5 m   **e)** diameter $6\frac{1}{2}$'   **f)** radius 12 yards

6. Communication A student comments that the formulas for circumference, $C = 2\pi r$ and $C = \pi d$, are basically the same formula. Do you agree or disagree with the statement? Explain your reasoning.

7. Application Gilles has a rectangular swimming pool with dimensions 16 feet by 32 feet. A 6-foot wide concrete deck surrounds the pool. What length of fencing is needed to enclose the pool and deck ?

8. Elaine is on the school cross-country running team. Last week's course was laid out as shown. Determine the length of the course in each unit.

    a) metres   **b)** kilometres   **c)** miles

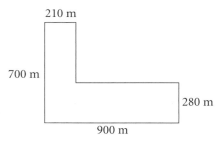

9. Refer to exercise 8. Elaine ran the course in 20 min. Recall, $\text{Speed} = \frac{\text{Distance}}{\text{Time}}$.

Determine her speed in each unit.

    a) metres per second   **b)** kilometres per hour   **c)** miles per hour

 10. A room is 11 feet wide and 15 feet long. A wallpaper border is to be pasted around the room. The wallpaper is sold in 18-foot rolls. How many rolls will be required for the border?

11. a) A rectangular park has a path around its perimeter. The park is 1500 m by 1200 m. Determine the length of the path in each unit.

    i) metres   **ii)** kilometres   **iii)** miles

    b) A diagonal path is to be constructed from one corner to the other. How long will the path be?

12. Calculate the perimeter of each right triangle.

    a) legs measure 14.0 cm and 9.0 cm

    b) hypotenuse length 17" and one leg 8"

13. A homeowner wants to purchase a garden hose for his rectangular-shaped yard. He wants to ensure that the hose will reach all areas of the yard. The dimensions of his yard are given, as well as the location of the tap for the hose. Is he able to purchase a 50-foot hose and reach all areas of the yard? Justify your answer.

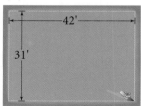

14. A Norman window has the shape of a combined semicircle and rectangle. Its dimensions are shown in the diagram. Determine the length of the border required around the window.

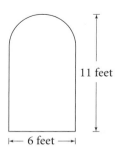

11 feet

← 6 feet →

15. A circular skating rink has a circumference of 145 m. Calculate the radius of the rink to the nearest tenth.

16. A regular hexagonal gazebo has perimeter 168 inches. Determine the length of one side of the gazebo.

17. A rectangular quilt is 180 cm by 150 cm. A bias ribbon is going to be used around the edge of the quilt to bind it. The ribbon is sold in 4-foot length packages. How many packages are needed?

18. A 5-foot wide deck is to be constructed around a circular swimming pool. The diameter of the pool is 18 feet.

a) Calculate the circumference of the outside edge of the deck.

b) How much longer is the outer edge of the deck compared to the inner edge of the deck?

19. Thinking/Inquiry/Problem Solving The cross section of a cottage roof is an isosceles triangle with height 4 m and base 6 m. Calculate the perimeter of the triangle.

C

20. Determine the perimeter of △ABC, given ∠B = 42°, $a = 8.5$ cm, and $c = 9.4$ cm.

21. A regular polygon has n sides, each of length s. Write a formula for the perimeter of the polygon. Explain your reasoning.

The urban planning students mentioned in Section 3.2 must include sport fields, swing sets, and other recreational facilities in their park design. They require sod for the fields and need to determine the area of the park.

Recall these area formulas from an earlier grade:

Rectangle: $A = lw$

rectangle

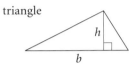

Triangle: $A = \frac{1}{2}bh$

triangle

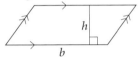

Parallelogram: $A = bh$

parallelogram

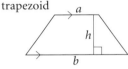

Trapezoid: $A = \frac{h(a + b)}{2}$

trapezoid

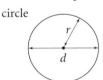

Circle: $A = \pi r^2$

circle

Since the park is irregular in shape, the area must be determined indirectly. Draw a dotted line as shown in the diagram.
The shape is now a trapezoid.

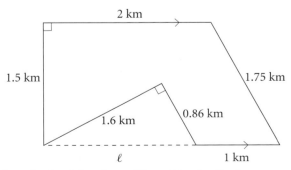

Calculate the length, ℓ, of the dotted line. Use the Pythagorean Theorem.

$$\ell^2 = 1.6^2 + 0.86^2$$
$$\ell = \sqrt{1.6^2 + 0.86^2}$$

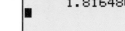

The length is approximately 1.8 km.

The length of the base of the trapezoid is 2.8 km.

To calculate the area of the park, determine the area of the trapezoid, $A_{trapezoid}$, then subtract the area of the triangle, $A_{triangle}$.

$$A_{trapezoid} = \frac{h(a + b)}{2}$$

$h = 1.5$, $a = 2.0$, $b = 2.8$

$$A_{trapezoid} = \frac{1.5(2.0 + 2.8)}{2}$$

Use a calculator.

Press: 1.5 $($ 2.0 $+$ 2.8 $)$ $\div$ 2 ENTER

$A_{trapezoid} = 3.6$

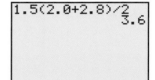

$$A_{triangle} = \frac{1}{2}bh$$

$b = 0.86$, $h = 1.6$

$$A_{triangle} = \frac{1}{2}(0.86)(1.6)$$
$$\doteq 0.69$$

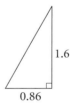

Area of the park $= A_{trapezoid} - A_{triangle}$
$$= 3.6 - 0.69$$
$$= 2.91$$

The area of the park is approximately 2.9 km^2.

Large areas of land are often expressed in hectares (ha).
Recall that 1 km^2 = 100 ha.
So, 2.9 km^2 = 2.9 × 100 ha
$$= 290\,ha$$

The area of the park is approximately 290 ha.

Discuss

How do we know which sides of the triangle are its base and height?

Sometimes we have to calculate dimensions before we can use a formula.

Example 1 Determine the area of each figure.
Round answers to the nearest tenth where appropriate.

a) a patio

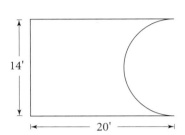

b) the side view of a rivet

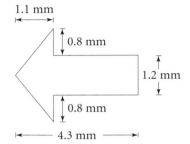

Solution

a) The area of the patio is the difference between the area of a rectangle and the area of a semicircle. Calculate the area of the rectangle, $A_{\text{rectangle}}$, then subtract the area of the semicircle, $A_{\text{semicircle}}$.

$A_{\text{rectangle}} = lw$
$l = 20,\ w = 14$
$A = (20)(14)$
$\quad = 280$

$A_{\text{semicircle}} = \dfrac{\pi r^2}{2}$

The width of the rectangle is equivalent to the diameter of the circle. The radius of the circle is half the diameter, so

$r = \dfrac{14}{2}$
$\quad = 7$

$A_{\text{semicircle}} = \dfrac{\pi(7)^2}{2}$ Press: [2nd] [∧] 7 [x^2] [÷] 2 [ENTER]

$\quad\doteq 77$

Area of the patio $= A_{\text{rectangle}} - A_{\text{semicircle}}$
$\qquad\qquad\qquad = 280 - 77$
$\qquad\qquad\qquad = 203$

So, the area of the patio is approximately 203 square feet.

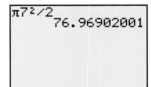

b) The total area is the sum of the area of a rectangle, $A_{\text{rectangle}}$, and the area of a triangle, A_{triangle}.

$A_{\text{rectangle}} = lw$

From the diagram,

$l = 4.3 - 1.1$

   $= 3.2$

$w = 1.2$

$A_{\text{rectangle}} = (3.2)(1.2)$

   $= 3.84$

$A_{\text{triangle}} = \frac{1}{2}bh$

From the diagram,

$b = 0.8 + 1.2 + 0.8$

   $= 2.8$

$h = 1.1$

$A_{\text{triangle}} = \frac{1}{2}(2.8)(1.1)$

   $= 1.54$

The total area $= A_{\text{rectangle}} + A_{\text{triangle}}$

   $= 3.84 + 1.54$

   $= 5.38$

So, the area of the rivet is 5.38 mm^2.

In the construction industry, materials are predominantly measured and sold in imperial units.

Example 2

Jane has decided to install a hardwood floor in her den. The flooring costs $9.49 per square foot installed. The den is 4.0 m by 4.5 m. Determine the cost of the floor.

Solution

Convert each metric dimension to feet.

Let x represent the width in feet.

4 m = x feet

0.3048 m $\doteq$ 1 foot

Write equal ratios.

$\frac{4}{0.3048} \doteq \frac{x}{1}$

   $x \doteq 13.12$

Let y represent the length in feet.

$4.5 \text{ m} = y \text{ feet}$

$0.3048 \text{ m} \doteq 1 \text{ foot}$

$\dfrac{4.5}{0.3048} \doteq \dfrac{y}{1}$

$\qquad y \doteq 14.76$

The dimensions of the room are approximately 13.12 feet by 14.76 feet.

$A = lw$

$\quad \doteq (13.12)(14.76)$

$\quad \doteq 193.65$

Since it is not possible to buy a partial square foot, round up.
So, Jane will require 194 square feet of hardwood.

To determine the cost, multiply the square feet by the cost per square foot.
$194 \times 9.49 = 1841.06$

The cost of the hardwood floor is $1841.06.

3.3 Exercises

A

✓ **1.** Determine the area of each figure. Round your answers to the nearest tenth where appropriate.

a)

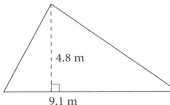

6"

4"

b)

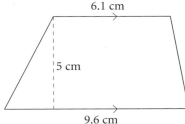

6.1 cm

5 cm

9.6 cm

c)

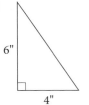

4.8 m

9.1 m

d)

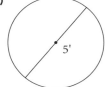

5'

2. Determine the area of each figure. Round your answers to the nearest tenth where appropriate.

a)

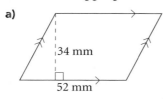

34 mm

52 mm

b)

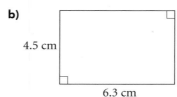

4.5 cm

6.3 cm

c)

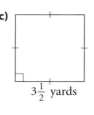

$3\frac{1}{2}$ yards

d)

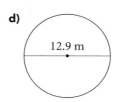

12.9 m

B

✓ **3. Knowledge/Understanding** Determine the area of each figure. Round your answer to the nearest tenth where appropriate.

a) A circle with radius 6 feet is painted around the free-throw line on a basketball court.

b) A wall is 7 feet high and $10\frac{1}{2}$ feet wide.

c) A trapezoid-shaped lot has parallel sides of length 7 m and 9 m, and depth 19 m.

d) A parallelogram-shaped advertising sign has a base $6\frac{1}{2}$ feet and height 5 feet.

e) A decorative circular window has diameter 17 cm.

✓ **4.** The hypotenuse of a right triangle is 10.8 cm. One leg is 6.1 cm. Calculate the area of the triangle to the nearest tenth.

✓ **5.** Calculate the area of each figure to the nearest tenth.

a)

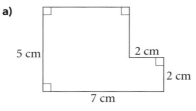

5 cm

2 cm

2 cm

7 cm

b)

2"

4"

5"

c)

85 mm

d)

6.1 m

3.4 m

4.7 m

8.2 m

e)

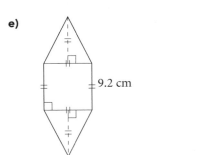

9.2 cm

f)

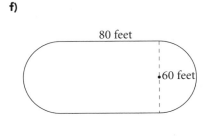

80 feet

60 feet

6. Two rectangular properties have these dimensions:
   Property A: 60 feet by 95 feet
   Property B: 27 feet by 200 feet
   Which property has a greater area?

7. Carol's backyard is the shape of a trapezoid with the parallel sides
   40 feet and 100 feet, and depth 120 feet. Carol is preparing to fertilize
   the lawn. A bag of fertilizer will cover 3000 square feet. How many bags
   of fertilizer must Carol buy?

✓ 8. A room is 12 feet by 14 feet. Jorge will buy carpet and underpad for the
   room from a discount supplier. He will contract a local installer to lay
   the carpet and underpad. Underpad is $7.95 per square yard and carpet
   is $49.85 per square yard. The installation costs $0.95 per square foot.
   Determine the total cost for the materials and installation.

✓ 9. Two pool designs are given. The shaded region in each diagram
   represents the decks. Determine the area of each deck.

a)

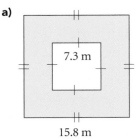

7.3 m

15.8 m

b)

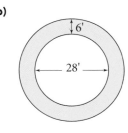

6'

28'

✓ 10. **Communication** Two rectangles with different dimensions have equal
   perimeters.

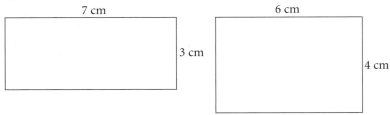

7 cm

3 cm

6 cm

4 cm

Will their areas also be equal? Explain your reasoning.

11. A circular-faced sander has an 8" diameter. A rectangular-faced sander is 3" by 18". Which sander covers a greater area? Justify your answer.

12. A Norman window has the shape of a rectangle and a semicircle. Its dimensions are given in the diagram. Determine the number of square feet of glass required for the window.

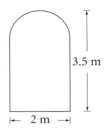

3.5 m

2 m

13. A carpet cleaning company advertised a three room special up to a maximum of 56 square yards, at $119.95. Mel is planning to have the carpet in three bedrooms cleaned. The rooms are rectangular and measure $8\frac{1}{2}$ feet by 11 feet, 13 feet by 15 feet, and 14 feet by 15 feet. Does Mel qualify for the special?

14. Application Calculate the required dimension for each circle.
   a) area = 227 m²; calculate the radius.
   b) area = 16 286 square inches; calculate the diameter.

15. Ron's driveway is 15 m long and 6 m wide. He plans to replace the asphalt he currently has with interlocking stone. Stone is sold by the square foot. How many square feet of stone must Ron order?

16. Isabel's shed roof requires new shingles. The roof resembles 4 congruent triangles with dimensions as shown. Approximately how many square feet is the roof?

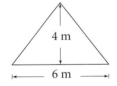

4 m

6 m

17. A landscaper is preparing a circular flowerbed. The bed has a 14-foot diameter. He will need 16 plants per square yard. How many plants should he buy?

18. Thinking/Inquiry/Problem Solving Tran and his family have moved into a new home. The family is building a patio at the back of the house. The rectangular patio is 20 feet by 30 feet. The patio stones are also rectangular and are 24 inches by 30 inches. What is the minimum number of patio stones that Tran will need?

19. Recall that 1 foot $\doteq$ 0.3048 m. Why is 1 square foot $\neq$ 0.3048 m²?

1. Convert each measure. Round your answers to the nearest tenth where appropriate.

   a) 5 feet to inches   **b)** 6.0 L to millilitres

   c) 14 yards to metres   **d)** 12 gallons to litres

   e) 7 kg to pounds and ounces   **f)** 120 cm to feet and inches

2. Calculate the perimeter of each figure.

   a) a triangle with sides 26.4 m, 29.6 m, and 18.3 m

   b) a regular octagon with sides $4\frac{1}{4}$ inches

   c) a circle with diameter 9 inches

   d) a parallelogram with sides $5\frac{1}{4}$ inches and $4\frac{1}{2}$ inches

3. The circumference of a circle is 54 cm. Calculate the radius of the circle to the nearest tenth.

4. Calculate the area of each figure. Round your answer to the nearest tenth where appropriate.

   a) a circle with radius 6.2 m

   b) a rectangle with length 9 feet and width $4\frac{1}{2}$ feet

   c) a parallelogram with base $4\frac{3}{4}$ inches and height 3 inches

   d) a right triangle with hypotenuse 15.4 cm and one leg 9.2 cm

Performance Assessment

5. Monica wants to install a wood floor in a 10' by 16' room. The 6' by 8' by $\frac{3}{4}$" thick boards will be cut to 6" by 4' by $\frac{3}{4}$" slats.

   a) What is the minimum number of slats required?

   b) At the shop, she has two options to get the boards cut to 6" by 4'.

        i) Have cuts done on the $8\frac{1}{4}$" diameter circular table saw.

        ii) Have cuts done on the 10" diameter circular table saw.

   Each cut on the smaller saw is $1.00, though more than one board can be placed on the table saw at a time. Each cut on the large saw is $1.20. To determine the thickness of wood a circular saw can cut, divide the diameter of the blade by 2. Which saw is the most economical choice? Justify your answer.

   c) To seal the floor, Urethane will be applied. Brand A costs $22/gallon and requires 2 coats. Brand B costs $40/gallon and requires 1 coat. Which brand would you advise Monica to buy? Explain.

The student group has included a rectangular sandbox in the park's recreational facilities. The sandbox is 3.8 m by 4.2 m and will be dug to 0.5 m deep. The students must determine how much sand is needed to fill the sandbox. The amount of space an object occupies is its volume.

A rectangular box is a prism. Recall from an earlier grade:

Volume of a prism = Area of base × Height

To calculate the volume of the sandbox,

Area of base = ℓw
$$= (3.8)(4.2)$$
$$= 15.96$$

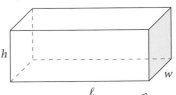

So, Volume = $(15.96)(0.5)$
$$= 7.98$$

The sandbox will need about 8 m³ of sand.

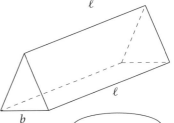

To determine the volume of a cylinder, we use a similar formula.

Volume of a cylinder, $V_{cylinder}$, = Area of base × Height
Since the base of a cylinder is a circle,
Area of base = πr^2.
So, $V_{cylinder} = \pi r^2 h$

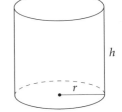

Here are some useful formulas for surface areas.

Surface Area

To calculate the surface area of a prism or cylinder, add the area of the plane figures of each side. We use the net diagram.

Rectangular Prism:
$$SA = \ell w + \ell w + \ell h + \ell h + wh + wh$$
$$= 2(\ell w + \ell h + wh)$$

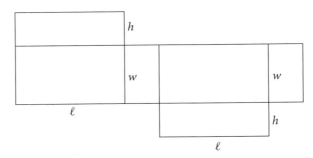

Triangular Prism:

$$SA = \ell b + \ell s + \ell s + \frac{1}{2}bh + \frac{1}{2}bh$$
$$= \ell b + 2\ell s + 2\left(\frac{1}{2}bh\right)$$
$$= \ell b + 2\ell s + bh$$

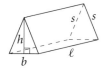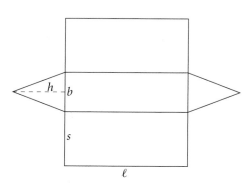

Use the Pythagorean Theorem to calculate s.

$$s^2 = \left(\frac{b}{2}\right)^2 + h^2$$
$$s = \sqrt{\left(\frac{b}{2}\right)^2 + h^2}$$

Cylinder:

$$SA = \pi r^2 + \pi r^2 + 2\pi rh$$
$$= 2\pi r^2 + 2\pi rh$$

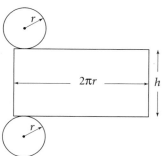

Example

Determine the volume and surface area of each prism.

a)

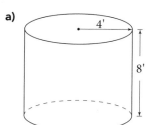

b)

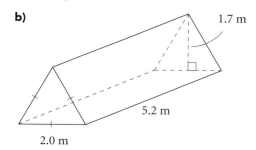

Solution

a) Volume of a cylinder = Area of base × Height
$$V_{\text{cylinder}} = \pi r^2 h \quad r = 4, h = 8$$
$$= \pi(4)^2(8)$$
$$\doteq 402.1$$

The volume of the cylinder is approximately 402 cubic feet.

$$SA = 2\pi r^2 + 2\pi rh$$
$$= 2\pi(4)^2 + 2\pi(4)(8)$$
$$\doteq 301.6$$

The surface area of the cylinder is approximately 302 square feet.

b) Use the triangular face of the prism as the base.
Height then refers to length of the prism.
So, Volume = Area of base × Length

$$V = \frac{1}{2}bh\ell$$

$b = 2.0, h = 1.7, \ell = 5.2.$

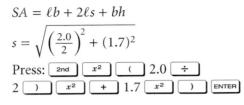
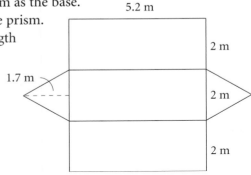

5.2 m

2 m

1.7 m

2 m

2 m

$$= \frac{1}{2}(2.0)(1.7)(5.2)$$

$$= 8.84$$

The volume of the prism
is approximately 8.8 m³.

$$SA = \ell b + 2\ell s + bh$$

$$s = \sqrt{\left(\frac{2.0}{2}\right)^2 + (1.7)^2}$$

Press: [2nd] [x²] [( ] 2.0 [÷]
2 [ )] [x²] [+] 1.7 [x²] [ )] [ENTER]

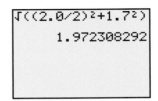

√((2.0/2)²+1.7²)
      1.972308292

$$SA = \ell b + 2\ell s + bh$$
$$= (5.2)(2.0) + 2(5.2)s + (2.0)(1.7)$$

Use your calculator's memory to
input the value for s, above.

Press: 5.2 [×] 2.0 [+] 2 [×] 5.2 [×]
[2nd] [(-)] [+] 2.0 [×] 1.7 [ENTER]

So, the surface area of the prism is
approximately 34.3 m².

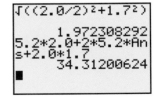

√((2.0/2)²+1.7²)
      1.972308292
5.2*2.0+2*5.2*An
s+2.0*1.7
      34.31200624
■

Discuss

Why do we use the calculator's memory for the value of s and not round to one
decimal place?

A

1. Calculate the volume of each prism.

   a) a hexagonal prism with area of base 17.6 cm^2 and height 3.6 cm

   b) a square-based rectangular prism with area of base 15.3 cm^2 and height 42.5 cm

   c) a cylinder with area of base $25\frac{1}{2}$ square feet and height 7 feet

2. **Knowledge/Understanding** Calculate the volume and surface area of each figure.

   a)

   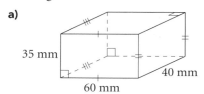

   35 mm
   60 mm
   40 mm

   b)

   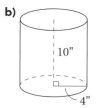

   10"
   4"

   c)

   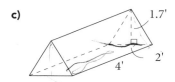

   1.7'
   2'
   4'

B

3. Calculate the volume of each prism.

   a) a rectangular prism 4' by 3' by 8'

   b) a cylinder with diameter 9.8 cm and height 6.3 cm

   c) a triangular prism 3 m long with triangular height 1.2 m and triangular base 1.8 m

4. A cylindrical tank with outside radius 15' and height 20' is to be painted. Determine the surface area to be painted in square feet.

5. A rectangular swimming pool is 18' by 32' by 4' deep. The pool is to be filled to a depth 6" from the top. How many cubic feet of water are needed to fill the pool?

6. **Communication** The students in this section's opening exercises were able to fill the sandbox with 9.5 m^3 of sand. Explain how this was possible.

7. A room is 3.8 m by 4.7 m by 2.4 m high. All surfaces except the floor are to be painted. Ignoring doors and windows, how many square metres of surface are to be painted?

8. A cylindrical tank with diameter 1.0 m and height 1.5 m is to be filled with water. How many litres of water are needed to fill the tank? $1000 \text{ cm}^3 = 1 \text{ L}$

9. A tent in the shape of a triangular prism is being made. The same material will be used for the walls and the floor. The floor is 6 feet by 12 feet. The tent height is 4 feet. Determine the minimum number of square yards of material required to make the tent.

10. Application Calculate the height of each rectangular prism.
  a) volume 2040 cm^3; area of the base 120 cm^2
  b) volume 107.5 m^3; base 9.4 m by 5.2 m

11. The volume of a cylinder is 31 808 mm^3. The radius is 15 mm. Determine the height of the cylinder.

12. Bob is a stonemason and is preparing to build a rectangular walk with fieldstone. Before laying the stone he must have a base of screenings. This base is to be 6 inches deep. The walk measures 2 feet by 44 feet. How many cubic feet of screenings must Bob order so that he can prepare the walk for the stone?

13. A garage floor is to be constructed of poured concrete. The floor is rectangular and measures 12 m wide by 8 m deep. The concrete will be poured to a depth of 30 cm. What amount of concrete will be required?

14. A building is a rectangular prism with base measuring 15 yards by 12 yards and height 4 yards. The exterior of the building is to be covered by a stucco-like material. The material costs $2.50 per square foot installed. Ignore the doors and windows in your calculations. How much will it cost to cover the walls?

15. The box of a dump truck measures 30 feet by 9 feet by 6 feet. How many cubic yards of gravel will the dump truck hold?

16. A water trough is the shape of a triangular prism. The ends are equilateral triangles. Each side of the triangle is 1 foot in length. The trough is 8 feet long. How many litres of water will the trough hold?

17. Thinking/Inquiry/Problem Solving A cylindrical aluminum can has height 14 cm and diameter 12 cm. Determine the dimensions of a can that has equal volume but uses less material (has less surface area).

C

18. Determine the volume of a triangular prism with sides of the triangular base measuring 10 cm, 14 cm, and 21 cm and having height 30 cm. Hint: Use trigonometry.

Cones and cylinders, and pyramids and prisms have related volumes. You will determine how the volumes of these shapes are related.

Investigation

Volume of a Cone and a Pyramid

1. Consider these cones.
Cone A: radius 3 cm and height 5 cm with volume 47.1 cm^3
Cone B: radius 7 cm and height 11 cm with volume 564.4 cm^3

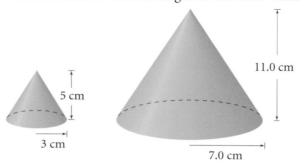

5 cm
3 cm
11.0 cm
7.0 cm

a) Calculate the volume of a cylinder that has equal height and radius to cone A.

b) Calculate the volume of a cylinder that has equal height and radius to cone B.

2. Compare the volume of each cylinder and cone with equal height and radius.

3. Based on your comparison, write a formula for the volume of a cone in terms of the volume of a cylinder.

4. A square-based prism has a volume of 105 m^3. An equal base, equal height pyramid has a volume of 35 m^3.
a) Compare the volumes of the two figures.
b) Write a formula for the volume of a pyramid.

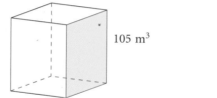

105 m^3

35 m^3

Volume of a Cone and a Pyramid

The volume of a cone, V_{cone}, with base radius r and height h is:

$V_{cone} = \frac{1}{3}$(area of base)(height)

Since the base of the cone is always a circle,

$V_{cone} = \frac{1}{3}\pi r^2 h$

The volume of a pyramid, $V_{pyramid}$, is:

$V_{pyramid} = \frac{1}{3}$(area of base)(height)

Example 1 Determine the volume of each figure. Round your answer to the nearest tenth.

a)

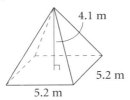

4.1 m

5.2 m

5.2 m

b)

9.5 cm

6.0 cm

Solution

a) The figure is a square-based pyramid.

$V_{pyramid} = \frac{1}{3}$(area of base)(height)   Substitute the values.

$= \frac{1}{3}(5.2)(5.2)(4.1)$ Use a calculator.

$\doteq 37.0$

The volume of the pyramid is approximately 37.0 m³.

b) The figure is a cone.

$V_{cone} = \frac{1}{3}\pi r^2 h$ Substitute the values.

$= \frac{1}{3}\pi(6.0)^2(9.5)$ Use a calculator.

$\doteq 358.1$

The volume of the cone is approximately 358.1 cm³.

Surface Area

The surface area of a pyramid is the sum of the area of the faces of the pyramid. The faces can best be visualized from the net.

In a square-based pyramid, we need the altitude, s, of the triangle. This distance is known as the slant height.

If only the base and height of the pyramid are known, the slant height, s, is calculated using the Pythagorean Theorem.

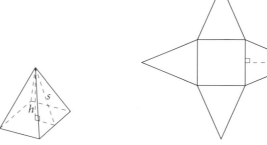

The lateral surface area of a cone is the area of the slanted surface. The total surface area is the sum of the area of the lateral surface and the base.

The lateral surface area of a pyramid is the sum of the triangular faces. The total surface area is the sum of the area of the lateral surface and the base.

TAKE NOTE

Surface Area of a Cone and a Pyramid

Cone	Square-Based Pyramid
$SA_{total} = A_{cone} + A_{base}$	$SA_{total} = 4 \times A_{triangle} + A_{base}$
$SA_{cone} = \pi rs$	$A_{triangle} = \frac{1}{2}bs$
$A_{base} = \pi r^2$	$A_{base} = b^2$
$SA_{total} = \pi rs + \pi r^2$	$SA_{total} = (4)\frac{1}{2}bs + b^2$

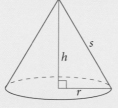

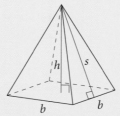

Example 2 Determine the total surface area of each figure. Round your answer to the nearest tenth.

a)

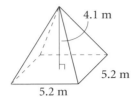

4.1 m

5.2 m

5.2 m

b)

9.5 cm

6.0 cm

Solution

a) Draw the net.

$SA_{total} = 4 \times A_{triangle} + A_{base}$

Use the Pythagorean Theorem to calculate s.

s

5.2 m

$s^2 = 2.6^2 + 4.1^2$ Use a calculator.

$s \doteq 4.8549$

$A_{triangle} = \frac{1}{2}bs$ Substitute the values.

$\quad = \frac{1}{2}(5.2)(4.8549)$

$\quad = 12.6227$

$A_{base} = b^2$ Substitute the values.

$\quad = (5.2)^2$

$\quad = 27.04$

$SA_{total} = (4)(12.6227) + (27.04)$

$\quad\quad = 77.5308$

The surface area of the pyramid is approximately 77.5 m^2.

b) Use the formula for surface area of a cone.

$SA_{total} = A_{cone} + A_{base}$

Use the Pythagorean Theorem to calculate the slant height, s.

$s^2 = 9.5^2 + 6.0^2$

$s \doteq 11.2361$

$SA_{cone} = \pi r s$

$\quad\quad = \pi(6.0)(11.2361)$

$\quad\quad \doteq 211.7955$

$A_{base} = \pi r^2$

$\quad\quad = \pi(6.0)^2$

$\quad\quad \doteq 113.0973$

$SA_{total} = 211.7955 + 113.0973$

$\quad\quad = 324.8928$

The surface area of the cone is approximately 324.9 cm^2.

Spheres

Recall from an earlier grade the formula for volume, V_{sphere}, and surface area, SA_{sphere}, of a sphere, with radius, r.

$$V_{sphere} = \frac{4}{3}\pi r^3 \qquad\qquad SA_{sphere} = 4\pi r^2$$

Example 3

Calculate the volume and surface area of the given sphere. Round your answers to the nearest tenth.

$V = \frac{4}{3}\pi r^3$

$ = \frac{4}{3}\pi(6.0)^3$

$ \doteq 904.8$

The volume of the sphere is approximately 904.8 mm^3.

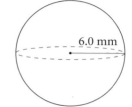

6.0 mm

$SA = 4\pi r^2$

$ = 4\pi(6.0)^2$

$ \doteq 452.4$

The surface area of the sphere is approximately 452.4 mm^2.

3.5 Exercises

A

1. Calculate the volume of each figure.

   a) a square-based pyramid, area of base 49 cm^2 and height 5 cm

   b) a cone, area of base 56.8 square inches and height 7 inches

   c) a hexagonal-based pyramid, area of base 650 mm^2 and height 44 mm

   d) a rectangular-based pyramid, area of base 180 square feet and height 10 feet

   e) a triangular-based pyramid, area of base 310 m^2 and height 12 m

   f) a cone, area of base 460 cm^2 and height 15.6 cm

2. Calculate the surface area of a cone with radius 6 inches and slant height 8 inches.

3. Calculate the lateral surface area of the pyramids with nets shown.

a)

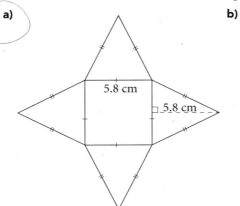

5.8 cm

5.8 cm

b)

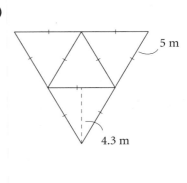

5 m

4.3 m

4. Calculate the lateral surface area of each cone.

a)

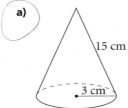

15 cm

3 cm

b)

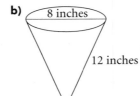

8 inches

12 inches

c)

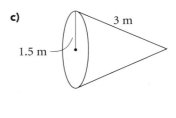

3 m

1.5 m

5. Calculate the total surface area of each cone in exercise 4.

6. Calculate the surface area of each sphere.

a)

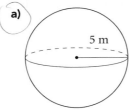

5 m

b)

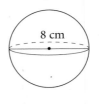

8 cm

c)

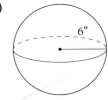

6"

7. Calculate the volume of each sphere.

a)

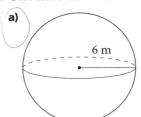

6 m

b)

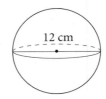

12 cm

c)

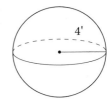

4'

8. Knowledge/Understanding Determine the volume and lateral surface area of each figure.

a)

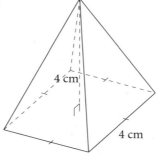

4 cm

4 cm

b)

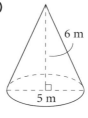

6 m

5 m

c)

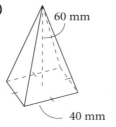

60 mm

40 mm

d)

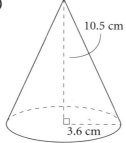

10.5 cm

3.6 cm

9. A certain type of ball bearing is 0.5 cm in diameter and has a density of 7.9 g/cm^3. Calculate the mass of each bearing. (Recall, $D = \frac{M}{V}$.)

✓ 10. An official NBA basketball has a diameter of 9 inches. Calculate the surface area and volume of the basketball.

11. Thinking/Inquiry/Problem Solving Joanne wants to create a scale model of an ancient pyramid. The actual dimensions of the pyramid are given. The scale she will use is 10 m = 1 cm. She will create the pyramid out of popsicle sticks and cover it with tissue paper. Calculate the minimum area of tissue paper she will need.

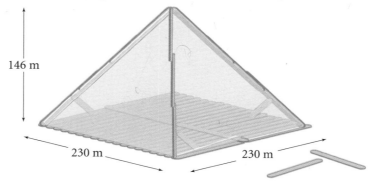

146 m

230 m

230 m

✓ 12. An office water dispenser holds 18.9 L of water. The paper cones from which people drink are 9.5 cm high with radius 3.5 cm.

   a) How many full cones of water can be dispensed from the container?

   b) What is the minimum amount of paper needed to construct the number of cones in part a?

✓ 13. a) **Application** The Earth is approximately a sphere. Its diameter is about 12 730 km. Water covers about 70% of Earth's surface. How many square kilometres of land cover the Earth?

   b) Canada is approximately 9.2 million km^2. What percentage of the Earth's land is Canada?

14. Coke is one by-product of crude oil. At a crude oil plant, large quantities of coke are produced. They are stored in large conical piles. Engineers assess how much coke is in a pile by measuring the height of the pile and diameter of the base. With this information they can calculate the volume. Calculate the volume of coke in a pile 10 m high with diameter 22 m.

15. A tent is the shape of a square-based pyramid. The tent is 2 m in height with a base 4 m long. The tent floor is made of the same material as the walls. Calculate the amount of material required to make the tent.

✓ 16. A pile of sand is approximately the shape of a cone. The pile is 35 feet in diameter and 40 feet high. Calculate the amount of sand to the nearest cubic foot.

17. Calculate the slant height of a cone-shaped pilon that has a lateral surface area of 283 cm^2 and radius 7.5 cm.

✓ 18. A square-based pyramid has a volume of 1261.5 mm^3. Its height is 18 mm. Calculate the dimensions of the base of the pyramid.

Ⓒ

19. A tetrahedron is a triangular-based pyramid consisting of four equilateral triangles. The sides of the triangles measure 12 cm. Calculate the total surface area and volume of the tetrahedron.

In this section you will use material from Sections 3.1–3.5 to solve multistep problems. You will also use your algebra skills to write formulas for areas and volumes of figures.

Example 1

Manuel is installing interlocking stone on his driveway, walk, and patio. The preparation work is complete. He will do the final levelling and laying of the stones himself. He must install a levelling bed of screenings 4 inches deep, then lay the stones on this bed. Screenings costs $25 per cubic yard, tax included. The stones come on skids, each with enough to cover 94 square feet. The cost of a skid is $210, tax and delivery included.

a) Calculate the cost of the material to complete the job.

b) If 4.5 stones cover 1 square foot, how many stones will Manuel lay?

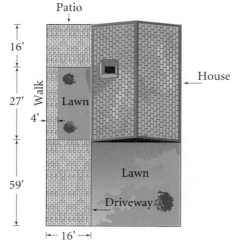

Solution

a) i) Calculate the total area.

Total area = Area of driveway + Area of walk + Area of patio
$$= 59 \times 16 + 27 \times 4 + 16 \times 16$$
$$= 1308$$

The total area is 1308 square feet.

ii) Calculate the cost of the screenings.

The depth is 4 inches. Convert inches to feet.

12 inches = 1 foot

4 inches = $\frac{1}{3}$ foot

Volume of screenings = Area of base × Depth

$$= 1308 \times \frac{1}{3}$$

$$= 436$$

The volume of screenings required is 436 cubic feet.

Screenings is sold in cubic yards; convert cubic feet to cubic yards.

1 yard = 3 feet

So, $(1 \text{ yard})^3 = (3 \text{ feet})^3$

So, 1 cubic yard = 27 cubic feet

Volume of screenings required = 436 ÷ 27

$$\doteq 16.1481$$

Manuel will need to buy 17 cubic yards of screenings, since 16 cubic yards will not be enough.

Cost = 17 × 25

$$= 425$$

The screenings will cost $425.

iii) Calculate the cost of the stones.

Determine the number of skids needed.

Number of skids = Total area ÷ Area of stones per skid

$$= 1308 \div 94$$

$$\doteq 13.9149$$

Manuel will need 14 skids of stone.

Cost of stone = 210 × 14

$$= 2940$$

The stone will cost $2940.

iv) Calculate the total cost.

Total cost = 425 + 2940

$$= 3365$$

The total cost of the job is $3365.

b) Number of stones = Area in square feet × Stones per square feet

$$= 1308 \times 4.5$$

$$= 5886$$

Manuel will lay 5886 stones.

Example 2

a) Determine, in terms of r and h, a formula for the volume of the figure shown below.

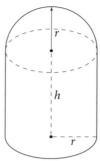

b) Calculate the volume of grain that could fit into a grain silo with radius 4.05 m and height 8.12 m.

Solution

a) Volume = Volume of cylinder + Volume of semisphere

$$V = \pi r^2 h + \frac{\frac{4}{3}\pi r^3}{2}$$

Simplify $\frac{\frac{4}{3}\pi r^3}{2}$.

Recall that to divide a fraction by a fraction, multiply by the reciprocal.

$$\frac{\frac{4}{3}\pi r^3}{2} = \frac{4}{3}\pi r^3 \div 2$$

$$= \frac{4}{3}\pi r^3 \times \frac{1}{2} \qquad \text{Multiply by the reciprocal.}$$

$$= \frac{4}{6}\pi r^3$$

$$= \frac{2}{3}\pi r^3 \qquad \text{Reduce.}$$

So, $V = \pi r^2 h + \frac{2}{3}\pi r^3$

Take out a common factor, πr^2.

$$V = \pi r^2(h + \frac{2}{3}r)$$

b) $V = \pi r^2(h + \frac{2}{3}r)$

Substitute $r = 4.05$ and $h = 8.12$ m.

$$V = \pi(4.05)^2(8.12 + \frac{2}{3}(4.05))$$

Use a calculator.

Press: (π) 4.05 (x²) (( ) 8.12 (+) 2 (A%) 3 (( ) 4.05 ( )) ( )) (ENTER =)

$$V \doteq 557.55$$

So, approximately 558 m³ of grain could fit in the silo.

Example 3   Gene has started his own business making gourmet spaghetti sauce. The sauce is packed in cans 10 cm in diameter and 15 cm high. The cans are packed 2 by 8 as shown.

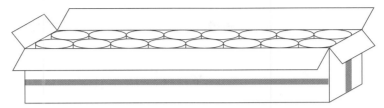

a) Calculate the surface area of the box used, assuming there is no cardboard overlap.

b) How could the same number of cans be packaged in order to use the least amount of cardboard?

Solution

a) The minimum dimensions of the box are 80 cm by 20 cm by 15 cm.

$SA = 2(\text{area of base}) + 2(\text{front face}) + 2(\text{side face})$
$ = 2(80 \times 20) + 2(80 \times 15) + 2(20 \times 15)$
$ = 6200 \text{ cm}^2$

The surface area of the box is 6200 cm^2.

b) To package 16 cans in a box, Gene can arrange the cans so they are 1 by 16, 2 by 8 (which he presently uses), or 4 by 4.

A box with cans arranged 1 by 16 has dimensions 10 cm by 160 cm by 15 cm high.

$SA = 2(10 \times 160) + 2(10 \times 15) + 2(160 \times 15)$
$ = 8300 \text{ cm}^2$

A box with cans arranged 4 by 4 has dimensions 40 cm by 40 cm by 15 cm high.

$SA = 2(40 \times 40) + 2(40 \times 15) + 2(40 \times 15)$
$ = 5600 \text{ cm}^2$

So, the arrangement that uses the least amount of cardboard is the 4 by 4 arrangement with box dimensions 40 cm by 40 cm by 15 cm.

When volume is fixed, a prism that incorporates a square will have the least surface area.

A

✓ **1.** Calculate the area of the shaded region.

a)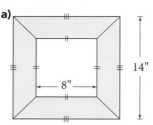

b)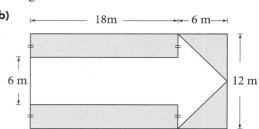

B

✓ **2.** A tent is in the shape shown. Calculate each measure.

  a) the volume of the tent

  b) the surface area excluding the floor

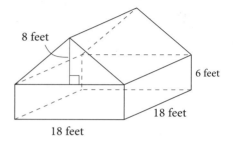

✓ **3. Knowledge/Understanding** Calculate the volume and surface area of the figure shown.

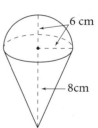

✓ **4.** Determine a formula, in terms of s, r, and h for the surface area of the figure shown.

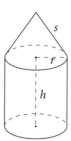

5. Neil is building a patio with interlocking stone in the shape shown. The preparation work is complete. He will do the final levelling work and lay the stones himself. He must install a levelling bed of screenings 6 inches deep, then lay the stones on this bed. Screenings costs $30 per cubic yard, tax included. The stones come on skids, each skid having enough stones to cover 74 square feet. The cost of a skid is $165, tax and delivery included. Calculate the cost of the patio.

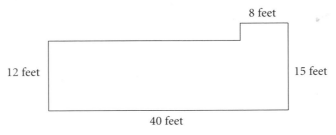

6. Application The walls and ceiling of a room are to be drywalled. The room is 12' by 16' by 8' high. Drywall comes in 4' by 8' sheets. How many sheets are needed to complete the job?

7. A swimming pool, 18' by 36', is filled with water to an average depth of 5' 10". A tanker truck will transport the water for the pool. The truck has a cylindrical tank 20' long with a diameter of 10'. How many truckloads of water are required to fill the pool?

8. A flat-topped silo is cylindrical. Its concrete walls, floor, and ceiling are 18 inches thick. The inside radius and height are 12 feet and 75 feet, respectively. Cement is required for the floor, walls, and ceiling. What volume of cement is needed to build the silo?

9. An oil tank has dimensions shown. Determine the volume of oil it can hold.

$1000 \text{ cm}^3 = 1 \text{ L}$

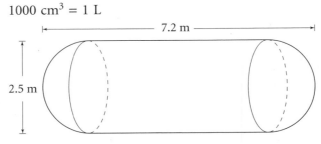

10. Jeff is in the lawn care business. He applies weed control to a customer's lawn shown on top of page 218. All areas other than the driveway, patio, house, and walk will be sprayed. If Jeff applies the spray at a rate of 5 L per 1000 square feet, how many litres will he use?

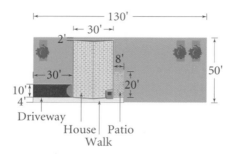

11. Refer to exercise 10. Jeff's truck has a cylindrical tank with radius 1.8 m and length 3 m. How many square feet of lawn can Jeff spray with a full tank?

✓ **12.** Melanie works as an estimator for a driveway paving company. She measures the area to be paved and provides an estimate for the customer. How much would it cost to pave the driveway shown if the company charges $5 per square foot?

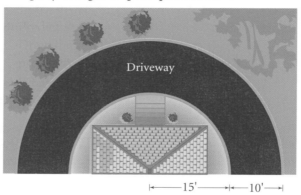

13. A concrete path is to be built around a circular wading pool. The diameter of the pool is 150 feet and the path is to be 10 feet wide. The concrete will be poured to a depth of 4 inches. Concrete costs $102.50/m³, delivered. Calculate the cost of concrete for the path.

14. Hal installs drywall. On this job he is using sheets that measure 4 feet by 8 feet. A room 18 feet by 14 feet by 8 feet high is his next task. Can Hal complete the room without cutting 1 or more of the sheets? Explain your reasoning.

✓ **15.** Miriam is putting up a fence and will need 8 posts. The posts have a 4" by 4" base and are 8' long. Her neighbour advises her to dig holes that are 2' in diameter and 3' deep. How many cubic feet of concrete will she require to fill all the holes once the posts are in?

16. The basement walls of a custom-built house are constructed of poured concrete. The walls stand 8 feet in height and must be at least 8 inches thick according to the building code. The basement has dimensions shown below. Concrete costs $95.60/m^3$, taxes and delivery included. Assume the minimum thickness is used. Calculate the cost of the concrete for the walls, ignoring any overlap at corners.

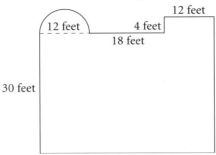

17. Refer to exercise 16. Many two-story homes are built with basement walls 10 inches thick. Calculate the difference in the cost of concrete to construct a basement with walls of minimum thickness and one with walls 10 inches thick.

18. Thinking/Inquiry/Problem Solving Troy is starting a catering business. He will be serving punch for an upcoming job. His punch recipe is in imperial units. It calls for 5 pints pineapple juice, 6 pints orange juice, and 2 pints cranberry juice. Troy has 1 large semisphere punch bowl, 60 cm in diameter. How many batches of the recipe must Troy prepare to fill the punch bowl? $1000 \text{ cm}^3 = 1 \text{ L}$

19. a) A hollow chocolate sphere is 12 cm in diameter and 1 cm thick. Calculate the volume of chocolate in the sphere.

b) Calculate the radius of a solid chocolate sphere that contains an equal volume of chocolate.

20. Communication Refer to exercise 19. If you were a chocolate manufacturer, which type of chocolate sphere would you market? Explain your reasoning.

21. A regulation baseball diamond is being built. Sod will be used for part of the play area as shown. Calculate the amount of sod needed.

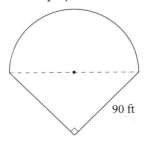

90 ft

1. A spherical gas tank is 16 m in diameter.

   a) What is the capacity of the tank in litres?

   b) The exterior of the tank is to be painted. Each can of paint covers 400 square feet. How many cans are required to complete the job?

2. A mass of 2.58 g of cast aluminum has a volume of 100 mm^3. What is the mass of a cast aluminum bar 12 cm by 7 cm by 4 cm?

3. a) What is the capacity of the can, below left?

   b) How much material is required for each washer, below middle?

   c) How much material is required for each metal support, below right?

4. The concrete base for a light pole is the shape of a square-based pyramid with the top cut as shown. Determine the amount of concrete required to construct the light pole base.

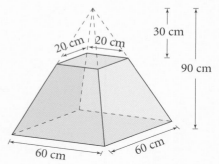

Performance Assessment

5. The first coat of paint for the outside walls of a building requires 1 L of paint for each 10 m^2 of wall surface. The second coat requires 1 L for every 15 m^2. Paint costs $3.50/L. Angie has to determine the cost of two coats of paint for the four outside walls of a building 60 feet long, 15 feet wide, and 12 feet high.

   a) How much will it cost for the required paint?

   b) When should she do her unit conversions? Explain your reasoning.

Many occasions arise where it is extremely difficult or impossible to obtain exact measurements to complete a task. For example, it is a challenge to determine the number of gallons of water a pond contains, the amount of topsoil required for a garden with an irregular shape, or the amount of fertilizer that should be applied to an area. In this project, you will investigate some techniques used to overcome these difficulties.

- Work with a partner.
- Each person should complete either *Investigation 1* or *Investigation 2*.
- Once you have completed your investigation, use your partner's description to estimate the area in the other investigation.
- Compare your results for each case study with your partner's results.
- When you have completed *Investigations 1* and *2*, complete *Investigation 3* with your partner.

Investigation 1

Landscape Designer

Misook works as a landscape designer. She designs a site and provides the customer with a contract price for the job. Since the company aims to make a profit, Misook must be careful not to undercharge for a job. She knows if she quotes a price too high, the company will likely lose the client.

When a flowerbed, walk, or patio has an irregular shape, Misook draws a scale diagram. For a flowerbed with given shape and dimensions, Misook drew the following scale diagram.

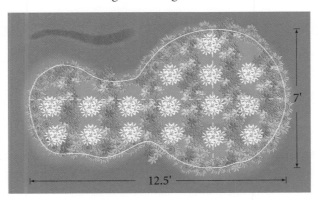

For this flowerbed, Misook will need topsoil to a depth of 15 inches.

1. Use grid paper. Trace the diagram above or obtain a copy of it from your teacher.

2. Estimate the area of the flowerbed.

3. Determine the volume of topsoil required for the flowerbed.

4. Write a report to explain your thinking. Describe the method you used to estimate the area of the flowerbed and the amount of topsoil required. Be as clear as possible as your partner will rely on this to determine the area and volume of the flowerbed.

Golf Course Superintendent

Kenji is a golf course superintendent. He is responsible for the maintenance of the course, making sure it is playable at all times. His job includes budgeting, fertilizer and pesticide application, irrigation, application of topdressing to the greens, and maintaining sand in the bunkers.

Kenji must be able to calculate area in order to top dress greens, fertilize fairways, or over-seed tees. Accurate calculations save time and money and prevent disasters such as the over application of fertilizer which will burn the grass on tees, fairways, and greens.

Kenji uses different methods to calculate areas depending upon the situation. Here is a plan of part of the golf course. The fairway has a stream crossing it.

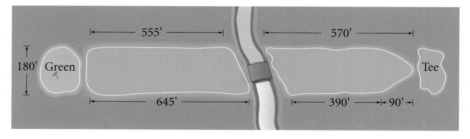

1. Use grid paper. Trace the diagram above or obtain a copy of it from your teacher.

2. Subdivide the diagram into shapes whose areas you can calculate using known formulas.

3. Calculate the area of the entire fairway.

4. Write a report to explain your thinking. Describe the method you used to estimate the area of the fairway. Be as clear as possible, as your partner will rely on this description to determine the area of the fairway.

Offset Method

Kenji uses the offset method to determine area when he is unable to subdivide the plan of the fairway into known shapes.

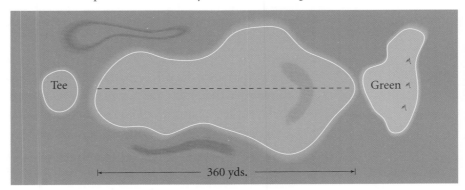

The offset method uses a series of measures taken at equal intervals. The number taken depends on the distances involved. In this case, Kenji decided that since the fairway's shape was not erratic, he would measure the width at 12 intervals. He chose 12 because it gave him a large enough number of intervals and also because it divides into 360 without a remainder. Since $360 \div 12 = 30$, he measured the width of the fairway at 30-yard intervals. He recorded the distances as shown.

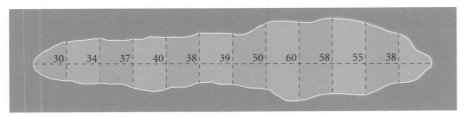

To determine an approximation of the area, add the measured distances (there are 11 in this example) and multiply by the width of the intervals (30 yards in this example).

1. Use grid paper. Trace the plan of the fairway below or obtain a copy from your teacher.

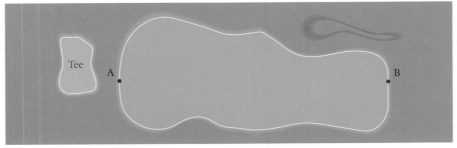

AB $\doteq$ 200 yards   Scale: $\frac{1}{4}$" represents 15 yards.

2. Select two different sets of intervals to determine the area of the fairway using the offset method.

3. Each group member should use a different set of intervals. Calculate the area of the fairway using the offset method.

4. Compare your results. Which calculation produces the more accurate area? How could you verify this?

5. Suppose an irregular shape is closer to a circle than a rectangle. How might you modify the offset method to calculate the area? Discuss this with your partner and write a report on your findings. Be sure to include worked examples and an explanation of what you did and why. Use your method to determine the area of the green below.

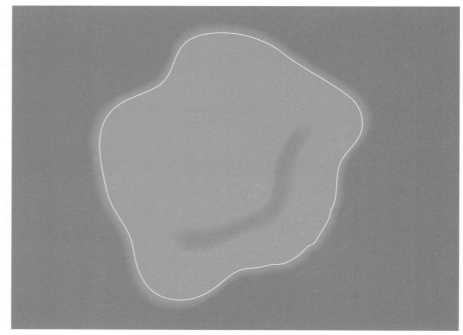

Scale: $\frac{1}{4}$" represents 10 feet.

Horticulturist

Serge wants to run his own business and knows he wants to work outdoors. Having enjoyed a summer job with a landscaper, he decided to take a horticulturist course at community college.

Job Description

- Plan gardens, parks, and golf courses
- Prepare soil for planting
- Plant and cultivate trees, shrubs, flowers, vegetables, and other plants
- Monitor growing conditions, fertilizers, and pesticides for plants
- Develop marketing plans for nurseries, landscaping companies, and greenhouses
- Manage nurseries and greenhouses

Working Conditions

- Outdoor work usually required, although some work may be done in greenhouses or research facilities
- Long working hours during the spring and summer
- Seasonal work
- Some physical labour

Qualifications and Training

- High school diploma
- College diploma in horticulture
- Good spatial sense and an eye for detail
- Physical strength and the ability to work as part of a team

Where's the Math?

To plan a garden, park, or golf course, horticulturists have to calculate how many plants will be needed for particular areas. They must be able to take accurate measurements and understand both the metric and imperial systems of measurement. They also calculate the quantities of soil, fertilizer, and pesticides to apply to different types of growing areas.

MATHEMATICS TOOLKIT

Measurement Systems

Length		
Metric System	Imperial System	Conversions
10 mm = 1 cm	12 inch = 1 foot	1 inch $\doteq$ 25.4 mm
100 cm = 1 m	3 feet = 1 yard	1 foot $\doteq$ 30.48 cm
1000 m = 1 km	1760 yards = 1 mile	1 yard $\doteq$ 0.9144 m
	5280 feet = 1 mile	1 mile $\doteq$ 1.609 km

Volume		
Metric System	Imperial System	Conversions
	16 fluid ounces = 1 pint	1 fluid ounce $\doteq$ 29.574 mL
1000 mL = 1 L	2 pints = 1 quart	1 pint $\doteq$ 0.473 L
	4 quarts = 1 gallon	1 gallon $\doteq$ 3.785 L

Mass		
Metric System	Imperial System	Conversions
1000 g = 1 kg	16 ounces = 1 pound	1 ounce $\doteq$ 28.35 g
1000 kg = 1 t	2000 pounds = 1 ton (US)	1 pound $\doteq$ 0.454 kg
		1 ton $\doteq$ 0.907 t

Measurement Tools

Perimeter

> The perimeter of a polygon is calculated by adding the lengths of its sides.

Circumference

> The circumference, C, of a circle: $C = \pi d$ or $C = 2\pi r$.

Area Formulas				
rectangle	triangle	parallelogram	trapezoid	circle
$A = \ell w$	$A = \frac{1}{2}bh$	$A = bh$	$A = \frac{a+b}{2}h$	$A = \pi r^2$

Figure	Volume	Surface Area
	$V =$ Area of base × Height $= \ell wh$	$SA =$ Sum of area of faces or $SA = 2(wh + \ell w + \ell h)$
	$V =$ Area of base × Height $= \pi r^2 h$	$SA = 2\pi r^2 + 2\pi rh$
	$V = \frac{4}{3}\pi r^3$	$SA = 4\pi r^2$
	$V = \frac{1}{3} \times$ Area of base × Height $= \frac{1}{3}\pi r^2 h$	$SA_{\text{lateral}} = \pi rs$ $SA_{\text{base}} = \pi r^2$ $SA_{\text{total}} = \pi rs + \pi r^2$
	$V = \frac{1}{3} \times$ Area of base × Height $= \frac{1}{3}b^2 h$	$SA_{\text{each triangle}} = \frac{1}{2}bs$ $SA_{\text{base}} = b^2$ $SA_{\text{total}} = 4\left(\frac{1}{2}bs\right) + b^2$

3.1   **1.** Which imperial unit would you use to take each measure?

    a) the length of your calculator

    b) the mass of an apple

    c) the distance from the school to your home

    d) the volume of oil an oil tanker can carry

2. Convert each measure.

    a) 8 feet of wood to inches   **b)** 2 kg of cheese to grams

    c) $3\frac{1}{4}$ miles of trails to yards   **d)** 3.75 L of milk to millilitres

3. Convert each measure. Round your answers to the nearest tenth.

    a) 12 yards of ribbon to metres   **b)** 2 gallons of paint to litres

    c) 19 feet of rope to centimetres   **d)** 2 pounds of flour to kilograms

4. Convert each measure.

    a) 70 mm to inches   **b)** 5 kg to pounds and ounces

    c) 3 L to fluid ounces   **d)** 65 m to yards, feet, and inches

3.2   **5.** Calculate the perimeter of each figure.

    a) a rectangular patio with sides 15 feet by 8 feet

    b) a triangular tile pattern with sides 22.4 m, 8.6 m, and 19.5 m

    c) a pentagon-shaped garden with each side $5\frac{1}{4}$ feet

    d) a parallelogram quilt piece with sides $6\frac{3}{4}$ inches and $5\frac{1}{4}$ inches

6. Calculate the circumference of each circular table.

    a) radius = 26.0 cm   **b)** diameter = 9 feet   **c)** radius = $3\frac{1}{2}$ yards

7. The legs of a right triangle are 17 cm and 12 cm. Calculate the perimeter of the triangle.

8. The circumference of a circle is 143 cm. Determine the diameter of the circle to the nearest tenth.

3.3   **9.** Calculate the area of each figure.

    a) circle; radius 15.4 m

    b) rectangle; length 9' by $4\frac{1}{2}$'

    c) trapezoid; parallel sides 8" and 16", and height 12"

    d) triangle; base 15 cm and height 12.5 cm

10. The hypotenuse of a right triangle is 14.6 cm. One leg is 9.3 cm. Calculate the area of the triangle.

11. Calculate the area of each figure. Round your answer to the nearest tenth where appropriate.

a)

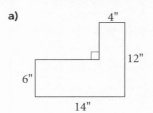

b)

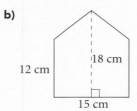

c)

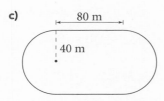

12. Chun is replacing the ceramic tiles in each of his two bathroom floors. The bathrooms are 2 m by 2.5 m and 3 m by 4 m. At the tile supplier, Chun discovered a discontinued tile pattern that he would like to use. The discontinued tile will cover 130 square feet. Is this tile sufficient for Chun's two bathrooms? Justify your answer.

3.4 **13.** Calculate the volume and surface area of each object.
  a) a box 8 feet by 5 feet by 4 feet
  b) a can with radius 4 m and height 6 m
  c) an ice cube with side length 3.2 cm
  d) a triangular prism-shaped trough with length 19 inches, and triangular base 11 inches with height 8 inches

14. A landscaper is preparing a rectangular flowerbed for planting. The bed measures 5 m by 3.5 m and will have topsoil to a depth of 12 cm. Topsoil is bought by the cubic yard. How much must be ordered for the bed?

15. A room is 3.9 m by 4.8 m by 2.5 m. All surfaces except the floor are to be painted. Ignoring doors and windows, how many cans of paint are required for two coats of paint? A 1-gallon can of paint will cover approximately 475 square feet.

3.5   **16.** Calculate the volume of each figure.

     a) a square-based pyramid, area of the base 81 square inches and height 6 inches

     b) a cone, area of the base 64.75 cm^2 and height 8.5 cm

     c) a pentagonal-based pyramid, area of the base 840 mm^2 and height 62 mm

     d) a triangular-based pyramid, area of the base 295 m^2 and height 15 m

17. Calculate the total surface area of a cone with radius 6 inches and height 8 inches.

18. A volleyball has a radius of 9.0 cm. Calculate the surface area and volume of the ball.

19. Calculate the surface area and volume of the figure below.

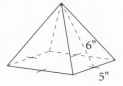

20. Calculate the volume and surface area (excluding the floor) of the tent shown.

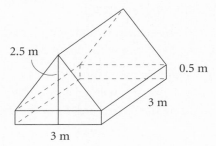

3.6 **21.** A swimming pool is 4 m by 10 m with an average depth of 2 m. The pool owner will purchase a chemical kit from an online store. The super kit is for pools up to 35 000 gallons, the deluxe kit is for pools up to 15 000 gallons, and the small kit is for pools up to 7500 gallons. Which kit should the pool owner purchase? Explain your reasoning.

22. A trophy is constructed of a sphere mounted on a cube. The diameter of the sphere and the length of a side of the cube are equal. Let s represent the length of the side of the cube. Write a formula for the volume of the trophy in terms of s.

23. The Khans are finishing their basement laundry room and intend to install a vinyl floor. The dimensions of the room are 5 m by 3.5 m. Self-adhesive vinyl tiles cost $1.53 per (12" by 12") tile. Vinyl flooring is cut from a roll and is $10.99 per square yard. For the roll-cut vinyl flooring, a $14.99 can of floor adhesive is required. Each can covers approximately 40 square yards. Which type of vinyl flooring is the more economical choice?

Maintaining Your Mastery

Review the algebraic skills that form part of the college admission process.

1. Expand and simplify.

  a) $4(x + 2)$ **b)** $-7(w^2 - 3w + 1)$ **c)** $5(y + 4)^2$

2. Factor.

  a) $6xw + 8xy - 4xz$ **b)** $3b^2 - 9$ **c)** $m^2 + 11m + 28$

  d) $x^2 - 4$ **e)** $x^2 - x - 20$ **f)** $16w^2 - 25z^2$

3. Factor.

  a) $2x^2 + 5x + 3$ **b)** $6x^2 - 5x - 4$ **c)** $12x^2 - 29x + 15$

4. Solve.

  a) $5x = 20$ **b)** $7b - 4 = 5b + 12$ **c)** $2(y - 5) = 3(y + 2)$

  d) $x^2 + 3x + 2 = 0$ **e)** $m^2 - 2m - 24 = 0$ **f)** $4x^2 - 4x - 3 = 0$

1. Convert each measure. Round your answers to the nearest tenth where appropriate.

   a) 9 feet to inches
   b) 25 pounds to ounces
   c) 50 pints to gallons and fluid ounces
   d) 4 yards to feet and inches
   e) 11 gallons to litres
   f) 100 miles to kilometres
   g) 15 kg to pounds and ounces

2. **Knowledge/Understanding** Calculate the perimeter of each figure.

   a)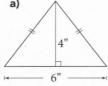
   b)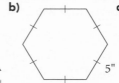
   c)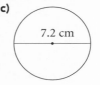
   d)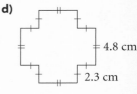

3. **Communication** Choose one figure. Explain how to calculate the area of the shaded region. Verify by calculating the area. Round your answer to the nearest tenth where appropriate.

   a)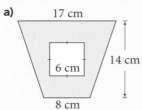
   b)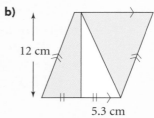

4. **Application** A circular in-ground garden pond has a radius 7.5 m. A 2-m concrete deck will be constructed around the pond. The concrete should be at least 15 cm thick. Calculate the minimum volume of concrete required to construct the deck.

5. **Thinking/Inquiry/Problem Solving** A tent manufacturer is investigating two tents. One tent is a square-based pyramid with base 2 m and height 2 m. The other is a dome tent (semisphere) with diameter 2 m. The manufacturer prefers the tent design that uses the least amount of material, to keep costs down. Which tent design is the better choice?

6. Lise Gaudreau and her family have recently built a new home on a large lot in the country. The lot measures 100 feet by 200 feet. Before they move in, Lise and some friends are going to prepare two gardens and sod the rest of the lot. Lise must order the necessary materials. She has decided that the gardens will require topsoil to a depth of 18 inches and the area to be sodded will need a topsoil base of 3 inches. Sod comes in rolls that measure 1 foot by 6 feet when opened flat. Topsoil is sold by the cubic yard. Determine the amount of sod and topsoil Lise must order.

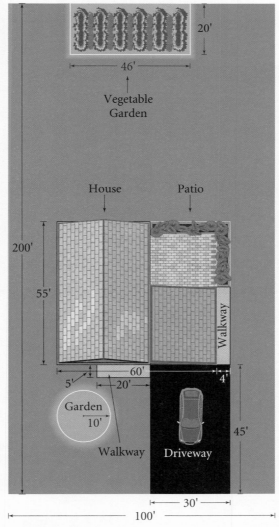

Geometry in Design

Designing and Constructing a Model

Geometric figures are all around us. They decorate walls, floors, and fabric. They form objects, both beautiful and useful. You will investigate how geometric figures are used in particular applications.

Curriculum Expectations

By the end of this chapter, you will:

> Identify, through observation and measurement, the uses of geometric shapes and the reasons for those uses, in a variety of applications.

> Represent three-dimensional objects in a variety of ways, using concrete materials and design or drawing software.

> Create nets, plans, and patterns from physical models related to a variety of applications, using design or drawing software.

> Design and construct physical models of things, satisfying given constraints and using concrete materials, design software, or drawing software.

1 Review: Translations

A figure is translated when it is moved in a straight line to another location. In the diagram below, A′B′ is the image of AB after a translation 2 units right and 3 units down.

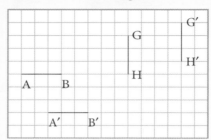

G′H′ is the image of GH after a translation 4 units right and 1 unit up.

Although the motion is in a straight line, it is described by horizontal and vertical changes. When a figure is translated, its size, shape, and orientation are unchanged.

Example

Describe the translation that would move polygon BCDEF to polygon B′C′D′E′F′.

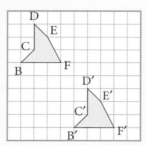

Solution

To move from D to D′, move 4 units right and 5 units down. The translation is 4 right, 5 down.

1. Copy △LMN on grid paper.
   Draw image △L′M′N′ after each translation.
   a) 4 left and 2 up
   b) 3 right and 1 down

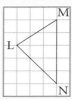

2 Review: Reflections

When a figure is reflected in a line, the figure and its image have certain properties. For example, consider △ABC reflected in line ℓ to form △A′B′C′.

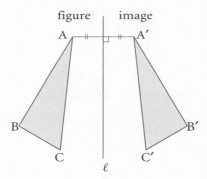

Each point on the figure has a corresponding point on the image. Consider points A and A′. Line ℓ is the perpendicular bisector of line segment AA′.

Similarly, line ℓ is the perpendicular bisector of the segment that joins any point on the figure to the corresponding point on the image.

When a figure is reflected in a line, its size and shape are unchanged, but its orientation changes.

Example

Does each diagram illustrate a reflection? Explain.

a)

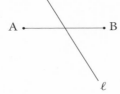

b)

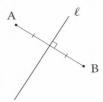

Solution

a) This diagram does not illustrate a reflection. The line segment joining points A and B is not perpendicular to the line of reflection.

b) This diagram illustrates a reflection. Points A and B are equidistant from the line, and the line joining A and B is perpendicular to the reflection line.

Exercises

1. Is each segment a reflection of AB in line ℓ? Explain.

a)

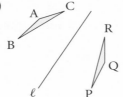

b)

2. Does each diagram illustrate a reflection in line ℓ? Explain.

a)

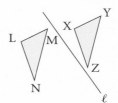

b)

3. Review: Rotations

A figure can be rotated about a point, the centre of rotation. For example, the tip of the minute hand rotates about the centre of a clock.

To specify a rotation we must give a centre of rotation, an angle of rotation, and a direction.

In the diagram below, A′ is the image of A under a rotation of 60° counter clockwise about O, the centre of rotation. Line segment OA and OA′ are equal, and ∠AOA′ = 60°.

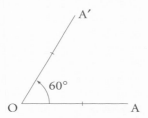

In the diagram below, △A′B′C′ is the image of △ABC under a rotation of 60° counter clockwise about O. Rotating a figure does not change its shape or size.

OA = OA′, OB = OB′, OC = OC′, ∠A = ∠A′, ∠B = ∠B′, and ∠C = ∠C′

So, △ABC is congruent to △A′B′C′.

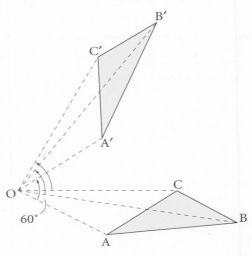

Example

Determine which triangle is the rotation image of △PQR after a rotation about O. Explain your reasoning.

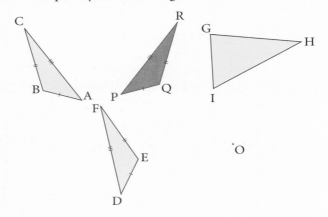

Solution

Triangle ABC is the reflection image of △PQR in a line that is the perpendicular bisector of segment AP. Triangle DEF is the rotation image of △PQR. Triangle DEF is congruent to △PQR and EO = QO. Triangle GHI is not congruent to △PQR, so △GHI is not related to △PQR by a reflection or rotation.

Exercises

1. This design was made by repeatedly rotating a triangle about a point until the last triangle coincides with the original triangle. What was the angle of each rotation?

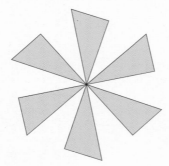

Since ancient times, people have used tiles to cover floors, walls, and furniture. We still use tiles today. The tiles are attached with cement or glue. Spaces between tiles are filled with grout to give a solid surface.

Tiles are made from ceramic, stone, clay, wood, leather, and glass.

Insetting geometric figures of wood is another method of tiling. It is known as *parquetry*. Basketball is often played on a parquet floor (below left).

The floor in the photo (above right), shows how parquetry can produce beautiful and complex patterns. This floor is in a Russian palace built hundreds of years ago for Catherine I.

Although tiles with different shapes can fit together, it is cheaper and easier to install tiles that have the same size and shape; that is, congruent tiles. Tiles are often square or hexagonal, like the ones below.

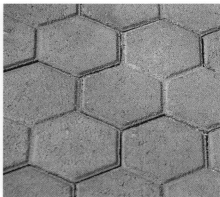

Examine the tiled sections below. In each case, the tiles do not *tessellate*, that is, they do not cover the surface without gaps or overlaps. When octagonal tiles are used (below left), small square tiles are needed to fill the holes. Pentagonal tiles (below right) do not tessellate either. A diamond-shaped tile is required to fit the gap.

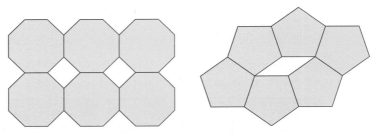

You will investigate why squares and hexagons tessellate, but regular octagons and regular pentagons do not.

Tessellating Regular Polygons

1. Six congruent equilateral triangles tessellate around point A, below left.

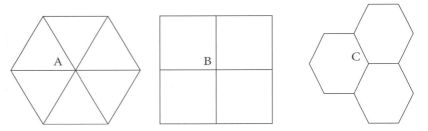

Recall that 1 complete turn at any point is 360°. What is the interior angle of an equilateral triangle? Explain why this interior angle allows 6 equilateral triangles to "fit" around point A.

2. Four congruent squares tessellate around point B, above middle. What is the interior angle of a square? Explain why this interior angle allows four squares to "fit" around point B.

3. Three congruent regular hexagons tessellate around point C, above right. Since 3 hexagons "fit" around point C, what is the measure of the interior angle of a regular hexagon?

4. Use the results of exercises 1, 2, and 3 to make a conjecture about the interior angle of a polygon that tessellates around a point.

5. A regular pentagon can be divided into 3 triangles, as on the right. Use the sum of the angles in a triangle to determine the sum of all five interior angles of the pentagon. What is the measure of one interior angle?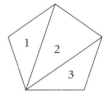

6. Use your answer from exercise 5 to test the conjecture you made in exercise 4.

7. Explain why a congruent regular octagon cannot tessellate.

TAKE NOTE

Tessellating Regular Polygons

For a congruent regular polygon to tessellate around a point, the measure of the interior angle must divide evenly into 360°.

Some non-regular polygons tessellate. These figures are often specially designed. For example, interlocking bricks fit together like puzzle pieces. This prevents shifting.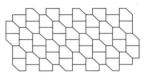

To ensure that one brick fits snugly against another, the sides must be translated images of each other.

You can design your own tessellating figure. If you have access to a computer with *The Geometer's Sketchpad*, do *Investigation 2*. Otherwise, do *Investigation 3*.

Investigation 2 Designing a Tile that Tessellates

In this Investigation, you will use the Mark Vector tool to translate a segment.

Use The Geometer's Sketchpad.

SET-UP

- From the File menu, choose New Sketch.
- From the Display menu, choose Preferences. Make sure that Autoshow Labels for Points is selected. This automatically labels points. Click OK.

Recall that you can change any label by using the Text tool . Double-click on the label and type a new letter.

1. Construct a parallelogram:

Click on this tool...   ...and do this:

a) Use the Segment tool to draw segment AB.

b) Use the Point tool to draw a point C anywhere on the screen. Check that point C is marked. Shift-click A.

c) From the Transform menu, choose Mark Vector.

d) Points A and C are marked. Shift-click B, segment AB, and C. Now, points A, B, and segment AB are marked. From the Transform menu, choose Translate. Click OK.

e) Use the Segment tool to join the points to form the sides of the parallelogram. Label the fourth vertex D.

2. To transform the parallelogram:

a) Use the Point tool to construct two points E and F between A and C as shown.

b) Construct segments CF, FE, and EA.

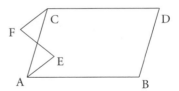

c) Shift-click point A, then point B. From the Transform menu, choose Mark Vector. Points A and B are marked.

d) Shift-click B to unmark B, then shift-click E, F, C, and the segments AE, EF, and FC. From the Transform menu, choose Translate...By Marked Vector.

e) Shift-click (in order) A, E, F, C, D, F′, E′, and B. From the Construct menu, choose Polygon Interior.

f) Select segments AC and BD. From the Display menu, choose Hide Segments.
You can also hide the labels by selecting the Text tool, then clicking on each point.

Since the sides of your figure are translated images of one another, the figure you have constructed will tessellate.

3. To tessellate the new figure:

a) Shift-click point A, then point B. From the Transform menu, choose Mark Vector.

b) Select your figure by clicking on its interior. From the Transform menu, choose Translate. Change the colour of the new figure by using the Display menu.

c) Repeat this process once more, shift-clicking B, then A.

d) To translate the figure down, use CA as the vector.

When the copies of your figure have covered the screen, you can drag points E and F to form a new figure and add details or different colours.

To make more complex figures, construct points between A and B, then translate these points using vector AC.

Investigation 3 **Design a Tile That Tessellates**

Use pencil and paper.

Design your own tessellation. You will need a pencil, pen, paper, and ruler.

1. Use a pencil to draw a rectangle, a parallelogram, or a hexagon.

2. Use a pen to draw a simple shape on one side of your polygon. Trace the simple shape onto another piece of paper.

3. Use the tracing on the second piece of paper and a pen to trace the shape onto the opposite side of your polygon.

4. Use a pen to draw a simple shape along another side of the polygon. Trace it onto another piece of paper. Use this traced copy and a pen to trace it onto the opposite side of the polygon.

5. Erase all pencil lines. Add details to your design.

6. Copy the design by making tracings and tessellate.

A

1. Use magazines, brochures, or the Internet to find examples of tiling with geometric figures. For each example, identify the figure or figures and describe the material used. Your collection should include:

   a) a ceramic or stone design that uses congruent tiles

   b) a ceramic or stone pattern that uses tiles with two different geometric shapes

   c) an example of mosaic tiling

   d) a parquet design in wood

   e) a piece of furniture that includes tile or wood inlay

✓ **2. Knowledge/Understanding**

   a) Identify the geometric figures in each design.

   b) State whether or not each design represents a tessellation and explain why.

i)

ii)

iii)

iv)

v)
vi)

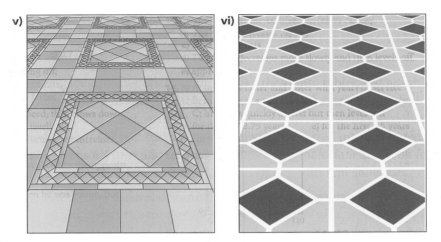

B

3. In *Investigation 1* you examined why pentagons do not tessellate. Use the same method to check whether a regular decagon tessellates.

4. Thinking/Inquiry/Problem Solving In the illustration, rectangular tiles of different sizes cover the patio.

a) Use a word processor or drawing program.
- Construct a regular hexagon. Make several copies of this figure.
- Construct a smaller regular hexagon. Make several copies.
  Note: In Word you can create a regular hexagon by clicking on autoshapes.

b) Use the figures from part a. Is it possible to use regular hexagons of two different sizes to cover a surface? Explain your reasoning.

5. **Application** Complete steps i to iii, then complete parts a to e.
   i) Cut a triangle out of cardboard.
   ii) Trace the triangle on paper and cut out 10 copies to represent tiles. Colour 5 of them.
   iii) Place the tiles on a plain piece of paper.

   a) Can you arrange the tiles to cover the surface? Explain.
   b) Does it matter which vertices of the triangles meet at one point?
   c) Compare your results with those of a classmate.
   d) Experiment with one of your classmate's triangles in your tiling pattern.
   e) Explain what you discovered.

6. **Communication** Patchwork quilts are made from pieces of cloth sewn together to create larger pieces that combine to form the quilt top. Each quilt square shown is a Four Patch Block. It is made by joining four identical square patches. Examine each photo. Complete parts a to c for each block.

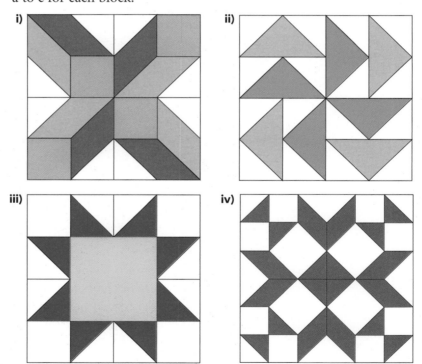

i)   ii)   iii)   iv)

   a) Identify the figures that form one patch in the Four Patch Block. Consider that figures are different if they have different sizes.

b) How many of each figure must be cut out of each colour of fabric to create the Four Patch Block?

c) Copy each design on grid paper. Cut the four patches apart. By joining the four patches along different edges you can create other quilt designs. With each set of patches design one new quilt block.

7. a) Use geometric figures to design a Four Patch Block on grid paper. Complete part b or part c.

b) Cut out the figures, then trace them on coloured paper. Glue the design on plain paper.

c) Mini-Project Cut out the figures, then trace them on fabric. Figures used for quilting require a seam allowance. Extra material must be added along each side of the figure so the pieces can be sewn together. The usual allowance is $\frac{1}{4}$". To sew pieces together, put right sides facing one another, match edges, and sew along the $\frac{1}{4}$" line. Turn faces open and iron flat.

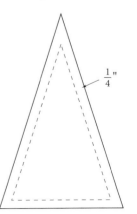

A figure, an object, or a pattern is *symmetrical* if it can be *reflected*, *rotated*, or *translated* and remain unchanged. Symmetry is used to create many patterns and designs.

Reflection Symmetry

A figure has reflection symmetry if a line divides it into two identical parts. For example, the letter A has reflection symmetry. A 3-dimensional object has reflection symmetry if a mirror divides it into two identical parts. For example, the stool has reflection symmetry.

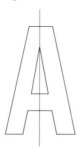

Rotation Symmetry

An object has rotation symmetry if it looks the same after being rotated about a point.

Discuss

All figures have 360° symmetry. Can you explain why?

Some figures look the same when rotated through angles that are between 0° and 360°. For example, in the pictures below left, only the blue dot at the corner shows that the square was rotated 90°. Without the dot we could not tell the angle of rotation.

We can see that the rectangle, below right, was rotated through 90°. To match the original it would need to be turned 180°.

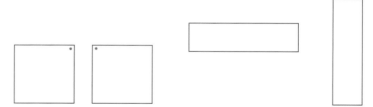

Translation Symmetry

A pattern has translation symmetry if a section of it can be moved, without rotating or reflecting, to exactly match another section of the pattern. Borders often make use of this type of symmetry.

Translations can also create patterns with 3-dimensional objects. In the illustration below, the two lights on the left can be translated to exactly match the two on the right.

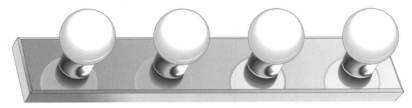

Glide Reflection Symmetry

A glide reflection is a combination of a translation and a reflection. Here, the heart shape has been translated and then reflected to form a border.

Glide reflections can be seen in packing. Space can be saved when items are packed by making use of a glide reflection.

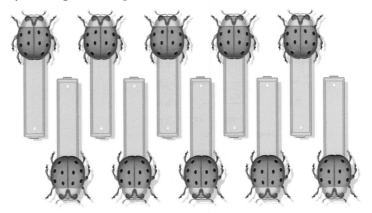

Examine each pattern. Identify the type of symmetry used in each design.

a)

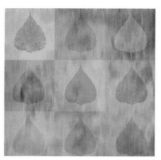

b)

c)

d)

Solution

a) This design has translation symmetry. The row of leaves has been translated down to form the next row.

b) This design has rotation symmetry. The blades show a pattern of repeated 90° rotations.

c) This design has reflection symmetry. A vertical line can be drawn so that the left side of the anchor is identical to the right side.

d) This bracelet design has glide reflection symmetry. The hearts have been translated and reflected in the pattern.

4.2 Exercises

A

1. Examine the capital letters of the alphabet.

A B C D E F G H I J K L M N O P Q R S T U V W X Y Z

Write each letter under the correct table heading.

Rotation Symmetry	Reflection Symmetry	No Symmetry

For rotation symmetry, only include those letters that can be rotated through angles other than 0° or 360°.

✓ 2. **Knowledge/Understanding** Identify the type of symmetry in each pattern.

a)

b)

c)

d)

e)

f)

3. Look through magazines, catalogues, books, or the Internet. Collect symmetry patterns and label each with the type of symmetry. Choose examples created from fabric, china, wood, and metal.

4. Thinking/Inquiry/Problem Solving The hubcaps in the photos all have rotation symmetry.

a) By what angle would you rotate each hubcap for its appearance to be unchanged?

b) Some hubcaps have reflection symmetry. Is it possible for a hubcap to have rotation symmetry but not reflection symmetry? Explain your reasoning using a diagram.

5. Although some items are not symmetrical, photographers, artists, cooks, and advertisers often make use of symmetry to display them.

a) Look through magazines, catalogues, books, or the Internet. Collect at least six examples of symmetry used to display a variety of items.

b) Identify the type of symmetry used.

6. Application Borders on wallpaper, fabric, and metal work often incorporate repeated motifs.

Make a symmetric design suitable for a wallpaper border.

- Cut a strip of paper 50 cm long and 10 cm wide.

- Draw a motif.

- Use a combination of translations, reflections, and rotations of your motif to create the border.

7. **Communication** Architects and builders use both geometric figures and symmetry concepts. Examine each photo.

a) Identify at least three geometric figures in each design.

b) In the photos below, find and describe instances of reflection, rotation, and translation symmetry.

i)

ii)

iii)

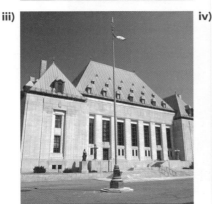

iv)

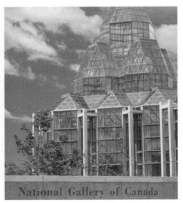

National Gallery of Canada

v)

Antiques-things
BY CHANCE

vi)

vii)

viii)

8. Artisans work with many different materials to create objects that display symmetry.

a) Identify the symmetry in each picture.

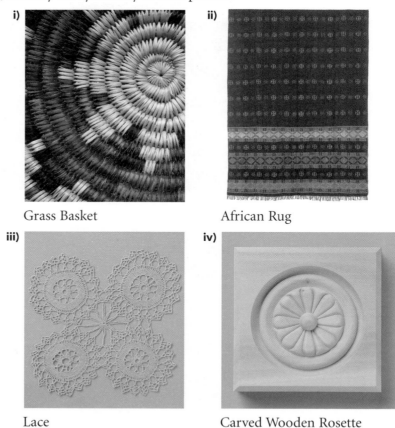

i)

Grass Basket

ii)

African Rug

iii)

Lace

iv)

Carved Wooden Rosette

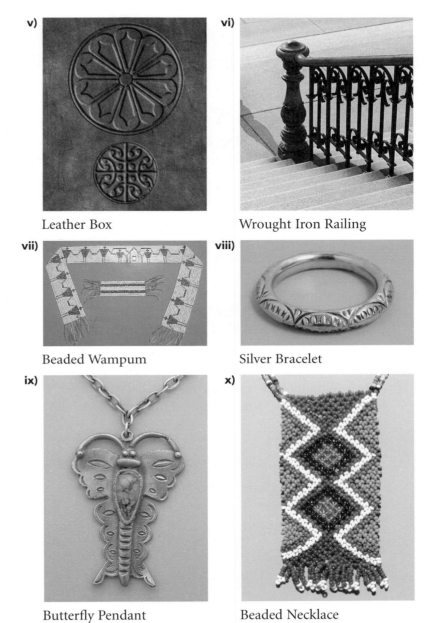

v) Leather Box

vi) Wrought Iron Railing

vii) Beaded Wampum

viii) Silver Bracelet

ix) Butterfly Pendant

x) Beaded Necklace

b) Choose one of the pictured items in part a, then complete each task.

- Using grid paper, plan a design suitable for a similar object made of the same material. Include at least one symmetry concept in your design.
- Use magazines, books, newspapers, or the Internet to find four additional objects made of the same material and illustrating one or more of the symmetry concepts. Sketch and describe the items you found.

When designing products, containers, or structures, it is necessary to represent 3-dimensional objects on paper. The drawings are usually created to scale and may also use perspective, or include different views. From the drawings, a scale model may be produced.

Perspective

Perspective helps us "see" a 3-dimensional object that is drawn on a 2-dimensional surface. It uses the idea that parallel lines moving away from us appear to meet at a point, which we call a *point at infinity*. This causes objects far away to look smaller.

Railway tracks are parallel, but they appear to get closer together in the distance.

Investigation 1 | ### Making a Perspective Drawing of a Rectangular Prism

If you have access to a computer, complete part 1, otherwise complete part 2.

1. Use *The Geometer's Sketchpad.*

• From the File menu, choose New Sketch.

• From the Graph menu, choose Show Grid, then choose Hide Axes.

    a) Construct 4 points to form a rectangle. Label the points A, B, C, and D. Join the sides of the rectangle.

    b) Construct a point near the top of the screen and label it O. This will be the point at infinity.

    c) Construct segments AO, BO, CO, and DO.

    d) Select AO and choose Point on Object from the Construct menu. Label this point E and move it so that it is closer to A than to O. Deselect any points.

e) Shift-click to select segment AB and point E. Choose Parallel Line from the Construct menu. Shift-click the new line and segment BO. Construct the intersection point by choosing Point at Intersection from the Construct menu. Label the point F. Hide the new line by selecting it and choosing Hide Line from the Display menu.

f) Shift-click to select segment AD and point E. Choose Parallel Line from the Construct menu. Construct the intersection point of the new line and segment DO. Label the point H. Hide the new line.

g) Shift-click to select segment BC and point F. Choose Parallel Line from the Construct menu. Construct the intersection point of the new line and segment CO. Label the point G. Hide the new line.

h) Shift-click E, F, G, and H and choose Segment from the Construct menu.

i) Shift-click A and E. From the Construct menu, choose Segment. This constructs a segment over part of the line AO. Right-click AE and choose Line Style, then Thick. Construct segments BF, CG, and DH. This will help the prism stand out.

Experiment with the sketch and answer the following questions:

1. What is the effect of dragging point O to the right? To the left? Closer to rectangle ABCD?

2. Why might a designer want to use a different position for the point at infinity?

3. Move point E closer to A, then farther away. What effect does this have on the prism?

4. Drag one of the points on ABCD.
- What is the relationship between the new shape of ABCD and the new shape of EFGH?
- Is the shape still a prism? Explain your reasoning.

2. Use a ruler and grid paper.

a) About halfway down a sheet of grid paper draw a rectangle ABCD to represent the front of the prism.

b) Near the top of the page draw a point O. This will be your point at infinity.

c) Draw dotted lines to join each vertex of the rectangle to point O. These lines represent parallel lines moving away from the viewer.

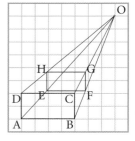

d) Use the grid to draw a line parallel to the top of the rectangle, that intersects DO at H and CO at G. Repeat for the other three sides of the rectangle as shown.

e) You now have the original rectangle and a smaller copy that represents the back face of the prism. In a prism these two faces are identical, but in a 3-dimensional perspective drawing the back face is smaller to help us understand that it is farther away.

Draw over the dotted lines to join the front rectangle to the back rectangle.

f) Investigate to see what happens to the prism when the position of point O is changed, or if the small rectangle is drawn further back. Repeat exercises 1 to 5 for 2 different positions of point O and 2 different small rectangles.

Views

Another method of representing an object is to show front, top, side, or rear views. No perspective techniques are used.

Investigation **2** **Using Views to Understand a 3-Dimensional Object**

A. The sketches show the side and top views of a set of stairs.

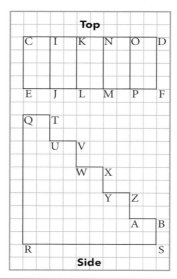

1. Use interlocking blocks or folded cardboard to create a model of this set of stairs.

2. Based on your model and the information in the sketches, draw the view of the front of the set of stairs.

3. Which points on the side view relate to points L and M on the top view? Improve the diagrams by using the same label for points that are repeated in other views.

B

✓ 1. **Knowledge/Understanding** A roof is often in the shape of a triangular prism.

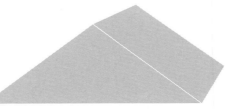

a) Draw a triangular prism in perspective, using technology, or pencil and paper.

b) Name and sketch one other familiar object that is in the shape of a triangular prism.

 2. A trough is often in the shape of a trapezoid-based prism.

a) Use *The Geometer's Sketchpad* to construct a trapezoid-based prism in perspective.

b) Name and sketch one other familiar object that is in the shape of a trapezoid-based prism.

✓ 3. Create 3-dimensional initials, using this illustration as a guide.

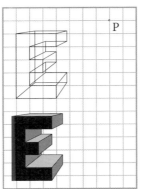

If you use *The Geometer's Sketchpad,* experiment with moving point P. When you are satisfied with the design, hide all the extra lines and the grid. Print the completed sketch.

If you have an initial such as P or D, construct 3 points and choose Arc through Three Points from the Construct menu. Then move the points until the curve looks right.

4. Communication If you look at a circular object from an angle it appears oval. To draw an upright cylinder in perspective, we represent the circular ends using ovals.

Select a cylindrical object such as a large can of soup. Set it approximately 50 cm in front of you and sketch the shape. Raise the can about 20 cm by putting a box or a pile of books under it, and make another sketch. Raise the can to approximately 40 cm and make a third sketch.

a) Compare the three drawings. How does the shape of the top face change as the can is raised?

b) If the top of the cylinder in a drawing is a thin ellipse, what can you say about the position of the observer? If the top of a cylinder is almost circular, what can you say?

5. The sketches show the front, top, and rear views of a building.

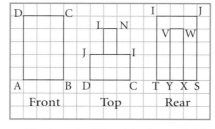

a) Use interlocking blocks or folded cardboard to create a model of this building.

b) Based on your model and the information contained in the sketches, draw the view of the right side of the building.

c) What does the rear view tell you about edge VW that is not clear from the top view?

d) Which point on the rear view is the same as point L on the top view? Look for other mislabelled related points. Use this information to make the sketches more understandable to the reader.

6. Application Use the top, front, and left- and right-side views shown to complete parts a to c.

   a) Use blocks or folded cardboard to construct a model of the building.

   b) Use your model and the information in the views to produce a side view of the shape of the building.

   c) Improve the diagrams by using the same label for points that are repeated in other views.

```
                    Top
          A D       H G
          ┌──┐
          B C       E F

   T  U   K  L       I  J

             N O     N  K
   W  V  P M

   X  Y  Q      R  M  L
  Left side   Front   Right side
```

7. Draw front, side, and top views of each 3-dimensional object listed below. You may use a set of geometric solids to work from. If you do not have a set of geometric solids, use one of the suggested items as a model.

   a) A rectangular prism: Suitable items include a cereal box, a detergent box, a fish tank

   b) A triangular prism: Cut a triangle out of a piece of styrofoam or wood

   c) A triangular-based pyramid: A tripod

8. Thinking/Inquiry/Problem Solving An *orthographic diagram* shows up to six views of an object in positions relative to each other. Usually three views are sufficient: the top, front, and side views. Broken lines show internal holes or indentations in objects. They also show how the holes extend through the object. Solid lines indicate the external features. Use the orthographic diagram given to create a perspective diagram of the object.

top

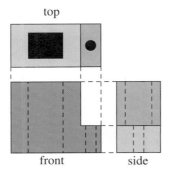

front   side

Perspective drawings and views are usually drawn to scale. Scale drawings may be smaller or larger than the original object.

There are several ways to produce a scale drawing.

Measure, Convert, and Draw Method

Decide how large the object will be, choose a suitable scale, and complete the drawing by converting each measurement. For example, if you are drawing the front view of a set of kitchen cupboards 2 m long, you might choose a scale of 1 cm to 10 cm. If the height of a cupboard is 62 cm, its height in the sketch will be 6.2 cm. Once you choose your scale, draw everything to scale including details like knobs or hinges.

Angles do not change in scale drawings; any angles in the actual object remain the same in the scale diagram.

Investigation **1** **Producing a Scaled Front View by Choosing a Suitable Scale**

You will need a measuring tape, ruler, rough paper, and grid paper.

Select a subject for your sketch, such as one wall of a kitchen, or the front wall of your classroom.

1. Prepare a very rough sketch of your subject.

Take measurements of the length and height of the wall, cupboards, shelves, appliances, decorations, or other items. Remember that this is a front view, so it is not necessary to measure the depth of the objects.

Label items on your sketch and record the measurements in the appropriate locations.

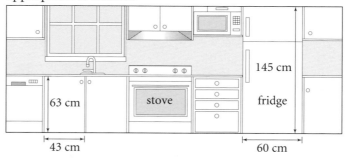

2. Choose a suitable scale.

To start, divide the total length of the subject by the length of the grid paper you are using.

Length of wall = 3.5 m
Length of grid paper = 27 cm or 0.27 m
3.5 divided by 0.27 is approximately 12.96.
The wall is almost 13 times the length of the grid paper, so a scale of 1 cm to 13 cm will ensure that the scaled length of the subject fits on the page.
Repeat this process with the other dimension.
Height of wall = 2.8 m
Width of grid paper = 21 cm or 0.21 m
2.8 divided by 0.21 is approximately 13.33.
The height of the wall is more than 13 times the width of the grid paper, so a scale of 1 cm to 13 cm will not work.
To fit the diagram on the page, choose another scale, for example: 1 cm to 15 cm, or 1 cm to 20 cm. These scales also provide more convenient numbers for calculations.

3. Convert each measurement: Divide each measurement by the scale factor and record the result.
For example, using a scale of 1 cm to 20 cm:
Width of stove = 60 cm
Width of stove on diagram $= \frac{60 \text{ cm}}{20}$
$= 3$ cm

4. Construct the diagram. Always use a ruler and write measurements clearly. Comment on the importance of careful measurement when constructing the diagram.

The Grid Method

If you have a small flat object or a photo, you can use a grid method to enlarge or reduce it. This is useful for creating scaled diagrams of curved designs.

Investigation 2 **Enlarging the Design Using a Grid**

1. Draw a grid with 1-cm by 1-cm squares on a piece of plastic, overhead transparency, or tracing paper. Lay the grid over the design.

2. Use 1-cm by 1-cm grid paper. Lightly outline every second line on the grid paper to produce a 2-cm by 2-cm grid. One block on the grid paper now contains 4 smaller squares.
Read from each block on the original grid; re-create the details in the corresponding block on the 2-cm grid.

3. Measure the total length of each design. What do you notice?

4. Explain how you could make the design 3 times as long and 3 times as wide as the original.

The Dilatation Method

You can reduce or enlarge figures by using a method similar to the method we used for perspective drawing.

Investigation 3 Creating a Scaled Copy of a Figure

If you have access to a computer, complete part 1. Otherwise, complete part 2.

1. Use *The Geometer's Sketchpad.*

   In this activity you will make a scaled copy of a triangle. The same method can be used to dilatate any design that you create using *The Geometer's Sketchpad.*

   • From the File menu, choose New Sketch.
   • Construct a triangle and label it QRS.
   • Construct a point near the top of the screen. Label it P.
   • Double-click point P to mark P as a centre for rotation or dilatation.
   • Select $\triangle$QRS by clicking and dragging a box around it.
   • From the Transform menu choose Dilate. A dialog box will appear. Enter a Scale Factor for the new triangle. To make the triangle sides half of those in $\triangle$QRS, enter 0.5. Click OK.
   • A new triangle, Q'R'S' will appear.

   a) Use the Measure tool to determine the lengths of the sides of both triangles.

   b) Shift-click P and Q. From the Measure menu, choose Distance. Repeat to find each distance: PQ', PR, PR', PS, and PS'.

   c) Check the relationship between the following pairs of measurements as P moves: PQ and PQ', PS and PS', PR and PR'
   QR and Q'R', RS and R'S', SQ and S'Q'
   Record your results.

d) Drag point Q and observe the new measurements. What do you notice about the relationships between the segments in question 1?

e) Select △QRS, then select Dilate and use scale factor 3. Drag △QRS closer to P if you cannot see the new triangle on the screen. Find the side lengths of the new triangle and the distances to P as before. Describe the relationship between the sides of △QRS and the sides of the new triangle.

2. **Use a ruler and grid paper.**

   a) Draw any △ABC. Join A, B, and C to O, the point at infinity.

   b) Find the midpoints of AO, BO, and CO. Label them E, F, and G. Join the points to form △EFG.

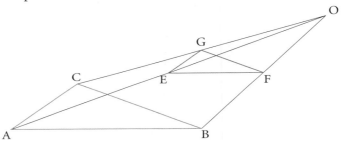

   c) Measure the lengths of corresponding sides in △ABC and △EFG. What do you notice?

   d) Describe △EFG in terms of △ABC.

This method is called *dilatation*. It is based on the idea that reducing or enlarging a figure affects all its parts. If EO and FO are half of AO and BO, then EF will be half of AB.
We say that △ABC was dilatated about point O by a factor of $\frac{1}{2}$.

When a 3-dimensional object is drawn without using perspective techniques, we have difficulty understanding what we see.
Try the following experiment.
Look at the drawing of the cube. Can you see that the dot on the corner is at the front left? Now try to see the cube so that the dot is at the back left.
If you can't see it immediately, try turning the page until your perspective shifts.

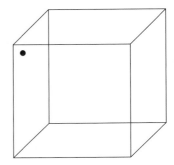

The effect works because the drawing is not really a perspective drawing. When we try to see what we expect to see – a cube – our brain needs to decide which corner is closer.

B

1. Choose one subject and produce a scaled, front-view diagram. Include all details, label objects, and clearly show measurements and the scale.
   - a wall in your home, school, or place of work
   - the front wall of a garage
   - the front section of a fence and gate

2. **Knowledge/Understanding** Choose one subject from the list below. Take and record measurements, then produce scaled front-, side-, and top-view diagrams. Include all details and labels, and clearly show measurements and the scale on your diagram.
   - a microwave oven
   - a deck, dock, or porch
   - another object approved by your teacher
   - a buffet, hutch, dresser, or cabinet
   - a desk

3. **Application** Enlarge the design below by a scale factor of 4 using the grid method.

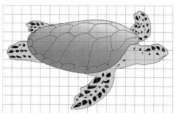

4. Use *The Geometer's Sketchpad* to construct and dilatate a quadrilateral by a factor of 1.5.

5. **Communication** State some uses of each (non-technological) method of enlarging and reducing. Explain how each method is used in its applications.

6. Construct a star, or other interesting figure, using *The Geometer's Sketchpad*. Dilatate the figure by a scale factor of 0.75.

7. **Thinking/Inquiry/Problem Solving**
   a) Draw an outline of your hand on a sheet of paper. Give the outline to your teacher to reduce or enlarge on a photocopier. Determine the scale of the image by taking measurements.
   b) Use a similar method to determine the scale of your photo on your driver's licence or student card. Compare your solution with a peer.

1. a) Identify the figures in the patch blocks below.

b) Choose one of the blocks. If the block is 40 cm on each edge, calculate how many of each figure you would need to make a quilt 200 cm by 240 cm. Specify how many of each colour.

2. Identify the type of symmetry used in each design. Specify the location of the line of symmetry, the angle of rotation, or the direction and size of the translation.

a)  **b)**

3. Create a perspective diagram of a triangular prism.

4. a) Use the grid method to enlarge the design, below left, by a factor of 2.

b) Use dilatation to reduce the object, below right, to half its size.

5. a) Copy each figure and draw all possible lines of reflection symmetry.

b) All regular polygons have reflection symmetry. What is the minimum number of mirror lines that can be drawn on any regular polygon? Explain.

Many 3-dimensional objects are constructed from flat material, such as fabric, cardboard, and sheet metal. The material is cut according to a pattern. It is folded or bent, then joined to form the object. In this section we will investigate this technique and use it to construct 3-dimensional models.

A *net* is a 2-dimensional figure that can be folded to produce a 3-dimensional object.

To make a cube, you can cut out 6 squares and tape the edges together.

You can also produce a cube from a net.

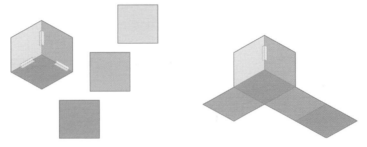

Nets can be used to produce objects with bendable materials, such as sheet metal or cardboard. By using nets, it is possible to eliminate some joins. The cube on the left has 12 joins. The one on the right has only 7. Joins use extra material and time, and can weaken the structure.

Investigation 1 Nets of Some 3-Dimensional Objects

For this activity you will need grid paper, a ruler, and scissors.

1. Examine the given nets. Predict the object produced by each net.
2. Enlarge each net by reproducing it on 1 cm by 1 cm grid paper. Draw dotted lines as shown.
3. Cut around the outside of each net. *Do not cut dotted lines.*
4. Fold on dotted lines to produce each object.
5. Verify your predictions from exercise 1 by identifying each object. You may need to refer to chapter 3.

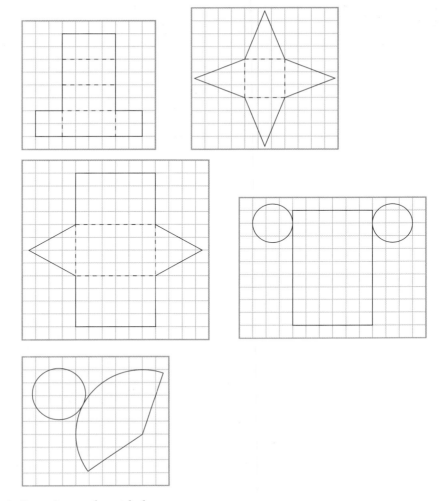

6. Examine each net below.

7. Identify the nets that produce closed objects. Explain why the other patterns are not nets of objects.

8. Notice that the same geometric shape can be constructed from different nets. Design a net different from the one previously given, to create a triangular prism.

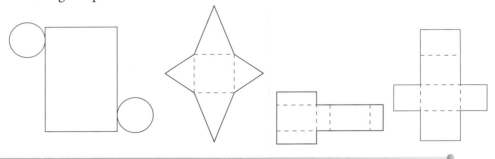

Using Technology to Construct Nets for Some Common 3-Dimensional Shapes

Use *The Geometer's Sketchpad* or a draw program and your nets from *Investigation 1* as guides.

1. Produce nets for each object below.
2. Print, then cut out and assemble your objects.

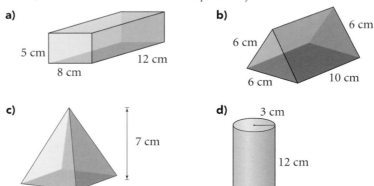

a) 5 cm, 8 cm, 12 cm

b) 6 cm, 6 cm, 6 cm, 10 cm

c) 7 cm, 6 cm

d) 3 cm, 12 cm

3. Describe how well your nets fit together. Describe any modifications you could make to improve your models.

Patterns are often complex. They have to accommodate how the edges will link to one another. In the next activity, you will investigate how particular objects are made from fabric, cardboard, and sheet metal or tin.

Investigation 3 **Making Patterns**

You will need work gloves, utility scissors, a staple remover, pliers, a tape measure, grid paper, and a variety of objects to take apart. Some suggested items are:
- cardboard containers, such as milk cartons and juice containers
- an old short-sleeved T-shirt

1. Carefully take apart each object at the joined edges.
   In the case of the T-shirt, cut carefully along the seam line.
2. Flatten out the material and make a scale drawing of the shape or shapes used to create the object.
3. Assume that the scale diagram shows the outside surface. Shade the areas that could not be seen when the object was assembled. Explain the purpose of these shaded areas.

B

✓ **1. Knowledge/Understanding and Communication** Identify the patterns that will produce a closed 3-dimensional object when folded. Explain your reasoning.

a)

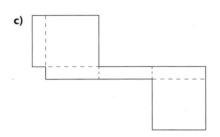

b)

c)

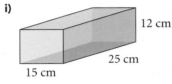

d)

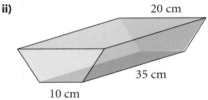

✓ **2. Application** Complete parts a and b for each object depicted.

i)

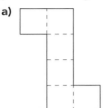

12 cm
25 cm
15 cm

ii)

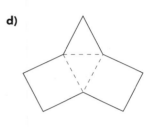

20 cm
35 cm
10 cm

iii)

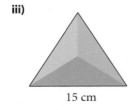

15 cm

iv) 15 cm

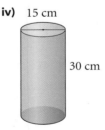

30 cm

a) Design a one-piece pattern that can be cut and folded to form the object. Include allowances for joins in the pattern.

b) Make a scale model of each object out of cardboard or heavy paper.

3. Tabs that fit into slots are sometimes used to join sections of cardboard to produce models. You can add tabs and slots to any net. Software such as Tabs will create nets with tabs attached. Modify one of the net patterns in *Investigation 1* to include tabs and slots.

Remember: The tab on one edge must line up with the slot on the matching edge. Allow at least 1 cm extra all along the slotted edge to prevent tearing. Long edges may need more than one tab. Tabs will stay in their slots if they hook in. A possible shape is shown.

✓ **4. Communication** Metal or cardboard must be cut so that edges that join are the same length. In clothing construction, an edge is sometimes cut larger than the edge it is to join. Before sewing the pieces together, the larger edge is altered to make it fit the smaller edge. Gathering and taking darts are two techniques that are used.
List examples of clothing that use these techniques. Explain what the function is in each piece of clothing.

5. Using a 2-cm by 2-cm grid, enlarge and cut out each pattern below. The dotted line marks the seam line. Pin the pattern pieces to fabric, and cut around the edges.

For the two pieces in a, sew the dart and join edges AB and CD.

For the two pieces in b, gather the edge of EF until it matches GH in length.

Display your samples by pinning them to heavy cardboard.

a)

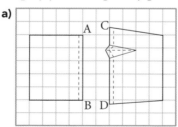

b)

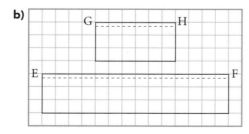

6. Thinking/Inquiry/Problem Solving Create a net of a sphere.

Layouts, plans, and scale models are some tools a designer or architect uses to provide information about a project. Careful planning can prevent costly mistakes.

Whether you are planning to landscape a garden, remodel a kitchen, construct a deck, build a house or apartment building, or decorate an office, preparing one or more of these is an essential first step.

Layouts

A *layout* is a scale diagram that shows the placement of objects, walls, stairs, and openings, as viewed from above. Layouts show how each floor of a house is divided into rooms, where shrubs and flowers are planted in a garden, or where the appliances and cupboards are located in a kitchen.

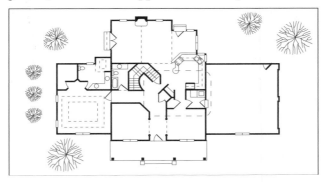

Layouts are used by interior decorators to model various scenarios – to observe the results of moving a desk, sink, fridge, or shrub to another location. To make wise decisions, a designer thinks about how the space will be used, then considers factors, such as available light, space for walking, and location of pipes and wiring.

Investigation 1 Using a Layout to Make Decisions

You will need a tape measure, paper on a clipboard or binder, a ruler, and grid paper.

1. Draw a rough top view of a room in your school or home.

2. Mark approximate locations of doors, windows, and objects.
   - A slanted segment in the direction of opening represents a door; a space indicates an opening or archway.

- Use small segments perpendicular to a wall edge to mark the location of windows.
- Draw squares, rectangles, or circles to represent objects. It is helpful to write the name of the object within the figure.

3. With a partner, take measurements of the room, and the objects in the room. Record these on the sketch.

Discuss

Why is it not necessary to measure heights of doors, walls, and objects?

4. Take measurements to locate items on your layout. For example, the top of a desk may be 55 cm by 45 cm, but to place it on the diagram, you need to measure its distance from the walls.

5. Transfer your information to grid paper.
- Choose a suitable scale. Include this information at the lower right corner of the page.
- Convert each measurement using the scale factor.
- Using a ruler, draw the room, openings, and objects. Label all details.

The layout can also be completed using drawing software or *The Geometer's Sketchpad.*

6. Experiment with changing the layout. Redraw the room to scale on a fresh sheet of grid paper. Include details that will not change, such as locations of doors and windows.

a) Trace, then cut out the figures in your original layout that represent objects in the room.

b) Move the cut outs around the new layout diagram. Remember to consider how the room is used and how people will move around. When you are satisfied with the results, tape the objects in their new locations.

If you have used drawing software or *The Geometer's Sketchpad* you can try different options by dragging the shapes that represent the objects to new locations on the screen.

The Geometer's Sketchpad:
- Construct polygon interiors for each object. Do this by using the point tool to create the vertices and then shift-clicking each point in order. Under the Construct menu, click on Polygon Interior.
- You can move the object around by clicking on the shaded area and dragging.

- To turn a rectangle, double-click on a vertex. Select the rectangle, then choose Rotate from the Transform menu. Enter the angle measurement and click OK. Select the original rectangle and choose Hide Object from the Display menu.

Scale Models

Scale models are 3-dimensional representations of one object or a collection of objects. They can be constructed from interlocking blocks, cardboard, and other materials. Elaborate scale models of houses may include lights, shingles, windows, miniature furniture, and even shrubs and fountains. Architects and builders use scale models to show what a finished project will look like; some people build them as a hobby.

Investigation 2 **Constructing Scale Model Frames**

In the previous section you made models of various 3-dimensional solids using nets. In this Investigation, you will use wooden sticks to construct a tetrahedron, a square-based pyramid, and a pentagonal prism. This method is useful for producing unusual 3-dimensional shapes. The frame can later be covered with paper or fabric.

You will need a ruler, wooden sticks (shish kebab skewers work well), and modelling clay or small pieces of foam.

A tetrahedron or triangular-based pyramid

Use 6 skewers of equal length. Construct one triangular face by connecting the skewers at the vertices using clay (or a small chunk of foam). Lay the triangle flat.

Push each of the other skewers into one of the vertices. Join their other ends together with clay.

1. How many faces does this shape have? How many edges? How many vertices?

2. Make another model in which the base is an isosceles triangle formed by 2 regular-length skewers and 1 half-length skewer. How many faces, edges, and vertices does this model have? Are the faces congruent?

3. Explain how the design of the base affected the other faces in the tetrahedron.

A square-based pyramid

1. Look at the diagram of the square-based pyramid on page 206. Calculate the number of skewers and pieces of clay you will need. Construct the frame of the pyramid.

2. How many faces does this shape have? How many edges? How many vertices?
   This model has 4 equilateral triangle faces. Make a second model that has four congruent triangle faces—each one formed from 2 regular-length skewers and 1 half-length skewer.

3. How many faces, edges, and vertices does this model have? How did the change in the triangular faces affect the base of the pyramid?
   Construct a rectangle using 2 regular length-skewers and 2 half-length skewers. Using this base, construct a pyramid.

4. How many faces, edges, and vertices does this rectangular-based pyramid have? What is the relationship between the 4 triangular faces?

A pentagonal prism

1. A pentagonal prism has two parallel pentagons joined by rectangles. Make a sketch of the prism and count the number of skewers and pieces of clay that you will need. Form the two pentagons. Join the pentagon ends with the remaining skewers to form the sides.

2. How many faces, edges, and vertices does the model have? What do you notice about the rectangular faces?

3. If the pentagons are the top and bottom, make a pentagonal prism that is half as tall.
   How many faces, edges, and vertices does the model have? What is the relationship between the rectangular faces?

4. Make a pentagon that is not regular. Using this as the base, construct a pentagonal prism.
   How many faces, edges, and vertices does the model have? What is the relationship between the rectangular faces?

B

✓ 1. **Communication** Layouts are important in areas other than interior decorating. A good layout helps people use objects more efficiently.

   a) Use the method from *Investigation 1*. Take measurements and draw the layouts for:

     i) the instrument panel of a car or appliance

     ii) a remote control or telephone handset

     iii) a table set for dinner for four people

   b) For one of the above layouts, explain how the placement of items in the layout promotes ease of use.

   c) For one of the above layouts, suggest a possible rationale for the size of items in the layout. Explain how reducing or enlarging the items would affect use.

✓ 2. **Application** Choose one subject from the list below. Make a rough sketch, pace out distances, and estimate locations and sizes of objects. Produce a layout diagram using a suitable scale.

   • a local supermarket

   • one floor of your school

   • a local playground, containing equipment

✓ 3. **Knowledge/Understanding** Collect 3 examples of layouts from newspapers or magazines. Renovation magazines, advertisements for new homes, and decorating magazines are possible sources.

   a) Calculate the scale used to produce the drawing.

   b) Enlarge each layout using the grid method.

4. Use the method from *Investigation 2*. Choose a suitable scale and construct scale models of each figure.

   a) a rectangular prism

Length	Width	Height
125 cm	85 cm	70 cm

   b) a trapezoid-based prism

Length	Width at top	Width at bottom
60 cm	25 cm	12 cm

   c) a cube, 40 cm on each edge

5. Select a simple piece of furniture in your home or school. Take measurements and construct a frame for a scale model as in *Investigation 2*. Cover with paper or fabric and add details to scale as necessary.

Wood sizes are always quoted before planing. Planing removes a thin layer of wood. The following chart shows some common sizes and their finished dimensions.

Name	Dimensions Before Planing	Finished Dimensions (dry)
2 by 4	2" by 4"	$1\frac{1}{2}$" by $3\frac{1}{2}$"
2 by 2	2" by 2"	$1\frac{1}{2}$" by $1\frac{1}{2}$"
1 by 2	1" by 2"	$\frac{3}{4}$" by $1\frac{1}{2}$"

6. You will need a ruler, scissors, tape, and heavy cardboard. Examine the plans for the picnic table.

6 feet

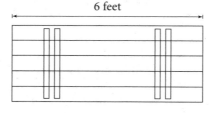

TOP VIEW
5 pieces of 2 by 6 cedar, 6 feet long, spaced $\frac{1}{4}$ inch apart.

6 feet

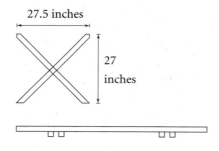

UNDERSIDE OF TOP
At each end, attach 2 pieces of 2 by 2 cedar 27.5 inches long to the underside of the top. Set pieces 2 inches apart and inset 1 inch from each side.

27.5 inches

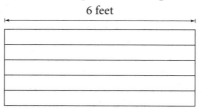

27 inches

ONE SET OF LEGS
2 pieces of 2 by 6 cedar, crossed. Set into the 2-inch groove on the underside of the table.

TABLE TOP
Side view showing grooves for legs.

LEG BRACE
2 by 6 cedar, 44.5 inches long. Butt each end to middle of the cross on legs.

a) From the information in the diagrams, use heavy cardboard to construct a scale model of the table that can fit on your desk.

b) Using the diagrams as a guide, draw plans for a bench to match the table. The bench should be 20" high, 12" wide, and the same length as the table. The leg style should match the table's.

7. Select a room in your house. Take measurements. Produce a layout diagram and a scale model. Cardboard walls can be designed using a net. Scale models of furniture and other objects can be constructed using frames, nets, interlocking blocks, or other materials.

8. Use the method from *Investigation 2*. Construct a scale model of a soccer ball.

9. **Thinking/Inquiry/Problem Solving** Props, sets, and costumes are often constructed from inexpensive materials. They must be carefully designed to look like the real thing and to stand up during a performance. Prepare plans similar to those in exercise 6 for **one** item from options i to iv.

   i) A top hat to be constructed of bristol board
   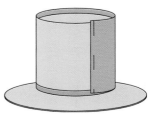
   - overall height 30 cm
   - diameter at top 15 cm
   - brim width 6 cm

   The design calls for the brim to have tabs that fold up into the cylinder portion of the hat so that tape joins are not visible.

   ii) A giant cone to be made of paper on a pre-constructed wire frame
   The wire frame is 2 m tall. The diameter of the circular end is 0.75 m. The art department needs a diagram that shows the exact dimensions of the paper, in order to paint designs before attaching the paper to the cone. The paper available is in rolls 1 m wide. It can be joined on the back with tape.

   iii) A frame for a backdrop to be constructed of 2 by 2 spruce
   The wood is available in 8-foot lengths.
   The backdrop is painted on paper 5 m long and 3 m high.
   The design calls for a rectangular frame with vertical pieces placed every 0.5 m for strength. Triangle supports will be attached at right angles to the back so the backdrop will be freestanding.

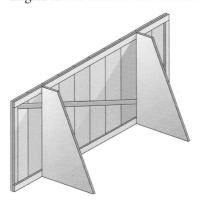

iv) A frame for a fake fireplace constructed of $\frac{1}{2}$" plywood

The wood is available in 8-foot by 4-foot sheets. The shelf on top of the fireplace will be constructed from 2 by 4 spruce. The "fire" will be constructed separately out of tissue and hidden lights. Paper painted to look like bricks will cover the frame.

The design calls for the following:
Fireplace: height 160 cm, width 180 cm
Shelf on top: width 180 cm, depth 10 cm
Fireplace opening: 40 cm wide and 40 cm high
A cardboard box containing the "fire" will sit in the opening.

The frame will be supported by two pieces of 2 by 2 lumber attached to the back at the middle of the right and left edges with hinges. Be careful to calculate the length of these legs to make sure that the fireplace stands perpendicular to the floor.

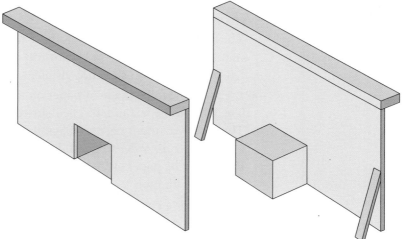

The draftsperson or designer must know how materials can be cut, shaped, and connected in order to draw a plan or produce a pattern. In the following activities, you will investigate how some of these factors affect design decisions.

Joints

Most manufactured objects have at least one joint. Joints can be mortared, glued, nailed, welded, or sewn. Plans must take into account the sizes of joints and provide for extra material, if necessary.

Investigation 1

Exploring Allowances for Butt Joints and Interlocking Joints

You will need 1-cm grid paper, scissors, and a ruler.

A carpenter has many ways to connect two pieces of wood. Butt joints in rough carpentry, mitred joints at the corners of picture frames, tongue-and-groove joints in hardwood flooring, and dovetail joints in furniture construction are just a few examples.

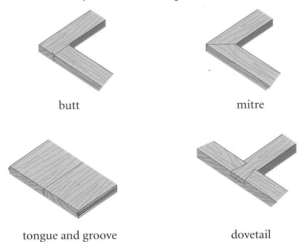

butt   mitre

tongue and groove   dovetail

The carpenter must allow for any overlap at the joints, so the finished object will be the correct size.

A. Work with butt joints

On grid paper, draw 4 rectangles 1 cm wide and 20 cm long, and
4 rectangles 1 cm wide and 15 cm long.
Cut out the rectangles. These will be your "boards."
A butt joint, as shown, will be used to connect two boards at right angles.

a) Lay out the boards to form the following:
  i) a rectangle 20 cm by 17 cm on the outside
    What are the dimensions on the inside?
  ii) a rectangle 22 cm by 15 cm on the outside
    What are the dimensions on the inside?

b) What is the largest rectangle you can construct with the boards? What is the smallest rectangle?

c) Using a width of your choice, make more "boards" out of grid paper to form:
  i) a rectangle 10" by 10" on the outside
  ii) a rectangle 10" by 10" on the inside

d) Make 2 boards 2 cm wide by 15 cm long, and 2 boards, 2 cm wide by 18 cm long.
  • Join them to make a rectangle that is 15 cm by 22 cm.
    What are the inside dimensions?
  • Join them to make a rectangle that is 18 cm long.
    What are the inside dimensions?

Explain how the outside and inside dimensions will be related if the rectangle is constructed with boards 3 cm wide.

B. Work with interlocking joints

Dovetail joints that interlock two pieces of wood are stronger than butt joints. In this section we will use an interlocking pattern, as shown, to join the boards.

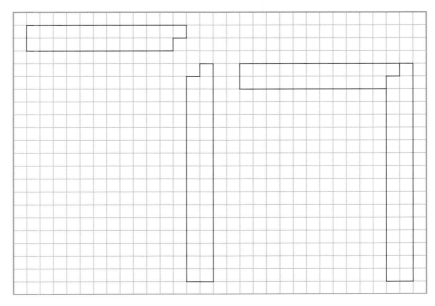

Each square on the grid is 0.5 cm by 0.5 cm.

a) Make "boards" out of grid paper and cut the ends in the interlock pattern. Construct the following:

   i) a rectangle 20 cm by 20 cm on the outside

   ii) a rectangle 20 cm by 20 cm on the inside

b) Without constructing the figures, calculate the sizes of boards necessary to construct the following:

   i) a rectangle 6" by 4" on the outside

   ii) a rectangle 6" by 4" on the inside

   iii) a rectangle 16 cm by 30 cm on the outside

c) What will the inside dimensions be of each rectangle in part b?

d) Make 2 boards 2 cm wide by 18 cm long, and 2 boards 2 cm wide by 15 cm long. Adapt the interlocking pattern by assuming that the squares on the grid are 1 cm by 1 cm.

   i) Join the boards to make a rectangle 18 cm by 17 cm on the outside. What are the inside dimensions?

   ii) Join the boards to make a rectangle 15 cm wide. What are the inside dimensions?

e) Explain how the inside and outside dimensions of the rectangle are related when this type of interlocking joint is used.

Joining Cylinders

Pipes are usually joined with couplings. A coupling may make the pipe longer, or change its direction by 90° or 45°. When a coupling is used, each pipe is cut and then inserted into the coupling.

Sometimes, it is necessary to join cylindrical objects without a coupling. The joint may then be taped or welded.

You will need several cardboard tubes of the same diameter, scissors, tape, a ruler, and a protractor.

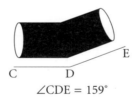

∠CDE = 159°

- Cut through one cardboard tube at an angle, as shown.
- Rotate a section of the cut tube one-half turn or 180°. Join the tubes and tape in place.
- Lay the joined tubes on a piece of grid paper and trace the angle. Use the protractor to measure the angle.

a) Use the same procedure to construct pipes that turn at the given angle.
 i) 100° **ii)** 140°

b) Explain how the angle of the bend is related to the angle at which the tube is cut.

Spans

To construct doorways and window openings it is necessary to place supports further than 16 inches apart. The carpenter uses an additional plate to span the distance. The plate rests on vertical pieces and supports the weight of the wall above the door or window. Some bridges are constructed in this way. Concrete pillars at each end support beams of wood, steel, or reinforced concrete.

Another way to span a doorway, road, or river is with an arch. Compare these two methods by conducting the following experiment.

You will need some textbooks, light cardboard such as that used in cereal boxes, a ruler, and scissors.

1. Cut a strip of cardboard 5 cm wide by 25 cm long.
   - Stand two textbooks 10 cm apart and rest the cardboard strip on the books.
   - Place an object such as scissors or a small stapler on the cardboard bridge.
   - Move the books 15 cm apart and repeat the experiment. Continue moving the books 5 cm apart until the bridge collapses.

2. Cut another strip of cardboard 5 cm wide by 25 cm long.
   - Bend the strip into an arch and stand it on a desk. Pile textbooks 10 cm apart at each end as shown. These represent the abutments of the bridge. They prevent the arch from flattening out when weight is added.

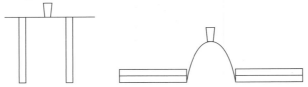

   - Put the object on top of the arch.
   - Move the books 15 cm apart and repeat the experiment. Continue moving the books 5 cm further apart until the bridge collapses.

3. Which shape supported the weight of the object across the widest span? Record your observations and conclusions.

4. The maximum span for a beam bridge is approximately 80 m. With modern materials arch bridges can span almost 600 m, although they are usually less than 250 m. If a longer bridge is needed, two or more beams or arch bridges can be joined in a row. From magazines or the Internet, collect examples of a beam bridge, an arch bridge, a connected series of beam bridges, and a connected series of arch bridges. For each bridge, describe the materials used and calculate the distance spanned by each beam or arch section.

B

1. A pattern is not a scale diagram. It is full size and is usually pinned or taped to the material so that the figures can be cut out. It usually includes dotted lines to show where the pieces are to be joined. Do one of the following:

   a) Make a pattern for a hand puppet. A hand puppet usually has three sections – one for the thumb, one for the little finger, and one for the middle three fingers.

   Trace around your hand, as shown, to get the basic shape.

   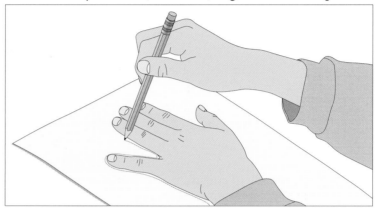

   Trace around the shape again, 1.5 cm outside the first line to allow for a comfortable fit. This will be the seam line.

   Allowing an additional 1 cm for a seam allowance, draw a pattern for the puppet.

   Mini-Project If you can sew, pin the pattern to fabric or felt and cut two copies. With right sides together, sew along the seam line. Do not sew the bottom edge! Clip close to the seam between each section. Turn the puppet right side out and decorate as you choose.

   b) Make a pattern for a pencil container. Cans covered with leather or suede make interesting containers.

   Choose an empty can without a lid. For pencils, a can should be about 15 cm high.

   The pattern for the section that covers the sides of the cylinder must allow approximately 1.5 cm to turn under at the seam, and 1 cm at the top and bottom.

   The pattern for the bottom must allow 1 cm to tuck under the sides. Draw the pattern for the sections. Pin to the fabric and cut the pieces. Glue pieces to the can, overlapping seams and hiding edges by turning material under. Decorate as desired.

✓ **2. Knowledge/Understanding** Since every joint could be a source of leakage, cylinders are often used to hold liquid. Cans and pipes can be formed from a flat piece of metal and joined by welding a single seam down the side.

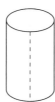

a) A seam requires extra material. If the seam allowance is 5 mm, draw a scale diagram of the pattern for a cylinder with the given finished dimensions.

	Height (cm)	Diameter (cm)
i)	20	15
ii)	16	10
iii)	12	8

b) The top and bottom of a can must also be welded. For each of the cylinders in part a, draw a scale diagram of the top using a seam allowance of 5 mm.

✓ **3. Application**

a) Draw a design for an open box made of plywood with the following specifications:
  • Exterior dimensions will be 3 feet by 2 feet by $1\frac{1}{2}$ feet high.
  • Butt joints will be used to join sections.

b) The plywood is $\frac{1}{2}$ inch thick and is available in 4 feet by 8 feet sheets. Draw a scale diagram to show how the pieces can be cut from the plywood. (Leave space between pieces in the layout since the saw cut removes some wood.)

4. A bricklayer uses an alternating pattern to lay bricks in rows. This technique prevents sections of the wall from collapsing. Since vertical mortar joints are not in a line, cracks cannot extend from top to bottom.

The thickness of the mortar joint must be included in any calculations. In counting mortar joints, many small vertical ones are equivalent to one that extends from top to bottom.

A bricklayer is building a wall with bricks 90 mm by 230 mm by 70 mm, as shown.

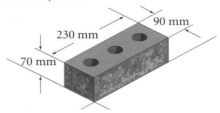

- The mortar joints will be 9.5 mm thick.
- There will be a mortar joint at the bottom where the bricks meet the concrete block foundation, but there will not be mortar on the top course of bricks.

Calculate the number of bricks needed for a wall 4 m long that extends 3 m above the concrete block foundation.

5. **Thinking/Inquiry/Problem Solving** Some houses have a single layer of brick on the outside. This is called *brick veneer* construction. Other houses have two layers of brick with an airspace between. This is called *solid brick*. In solid brick construction, the two layers are linked by laying bricks at right angles to the face, every sixth row as shown.

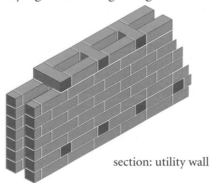

section: utility wall

A bricklayer is building a solid brick wall with bricks 90 mm by 230 mm by 70 mm.

- The mortar joints will be 9.5 mm thick.
- There will be a mortar joint at the bottom but not at the top.

a) Calculate the number of bricks needed for a wall 4 m long that extends 3 m above the concrete block.

b) Calculate the width of the airspace between the two layers.

1. In this chapter, you have learned to:
   i) prepare a layout ii) draw front, rear, and side views
   iii) construct a scale model iv) construct a net
   v) prepare a blueprint sketch vi) make a pattern
   For each situation below, choose one action, from i to vi above, and explain why it is an appropriate choice.
   a) remodelling a bathroom
   b) constructing a deck
   c) studying the architecture of a famous building
   d) sewing a puppet
   e) preparing a presentation to convince a company to go with your design for a new head office building
   f) making tetrahedron decorations for a science fair in the school gym
   g) designing a remote control for a robot
   h) preparing diagrams for a parts list
   i) making a table and chairs for a doll house

2. Use *The Geometer's Sketchpad* or other drawing software to produce nets for each shape.

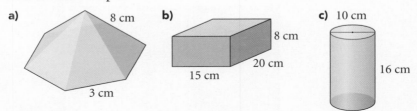

a) 8 cm, 3 cm
b) 8 cm, 20 cm, 15 cm
c) 10 cm, 16 cm

3. Choose a building or a large object. Use 1-cm by 1-cm grid paper to draw front, side, and rear views.

4. Collect 3 or more different-style envelopes. Carefully take each envelope apart to reveal the net. Using graph paper, make a scale diagram of each net. Shade the areas that are added to allow the envelopes to be glued.

Performance Assessment

5. Design a pattern for a box with a lid. The pattern must use no more than 2 sheets of $8\frac{1}{2}$" by 11" paper. In the pattern, include tabs to allow edges to be connected. Cut out and assemble the box. Explain how you determined the dimensions under the given constraints.

In this chapter you have investigated some of the properties of 2- and 3-dimensional objects and have developed many skills. You are now able to:

- Prepare scale diagrams and models.
- Draw layouts and views.
- Make nets, patterns, and plans.
- Construct frames for models.
- Provide allowances for joints in calculating materials.

In this section you will apply what you have learned to design and construct a model.

1. Choose a project topic from one of the lists below.

a) Fashion	b) Interior design	c) Construction	d) Landscape design
Hats	Kitchen	Bridges	Water gardens
Costumes	Floors	Chairs	Golf courses
Motifs in fabric	Layout of a 100 m² living space	Dog houses	Playgrounds

You may want to concentrate on a subtopic rather than the entire area. For example, if you choose costumes, you might focus on animal costumes.

2. Investigate your topic or subtopic. Use books, magazines, and the Internet. The results of your investigation should be presented in a booklet. Include:

- a description of how either 2- or 3-dimensional shapes are involved in your topic area
- photos of at least four objects to illustrate the variety of possibilities for design in your topic area
- at least one pattern, layout, or plan obtained from a book or other reliable source for an object in your topic area
- facts about the construction of objects in your area, such as choice of materials, methods of cutting and joining, size constraints, allowances for joints, and/or requirements for strength

Constructing the model

Choose an object or item within your area to design and construct according to these criteria:

- The design must be drawn to scale on 1-cm grid paper. It must include the scale in the lower right corner.
- All labels and measurements must be included.
- All views necessary to give the observer a clear understanding of construction details must be included.
- The design must take into account the construction requirements mentioned in your booklet. For example, if you are designing a lawn chair and your research shows that the seat must be 45 cm above the ground for comfort, your design should reflect this fact.
- The model must be to scale, must follow the design, and must include as many correct details as possible.

Include a one-page explanation of how the model was constructed and your reasons for making particular design or construction decisions. Include the model.

Interior Designer

Chris wanted a career where she could use her artistic ability in a practical setting. She decided to train as an interior designer at community college.

Job Description

- Design the interior of new homes, offices, restaurants, hotels, and theatres
- Plan renovations of existing interior spaces
- Meet with clients to coordinate their needs with the designer's ideas
- Coordinate the work of tradespeople who carry out design plans

Working Conditions

- Much of the work is freelance
- Evening and weekend work may be necessary for meeting with clients
- Hours can be irregular with 80-hour work weeks when deadlines are approaching

Qualifications and Training

- Graduation from high school
- Successful completion of an interior design program at a community college or university
- Artistic ability

- Self-discipline to budget time and money and meet production deadlines
- Good communication skills and an ability to listen to people

Where's the Math?

Interior designers must be able to visualize and make two- and three-dimensional drawings and models of the interiors they design. A good visual sense of two- and three-dimensional figures will enable the designer to plan imaginative and functional interiors. In the early stages of a project, the designer estimates the costs of the design plan. When plans are finalized, the exact cost of materials and labour is calculated so the designer can charge the client appropriately.

Review Exercises

MATHEMATICS TOOLKIT

Geometry and Design Tools

> Reflection symmetry: A 2-dimensional figure has reflection symmetry if a mirror line divides it into two identical parts.

> Rotation symmetry: A 2-dimensional figure has rotation symmetry if there is a centre point about which an object is turned a certain number of degrees and still looks the same.

> Translation symmetry: A pattern has translation symmetry if a section of it can be moved without rotating or reflecting to exactly match another section of the pattern.

> Glide reflection symmetry: A glide reflection is a combination of a translation and a reflection.

> Perspective drawings: Perspective uses the idea that parallel lines moving away from us appear to meet at a point, which we call a *point at infinity*.

> Scale drawings: Scale drawings may be smaller or larger than the original object. All distances in the drawing are multiples of those in the original, but angles do not change. There are several ways to produce a scale drawing.

1. **Measure, Convert, and Draw:** Take measurements of the object, multiply each measurement by a conversion factor, and use the new values to make the drawing.

2. **The Grid Method:** Place a grid over a 2-dimensional object, then reproduce by sketching details on a smaller or larger grid.

3. **Dilatation:** Join points on the original to a centre of dilatation, divide the resulting join lines using the same factor, and connect the points of division to form the scaled image.

Layouts: A layout is a scale diagram that shows the placement of objects, walls, stairs, and openings as viewed from above.

4.1   **1.** The Arabic Star, right, is a quilt block that is made up of tessellated diamonds. A diamond has four sides of equal length and opposite angles of equal measure. What must the measure be of each interior angle of the diamonds in order for them to tessellate?

4.2   **2. a)** Some designs can illustrate more than one type of transformation. Examine the rows of hearts, ii to vi. Determine which row shows a transformation pattern that matches the top design, i. Describe the pattern in each case.

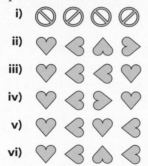

    b) On grid paper, create a wallpaper border pattern 25 cm long and 15 cm wide that uses at least two of the following transformations: reflection, rotation, translation, glide reflection.

3. In magazines or on the Internet, search for company logos that illustrate reflections, translations, or rotations. Sketch or copy the logos and identify:

    a) the type of transformation in each design

    b) the location of the mirror line, the direction and size of the translation, or the angle of rotation, as appropriate

4.3   **4.** Choose *one* object and produce top-, front-, and side-view diagrams, using an appropriate scale.

    a) a step ladder

    b) a stapler

    c) a desk or dresser

5. On grid paper, draw a trapezoid. Use the trapezoid and the idea of a point at infinity to create a perspective diagram of a prism with trapezoids at each end.

4.4   **6.** Use dilatation to enlarge the object, below left, to 2 times its size.

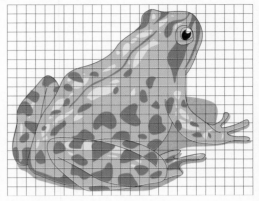

7. Use the grid method to reduce the object, above right, to one half of its size.

4.5   **8.** Produce nets for each object. Use *The Geometer's Sketchpad* or a draw program.
Print, cut out, and assemble your objects.

a)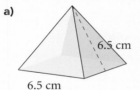
6.5 cm
6.5 cm

b)
2.5 cm
10.5 cm

c)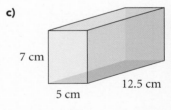
7 cm
5 cm
12.5 cm

9. Identify the patterns that will produce a closed object when folded. Explain your reasoning.

a)

b)

c)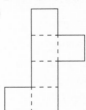

4.6   **10.** Design a one-piece pattern that can be cut and folded to form a wallet in the shape of a rectangular prism. The wallet should be 14 cm long, 6 cm wide, and 1 cm thick. Include:
   • a rectangular flap that overlaps the front face by 3 cm
   • allowances for joins in the pattern
   • a scale model made of paper or fabric

11. a) Take measurements and draw the layouts for either i, ii, or iii.
- **i)** two different models of scientific calculator
- **ii)** opening web pages for two online banking services
- **iii)** the design on the soles of two makes of running shoes

b) Compare the placement of items in the layouts and suggest possible advantages of one layout over the other.

12. a) Draw a design for an open box made of plywood with given specifications.
- Exterior dimensions: 3.5' by 1' by 18" high
- Butt joints will be used to join sections.

b) The plywood is $\frac{1}{2}$" thick and is available in 4' by 8' sheets. Draw a scale diagram to show how the pieces can be cut from the plywood.

13. For each object from i to iv complete parts a to c.
- **i)** a triangular prism 12 cm long, with equilateral triangle ends of side length 5 cm
- **ii)** a rectangular prism 20 cm long, 13.5 cm wide, and 12.5 cm high
- **iii)** a cylindrical box 18 cm tall, with diameter 7.5 cm
- **iv)** a trapezoid-based prism 22 cm long, 14 cm wide at the top, and 17 cm wide at the bottom

a) Design a one-piece pattern that can be cut and folded to form the object.

b) Include allowances for joins in the pattern.

c) Make a scale model of each object out of cardboard or heavy paper.

4.7 **14.** A bricklayer is building a garden wall with bricks 90 mm by 230 mm by 70 mm, as shown.

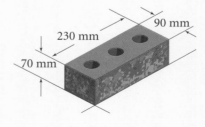

- The mortar joints will be 9.5 mm thick. No mortar is required at the bottom, but there will be mortar on the top course to attach a decorative stone cap 10 cm thick.

a) Calculate the number of bricks needed for a wall 10 m long, which extends approximately 1.5 m above the ground, including the cap.

b) Explain why it may not be possible to make the wall exactly 1.5 m high using full bricks.

15. On grid paper, use butt joints and "boards" 1 cm wide to produce each shape.

    i) a rectangle 15 cm by 16 cm on the outside

    ii) a rectangle 12 cm by 9 cm on the inside

16. Calculate the outside dimensions of a cylindrical concrete well. The concrete top and sides are 10 cm thick, the inside radius is 34 cm, and the inside height is 10 m.

17. Produce a tube from cardboard that bends at an angle of 168°.

18. a) Draw a scale diagram of the pattern for a cylindrical can with each finished dimension if the seam allowance is 5 mm.

	Height (cm)	Diameter (cm)
i)	35	7.5
ii)	20.25	9.5
iii)	10.75	14

    b) The top and bottom of a can must also be welded. For each cylinder in part a, draw a scale diagram of the top using a seam allowance of 5 mm.

Maintaining Your Mastery

Review the algebraic skills that form part of the college admission process.

1. Solve.

    a) $4x = 12$ **b)** $-5y = 20$ **c)** $8y = 22$

    d) $x + 7 = 3 - x$ **e)** $3p - 8 = 7p + 12$ **f)** $6m - 1 = m + 3$

2. Expand and simplify.

    a) $3(b + 1)$ **b)** $4x(x - 2)$ **c)** $-3q(2q - 3)$

    d) $4w(w^2 + 3w - 1)$ **e)** $-7(k - 3) + 5(k + 2) - 9(k - 1)$

3. Factor.

    a) $5x - 15$ **b)** $-3z + 12$ **c)** $7x^2y^2 + 14x^2y - 4xy$

    d) $(w^2 + 6w + 8)$ **e)** $(m^2 - 6m + 9)$ **f)** $(h^2 - 4h - 21)$

4. Solve.

    a) $3x^2 + 7x + 2 = 0$ **b)** $2x^2 - 9x - 5 = 0$ **c)** $5x^2 - 13x + 6 = 0$

1. **Knowledge/Understanding**
   a) Explain, with reference to the size of the interior angles, why you cannot cover a floor without gaps using only regular octagonal tiles.
   b) Explain, with reference to the size of the interior angles, why you can cover a floor without gaps using copies of any triangle.

2. **Communication**
   a) On grid paper, draw a right-angled triangle with acute angles 30° and 60°. Use the triangle and the idea of a point at infinity to create a perspective diagram of a triangular prism.
   b) Explain why the triangle at the other end of the prism also has angles of 30°, 60°, and 90°.

3. Use the grid method to enlarge the object by a factor of 3.

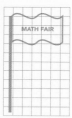

4. **Application** Draw front, left, right, and rear views of the following block sculpture, using 1-cm by 1-cm graph paper. You may find it helpful to build the model with blocks first.

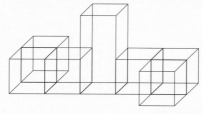

5. Design a pattern for a cylindrical box with a lid. The pattern must use no more than 2 sheets of 8.5" by 11" paper. Edges can be taped. Cut out and assemble the box.

6. **Thinking/Inquiry/Problem Solving** Position the letters U, B, E on this net so that, when folded into a cube, it will read CUBE as it is rotated forward.

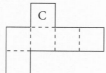

7. Design a scale diagram of a living area, a garden, a building, or similar space according to the listed specifications.

Specifications

1. At least 2 floor or object surfaces must be covered with geometric figures or symmetry patterns. For example, a section of flooring could be covered with a combination of octagonal and square tiles. You may choose to sketch these on a separate page instead of on your scale diagram.

2. On a separate diagram show 2 or more views of at least one 3-dimensional object such as a piece of furniture. Be sure to include information outlining the type of joins used, as well as the reasons for each join.

Presentation

Include with your scale diagram:

- A brief description of the covered floor of object surfaces, including the names of the shapes used, as well as information about the arrangement of the shapes
- Views of the 3-dimensional object with information about how the object is joined, and reasons for the joins

Be creative in your choices.

CUMULATIVE REVIEW

1. Solve each triangle. Round angles and lengths to the nearest tenth.
   a) $\triangle ABC$: $\angle B = 90°$, $\angle C = 30°$, $a = 3.7$ cm
   b) $\triangle DEF$: $\angle F = 36°$, $d = 6$ mm, $e = 7$ mm
   c) $\triangle KMN$: $\angle K = 46°$, $\angle M = 62°$, $n = 10.0$ m

2. Expand and simplify.
   a) $(x + 3)(x - 4)$
   b) $(3y + 1)(2y^2 - 5y + 1)$
   c) $(3x + 4)(2x - 1)$
   d) $2(y + 1)(y - 2) + (3y + 1)(2y + 4)$

3. Factor.
   a) $x^2 - 7x + 12$
   b) $4y^2 - 81$
   c) $4x^2 + 2x - 30$

4. Solve.
   a) $x^2 + x - 12 = 0$
   b) $10y^2 - 11y - 6 = 0$

5. Convert each measure. Round your answer to the nearest tenth where appropriate.
   a) 8 feet to inches
   b) 40 pounds to ounces
   c) 256 mm to inches
   d) 12 L to gallons
   e) 150 pounds to kilograms
   f) 80 miles to kilometres

6. Calculate each perimeter.
   a) a regular octagon with sides 9 feet
   b) a right triangle with hypotenuse 5 km and one leg 3 km

7. Calculate each surface area and volume.
   a) a rectangular prism with length 70 mm, height 120 mm, and width 30 mm
   b) a cone with radius 5 cm and height 8.5 cm

8. A cylinder with a radius of 2 m is cut out of a cube with side length 5 m. Determine the surface area and volume of the solid.

9. A rectangular deck, 15' by 10', is to be constructed using 1' by 8' by 2" lumber.
   a) What is the surface area of the deck?
   b) Assume there will be no gaps between the wood. How many pieces of wood are required to complete the project?
   c) What is the total volume of wood?

10. The walls and ceiling of a room require 2 coats of paint. The room is 14' by 20', and is $7\frac{1}{2}$' high. The window in the room is 2' by 4', and the door is $2\frac{3}{4}$' by $6\frac{3}{4}$'. How many gallons of paint are required if 1 gallon of paint covers 350 square feet?

11. Copy the table below. Write the numbers from 1–20 in the appropriate column.

Rotation Symmetry (other than 0° and 360°)	Reflection Symmetry	No Symmetry

12. Copy the figure, below left.
  a) Draw all possible lines of reflection symmetry.
  b) Determine all the possible angles of rotation symmetry other than 0° and 360°.

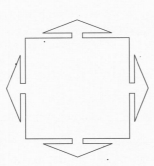

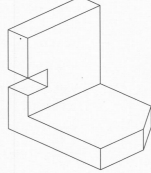

13. Provide a top, front, and side view of the isometric drawing, above right.

14. Complete each step on grid paper.
  a) Draw a square.
  b) Use the square and the idea of a point at infinity to create a perspective diagram of a cube.
  c) Use the grid method to enlarge your drawing by a factor of 2.

15. Create a scale diagram of a net for a box of cereal 42 cm high, 15 cm long, and 2 cm wide.

16. Construct a scale model of your box of cereal using only 2 sheets of $8\frac{1}{2}$" by 11" paper.

Planning an Apartment

Background

Many students in grade 12 are looking forward to moving into their own apartment. Before taking such a step, you need to ask yourself many questions.

- What kind of an apartment would you like?
- How large an apartment do you hope to have?
- What furniture would you like to buy for an apartment, and how much will it cost?
- What changes in the paint, wallpaper, or floor covering of an apartment might you make?

Recall, from Chapter 3, that Canada uses the metric system. However, the United States still uses the imperial system of measurement; so, many products used in building and interior design are given in imperial units.

Suppose a wall measures 4.2 m by 3.8 m. How many square feet is this?

Refer to page 226 for metric-imperial equivalencies.

We can solve this problem by using ratios to find each measurement in feet, then multiplying to determine the area.

> Convert 4.2 m to feet.
> Let x represent the number of feet.
> $$\frac{1}{x} = \frac{0.3048}{4.2}$$
> $x \doteq 13.78$ feet
> Similarly, we find that 3.8 m $\doteq$ 12.47 feet.
> The wall is 13.78 by 12.47 square feet.
> $A = 3.78 \times 12.47$
> $\quad = 171.84$ square feet

Another way to solve this problem is to multiply 4.2 m by 3.8 m to give 15.96 m^2, then divide this answer by 0.3048^2, to give 171.84 square feet, the same answer.

Suggested Group Size: Work in pairs

Suggested Materials:

Graphing calculators, grid paper, decorating magazines and catalogues, computer spreadsheet (optional), Internet access (optional)

Curriculum Expectations

By the end of *Explore*, *Research*, *Report* you will:

> Solve problems related to the perimeter and area of plane figures.

> Demonstrate accuracy and precision in working with metric measures.

> Demonstrate a working knowledge of the measurement of length and area in the imperial system, in relation to applications, for example design, and in construction.

> Perform required conversions between the imperial and the metric system, as necessary within projects and applications.

> Use calculators effectively to solve problems involving measurement, and judge the reasonableness of answers.

305

Planning an Apartment

1. Painting a Room

Suppose you decide to paint the walls of your apartment living room. The room is 5.7 m long, 3.5 m wide, and 2.4 m high.

a) Paint is usually sold in US-gallon and US-quart cans. If a gallon covers approximately 400 square feet, how many square feet will a quart cover?

b) If you need two coats of paint on the walls, how many cans of paint will you need?

c) If a gallon of paint is $23.99 and a quart is $9.99, how much will the paint cost? Remember to include the taxes.

2. Putting a Wallpaper Border around a Room

Use the dimensions of the room in exercise 1. Wallpaper border is sold in 5-yard rolls. How many rolls of wallpaper border are needed to put a border around the room?

3. Putting Carpet in a Room

Carpet is usually priced by the square foot or the square yard. Carpet comes in rolls of 12'. Suppose you decide to carpet the room in exercise 1.

If carpet costs $27.09 per square yard installed, how much will it cost to carpet the room? Include taxes.

4. Putting Vinyl Tiles in a Bathroom

You redo the bathroom floor (2 m × 1.75 m) with 8" tiles. If the tiles come in boxes of 12, how many boxes do you need?

5. Making a Scale Diagram

a) The scale on this diagram of a dining room is 1 cm to 0.5 m.

   i) What are the dimensions of the room?

   ii) How wide is the door and the window?

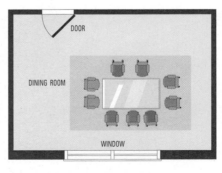

b) Make a scale diagram of your classroom.

   i) Measure the length and width of the room, and the width of the windows and doors.

   ii) Make a scale diagram of the room using the scale 1 cm = 1 m. Show the windows and doors. Repeat, using the scale 1 cm = 0.5 cm.

Now you are ready to design your dream apartment. Together, you and your partner can decide whether to plan a small apartment with one or two rooms, or something more lavish. Make a rough sketch of the rooms. Be sure to include a bathroom, a kitchen or kitchen area, and closets. To complete the activities described below, you may decide to divide the responsibilities between an interior designer and a painter/decorator.

Interior Designer – Your job includes:

- making an accurate diagram of the apartment—drawn to scale
- furnishing the apartment
- using a spreadsheet or chart to keep track of the costs of furnishing and decorating the apartment

Painter/Decorator – Your job includes:

- visiting home improvement, furniture, or decorating stores
- choosing colours and getting swatches or pictures of paint, wallpaper, carpeting, and tile
- completing the exercises in *Explore*, page 306
- calculating the costs of the decorating which you plan to do

Complete exercises 1–7.

1. Designing the Apartment

a) Decide on a scale that is large enough for you to clearly show all the features of your apartment, including the height of the walls, windows, and doors. Show placement of furniture and an audio system on your diagram.

b) Make a scale diagram of the apartment. Show the dimensions of all rooms. Refer to home improvement and decorating books and magazines for ideas on how to make a professional-looking diagram. For example, kitchens and bathrooms are often shown with a grid pattern to indicate tiling. You may decide to finalize the measurements of the rooms after you have chosen your furniture. All measurements should be metric.

2. Choosing the Furniture for Your Apartment

a) Make a list of the furniture you will need. You may wish to consider items such as lamps, an audio system or home entertainment centre. Make sure you have measurements and prices for everything you will need. Visit local stores and choose your furniture. You can refer to home decorating magazines, books, and the Internet for ideas. You can also get ideas from your own home, or from friends and relatives.

b) Begin a spreadsheet or *cost sheet* to keep track of all costs. Be sure to include descriptions of the furniture and materials you choose.

3. Wallpapering a Room

a) Choose at least one room to be wallpapered.

b) If possible, visit a local home improvement store and discuss with store personnel the type of wallpaper that would be appropriate for your room. Ask for prices and a swatch of a wallpaper that you like.

c) The dimensions of the room from your scale diagram will determine how many rolls of wallpaper to buy. Determine the total cost of the wallpaper, including the taxes.

4. Painting a Room

a) Choose at least one room to be painted.

b) Visit a local store and ask store personnel for advice to help you decide on the type and colour of paint. Ask for paint colour swatches and prices.

c) Using the dimensions of the room from your scale diagram, show the calculations that will determine how much paint to buy. Determine the total cost of the paint, including taxes, and add it to your cost sheet.

5. Carpeting a Room

a) Plan on carpeting at least one room in your apartment.

b) Visit a local carpet store to get ideas for types and colours of carpet. Remember that even though your room is not 12' wide, you will probably have to buy a 12-foot wide piece of carpet.

c) The dimensions of the room from your scale diagram will determine how much carpet to buy. Determine the total cost of the carpet, including the taxes. Show your calculations.

6. Tiling a Room

a) Choose a room to be tiled. This may be your bathroom or kitchen.

b) Visit a local home improvement store for ideas about the types, colours, and sizes of tile. Exercise 4 in the *Explore* section used 8-inch vinyl tiles, but you may decide to choose another size or type. Obtain information about cost.

c) Use the dimensions of your room to determine how much tile you need to purchase. Determine the amount and cost of the tile, including the taxes. Show your calculations.

7. Completing Your Apartment Plans

a) Consolidate your findings. Complete your scale diagram. Show the measurements of each room and the placement of all furniture. Research books or magazines to make your apartment attractive.

b) Collect all the calculations you have done, as well as the pictures and samples of materials you have used for your report.

Report

Make a portfolio of the work you have completed planning your apartment. Include:

- your answers to the exercises in the *Explore* section
- the rough sketch of the apartment layout
- the scale diagram you have made, showing all features, including furniture placement
- wallpaper and paint swatches, and pictures or drawings of the furniture and audio equipment you have bought
- your completed *cost sheet*
- a detailed report on what you have learned in planning your apartment

Present your apartment plans to the class. Show your scale diagram, describe particular features of the apartment, and explain why you have designed the apartment the way you have.

5 Sampling

Curriculum Expectations

By the end of this chapter, you will:

> Determine appropriate methods for collecting, storing, and retrieving, from primary or secondary sources, data involving one and two variables.

> Design questionnaires for gathering data through surveys, giving consideration to possible sources of bias.

> Demonstrate an understanding of the distinction between the terms *population* and *sample*.

> Choose from and apply a variety of sampling techniques.

> Represent data in appropriate graphical forms, using technology.

> Construct a scatter plot to represent data, using technology.

> Formulate extending questions related to the conclusion reached in the investigation of a problem or an issue.

> Communicate the process used and the conclusions reached in the investigation of a problem or an issue, using appropriate mathematical forms.

> Make and justify statements about a population on the basis of sample data.

> Explain the use and misuse in the media of graphs and commonly used statistical terms and expressions.

> Assess the validity of conclusions made on the basis of statistical studies, by analysing possible sources of bias in the studies.

> Explain the meaning, and the use in the media, of indices based on surveys.

Necessary Skills

1 Review: Frequency Tables

When we collect a set of data, it may contain a wide range of numbers. To present the data clearly, we group the data and display them in a frequency table or histogram.

Here are some points to consider when you group data.

- All the intervals should be the same width.
- There should be between 5 and 20 intervals. The exact number will depend on the type of data.
- There should be no gaps between the intervals.

To choose an appropriate interval width, calculate the range. This is the difference between the maximum and minimum values. Then divide the range by 5 and by 20. The interval width should be between these values.

Example

These are the final mathematics marks for a class of grade 12 students. Group these data in a frequency table.

73, 34, 12, 63, 42, 65, 23, 74, 85, 60, 80, 56, 64, 64, 74, 21, 54, 56, 64, 76, 78, 80, 50, 45, 85, 66, 67, 65, 75, 25

Solution

The maximum value is 85. The minimum value is 12. The range is $85 - 12 = 73$.

$$\frac{73}{5} = 14.6 \qquad \frac{73}{20} = 3.65$$

A suitable interval width between 3.65 and 14.6 is 10. Since the minimum value is 12, the first interval will be 10–20. Set up a table like the one on the following page.

Make a tally mark in the Tally column for each data value in each interval. Data values that occur on a boundary belong in the higher interval. For example, a mark of 60 belongs in the 60–70 interval.

Count up the tally marks and enter the frequency.

Interval	Tally	Frequency
10–20	|	1
20–30	|||	3
30–40	|	1
40–50	||	2
50–60	||||	4
60–70	⫴⫴ ||||	9
70–80	⫴⫴ |	6
80–90	||||	4

Exercises

1. Suggest an appropriate interval width for each set of data.

   a) Data were collected on the maximum monthly temperature each month for 2 years. The maximum temperature recorded was 35°C and the minimum was 4°C.

   b) Data were collected on the prices of 30 different styles of running shoes. The maximum price was $145 and the minimum price was $56.

   c) Data were collected on the lengths in centimetres of 100 different bolts. The maximum length was 5.60 cm and the minimum was 2.44 cm.

2. Copy the table below. Group these data into the table.

   3.2, 5.4, 11.2, 1.3, 6.4, 7.0, 8.0, 4.4, 6.0, 8.1, 6.0, 4.2, 7.0, 9.8, 6.8, 3.9, 2.0, 4.7, 5.0, 5.5, 7.7, 8.2, 11.4, 11.8, 2.0, 1.8

Interval	Tally	Frequency
0–2		
2–4		
4–6		
6–8		
8–10		
10–12		

2 Review: Graphing Data

Data are frequently displayed as graphs. Three types of graphs are bar graphs, histograms, and circle graphs.

- We use a bar graph when the data are *discrete* (counted). For example, we would use a bar graph to show data on the numbers of oranges in different-sized crates.

- We use a histogram when the data are *continuous* (measured). For example, we would use a histogram to graph data on the lengths of different pieces of lumber.

- We use a circle graph to show how something is broken into parts. For example, we would use a circle graph to display data on how the government spends our tax dollars.

Example 1

Bozena collected these data on the number of students in her class born in each season.

Spring: 12   Summer: 8   Autumn: 9   Winter: 3

Choose an appropriate graph and use it to display these data.

Solution

These data are discrete. Use a bar graph.

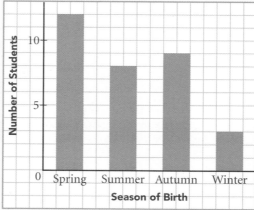

Example 2   An 80-kg load of recyclables contains these materials:

         Paper: 40 kg   Plastic: 8 kg   Other: 32 kg

Display these data in an appropriate graph.

Solution

These data can be displayed in a circle graph or a bar graph. We will use a circle graph.

There are 360° in a circle. Find the number of degrees in each segment.

     Paper: $\frac{40}{80} \times 360° = 180°$

     Plastic: $\frac{8}{80} \times 360° = 36°$

     Other: $\frac{32}{80} \times 360° = 144°$

Use compasses to draw the circle
and a protractor to draw the graph.

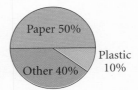

Example 3   This frequency table shows the time in minutes it took some athletes to complete a 5-km run.

Choose an appropriate graph and use it to display these data.

Interval	Frequency
12–14	1
14–16	3
16–18	5
18–20	7
20–22	2
22–24	1

Solution

These data are continuous. Use a histogram. The lowest value of the lowest interval is 12. Use a horizontal scale from 12 to 24.

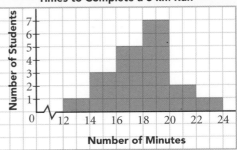

Exercises

1. These data represent the total points in the 2000–2001 NHL hockey season for 4 players on the Ottawa Senators. Choose an appropriate graph and use it to display these data.

Player	Total Points
Hossa	75
McEachern	72
Smyth	70
Yashin	88

2. The heights, in centimetres, of students in a grade 11 class are given below.

165, 183, 196, 163, 176, 156, 178, 180, 158, 184, 203, 159, 168, 171, 185, 186, 162, 167, 173, 192, 188, 182, 174, 161, 166, 189, 182, 183, 200, 181

a) Copy and complete this table.

Interval	Frequency
155–160	
160–165	
165–170	
170–175	
175–180	
180–185	
185–190	
190–195	
195–200	
200–205	

b) Use the table to draw an appropriate graph.

c) What is the most frequent range of heights in the class?

3 Review: Drawing Scatter Plots and Lines of Best Fit

Sometimes we are not interested in how often a number occurs; instead, we want to examine its relationship to a second number. For example, we may want to compare the heights and masses of a group of people, or we may want to investigate how the height of a ball thrown in the air changes over time. To display such data, we use a *scatter plot* — a series of points plotted from a set of ordered pairs.

If the data appear to be linear, we can draw a *line of best fit* to represent the data. A line of best fit is a line that passes as close as possible to a set of plotted points. When drawn by hand, more than one line of best fit is possible.

Example

Simeon records the temperature outside his house every hour from 1:00 P.M. to 10:00 P.M. Here are his data; times are expressed using the 24-h clock:

Time	Temperature (°C)
13:00	20
14:00	21
15:00	21
16:00	19
17:00	18
18:00	18
19:00	17
20:00	15
21:00	14
22:00	12

Display these data in a scatter plot. Draw a line of best fit for the data.

Necessary Skills

Solution

Use a horizontal scale from 12:00 to 23:00 and a vertical scale from 10°C to 22°C. Use a clear ruler to draw a line that passes as closely as possible to all the points on the graph.

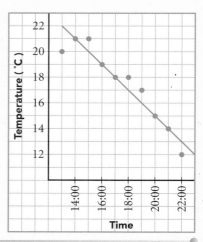

Exercises

1. Data are collected on the heights in centimetres and the ages in years for 10 students.

Age (years)	14	14	16	18	19	17	18	15	13	18
Height (cm)	160	190	183	194	176	183	203	172	148	151

   a) Display these data in a scatter plot.

   b) Does there appear to be a relationship between age and height? Explain.

   c) Draw a line of best fit for these data.

2. These data were collected for shoe size and mathematics mark for 8 students.

Shoe Size	11	7	$8\frac{1}{2}$	10	13	6	$9\frac{1}{2}$	9
Mark	72	57	81	57	64	80	70	88

   a) Display these data in a scatter plot.

   b) Do you expect a relationship between shoe size and mathematics mark? Explain.

   c) Draw a line of best fit for these data.

   d) Is there a relationship between shoe size and mathematics mark? Explain.

People collect data because they need information. Often, instead of surveying the entire *population*, a small portion, called a *sample*, is consulted. Sampling is also used for product testing. For example, a manufacturer wishes to test the lifespan of its light bulbs. It cannot test each light bulb, because testing destroys the product.

Sampling is used to gain information about a population by testing or observing only a portion of it. A population may be composed of people or items.

Discuss

Why may an entire population not be surveyed?

A *census* is a survey of the entire population. Statistics Canada conducts a census every five years. During the census, information is collected about every person living in Canada. A sample that comprises 20% of the population is given a longer, more detailed survey to complete.

A census is one example of data collected from a *primary source*. The most popular methods of collecting data from a primary source include:

- personal and telephone interviews
- surveys
- observation and measurements
- product testing

Suppose we wish to collect data about household income in 1900. It is not possible to gather these data from primary sources, so we must use *secondary sources*. Secondary sources of data include Statistics Canada, reference books, the media, the Internet, and publications from polling firms.

TAKE NOTE

Some Survey Terms

Population: the entire group of items or individuals being considered

Sample: a small group of items or individuals chosen to represent the total population

Primary source data: data collected directly by the person or group who will use the information

Secondary source data: data that have already been collected and are made available to the public

What Percent of Children Are Only Children?

1. Use your class as a sample of the school population.

    a) Count the number of students who are only children.

    b) Count the number of students in the class.

    c) Write the number of only children as a percent of the number of students in the class.

2. **Σ-STAT** If you have Internet access, you can use E-Stat from Statistics Canada to determine the percent of families in Ontario with only one child. The E-Stat website address is: http://estat.statcan.ca Get your school's user name and password and instructions on how to proceed from your teacher.

3. How do the results for your class compare with the results for Ontario? Suggest reasons for any differences.

4. Why might you use Statistics Canada data or other secondary data rather than your own sample?

Example 1 Identify the population about which the information is sought.

    a) The management team at a shopping mall in Sudbury wants to know how to attract more people between the ages of 18 and 24 to the mall.

    b) A soft drink bottler wants to determine the actual volume of pop in 1-L bottles.

    c) The school cafeteria wants to determine which items should be added to the menu.

    d) A polling firm wishes to determine which political party is expected to win the next federal election.

Solution

    a) People from Sudbury between the ages of 18 and 24

    b) All 1-L bottles of pop bottled by this company

    c) All students who purchase their lunch at the school cafeteria

    d) All Canadians over the age of 18 who are eligible to vote

---

When a sample is not representative of a population, we say the sample is *biased*. For example, if the population consists of 14 girls and 15 boys, a sample of this population should have approximately equal numbers of girls and boys. A sample of 7 girls only would be a biased sample.

Example 2 In each case, state how the sample may be biased.

a) To determine which team Canadians expect to win the Stanley Cup, researchers conducted a survey of 1000 people selected from a Barrie telephone book.

b) To assess the opinions of the Canadian people on an increase in funding for health care, researchers counted the number of callers for and against to a radio call-in show.

c) To determine what legal driving age is preferred by Canadian teenagers, researchers interviewed 2000 high school students from across Canada.

d) To determine how long a brand of batteries will last, the last 1000 batteries of a particular production run are removed and tested.

Solution

a) Since the opinions of Canadians are required, a survey restricted to people in Barrie may produce a bias toward the local team, the Toronto Maple Leafs.

b) Since the people surveyed were required to phone in, there is a bias toward the members of the population who listen to that radio station. Also, people with strong opinions about this issue are more likely to call in.

c) There does not appear to be any bias in this survey.

d) There may be a bias since all 1000 batteries are taken from the same production run.

A survey is *reliable* if the results can be duplicated in another survey. A biased sample may not produce reliable results. For example, a researcher asks 100 spectators at a football game to name their favourite sport. This sample is biased. Spectators at a football game are more likely to choose football as their favourite sport. A second researcher poses the same question to 100 randomly selected people at a shopping mall. This sample is not biased. These surveys would likely produce different results.

Discuss
Explain why a biased sample may not produce reliable results.

A survey is *valid* if the results represent the entire population. Sonia wants to find out what percent of students in her school have a driver's licence. She polls her class and determines that 47% of the students have a driver's licence. Sonia concludes that approximately 47% of students in her school have a driver's licence. Yet according to office records, 28% of the students in the school have a driver's licence. Sonia's poll is not valid because her sample result does not represent the school population.

Discuss

Explain the difference between a reliable result and a valid result.

Example 3

In each case, state whether the results are reliable and/or valid. Explain.

a) A set of bathroom scales consistently indicate a mass that is 2 kg greater than the true mass.

b) The results of a phone-in survey conducted in Calgary show that 80% of residents are in favour of having a Formula One race through the streets of the city.

Solution

a) The results are reliable because the scales consistently indicate the same mass for the same object. The results are not valid because the measured mass is always 2 kg greater than the true mass.

b) For reliability, the sample of the population surveyed should be representative of all the people living in Calgary. This may not be the case with a phone-in survey. Only people who are interested in the race will respond by phone. Also, the results may not be valid if the number of people surveyed was too small. For example, the results from a sample size of 5 may not be an accurate indication of the result for the whole population of Calgary.

5.1 Exercises

A

1. Identify the population you would sample for an opinion on each topic.

a) VIA rail fares

b) Provincial tax rebates

c) The cost of daycare in Ontario

2. Identify the population you would sample for an opinion on each topic.
   a) The availability of student parking at urban high schools
   b) The quality of food served in your school's cafeteria
   c) Fees students pay to be members of athletic teams

3. In each case, state whether the source of data is primary or secondary.
   a) Michel surveys students in his class about their favourite music.
   b) Susan used information from a national newspaper to determine the top ten movies this past weekend.
   c) An automobile manufacturer surveys local car dealerships to determine the number of sport utility vehicles sold.
   d) To determine which type of vehicle is most popular, Kevin examines Statistics Canada data on automobiles.

B

4. **Knowledge/Understanding** Would you use a primary source or a secondary source of data to answer each question? Explain.
   a) Have the number of marriages in your town increased or decreased over the last 50 years?
   b) Which political party is expected to win the next provincial election?
   c) What is the favourite car colour of teachers in your school?
   d) What is the favourite car colour in Canada?

5. **Application** In each situation, explain why you would collect data from a sample instead of the population.
   a) To find the average age when drivers got their licences
   b) To find the number of hours a battery will last
   c) To find the average volume of milk in a 2-L carton
   d) To find the average mass of a full-term, newborn baby

6. Refer to exercise 5. Would you use a primary or secondary source of data in each situation? Explain.

7. Explain what it means when the results of a survey of a sample of a population are valid.

8. A magazine asks its readers for their opinions on the spending habits of teenagers.
   a) Do you think the results of the survey would be valid? Explain.
   b) Do you think the results are reliable? Explain.

9. Describe the advantages and disadvantages of each method of gathering primary data. Describe a situation in which each method may be used to collect data.

   a) Personal or telephone interviews

   b) Written surveys

   c) Observation of the population

   d) Measurement taking

   e) Product testing

10. **Communication** Explain the difference between a population and a sample.

    a) What are the advantages and disadvantages of surveying a sample of the population?

    b) What are the advantages and disadvantages of surveying the population?

 11. Search E-Stat, the Internet, or the library for data on the average number of people in a household in Ontario. Describe the process you used to find these data.

12. The students' council wanted to find out if there was enough support from students for a talent contest. The council surveyed students in two grade 12 classes.

    a) Would the results of this survey be valid? Explain.

    b) Would the results be reliable? Explain.

13. **Thinking/Inquiry/Problem Solving** Collect data on the height and scoring averages of at least 20 professional or high school basketball players.

    a) Create a scatter plot of height against points per game. Draw a line of best fit.

    b) Can a player's height be used to predict her or his scoring average? Explain.

    c) Could the team's success be predicted by the heights of the players on the team? Explain.

14. Visit your school library or your town's public library. Research the sources of secondary data that are available. What types of secondary data do you have access to? What organizations collected the data?

Selecting a Sample

A critical part of survey design is the method of sample selection. A carefully selected sample of 1000 people can be used to represent the Canadian population. For the results of a survey to be valid, the sample must be *representative* of the population. This means the sample must contain the same characteristics as the population in the same proportion. The sample must also be *random*; every member of the population must have an equal chance of being selected.

TAKE NOTE

Samples

- A sample is representative of the population if it contains the same characteristics in the same proportion.
- A sample is random if every member of the population has an equal chance of being selected.

Many sampling methods use a list of random numbers. This is a list of digits selected in such a way that each digit has an equal chance of being selected. Here are some methods for generating a list of random numbers.

- Put slips of paper with the digits 0 to 9 in a box. Draw a slip of paper, record the digit that appears on it, return the paper to the box, and repeat the procedure until you have enough random numbers.
- Use a telephone directory. Turn to any white page of a telephone directory. Without looking, put a pencil point on a number. Write down the last digit of this number. Repeat until you have enough random numbers.

- Use the randInt command on a TI-83 graphing calculator. To choose an integer between 0 and 9, enter [MATH] [◄] 5 to display randInt(. Then press 0 [,] 9 [ )] [ENTER] to display a random number. Record the result. Press [ENTER] repeatedly until you have enough random numbers. Your screen should look similar to this.

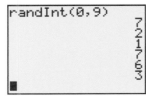

Here are some common sampling methods.

Simple Random Sample

Every member of the population has an equal chance of being selected. For example, a sample of 20 students is required from a school population of 865 students. Assign a distinct number between 1 and 865 to each member of the population. Then generate a list of 20 random numbers between 1 and 865. Eliminate the duplicates. Select the members of the population that correspond to these random numbers. This is the most reliable sampling method.

Discuss

Is it possible for a random sample to be biased? Explain.

Systematic Sample

Every nth member of the population is selected. For example, to maintain quality control, a company tests every 10th item from a production line.

Cluster Sample

Every member of a randomly chosen subgroup of the population is part of the sample. For example, the school board selects one of its secondary schools at random. Then every student within that school is in the sample. This method assumes that each cluster contains members who were randomly selected.

Stratified Random Sample

The population is divided into subgroups. A random sample is selected from each subgroup proportional to the size of that subgroup. For example, a middle school has 220 students in grade 7 and 320 students in grade 8. There are a total of 220 + 320, or 540 students. Determine the number of students from each grade to include in a sample of 20 students.

Grade 7 students

$$\frac{220}{540} \times 20 = 8.148$$

Grade 8 students

$$\frac{320}{540} \times 20 = 11.852$$

Round the answers to the nearest whole number; ensure the numbers add to 20. Eight grade 7 students and twelve grade 8 students would be selected at random.

Convenience Sample

Convenient members or subgroups of the population are chosen. For example, your friends, teammates, or family are surveyed.

Self-Selected Sample

Only volunteers participate in this sample. For example, a magazine publishes a questionnaire. Only those interested will complete and return the questionnaire.

Discuss
Which sampling methods are most likely to be biased? Explain.

Investigation

Frequency of Letters in the English Language

Work with a partner.

1. Which 5 letters do you think are used most frequently in the English language?

2. Decide how to select a random sample of 50 words in the English language. Select the sample.

3. Determine the numbers of the different letters in your 50 words. Copy and complete this frequency table.

Letter	Tally	Frequency
A		
B		
C		
X		
Y		
Z		

4. a) Which 5 letters occurred most often in your sample?

   b) How do your results in part a compare with your answer to exercise 1?

5. Compare your answers with those of other students. Which 5 letters occur most frequently in the English language?

6. Use the table you completed in exercise 3. What other question(s) does your analysis of the data lead you to ask? Can you use the data you collected to answer this question? If not, describe the information you need to answer this question.

7. Write to explain how you selected your random sample and the conclusions you reached about the frequency of letters in the English language.

In each case,

    i) State the population about which the information is sought.

    ii) Name the sampling method.

    iii) Explain whether the sample is random and/or biased.

a) Researchers wish to determine which team Canadians think will win the World Series this season. They send out questionnaires to 100 companies chosen randomly from a list of Canadian businesses. Anyone who works at the company can complete the questionnaire.

b) To determine which candidate students at a local high school will support for Student Council president, you use random numbers to select one class from each grade, then use random numbers again to pick 5 students from each class to complete a survey.

c) To determine the strength of aluminum extension ladders produced by a company, every 100th ladder is tested.

Solution

a) **i)** The population is all Canadians.

    ii) This is a convenience sample.

    iii) It is not a random sample. It excludes many groups in the population, such as farmers, homemakers, or senior citizens. The sample is biased.

b) **i)** The population is all students at this high school.

    ii) This is a stratified random sample.

    iii) The sample is random and representative of the population. The sample is not biased.

c) **i)** The population is all aluminum extension ladders produced by this company.

    ii) This is a systematic sample.

    iii) The sample is not random, but should be representative of the population. The sample is not biased.

Once data have been collected, we need to store the raw data so we can refer to them later. We can store data using pencil and paper, a spreadsheet, or lists on a graphing calculator.

Discuss

List the advantages and disadvantages of each method of storing data.

A

✓ **1.** A suggestion box is placed in the school hallway to obtain students' reactions to a new school policy.

a) What population is being surveyed?

b) What type of sample is this?

c) Is this sample biased? Explain.

✓ **2. Knowledge/Understanding** The computer system of a large hospital contains the records for 60 000 patients. The records are numbered sequentially from 1 to 60 000. The hospital administrator wishes to determine patients' level of satisfaction with hospital food. For her sample, she selects the records numbered 100, 200, 300, and so on.

a) What is the population for this survey?

b) What type of sampling was used?

c) Will this sample be representative of the population? Explain.

3. Explain why a sample obtained from approachable people, such as friends and family members, is not representative of the population.

4. A television program chooses its Movie of the Week according to the votes cast by viewers. They phone one of two 1-900 phone numbers at $0.75 per call. Is this a random sample? Explain.

5. Identify the segment of the population who would strongly bias a survey on each topic.

a) Whether fur from animals should be made into coats

b) Whether people should be allowed to keep exotic animals as pets

6. To provide quality control, a supervisor inspects a random sample of items from the assembly line. The items are taken from the first hour's production each day. Is this sample representative of the population? Explain.

B

7. Many surveys gather information from 500 to 1000 respondents.

a) Do you think these numbers are adequate for valid results? Explain.

b) What factors do you think should be considered when deciding on the size of the sample?

8. Drug manufacturers frequently use young and middle-aged men in their clinical trials.

   a) Give reasons why women, children, and senior citizens may be excluded from clinical trials.

   b) Will the results of clinical trials that exclude women, children, and senior citizens be valid? Explain.

9. Generate a set of ten random numbers from 0 to 9.

   a) Compare your set of numbers with that of another student. Are there any similarities or patterns? Explain.

   b) Do your numbers appear to be random? Explain.

10. Application

   a) Generate a list of random numbers. Use it to select a random sample of 5 students from your class.

   b) Compare your sample to a classmate's sample. Explain any differences.

11. Communication Describe how you might obtain each sample.

   a) A simple random sample from the school population

   b) A systematic sample of cars in a parking lot

   c) A cluster sample of residents in a city

   d) A stratified random sample of strawberries in a field

12. The school cafeteria would like to introduce a new vegetarian pizza. Which sampling technique would you recommend to determine which of 3 possible toppings should be used? Explain.

13. Suppose you plan to conduct a survey of your community or city.

   a) Describe how to select a cluster sample of this population.

   b) Describe how to select a stratified random sample of this population.

14. When buying wine, a person examines a small amount of the wine for bouquet, flavour, and taste. Is a mouthful a suitable random sample? Explain.

15. Which sampling methods are most likely to be used by a professional polling firm? Explain.

16. Describe how a manufacturer of calculators can use random sampling to maintain quality control.

17. Prior to the 1936 U.S. Presidential elections, the *Literary Digest*, a national magazine in America, conducted a poll to find out who people would vote for. The magazine sent out 10 million questionnaires to its readers and received 2.3 million responses. This poll predicted that Franklin Roosevelt would lose and get 43% of the vote. In fact, Roosevelt won with 62% of the vote.

    a) Only magazine subscribers were surveyed. How did this affect the sampling?

    b) Only 23% of people surveyed responded. How did this affect the sampling?

    c) Another pollster, George Gallup, polled only 50 000 randomly selected Americans. He correctly predicted the election results. Explain how this could have happened.

18. On May 26, 2001, the article "Bid official finds poll just too good" appeared in *The Globe and Mail*. Part of the article is reproduced below.

> Bob Richardson knows better than most people that you can't believe the results of every poll — even when it's news you want to believe.
>
> Richardson is the chief operating officer of the Toronto 2008 Olympic Bid committee and vice-president of professional pollster, Ipsos-Reid.
>
> When he learned yesterday of a poll that rated Toronto far in front of Paris and Bejing in the race for the 2008 Olympics, Richardson was the first to shoot it down.
>
> An ongoing Internet poll begun Tuesday on the Web site of Time magazine's European edition, asks which city should host the 2008 Olympics and gives Toronto the runaway lead. Of 1700 votes cast by yesterday afternoon, Toronto had pulled in 76.82 percent, Paris is far back at 14.17 percent and Beijing trails with 9 percent.

    a) Why would Richardson dismiss the results of the poll? Explain what is wrong with the poll.

    b) Describe how to select a sample that would be representative of the population for this survey.

    c) A survey of 32 sports editors in 28 countries picked Bejing to win. Is this sample more representative of the population? Explain.

19. Suppose you were asked to sample the population about an issue that may be controversial. Examples might include human cloning or using agricultural land for housing. Is it possible to obtain an unbiased sample? Explain.

20. The population of a grade 9–12 high school is given in the table.

Grade	9	10	11	12
Number of Students	400	450	350	300

The school council wishes to conduct a survey to determine the number of hours of television students watch per week.

a) How would you advise the council to choose a sample of the school population?

b) Explain why you chose that method rather than any other.

✓ **21. Thinking/Inquiry/Problem Solving**

a) Collect data on any one of these topics. Describe the population you are studying, determine the size of sample required, and select a representative sample.

   i) The most popular brand of toothpaste used by students in your school

   ii) The average mass of backpacks or track bags (and their contents) carried by students in your school

   iii) The average number of letters in words in the English language

   iv) The percent of students in your school who work at a part-time job during the school year

   v) The average circumference of a basketball

b) Store these data. You will use them again in Section 5.4.

c) Write to explain how you selected your random sample and explain the conclusions you reached.

d) Does your analysis of the data lead you to ask any other questions about the population you studied? If you can answer these questions using the data you gathered, do so. If not, describe the information you need to answer these questions.

5.3 Survey Design

The two most important factors that affect the validity of a survey are:

- the sample of the population that was surveyed; and
- the design of the questionnaire used to collect the data.

In Section 5.2, we studied methods of selecting an unbiased sample. In this section, we will examine the steps involved with designing a high-quality questionnaire.

The first step in designing a questionnaire is to identify the population. This allows us to select a representative sample and to direct our questions to that population. Next, we need to identify the purpose of the survey so we can ask questions that will give us the information we need. Finally, we must design the questionnaire itself. Here are some points to consider when composing the questions:

- Decide whether the questions will be open, closed, or a combination. An *open question* is answered by the respondent in her or his own words. For example: "How should the Ontario government spend any budget surplus?"

  A *closed question* is answered by checking a box or circling one of several given responses. For example:

  How should the Ontario government spend any budget surplus? Check the category you think is most important.

  _____ Reduce taxes   _____ Increase spending on education

  _____ Increase spending   _____ Reduce the provincial debt
         on health care
  _____ Other _____

- Be sure the questions are clear and precise. The question "What is your income?" is not precise. A better way to ask for this information is to say: "What was the amount of total income you reported on line 150 of your 2000 tax return?"

- Avoid leading questions. A leading question suggests an answer; for example: "Do you agree that free trade has been good for the Canadian economy?" This question would be better worded: "Do you think free trade has had a positive, negative, or neutral effect on the Canadian economy?"

- Avoid words that may raise strong emotions. For example: "Irresponsible dog owners should not be allowed to exercise their dogs in public parks. Circle one.   Agree   Disagree"

- Decide whether the respondents are to remain anonymous.

What are some advantages and disadvantages of asking open questions? closed questions?

Give some reasons why respondents might want to remain anonymous.

Investigation 1 **Evaluating Survey Questions**

Work with a partner.

1. Select a random sample of at least 20 people from the school population.

2. Ask each person in the sample to answer these questions. Ask the questions <u>exactly</u> as they are written; do not explain or clarify the questions. Carefully record the answers.

   a) "How large is this mathematics textbook?" (Show your mathematics textbook as you ask this question.)

   b) How many hours of television do you watch?

   c) Do you think students are overburdened and the amount of homework assigned should be reduced?

   d) What is your favourite sport? Choose one.

   | Hockey | Golf | Baseball | Lacrosse |

3. Examine the answers you got for each question. Did the respondents interpret the questions in the same way? Compare your results with those of your classmates.

4. Describe the problems with each question.

5. Rewrite each question so it will produce reliable results. Ask each person in the sample to answer the new survey questions and record their answers.

6. How do your results from exercise 5 compare to your results from exercise 2? Explain.

In *Investigation 1*, you examined how poorly designed survey questions can give unreliable results. In *Investigation 2*, you will design your own questionnaire and survey a sample of the school population.

 Investigation 2

Using a Sample to Survey a Population

Work in a group of 3 or 4 students.

1. Decide what you want to find out about your school population. Some possibilities include: favourite music group, favourite sport as a spectator or player, or how far students live from school.

2. Select a sample of students. Make sure the sample is random, not biased.

3. Design a questionnaire. Have all the students in your sample respond to the questionnaire.

4. Store the raw data.

5. Organize the data you gathered in a chart, a table, or a graph.

6. Write a report of your findings. Include the sampling method you used, your questionnaire, your data, and your conclusion.

7. What other conclusions can you reach about the population, other than the answer to the question posed? Explain.

8. Make a statement about the population based on your sample data. Justify your statement.

5.3 Exercises

 B

1. Describe some flaws in each survey question. Suggest an alternative question.

   a) A survey is conducted to find out whether students should be offered optional mathematics courses. The question asked was: "Do you like mathematics?"

   b) A survey is conducted to find out the mother tongues of students. The question asked was: "Which is your mother tongue?"
   Circle one: English   French

 2. A survey is conducted in a laundromat. People are asked what brand of detergent they buy. Another survey is conducted in the laundromat. People are asked what brand of detergent they are using. Do you think the two surveys will reach similar conclusions? Explain.

3. **Knowledge/Understanding** Describe some flaws in each survey question. Suggest an alternative question.

   a) A survey is conducted to find out whether residents of a town support an increase in their municipal taxes. The question asked was: "Do you think your municipal taxes are too high?"

   b) A survey is conducted to find out whether people in Ontario are willing to donate blood. The question asked was: "Have you ever donated blood?"

4. In the early 1990s, there was a debate in Ontario about whether stores should be allowed to open on Sundays.

   One survey question asked: "Should stores that want to open on Sunday be allowed to open on Sunday?"

   Another survey question asked: "Should the government make Sunday the one uniform day a week when most people do not have to work?"

   a) Is each survey question valid? Explain.

   b) What results would you expect from the responses to each question? Explain.

   c) Write an unbiased question that addresses the issue of Sunday shopping.

5. The people who run the school cafeteria want to find out which type of food or drink is most popular. A survey of students is conducted. The survey asks:

   "The last time you visited the cafeteria, what did you purchase?" Circle all that apply.

   Hamburger   Hot dog   French fries   Beverage   Other

   a) Is this question valid? Explain.

   b) Write an alternative question that would produce valid data.

6. The owner of the local pizza parlour asks customers to fill out a response card. It says: "Are you satisfied with the quality of our food and service? Yes or No."

   a) What information do you think the owner of the pizza parlour is seeking?

   b) Do you think she will get the information she needs from the responses? Explain.

   c) Write an alternative question or set of questions that would provide her with the required information.

7. The school librarian wants to know if the school library has the resources students need to complete their projects and assignments. He asks every student who comes into the library: "Were you satisfied with the level of service when you last visited the library? Yes or No."

a) Will the librarian get the information he needs from this survey? Explain.

b) Design a new question or set of questions that will give the librarian the information he requires.

8. Thinking/Inquiry/Problem Solving In 2001, the Ontario government proposed giving tax credits to parents whose children attend private schools. The *National Post* newspaper commissioned a poll to find out how many people were in favour. It found 54% of Ontarians were in favour of the tax credit. The Ontario Secondary School Teachers' Federation commissioned a similar poll. It found 67% of Ontarians were opposed to the tax credit.

One poll asked: "Will the current publicly-funded education system be hurt because of the money taken out of the public system? 1) Yes or 2) No"

The other poll asked: "Parents with children in independent schools should: (choose one) 1) Get some tax relief to help with tuition fees, or 2) Have to pay the full cost without any tax relief."

a) Match each question with the organization that posed it. Explain your choice.

b) Design an unbiased question that could be asked.

9. This is part of the survey used for the 14th annual *Maclean's* year-end poll conducted in November 1997:

How much do you agree or disagree with each of the following statements?

Strongly Agree	Somewhat Agree	Neither Agree nor Disagree	Somewhat Disagree	Strongly Disagree

i) Only a fool would turn a wallet they found with money in it over to the police.

ii) The next generation will probably not be as dedicated to hard work as were previous generations.

a) What do you think is the purpose of each question?

b) Do you think these questions are valid? Explain.

10. Communication Suppose you wish to use secondary data to answer a question about a population. Describe what you need to know about the methods used to collect the data before you can determine the quality of secondary data.

11. Application Choose one of these issues.

    A Should the school cafeteria be run by a franchise?

    B Should students be required to wear a uniform to school?

    C Should year-round schooling replace the current September to June model?

Design a survey to determine the opinions of your school population on the issue. You should include:

a) The question or questions you would ask

b) A description of how you would select an unbiased sample

c) A description of the steps you would take to conduct the survey

d) A description of how you plan to store the raw data

12. Choose one of these issues.

    A Should people have to pay user fees for health care?

    B Should high school students be required to volunteer in the community?

    C Should inline skaters be required by law to wear helmets and knee, elbow, and wrist protection?

Design a survey to determine the opinions of people in your city or region on the issue. You should include:

a) The question or questions you would ask

b) A description of how you would select an unbiased sample

c) A description of the steps you would take to conduct the survey

d) A description of how you plan to store the raw data

13. Decide what you want to find out about your classmates. Some possibilities include: their average age in years and months; the average number of siblings they have; or whether they were born in Ontario or elsewhere.

a) Design a clear, unbiased question that you can ask to gather the data you need.

b) Select an unbiased sample of the students in your class to respond to your question. Record their responses.

c) Store the raw data.

d) Organize the data you gathered. Use a tally chart, a table, a graph, or any other appropriate representation.

e) Write a report of your findings. Include the method of sample selection you used, the question you asked, your results, and your conclusion.

f) Is there another question that could be answered using the data you collected? Write the question and your answer.

1. Identify the population you would sample for an opinion on each topic.

   a) Building a new highway to bypass Metropolitan Toronto

   b) Increasing minimum wage

   c) Increasing property taxes in Burlington, Ontario

2. For each topic in exercise 1, describe how you would select a representative sample.

3. In each case, state whether the source of data is primary or secondary.

   a) Duan used data from the Canadian Real Estate Association to determine the average price of a house in Ottawa.

   b) To determine the average rate of unemployment in Canada for the last 5 years, Stephanie used data collected by Statistics Canada.

   c) Statistics Canada collected data from Canadian households on annual household income.

4. There were 20 contestants in a chili cook-off. The general public sampled as many of the 20 chili dishes as they wished. They then cast their votes for the best chili award. Does this sample produce valid results? Explain.

5. A survey is conducted to determine where students intend to go when they leave high school: the workplace, college, or university. The students are asked: "What are your future plans?"

   a) Identify the flaws in this survey question.

   b) Modify the question to improve its reliability.

Performance Assessment

6. Design a survey to determine the issues that teenagers in your town are most concerned about. Include:

   a) The question or questions you would ask

   b) A description of how you would select an unbiased sample

   c) A description of the steps you would take to conduct the survey

   d) A description of how you plan to store the data

Once we collect data, it is useful to organize them in a table or display them in a graph. In this section, we will examine ways to display data graphically using technology.

In *Investigation 1*, you will use a TI-83 graphing calculator to plot a histogram.

Investigation 1

Displaying Foot Lengths in a Histogram

1. Have each student in the class measure her or his foot length to the nearest centimetre and record the measure on the blackboard.

2. Enter the data.

   • To access the list editor, press [STAT] **1**.

   • Clear any data in list L1. Use the arrow keys to highlight L1, then press [CLEAR] [ENTER]. Ensure all other lists are clear.

   • Input each foot length in list L1. Press [ENTER] after each number.

3. Graph the data.

   • Press [Y=]. To clear an equation, use [▼] to highlight the equation, then press [CLEAR].

   • Press [2nd] [Y=] to access the STAT PLOT menu. Press **1** to select Plot 1. Highlight **On** and press [ENTER].

   • Press [▼] [►] [►] [ENTER] to select a histogram. Use the arrow key to move the cursor down to Xlist. Press [2nd] **1** to graph the data in list L1. Use the arrow key to move the cursor down to Freq. Press [ALPHA] **1**. Your screen should look like the one below.

   • Press [WINDOW]. For Xmin, input 10; for Xmax, input 40. Xscl is the width of the bar; input 1. For Ymin, input –5; for Ymax, input 15; for Yscl, input 1.

   • Press [GRAPH] to display the histogram. Press [TRACE] and use the left and right arrow keys to move from bar to bar. Explain the meaning of the display at the bottom of the graph.

4. What is the most frequent foot length? How can you tell this from the graph?

5. Describe the shape of the graph. Explain how it relates to the data.

6. Graph the data grouped in intervals of width 5.
- Use the data you entered in list L1 in exercise 2. Press [WINDOW]. Change the value of Xscl to 5; change Ymax to fit the new histogram on the screen.
- Press [GRAPH] to display the new histogram. Press [TRACE] and use the left and right arrow keys to move from bar to bar. What is the width of each bar?

7. a) Describe the shape of the graph in exercise 6. Explain how it relates to the data.

b) Can you tell the most frequent foot length from this graph? Explain.

c) Compare your graphs from exercises 3 and 6.

8. Copy and complete this tally chart to group the foot length data. Remember that a value that falls on the boundary between intervals goes into the higher interval. How do the frequencies in the third column compare to the values of "n" displayed when you used the TRACE command in exercise 6?

Foot Length (cm)	Tally	Frequency
0–5		
5–10		
10–15		
15–20		
20–25		
25–30		
30–35		
35–40		

9. Graph the data grouped in intervals of different widths. Change the value of Xscl to change the interval width. How does the histogram change as the interval changes?

10. Why might you choose to graph ungrouped data? Grouped data? If you choose to graph grouped data, what factors would you consider when determining the width of the intervals?

Grouping data makes the data appear more uniform. There is less variation in the heights of the bars on a graph of grouped data.

Consider these data on the average values of houses in various Canadian cities in 1997. Data for the territories were not available.

City	Average House Value in 1997 ($)
Calgary	143 305
Edmonton	111 587
Halifax	109 827
Montreal	112 362
Ottawa	143 866
Regina	82 643
Saint John	86 171
Saint John's	92 797
Toronto	211 307
Vancouver	287 094
Victoria	218 398
Winnipeg	86 040

We can enter these data in a spreadsheet and produce a bar graph. These instructions are for Microsoft Excel. If you use a different spreadsheet program, consult the manual. At the computer, open the spreadsheet program and start a new spreadsheet.

Enter the data.

- Enter the title "Average House Values in Canadian Cities in 1997" in cell A1. Enter the headings "City" and "Average House Value ($)" in cells A3 and B3.
- Enter the city names in cells A4 to A15 and the house values in cells B4 to B15. Your screen should look like this:

	A	B	C	D	E	F
1	Average House Values in Canadian Cities in 1997					
2						
3	City	Average House Value ($)				
4	Calgary	143305				
5	Edmonton	111587				
6	Halifax	109827				
7	Montreal	112362				
8	Ottawa	143866				
9	Regina	82643				
10	St John	86171				
11	St John's	92797				
12	Toronto	211307				
13	Vancouver	287094				
14	Victoria	218398				
15	Winnipeg	86040				

Construct the bar graph.

- From the Insert menu, select Chart. Click on Column to create a graph with vertical bars. Click Next.

- Click in the Data range box. On the spreadsheet, click on cell A4, then hold down the mouse button and drag to cell B15. This selects the cells that contain the data and labels we want in the chart. Click Next.
- Click the Titles tab.
  Click in the Chart title box and enter the title "Average House Values in Canadian Cities in 1997."
  Click in the Category (X) axis box and enter the label "City."
  Click in the Category (Y) axis box and enter the label "Average House Value ($)."
  Click on the Legend tab and deselect Show legend. Click Next.
- Select whether you want the chart placed in a new sheet or as an object in your current spreadsheet. Click Finish. Your graph should look like this:

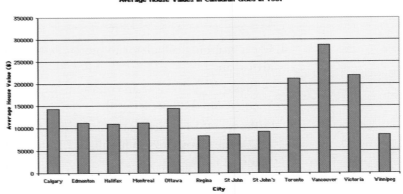

Discuss

Why did we display these data in a bar graph, not a histogram? What do we see from the graph that we did not see in the table?

In *Investigation 2*, you will collect data on arm span and hand span, then plot them in a scatter plot.

Investigation 2

Hand Span Versus Arm Span

Work with a partner. You will need a tape measure.

1. Do you think hand span and arm span are related? Explain.
2. Measure and record your hand span and arm span to the nearest half-centimetre. Your hand span is the greatest possible distance between the tips of your thumb and your fifth finger. Your arm span is the distance from fingertip to fingertip, with your arms stretched out sideways.

3. Combine your results with those of the other students in your class. Record the data in a table like the one below.

Name	Hand Span (cm)	Arm Span (cm)

4. Use a graphing calculator to plot a scatter plot of hand span versus arm span.

- Press [Y=]. To clear an equation, use the [▼] key to highlight the equation, then press [CLEAR].

- Press [STAT] **1** to access the list editor. Clear any data in lists L1 and L2. Use the arrow keys to highlight L1, then press [CLEAR] [ENTER]. Repeat for L2.

- Input the hand span data in list L1 and the arm span data in list L2.

- Press [2nd] [Y=] to access the STAT PLOT menu. Press **1** to select Plot 1. Highlight **On** and press [ENTER].

- To select a scatter plot, press [▼] [ENTER]. If L1 is not displayed beside Xlist, use the arrow key to move the cursor down to Xlist and press [2nd] **1**. If L2 is not displayed beside Ylist, use the arrow key to move the cursor down to Ylist and press [2nd] **2**. Use the arrow keys to highlight the + mark and press [ENTER]. Your screen should look like the one below.

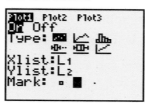

- To set the window, press [WINDOW]. For Xmin, input a value smaller than the smallest hand span; for Xmax, input a value larger than the largest hand span; for Xscl, input 1. For Ymin, input a value smaller than the smallest arm span; for Ymax, input a value larger than the largest arm span; for Yscl, input 20.

- Press [GRAPH] to display the scatter plot. Sketch or print the scatter plot.

5. Is there a relationship between hand span and arm span? Explain.

In *Investigation 2,* we used a graphing calculator to plot the scatter plot. We can also use a spreadsheet and these steps to plot a scatter plot.

- Open a new spreadsheet and enter the data.
- From the Insert menu, select Chart. Click on XY (Scatter). Click Next.
- Click in the Data range box. Select the cells that contain the hand span and arm span data. Click Next.
- Click the Titles tab. Click in the Chart title box and enter the title "Hand Span Versus Arm Span"; click in the Category (X) axis box and enter the label "Hand Span"; click in the Category (Y) axis box and enter the label "Arm Span." Click on the Legend tab and deselect Show legend. Click Next.
- Select whether you want the chart placed in a new sheet or as an object in your current spreadsheet. Click Finish.

5.4 Exercises

 B

Use a graphing calculator and/or a computer with a spreadsheet program to complete exercises 1 to 12.

 1. Application This table gives data on the top offensive teams in the National Football League for the 2000–2001 regular season.

Team	Total Yards	Total Points
St. Louis	7075	540
Denver	6567	485
Indianapolis	6141	429
San Francisco	6040	388
Minnesota	5961	397
Oakland	5776	479
Jacksonville	5690	367
Kansas City	5614	355
Buffalo	5498	315
New Orleans	5397	354

a) Construct a scatter plot of total points versus total yards.

b) Is there a relationship between total points and total yards? Explain.

2. These data from Statistics Canada show the number of babies born in Ontario every quarter from 1998 to 2000.

	I	II	III	IV
1998	32 364	35 133	34 516	30 646
1999	31 355	34 391	33 229	30 910
2000	30 994	33 897	33 198	30 359

a) Construct a bar graph of the data.

b) Describe any trends you see.

3. Create a scatter plot of the data from exercise 2 on a graphing calculator.

a) Describe how you will enter the quarters in list L1.

b) Sketch the scatter plot.

c) What conclusion, if any, can you draw from the scatter plot?

4. These data are from the Ministry of Training, Colleges and Universities. They show the enrolment in 5 Toronto area colleges on September 18, 2000, for ministry-funded programs.

College	Total Enrolment
Centennial	9 600
George Brown	8 990
Humber	11 780
Seneca	14 000
Sheridan	9 500

a) Display these data in a bar graph.

b) What do you learn from the graph that you did not see in the table? Explain.

5. Communication For each type of graph listed below, describe the characteristics of the graph and give an example of a situation in which it would be used.

a) histogram   **b)** bar graph   **c)** scatter plot

6. This table shows the games won as a percent of games played (PCT) and the average points scored per game (PF) for the teams in the Women's National Basketball Association (WNBA) in the 2000 season.

Team	PCT	PF
Los Angeles Sparks	87.5	75.5
New York Liberty	62.5	66.6
Cleveland Rockers	53.1	67.7
Houston Comets	84.4	77.3
Orlando Miracle	50.0	67.6
Sacramento Monarchs	65.6	73.2
Phoenix Mercury	59.4	69.2
Washington Mystics	43.8	68.0
Detroit Shock	43.8	72.8
Utah Starzz	58.1	77.9
Miami Sol	40.6	55.9
Minnesota Lynx	46.9	68.5
Indiana Fever	28.1	69.2
Portland Fire	31.2	67.3
Charlotte Sting	22.6	70.5
Seattle Storm	21.9	56.4

a) Construct a scatter plot of percent games won versus average points scored per game.

b) Is there a relationship between the percent of games won and the average number of points scored per game? Explain.

7. These data are from Statistics Canada. They show the average number of people in a family every 10 years from 1961 to 1991.

Year	1961	1971	1981	1991
Average Number of People	3.9	3.7	3.3	3.1

a) Choose an appropriate type of graph. Explain your choice.

b) Graph these data.

c) Can these data be graphed using a different type of graph than the type you used? Explain.

8. Knowledge/Understanding This table gives the total points earned in the 2000–2001 hockey season for 5 of the Pittsburgh Penguins.

Player	Total Points
Jagr	121
Kovalev	95
Lang	80
Lemieux	76
Straka	95

a) Display these data in an appropriate graph.

b) Which display is most informative, the table or the graph? Explain.

9. Retrieve the data you collected in Section 5.2, exercise 21. Display these data in an appropriate graph. Does the graph confirm the conclusions you reached about this population? Explain.

10. Thinking/Inquiry/Problem Solving Sandra polled her class to find out how much each person spent, in dollars, on fast food last month. Here are the data she collected.

0, 12, 15, 23, 35, 38, 35, 54, 58, 52, 42, 45, 41, 48, 44, 68,
0, 16, 30, 35, 30, 50, 55, 55, 59, 47, 40, 45, 43, 65, 93

a) Enter the data into list L1 on your calculator. Set an appropriate window.

b) Plot a histogram of the data for each group of window settings. Sketch or print each histogram.
   i) Xscl = 3, Ymax = 5, Yscl = 1
   ii) Xscl = 10, Ymax = 10, Yscl = 1
   iii) Xscl = 20, Ymax = 20, Yscl = 5
   iv) Xscl = 30, Ymax = 30, Yscl = 5

c) Which histogram is most difficult to read?

d) Which histogram(s) clearly and accurately represent the data?

e) Explain why the choice of horizontal scale is important when you draw a histogram.

f) What effect does changing the value Yscl have on the histogram?

11. The distribution of marks on a mathematics test is shown in the table.

Interval	Frequency
30–40	2
40–50	1
50–60	4
60–70	11
70–80	9
80–90	4
90–100	3

a) Calculate the midpoint of each interval. Enter the midpoints into list L1 on a graphing calculator. Enter the frequencies into list L2.

b) In the STAT PLOT menu, select histogram. Enter L1 for Xlist and L2 for Freq. Why is L1 used for Xlist and L2 used for Freq?

c) Set the window so Xmin = 30, Xmax = 100, Xscl = 10, Ymin = 0, Ymax = 12, and Yscl = 1. Explain how each value was determined.

d) Press (GRAPH) to display the histogram. Sketch or print the graph.

e) How was the process you used to plot this histogram different from the process you used in *Investigation 1*? Why was it necessary to use a different process?

12. a) Select a random sample of 10 classmates. Describe how you obtained your sample.

b) Collect data on the number of people in each person's immediate family.

c) Graph these data in a bar graph.

d) What is the most frequent number of people living in a household? Explain.

e) If you have access to the Internet, go to: http://estat.statcan.ca Compare your results with data collected by Statistics Canada. Explain any differences.

Σ-STAT

When we read reports of survey results, we need to assess the quality of the data and the truthfulness of any claims that are made.

Here are some questions to ask when you assess reported survey results.
- Was the sample representative of the population?
- Was the sample large enough?
- What question or questions were asked?
- Have the results been interpreted correctly and reported accurately?

Many polls reported in the media contain a statement similar to this: "This poll is accurate to within 4%, 19 times out of 20" or "The margin of error is 4%, 19 times out of 20." For example, on January 5, 1999, *The Toronto Star* published these poll results:

> Poll results show the Conservatives at 43 percent of decided voter support, the Liberals at 41 percent, and the New Democratic Party at just 14 percent.
>
> Environics questioned 1004 Ontario voters by telephone between December 11 and January 4. Such polls are said to be accurate within 3 percentage points, 19 times out of 20.

This means that if the survey was conducted many times, with different random samples of 1004 Ontario voters, on average the sample percents will estimate the true population percents to within 3%, 19 times out of 20. So, the percent that supported the Conservatives would be between 40% and 46%, and the percent that supported the Liberals would be between 38% and 44%. Since the ranges of support for the two political parties overlap, this survey is inconclusive. When the margin of error is not stated, we cannot assess the accuracy of the results. Larger sample sizes result in smaller margins of error.

Example 1

A survey was conducted to compare two brands of cola. The results indicated that 35% of the people surveyed preferred Quench Cola, 40% preferred Crown Cola, and 25% said the brands were equal.

This advertisement for Quench Cola referred to the survey results: "QUENCH BEATS CROWN — an amazing 60% said Quench Cola tastes as good as or better than Crown Cola."

a) Is Quench's claim truthful? Explain.

b) Is Quench's claim accurate? Explain.

c) Are these data valid? Explain.

Solution

a) Quench's claim is truthful. Sixty percent of the people surveyed did prefer Quench or thought the brands were equal.

b) Quench's claim is not accurate. It suggests that Quench is the more popular brand of cola when in fact 65% of the people surveyed thought Crown Cola tasted as good as or better than Quench Cola.

c) We cannot tell if these data are valid. We do not know the size of the sample or how it was selected.

Charts and graphs often appear with reports of surveys and in advertising. We should examine these carefully because sometimes they can be misleading.

Example 2 A construction company built twice as many houses in 1990 as it did in 1980. An employee drew this graph to represent these data.

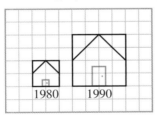

a) Explain how this graph is misleading.

b) Draw a graph that more accurately represents the data.

Solution

a) The house icon that represents the number of houses built in 1980 covers an area of 4 square units.

The house icon that represents the number of houses built in 1990 covers an area of 16 square units.
The area of the 1990 icon is 4 times the area of the 1980 icon.
This graph suggests that 4 times as many houses were built in 1990 as in 1980.

b) Draw a graph where the widths of the houses are equal, and the height represents the increase in the number of houses built.

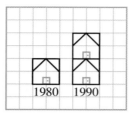

In the media, we frequently hear reports that mention indices, such as the Consumer Price Index (CPI) or the S&P/TSX Composite Index (which is now used instead of the TSE 300 Composite Index). An *index* is a sample of a particular population used to identify trends in that population.

The CPI is used to measure changes in retail prices by comparing, over time, the cost of a representative basket of goods and services. The CPI compares prices in any given period to prices in the base period (1992 at the time of printing). The value of the CPI in the base year is always 100.0. This table gives the value of the CPI each year from 1990 to 2000. The CPI data are percents.

Year	1990	1991	**1992**	1993	1994	1995	1996	1997	1998	1999	2000
CPI	93.3	98.5	**100.0**	101.8	102.0	104.2	105.9	107.6	108.6	110.5	113.5

The CPI in 2000 was 113.5. When we compare this to the base year, 1992, we see that prices in 2000 were 13.5% higher than in 1992. Prices in 1991 were 1.5% lower than in 1992.

Example 3 In August 2001, the CPI was 118.3 for Ontario and 121.2 for Saskatchewan.

a) Does this mean that prices were higher in Saskatchewan than in Ontario? Explain.

b) What information does this give us about prices in Ontario and Saskatchewan?

Solution

a) No, the CPI measures *changes* in prices, it does not give us any information about price levels.

b) Prices in Saskatchewan have increased more rapidly than prices in Ontario. Between 1992 (the base year) and 2001, prices in Saskatchewan increased 21.2%. During that same period, prices in Ontario increased 18.3%. Despite the more rapid growth in prices, it is possible that prices are lower in Saskatchewan than in Ontario.

5.5 Exercises

B

1. The results of a political poll are displayed in a circle graph (below left). Describe how the graph is misleading.

2. The pictograph (above right) illustrates the profits of a computer manufacturing company for two consecutive years. Explain why this graph is misleading.

3. The results of a poll indicate that 51% of Canadians think the Prime Minister is doing a good job. The poll is considered accurate to within 4%, 19 times out of 20.

a) Explain what this means.

b) Can we say that the majority of Canadians agree with the job the Prime Minister is doing? Explain.

4. These data from Statistics Canada show the number of unemployed people in Canada each year from 1995 to 2000.

Year	Number of Unemployed
1995	1 393 100
1996	1 436 900
1997	1 378 600
1998	1 277 300
1999	1 190 100
2000	1 089 600

a) Draw a graph that accurately represents these data.

b) Alter the graph to support a particular point of view. Explain the point of view.

✓ **5. Application** The value of the Canadian dollar in terms of U.S. dollars changes over time. This graph shows how the value of the Canadian dollar changed between 1998 and 2001. Each value was recorded at the close of trading on January 31 of the stated year.

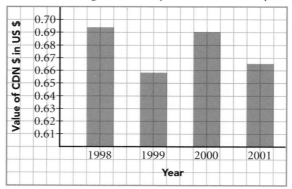

a) Examine the graph and explain why it may be misleading.

b) Draw a graph that more accurately represents the data.

✓ **6.** Look in newspapers and magazines to find an example of a graph that is misleading. Copy the graph into your notebook.

a) Explain how the graph is misleading.

b) Redraw the graph so it more accurately represents the data.

✓ **7.** The *Maclean's* year-end poll was published December 20, 1999. A random sample of 1200 Canadians was interviewed for this poll. The national sample is considered accurate to within 3.5%, 19 times out of 20.

Here is one of the questions from this poll, with the results.
　　Overall, do you think Canada would benefit or lose out from having a common currency with the United States?

Greatly benefit	17%
Somewhat benefit	27%
No impact either way	8%
Somewhat lose out	22%
Greatly lose out	20%

A student read these results and stated: "Canadians are evenly divided on the issue of entering into common currency with the United States." Has the student interpreted the results correctly? Explain.

8. An automobile safety handbook states that the majority of car accidents occur within 5 blocks of home.

   a) What incorrect conclusion might we draw from this claim?

   b) What other information do we need before we can accurately assess this claim?

9. **Knowledge/Understanding** The CPI for all items in June 2001 was 117.5 for Canada and 118.5 for Ontario.

   a) Describe how prices have changed in Ontario since the base year of 1992.

   b) Are prices increasing faster in Ontario or in all of Canada? Explain.

10. The CPI for energy for August 2001 was 133.4.

    a) In the base year of 1992, the CPI for energy was 100.0. What happened to energy prices from 1992 to 2001? Explain.

    b) The CPI for all products in August 2001 was 117.1. Suggest reasons why the CPI for energy is so much higher than the CPI for all items.

11. **Communication** The article "Opinion polls still valid" appeared in *The Calgary Herald* on February 3, 2000. Portions of the article are reproduced below.

> Can poll results be manipulated? Well, of course poll results can be manipulated.
>
> The real question is: why would you? The taking of a public opinion poll is, by definition, to get accurate public opinion — to get solid, accurate research.

a) List some organizations that rely on "solid, accurate research." Explain why each organization requires accurate information.

b) Suggest reasons why an organization may want to manipulate poll results. How might they do this?

12. The S&P/TSX Composite Index is a sample of the stock prices of Canadian companies traded on the Toronto Stock Exchange.

   a) Research newspapers and the Internet to determine what types of stocks are included in the S&P/TSX Composite Index.

   b) Look in the newspaper or on the Internet to find a graph of the closing values of the S&P/TSX Composite Index over the past several months. Describe any trends you see.

13. Thinking/Inquiry/Problem Solving Create an index of 20 of the largest technology stocks traded on the Toronto Stock Exchange.

   a) What is the population?

   b) Describe how you would obtain a representative sample for the index.

   c) Use your index of 20 technology stocks. Calculate the daily average price for the stocks in your sample each day for two days.

   d) Compare the change in your index to that of the S&P/TSX Composite Index over the same two days. Is your sample representative of the S&P/TSX Composite Index? Explain.

14. Every year from 1993 to 1998, Canada placed first in the United Nations Human Development Index (HDI). It measures quality of life. Some of the factors considered when calculating the index include income, life expectancy, literacy, and school enrolment. In 1999, Canada fell to third place behind Norway and Australia. Many members of the media expressed concern about budgetary issues affecting the quality of life of Canadians.

   a) What factors would you consider when measuring quality of life? Explain.

   b) Do you think the items considered in the United Nations index are valid indicators of quality of life? Explain.

   c) Here are the results for the top 3 countries: Norway 0.939, Australia 0.936, Canada 0.936. Norway and Australia were ahead because they had better life expectancy and educational enrolment. Do you think Canadians should be concerned about their ranking? Explain.

1. These data are from Statistics Canada. They show the percent of Canadian homes with telephones every 5 years from 1965.

Year	1965	1970	1975	1980	1985	1990	1995
Homes with Telephones (%)	89.4	93.9	96.4	97.6	98.2	98.5	98.7

a) Display these data in a scatter plot and a bar graph.

b) Compare your graphs from part a. Do they give the same information? Explain.

2. In August 2001, the CPI for clothing and footwear was 106.6 and the CPI for transportation was 130.9.

a) In 1992, the CPI for both categories was 100.0. Explain what happened to prices in both categories from 1992 to 2001.

b) Suggest reasons why the CPI for transportation was so much higher than the CPI for clothing and footwear in August 2001.

Performance Assessment

3. Suppose you were hired by Magic Inc. to prepare marketing materials. The company collected data on its annual sales and on the 2001 annual sales of three of its competitors.

	Annual Sales for Magic Inc.				
Year	1997	1998	1999	2000	2001
Annual Sales ($)	3 000 000	3 051 000	3 080 000	3 121 000	3 154 000

	2001 Annual Sales			
Company	Magic	Mirage	Illusion	Fantasy
Annual Sales ($)	3 154 000	6 503 000	5 000 500	2 002 000

An independent survey of consumers found that 30% prefer Magic, 27% prefer Mirage, 25% prefer Illusion, and 18% prefer Fantasy. This survey is considered accurate to within 3%, 19 times out of 20.

Without altering any data, construct a scatter plot of the sales data, a bar graph of the 2001 annual sales, and a summary of the survey results that portrays Magic Inc. in as favourable a light as possible.

Project: Collecting Data

You will collect secondary data on an issue of interest to you. You will also design and conduct a survey to estimate public opinion about a different issue. In each case, you will display the data graphically, make a statement or draw a conclusion about the population you studied, and write a report.

Collect and Analyse Secondary Data

1. Research the library or the Internet to collect secondary data on one of the topics listed below, or a topic of your choice.

   - Unemployment by age, gender, or province
   - A comparison of average home values in various cities in Ontario
   - A comparison of average household or personal income of individuals living in different parts of Ontario or Canada
   - The percentage of the population with each blood type

2. Evaluate the quality of the data by answering these questions.

   a) Who collected the data? Does the person or organization have an established reputation?

   b) Were the data collected from a sample or from the population? What was the population? If the data were collected from a sample, how was the sample selected?

   c) What question or questions were asked?

3. Store the raw data.

4. Organize the data into a table or a graph.

5. Analyse the data and draw a conclusion about the population.

6. Write a report. Include the topic you selected, the data you collected, and the source of the data, as well as your analysis of the source, your table or graph, and your conclusion.

Collect and Analyse Primary Data

1. Select an issue that interests you. You may use one from this list or you may select one of your own.

   - How people spend their leisure time
   - What people think of federal, provincial, or municipal government policies
   - What household products people use
   - What charities people support

2. Clearly define the population you will sample.

3. Decide on a sample size and method of sample selection. Select a representative sample.

4. Clearly define the purpose of your survey. What do you want to find out about the population? What data do you need to collect to get that information? Construct your questionnaire. Be careful to construct clear, precise, unbiased questions. Field-test your questions with classmates.

5. Conduct the survey and record the results. Store the raw data.

6. Organize the data into tables and/or graphs.

7. Analyse the results, then use the data to draw conclusions about the population.

8. Write a report of your survey. Include in your questionnaire a description of how you selected your sample, the data you collected from the survey, your tables and graphs, and your conclusions. Also include answers to these questions:

   a) Were there any flaws in or problems with the survey? Explain.

   b) What other conclusions can you draw about the population using the data you collected? Explain.

Observers view a focus group through a one-way mirror.

Marketing Specialist

Fatima wanted the excitement of a job on the cutting edge of new ideas. Training at community college as a marketing specialist was a good decision for her.

Job Description

- Determine the type and quantity of advertising a company should do
- Develop and implement marketing strategies
- Plan studies to research public opinion
- Tabulate and analyze research data
- Prepare written materials for sales campaigns

Working Conditions

- Can be a high-stress job
- Evening, weekend, and overtime work required when ad campaigns are under way
- Job opportunities available in many different types of companies
- Travel may be necessary
- Good job mobility

Qualifications and Training

- Graduation from high school
- Community college training in marketing
- Computer skills
- Creativity
- Good communication and writing skills

Where's the Math?

Marketing specialists must be able to understand and interpret statistics. They often design statistical studies and use the results to plan advertising campaigns. Because marketers cannot interview all members of a given population, it is especially important for them to understand the concept of sampling.

Review Exercises

MATHEMATICS TOOLKIT

Sampling Tools

Consider these points when you collect data:
> Will data be collected from a primary source or a secondary source?
> What is the population?
> What is the purpose of the survey?
> Will you conduct a census or survey a sample of the population?
> What type of sample will be used?
  • simple random sample
  • systematic sample
  • cluster sample
  • stratified random sample
  • convenience sample
  • self-selected sample
> Are the survey questions clear, precise, and unbiased?

Decide how the data will be organized and displayed:
> Frequency table
> Bar graph
> Histogram
> Scatter plot

Consider these points when you assess reported data:
> Who collected the data?
> What population was studied?
> How was the sample selected?
> What question or questions were asked?
> Do the data support any claims that are made?

5.1 **1.** Identify the population you would survey to obtain data on each topic.
  a) The types of crimes committed by people aged 15 to 25
  b) The number of school children of each age from 5 to 19 years
  c) The countries of origin of new immigrants to Canada in 2001

2. State how each sample may be biased.

 a) To assess the opinions of people in his community on a proposed municipal bylaw, Kamil asked every 5th person entering the library whether he or she supported or opposed the legislation.

 b) To find the most popular brand of jeans among teenage girls, Pattijo asked the girls in her class to name their favourite brand.

3. Would you use a primary or secondary source of data to answer each question? Explain.

 a) What percent of Canadian families own more than one vehicle?

 b) What is the average height of teenagers in your school?

 c) What is the average height of Canadian teenagers?

4. In each case, would you collect data from a sample or the population? Explain.

 a) What is the average diameter of a Canadian quarter?

 b) What is the average distance travelled before a particular brand of tire needs to be replaced?

5.2 **5.** Health and Welfare Canada samples food to test for contamination.

 a) Describe how the Ministry could select a sample of each type.

 i) cluster sample **ii)** systematic sample

 iii) simple random sample **iv)** stratified random sample

 b) Which sampling method would you recommend? Explain.

6. Each year, sportswriters vote on the most valuable player in major league baseball. A newspaper conducts a mail-in poll of coaches and managers of the teams. Will this result in a representative sample? Explain.

7. A radio phone-in show surveys listeners about their favourite song by answering every second call to the station.

 a) Identify the type of sample.

 b) Will the results of this survey be valid? Explain.

8. A survey asks Canadians to respond by calling a 1-900 number at a cost of $1 per call to answer the question "Have you ever stolen?" Each caller's telephone number will be recorded so people cannot call in twice. Explain the weaknesses with this survey.

9. A polling firm plans to assess the level of satisfaction Canadian adults have with government services. Explain why a carefully selected sample of 1000 Canadians will give more reliable results than a biased sample of 50 000 Canadians.

5.3 10. A school is considering cancelling the rugby team. Supporters of the team conduct a survey. They ask: "Are you against not having a rugby team?"

a) Identify the flaws in this question.

b) Do you think the results of this survey will be valid? Explain.

c) Suggest a suitable question that could be asked.

11. Select two different random samples of 10 students each. Ask all the students in the first sample to respond to question 1 and all the students in the second sample to respond to question 2. Record the responses.

Question 1: Do you believe the number of days in a school year should be increased? Choose one. Yes   No

Question 2: Statistics show that students in countries where the school year is longer receive a better education and obtain better-paying jobs. Would you support increasing the length of the school year? Choose one. Yes   No

a) What was the survey attempting to find out?

b) Compare the results of the two surveys. Explain any differences in the results.

c) What would be a suitable question to ask? Explain.

12. A survey is conducted to determine the types of heart problems Canadians have. Each person in the sample has to record her or his name and answer this question: "Do you have heart trouble?" Describe the weaknesses in the survey.

13. A survey was conducted to determine which sport people most like to participate in. The question asked was: "What is the first sport you learned to play and still play?"

a) Is this question valid?

b) Write an alternative question that would produce more valid results.

14. Suppose you are hired by the Ontario government to conduct a survey to determine the opinions of people in Ontario on this issue: Should all secondary schools in Ontario receive equal funding?

a) What question or questions would you ask?

b) Describe how you would select an unbiased sample.

c) Describe how you would conduct the survey.

5.4 **15.** A company sells hockey equipment. This table shows the annual sales for the years 1998 to 2001.

Year	1998	1999	2000	2001
Sales ($)	105 923	98 263	143 829	149 066

a) Draw a bar graph to represent these data.

b) What information does the graph give you that the table did not?

16. These are the final marks on a history exam.

89, 65, 76, 45, 80, 86, 76, 66, 57, 53, 79, 84, 90, 64, 77, 78, 72, 65, 68, 84, 52, 56, 68, 65, 75, 76, 77, 87, 83, 74

a) Display these data in a frequency table. Group the marks in intervals of width 10, beginning at 40.

b) Display the data as a histogram. Sketch the histogram.

c) What range of marks occurs most frequently in the class? Did the class perform well on this exam? Explain.

17. These data from the Bank of Canada show the bank rate and the exchange rate on January 31 each year from 1996 to 2001.

Date	Bank Rate (%)	Exchange Rate: US$1 in $CDN
1996	5.37	1.37
1997	3.25	1.35
1998	4.50	1.44
1999	5.25	1.52
2000	5.00	1.45
2001	5.75	1.50

a) Draw a scatter plot of the bank rate versus the exchange rate.

b) Does there appear to be a relationship between the bank rate and the exchange rate? Explain.

18. Ingrid collected these data on mass in kilograms and total points for the players on her school's girls' basketball team.

Mass (kg)	69	74	68	56	66	56	75	66	70	65	65	73	62
Points	74	52	64	68	57	72	69	78	74	62	64	67	55

a) Which type of graph would best display these data? Explain.

b) Construct a graph to represent these data.

5.5 **19.** An article published in the August 27, 2001 edition of *The Toronto Star* says: "Families spend $1100 on school gear." The margin of error was reported to be 2.5%, 19 times out of 20. What is the range of amounts Canadian families expect to pay for school gear?

20. Sonja researched accident statistics in her community. In the past year, 6 people were killed in car accidents and 1 person was killed in a motorcycle accident. Sonja concluded that it is safer to ride a motorcycle than it is to drive a car. Explain her error.

21. Samuel established a student price index (SPI) to measure changes in prices for school supplies, bus tickets, and cafeteria lunches. He established 1998 as the base year. Here is Samuel's index for 1997 to 2000.

Year	1997	**1998**	1999	2000
SPI	100.9	**100.0**	101.1	104.7

a) According to Samuel's index, what happened to prices for student goods and services from 1997 to 1998?

b) How are prices in 2000 related to prices in 1998?

Maintaining Your Mastery

Review the algebraic skills that form part of the college admission process.

1. Expand and simplify.

  a) $5(x - 4)(x + 7)$ **b)** $6(x - 3)^2$

  c) $3x(x + 9) - (x + 1)(x - 1)$

2. Factor.

  a) $x^2 + 8x + 7$ **b)** $4x^2 - 28x + 40$ **c)** $3x^2 - 27$

3. Factor.

  a) $4x^2 + 11x + 7$ **b)** $25x^2 + 30x + 9$ **c)** $15x^2 + 10x - 5$

4. Solve each equation.

  a) $15x + 17 = 5(x + 24) - 3$ **b)** $9x^2 - 1 = 3x^2 + x$

1. **Knowledge/Understanding** Identify the population you would sample for an opinion on each topic.

   a) The quality of school cafeteria food

   b) Fees paid to apply for your driver's licence

2. **Communication** Suppose you wish to determine the attitudes of Canadian students toward the environment.

   a) Describe how you would select a random sample.

   b) What question or questions would you ask?

   c) Describe the method you would use to conduct the survey.

3. **Application**

   a) Draw a histogram of these data. Use intervals of width 10 beginning at 10.

   25, 35, 85, 67, 46, 38, 45, 30, 20, 78, 76, 64, 36, 44, 21,

   14, 24, 64, 36, 80, 40, 35, 74, 33, 65, 42, 23, 12, 34, 23

   b) How would changing the width of the interval change the histogram?

4. This graph shows the level of the Bank of Canada bank rate semi-annually from January 1998 to January 2001.

   a) Explain why this graph is misleading.

   b) Draw a new graph that more accurately represents these data.

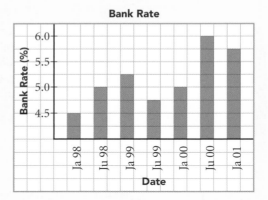

5. **Thinking/Inquiry/Problem Solving** A company surveyed 1000 randomly selected consumers to determine which type of dishwasher detergent people prefer: liquid or powder. Forty-nine percent of people surveyed preferred liquid and 51% preferred powder. The margin of error for this survey is 5%, 19 times out of 20. Sandra conducted her own survey of 200 randomly selected consumers and found that 53% prefer liquid and 47% prefer powder. Are the results of Sandra's survey consistent with the results of the company's survey? Explain.

6. On November 25, 2000, each major Toronto daily newspaper published the results of a different opinion poll. Each poll was about the voting intentions for the November 27 federal election. These were the headlines of the articles:

"Liberal majority, poll says" (*The Toronto Star*)

"PM's majority on razor's edge" (*The Globe and Mail*)

"Grits fear minority, attack Clark" (*National Post*)

The results of each newspaper's poll are summarized in the table.

Newspaper	Polling Firm	Sample Size	Margin of Error
The Toronto Star	Ekos Research Associates Inc.	3910	1.6%
The Globe and Mail	Ipsos-Reid	4102	1.5%
National Post	COMPAS Inc.	1032	3.2%

Newspaper	Popular Vote (% of decided voters)				
	Liberal	Canadian Alliance	Bloc Quebecois	Progressive Conservative	NDP
The Toronto Star	42.8	24.7	9.2	10.9	9.1
The Globe and Mail	39	27	10	12	10
National Post	40.6	25.1	10.0	11.6	8.9

a) Does each newspaper's headline accurately report the results of its poll? Explain.

b) Examine the data in the columns titled "Sample Size" and "Margin of Error." What happens to the margin of error as the sample size increases? Do you think this is always true? Explain.

Chapter Project

Choosing a Franchise

Many entrepreneurs choose to minimize the risk involved with owning a business by purchasing a franchise. When choosing a franchise, it is important to analyse the data carefully to make the best investment.

Curriculum Expectations

By the end of this chapter, you will:

> Identify and describe properties of common distributions of data.

> Calculate the mean, median, mode, range, variance, and standard deviation of a data set, using standard statistical notation and technology.

> Describe the significance of results drawn from analysed data.

> Make and justify statements about a population on the basis of sample data.

> Determine an equation of a line of best fit, using the regression capabilities of graphing technology.

> Calculate and interpret the correlation coefficient, using appropriate technology.

> Describe possible misuses of regression.

> Describe the relationship between two variables suggested by a scatter plot.

> Collect, organize, and analyse data to address problems or issues, and calculate relevant statistical measures.

> Formulate a summary conclusion to a problem or an issue, by synthesizing interpretations of individual statistical measures.

> Formulate extending questions related to the conclusion reached in the investigation of a problem or an issue.

> Communicate the process used and the conclusions reached in the investigation of a problem or an issue, using appropriate mathematical forms.

> Enter data or a formula into a graphing calculator and retrieve other forms of the model.

> Describe the effect on a given graph of new information about the circumstances represented by the graph.

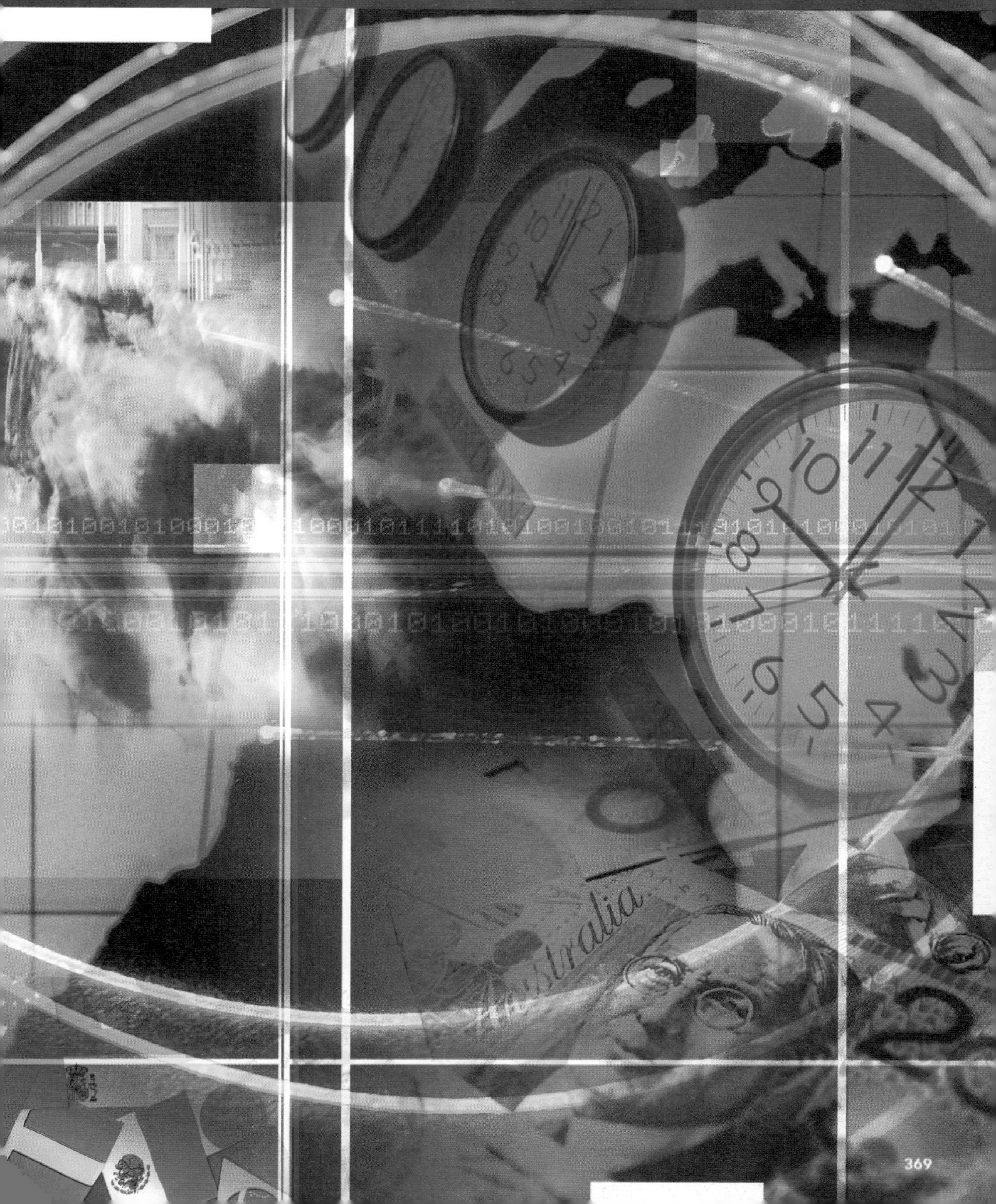
Australia

Review: Measures of Central Tendency

The *mean*, the *median*, and the *mode* are three measures of central tendency. They give us information about the "centre" of a set of data. All three measures of central tendency lie between the smallest and largest numbers in the data set.

Heather got these test marks out of 100 in mathematics:

| 63 | 74 | 77 | 68 | 71 | 74 | 70 | 65 |

To calculate the *mean*, add the numbers, then divide by the number of numbers.

Heather's mean mark is $\dfrac{63 + 74 + 77 + 68 + 71 + 74 + 70 + 65}{8} = 70.25$.

The mean of a sample is represented by $\overline{x}$ (read *x*-bar).

For a set of data $x_1, x_2, x_3, ..., x_n$, the mean is: $\overline{x} = \dfrac{x_1 + x_2 + x_3 + ... + x_n}{n}$

To find the *median*, arrange the numbers in order and find the middle number. If there is an even number of numbers, the median is the mean of the two middle numbers.

Here are Heather's marks in order from lowest to highest:

| 63 | 65 | 68 | 70 | 71 | 74 | 74 | 77 |

Heather's median mark is $\dfrac{70 + 71}{2} = 70.5$.

To find the *mode*, determine which number occurs most frequently. There may be more than one mode, or there may be no mode.

Heather's mode mark is 74.

If the data are displayed in a frequency table, we calculate the mean by calculating the product of each value and its frequency, adding the products, then dividing by the number of numbers (the total frequency).

Example

This table shows the annual salaries earned by employees of a small company.

Annual salary ($)	Frequency
35 500	3
42 750	5
51 000	5
99 000	1
150 000	1

a) Determine each measure of central tendency.
  i) the mean   **ii)** the median   **iii)** the mode
b) Which measure most fairly represents the average annual salary? Explain.

Solution

a) i) To calculate the mean salary, multiply each salary by its frequency, add the products, then divide by the total frequency (in this case, 15).

$$\bar{x} = \frac{(3 \times 35\ 500) + (5 \times 42\ 750) + (5 \times 51\ 000) + (1 \times 99\ 000) + (1 \times 150\ 000)}{15}$$

$$= 54\ 950$$

The mean annual salary is $54 950.

ii) The median salary is the middle salary. Since there are 15 employees, the salary of the 8th employee is the median.
The median salary is $42 750.

iii) There are two mode salaries. They are $42 750 and $51 000.

b) Only 2 of the 15 employees earn more than the mean salary of $54 950; it is too high to be representative. The mean has been pulled up by two very high salaries. There are two mode salaries. One of the mode salaries is the same as the median salary of $42 750. The median salary probably best represents the average annual salary.

If the data are grouped into intervals, the calculated values for the mean, the median, and the mode will only be estimates. Suppose you were given these data about the amounts of charitable donations.

Amount of donation ($)	Frequency
0–10	26
10–20	32
20–30	14
30–40	8
40–50	4
50–60	1

Since we do not have the raw data, we do not know the actual amount of each donation. We assume that each donation in an interval was for the mean amount of that interval. Thus, we assume there were 26 donations of $5, 32 donations of $15, 14 donations of $25, and so on.

To find the estimated mean donation, we multiply the mean of each interval by the frequency, add the products, then divide by the total frequency.

$$\bar{x} = \frac{(26 \times 5) + (32 \times 15) + (14 \times 25) + (8 \times 35) + (4 \times 45) + (1 \times 55)}{85}$$
$$\doteq 17.35$$

The mean donation is approximately $17.35.

There were 85 donations altogether. The 43rd donation is the median. This is in the interval 10–20, so the median donation is approximately $15.

The mode interval is 10–20, so the mode donation is approximately $15. In this case, the measures of central tendency are all close to $15. They are all representative of the average donation.

Exercises

1. Sophie collected these data on the ages of participants in an intramural basketball league. Determine the mean, the median, and the mode for these data. Which measure best represents the average age of participants? Explain.

Age (years)	Frequency
15	3
16	5
17	9
18	11
19	8

2. A running club recorded the distance in kilometres that each of its members ran. Determine the mean, median, and mode distances. Which measure best represents the average distance? Explain.

Distance run (km)	Frequency
0–2	5
2–4	7
4–6	10
6–8	6
8–10	2

In Chapter 5, we collected data and organized them into tables and graphs. In this chapter, we will analyse data. In Sections 6.1 to 6.3, we will analyse *single-variable data*. Single-variable data are data collected on one variable, such as heights of college students, which can be organized into a frequency table. In Sections 6.4 and 6.5, we will analyse *two-variable data* and look for a relationship between two variables, for example, height and shoe size.

We reviewed three measures of central tendency in Necessary Skills: the mean, the median and the mode. These three measures give us information about the centre of the data, but they do not tell us anything about the *spread* of the data.

Anne and Michael collected pledges for the Terry Fox Run. Consider the histograms of their pledges.

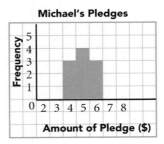

Both of these data sets have mean 5 and median 5, but Anne's pledges are more spread out. When the data are widely spread, the measures of central tendency are less likely to be representative of the population. We will examine three measures of the spread of data: the *range*, the *variance*, and the *standard deviation*.

The *range* is the difference between the largest value and the smallest value in a data set.

    The range of Anne's pledges is $8 - 2 = 6$.
    The range of Michael's pledges is $6 - 4 = 2$.

The range is simple to calculate, but it relies only on the largest and smallest values. It does not give any information about the spread of the other data.

To calculate the *variance* of a data set:
- Calculate the mean.
- Subtract the mean from each data value, then square the result.
- Add the squared numbers.
- Divide by one less than the number of data items.

The variance of a data set is the mean of the squared differences between the data values and the mean of the data. We use the symbol s^2 to represent the variance.

Given any data set, $x_1,\ x_2,\ x_3, ..., x_n$, the variance is:

$$s^2 = \frac{(x_1 - \bar{x})^2 + (x_2 - \bar{x})^2 + (x_3 - \bar{x})^2 + ... + (x_n - \bar{x})^2}{n - 1}$$

The most common measure of spread is the *standard deviation*. The standard deviation of a data set is the square root of the variance. We use s to represent the standard deviation. To calculate the standard deviation of a data set:

- Calculate the variance, s^2.
- Take the square root of the variance.

Given any data set, $x_1, x_2, x_3, ..., x_n$, the standard deviation is:

$$s = \sqrt{\frac{(x_1 - \bar{x})^2 + (x_2 - \bar{x})^2 + (x_3 - \bar{x})^2 + ... + (x_n - \bar{x})^2}{n - 1}}$$

We can calculate the variance and standard deviation of Anne's and Michael's pledge data. The first step is to calculate the mean. In this case, we know that Anne's mean pledge is $5.

Complete the table to calculate the variance of Anne's pledges.

Pledge amount ($)	Mean pledge	Difference from mean	Square of difference
2	5	−3	9
3	5	−2	4
4	5	−1	1
4	5	−1	1
5	5	0	0
5	5	0	0
6	5	1	1
6	5	1	1
7	5	2	4
8	5	3	9
		TOTAL	30

$$s^2 = \frac{30}{9}$$
$$= 3.\dot{3}$$

The standard deviation of Anne's pledges is the square root of the variance,
$$s = \sqrt{3.\dot{3}}$$
$$\doteq 1.83$$

Anne's mean pledge was $5 with a standard deviation of about 1.83.

Michael's mean pledge is also $5.

Complete the table to calculate the variance of Michael's pledges.

Pledge amount ($)	Mean pledge	Difference from mean	Square of difference
4	5	−1	1
4	5	−1	1
4	5	−1	1
5	5	0	0
5	5	0	0
5	5	0	0
5	5	0	0
6	5	1	1
6	5	1	1
6	5	1	1
		TOTAL	6

$$s^2 = \frac{6}{9}$$
$$= 0.\dot{6}$$

The standard deviation of Michael's pledges is the square root of the variance,

$$s = \sqrt{0.\dot{6}}$$
$$\doteq 0.82$$

Michael's mean pledge was $5 with a standard deviation of about 0.82.

Anne's mean pledge was $5 with a standard deviation of 1.83; Michael's mean pledge was also $5, but the standard deviation of his pledges was only 0.82. The bars in the histogram of Michael's pledges are tightly packed about the mean. In the histogram of Anne's pledges, the bars are more spread out. A higher standard deviation tells us the data are more spread out.

TAKE NOTE

Standard Deviation

- Just as the mean represents the typical value of a variable for a population, the standard deviation represents the typical distance of a particular data value from the mean.
- The larger the standard deviation, the more spread out the data; the smaller the standard deviation, the less spread out the data.

Calculating the variance and standard deviation by hand is tedious, and there is a good chance of making an error. We can use technology to calculate the measures of central tendency and spread of the data. The instructions given here are for a TI-83 graphing calculator. If you use a different calculator, consult the user's manual.

Follow these steps to calculate the mean and standard deviation of Anne's pledge data. The data are reproduced in a frequency table for convenience.

Anne's Pledges	
Amount of pledge ($)	Frequency
2	1
3	1
4	2
5	2
6	2
7	1
8	1

- Press [STAT] [ENTER] to access the lists. To clear data from list L1, use the arrow keys to highlight L1 and press [CLEAR] [ENTER]. Repeat for list L2.
- Enter the pledge amounts in list L1. Press [ENTER] after each amount. Enter the frequencies in list L2. Your screen should look like this:

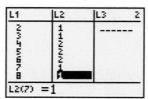

- This is single-variable data; press [STAT] [►] 1 to select 1-Var Stats. Press [2nd] 1 [,] [2nd] 2. This tells the calculator to use the values from list L1 and the frequencies from list L2. If no frequency list is specified, the calculator will assume all the frequencies are 1.

Press [ENTER] to execute the command. Your screen should look like the one below.

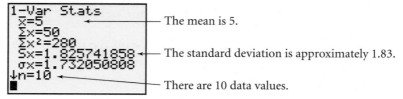

The arrow beside n=10 indicates there is more information. If you scroll down to the bottom, your screen will look like the one at the top of the next page.

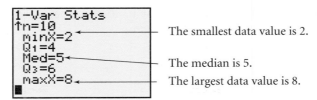

The smallest data value is 2.

The median is 5.

The largest data value is 8.

- Anne's mean pledge was $5 with a standard deviation of about 1.83.

Discuss

Describe how to use the results of the 1-Var Stats command to calculate the range and the variance for Anne's pledge data.

Example

Cameron collected these data about the number of hours her classmates spent working at part-time jobs last week.

| 0 | 5 | 3 | 0 | 4 | 16 | 3 | 5 | 17 | 5 |
| 14 | 2 | 3 | 4 | 1 | 0 | 6 | 5 | 3 | 7 |

a) Display these data in a histogram.

b) Determine the mean, the median, the mode, the range, and the standard deviation.

c) How well does the mean represent the typical number of hours of part-time work? Explain.

Solution

a) Clear any data in list L1.

Enter the data on number of hours worked into list L1.

Press [2nd] [Y=] 1 [ENTER] to access STAT PLOT and turn on Plot 1.

Press [▼] [►] [►] [ENTER] to select the histogram.

Enter L1 next to Xlist and 1 next to Freq.

Your screen should look like the one below left.

 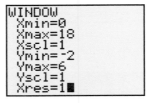

Use the window settings shown above right.

Press GRAPH to display the histogram (below left).

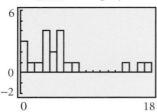

b) We can see from the histogram that there are two modes (represented by the tallest bars). Press TRACE and use the arrow keys to determine the modes. The modes are 3 h and 5 h.

Use the 1-Var Stats command to calculate the other measures.

Press STAT ▶ 1 to access 1-Var Stats.

Press 2nd 1 ENTER.

You should get the screen shown below left; you can use the arrow keys to view the rest of the results (below right).

```
1-Var Stats      1-Var Stats
 x̄=5.15           ↑n=20
 Σx=103            minX=0
 Σx²=999           Q₁=2.5
 Sx=4.9659366      Med=4
 σx=4.840196277    Q₃=5.5
↓n=20             ■ maxX=17
```

The mean is 5.15, the median is 4, and the modes are 3 and 5.

The range is the difference between maxX and minX, $17 - 0 = 17$.

The standard deviation is approximately 4.97.

c) The standard deviation of 4.97 is almost as large as the mean 5.15. This tells us that the mean is not representative of the population. Of the 20 people surveyed, only 5 worked more than the mean number of hours. Three of Cameron's classmates worked 14 or more hours last week. These large values pulled the mean up. In this case, the median is a better indicator of the typical number of hours of work.

6.1 Exercises

A

1. Calculate the mean, the range, the variance, and the standard deviation for each data set.

   a) 20, 30, 30, 40

   b) 18, 21, 24, 27, 30

c) 14, 19, 22, 22, 23, 23, 24, 24, 24

d) 17, 19, 19, 27, 27, 50

2. Calculate the mean, the range, and the standard deviation for each data set.

a)

Value	Frequency
27	3
28	5
29	9
30	6
31	1

b)

Value	Frequency
55	7
60	9
65	10
70	15
75	22
80	12
85	5

B

3. Last year, Joe bought 3 CDs at $18.99, 5 CDs at $14.99, and 1 CD at $10.

a) Find the mean price, the median price, and the standard deviation.

b) What does the standard deviation tell you about the prices Joe paid for CDs last year? Explain.

4. Knowledge/Understanding The table gives data on the lengths of 120 randomly selected bolts.

Length (mm)	4	5	6	7	8
Frequency	20	30	10	40	20

a) Calculate the mean and median lengths and the standard deviation.

b) How well does the mean length represent the typical length of a bolt from this population? Explain.

5. Without calculation, predict which data set will have the largest standard deviation and which will have the smallest. Explain.

a)
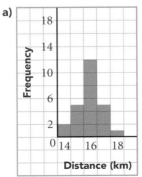

b)
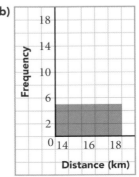

c)
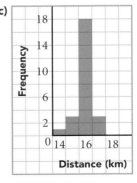

6. Refer to exercise 5. Calculate the standard deviation of each data set. How do the results compare to your predictions?

7. Without calculation, predict which data set will have the largest standard deviation and which will have the smallest. Explain.

a)
Height (cm)	Frequency
155	2
160	6
165	12
170	11
175	7
180	3
185	1

b)
Height (cm)	Frequency
155	3
160	6
165	22
170	7
175	2
180	1
185	1

c)
Height (cm)	Frequency
155	5
160	6
165	7
170	6
175	6
180	6
185	6

8. Refer to exercise 7. Calculate the standard deviation of each data set. How do the results compare to your predictions?

9. Forty soccer players from a high school league were asked to make 10 penalty kicks. The rate of success for each player was recorded and the standard deviation was calculated for the group. The experiment was repeated using 40 people randomly selected at a movie theatre. Which group do you expect would have the greater standard deviation? Explain.

10. Application The table gives the hourly wages, in dollars, of 20 randomly selected employees at a fast food restaurant.

9.71	9.12	10.37	10.58	10.74	8.95	10.14	10.57	9.74	10.54
10.69	10.67	10.67	10.85	8.90	10.76	9.55	10.00	8.83	9.72

a) Calculate the mean wage.

b) Calculate the standard deviation of the wages.

c) Make a statement about the typical hourly wage of an employee at this restaurant. Use the statistics you calculated in parts a and b to support your statement.

11. Describe how to determine the mode(s) of a data set by examining a histogram of the data.

12. Thinking/Inquiry/Problem Solving These data represent the lengths, in centimetres, of different pieces of string.
80, 25, 25, 25, 45, 35, 35, 25, 25, 35

a) Determine the mean, median, and mode lengths, and the standard deviation.

b) Suppose you measured incorrectly and the first length was 150 cm rather than 80 cm. Predict the effect on each of the three measures of central tendency and the standard deviation.

c) Enter the corrected length, that is, change the first length from 80 cm to 150 cm. Determine the new mean, median, mode, and standard deviation. Compare these results to your results in part a.

d) Which measure of central tendency is most affected by large changes in an extreme value? Explain.

13. A teacher has two classes in the same course and wishes to compare their performances. The marks for each class are given in the tables.

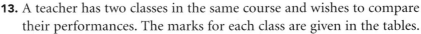

Class A	50	55	65	54	75	78	79	80	45	54	45
	67	76	62	81	55	65	75	80	60	70	

Class B	96	40	44	97	83	88	54	93	55	70	55
	98	57	42	67	68	91	55	53	55	58	

a) Calculate the mean, the median, the mode, the range, the variance, and the standard deviation for each class.

b) Which class is doing better? Use your statistics from part a to justify your choice.

14. These data represent the prices in dollars of various sweatshirts.
40, 42, 43, 44, 45, 46, 47, 48, 49, 50, 52

Determine the effect on the mean, the median, and the standard deviation in each case.

a) Each price is increased by $5.

b) Each price is doubled.

c) The lowest price is increased by $2 and the highest price is decreased by $2.

15. Communication The means and the standard deviations of two data sets are given in the table.

Data set	Mean	Standard deviation
A	25	8
B	2500	8

Explain how well each mean represents a typical member of the population it represents.

16. Work with a partner. Choose a human characteristic that can be measured, such as length of arm from elbow to fingertip, height, mass, or body temperature.

a) Collect data from each member of your class.

b) Graph the distribution of the data.

c) Calculate the mean and the standard deviation of the data.

d) Make a statement about the characteristic you measured. Use your work from parts a to c to justify your statement.

e) What questions can you ask about the characteristic you studied? Can you answer these questions with the data you gathered, or do you need to collect more data? Explain.

17. When bidding for the 1996 Summer Olympic Games, representatives from the city of Atlanta stated that the average temperature in July, measured in degrees Celsius, was in the mid-20s. When the games took place, the temperature was often in the mid-30s. The representatives from Atlanta referred to a mean temperature that was calculated using temperatures taken in the morning and evening. What measure would have been more helpful for the International Olympic Committee when making its decision? Explain.

18. A manufacturer of light bulbs collected these data on the measured lifetimes (in hours) of two brands of light bulbs.

Measured lifetimes, in hours, of 24 randomly selected Brand A light bulbs

1060	1017	854	1105	1191	876	925	976	917	948	1010	1137
1124	1027	968	977	858	1172	1142	1004	1036	1071	833	1117

Measured lifetimes, in hours, of 24 randomly selected Brand B light bulbs

1067	1005	938	1048	1015	983	978	1046	939	1120	1080	1138
993	942	945	1146	968	1025	1001	954	1119	1138	1033	963

a) Calculate the mean lifetime and the standard deviation for each brand.

b) Which is the better light bulb? Explain.

In Chapter 5, we organized data into frequency tables and histograms. These are examples of *frequency distributions*. A frequency distribution gives the number of occurrences of each of the possible values of a variable. In this section, we will examine several common frequency distributions.

Exploring Distributions of Data

Work in a group of 4. Each group member should complete exercises 1 to 8 for one of the data sets, then share the results with the rest of the group.

These 4 sets of data were collected:

Set A: mass in kilograms of 44 adult women rounded to the nearest 5 kg
40, 45, 45, 50, 50, 50, 50, 50, 55, 55, 55, 55, 55, 55, 55, 55, 55, 60, 60, 60, 60, 60, 60, 60, 60, 60, 60, 65, 65, 65, 65, 65, 65, 65, 65, 65, 70, 70, 70, 70, 70, 75, 75, 80

Set B: mass in kilograms of 55 adult men and women rounded to the nearest 5 kg
45, 45, 50, 50, 50, 55, 55, 55, 55, 55, 55, 60, 60, 60, 60, 60, 60, 60, 65, 65, 65, 65, 65, 65, 70, 70, 70, 70, 75, 75, 75, 80, 80, 80, 80, 80, 80, 85, 85, 85, 85, 85, 85, 85, 90, 90, 90, 90, 90, 90, 95, 95, 95, 100, 100

Set C: mass in kilograms of 44 male members of a social club for tall adults rounded to the nearest 5 kg
65, 70, 75, 75, 80, 80, 85, 85, 85, 85, 90, 90, 90, 90, 90, 90, 90, 90, 95, 95, 95, 95, 95, 95, 95, 95, 95, 100, 100, 100, 100, 100, 100, 100, 100, 105, 105, 105, 105, 105, 105, 110, 110, 110

Set D: mass in kilograms of 48 members of the Ontario Jockey Club rounded to the nearest 5 kg
45, 45, 45, 50, 50, 50, 50, 50, 55, 55, 55, 55, 55, 55, 55, 55, 60, 60, 60, 60, 60, 60, 60, 60, 60, 65, 65, 65, 65, 65, 65, 65, 65, 70, 70, 70, 70, 70, 75, 75, 75, 80, 80, 80, 85, 85, 90, 90

1. Organize the data into a frequency table.

2. Follow these steps to graph the frequency distribution.
   - Press STAT ENTER to access the lists. Clear any data in lists L1 and L2. Enter the masses in L1 and enter the frequencies in L2.

- Press [2nd] [Y=] 1 [ENTER] to turn on the STAT PLOT. Press [▼] [►] [ENTER] to select the broken-line graph. Enter L1 next to Xlist and L2 next to Ylist. Press [▼] [►] [ENTER] to select the + mark. Your screen should look like the one below left.

 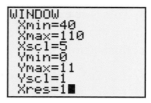

- Use the window settings shown above right.
- Press [GRAPH] to display the distribution.

3. Carefully sketch the distribution in your notebook. Label the axes and indicate the scale.

4. Use the frequency table from exercise 1 or the histogram from exercise 2 to determine the mode(s).

5. Follow these steps to calculate the mean and the median of the data.
   - Press [STAT] [►] 1 to access 1-Var Stats.
   - Press [2nd] 1 [,] [2nd] 2 [ENTER] to display the statistics. Use the [▼] key to scroll down to view the median. Record the mean and the median in your notebook.

6. Press [GRAPH] to display the frequency distribution again. Press [TRACE] and use the arrow keys to scroll along the graph, until you find the locations of the mean, the median, and the mode. Record these locations on the graph in your notebook.

7. Describe the shape of the distribution, mentioning the location(s) of any peaks and the locations of the mean, the median, and the mode in relation to the peak(s).

8. What conclusions can you make about the population based on the shape of the distribution and the measures of central tendency? Explain.

In the *Investigation*, we graphed four common distributions of data.

Normal Distribution

The data in Set A approximate a *normal distribution*. This distribution is often referred to as a "bell curve" because of its bell shape.

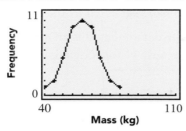

The mean, the median and the mode are equal and are located at the centre of the distribution. The normal distribution is symmetrical around the mean (the highest point).

Bimodal Distribution

The data in Set B follow a *bimodal distribution*. This distribution has two high peaks and, if the peaks are of equal height, two modes.

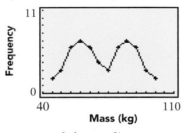

The mean and the median are not necessarily equal and are located between the two peaks. A bimodal distribution often indicates there are two subgroups in the data, which should be examined independently. In this case, the data on masses of adult men should be considered separately from the data on masses of adult women.

Skewed Distribution

The distributions of data sets C and D are both skewed. A *skewed distribution* is not symmetrical. The data tend to be clustered at one end.

The distribution of the data in Set C is an example of a distribution that is *skewed left*. Although the peak of the distribution is on the right, it is skewed left because there is a long tail to the left.

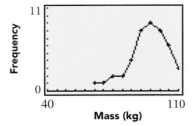

In a distribution that is skewed left, the mode is located at the peak, the median is less than the mode, and the mean is less than the median. The mean is affected by extreme values. The mean is less than the median because the mean is affected by the very low values in the tail.

The distribution of the data in Set D is an example of a distribution that is *skewed right* because of the long tail to the right.

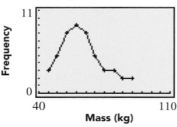

In a distribution that is skewed right, the mode is at the peak, the median is greater than the mode, and the mean is greater than the median. In this case, the mean is affected by the large values in the tail that make the mean greater than the median.

Example

Elliot plans to collect data on the heights of all the people in each of these groups at his school.

a) the members of the senior girls' basketball team

b) the males in grade 12

c) all grade 12 students

In each case, predict the shape of the distribution of data. Explain.

Solution

a) The data on the heights of the members of the senior girls' basketball team will likely be skewed left. We expect most of the girls will be tall.

b) Data on the heights of all the males in grade 12 will likely be normally distributed. Some of the boys will be tall and some will be short.

c) Data on the heights of all grade 12 students will likely be bimodal. Most of the students in grade 12 will be between the ages of 17 and 19. On average, boys in this age group are taller than girls.

A

✓ **1. Knowledge/Understanding** Match each label with its graph.

    i) normal   **ii)** bimodal   **iii)** skewed right   **iv)** skewed left

a)
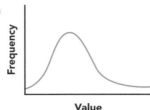

b)
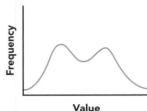

c)
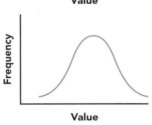

d)
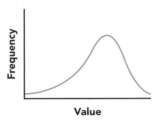

✓ **2.** Sketch a copy of each distribution in exercise 1 in your notebook. Indicate on the graph where the mean, the median, and the mode are likely to occur.

B

✓ **3.** These are the marks out of 10 on the latest quiz for a math class.
    9, 3, 4, 5, 9, 5, 9, 8, 6, 10, 7, 8, 6, 9, 9, 7, 8, 10, 8, 9, 9, 10, 9, 10, 10, 7

    a) Graph the distribution of the marks.

    b) Identify the type of distribution.

    c) Predict the locations of the mean, the median, and the mode on the distribution.

    d) Calculate the mean, the median, and the mode to verify your predictions in part c.

    e) Which measure of central tendency best represents the data? Explain.

✓ **4. Application** The table gives the frequency distribution of annual salaries of employees in a company.

Salary ($)	15 000	25 000	35 000	50 000	70 000	90 000
Frequency	28	36	26	14	8	3

    a) Graph the frequency distribution and identify it.

    b) Calculate the mean, the median, and the mode and indicate their locations on the graph.

c) Which measure of central tendency best represents the data? Explain.

d) Based on the distribution of data and the measures of central tendency, what conclusions can you draw about the salaries of employees at this company?

✓ **5.** A quality control supervisor measures the actual lengths of 5-cm bolts produced on an assembly line on a particular day.

Length (cm)	4.80	4.85	4.90	4.95	5.00	5.05	5.10	5.15	5.20
Frequency	5	7	10	14	16	14	11	7	4

a) Graph the distribution of lengths.

b) What type of distribution is it? Explain.

c) The mean length of the bolts is supposed to be 5.00 cm. Is this the case?

d) Does there appear to be a problem with the production process? Explain.

✓ **6.** The measures of central tendency are given for 4 data sets. In each case, identify a likely distribution for the data. Explain.

a) mean = 49.8   median = 50   mode = 50

b) mean = 35   median = 40   mode = 45

c) mean = 50   median = 51   mode = 38, 58

d) mean = 50   median = 46   mode = 42

✓ **7.** Refer to exercise 6. Explain how you used the mean, the median, and the mode of a data set to identify how the data were distributed, without graphing them.

✓ **8.** Data were collected on the ages of students enrolled at an elementary school. Here is the graph of the frequency distribution.

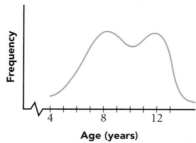

a) Describe the characteristics of the population.

b) Why might the principal of this elementary school need this information? Explain.

c) In what range of values will the mean lie? the median lie? Explain.

✓ **9. Communication** Data were collected on the prices of houses sold in the last year in a suburban area. Here is the frequency distribution of house prices.

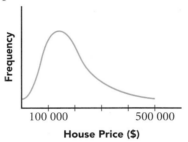

a) What conclusions can you draw about the prices of houses in this area? Explain.

b) Suppose you are a real estate agent trying to entice people to buy in the area. Which measure of central tendency would you use? Explain.

c) Suppose you are a real estate agent trying to encourage people to sell their homes. Which measure of central tendency would you use? Explain.

✓ **10.** Suppose you collected data on the annual income of workers in each group listed below. In each case, predict the shape of the distribution. Explain.

a) executives of Fortune 500 companies

b) child-care providers

c) all the employees of McDonald's

✓ **11.** Describe a set of data for each distribution.

a) normal   **b)** bimodal

c) skewed left   **d)** skewed right

✓ **12. Thinking/Inquiry/Problem Solving** Suppose you measure the time it takes students in your class to run 1 km. How do you expect the data to be distributed? Explain.

In Section 6.2, we learned about different distributions of data. In this section, we will study the normal distribution in more detail. Many characteristics of manufactured products have frequency graphs that closely approximate a normal distribution. Human characteristics such as height, mass, and intelligence have frequency distributions that closely approximate a normal distribution.

A manufacturer of light bulbs measured the usable lifetimes of 60-W light bulbs to the nearest hour. The data are displayed below.

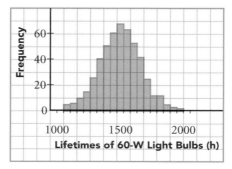

This manufacturer produces thousands of 60-W light bulbs every year. Suppose we measured the usable lifetime of every 60-W light bulb produced in the last 5 years and graphed the frequency distribution. The midpoints of the tops of the bars would form a curve similar to the one below.

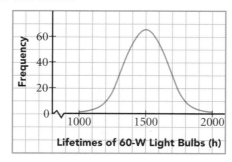

This smooth, bell-shaped curve is the graph of a normal distribution; it is called the *normal curve*.

Comparing Standard Deviations

In this *Investigation*, you will examine how changing the standard deviation affects the graph of the normal distribution.

The Crispy Chip Company needs to purchase a new machine to be used in the production of its 50-g snack-size bags. The company tests three different machines and records the mass of each bag produced by each machine to the nearest gram. Here are the results:

Machine A

Mass (g)	40	41	42	43	44	45	46	47	48	49
Frequency	1	2	3	5	7	10	13	17	22	26

Mass (g)	50	51	52	53	54	55	56	57	58	59	60
Frequency	28	26	22	17	13	10	7	5	3	2	1

Machine B

Mass (g)	40	41	42	43	44	45	46	47	48	49
Frequency	5	6	7	8	9	11	13	15	17	19

Mass (g)	50	51	52	53	54	55	56	57	58	59	60
Frequency	20	19	17	15	13	11	9	8	7	6	5

Machine C

Mass (g)	40	41	42	43	44	45	46	47	48	49
Frequency	0	0	0	1	2	3	8	20	30	37

Mass (g)	50	51	52	53	54	55	56	57	58	59	60
Frequency	38	37	30	20	8	3	2	1	0	0	0

1. Enter the data into a calculator.

- Press STAT ENTER to access the lists. Clear any data from the lists.

  For Machine A, enter the masses into list L1 and the frequencies into list L2.

  For Machine B, enter the masses into list L3 and the frequencies into list L4.

  For Machine C, enter the masses into list L5 and the frequencies into list L6.

2. Calculate the mean, the median, and the standard deviation for each data set and record the values.

- Press [STAT] [►] 1 to access 1-Var Stats.
- Press [2nd] 1 [,] [2nd] 2 [ENTER] to display the statistics for Machine A. Use the arrow keys to scroll down to view the median. Repeat for Machines B and C. Remember, the data for Machine B are in lists L3 and L4 and the data for Machine C are in lists L5 and L6.

3. Determine the mode for each data set.

4. Plot the frequency distribution for each data set on the same graph.

- Press [2nd] [Y=] 1 [ENTER] to access STAT PLOT and turn on Plot1. Select the broken-line graph. Enter L1 for Xlist and L2 for Ylist. Select the + mark. Your screen should look like the one below left.

- Use the arrow keys to highlight Plot2, press [ENTER]. Set Plot2 as shown above right.
- Use the arrow keys to highlight Plot3, press [ENTER]. Set Plot3 as shown below left.

 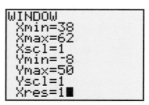

- Set your window. Appropriate settings are shown above right.
- Press [GRAPH] to display all three distributions on the same screen. Copy the graphs into your notebook and label them.

5. Refer to exercises 2 and 3.

a) Which statistics are the same for each set of data? How is this illustrated on the graphs of the distributions?

b) Which statistics are different for each set of data? How is this illustrated on the graphs of the distributions?

6. Does the mean, the median, the mode, and/or the standard deviation affect the shape of the graph of the normal distribution? Explain.

7. Which machine will produce bags that are more likely to have a mass of 50 g? Which machine should the company purchase? Explain.

The location of the normal curve is determined by the mean. A change in the mean causes the normal curve to shift right or left.

The width of the normal curve is determined by the standard deviation. A change in the standard deviation causes the normal curve to become broader or narrower.

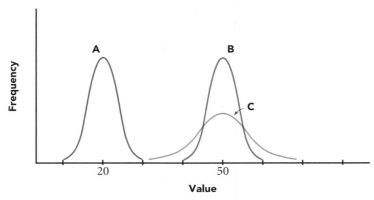

In the graph, data sets A and B have the same standard deviation (and the same width), but the mean of data set B is larger. Data sets B and C have the same mean, but the standard deviation of data set C is larger.

TAKE NOTE

Properties of a Normal Distribution

- Every normal distribution has a mean, $\bar{x}$, and a standard deviation s.
- The mean, the median, and the mode are equal.
- The graph is symmetrical about the mean.
- Almost all the data lie within 3 standard deviations of the mean.

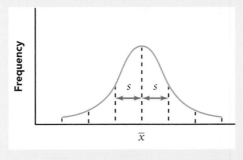

The normal distribution is useful because certain percents of data fall within specific distances from the mean.

TAKE NOTE
68-95-99 Rule

- About 68% of the data are within 1 standard deviation to the left and right of the mean.
- About 95% of the data are within 2 standard deviations to the left and right of the mean.
- About 99.7% of the data are within 3 standard deviations to the left and right of the mean.

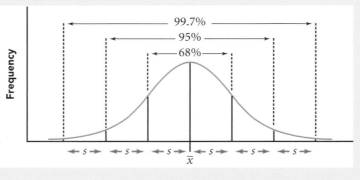

The graph of the normal distribution is symmetrical, so we redraw the distribution to show the percent of data that lie in each interval.

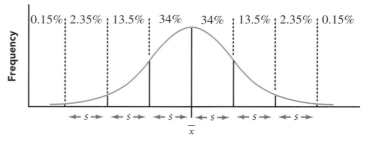

Example

Cadbury produces 43-g bags of Mini Eggs. Every hour, 10 bags are taken from the production line and weighed. Here are some of the results.

Time	Mass (g)									
7:00	44.8	44.9	44.7	43.5	44.9	43.1	44.8	43.3	45.0	44.8
8:00	43.6	43.7	43.2	43.6	43.1	43.1	43.2	43.2	43.6	44.8
9:00	43.3	43.4	43.1	43.3	44.0	45.0	43.2	43.2	43.2	45.2

a) Enter the data in list L1 of your calculator. Calculate the mean and the standard deviation. Round your answers to two decimal places.

b) Assume the distribution is normal. Determine the masses that are each distance away from the mean.
i) 1 standard deviation
ii) 2 standard deviations
iii) 3 standard deviations

c) Sketch a normal curve. Label the mean and the masses that are 1, 2, and 3 standard deviations from the mean. Show the percent of data that lie within each interval.

d) Find the proportion of bags of Mini Eggs with mass that is:
i) less than 42.32 g
ii) greater than 44.63 g
iii) between 43.09 g and 45.40 g

e) Estimate the range of masses of 43-g bags of Cadbury Mini Eggs.

Solution

a) Press $\boxed{\text{STAT}}$ $\boxed{\blacktriangleright}$ 1 to access 1-Var Stat. Press $\boxed{\text{2nd}}$ 1 $\boxed{\text{ENTER}}$ to display this screen.

```
1-Var Stats
 x̄=43.86
 Σx=1315.8
 Σx²=57728.24
 Sx=.7712953726
 σx=.7583315018
↓n=30
■
```

The mean is 43.86 and the standard deviation is approximately 0.77.

b) The mean mass is 43.86 g.
The masses that are 1 standard deviation from the mean are:
$43.86 + 0.77 = 44.63$ g, and
$43.86 - 0.77 = 43.09$ g

The masses that are 2 standard deviations from the mean are:
$43.86 + 2(0.77) = 45.40$ g, and
$43.86 - 2(0.77) = 42.32$ g

The masses that are 3 standard deviations from the mean are:
$43.86 + 3(0.77) = 46.17$ g, and
$43.86 - 3(0.77) = 41.55$ g

c)

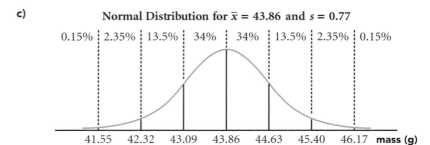

Normal Distribution for $\bar{x} = 43.86$ and $s = 0.77$

0.15% ⋮ 2.35% ⋮ 13.5% ⋮ 34% ⋮ 34% ⋮ 13.5% ⋮ 2.35% ⋮ 0.15%

41.55 42.32 43.09 43.86 44.63 45.40 46.17 **mass (g)**

d) i)

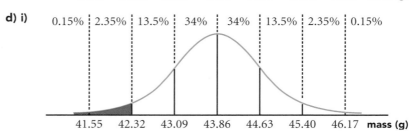

0.15% ⋮ 2.35% ⋮ 13.5% ⋮ 34% ⋮ 34% ⋮ 13.5% ⋮ 2.35% ⋮ 0.15%

41.55 42.32 43.09 43.86 44.63 45.40 46.17 **mass (g)**

About 2.35% + 0.15% = 2.5% of bags of Mini Eggs have a mass less than 42.32 g.

ii)

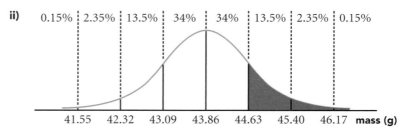

0.15% ⋮ 2.35% ⋮ 13.5% ⋮ 34% ⋮ 34% ⋮ 13.5% ⋮ 2.35% ⋮ 0.15%

41.55 42.32 43.09 43.86 44.63 45.40 46.17 **mass (g)**

About 13.5% + 2.35% + 0.15% = 16% of bags of Mini Eggs have a mass greater than 44.63 g.

iii)

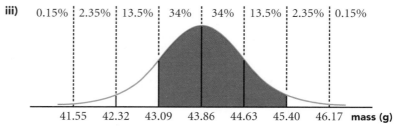

0.15% ⋮ 2.35% ⋮ 13.5% ⋮ 34% ⋮ 34% ⋮ 13.5% ⋮ 2.35% ⋮ 0.15%

41.55 42.32 43.09 43.86 44.63 45.40 46.17 **mass (g)**

About 34% + 34% + 13.5% = 81.5% of bags of Mini Eggs have a mass between 43.09 g and 45.40 g.

e) We know that about 99.7% of the data lie within 3 standard deviations of the mean. We can use this to estimate the range of masses of Mini Eggs.

46.17 − 41.55 = 4.62 g

A reasonable estimate of the range of masses is 4.62 g.

Discuss

Describe a different way to estimate the range of masses of bags of Mini Eggs in the Example. Explain why the range cannot be determined exactly.

Exercises

A

1. Which normal distribution has the highest standard deviation and which has the lowest? Explain.

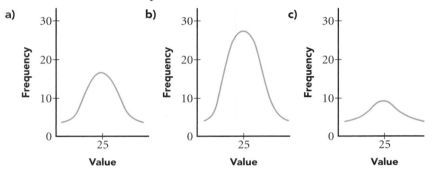

2. The marks on a recent test are normally distributed, with mean 72 and standard deviation 6.
   a) Determine the marks that are each distance away from the mean:
      i) 1 standard deviation
      ii) 2 standard deviations
      iii) 3 standard deviations
   b) Sketch a normal curve. Label the mean and the marks that are 1, 2, and 3 standard deviations from the mean. Show the percent of data that lie in each interval.

3. **Knowledge/Understanding** Three sets of data are described. Match each data set with the graph most likely to represent its distribution. Use each graph only once. Explain your pairings.
   a) the actual volume of pop in a 1-L bottle
   b) the annual incomes of all Canadians over the age of 15
   c) the marks received by a group of mathematics students on a chapter test

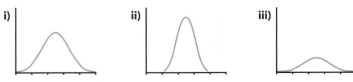

4. The usable lifetimes of 10 000 AA batteries are normally distributed with a mean lifetime of 25 h and a standard deviation of 2 h.

a) Determine the lifetimes that are within 1, 2, and 3 standard deviations of the mean.

b) What percent of batteries have a usable lifetime in each range?
   i) between 23 h and 27 h
   ii) between 29 h and 31 h
   iii) between 19 h and 27 h

5. The masses of the stones in a load of gravel are normally distributed, with mean 4.8 g and standard deviation 0.4 g.

a) Sketch the normal distribution of the masses of the stones. Label the mean and the points that are 1, 2, and 3 standard deviations from the mean.

b) What percent of the stones have mass in each range?
   i) less than 3.6 g   **ii)** greater than 3.6 g
   iii) greater than 4.4 g   **iv)** between 4.8 g and 5.2 g
   v) between 3.6 g and 6.0 g

c) Estimate the range of masses of the stones.

6. Application The results of a standardized test were normally distributed, with mean 504 and standard deviation 110.

a) Sketch the normal distribution of the test scores. Label the mean and the points that are 1, 2, and 3 standard deviations from the mean.

b) What percent of students had scores in each range?
   i) less than 614   **ii)** greater than 504
   iii) greater than 284   **iv)** between 394 and 724

c) Estimate the range of test scores.

7. Sketch each pair of normal distributions on the same grid. How are the sketches similar? How are they different?

a) mean 50, standard deviation 10   **b)** mean 40, standard deviation 5
   mean 50, standard deviation 20   mean 50, standard deviation 5

8. The Stanford-Binet Intelligence Quotient (IQ) test scores of Canadians are normally distributed, with mean 100 and standard deviation 16.

a) What percent of people have an IQ greater than 132 as measured by this test?

b) The label "genius" applies to a person who scores in the top 2% of all those taking the test. What score would a person need to be classified a genius?

9. **Communication** Here is a graph of a normal distribution, with mean 50 and standard deviation 4. In each case, explain how the graph would change, then sketch a new graph.

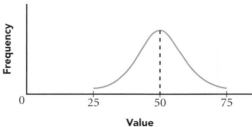

Value

a) The mean remains the same and the standard deviation is 8.

b) The mean is 75 and the standard deviation is the same.

c) The mean is 25 and the standard deviation is 2.

10. A manufacturer of light bulbs advertises that its light bulbs have a lifetime of 2000 h. An independent research agency tests the light bulbs and finds the lifetimes are normally distributed, with mean 2066.8 h and standard deviation 84.4 h. Is the manufacturer's claim reasonable? Explain.

11. **Thinking/Inquiry/Problem Solving** Here are the results of a standardized test for students from two school districts.

District	Mean score	Standard deviation
A	600	50
B	500	100

a) Compare the results for the two districts. Which district did better? Explain.

b) Which district had more uniform results? Explain.

12. A group of adults had their reaction times tested. Then, after taking cold medication their reaction time was tested again. How would you expect the distribution of reaction times to change? Use diagrams in your explanation.

13. Sacks of grain packed by an automatic loader have a mean mass of 61.0 kg. Ninety-five percent of the sacks have masses between 56.4 kg and 65.6 kg.

a) Explain how to determine the standard deviation.

b) Calculate the standard deviation.

14. We can use a graphing calculator to sketch a normal distribution. Follow these steps to graph a normal distribution with mean 25 and standard deviation 2:

- Turn off all STAT PLOTs.
- Press ☐ Y= ☐. Press ☐ 2nd ☐ ☐ VARS ☐ **1** to select normalpdf(. The syntax for the normalpdf function is normalpdf(variable, mean, standard deviation).
- Press ☐ X,T,θ,n ☐ ☐ , ☐ **25** ☐ , ☐ **2** ☐) ☐ ☐ ENTER ☐. You should get the screen shown below left.

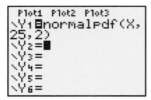 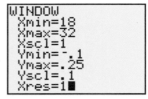

- Set the window. In this case the mean is 25 and the standard deviation is 2, so virtually all the data will be between 19 and 31. Appropriate window settings are shown above right.
- Press ☐ GRAPH ☐ to display the distribution. The *y*-values are relative frequencies — the frequency of each value divided by the total frequency.

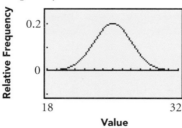

a) Graph a normal distribution with mean 50 and standard deviation 3.

b) What are appropriate window settings?

c) Use the calculator to graph the distributions in exercise 7. To graph two distributions on the same screen, define the first distribution in Y1 and the second distribution in Y2.

15. We can use a graphing calculator to shade a range on the normal curve and determine the percent of the data that lie within that range. This allows us to find proportions of data that are not 1, 2, or 3 standard deviations from the mean.

We will use the normal distribution from exercise 14. Follow these steps to determine the percent of data that are between 23 and 27.

- Turn off all STAT PLOTs.

- Set an appropriate window. In this case, use the window settings shown in exercise 14.
- Press [2nd] [VARS] [▶] 1 to select ShadeNorm(. The syntax for the ShadeNorm command is ShadeNorm(lower bound, upper bound, mean, standard deviation).
- Enter 23 [,] 27 [,] 25 [,] 2 [ )] [ENTER]. You will get this screen.

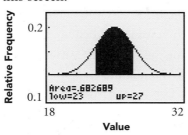

When we graph a normal distribution with relative frequency on the vertical axis, the total area under the curve is 1. The area of the shaded region represents the proportion of the data that lie within this range. We can express this value as a percent. Approximately 68.3% of the data are between 23 and 27.

a) The masses of fish in a load of cod were distributed normally, with mean 2.7 kg and standard deviation 0.3 kg. Determine the percent of fish with masses between 2.3 kg and 3.1 kg.

b) Refer to part a. Determine the percent of fish with masses greater than 3.2 kg. Since almost all of the data lie within 3 standard deviations of the mean, enter a value for the upper bound that is 4 or more standard deviations from the mean.

C

16. Frequently, individual results of a standardized test are reported as *percentiles*. The test scores are ordered from smallest to largest, then divided into 100 groups. The first percentile is the score such that 1% of the data are less than that score. The second percentile is the score such that 2% of the data are less than that score, and so on. The 50th percentile is the median — 50% of the data lie below this value.

The scores on a standardized test were distributed normally, with mean 650 and standard deviation 30.

a) Sketch the normal distribution of the test scores. Label the mean and the points that are 1, 2, and 3 standard deviations from the mean.

b) What percent of students received a score greater than 680?

c) Susan's score was in the 84th percentile. What is the minimum score she could have received? Explain.

1. These data represent the number of children in each of 24 households.
   2, 0, 3, 2, 1, 3, 1, 3, 4, 1, 4, 2, 2, 3, 2, 3, 2, 1, 0, 0, 1, 2, 3, 2
   a) Organize the data into a frequency table.
   b) Use the table from part a to determine the mode number of children.
   c) Calculate the mean, the median, and the standard deviation.
   d) Calculate the range and the variance.
   e) Make a statement about the typical number of children in a household. Use the statistics you calculated in parts b to d to support your statement.

2. The measures of central tendency are given for 3 data sets. In each case, identify a likely distribution for the data. Explain.
   a) mean = 100   median = 98   mode = 94
   b) mean = 98   median = 103   mode = 106
   c) mean = 100   median = 100   mode = 97, 104

3. These data represent the marks out of 15 on a mathematics quiz.
   12, 15, 6, 13, 11, 9, 12, 8, 10, 10, 11, 14, 12, 13,
   14, 13, 13, 11, 13, 14, 12, 14, 15, 9, 15, 13, 7
   a) Graph the distribution of the marks. Identify the type of distribution.
   b) Calculate the mean, the median, and the mode and indicate their locations on the distribution.
   c) Which measure of central tendency best represents the typical mark on this quiz? Explain.
   d) Did the class do well on this quiz? Explain.

Performance Assessment

4. One hundred squash balls are dropped from a height of 250 cm. The height of the first bounce for each ball is recorded. The bounce heights were normally distributed, with mean 75 cm and standard deviation 1.9 cm.
   a) What percent of balls have bounce heights in each range?
      i) less than 78.8 cm   ii) between 69.3 cm and 75 cm
   b) A ball is considered "fast" if it bounces above 80.7 cm. How many of the balls are fast?
   c) What is the approximate range of bounce heights?

In Sections 6.1 to 6.3, we analysed single-variable data. In this section and Section 6.5, we will introduce some techniques for analysing two-variable data.

Researchers collect and analyse two-variable data to answer questions such as these:

- If parents are tall, will their children be tall too?
- Do people with more education earn higher salaries?
- Will lowering taxes increase consumer spending?
- Do people who study longer earn higher marks?
- Does the correct use of a booster seat reduce the risk of death or serious injury to a child involved in a car accident?

Once we collect two-variable data, it is useful to display them in a scatter plot. From the scatter plot, we can determine if there are any trends in the data. Consider the following examples.

This graph shows goals scored versus shots on goal for the top 16 players in the NHL for the 2000–2001 regular season.

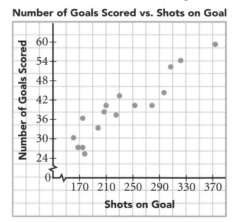

Number of Goals Scored vs. Shots on Goal

The points show an upward trend from left to right, so these variables are *positively correlated*. In other words, the number of goals scored increases as the number of shots on goal increases.

This graph shows the cost in dollars versus the annual energy requirement in kilowatt-hours (kWh) for various models of dishwashers.

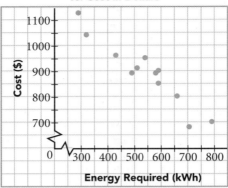

The points show a downward trend from left to right. We say these variables are *negatively correlated*. Dishwashers that are more energy efficient (use less energy) cost more money.

This graph shows height in centimetres versus number of siblings.

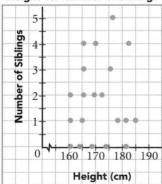

There is no pattern in the data, so we say there is *no correlation*. In other words, the two variables are not related.

The relationship between two variables must be analysed carefully. It is possible for two variables to be positively or negatively correlated, even if a change in the value of one of the variables has no effect on the value of the other variable. If this is the case, we say there is no *causal relationship*.

Examine this graph that shows total points scored versus jersey number for the members of a senior girls' basketball team.

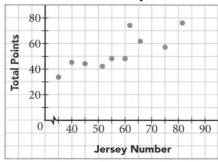

Total Points vs. Jersey Number

According to these data, the two variables are positively correlated. However, having a player wear a jersey with a higher number will not cause her to score more points.

Example 1

Consider these data sets.

i)

Arm span (cm)	Height (cm)
70	70
110	108
118	120
124	123
140	141
155	160
168	165
177	178
188	185
195	195

ii)

Weeks dieting	Mass (kg)
1	65
2	64
3	64
4	62
5	61
6	60
7	58
8	57
9	57
10	56

iii)

Height (cm)	Grade 12 math mark (%)
165	54
170	88
174	67
180	74
182	50
185	60
187	90
190	45
192	75
195	72

For each data set:

  a) Plot the data on a scatter plot.

  b) Identify whether the variables are positively correlated, negatively correlated, or not correlated.

  c) If the variables are correlated, state whether there might be a causal relationship. Explain.

Solution

a) For each data set:

- Press [STAT] [ENTER] to access the lists. Clear any data in lists L1 and L2. Enter the data into lists L1 and L2.
- Press [2nd] [Y=] 1 [ENTER] to access STAT PLOT and turn on Plot1.
- Press [▼] [ENTER] to select the scatter plot. Enter L1 for Xlist and L2 for Ylist.
- Set an appropriate window.
- Press [GRAPH] to display the scatter plot. Copy the scatter plot into your notebook.

i)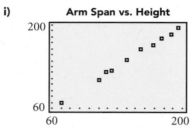

Arm Span vs. Height

ii)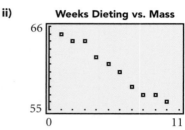

Weeks Dieting vs. Mass

iii)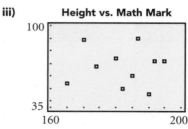

Height vs. Math Mark

b) i) There is a positive correlation between arm span and height. According to these data, a person with a large arm span will be tall and a person with a small arm span will be short.

ii) There is a negative correlation between the number of weeks dieting and mass. According to these data, the more time a person spends dieting, the lower is her or his mass.

iii) According to these data, there is no correlation between a person's height and her or his mark in grade 12 mathematics.

c) i) There is a causal relationship between arm span and height. Our bodies are in proportion. A tall person will have a larger arm span than a short person.

ii) There may be a causal relationship between the number of weeks a person diets and his or her mass. If the person burns more calories than he or she consumes, he or she will lose weight.

iii) There is no causal relationship between the height of a grade 12 student and her or his mark in grade 12 mathematics.

If the variables are correlated, we can determine the equation of the line of best fit. We can then use this equation and its graph to make predictions.

In Chapter 5, Necessary Skills 3, you reviewed drawing a line of best fit by hand. You may have found that it was often difficult to determine which line best fit the data. One method that avoids guessing is the method of least squares.

The *least squares line* or *regression line* is the line such that the sum of the squares of the vertical distances between the data points and the line are a minimum. In this section, we will use the regression capabilities of a graphing calculator to determine the equation of the line of best fit.

These instructions are for a TI-83 graphing calculator. If you use a different graphing calculator, consult the user's manual. Follow these steps to find the regression line of best fit for the data on weeks dieting versus mass from *Example 1*.

- Press $\boxed{\text{STAT}}$ $\boxed{\text{ENTER}}$ to access the lists. Clear any data in lists L1 and L2. Enter the number of weeks' data into list L1 and the mass data into list L2.

- Press $\boxed{\text{STAT}}$ $\boxed{\blacktriangleright}$ 4 to select LinReg(ax+b). The command LinReg(ax+b) will give the equation of the line of best fit in the form $y = ax + b$, where a is the slope of the line and b is the y-intercept.

- Press $\boxed{\text{2nd}}$ 1 $\boxed{,}$ $\boxed{\text{2nd}}$ 2 $\boxed{,}$ $\boxed{\text{VARS}}$ $\boxed{\blacktriangleright}$ 1 1. This tells the calculator to perform the regression on the data stored in lists L1 and L2 and to paste the equation into Y1 in the Y= list. Press $\boxed{\text{ENTER}}$ to execute the regression.

- Your screen should look like the one at right. The values for r^2 and r may or may not be displayed. The equation of the line of best fit is approximately $y = -1.08x + 66.33$. The slope, -1.08, represents the weekly mass loss in kilograms. The y-intercept, 66.33, represents the person's mass in kilograms before starting to diet (in week 0).

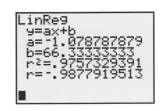

- Set up Plot1 in STAT PLOT to display a scatter plot of the data. Set an appropriate window. Press $\boxed{\text{GRAPH}}$ to display the scatter plot and the line of best fit.

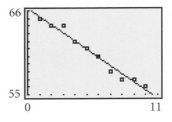

Discuss

Explain why it is important to determine whether the variables are correlated before determining the equation of the regression line of best fit.

Example 2

The table shows the Consumer Price Index (CPI) with base year 1992, and the number of Canadians, in thousands, 15 years of age and over who were unemployed (U) every year from 1991 to 2000. Recall that the CPI is an index that measures changes in prices of consumer goods.

Year	1991	1992	1993	1994	1995	1996	1997	1998	1999	2000
CPI	98.5	100.0	101.8	102.0	104.2	105.9	107.6	108.6	110.5	113.5
U (1000s)	1479.5	1602.3	1647.0	1514.9	1393.1	1436.9	1378.6	1277.3	1190.1	1089.6

a) Draw a scatter plot of the CPI versus unemployment.

b) Describe any trends in the graph. Is there a correlation between changes in prices and unemployment?

c) Determine the equation of the line of best fit. Interpret the meaning of the slope and the y-intercept in terms of the data.

d) Graph the line of best fit and the scatter plot on the same screen. Use the graph of the line of best fit to predict the number of Canadians who would be unemployed if the CPI were 117.0.

Solution

a) Enter the CPI data in list L1 and the unemployment data in list L2. Access STAT PLOT and turn on Plot 1. Select the scatter plot. Enter L1 for Xlist and L2 for Ylist.
Use these window settings:
Xmin = 95, Xmax = 118, Xscl = 1,
Ymin = 900, Ymax = 1675, Yscl = 100.
Clear all equations from the Y= list.
Press [GRAPH] to display the screen shown at right.

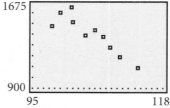

b) There is a downward trend in the data. As the CPI increases, unemployment decreases. These data are negatively correlated.

c) Press [STAT] [▶] 4 to select LinReg(ax+b).
Press: [2nd] 1 [,] [2nd] 2 [,] [VARS]
[▶] 1 1 [ENTER]

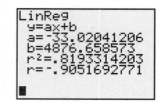

The equation of the line of best fit is approximately $y = -33.02x + 4876.66$. The slope, -33.02, represents the average decrease, in thousands, in unemployment for a 1% increase in the CPI. The y-intercept, 4876.66, represents the number of Canadians, in thousands, who would be unemployed if the CPI were 0.

d) Press GRAPH to display the graph. Press TRACE ▲, then press ► repeatedly, until the value of X in the bottom left corner of the screen is as close as possible to 117.0.

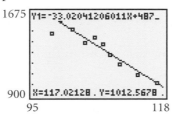

If the CPI were 117.0, approximately 1 012 568 Canadians would be unemployed.

Discuss

Suppose the CPI were 0. What does that tell us about price levels?

6.4 Exercises

A

 1. Classify each data set as single-variable or two-variable. Explain.

a)

Length	Frequency
10	1
12	3
14	7
16	4

b)

Length	Width
10	3
12	5
14	7
16	12

 2. In each scatter plot, are the variables positively correlated, negatively correlated, or not correlated? Explain.

a)
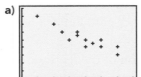

b)
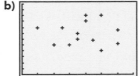

c)
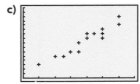

3. **Communication** Suppose you collected data to compare each pair of variables. In each case, do you think the variables will be positively correlated, negatively correlated, or not correlated? Explain.
   a) foot size versus height
   b) height of a dropped ball versus time
   c) height versus number of shirts owned

4. In each case, state whether there is a causal relationship between the variables. Explain.
   a) number of hours spent studying mathematics; mark on mathematics test
   b) amount of money spent to hire a tutor in mathematics; mark on mathematics test
   c) foot length; amount of money saved in RRSPs
   d) the surface area of an ice cube; the time the ice cube has been sitting at room temperature

B

5. **Application** The table shows the age in years and the diameter in centimetres of a particular species of tree.

Age (years)	8	19	11	4	16	18	12	22	5
Diameter (cm)	9	12	10	1	19	9	6	15	5

   a) Draw a scatter plot of the data. Put age on the horizontal axis and diameter on the vertical axis. Copy the graph.
   b) Describe any trends in the graph. Is there a correlation between the diameter of a tree and its age?
   c) Determine the equation of the line of best fit.
   d) Graph the equation of the line of best fit and the scatter plot on the same screen. How well does the line fit the data? Explain.
   e) Estimate the age of a tree that has a diameter of 25 cm.
   f) Estimate the diameter of a 10-year-old tree.

6. The table gives the heights and masses of 13 students.

Height (cm)	150	151	152	154	156	158	160	161	164	165	166	170	172
Mass (kg)	51	56	54	58	56	62	91	65	66	70	71	74	74

   a) Plot the data in a scatter plot. Put height on the horizontal axis and mass on the vertical axis.
   b) Determine the equation of the regression line of best fit.
   c) Graph the equation of the line of best fit on the same screen as the scatter plot. Does it appear to be a good fit? Explain.

d) Predict the height of a student with mass 80 kg.

e) Predict the mass of a student who is 2 m tall.

 7. Suppose you collect data on the ages of members of the population and a second variable to determine whether they are correlated. Give an example of a second variable that would be:

a) positively correlated with age

b) negatively correlated with age

c) not correlated with age

 8. Knowledge/Understanding The table gives data for the top ten money leaders in the Ladies Professional Golf Association (LPGA) for the 2001 golf season.

Rank	Player	Events	Earnings ($)
1	Annika Sorenstam	18	1 326 209
2	Se Ri Pak	17	1 257 048
3	Karrie Webb	16	1 191 019
4	Maria Hjorth	22	735 230
5	Dottie Pepper	19	707 411
6	Laura Diaz	22	653 040
7	Mi Hyun Kim	23	629 624
8	Rosie Jones	16	622 531
9	Catriona Matthew	21	620 563
10	Lorie Kane	19	614 909

a) Draw a scatter plot of earnings versus number of events played. Copy the graph.

b) Describe any trends in the graph. Is there a correlation between a player's earnings and the number of events she played?

c) Is it appropriate to find a line of best fit for earnings versus number of events played? Explain.

 9. The table gives the winning times in seconds for the men's Olympic 100-m dash.

Year	1960	1964	1968	1972	1976	1980	1984	1988	1992	1996	2000
Time (s)	10.2	10.0	9.95	10.14	10.06	10.25	9.99	9.92	9.96	9.84	9.87

a) Enter the years in list L1 and the times in list L2. Find the equation of the regression line of best fit.

b) Use the equation to predict the winning time in the 100-m dash in 2008.

10. An obstetrician checks the measurements of various parts of a fetus using ultrasound technology. She determines whether the baby is developing at a healthy rate by comparing the baby's measurements to a table that shows average sizes for particular stages of development. A portion of this table is reproduced here.

Age (weeks)	12	16	20	24	28	32	36	40
Head circumference (cm)	7.1	12.4	17.5	22.1	26.2	29.7	32.5	34.5

a) Enter the ages in list L1 and the head circumferences in list L2. Find the equation of the line of best fit.

b) Use the equation to estimate an average measurement of head circumference for a fetus aged 30 weeks.

c) A pregnant woman has an ultrasound examination. The head circumference of the fetus is 20.6 cm. What age in weeks does the doctor predict for the fetus?

11. Refer to exercise 10. Doctors are concerned if the growth rate is ahead or behind by more than two weeks. Suppose a woman is 33 weeks pregnant and the fetal head circumference measures 28.3 cm. Will the doctor be concerned? Explain.

12. To investigate the resistance in an electrical circuit, Rose measured the voltages when different currents passed through the circuit. Her data are given in the table.

Current (A)	0.5	1	1.5	2	2.5	3	3.5	4	4.5
Voltage (V)	5.0	10.3	15.2	20.4	25.5	30.5	35.8	40.7	46.0

a) Enter the currents in list L1 and the voltages in list L2. Draw a scatter plot of the data and determine the equation of the line of best fit. Copy the graph and equation.

b) Estimate the voltage when the current is 5 A.

c) Use the equation of the line of best fit to estimate the voltage when the current is 0 A. Does your answer make sense? Explain.

13. Give an example of a pair of two-variable data that would display each type of correlation. Explain.

a) a positive correlation

b) a negative correlation

c) no correlation

✓

14. **Thinking/Inquiry/Problem Solving** Choose a topic from the list below or select your own topic.

- the number of hours per week spent studying mathematics versus the current mark in mathematics
- the number of hours per week spent working at a part-time job versus the average weekly income
- the average number of hours per week spent watching television versus the number of hours per week spent playing sports

a) Conduct a survey to determine whether there is a relationship between the two variables.

- Identify the population, then select a random sample of 20 or more members of the population.
- Design two survey questions.
- Ask each person in your sample to answer both questions.
- Record their responses.

b) What type of correlation do you expect? Explain.

c) Plot the data in a scatter plot.

d) What type of correlation does the graph show? How does this compare to your prediction in part b? Explain.

e) Determine the equation of the line of best fit.

f) Make a statement about the population based on your analysis.

g) Ask a question about the population that you can answer using the data you collected.

✓

15. Research E-Stat, the Internet, or the library to collect data on the unemployment rate in Ontario over time.

a) Plot the data in a scatter plot.

b) Determine the equation of the line of best fit.

c) Graph the line of best fit and the scatter plot on the same screen.

d) Can you use the graph to predict the unemployment rate in Ontario in 2020? How reliable would the prediction be? Explain.

e) Make a statement about the unemployment rate in Ontario over time. Use the results of your analysis to support your statement.

In Section 6.4, we plotted scatter plots of two-variable data. Some data sets had graphs that were very close to linear; other data sets showed a weak linear trend or no trend.

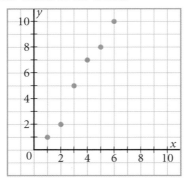 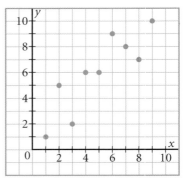

The graph above left shows data points that are very close to a line. The graph above right shows points with a linear trend.

Statisticians assign a number to indicate how close the points in a scatter plot are to forming a line. This is the *correlation coefficient, r*.

Some graphing calculators determine *r* when they find the equation of the regression line of best fit. For the calculator to display the correlation coefficient with the equation of the line of best fit, the diagnostic feature must be turned on. This must be done before the data are entered and the window is set.

Follow these steps to turn on the diagnostic feature of a TI-83 graphing calculator.

- Press 2nd 0 to select CATALOG.
- Press ▼ repeatedly until the cursor points to DiagnosticOn.
- Press ENTER ENTER.

When the results of the linear regression are displayed, the value of *r* appears at the bottom of the display.

In *Investigation 1*, you will determine the correlation coefficient for various data sets and examine how the value of the correlation coefficient is related to the shape of data in a scatter plot.

Investigation 1

The Correlation Coefficient

Work in a group of 5. Each group member should complete exercises 1 and 2 for two data sets, then share the results with the rest of the group. You may work together or individually to complete exercises 3 and 4.

All the x and y-values are in the range from 0 to 10. Use these window settings throughout the Investigation.

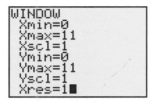

```
WINDOW
 Xmin=0
 Xmax=11
 Xscl=1
 Ymin=0
 Ymax=11
 Yscl=1
 Xres=1■
```

1. For each data set:

   a) Determine the equation of the regression line of best fit and the value of the correlation coefficient, r.

   - Press [STAT] [ENTER] to access the lists. Clear any data in lists L1 and L2. Enter the x-values in list L1 and the y-values in list L2.
   - Press [STAT] [▶] 4 to select LinReg(ax+b).
   - Press [2nd] 1 [,] [2nd] 2 [,] [VARS] [▶] 1 1 [ENTER]. Record the equation of the line of best fit and the correlation coefficient, r.

   b) Draw the line of best fit and the scatter plot on the same screen.

   - Press [2nd] [Y=] 1 [ENTER] to access STAT PLOT and turn on Plot1.
   - Press [▼] [ENTER] to select the scatter plot. Enter L1 for Xlist and L2 for Ylist.
   - Press [GRAPH] to display the graph. Copy the graph into your notebook and record the value of r underneath it.

Set A	x	1	2	4	5	8	8	10
	y	2	2	3	5	6	8	10

Set B	x	0	1	2	3	5	6	6
	y	0	2	4	6.5	8	9	10

Set C	x	1	2	3	4	7	8	10
	y	1	3	6	2	9	6	7

Set D	x	1	1.5	2	2.5	4	4.5	5
	y	2	3	4	5	8	9	10

Set E	x	1	3	4	5	7	8	10
	y	9	8	6	5.5	6	3	2

Set F	x	1	2	4	6	7	9	10
	y	1	2	4.5	6	7.5	1	10

Set G	x	1	1	3	4	7	8	10
	y	5	8	2	6	5	2	1

Set H	x	1	2	4	5	5	8	8
	y	1	6	5	7	2	5	8

Set I	x	0	1	2	3	6	8	10
	y	8	7.5	7	6.5	5	4	3

Set J	x	2	2	3	5	5	8	10
	y	2	7	4	2	8	7	1

2. For each graph, describe how closely the line fits the data. Use these terms: exactly, very closely, somewhat closely, weakly, not at all.

3. Compare the descriptions in exercise 2 to the value of r for each graph. What is the connection between how close a set of points is to being linear and its correlation coefficient?

4. Which lines have a negative slope and which have a positive slope? What is the connection between the sign of r and the slope of the line of best fit?

In *Investigation 1*, you should have found that the closer r is to 1 or −1, the better the line fits the data.

TAKE NOTE

Correlation Coefficient

- The correlation coefficient, r, is a measure of how well data can be described by the equation of a line. The closer r is to 1 or −1, the better the line fits the data.
- When r is positive, the variables are positively correlated and the slope of the line of best fit is positive.
- When r is negative, the variables are negatively correlated and the slope of the line of best fit is negative.

In data Set F from *Investigation 1*, most of the data lie in a line. However one point (9, 1) differs greatly from the rest of the data. This point is called an *outlier*. An outlier is an observed value that differs markedly from the pattern established by most of the data.

Investigation 2

Examining the Effects of Outliers

In this Investigation, you will remove an outlier from a data set and examine the effect on the correlation coefficient.

Consider these data.

x	1	2	3	4	5	6
y	3	5	7	10	31	13

1. Determine the equation of the regression line of best fit and the value of the correlation coefficient, r.
   - Press [STAT] [ENTER] to access the lists. Clear any data in lists L1 and L2. Enter the x-values in list L1 and the y-values in list L2.
   - Press [STAT] [▶] 4 to select LinReg(ax+b).
   - Press [2nd] 1 [,] [2nd] 2 [,] [VARS] [▶] 1 1 [ENTER]. Record the equation of the line of best fit and the correlation coefficient, r.

2. Does the correlation coefficient indicate a line of best fit that fits the data well? Explain.

3. Draw the line of best fit and the scatter plot on the same screen.
   - Press [2nd] [Y=] 1 [ENTER] to access STAT PLOT and turn on Plot1.
   - Press [▼] [ENTER] to select the scatter plot. Enter L1 for Xlist and L2 for Ylist.
   - Use these window settings.
   - Press [GRAPH] to display the graph. Copy the graph. Does the line fit the data well? Explain.

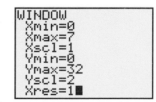

```
WINDOW
 Xmin=0
 Xmax=7
 Xscl=1
 Ymin=0
 Ymax=32
 Yscl=2
 Xres=1■
```

4. Use the equation of the line of best fit to predict the value of y when x is 10. Is this a good prediction? Explain.

5. Examine the scatter plot. Does there appear to be a correlation? Explain.

6. The point (5, 31) is an outlier. Remove the point (5, 31) from the data and repeat exercises 1 to 4.

7. Explain the effect an outlier such as (5, 31) has on the line of best fit.

In *Investigation 2*, we discovered that when we fit a regression line to a data set that contains an outlier, the line does not fit the data well and the value of the correlation coefficient, r, is not close to 1 or −1.

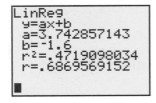
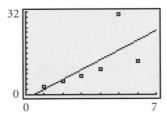

When we remove the outlier, the regression line fits the data well and the value of the correlation coefficient, r, is much closer to 1.

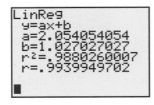
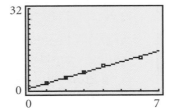

It is good practice to examine the scatter plot for outliers. But, we must remember that in any scatter plot there may be some points that do not precisely follow the trend.

Points should only be rejected as outliers with good reason. A point can be rejected as an outlier if there was an error in collecting the data or if outside factors affected the data. For example:

- Katherine collected data on the heights of students and their arm spans. When she recorded the data, she mistakenly recorded a height of 181 cm as 101 cm. She would reject the point containing this value.
- A company records its total revenue each month. Last month, the workers at the company went on strike for two weeks. The month in which the strike occurred would not be included in an analysis of revenue over time.

The presence of an outlier can affect the analysis of data. Other factors, such as sample size and composition, also need to be considered when analysing data. Recall, from Chapter 5, that a carefully selected sample of 1000 people can be used to represent the population of Canada. A sample that is too small may yield results that are not valid.

A scatter plot helps to determine whether the data support a linear relationship. Linear regression is only appropriate if the data appear to be linear.

A reporter gathered these data from Statistics Canada.

Year	1961	1971	1981	1991
Average size of a family	3.9	3.7	3.3	3.1

The reporter calculated the equation of the line of best fit to be $y = -0.028x + 58.828$, where x represents the year and y represents the average size of a family. Based on this equation, he reported that the Canadian family will disappear in the year 2100.

What errors has the reporter made in drawing this conclusion?

Solution

The reporter has made two errors.

First, the sample size is too small. Four points are not enough to establish a trend. If one or more of these points is an outlier, the line of best fit will not be representative of the overall trend in changes in family size over time. It is possible that the overall pattern is not linear. If this is the case, linear regression is not appropriate.

Second, when the reporter used the line of best fit to predict the average family size in 2100, he did not keep in mind the context of the data.

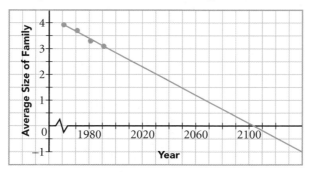

From the equation, the y-intercept of 58.828 tells us that 2000 years ago, the average family size was almost 59 people!

The equation $y = -0.028x + 58.828$ is not an appropriate model of the average size of a Canadian family over time.

A

✓ **1.** Estimate the value of *r* for each graph.

a)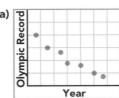

b)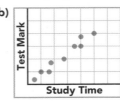

c)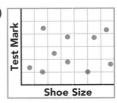

✓ **2. Knowledge/Understanding** Describe the characteristics of a scatter plot that has each correlation coefficient.

a) $r = -0.95$ **b)** $r = 1$ **c)** $r = 0.25$ **d)** $r = 0.65$

✓ **3.** Which of the following relations would you expect to most closely fit a linear model for professional basketball players? Explain.

a) height versus number of rebounds

b) height versus number of fouls

B

✓ **4. Application** The table shows a patient's temperature taken over a period of 14 h.

Time	08:00	10:00	12:00	14:00	16:00	18:00	20:00	22:00
Temperature (°C)	39.0	39.5	39.5	40.0	40.5	38.0	37.5	38.0

a) Draw a scatter plot of temperature versus time. Predict a value for the correlation coefficient, *r*.

b) Determine the equation of the line of best fit and calculate the correlation coefficient, *r*.

c) Explain why you should not use the equation from part b to predict the patient's temperature at midnight.

✓ **5.** These data show the fuel consumption in litres per 100 km for engines of various sizes.

Engine size (L)	2.2	3.0	3.8	4.6
Fuel consumption (L/100 km)	6.4	7.5	8.6	9.7

a) Enter the engine sizes in list L1 and the fuel consumptions in list L2. Determine the equation of the line of best fit.

b) Graph the line of best fit and the scatter plot on the same screen. How well does the line fit the data? Explain.

c) Use the equation from part a to predict the fuel consumption for an engine of 2.5 L and 5.0 L.

6. Refer to exercise 5.

   a) Determine the correlation coefficient.

   b) How well does the line of best fit calculated in part a of exercise
   5 model the relationship between engine size and fuel consumption?
   Explain.

7. Communication Describe the relationship between the value of r and
the shape of a scatter plot. Use diagrams in your explanation.

8. A college administrator wants to determine whether an entrance test is
a good predictor of success in a college engineering program. She selects
12 students at random and compares their marks on the entrance test
to their marks at the end of the first term.

Student	A	B	C	D	E	F	G	H	I	J	K	L
Entrance test mark (%), x	73	83	55	43	65	93	75	80	58	75	64	77
First term mark (%), y	63	88	77	67	70	93	72	81	47	74	66	73

   a) Determine the equation of the line of best fit.

   b) How well does the line fit the data? Explain.

   c) Can the entrance test be used as a predictor of success in the college
   program? Explain.

9. Explain why a scatter plot with only two points will always have an
r-value of 1, −1, or undefined.

10. Thinking/Inquiry/Problem Solving Everton conducts a study of the
relationship between the average number of hours a student works at
a part-time job each week and her or his average mark. He collects data
from a random sample of 5 students. His data are given in the table.

Hours worked, x	3	8	5	10	15
Average mark (%), y	56	80	63	78	90

Everton plots the data on a scatter plot and notes there is a positive
correlation. He calculates the line of best fit as $y = 2.806x + 50.387$,
where x is the number of hours of part-time work and y is the average
mark. The correlation coefficient is 0.954. Everton concludes that the
line fits the data well.

   a) Draw Everton's line of best fit and a scatterplot of the data on the
   same grid. Does the line fit the data well? Explain.

   b) Everton concluded that the greater the number of hours of part-
   time work, the higher a student's marks. Do you agree? Explain.

c) According to the equation of the line of best fit, how many hours should a student work each week to have an average mark of 100%?

d) According to Everton's equation, what mark would you receive if you did not work part-time after school?

e) Explain the errors Everton has made.

11. Tran examined Everton's data from exercise 10. He believes the data point (8, 80) is an outlier. He recalculates the equation of the line of best fit as $y = 2.827x + 48.427$ with a correlation coefficient 0.998.

a) Tran concluded that there is even stronger evidence of a positive correlation. The more you work part-time after school, the higher your marks will be. Do you agree? Explain.

b) According to Tran's equation of the line of best fit, how many hours should a student work each week to have an average mark of 100%?

c) According to Tran's equation, what would your average mark be if you did not work part-time after school?

d) What errors has Tran made?

12. Ayesha used a CBR to collect data on the heights of successive bounces of a ball. She recorded the bounce number and the height of the ball in centimetres.

Bounce number, x	1	2	3	4	5
Height (cm), y	90	54	33	20	11

a) Predict the height of the ball on the 7th bounce.

b) Draw a scatter plot of the data.

c) What type of correlation does there appear to be?

d) Determine the equation of the line of best fit and the correlation coefficient.

e) Does the line fit the data well? Explain.

f) According to the equation of the line of best fit, how high will the ball bounce on the 7th bounce? How does this compare with your prediction in part a? Explain.

13. *The Geometer's Sketchpad* **and Lines of Best Fit**

The Geometer's Sketchpad contains a built-in sample sketch that allows us to work with the line of best fit. The line of best fit is the line that minimizes the sum of the squares of the distances between the points and the line.

• Open *The Geometer's Sketchpad*.

• Click on File and Open.

• Double-click on the samples directory, then sketches, and finally the analytic directory.

• Double-click on leastsqr.gsp to open the file.

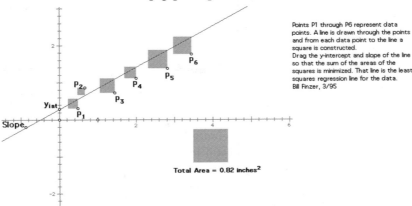

Points P1 through P6 represent data points. A line is drawn through the points and from each data point to the line a square is constructed.
Drag the y-intercept and slope of the line so that the sum of the areas of the squares is minimized. That line is the least squares regression line for the data.
Bill Finzer, 3/95

Total Area = 0.82 inches²

• The sketch consists of 6 data points and a line. You can change the slope and y-intercept of the line by clicking and dragging the points labelled "Slope" and "Y_{int}."

• From the Display menu, select Preferences and set the distance unit to centimetres and the precision to hundredths.

• To find the line of best fit, minimize the area of the square labelled "Total Area." This square represents the sum of the squares of the distances from the points to the line. Adjust the slope and the y-intercept of the line until the Total Area is a minimum. This gives the regression line.

• To find the equation of the line of best fit, click on the line to select it. From the Measure menu, select Equation. The equation of the line will be displayed underneath the total area.

• To find the coordinates of a point, click on the point to select it. From the Measure menu, select Coordinates. The coordinates of the point will be displayed under the total area.

• You can click and drag the points to new locations to find the equations of lines of best fit for different data sets.

Use *The Geometer's Sketchpad* to find the equation of the line of best fit for each data set. You may want to use a graphing calculator to find the equation of the line of best fit and compare your results.

a)

x	1.01	0.56	0.19	1.89	2.96	5.01
y	1.24	0.61	0.29	0.86	−0.49	0.05

b)

x	1.38	1.68	0.19	2.24	3.14	3.61
y	1.85	0.38	1.28	1.36	0.86	1.60

1. How do you expect each pair of variables to be correlated? Explain.
   a) distance driven versus amount of fuel remaining
   b) years of education versus number of children
   c) distance driven versus number of oil changes

2. Your maximum heart rate depends on your age. These data were collected from a medical journal.

Age (years), x	30	40	50
Maximum heart rate (beats/min), y	194	182	170

   a) Determine the equation of the line of best fit.
   b) Graph the line of best fit and the scatter plot on the same screen. How well does the line fit the data? Explain.
   c) Use the equation from part a to predict the maximum heart rate for a person of each age.
      i) 20 years   ii) 70 years   iii) 35 years
   d) Determine the correlation coefficient.
   e) Is it reasonable to use the line of best fit from part a to make predictions? Explain.

Performance Assessment

3. These data were collected on the heights of 19-year-old girls and the heights of their parents. The heights are in centimetres.

Father's height (cm)	201	190	185	180	178	177	180	184	172	180
Mother's height (cm)	185	166	160	176	167	181	174	190	166	152
Daughter's height (cm)	200	170	185	170	171	172	170	178	163	160

   a) Draw a scatter plot of each pair of variables. Describe the correlation in each graph.
      i) daughter's height versus father's height
      ii) daughter's height versus mother's height
   b) Determine the equation of the line of best fit and the correlation coefficient for each graph in part a. Which relationship has the stronger correlation, that is, the value of r closest to 1 or −1? Explain.
   c) Research suggests that a good predictor of a daughter's height is the mean of the heights of her parents. Do these data support that research? Explain.

Fathom is a powerful dynamic statistics program. In this section, we will use *Fathom* to set up a scatter plot and calculate the equation of the line of best fit.

Follow these steps to find the equation of the line of best fit for the data on height versus foot size.

Foot size (cm)	Height (cm)
30	180
25	165
35	205
28	172
32	186

- Open *Fathom*. From the File menu, select New.
- To enter the data, click on Insert, then Case Table. An empty table will appear on the screen.

    Click on the word <new>. Key in FootSize and press Enter. Column titles can only include letters, numbers, and underscores.

    When you press Enter, another column appears. Click on the word <new> in the new column and key in Height. Press Enter.

    The table is titled "Collection 1" and there is a box on the screen that is also labelled "Collection 1." Double-click on the name under the box, key in "FootSize vs Height Data," then click OK. The name of the box and the table both change.

    Click on the first cell in the FootSize column of the table. Key in 30 and press Tab. The cursor moves to the first cell in the Height column. Key in 180 and press Tab. Continue to key in the data, pressing Tab after each entry.

    As you key in the data, the first column may shift out of sight. You can resize the box that contains the table. Click on the right side of the box and drag to the right.

- To create a scatter plot of the data, click Insert, then Graph. An empty graph will appear.

    Click on the FootSize column header and drag it to the horizontal axis of the graph. The FootSize data will appear as points on the horizontal axis.

Click on the Height column header and drag it to the vertical axis of the graph. The ordered pairs will be plotted. Your screen should look like this:

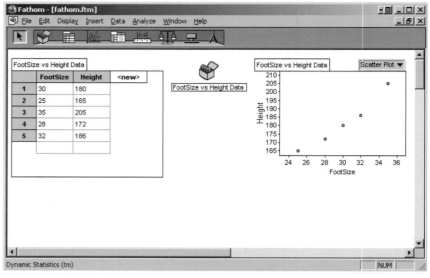

- To change the scale of the graph, click on the graph to select it. From the Graph menu, select Show Graph Info. The maximum and minimum values will be displayed in blue. To change a value, double-click on it and key in the new value. Press Enter.
- To calculate the equation of the line of best fit, click on the graph to select it. From the Graph menu, select Least-Squares Line. The line of best fit will be drawn in red. The equation of the line of best fit and the value of the correlation coefficient are displayed below the graph.
- You can click and drag points on the graph. The corresponding values in the table will change. You can also change entries in the table and the corresponding point on the graph will change.

Use *Fathom* to find the equation of the line of best fit for each data set.

a)

Distance from eye chart (m)	2	4	6	8	10	12
Percent of letters read correctly	100	97	93	93	88	85

b)

Current (mA)	15.0	10.9	9.2	3.6	4.7
Voltage (V)	3.1	4.0	5.5	8.1	10.5

You will use the skills developed in this chapter to analyse franchise information.

Franchising is a popular way to get into business. An established firm (the franchisor) sells the rights to other firms (franchisees) to use the franchisor's trade name and suppliers. There are more than 1300 franchised operations in Canada in sectors as diverse as fast food, dry cleaning, dollar stores, office supply stores, and video outlets.

The key to owning a successful franchise is research. In this project, you will analyse the growth of two franchise operations over time and use the results of your analysis to predict future growth. You will also examine the costs involved with each franchise. You may choose two franchises of interest to you and collect your own data from the Internet or the library, or you may use the data provided here.

According to a CBC news report, Canada has more coffee shops per capita than any other nation. Two Canadian franchises are The Java Hut and Grinds.

The Java Hut

The Java Hut began franchising in 1980.

The table gives the number of franchises every year from 1989 to 2001.

Year	1989	1990	1991	1992	1993	1994	1995
Number of franchises	138	154	169	174	182	193	220

Year	1996	1997	1998	1999	2000	2001
Number of franchises	243	299	354	380	398	391

This table shows the costs and fees required to own a Java Hut franchise.

Total investment	Between $280 000 and $350 000
Franchise fee	$25 000
Ongoing royalty fee	9%

Grinds

Grinds began franchising in 1965. Currently, 95% of Canadian stores are franchise-owned and -operated. The table gives the total number of stores — corporate and franchise — in Canada from 1978 to 1995.

Year	1978	1984	1987	1989	1991	1993	1995
Number of stores	100	200	300	400	500	700	1200

This table gives the total number of Canadian franchises from 1996 to 1999.

Year	1996	1997	1998	1999
Number of franchises	1277	1401	1515	1630

This table shows the costs and fees required to own a Grinds franchise.

Total investment	Between $434 700 and $775 100
Franchise fee	$35 000
Ongoing royalty fee	4.5%

1. Research the advantages and disadvantages of purchasing a franchise instead of starting your own business.

2. Develop a model for each franchise to predict the number of franchises in 2010. Describe the process you used to develop the model and assess how reliable the model will be as a predictor of growth.

3. Compare the growth of the two operations over time. Which franchise is growing more rapidly?

4. Compare the investments required to purchase each franchise.

5. What other information do you need before deciding which franchise to purchase?

Write a report stating which franchise you would purchase. The report should include:
- your rationale for investing in a franchise
- your analysis of the franchise data
- any other information that contributed to your decision

Paralegal

Kevin has an analytical mind and has always been fascinated by law. Training as a paralegal at community college seemed like an excellent choice for him.

Job Description

Work under the supervision of a lawyer to assist with trial preparation

- Prepare legal documents such as wills
- Mediate disputes
- Do legal research
- Represent clients in court

Working Conditions

- 8- to 10-hour days, 5 days a week
- Evening and weekend work may be required
- Work can be stressful
- Work can be done for law firms, corporations, or the civil service

Qualifications and Training

- Graduation from high school
- Successful completion of a two-year paralegal program at community college
- Good analytical skills
- Ability to communicate clearly and persuasively, both in speaking and writing
- Computer skills

Where's the Math?

Studying math develops the analytical skills needed in legal work. Statistics is an important tool for making legal arguments. It is also important that paralegals be knowledgeable about how arguments can be made by misusing statistics. Paralegals also use math to calculate expenses for clients and law firms and estimate the costs of bringing a case to court.

MATHEMATICS TOOLKIT

Single-Variable Tools

> Measures of central tendency

Mean: the sum of the numbers divided by the number of numbers

Median: the middle number when the numbers are arranged in order

Mode: the most frequently occurring number

> Measures of spread, for any data set $x_1, x_2, x_3, ..., x_n$

Range: the difference between the highest and lowest values

Variance: the mean of the squared differences between the points and the mean

$$s^2 = \frac{(x_1 - \bar{x})^2 + (x_2 - \bar{x})^2 + (x_3 - \bar{x})^2 + ... + (x_n - \bar{x})^2}{n - 1}$$

Standard deviation: the square root of the variance

$$s = \sqrt{\frac{(x_1 - \bar{x})^2 + (x_2 - \bar{x})^2 + (x_3 - \bar{x})^2 + ... + (x_n - \bar{x})^2}{n - 1}}$$

> Common distributions of data

Normal Distribution

The mean, the median, and the mode are equal.

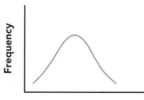

Bimodal Distribution

There may be more than one mode. The mean and the median are between the modes.

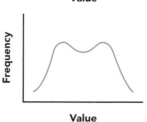

Skewed Left

The mode is at the peak, the median is less than the mode, and the mean is less the median.

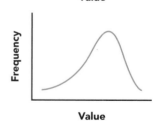

Skewed Right
The mode is at the peak, the median is greater than the mode, and the mean is larger the median.

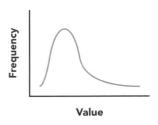

> In a normal distribution:
>> 68% of the data lie within 1 standard deviation of the mean.
>> 95% of the data lie within 2 standard deviations of the mean.
>> 99.7% of the data lie within 3 standard deviations of the mean.

Two-Variable Tools

> Correlation

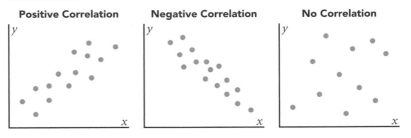

> The regression line of best fit is the line that minimizes the sum of the squares of the differences between the points and the line.

> The correlation coefficient, r, is a measure of how well data can be described by the equation of a line.
>> If r is close to 1 or -1, the line fits the data very well.
>> If r is positive, the variables are positively correlated.
>> If r is negative, the variables are negatively correlated.

> An outlier is an observed value that differs markedly from the pattern established by most of the data.

6.1

1. The golf scores of 25 students are compared to the scores of 25 professional golfers. Which group do you think will have the greater standard deviation in their scores? Explain.

2. A shoe company is analysing data on shoe sizes sold to determine the sizes of shoes it should produce. Which measure of central tendency should the company use in its analysis? Explain.

3. Three schools competed in a trivia competition. Each team has five members. Their scores are given in the table.

Team A	21	42	25	62	32
Team B	42	12	62	52	32
Team C	32	24	16	62	52

a) Calculate the mean, the median, the mode, the range, the variance and the standard deviation of each team's scores.

b) Which team do you think had the best performance? What criteria did you use? Explain.

c) Which team had the most consistent performance? Which measure did you use? Explain.

4. Create two sets of numbers that fit these criteria:
   • Each set contains 10 numbers.
   • Both sets have the same mean.
   • The standard deviations of the sets are significantly different.
   Describe the process you used to create these sets.

5. An inspector at a packaging facility selected a sample of 20 150-g packages of corn chips from the day shift and 20 from the afternoon shift. The packages had these masses in grams.

Day shift masses (g)									
142	148	141	148	149	153	160	142	153	146
148	149	150	146	151	156	141	148	159	156

Afternoon shift masses (g)									
146	158	145	166	158	164	154	158	150	140
147	166	167	151	148	155	154	146	153	160

a) Calculate the mean and the standard deviation for each shift.

b) Which shift has the smaller standard deviation?

c) Which shift is doing the best job? Explain.

6.2 **6.** Conduct each experiment 10 times. Record your results in your notebook and on the blackboard. Collect data from 9 of your classmates so you have a total of 100 results for each experiment.

Experiment 1: Roll a pair of dice and record the sum of the numbers on the faces of the dice.

Experiment 2: Roll a single die 4 times and record the number of 6s.

Graph the frequency distributions for experiments 1 and 2. In each case, state the type of distribution. Explain.

7. The measures of central tendency are given for 3 data sets. How are the data distributed? Explain.

a) mean = 28   median = 42   mode = 50

b) mean = 33   median = 33   mode = 33

c) mean = 15   median = 14   mode = 12, 16

8. Suppose you collected data on the masses of athletes in each group. Predict the shape of each distribution.

a) female gymnasts

b) male weight lifters

c) sprinters

6.3 **9.** Describe the effect on the graph of the normal distribution in each case.

a) The mean increases and the standard deviation remains the same.

b) The mean does not change but the standard deviation decreases.

10. An inspector measures the actual volume of milk in 250-mL cartons. The volumes are distributed normally, with mean 250 mL and standard deviation 1.5 mL.

a) Sketch the normal distribution of volumes. Label the mean and the points that are 1, 2, and 3 standard deviations from the mean.

b) What percent of the cartons have volumes in each range?
   i) less than 247 mL   **ii)** between 243.5 mL and 253 mL

c) Cartons of milk are rejected if the actual volume of milk is less than 247 mL or greater than 253 mL. In a run of 5000 cartons of milk, how many will be rejected?

11. A manufacturer of electric pencil sharpeners has found that the average life of its product is 3.5 years, with a standard deviation of 1.5 years. Pencil sharpeners that break within the first 6 months are replaced free. Assuming the lifetimes are distributed normally, determine the percent of pencil sharpeners the manufacturer can expect to replace.

12. The mean score on a standardized test was 575. Ninety-five percent of the people who wrote the test got scores between 505 and 645. What is the standard deviation of test scores?

6.4 **13.** In each case, are the data single-variable or two-variable? Explain.

a) Data on annual income versus years of service are graphed on a scatterplot.

b) Data on the frequencies of various annual incomes are displayed in a histogram.

14. Suppose you collected data to compare each pair of variables.

i) speed travelled versus number of accidents

ii) the amount of money spent on vehicle repairs versus the number of mornings the vehicle starts on the first attempt

iii) heat loss versus thickness of insulation

a) In each case, do you think the variables will be positively correlated, negatively correlated, or not correlated? Explain.

b) Do you think there is a causal relationship between the variables? Explain.

15. These data on a particular model of used car were collected from the classified section of a newspaper.

Age (years), x	6	1	9	3	5	4
Asking price ($), y	7000	15 000	1500	13 500	11 900	6200

a) How do you expect the age of a car and the asking price to be correlated? Explain.

b) Draw a scatter plot of the data.

c) How are the data correlated? How does your answer compare to your answer to part a? Explain.

d) Determine the equation of the line of best fit and the correlation coefficient, r.

e) According to the correlation coefficient, how well does the line fit the data? Explain.

f) Graph the line of best fit and the scatter plot on the same screen. How well does the line fit the data? Explain.

g) Use the equation of the line of best fit to predict the asking price for a 2-year-old car.

6.5 **16.** Explain how to interpret the value of the correlation coefficient.

17. What factors should we consider when deciding whether to exclude a data point from an analysis of the data? Explain.

18. Refer to exercise 15.

a) Remove the outlier and calculate the equation of the new line of best fit. How does the correlation coefficient for this line compare to the correlation coefficient from exercise 15?

b) Which line will be the better predictor of the asking price? Explain.

19. The table shows the mass of a drug in milligrams that remains in the bloodstream over time in hours.

Time since dose (h)	1.0	2.0	4.0	8.0	10.0	12.0
Amount in bloodstream (mg)	7.7	7.1	6.0	3.9	2.8	1.9

a) Determine the equation of the line of best fit and the value of the correlation coefficient.

b) How reliable is this model in predicting the amount of the drug that remains in the bloodstream at a given time? Explain.

Maintaining Your Mastery

Review the algebraic skills that form part of the college admission process.

1. Expand and simplify.

a) $7x(2x - 1) + 3(x^2 + 6)$

b) $9(x + 4) - 3(x - 3) - (x + 12)^4$

2. Factor.

a) $3x^2 + 3x - 36$

b) $4x^2 + 4x - 15$

3. Rearrange each formula to isolate the variable indicated.

a) $T = -0.0034H + 100$ for H

b) $S = 2\pi r^2 + 2\pi rh$ for h

4. Solve by elimination.

a) $5x - 3y = 12$
$2x - 3y = 3$

b) $2x + 5y = 4$
$6x - 2y = -5$

Self - Test

1. **Knowledge/Understanding** A soft-drink company uses an automated device to fill 355-mL cans of soda pop. The machine must be checked frequently to see whether it is putting exactly 355 mL in each can. In a sample of 30 cans of pop, these volumes in millilitres were measured:

352	354	353	351	357	358	358	358	354	356
352	356	354	352	353	351	352	357	354	356
353	355	351	353	353	350	356	358	355	355

a) Calculate the mean, the median, and the standard deviation of these volumes. Interpret these statistics in terms of the filling process.

b) What problems will be encountered if the standard deviation gets too high? Explain.

2. **Communication** A teacher remarks to the principal that the marks of students in one of his classes follow a bimodal distribution. Describe how the marks are distributed in the class. What does this tell you about the performance of the class? Explain.

3. **Application** The heights of tomato plants in a particular crop are distributed normally, with mean 63 cm and standard deviation 6 cm.

a) Sketch the normal distribution. Label the mean and the points that are 1, 2, and 3 standard deviations away from the mean.

b) What percent of tomato plants in this crop are taller than 57 cm?

c) Estimate the range of heights of the tomato plants in this crop.

4. **Thinking/Inquiry/Problem Solving** A science student measured the temperature at which water boils at different heights above sea level. The data she collected are given in the table.

Height (m)	0	100	655	1380	2100	2850	4012	5950
Temperature (°C)	99.8	100.0	97.2	95.3	100.4	91.0	85.8	78.2

a) Graph the data in a scatter plot and describe the type of correlation.

b) Determine the equation of the line of best fit and the correlation coefficient, r. How well does the line fit the data? Explain.

c) Estimate the boiling point of water at the Dead Sea, 399 m below sea level. How reliable is this estimate? Explain.

d) Which point is an outlier? Remove the outlier from the data set and repeat parts a to c. How do these results compare to your original answers?

5. Christine is doing a science report on the effectiveness of sunscreen as indicated by its Sunscreen Protection Factor (SPF). She has found that the percent of the sun's ultraviolet light that passes through the sunscreen can be calculated using the SPF number. She created a table showing her data, but did not get the percent for SPF 2 or for SPF 45.

Sunscreen Protection Factor (SPF)	Percent of Ultraviolet Light Passing Through
2	?
5	20
8	12.5
15	6.7
25	4.0
45	?

a) Describe how you can use the existing data to estimate the percents for SPF 2 and SPF 45.

b) Use the process you described in part a to estimate the percents for SPF 2 and SPF 45. How confident are you about these estimates? Explain.

c) Christine later discovers the percents for SPF 2 and SPF 45 are 50 and 2.2, respectively. How do these values compare to your estimates from part b?

d) Is a line of best fit a good representation of these data? Explain.

Analysis of Graphical Models

Canada's Population Growth

The population of Canada is growing rapidly. You will use the skills developed in this chapter to analyse the populations of Canada, the provinces, and some cities over time. You will connect trends in the population graphs to historic events.

Curriculum Expectations

By the end of this chapter, you will:

> Interpret a given linear, quadratic, or exponential graph to answer questions, using language and units appropriate to the context from which the graph was drawn.

> Interpret the rate of change and initial conditions of a linear model given within a context.

> Make and justify a decision or prediction and discuss trends based on a given graph.

> Describe the effect on a given graph of new information about the circumstances represented by the graph.

> Communicate the results of an analysis orally, in a written report, and graphically.

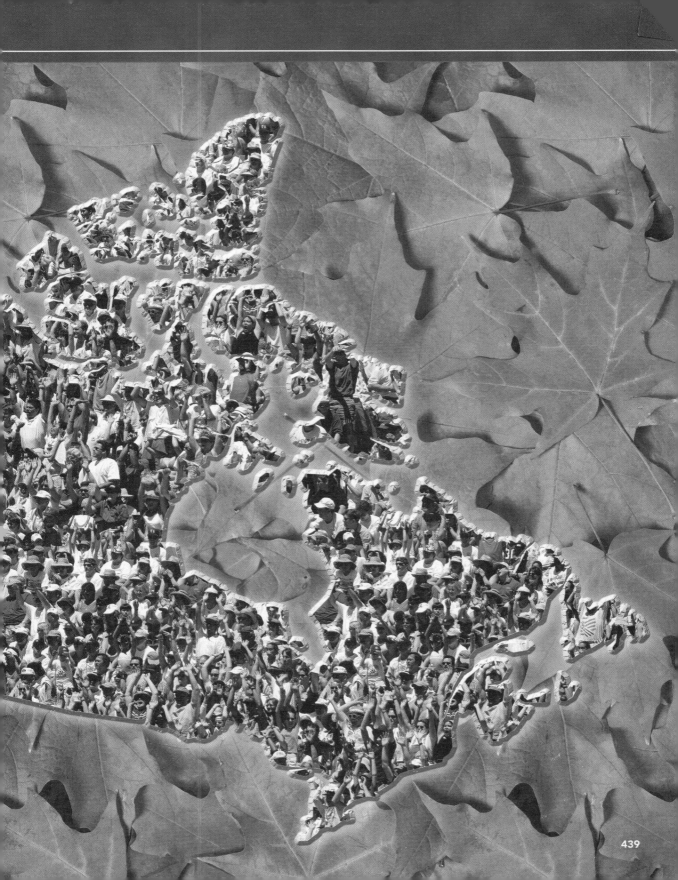

1 Review: Arithmetic and Geometric Sequences

In grade 11, you studied arithmetic and geometric sequences.

Arithmetic Sequences

- In an arithmetic sequence, the same number is added to each term to get the next term. This number is called the *common difference*. It is found by subtracting any term in the sequence from the next term. Here is an example:

Arithmetic sequence	*Common difference*
1, 5, 9, 13, …	$5 - 1 = 4$
	$9 - 5 = 4$
	$13 - 9 = 4$

- If we graph the terms of an arithmetic sequence, the points follow the path of a straight line.

- An arithmetic sequence with a positive common difference represents linear growth. The graph slopes up from left to right.

- If the common difference is negative, the arithmetic sequence represents linear decay and the graph slopes down from left to right.

Example 1

a) Write the first 5 terms of each arithmetic sequence.
   i) The first term is 5 and the common difference is 2.
   ii) The first term is 14 and the common difference is −3.

b) Graph each sequence from part a. Put the term number on the horizontal axis and the term value on the vertical axis.

Solution

a) i) 5, 7, 9, 11, 13
   ii) 14, 11, 8, 5, 2

b) i)

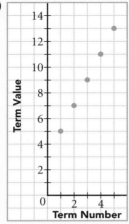

ii)

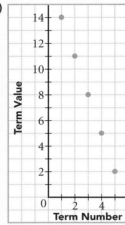

Discuss

In the graph of each sequence, explain why the points are not joined with a straight line.

Geometric Sequences

- In a geometric sequence, each term is multiplied by the same number to find the next term. This number is called the *common ratio*. It is found by dividing any term in the sequence by the preceding term. Here is an example:

Geometric sequence
  2, 10, 50, 250, …

Common ratio
$$\frac{10}{2} = 5$$
$$\frac{50}{10} = 5$$
$$\frac{250}{50} = 5$$

- If we graph the terms of a geometric sequence, the points follow the path of a curve.

- If the common ratio is greater than 1, the geometric sequence represents exponential growth. The graph curves up from left to right.

- If the common ratio is between 0 and 1, the geometric sequence represents exponential decay. The graph curves down from left to right.

Example 2

a) Write the first 5 terms of each geometric sequence.
   i) The first term is 3 and the common ratio is 2.
   ii) The first term is 64 and the common ratio is $\frac{1}{2}$.

b) Graph each sequence from part a. Put the term number on the horizontal axis and the term value on the vertical axis.

Solution

a) i) 3, 6, 12, 24, 48

   ii) 64, 32, 16, 8, 4

b) i) 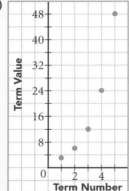   ii)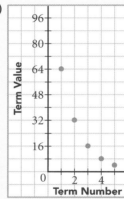

1. Classify each sequence as arithmetic or geometric. Determine the common difference or the common ratio.

   a) 100, 110, 121, 133.1, ...   **b)** 3, 7, 11, 15, ...

   c) 20, 18, 16, 14, ...   **d)** 1000, 100, 10, 1, ...

2. Write the first 5 terms of each sequence, then graph the sequence.

   a) The first term is 100 and the common ratio is 0.5.

   b) The first term is 7 and the common difference is 2.

2 Review: Characteristics of Linear, Quadratic, and Exponential Graphs

In grade 10, you studied linear and quadratic functions. In grade 11, you studied exponential functions. Each type of function has its own shape of graph. We can examine the graph to determine the type of function it represents.

Linear Graphs

Examine these graphs of linear functions.

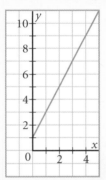
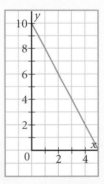

We can make a table of values for each graph.

x	y	Difference
0	1	
		2
1	3	
		2
2	5	
		2
3	7	

x	y	Difference
0	10	
		−2
1	8	
		−2
2	6	
		−2
3	4	

Successive *y*-values form an arithmetic sequence.   The rate of growth is constant.   Successive *y*-values form an arithmetic sequence.   The rate of decay is constant.

For any linear function:
- The graph is a straight line.
- The rate of growth or decay is constant.
- Successive *y*-values form an arithmetic sequence. If the *x*-values are consecutive, the common difference of the sequence of *y*-values is the slope.

- The function is defined by an equation of the form $y = mx + b$; where m is the slope and b is the y-intercept.
- If m is positive, the function represents linear growth; if m is negative, the function represents linear decay.

Quadratic Graphs

Examine these graphs of quadratic functions.

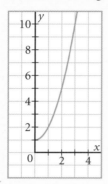
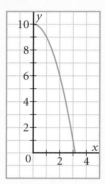

We can make a table of values for each graph.

x	y	Difference
0	1	
		1
1	2	
		3
2	5	
		5
3	10	

The differences form an arithmetic sequence.

x	y	Difference
0	10	
		−1
1	9	
		−3
2	6	
		−5
3	1	

The differences form an arithmetic sequence.

For any quadratic function:
- The graph is a curve called a *parabola*.
- The rate of growth or decay is not constant, but increases or decreases by a constant amount.
- The differences in successive y-values form an arithmetic sequence.
- The function is defined by an equation of the form $y = ax^2 + bx + c$.
- If a is positive, the parabola opens up; if a is negative, the parabola opens down.

Exponential Graphs

Examine these graphs of exponential functions.

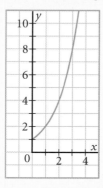

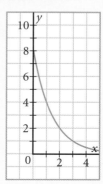

We can make a table of values for each graph.

x	y	Difference	Ratio
0	1		
		1	2
1	2		
		2	2
2	4		
		4	2
3	8		

x	y	Difference	Ratio
0	8		
		-4	$\frac{1}{2}$
1	4		
		-2	$\frac{1}{2}$
2	2		
		-1	$\frac{1}{2}$
3	1		

Successive *y*-values form
a geometric sequence.

Successive *y*-values form
a geometric sequence.

- The graph is a curve.
- The rate of growth or decay increases or decreases by a changing amount.
- Successive *y*-values form a geometric sequence.
- The function is defined by an equation of the form $y = a(b)^x$.
- If *b* is greater than 1, the function represents exponential growth; if *b* is between 0 and 1, the function represents exponential decay.

Necessary Skills

Example

The graphs of three functions, A, B, and C, are shown on the same grid. For each graph, determine if it is linear, quadratic, or exponential.

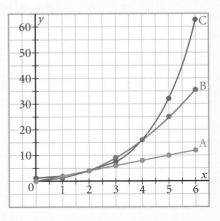

Solution

Examine the rates of growth of the graphs. Make a table of values for each function and examine the differences in successive y-values.

Function A

x	y	Difference
0	0	
		2
1	2	
		2
2	4	
		2
3	6	
		2
4	8	
		2
5	10	
		2
6	12	

Function B

x	y	Difference
0	0	
		1
1	1	
		3
2	4	
		5
3	9	
		7
4	16	
		9
5	25	
		11
6	36	

Function C

x	y	Difference	Ratio
0	1		
		1	2
1	2		
		2	2
2	4		
		4	2
3	8		
		8	2
4	16		
		16	2
5	32		
		32	2
6	64		

The graph of function A is a straight line so this is a *linear graph*. From the table, there is a constant difference of 2 between successive y-values.

The graph of function B curves up. Its growth rate increases, so it is not linear. The differences in successive y-values increase by 2. Function B is a quadratic function; its graph is a *parabola*.

The graph of function C curves up and is similar to the graph of function B for small values of x. For large values of x, the graph of function C grows faster and faster. From the table of values, the differences between successive y-values increase by increasing amounts. Function C is neither linear nor quadratic. If we calculate the ratio of successive y-values, there is a constant ratio of 2. Function C is exponential and its graph is an *exponential graph*.

1. Classify each graph as linear, quadratic, or exponential. Explain.

a)
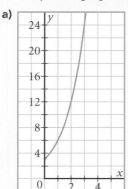

b)
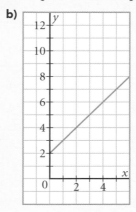

c)
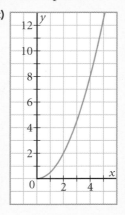

2. For each table of values:
  i) Graph the data.
  ii) Describe the shape of the graph.
  iii) Classify the graph as linear, quadratic, or exponential.

a)

x	0	1	2	3	4	5	6
y	100	200	400	800	1600	3200	6400

b)

x	0	1	2	3	4	5	6
y	50	40	20	−10	−50	−100	−160

c)

x	0	1	2	3	4	5	6
y	2.6	2.8	3.0	3.2	3.4	3.6	3.8

d)

x	0	1	2	3	4	5	6
y	5555	1666	500	150	45	13.5	4.05

e)

x	0	1	2	3	4	5	6
y	−5	−2	7	22	43	70	103

Graphs are a great way to present information. Previously, you plotted data from experiments, displayed survey results in a graph, and graphed functions.

In this Chapter, we will work in the opposite direction. We will retrieve information from graphs and use that information to make predictions.

You reviewed graphing a linear function in Chapter 2, Section 2.3, and slope in Chapter 2, Necessary Skills 6. In this section, we will interpret the graph of a linear function.

Jorge's Drive-a-Jag rents luxury cars. The amount charged is determined by the distance driven. The price structure is displayed in the graph.

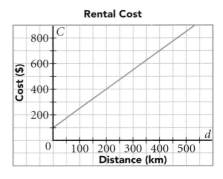

The first step in reading a graph is to determine how the information is plotted. The distance driven, d, in kilometres, is plotted horizontally and the cost, C, in dollars, is plotted vertically.

Some questions can be answered directly from the graph. For example, if you drive 300 km, how much does it cost to rent a car? Find the point on the line with $d = 300$ km and read off the cost, $C = \$550$.

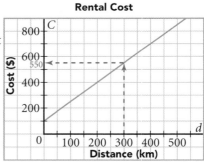

Jorge's price structure is *linear*. We can determine the slope from the graph.

Choose any two points on the graph.

$$\text{slope} = \frac{\text{rise}}{\text{run}}$$
$$= \frac{300}{200}$$
$$= 1.50$$

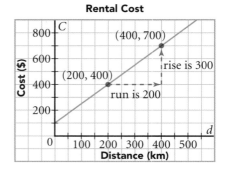

Slope is a *rate*. From the scales on the graph, we can determine the units for the slope of this line. This will help us to interpret the meaning of the slope.

- The rise represents a change in cost, in dollars.
- The run represents a change in distance, in kilometres.
- Since slope is $\frac{\text{rise}}{\text{run}}$, the units for slope are \$/km. The slope is \$1.50/km; this is the rate charged per kilometre.

Slope is calculated by comparing how two amounts change. Slope is always a rate associated with the problem.

Another important feature of any linear graph is its vertical intercept.

The C-intercept of this graph is the value of C where the line crosses the vertical axis. For this graph, the C-intercept is \$100. If you rent a car and drive it 0 km, you owe \$100. This is the flat fee.

How much would it cost to drive 273 km?

How much would it cost to drive 1500 km?

It is hard to read 273 km accurately on the graph, and 1500 km is not even on the graph! We can answer these questions using the equation that defines the graph.

Recall, the equation of a line is $y = mx + b$, where m is the slope and b is the y-intercept. Rewrite $y = mx + b$ for Jorge's price structure:

- x is now d.
- y is now C.
- m is 1.50.
- b is 100.

The equation is $C = 1.50d + 100$, where d is distance in kilometres and C is cost in dollars.

The cost for 273 km is $C = 1.50(273) + 100$ or \$509.50.
The cost for 1500 km is $C = 1.50(1500) + 100$ or \$2350.00.

Discuss
Describe how to use the graph to determine the cost to drive 1500 km.

TAKE NOTE

Linear Graphs

The slope of a linear graph is a rate.
The vertical intercept is a starting value or flat fee.

Example 1

Asha decided to let her hair grow. The graph shows her hair length over the next year.

a) How long was Asha's hair when she started to let it grow? Explain.

b) Determine the rate at which Asha's hair grew.

c) Write an equation that relates the length, L, of Asha's hair to the length of time, t, she has been growing her hair.

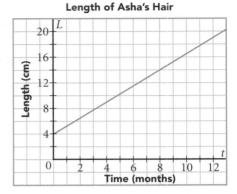
Length of Asha's Hair

d) i) Use the graph to estimate her hair length after 5 months.
   ii) Use the equation to estimate her hair length after 5 months.
   iii) Compare your estimates from parts i and ii. Which estimate is more reliable? Explain.

e) Predict the length of Asha's hair after 2 years. What assumptions did you make?

Solution

a) The vertical intercept is 4. This is the starting value. Asha's hair was 4 cm long when she started to let it grow.

b) Calculate the slope to determine the rate at which Asha's hair grew. From the graph,

$$\text{Slope} = \frac{\text{Rise}}{\text{Run}}$$
$$= \frac{10}{8}$$
$$= 1.25$$

Asha's hair grew 1.25 cm per month.

Length of Asha's Hair

c) The general equation of a line is $y = mx + b$.
   - x is now t.
   - y is now L.
   - m is 1.25.
   - b is 4.

The equation is $L = 1.25t + 4$.

d) i) From the graph, the length of Asha's hair after 5 months was approximately 10.2 cm.

ii) $L = 1.25(5) + 4$
$= 10.25$
From the equation, Asha's hair was 10.25 cm long after 5 months.

iii) The estimate from the equation is more reliable. On the graph, the length of Asha's hair after 5 months is between grid lines.

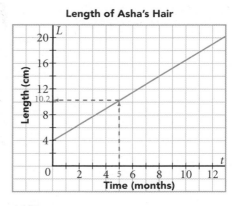

Length of Asha's Hair

e) Substitute $t = 24$ months into the equation and solve for L.
$L = 1.25(24) + 4$
$= 34$

After 2 years, Asha's hair will be 34 cm long, assuming she does not cut it.

Discuss

When determining slope or estimating values, why should you choose points that lie on the grid lines?

Sometimes we cannot get the information we need directly from the graph.

Don works at a grocery store stocking shelves. For a display, he stacked soup cans in a pyramid over 2 m high. The graph shows how the height of the pyramid increased with additional layers of cans.

a) Determine the height of one soup can.

b) Write an equation to describe the graph.

c) How many layers of cans did Don need for his 2-m pyramid?

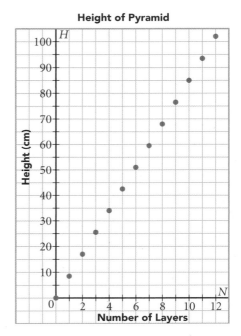

Height of Pyramid

Solution

a) The height of 1 soup can is the height of 1 layer. We cannot determine this height exactly from the graph because it is between grid lines.

The slope of the graph is the number of centimetres per layer, so the slope represents the height of one soup can.

From the graph:

$$\text{Slope} = \frac{\text{Rise}}{\text{Run}}$$

$$= \frac{85}{10}$$

$$= 8.5$$

Each layer adds 8.5 cm, so the height of one soup can is 8.5 cm.

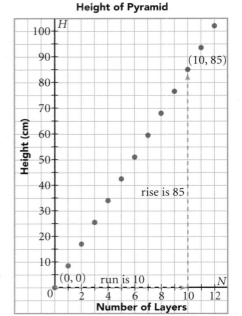

Height of Pyramid

b) The general equation of a line is $y = mx + b$.

- x is now N.
- y is now H.
- m is 8.5.
- b is 0.

The equation is $H = 8.5N$.

c) Substitute $H = 200$ cm in the equation and solve for N.

$$200 = 8.5N$$

$$\frac{200}{8.5} = N$$

$$23.53 = N$$

The number of layers must be a whole number. A pyramid with 24 layers is 204 cm tall, just over 2 m as required.

Discuss

Explain why the points are not joined on the graph.

Discuss

In Section 2.3, you used the terms *direct variation* and *partial variation* to describe linear functions. Both have linear graphs. How can you tell the difference between direct and partial variation on a graph?

A

1. Determine the slope and *y*-intercept of each linear graph.

a)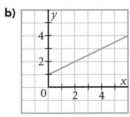

b)

c)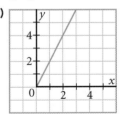

 2. For each graph:

  i) Calculate the slope.

  ii) Give the units of the slope.

  iii) Explain what the slope represents.

a)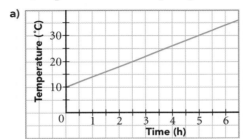

b)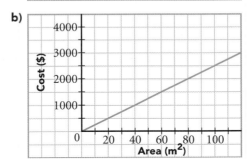

c)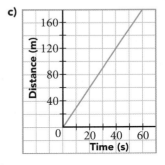

3. Determine the equation of each line.

a)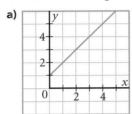

b)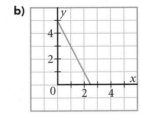

c)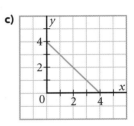

✓ **4.** A landscaping company pays its workers an hourly wage. A worker with no experience earns $8.50 per hour. A worker with 5 years' experience earns $12.50 per hour.

    a) Draw a graph of hourly wage against years of experience. Use the two given points and assume the graph is a line.

    b) Determine the slope of the line. Include appropriate units. Explain the meaning of the slope.

    c) Determine the hourly wage of a worker with 3 years' experience.

5. An energy auditor checks the temperature at different places in a thick concrete wall. At a distance, d metres, into the wall, the temperature, T, in degrees Celsius is given by $T = -15d + 25$.

    a) Plot a graph of T against d. Start at $d = 0$ m, the inside face of the wall. Plot up to $d = 1.2$ m, the outside face of the wall.

    b) What is the temperature on the inside face? on the outside face?

    c) Describe two methods to find the slope of the line, then determine the slope.

    d) What information does the slope give?

6. The graph shows the temperature of a container of yogurt that was left on the kitchen counter.

    a) What value is plotted on the horizontal axis?

    b) What value is plotted on the vertical axis?

    c) Determine the slope of the line. Include the units in your answer.

    d) Explain the meaning of the slope.

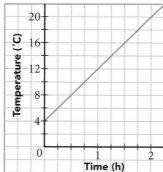

7. **Knowledge/Understanding** Jaime tracks the price of a set of skis over the winter. The changing price is shown in the graph.

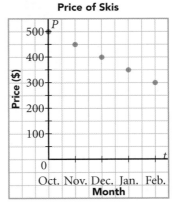

Price of Skis

a) What was the price in October?

b) What was the price in January?

c) Determine the slope of the line. Include the units in your answer. How did you quantify the months?

d) Write the equation of the line.

e) When the price of the skis was $250, Jaime asked her parents if she could buy them. When was the price $250?

8. The graph shows how to convert temperatures in degrees Celsius, T_C, to temperatures in degrees Fahrenheit, T_F.

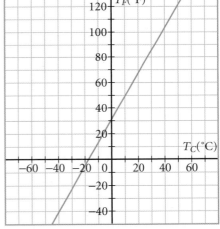

a) Convert 0°C to degrees F.

b) Convert 0°F to degrees C.

c) Write an equation for T_F.

d) What is T_F when $T_C = 200°C$?

e) What is T_C when $T_F = -100°F$?

9. Many towns have reservoirs to store water for future use. The graph shows the height of water in one town's reservoir during a dry summer.

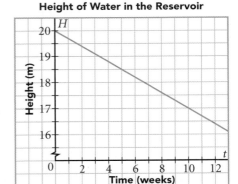

Height of Water in the Reservoir

a) What was the water level at the beginning of the summer?

b) Determine the rate of fall of the water level.

c) Write an equation to describe the water level over time.

d) Is it reasonable to expect the water level to fall at a constant rate? Explain.

10. **Application** A car owner keeps a logbook of how much gasoline he uses and how far he drives between fill-ups. The information is shown on the graph.

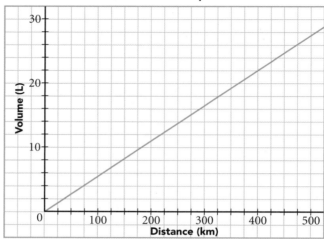

Volume of Fuel Required

a) How far can he drive on 20 L of gasoline?

b) How much gasoline does he require to travel 450 km?

c) Calculate the slope of the graph. What are the units?

d) How many kilometres can he drive on 1 L of gasoline?

e) Fuel consumption is expressed as litres per 100 km (L/100 km). What is the car's fuel consumption?

11. Marie-France's chequing account does not pay interest. She deposits the same amount each month. The balance of Marie-France's account over time is shown in the graph.

Balance of Marie-France's Chequing Account

a) How much was in Marie-France's account to start?

b) How much does she deposit each month?

c) Estimate when Marie-France will have $2000 in her account.

12. Marla walks 500 m, about 5 blocks, to school every day. The graph shows her distance from home, in metres, with time, in minutes, for a typical day.

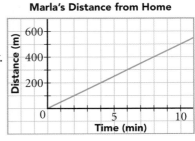
Marla's Distance from Home

a) Calculate the slope of the graph. What does the slope mean?

b) Sketch a graph of Marla running to school.

c) Sketch a graph of Marla walking halfway to school and then walking back home to get her math project.

13. Thinking/Inquiry/Problem Solving
Sairah's job around the house is to monitor the supply of cookies and to buy more when necessary. The graph shows the number of cookies over time for a normal week. For each situation, sketch a revised graph.

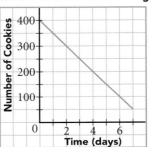
Number of Cookies Remaining

a) Sairah buys more cookies one week.

b) Sairah's uncle, a known cookie eater, comes to stay.

c) Sairah restocks the cookie cupboard part way through the week.

d) Sairah buys a brand of cookies that nobody likes.

14. A gecko is a small lizard. Students in a grade 9 mathematics class used a CBR to record the motion of a gecko. The gecko slipped out of range of the CBR after 3.5 s. The graph shows the distance of the gecko from the CBR, in metres, over time, in seconds.

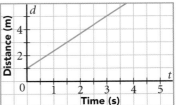
Motion of a Gecko

a) How far was the gecko from the CBR when it slipped out of range?

b) What was the gecko's speed?

c) Write an equation for the gecko's motion.

d) When was the gecko 3.2 m away from the CBR?

15. Communication Tim and Zack run a race. Tim always runs faster, so he gives Zack a head-start. Sketch a graph of distance versus time for the boys' race. Explain the important features of your graph.

16. Students in an environmental science class collected 8 samples of sand from a streambed. They measured the volume, V, in millilitres and the mass, m, in grams for each sample.

V (mL)	5	12	14	20	25	37	41	53
m (g)	21	50	59	84	105	155	172	223

a) The values for mass do not increase by a constant amount. Explain why the graph of m against V might still be linear.

b) Draw a scatter plot of the data.
- Press [Y=] and clear any equations.
- Press [STAT] [ENTER] to access the lists. Clear any data in lists L1 and L2. Enter the volume data in list L1 and the mass data in list L2.
- Press [2nd] [Y=] 1 [ENTER] to access and turn on Plot1 in STATPLOT.
- Press [▼] [ENTER] to select the scatter plot. Enter L1 for Xlist and L2 for Ylist.
- Set an appropriate window.
- Press [GRAPH] to display the scatter plot. Copy the scatter plot into your notebook.

c) Describe the shape of the graph.

d) Determine the equation of the regression line of best fit.
- Press [STAT] [▶] 4 to select LinReg(ax+b).
- Press: [2nd] 1 [,] [2nd] 2 [,] [VARS] [▶] 1 1 [ENTER]

e) Graph the line of best fit on the same screen as the scatter plot. How well does the line fit the data? Explain.

f) What is the slope of the line of best fit? Explain the meaning of the slope. Make reference to the units in your explanation.

g) What is the m-intercept of the line of best fit? Explain the meaning of the m-intercept; include the units in your explanation.

h) The *density* of a substance is found by dividing the mass of the substance by its volume. Another unit for 1 mL is 1 cm^3 (1 cubic centimetre). What is the density of the sand from the streambed in grams per cubic centimetre?

The arc of a pop-fly, the curve of a satellite dish, the frightening dip in the track of a roller coaster—these all take the shape of a parabola.

In this section, you will examine quadratic graphs. A quadratic graph is a piece of a parabola.

The graph shows the cross-section of part of a roller-coaster track. The horizontal and vertical distances are both measured in metres.

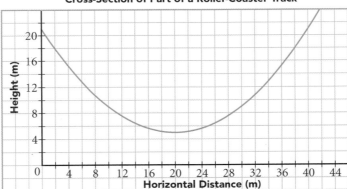

Cross-Section of Part of a Roller-Coaster Track

The graph starts when the track is 21 m above the ground. The track slopes down steeply at first, then not so steeply. After a horizontal distance of 20 m, it levels off at a height of 5 m. The track then starts to slope up more and more steeply.

This curve is quadratic if the differences in successive heights form an arithmetic sequence.

Horizontal distance (m)	Vertical distance (m)	Difference (m)
0	21	
		−7
5	14	
		−5
10	9	
		−3
15	6	
		−1
20	5	
		1
25	6	
		3
30	9	
		5
35	14	
		7
40	21	

The differences increase by a constant amount. The differences form an *arithmetic sequence*. This graph is quadratic.

The first few differences in height are negative. The track is going down.

The track is at a minimum height of 5 m when *d* is 20 m.

The differences are positive for larger values of *d*. The track is now going up.

This quadratic graph *opens up*—its two arms point up. It has a lowest point, or *minimum*, at (20, 5). The lowest point on this section of track is 5 m above the ground. Before the minimum, the track is going down; after the minimum, it is going up.

The laws of gravity control how apples fall and how fly balls soar. Many situations that involve gravity can be represented by quadratic graphs. Even though an apple falls straight down, the graph of the height of the apple over time is quadratic. This is because gravity causes the apple to accelerate; it falls slowly at first and then more and more quickly.

Example 1

A tennis ball is shot into the air from a tennis cannon. The graph shows the ball's height above the ground compared to the time from launch.

a) How high is the ball immediately after it leaves the cannon?

b) When does the ball hit the ground?

c) What is the maximum height of the ball? When is the ball at its maximum height?

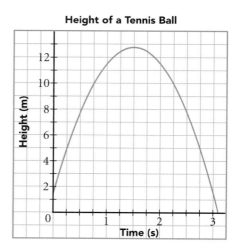

Height of a Tennis Ball

Solution

a) The ball leaves the cannon at 0 s at a height of 1.5 m.

b) The height is 0 m when the ball hits the ground. This occurs at 3.1 s. The ball hits the ground about 3.1 s after launch.

c) The maximum point of the curve is (1.5, 12.8). The ball reaches a maximum height of approximately 12.8 m after 1.5 s.

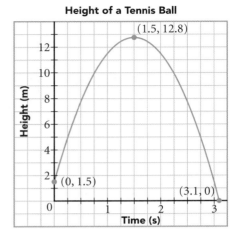

Height of a Tennis Ball

Discuss

Explain why the graph does not include any negative values for time or height.

The next situation is an example of quadratic growth.

Example 2

Jesse has designed an advertising logo in art class.

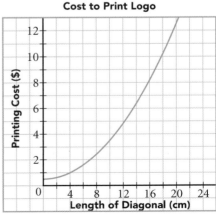

The price to print the logo depends on its size. The graph gives the printing price for a range of diagonal measurements.

a) What is the value of the vertical intercept? What does the vertical intercept represent?

b) How much does it cost to print a logo with a 10-cm diagonal?

c) How much does it cost to print a logo with a 20-cm diagonal?

d) Explain why it is reasonable that a larger logo costs so much more to print.

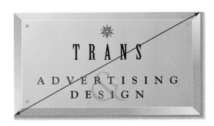

Cost to Print Logo

Solution

a) The vertical intercept is $0.50. This represents a flat fee for the printing. It could include the cost of the glossy paper and the use of the printing machine.

b) The cost of a logo with a 10-cm diagonal is $3.50.

c) The cost of a logo with a 20-cm diagonal is $12.50.

e) The amount of ink used on a logo depends on the area of the design. The area of a logo with a 20-cm diagonal is about 4 times larger than the area of a logo with a 10-cm diagonal.

TAKE NOTE

Quadratic Graphs

A quadratic graph is a section of parabola. There are two basic types.

Opening Up:

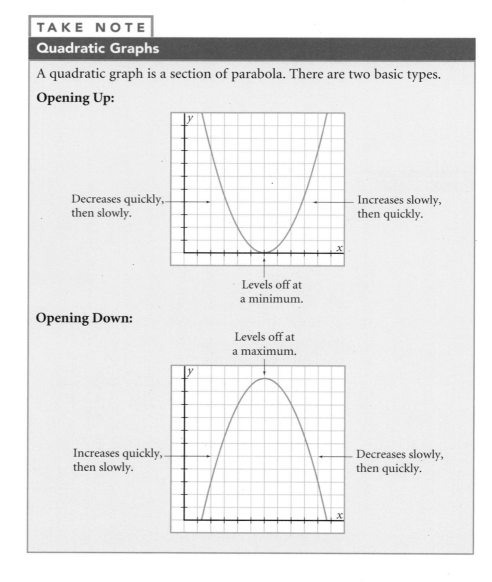

Decreases quickly, then slowly.

Increases slowly, then quickly.

Levels off at a minimum.

Opening Down:

Levels off at a maximum.

Increases quickly, then slowly.

Decreases slowly, then quickly.

A

1. Each of these quadratic graphs is a piece of a parabola. For each graph, state whether the parabola opens up or down.

a)

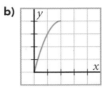

b)

c)

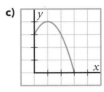

2. For each quadratic graph:
   i) State whether it has a maximum or minimum.
   ii) Give the coordinates of the maximum or minimum point.

a)

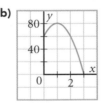

b)

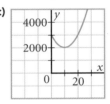

c)

3. a) In the graph below left, which curve represents quadratic growth? Explain.

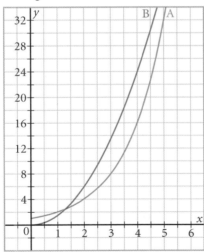
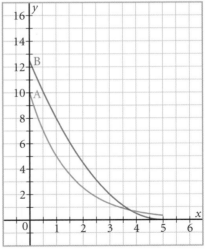

b) In the graph above right, which curve represents quadratic decay? Explain.

✓ **4.** Televisions are priced according to screen size. One manufacturer suggests retailers use the formula $C = 200 + 0.42D^2$, where C is the cost in dollars and D is the screen size in inches.

   a) Draw a graph of cost against screen size. Use screen sizes from 14" to 34".

   b) Explain why the graph is quadratic.

   c) Explain the meaning of the term "200" in the formula.

   d) Explain the meaning of the term "$0.42D^2$" in the formula.

5. The graph in exercise 4 is quadratic but not very curved.

   a) Draw a straight line to join your data points for televisions with 14" and 34" screens.

   b) Find the equation of this line.

   c) i) Calculate the cost for a 24" television set using the formula in exercise 4.

   ii) Calculate the cost for a 24" television set using the equation of the line from exercise 5.

   d) Which formula is more practical? Explain.

✓ **6. Knowledge/Understanding** TinCanCo manufactures tin cans. One product line includes cans that are all 20 cm tall. The graph shows how the volume in millilitres depends on the radius in centimetres.

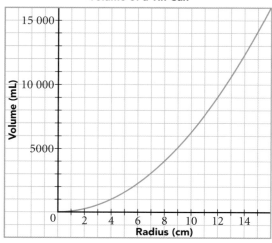

   a) What is the volume of a can with radius 4 cm?

   b) What is the radius of a can with volume 2.50 L?

c) Copy and complete the table.

Radius (cm)	Volume (L)	Difference
0		
5		
10		
15		

d) Determine if the graph is quadratic.

e) Predict the volume of a can with radius 20 cm. Explain your method.

7. A car travelling 50 km/h will stop in about 23 m. A car travelling 100 km/h will stop in about 93 m. The graph shows how stopping distance depends on speed.

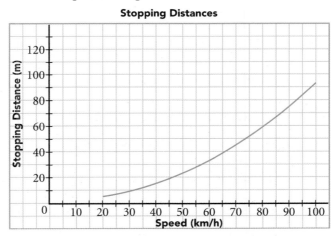

Stopping Distances

a) Determine the stopping distances for speeds of 20 km/h and 30 km/h. What is the difference?

b) Determine the stopping distances for speeds of 90 km/h and 100 km/h. What is the difference?

c) From your own experience, explain why stopping distance increases as speed increases.

d) According to the graph, what is the minimum stopping distance? Does this make sense? Explain.

e) Estimate the stopping distance for a car travelling 110 km/h. Explain your method.

8. **Application** The amount of drag, or air resistance, on a moving car depends on many factors. One important factor is the speed of the car. The graph shows how the drag, in kiloNewtons, depends on the speed, in kilometres per hour.

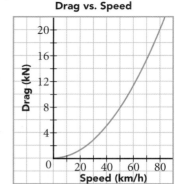
Drag vs. Speed

   a) Determine the drag at each speed:
      i) 20 km/h
      ii) 40 km/h
      iii) 60 km/h
      iv) 80 km/h
   b) Is the graph quadratic? Explain.

9. The graph shows how the cost of a pizza at a particular restaurant depends on the size of the pizza.

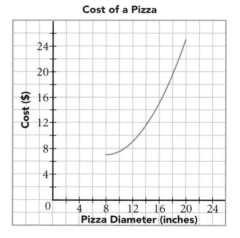
Cost of a Pizza

   a) Verify that the graph is quadratic. Explain.
   b) Why is it reasonable that pizza pricing is not linear?
   c) Locate the vertex of the parabola. What does the vertex represent?
   d) Explain why it is reasonable that the vertex is not at the origin.

10. A plastic 2-L pop bottle is filled with water. A hole is made near the bottom of the bottle. As the water drains out, the height of the water level in the bottle drops. One student records the height of the water level at 20-s intervals.

Time (s)	0	20	40	60	80	100	120	140	160	180	200
Height (mm)	130	105	83	64	48	34	22	13	6	2	0

   a) Graph the data.
   b) Explain why the graph is quadratic.
   c) At what time is the water draining fastest? Explain.
   d) State the coordinates of the minimum point.

11. **Thinking/Inquiry/Problem Solving** Jan repeated the pop bottle experiment of exercise 10, trying out some variations. For each variation:

    i) Sketch the graph you would expect.

    ii) Explain the shape you chose.

a) Jan started with a partly full bottle.

b) Jan punched a larger hole in the bottle.

c) Jan used a 750-mL bottle, which has a smaller diameter than a 2-L bottle.

12. The graph shows the distance travelled by a skateboarder rolling down a straight slope.

    a) Explain the shape of the graph in terms of the motion of the skateboarder.

    b) Sketch a distance-time graph for a skateboarder on:

        i) a steeper slope

        ii) a shallower slope

        iii) a level sidewalk

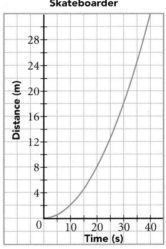

Distance Travelled by Skateboarder

13. **Communication** The graph shows the motion of a cyclist going from one stop sign to another. For each time interval, describe the shape of the graph and the speed of the cyclist.

    a) the first 10 s

    b) between 10 s and 30 s

    c) the last 10 s

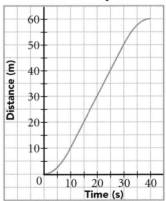

Motion of a Cyclist

14. The graph shows the motion of two cars, A and B, leaving a stop sign.

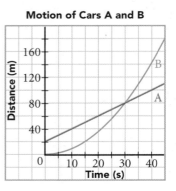

Motion of Cars A and B

a) Explain how you can tell from the graph that car A is moving at constant speed.

b) Calculate the speed of car A.

c) Describe the motion of car B.

d) When does car B catch up to car A?

e) Over what times is car B moving faster than car A? Explain.

15. A skydiver steps out of an airplane 3000 m above the ground. The skydiver falls freely to 1000 m above ground level, then the parachute opens. The table gives the height above the ground for several times after exiting the plane.

Time (s)	0	2	4	6	8	10
Height (m)	3000	2980	2920	2820	2680	2500

a) Graph the data on a coordinate grid.

b) Use your graph to estimate the time when the skydiver reaches a height of 1000 m.

c) Draw a scatter plot of the data.
- Press [Y=] and clear any equations.
- Press [STAT] [ENTER] to access the lists. Clear any data in lists L1 and L2. Enter the time data in list L1 and the height data in list L2.
- Press [2nd] [Y=] 1 [ENTER] to access and turn on Plot1 in STATPLOT.
- Press [▼] [ENTER] to select the scatter plot. Enter L1 for Xlist and L2 for Ylist.
- Set an appropriate window.
- Press [GRAPH] to display the scatter plot. Copy the scatter plot into your notebook.

d) Determine the quadratic regression equation of best fit.
- Press [STAT] [▶] 5 to select QuadReg.
- Press [2nd] 1 [,] [2nd] 2 [,] [VARS] [▶] 1 1 [ENTER].

e) Graph the regression equation on the same screen as the scatter plot. How well does the function fit the data? Explain.

f) Press [Y=] [▲] [ENTER] to turn off Plot 1. Use the TRACE command to determine when the skydiver is 1000 m above the ground.

g) Compare your answers from parts b and f. Explain any differences.

Compound interest, population growth, and radioactive decay all show exponential behaviour. In grade 11, *Mathematics of Personal Finance,* you worked with exponential functions and drew exponential graphs.

In this section, we will do the opposite—we will examine exponential graphs and see what information we can uncover.

Have you ever watched bread dough rise? Many recipes say "Let the dough rise until double in bulk." You are supposed to wait until the volume of the bread dough is twice the starting volume.

Kayla works in a commercial bakery that uses huge volumes of dough. The graph shows the volume of one batch of dough over time.

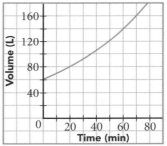

Volume of Bread Dough

Time, in minutes, is plotted on the horizontal axis. The volume of the dough, in litres, is plotted on the vertical axis.

How can we find the *doubling time* for this type of dough? From the graph, the starting volume is 60 L. This is the volume at time = 0 min. Now look for when the volume is 2 × 60 L = 120 L. This happens at about 50 min. The doubling time is about 50 min.

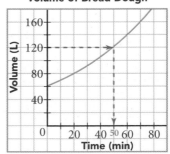

Volume of Bread Dough

Discuss

From the graph, it looks like someone forgot this batch of dough. Explain.

We can start at *any* place on the graph to find the doubling time (as long as we do not run off the end). The graph shows how to calculate the doubling time starting at time = 10 min.

The volume at 10 min is about 69 L. The volume is 2 × 69 L = 138 L at about 60 min. The doubling time is about:
60 min − 10 min = 50 min

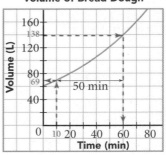

Volume of Bread Dough

Is the graph really exponential? By what percent does the bread dough increase every 10 min? We need to make a table of values to answer detailed questions like these.

It is difficult to read the volumes accurately from the graph. This is always a problem when interpreting a graph.

Recall, a graph of exponential growth increases more and more quickly. If the differences in the *x*-values are constant, there is a common ratio between successive *y*-values.

The graph of the volume of bread dough over time does increase more and more quickly. This is confirmed by the volumes in the table. The volumes form a geometric sequence with a common ratio of about 1.15.

Time (min)	Volume (L)	Ratio
0	60	
		1.150
10	69	
		1.145
20	79	
		1.152
30	91	
		1.154
40	105	
		1.143
50	121	
		1.149
60	139	
		1.151
70	160	
		1.150
80	184	

Every 10 min, the volume of dough increases by a factor of 1.15.

Recall, the growth factor, *b*, for exponential growth is given by $1 + r$, where *r* is the percent rate of increase expressed as a decimal. Since the growth factor is 1.15, the dough increases by 15% every 10 min.

Discuss

In the table, explain why the ratios are not exactly 1.15.
How did we know the time required for the volume of dough to increase by 15% was 10 min?

A graph of exponential decay decreases quickly at first and then more gradually. Recall, the *half-life* of a substance is the time it takes for the amount of that substance to be reduced by one-half. We used the graph of the volume of bread dough over time to determine the doubling time. We can use a similar process to find the half-life for exponential decay.

Investigation

Determining the Blood Level of an Antihistamine

When hay-fever season arrives, we all see the advertisements for allergy medicines: 8-Hour Relief! 12-Hour Relief! 24-Hour Relief!

Different drugs are processed by our bodies at different rates. The graph shows the amount of antihistamine remaining in a person's bloodstream. The first measurement is taken 1 h after the capsule is swallowed.

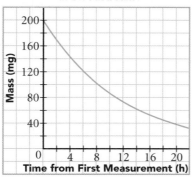

Amount of Drug Remaining in Bloodstream

1. Explain why the first measurement was made 1 h after the drug was swallowed.

2. How much antihistamine was in the blood at the time of the first measurement (0 h)?

3. Determine the half-life of the drug in the bloodstream.

4. Repeat your determination of the half-life using a different starting point. Compare your result to your answer to exercise 3. Did you get the same result? Explain.

5. Copy and complete this table.

Time (h)	Mass (mg)	Ratio
0		
4		
8		
12		
16		
20		

6. Is the graph exponential? Explain.

7. What is the common ratio? Explain the meaning of the common ratio in terms of the amount of the drug in the bloodstream. What is the time period?

8. Use the graph to determine the percent decrease of the drug each hour.

9. In exercise 7, you should have found a common ratio of 0.72 over 4 h. We can use this common ratio to find the hourly percent decrease. Recall, the decay factor, b, is given by $1 - r$, where r is the percent rate of decrease expressed as a decimal.

a) Explain why the exponent is 4 in this formula: $(1 - r)^4 = 0.72$.

b) By what percent does the blood level of antihistamine decrease each hour?

10. Compare your answers to exercises 8 and 9b. Which percent is more accurate? Explain.

11. Describe how changing the scales on the graph could allow you to determine the hourly percent decrease more accurately.

In the *Investigation*, you used the graph and an indirect method to determine the percent rate of increase for one unit of time. You will use the indirect method in *Example 1*.

Example 1

Grandma's old cookie jar is a valuable antique. The graph shows how its value increases with time.

a) How much is the cookie jar worth initially?

b) How much will it be worth in 10 years?

c) Determine the doubling time for its value.

d) Determine the annual percent increase in its value.

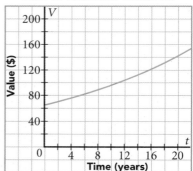
Value of Grandma's Cookie Jar

Solution

a) At $t = 0$ years, the cookie jar is worth about $65.

b) At $t = 10$ years, the cookie jar is worth about $95.

c) The cookie jar is worth $65 initially. To find the doubling time, determine the year in which its value is $2 \times \$65 = \$130$. From the graph, the value of the cookie jar is $130 at about $t = 18$ years. The doubling time is about 18 years.

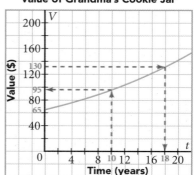
Value of Grandma's Cookie Jar

d) The scale on the graph is too small to accurately read the values of the cookie jar for 2 years in a row. We need to use a longer time interval to find the increase over 1 year.

From part c, we know the value doubles about every 18 years. Suppose the annual rate of increase is r.

$$(1 + r)^{18} = 2$$
$$(1 + r) = \sqrt[18]{2} \qquad \text{Press: } 18 \boxed{\text{2nd}} \boxed{\land} 2 \boxed{\text{ENTER}}$$
$$(1 + r) \doteq 1.039$$
$$r = 1.039 - 1$$
$$r = 0.039$$

The value of the cookie jar increases by approximately 4% each year.

Discuss

Some calculators do not have the $\sqrt[x]{}$ function. Describe how to use exponents to evaluate $\sqrt[18]{2}$.

Sometimes the graph does not extend far enough to give us the information we need. When this is the case, we need to use an indirect method.

Example 2

An imaging technologist must be cautious of the amount of radiation received over her or his working life. Sheets of lead shield the technologist's console to provide a safe working space. The amount, or flux, of radiation penetrating a given thickness of lead is shown in the graph.

a) What thickness of lead blocks 50% of the radiation?

b) What percent of radiation will pass through 3.0 cm of lead?

c) How much lead is needed to block 99% of the radiation?

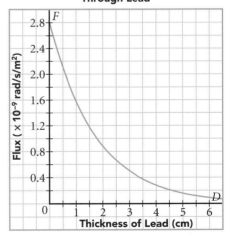

Flux of Radiation Passing Through Lead

Solution

a) In this problem, rather than finding the half-life, we are finding the half-thickness—the thickness of lead through which only half of the radiation can pass.

From the graph, for $D = 0$ cm, the flux of radiation is 2.8×10^{-9} rad/s/m^2.

Fifty percent of this value is:
$0.5 \times 2.8 \times 10^{-9}$ rad/s/m^2
$= 1.4 \times 10^{-9}$ rad/s/m^2

From the graph, the flux of radiation is 1.4×10^{-9} rad/s/m^2 when D is approximately 1.2 cm.

Lead about 1.2 cm thick reduces the flux of radiation by 50%.

Flux of Radiation Passing Through Lead

b) In part a, we determined that the flux of radiation is 2.8×10^{-9} rad/s/m^2 when the lead is 0 cm thick.

From the graph, when the lead is 3.0 cm thick, the flux of radiation is 0.5×10^{-9} rad/s/m^2.

Suppose the rate of decrease over 3.0 cm is r.

Then, $\qquad (1 - r) = \dfrac{0.5 \times 10^{-9}}{2.8 \times 10^{-9}}$

Solving for r, $\qquad 1 - r \doteq 0.82$

$\qquad\qquad 1 - 0.82 = r$

$\qquad\qquad\qquad r = 0.18$

So, 18% of the radiation passes through 3.0 cm of lead.

c) The graph does not extend far enough to find the thickness through which only 1% of the radiation passes. We need an indirect method.
In part a, we found that the flux of radiation drops by 50% for every 1.2 cm of lead. When the lead is 1.2 cm thick, $\frac{1}{2}$ of the radiation passes through.
When the lead is $2 \times 1.2 = 2.4$ cm thick, $\frac{1}{2} \times \frac{1}{2} = \frac{1}{4}$ of the radiation passes through.
When the lead is $3 \times 1.2 = 3.6$ cm thick, $\frac{1}{4} \times \frac{1}{2} = \frac{1}{8}$ of the radiation passes through. Remember that exponential decay is a geometric sequence. For every increase of 1.2 cm in the thickness of the lead, the amount of flux is halved.

So, we need to find the value of n that makes $\left(\frac{1}{2}\right)^n$ less than 1% or $\frac{1}{100}$.

By trial and error, the smallest value of n that works is $n = 7$.

For better than 99% shielding, the lead should be at least 7×1.2 cm or 8.4 cm thick.

Discuss

When would you calculate a percent increase or decrease directly from the data on the graph? When would you use a longer time or distance and solve an equation?

TAKE NOTE

Exponential Graphs

There are two types of exponential graphs.

Exponential Growth:

- Grows slowly, then quickly.
- Use doubling time or equivalent.

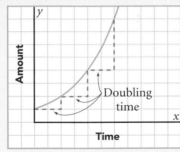

Exponential Decay:

- Falls quickly, then slowly.
- Use half-life or equivalent.

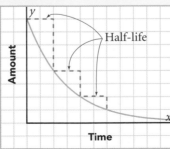

A

✓ **1.** For each exponential graph, state:
   i) the initial value of y
   ii) the doubling time

a) 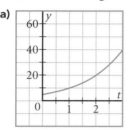   **b)** 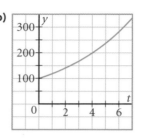   **c)**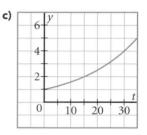

✓ **2.** For each exponential graph, state:
   i) the initial value of y
   ii) the half-life

a) 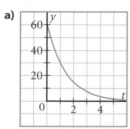   **b)** 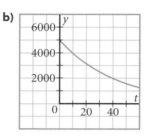   **c)**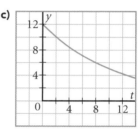

B

✓ **3. Knowledge/Understanding**
An antiseptic spray is used to clean the surfaces in a veterinary office. The percent of active bacteria is graphed over time.

a) Explain the vertical scale.

b) Determine the half-life of the bacteria.

c) What is the rate of decrease of bacteria each minute?

d) When is the level of active bacteria down to 5%?

Percent of Active Bacteria

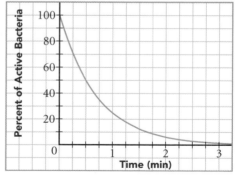

4. Sean has purchased a term deposit that earns compound interest. The value of the term deposit over time is shown in the graph.

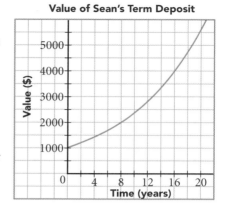
Value of Sean's Term Deposit

a) How much money did Sean deposit?

b) When will the term deposit be worth $4500?

c) Determine the doubling time for the deposit.

d) What is the annual interest rate?

5. Communication A biology class uses fruit flies for its genetics studies. The lab that supplies the fruit flies enclosed this graph with the shipment of flies.

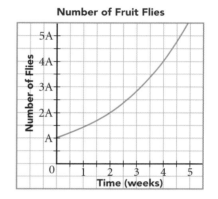
Number of Fruit Flies

a) Explain what is plotted.

b) What is the doubling time for the population?

c) What is the daily rate of increase in the population?

d) If you start with a population of 20 flies, when would you expect to have 50 flies?

6. Application The graph shows the number of infant deaths in Canada each year from 1972 to 2000. All infants were less than one year of age.

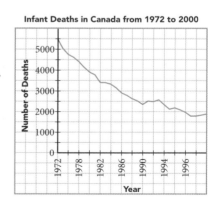
Infant Deaths in Canada from 1972 to 2000

a) How many infant deaths were there in 1983?

b) Estimate the time for the number of deaths to decrease by 50% from each year.
   i) 1974   **ii)** 1977
   iii) 1979

c) Estimate the average time required for the number of deaths to decrease by 50%.

d) Between 1972 and 2000, the number of infant deaths is decreasing exponentially.

   Predict the number of infant deaths in 2010. What assumptions did you make?

7. Canada's national debt grew substantially between 1970 and 1995.

a) What was the value of the debt in each year?

   i) 1970

   ii) 1995

b) Find the doubling time for the debt.

c) Calculate the annual rate of increase of the debt.

d) Estimate the value of the debt in 2010.

e) For part d, explain any assumptions you made and describe the method you used.

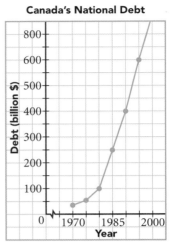

Canada's National Debt

8. Many cancer treatment facilities are located near the atomic accelerator laboratories that manufacture the radioisotopes used in therapy. A 600-mg sample of an experimental isotope decays according to the graph.

a) What is the half-life of the sample?

b) How much of the sample is left after 3 h?

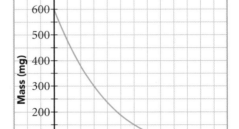

Mass of a Radioactive Isotope

c) Use your answers to parts a and b to explain why cancer treatment facilities are often located close to atomic accelerators.

9. Most VCRs and digital clocks contain a capacitor for power during a brief hydro outage. The graph shows how the voltage on a capacitor decreases with the duration of the hydro outage.

a) Estimate the half-voltage; that is, the time needed for the voltage to fall by a factor of 2.

b) What voltage remains after each time?

   i) 1 s   ii) 5 s   iii) 10 s

c) Estimate the voltage remaining after 0.1 s.

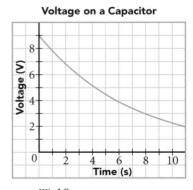

Voltage on a Capacitor

10. The higher you go up into the atmosphere, the lower the air pressure gets. This is why airplane cabins must be pressurized and why climbers need oxygen tanks to climb Mount Everest. The graph shows how air pressure, in kiloPascals, changes as the altitude, in kilometres, increases.

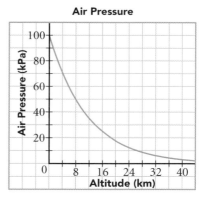

Air Pressure

a) Find the air pressure at sea level (altitude = 0 km).

b) Over what distance does air pressure decrease by a factor of 2?

c) Over what distance does air pressure decrease by a factor of 10?

d) Find the air pressure in these locations:
   i) Calgary, altitude 1084 m
   ii) Mount Logan, altitude 6050 m
   iii) Mount Everest, altitude 8848 m

e) Estimate the air pressure at an altitude of 100 km, a typical height for Space Shuttle flights. What percent of air pressure at sea level is this?

11. Scientists measure noise level or loudness in decibels (dB). The chart gives the loudness for some day-to-day sounds. It also gives the intensity of the sound waves that affect your ear in Watts per square metre (W/m^2).

Sound	Loudness (dB)	Intensity (W/m^2)
Hair dryer	70	0.000 01
Traffic noise	80	0.0001
Lawnmower	90	0.001
CD player on medium	100	0.01
Power saw	110	0.1

a) Plot intensity against loudness. For the vertical scale, use increments of $0.01 \ W/m^2$ to a maximum value of $0.1 \ W/m^2$.

b) Describe the shape of the graph.

c) What happens to the value of intensity if the loudness increases by 10 dB?

d) What increase in loudness causes the intensity to double?

e) Calculate the intensity for these common sounds:
   i) jet engine (140 dB)
   ii) shotgun firing (130 dB)
   iii) space rocket (160 dB)

f) Estimate the loudness associated with these intensities:

    i) threshold of pain (10 W/m^2)

    ii) instant perforation of the ear drum ($10\ 000$ W/m^2)

12. Five children in a school came down with chicken pox at the same time. The number of children with chicken pox increased for several weeks.

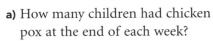

Number of Cases of Chicken Pox

a) How many children had chicken pox at the end of each week?

    i) week 2

    ii) week 4

    iii) week 6

b) What was the doubling time for the number of cases of chicken pox?

c) By what percent did the number of cases increase each week?

d) Explain the statement: "Contagious diseases spread exponentially."

✓ **13. Thinking/Inquiry/Problem Solving** Devi invests $2500 in an account that pays *simple interest*. After 8 years, she will have $3500. Sandhya claims she can start with less money and end up with more.

a) The value of Devi's account is a linear function. Explain.

b) Suppose the annual simple interest rate is r. Calculate r.

c) Find the equation for the amount in Devi's account over time.

d) Graph the amount in Devi's account over time.

e) If Sandhya invests $2500 at 4% compounded annually, the amount in her account is determined by $V = 2500(1.04)^t$. Explain.

f) Graph the function that represents the amount in Sandhya's account over time on the same screen as the graph of the amount in Devi's account over time.

g) When will there be more in Sandhya's account than in Devi's account?

h) Change the rate of interest on Sandhya's account so that the amount in her account equals the amount in Devi's account at $t = 8$ years.

i) In part h, did you increase or decrease Sandhya's rate from 4%? Explain.

j) Suppose Sandhya starts with $2000. Determine the rate of compound interest she would need so that the balance in her account equals the balance in Devi's account at $t = 8$ years.

1. The graph shows the distance, *D*, travelled by a jogger as a function of time, *t*.

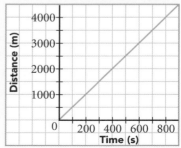

Distance Travelled by a Jogger

a) How long does it take the jogger to run 2500 m?

b) Calculate the slope of the graph.

c) Explain the meaning of the slope.

d) Write the equation relating distance to time.

2. A company has proposed two plans, A and B, for the number of vacation days an employee may take. Both plans depend on years of service.

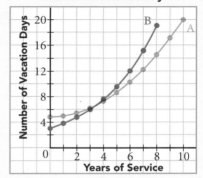

Number of Vacation Days

a) Which plan gives more vacation days for 3 years of service? 9 years of service?

b) Show that the graph for plan A is quadratic.

c) Show that the graph for plan B is exponential.

d) Find the doubling time for plan B.

3. The graph shows the growth of two types of coral over 50 years.

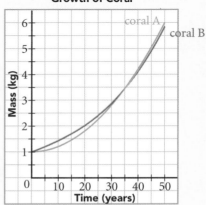

Growth of Coral

a) Which type of coral grows the fastest
   i) in the first 10 years?
   ii) after 50 years?
   Explain.

b) Which growth curve is exponential? Explain.

c) For the growth curve from part b,
   i) Find the doubling time.
   ii) Find the annual increase.

d) Identify the growth pattern of the other type of coral. Explain.

A graph is a visual tool to summarize the changes we observe. If used with care, a graph can provide insight into future events.

This graph appeared in *The Globe and Mail* on March 1, 1999. The change in the number of jobs every year from 1990 to 1998 is plotted for 4 groups of workers:

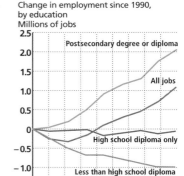

CLASS STRUGGLE

Change in employment since 1990, by education
Millions of jobs

Source: Statistics Canada   The Globe and Mail

- those with a post-secondary degree or diploma
- all workers
- those with a high school diploma only
- those without a high school diploma

Four separate trends appear on the graph.

- The number of new jobs for people with post-secondary education increased at a steady rate.
- The total number of new jobs available to all workers increased at a steady rate.
- The number of new jobs for people with a high school diploma only remained steady at close to 0.
- The number of new jobs for people without a high school diploma decreased at a relatively steady rate.

Will these trends continue? The graph does not give us that information. *If* there is no large change in the economy and *if* there is no large change in education levels, the trends *may* continue for *a while*. Some things cannot be predicted with great confidence.

Trends

Trends in graphs, as illustrated above, occur in three broad groups:

- *increasing* (more new jobs for post-secondary graduates)
- *constant* (no change in the number of new jobs for high school graduates)
- *decreasing* (fewer jobs for those without a high school diploma)

Sometimes, a finer description of a trend is needed.

Example 1 Most new jeans shrink when they are washed. The graph shows three possible curves to represent the effect of repeated washings on the length of a pair of jeans.

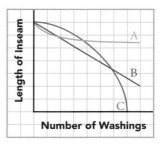

a) Describe the trend displayed by each curve.

b) Which curve best represents the effect of the number of washings on the length of a pair of jeans? Explain.

c) Describe the trend of length in relation to the number of washings.

d) Why is it important to know which of the 3 decreasing trends is the correct one?

Solution

a) All three curves show a decreasing trend. Curve A is decreasing at a decreasing rate; curve B is decreasing at a constant rate; and curve C is decreasing at an increasing rate.

b) Jeans shrink a lot the first time they are washed. They shrink less the second time they are washed and even less the third time. After a few washings, they stop shrinking. Curve A fits this description.

c) The trend is decreasing—quickly at first and then more slowly.

d) You do not want jeans that continue to shrink a lot every time they are washed. The other two decreasing trends shrink to nothing!

TAKE NOTE

Seven Basic Trends

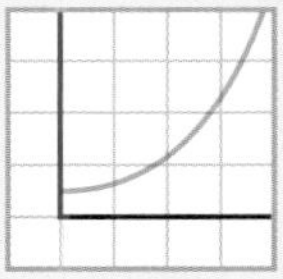

Increasing faster and faster

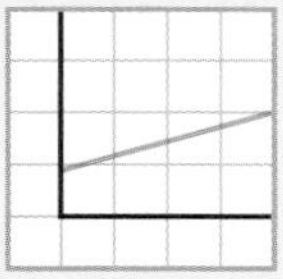

Increasing at a constant rate

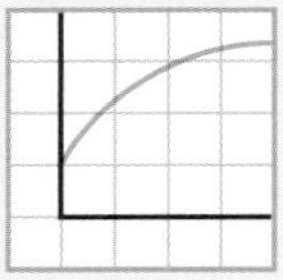

Increasing, but levelling off

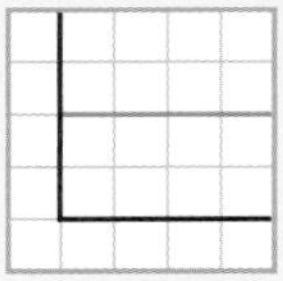

Constant

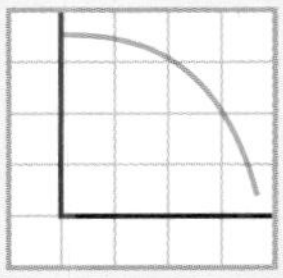

Decreasing faster and faster

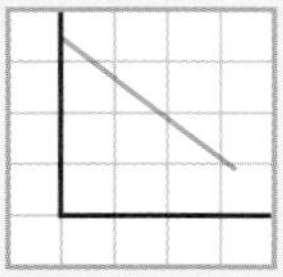

Decreasing at a constant rate

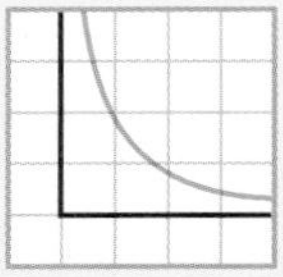

Decreasing, but levelling off

Predictions

Jose Cruz runs to centre field, opens his glove and casually catches a fly ball. Is this good luck? No, it is good prediction.

Developing an ability to anticipate the path of a fly ball takes years of observation and, at a subconscious level, analysis. The speed, angle, and spin of the ball as it leaves the bat, the air temperature and humidity, the wind speed and direction, special air circulation quirks of the stadium—all these contribute to the motion of the ball. Furthermore, the fielder continues to follow the ball and update its trajectory right until the ball is caught. Superb predictions are tricky, and are worth the big bucks!

Given only a graph with a trend, the best prediction you can make is to follow the trend. This is easy and reasonably reliable for a linear trend.

Example 2

One of Raba's household chores is filling the water softener with salt when the salt is down to the refill line. The graph shows the salt level with time.

a) Predict when Raba will have to refill the water softener with salt.

b) Discuss the factors that might affect the reliability of your prediction.

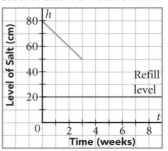

Level of Salt in a Water Softener

Solution

a) The trend in the graph is decreasing at a constant rate. Extend the line until it crosses the refill line at $h = 20$ cm. The time is $t = 6$ weeks. Raba will need to put salt in the water softener 6 weeks after the first time on the graph.

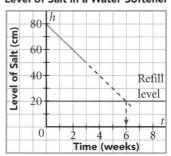

Level of Salt in a Water Softener

b) Most water softeners recycle with a fixed pattern. Unless the electricity or water is turned off for a week or more, the salt will continue to be used at the same rate. The prediction should be very reliable. It is easy to draw a line and there are not many factors that will affect the rate of salt use.

If the graph is a curve, predicting reliably becomes more difficult. We need a lot of information about the situation to know how to continue the curve. Often, only a short-term prediction is reasonable.

Example 3

Maria and Vlad used a CBR to record the position of a remote control car. They graphed their results for the first 4.0 s, before the car slipped out of range.

a) Estimate the position of the car at $t = 4.1$ s and at $t = 5.0$ s.

b) Another student answers part a: When $t = 4.1$ s, $d = 3.7$ m. When $t = 5.0$ s, $d = 3.5$ m. These answers may be different from your answers to part a. Explain why both answers can be considered correct.

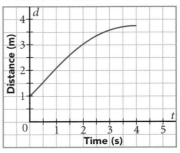

Position of a Remote Control Car

Solution

a) The trend of the graph is increasing but levelling off. Extend the curve as smoothly as possible. Reading from the extended graph (shown in orange), when $t = 4.1$ s, $d = 3.8$ m; when $t = 5.0$ s, $d = 3.9$ m.

b) There are many smooth curves that extend the given graph. They are quite close together at $t = 4.1$ s, so $d = 3.7$ m is reasonable. The curves spread out at later times, so $d = 3.5$ m is quite different from our result but still possible.

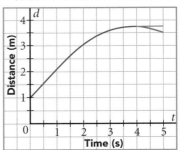

Position of a Remote Control Car

Discuss

Examine the two curves in the solution. Describe the motion of the car in the two predictions.

A

✓ **1.** Match each temperature forecast with its graph.

    i) cool all week

    ii) warm today, but cooling gradually over the next few days

    iii) cold today, but a warm front will arrive tonight

a) 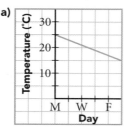   **b)** 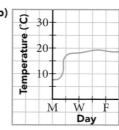   **c)**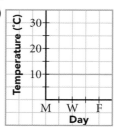

✓ **2.** Predict the value of y when $x = 10$.

a) 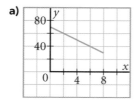   **b)** 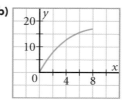   **c)**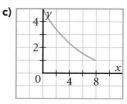

3. Look back at your linear, quadratic, and exponential graphs. Find an example of each of the seven basic trends.

B

4. For each graph of a stock index, describe the trend in stock prices.

a) 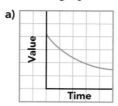   **b)** 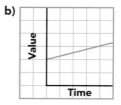   **c)**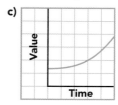

✓ **5.** Describe the motion represented by each position-time graph.

a) 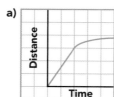   **b)** 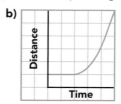   **c)**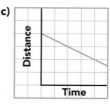

6. Knowledge/Understanding The graph shows Ola's height in inches as a function of his age in years.

a) Describe the trend in the graph.

b) Predict Ola's height at age 20. What assumptions did you make?

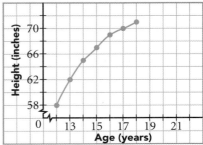

Ola's Height vs. Age in Years

7. Communication A friend shows you the graph at right and asks you to estimate the value of y when $x = 12$.

a) Describe how you would make the estimate.

b) You are told that the graph shows the amount of an investment that earns compound interest over time. How can you improve your estimate?

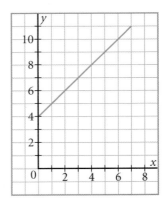

8. Two linear trends are shown.

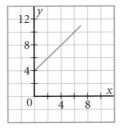

a) Describe the similarities in the graphs. What is the major difference between the graphs?

b) Compare the accuracy of predictions made from these graphs.

c) Describe a circumstance in which you would select each type of presentation.

9. A photographer measures the intensity of a bright flood lamp from various distances. The data are shown in the graph.

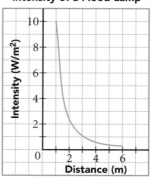

Intensity of a Flood Lamp

a) Describe the trend in the graph.

b) Estimate the intensity of the flood lamp from a distance of 6.5 m.

c) Estimate the intensity of the flood lamp from a distance of 0.5 m.

d) You estimated intensities in parts b and c. Which intensity estimate is likely to be more accurate? Explain.

10. City Council is developing a new Town Plan and requires a projection of the city's population. The graph shows the population of the city for the past 40 years.

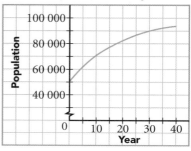

Population of a City

a) What is the population of the city now (year 40)?

b) How much has the population increased in the last 20 years?

c) Predict the population in year 50.

11. Thinking/Inquiry/Problem Solving For each scenario, sketch a graph of inside temperature with time and explain the shape. Suppose the initial inside temperature is 21°C and the outside temperature is 12°C.

a) Sam burns some toast and opens all the windows.

b) Sam's mother comes home, closes the windows, and sets the thermostat to 22°C.

c) Sam's father resets the thermostat to 18°C before going to bed.

12. Rozmin and Bashir take out a mortgage for $100 000 at 7%. The graph shows the total value of their payments for different lengths of the mortgage.

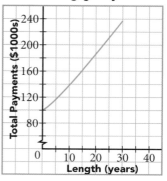

Total Mortgage Payments

a) Describe the trend in the graph.

b) Estimate the total payments for a 35-year mortgage.

c) How much extra would they pay if they extended the mortgage by 5 years?

13. The graph shows the speed of a skydiver over time.

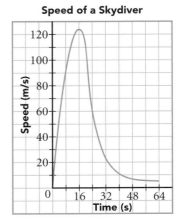

Speed of a Skydiver

a) The parachute opens after 16 s. Describe the trend in speed between the time the skydiver jumped and the time he opened his parachute.

b) What is happening to the speed between 16 s and 32 s?

c) What is the highest speed of the dive?

d) Describe the trend in the speed after 24 s.

e) Estimate the *terminal velocity*, the steady speed for the last part of the dive.

14. In many companies, the wage earned by an employee is related to the employee's years of service. The graph shows the pay scales for 3 companies.

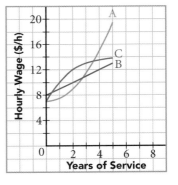

a) Describe the trend of each pay curve.

b) For what years is pay curve B higher than pay curve A?

c) For what years is pay curve C higher than pay curve A?

d) Which curve increases most between 0 years and 2 years?

15. Application A pot of water is placed on the stove. Its temperature, T, in degrees Celsius, satisfies this relation with time, t, in seconds:

$$T = \frac{120t + 400}{t + 20}$$

a) Graph the relation.

b) What is the starting temperature?

c) What is the temperature after 80 s?

d) When is the temperature changing fastest?

e) Describe the trend of the graph. Explain.

16. You have learned how to make predictions using formulas and graphs. Write a paragraph to compare the two techniques. Include a discussion of which technique is easiest and which is more accurate.

Kaaydah invests $1000 at 6% compounded annually and Jim invests $1000 at 7% compounded annually.

Car A accelerates quickly from a stop sign and car B accelerates slowly.

One hazardous waste site monitors 600 kg of radioactive waste with a half-life of 500 years, while a laboratory monitors 200 kg of the same material.

In each case, graphs representing the two stories are similar but not exactly the same. In this section, we will explore variations within a problem.

What do we know about the value of the investments Kaaydah and Jim made?

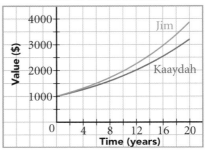

Values of the Investments

- Both investments start with $1000.
- Both investments show exponential growth.
- They have different rates of growth.

The graphs have the same starting point and the same general shape, but the curve representing Jim's investment increases faster than the curve representing Kaaydah's investment.

What will the graphs of distance over time look like for the two accelerating cars?

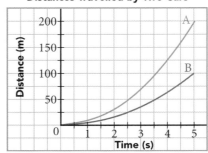

Distances Travelled by Two Cars

- Both cars start at the stop sign.
- Both graphs are quadratic.
- The graphs curve upward at different rates.

Again, the graphs have the same starting point and the same general shape, but the graph that represents the motion of car A curves up faster than the graph that represents the motion of car B.

What will the graphs of radioactive decay look like for the two batches of radioactive material?

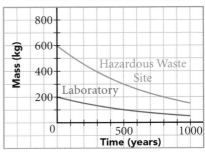

Amounts of Radioactive Waste

- Both batches of waste decay exponentially.
- Both batches decay at the same rate; they have the same half-life.
- The two starting amounts are different.

This time, the graphs have different starting points but the same rate of decrease.

TAKE NOTE

Variations in Trends

Watch for pairs of similar situations.

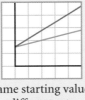

Same starting value, different rate

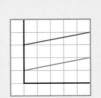

Different starting value, same rate

Example 1

Kelly, a long-distance runner, begins a 1500-m race. Her distance from the starting line is graphed for the first 20 s of the race. Debbie is a sprinter who runs the 200-m race.

a) Describe how Debbie's motion would differ from Kelly's in the first 20 s.

b) Copy the graph of Kelly's distance over time. Sketch the graph of Debbie's motion on the same axes.

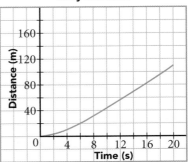

Kelly's Motion

Solution

a) Debbie, the sprinter, would run more quickly than Kelly, the long distance runner. Debbie will travel farther in the same time period.

b) The graph of Debbie's motion starts at the same place, the starting line. Since she runs faster, the graph of her motion will be steeper than the graph of Kelly's motion.

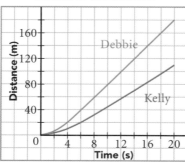

Example 2 The graph shows the lending rate for a secured loan at a particular bank for a 10-week period. The bank manager explained that lending rates for unsecured loans were about 2% higher. Copy the graph of secured lending rates. Sketch a graph of the unsecured rates over time on the same axes as the secured rates. What is similar about the two graphs?

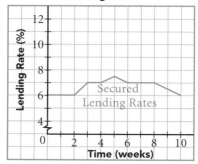

Solution

The unsecured lending rates have the same ups and downs as the secured rates. The graphs have the same shape, but the graph representing the unsecured lending rates is shifted up by 2 units, that is, 2%.

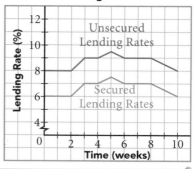

A

1. Compare each pair of curves. How are they similar? different?

a)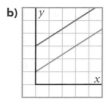

b)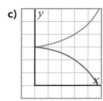

c)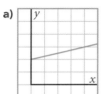

2. For each curve, sketch:

   i) a curve that has a different starting value

   ii) a curve that has a greater rate of change

a)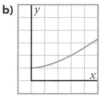

b)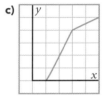

c)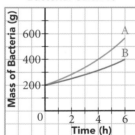

B

3. **Knowledge/Understanding** The graph shows the growth of two bacterial cultures, A and B.

   a) Which culture is growing more quickly? Explain how you can see this on the graph.

   b) What might cause such a difference in growth?

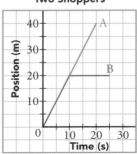

Masses of Two Bacterial Cultures

4. The graph shows the positions of two shoppers, A and B, over time.

   a) Compare their starting positions and speeds.

   b) Describe how their motions differ.

Positions of Two Shoppers

5. The graph shows the population growth of two towns, E and F.

Populations of Two Towns

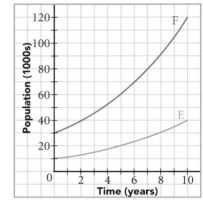

a) What is the initial population of each town?

b) Find the doubling time for the population of town E.

c) Find the doubling time for the population of town F.

d) What is the population increase in town E between year 5 and year 10?

e) What is the population increase in town F between year 5 and year 10?

f) The populations of these two towns are growing at the same rate. Explain why the graphs appear to have different shapes.

6. In exercise 12 of Section 7.4, Rozmin and Bashir had a $100 000 mortgage at 7%. The total of their mortgage payments increased with the length of the mortgage.

Total Mortgage Payments

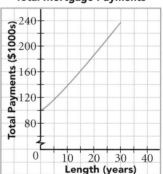

a) Copy the graph.

b) On the same axes, sketch the graph of the total payments for a $100 000 mortgage at a higher interest rate.

c) On the same axes, sketch the graph of the total payments for a $75 000 mortgage at 7%.

d) On the same axes, sketch the graph of the total payments for a $140 000 mortgage at a lower interest rate.

7. Each retail sector has a busy season. For each retail sector, sketch a possible graph of sales over time for one year. Explain.

a) toys

b) prescription drugs

c) clothing

d) office supplies

8. A potato takes about 1 h to cook in a hot oven. The graph shows the temperature of the outside of a potato during baking.

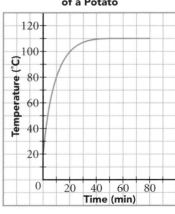

Temperature of the Outside of a Potato

a) Describe the graph. Relate the shape of the graph to what is happening to the potato.

b) Initially, the temperature at the centre of the potato is 20°C. After 1 h, the temperature at the centre of the potato is 100°C. Sketch a temperature-time graph for the centre of the potato. Explain the shape.

c) Describe how the temperature-time graphs for the outside and inside of the potato would change if the potato were cooked at a lower temperature for a longer period of time. Include sketches with your description.

9. Communication The graph shows the height of a tomato plant over the growing season. Describe and explain the two trends in the graph.

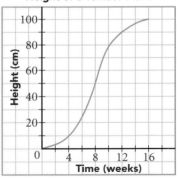

Height of a Tomato Plant

10. A capacitor with an initial voltage of 9 V discharges with a half-life of 5 s. The graph shows the voltage on a capacitor over time.

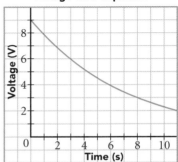

Voltage on a Capacitor

a) Copy the graph.

b) On the same axes as the graph in part a, sketch the voltage-time graph for each capacitor:

  i) initial voltage of 3 V, half-life of 5 s

  ii) initial voltage of 9 V, half-life of 10 s

  iii) initial voltage of 3 V, half-life of 10 s

11. In exercise 9, a tomato plant reached a full height of about 100 cm in about 16 weeks. Sketch a height-time graph for each variety of tomato.

    a) full height: 80 cm; time to mature: 16 weeks

    b) full height: 100 cm; time to mature: 20 weeks

    c) full height: 80 cm; time to mature: 14 weeks

12. Application Val's parents kept a record of his mass from birth until he was 30 months old.

Age (months)	0	3	6	9	12	15	18	21	24	27	30
Mass (kg)	3.4	5.5	7.2	8.5	9.5	10.3	11.0	11.5	12.0	12.5	12.9

    a) Draw a graph of Val's mass over time.

    b) Sketch a graph of each child's mass over time on the same set of axes as Val's mass-time graph.

      i) Steen had a birth mass of 3.9 kg and grew in a fashion similar to Val.

      ii) Norio had a birth mass of 3.1 kg but grew very quickly.

      iii) Dave had a birth mass of 3.4 kg and grew in a fashion similar to Val until he was 18 months old. Then he got a series of ear infections and did not eat well.

13. Some energetic students measured how far the centre of a trampoline dipped as more and more students climbed on.

Number of Students	1	2	3	4	5	6	7
Depth at Centre (cm)	15	31	45	59	74	91	105

    a) Graph the data. Describe the trend of the graph.

    b) Predict the depth at the centre if 10 students were on the trampoline.

    c) Suppose the springs around the edge of the trampoline were replaced by tighter springs. Describe how the graph of depth versus number of students would change. Sketch the new graph.

14. Thinking/Inquiry/Problem Solving There are many ways a quantity can decrease to zero. For each situation below:

      i) Sketch the decay curve.

      ii) Explain the shape you chose.

    a) The value of a car depreciates with time.

    b) The height above ground of a skydiver decreases with time.

    c) The level of gasoline in your car's fuel tank decreases with time.

    d) The temperature of a package of English muffins decreases when it is put in the freezer.

1. The graph gives the prices of coloured road signs and reflective, coloured road signs. The price of a sign depends on the measure of its diagonal.

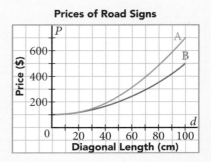

Prices of Road Signs

a) Describe the trends of the curves.

b) Which curve represents the prices for reflective, coloured signs? Explain.

Performance Assessment

2. Tourists, shoppers, and business people cross the border from the United States into Ontario. The graph shows the number of cars with American licence plates crossing into Ontario from January 1993 to April 2001.

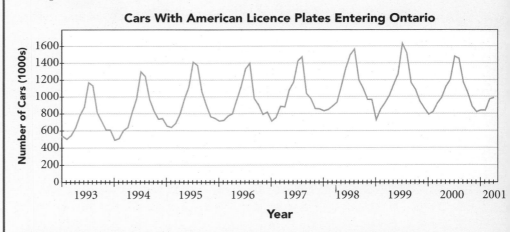

Cars With American Licence Plates Entering Ontario

a) Describe and explain the short- and long-term trends in the graph.

b) Describe the effect of these conditions on the number of American cars entering Ontario:

   i) There are no major changes in the economy.

   ii) The value of the Canadian dollar falls substantially relative to the American dollar.

   iii) There is a major recession in both countries.

c) For each situation in part b, sketch a graph of the number of American cars entering Ontario for 2002–2005.

We all have our own stories of how we came to live where we do. Some of us are new to Canada and some of us have had family here for hundreds or thousands of years. The 20th century brought change to all our lifestyles. As a nation, we have seen rural life and city life, peace and war, health and epidemic, depression and prosperity. These factors and others affect the number of people who choose to live in Canada and where in Canada they choose to live.

You will use the skills developed in this chapter to determine the rate of growth of Canada's population. You will see which provinces are growing and which are not. You can even compare your home region to Ontario or to Canada as a whole.

Canada's Population

Canada's population figures for over 140 years are given in the table.

Canada's Population (in thousands)

Year	Population
1851	2437
1861	3230
1871	3689
1881	4325
1891	4833
1901	5371
1911	7207
1921	8788
1931	10 377
1941	11 507
1951	13 648
1961	18 238
1971	21 568
1981	24 900
1991	28 111

1. a) Graph Canada's population over time on a full sheet of graph paper.

  b) The population growth looks like exponential growth, with a few flatter times and a few steeper times.

  i) When was the growth rate a bit low or a bit high?

ii) Identify what happened in Canada to cause these unusual growth rates.

2. **a)** Start with 1851.

   i) What was the population in 1851?

   ii) In what year was the population twice as large?

   iii) How many years did it take for the population to double?

   b) Now start from the year you found in part ii of exercise 2a. Find the next doubling time for the population.

   i) How many times has Canada's population doubled since 1851?

   ii) Compare the doubling times. Are they reasonably constant?

   iii) Explain why you might expect the doubling times to be equal.

   iv) Calculate the average doubling time for the population.

3. Suppose the population grew at a constant rate, r, from 1851 to 1991.

   a) Explain this formula: $2437(1 + r)^{140} = 28\ 111$

   b) Solve for r.

   c) What was the average annual percentage growth between 1851 and 1991?

4. Use the method of exercise 3 to calculate the average annual percentage growth in each period.

   a) between 1851 and 1901

   b) between 1901 and 1951

   c) between 1951 and 1991

5. Analyse the data using a graphing calculator.

   a) Draw a scatter plot of the data. Use this code for the years: $1851 = 0$; $1861 = 10$; $1871 = 20$; and so on.

   Press $\boxed{\text{Y=}}$ and clear any equations.

   Press $\boxed{\text{STAT}}$ $\boxed{\text{ENTER}}$ to access the lists. Clear any data in lists L1 and L2. Enter the years in list L1 and the population data in list L2.

   Press $\boxed{\text{2nd}}$ $\boxed{\text{Y=}}$ 1 $\boxed{\text{ENTER}}$ to access and turn on Plot1 in STATPLOT.

   Press $\boxed{\blacktriangledown}$ $\boxed{\text{ENTER}}$ to select the scatter plot. Enter L1 for Xlist and L2 for Ylist.

   Set an appropriate window.

   Press $\boxed{\text{GRAPH}}$ to display the scatter plot. Copy the scatter plot into your notebook.

   b) Press $\boxed{\text{Y=}}$. Enter the formula $y = 2437(1.0173)^x$ in Y1. Explain this formula.

   c) Press $\boxed{\text{GRAPH}}$. Describe how well the exponential curve fits the data.

   d) Determine the exponential regression equation of best fit.

   Press $\boxed{\text{STAT}}$ $\boxed{\blacktriangleright}$ 0 to select ExpReg.

Press 2nd 1 , 2nd 2 , VARS ▶ 1 2 ENTER.

e) Graph the regression equation on the same screen as the scatter plot and the equation from part b. How well does the regression equation fit the data? Explain.

6. Your answers to exercises 2 through 5 all provide information on how Canada's population grew between 1851 and 1991. Summarize what you learned about the growth pattern and the growth rate of our population.

7. Predict Canada's population in 2011 and in 2051. Explain your reasoning.

Provincial Populations

The table gives the populations of Canada, Newfoundland and Labrador, Ontario, and British Columbia from 1977 to 1997.

Canadian and Provincial Populations (in Thousands)

Year	Canada	Newfoundland and Labrador	Ontario	British Columbia
1977	23 796.4	566.6	8525.6	2581.2
1978	24 036.3	568.6	8613.3	2615.8
1979	24 276.9	571.0	8685.9	2675.0
1980	24 593.3	574.2	8770.1	2755.5
1981	24 900.0	576.5	8837.8	2836.5
1982	25 201.9	576.3	8951.4	2886.3
1983	25 456.3	581.2	9073.4	2919.6
1984	25 701.8	581.8	9206.2	2960.6
1985	25 941.6	580.9	9334.4	2990.0
1986	26 203.8	578.1	9477.2	3024.4
1987	26 549.7	576.5	9684.9	3064.6
1988	26 894.8	576.2	9884.4	3128.2
1989	27 379.3	577.4	10 151.0	3209.2
1990	27 790.6	578.9	10 341.4	3300.1
1991	28 120.1	580.3	10 471.5	3379.8
1992	28 542.2	583.6	10 646.8	3476.6
1993	28 946.8	584.5	10 814.1	3575.6
1994	29 255.6	581.8	10 936.5	3671.1
1995	29 617.4	577.5	11 098.1	3766.2
1996	29 969.2	571.7	11 258.4	3857.6
1997	30 286.6	563.6	11 407.7	3933.3

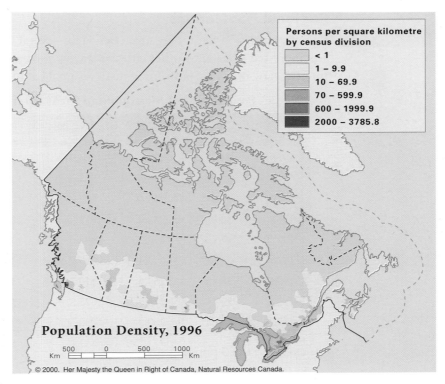

Population Density, 1996

Persons per square kilometre by census division

	< 1
	1 – 9.9
	10 – 69.9
	70 – 599.9
	600 – 1999.9
	2000 – 3785.8

500   0   500   1000
Km   Km

© 2000. Her Majesty the Queen in Right of Canada, Natural Resources Canada.

Σ-STAT If you are interested in data for other provinces or territories, you can find them on the Internet. Log on to E-Stat from Statistics Canada at http://estat.statcan.ca/.

1. a) i) Graph the 4 populations with time.

   ii) What are the advantages of plotting the 4 data sets on the same axes?

   iii) What are the disadvantages of plotting the 4 data sets on the same axes?

   b) Describe the trends in population growth for each of the 4 regions.

2. a) For each of the 4 regions, calculate the average annual growth rate of the population in each period.
   i) between 1977 and 1982
   ii) between 1982 and 1987
   iii) between 1987 and 1992
   iv) between 1992 and 1997

   b) For each population, describe its growth pattern over the 20-year period.

   c) Compare the growth in the different provinces.

3. Summarize your findings from exercises 1 and 2. Explain the changes in each province's population.

Regional Populations

 Recent population figures are given below for several Ontario cities. If you are interested in data for other cities or towns, you can find them on the Internet. Log on to E-Stat from Statistics Canada at http://estat.statcan.ca/.

Populations of Metropolitan Areas (in thousands)

Year	Kitchener-Waterloo	Oshawa	Ottawa-Hull	Thunder Bay	Windsor
1988	341.4	228.6	884.0	127.1	266.1
1989	353.8	239.5	907.5	127.5	268.4
1990	364.1	244.6	932.0	128.2	270.6
1991	369.5	248.9	952.2	129.0	271.7
1992	376.3	256.7	974.6	130.2	274.4
1993	382.3	263.4	997.7	130.6	277.7
1994	388.5	269.6	1110.7	130.7	281.5
1995	395.4	275.6	1023.2	131.0	285.9
1996	403.3	280.9	1030.5	131.3	291.7

1. a) Graph the 5 populations.

   b) Describe the trends in population growth for each of the 5 cities.

2. a) For each city, calculate the average annual growth rate between 1988 and 1996.

   b) For each city, predict the population in 2008.

3. Summarize your findings to exercises 1 and 2. Why have the populations of these cities changed in this way? What factors will affect the reliability of your predictions?

Ideas for Further Investigation

The Internet, the library, your Chamber of Commerce, and your local government (regional, municipal, town, city or county office) are good sources for population information.

Use your research and analysis skills to study population growth in:

- your region, town, or city
- another province or territory
- a country you have visited or where you have family

If you want the big picture, demographers have assembled information on whole continents and the whole world over the millennia. Try out a growth curve for the world since the year 1000.

Millwright

Rajiv enjoys working with machinery and was attracted to the idea of an apprenticeship program where you are paid to learn. He decided to go to a community college that offered apprenticeship training to become a millwright.

Job Description

- Install, repair, replace, and dismantle the machinery and heavy equipment used in many industries
- Read blueprints, pour concrete, diagnose and solve mechanical problems
- Move heavy machinery using rigging and hoisting devices, such as pulleys and cables

Working Conditions

- A 48-hour work week is average
- Most millwrights are employed by factories
- Contract work allows for variety in work environments
- Salaries are quite good

Qualifications and Training

- Grade 10 education a minimum, but most applicants have a high school degree
- Completion of a 3- to 4-year apprenticeship program connected with a community college
- Good people skills
- Physical strength and manual dexterity
- Ability to analyse problems in three dimensions

Where's the Math?

Millwrights must have good math skills so they can measure angles, material thickness, and small distances. They must know the load-bearing properties of ropes, cables, hoists, and cranes. As robotics and laser technology become more important in this work, the millwright must know how to interpret and analyse graphs of various kinds.

MATHEMATICS TOOLKIT

Graphical Models Toolkit

Linear Graphs

> Use your knowledge of $y = mx + b$.

> m is a rate, with units.

> b is the starting value.

> The differences between successive y-values are constant.

Quadratic Graphs

> Use your knowledge of parabolas, $y = ax^2 + bx + c$.

> Look for a minimum or a maximum point.

> The differences between successive y-values form an arithmetic sequence.

Exponential Graphs

> Use your knowledge of $y = a(b)^x$.

> Exponential growth has a doubling time.

> Exponential decay has a half-life.

> The ratios between successive y-values are constant.

Trends

> Look for variations on increasing, constant, or decreasing trends.

Predictions from Graphs

> Use the equation for the curve if you know it; otherwise, follow the trend of the graph.

> List any assumptions you made.

> Think about how reliable your estimate is.

Variations on Trends

> Different starting values

> Different rates of change

> Different functional shape

7.1   **1.** For each linear graph:
  i) Calculate the slope; include units.
  ii) Write the equation of the line.

a)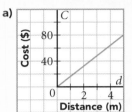

b)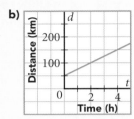

c)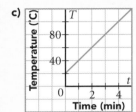

2. A landscaper installs flagstone pathways according to the price structure shown in the graph.

a) What is plotted on the horizontal axis?

b) What is plotted on the vertical axis?

c) Determine the slope of the graph. What are the units for the slope?

d) What does the slope represent?

e) What is the meaning of the P-intercept?

f) How much would it cost to install a 50-m² path?

g) Suppose a homeowner has a budget of $500. What is the maximum pathway area that can be installed?

Price of Flagstone

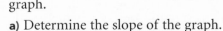

3. Marla owns a cafe. She has discovered that her weekly sales depend on the outside temperature, as shown in the graph.

a) Determine the slope of the graph.

b) Explain the meaning of the slope.

c) Suggest a reason why the slope is negative.

Marla's Weekly Sales vs. Temperature

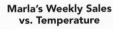

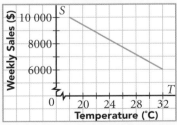

d) Write the equation relating weekly sales to outside temperature.

e) Predict Marla's weekly sales when the outside temperature is:
   i) 35°C
   ii) 10°C

4. Workers at an apple orchard pack apples into wooden crates for shipment to local grocery stores. The graph shows how the mass of a loaded crate depends on the number of apples inside.

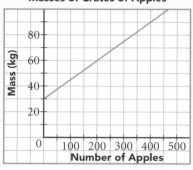

Masses of Crates of Apples

a) What is the mass of a crate containing 200 apples?

b) How many apples are in a crate that has a mass of 70 kg?

c) Determine the slope of the graph.

d) Explain the meaning of the slope.

e) What is the mass of 1 crate? Explain.

7.2   **5.** The graph shows the height of a bungee-jumper above the ground over time.

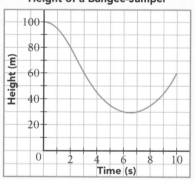

Height of a Bungee-Jumper

a) When is the jumper falling fastest?

b) When does the jumper reach the minimum height?

c) What is the minimum height?

d) Explain what happens after the jumper reaches the minimum height.

6. Seth receives a bonus each week he works overtime. The bonus scheme is shown in the graph.

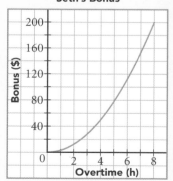

Seth's Bonus

a) This graph is a section of a parabola. Does the parabola open up or down?

b) How much more is Seth's bonus if he works 4 h overtime instead of 3 h?

c) How much more is Seth's bonus if he works 8 h overtime instead of 7 h?

d) Where is the graph increasing most quickly? What does this mean in terms of Seth's bonus?

7. Hal and Sara have to paint some large wooden cubes for Drama Club. The graph shows the volume, in millilitres, of paint needed to cover different cubes, according to the length, in metres, of a side of the cube.

a) How much paint is needed for a cube with side length 2.2 m?

b) What is the maximum side length of a cube that can be painted with 1500 mL of paint?

c) The graph is quadratic. Explain the shape of the graph in the context of the problem.

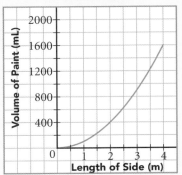

Volume of Paint

8. Ralph decides to raise rabbits. As the graph shows, rabbit populations grow amazingly quickly.

a) What is the initial rabbit population?

b) What is the doubling time?

c) By what percentage does the population increase each month?

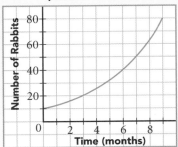

Population of Rabbits

7.3 **9.** The graph shows how much sunlight reaches different depths of seawater.

a) Find the depth of water at which 50% of the incoming light remains.

b) Find the depth of water at which 25% of the incoming light remains.

c) Compare your answers to parts a and b. Explain.

d) What percent of sunlight will reach a depth of 100 m?

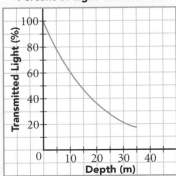

Percent of Light Transmitted

10. TestEx is a company that performs quality tests on manufactured items. It tested a line of plates to be used in hotels. The graph shows the number of plates expected to survive over time.

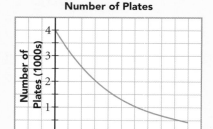

Number of Plates

a) Determine the number of usable plates at each time.

  i) initially

  ii) after 2 years

  iii) after 10 years

b) What is the half-life of the plates?

c) What percent of plates are lost or broken each year?

11. Todd invests in a bond. The graph shows the value of the bond over time.

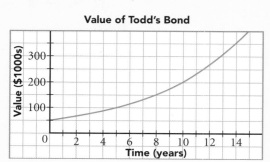

Value of Todd's Bond

a) What is Todd's initial investment?

b) How long will it take for the value of the bond to double?

c) Determine the annual interest rate.

12. The graph shows the average house price in a small town over a 12-month period.

a) Describe the general trend of the graph.

b) During which time interval did the average price rise fastest?

c) Predict the average house price

  i) in month 14

  ii) in month 16

d) Explain any assumptions you made in part c.

7.4 **13.** For each situation, select the graph that best illustrates how the temperature of a casserole changes over time.

  i) A casserole is taken from the fridge and left on the counter.

  ii) A casserole is taken from the oven and set on the table.

  iii) A casserole is taken from the freezer and thawed in the microwave.

a) 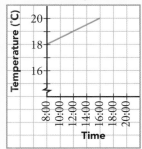 b) 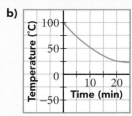 c)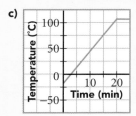

14. Students in an environmental studies class recorded the outside temperature every 2 h. Their results are shown in the graph.

  a) Describe the trend in the graph.

  b) Predict the outside temperature at 6:00 P.M.

  c) Describe any assumptions you made in part b.

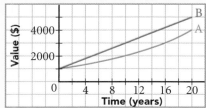

15. Leslie and Kayla each invest $1000. Leslie chooses an account that pays simple interest. Kayla's account pays compound interest. The balances for two accounts, A and B, are shown on the graph. Which account belongs to Leslie? Explain.

Values of Leslie's and Kayla's Investments

16. The graph shows the vacancy rate for rental housing over several years.

a) Describe the trend of the graph.

b) Predict the vacancy rate in year 6.

c) Predict the vacancy rate in year 7.

d) How reliable are your predictions in parts b and c? Explain.

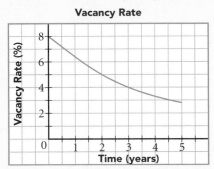

7.5 **17.** These graphs appeared in *The Toronto Star* on September 30, 2001. They show the levels of two stock market indices in July, August and September 2001.

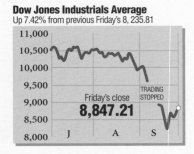

a) Describe the trends shown in the graphs.

b) How are the graphs similar? different?

18. Jacques and Stefan each bought new cars. Jacques' car cost $14 000 and Stefan's car cost $16 000. The value of both cars will depreciate 10% each year.

a) Sketch a graph of the values of the two cars over time.

b) How are the two curves similar? different?

19. The graph shows the distance from the start of a trail of a cyclist over time. The cyclist is riding at a relatively constant speed. Describe how the graph would change for each variation. Include a sketch in your description.

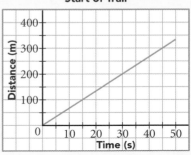

Distance of a Cyclist from Start of Trail

a) The cyclist rides at a higher constant speed.

b) The cyclist speeds up going downhill.

c) The cyclist slows and stops for a break.

Maintaining Your Mastery

Review the algebraic skills that form part of the college admission process.

1. Expand and simplify.

a) $5(x + 3) - 2(3x - 7)$ b) $x(2x - 1) + 4(x^2 - 3x)$

c) $6xy^2(x + y) - 8x^2y^2$

2. Expand and simplify.

a) $(x + 4y)(x - y)$ b) $(x + 2y + 1)(4x - 5y)$ c) $4(x - 5)(x + 3)$

3. Factor.

a) $6x^2 - 9xy$ b) $n^2 + 7n + 12$ c) $100 - 9z^2$

d) $4t^2 - 36t + 32$ e) $3x^2 - 48$ f) $y^3 + 13y^2 + 40y$

4. Solve.

a) $5c + 4 = -7c + 28$ b) $3s(s - 4) = 0$ c) $k^2 + 11k - 26 = 0$

5. Solve algebraically.

a) $5x + y = -17$
$3x - 4y = -1$

b) $x + 7y = 31$
$2x + y = 23$

c) $2x + 3y = 12$
$x - 2y = 6$

1. The graph shows the temperature on Maureen's deck over time.

   a) **Communication** Explain why the graph is quadratic. Use a table in your explanation.

   b) When is the temperature at a maximum?

   c) When is the temperature increasing fastest?

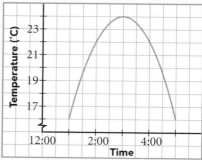

Temperature on Maureen's Deck

2. In 1965 Gordon Moore, co-founder of Intel, predicted that each new generation of computer chip would have about twice the capacity as the previous generation. He also predicted that the growth would be exponential. The graph shows the number of transistors per chip for recent years.

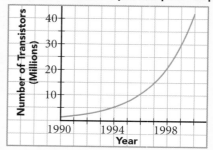

Number of Transistors per Computer Chip

   a) **Application** Determine the average doubling time for chip capacity.

   b) **Knowledge/Understanding** Intel released the Pentium 4 processor chip in 2000. It has over 42 million transistors. Predict the number of transistors per chip for computer chips that will be released in 2004 and 2010.

   c) In 1971, Intel's 4004-microprocessor had 2300 transistors. Is this consistent with the trend displayed in the graph? Explain.

3. **Thinking/Inquiry/Problem Solving**

   a) The mass of a Labrador Retriever puppy is about 1 pound at birth. Its mass increases at a reasonably constant rate, reaching its adult mass of about 72 pounds at 2 years. Sketch a graph of mass versus time for an average puppy. Explain the shape.

   b) Ottis had a normal birth mass but grew more slowly than usual. He reached his adult mass of 50 pounds at 18 months. Sketch a graph of Ottis' mass versus time on the same grid as the graph from part a. Explain the differences between the two curves.

4. a) A candy-maker pours a pan of hot sugar syrup onto an ice-cold marble slab to cool. The temperature of the syrup, T, in degrees Celsius, is recorded every 12 s for the first minute.

t (min)	0	0.2	0.4	0.6	0.8	1.0
T (°C)	116	115	114	113	112	111

  i) Graph the data. Describe any trends.

  ii) Write an equation for the temperature in terms of time.

  iii) Predict when the syrup will cool to 36°C, the temperature needed for the next step in the preparation.

b) A batch of syrup was left in the pot to cool. The temperature was recorded every 5 min for 40 min.

t (min)	0	5	10	15	20	25	30	35	40
T (°C)	116	93	75	60	48	39	31	25	20

  i) Graph the data. Describe any trends.

  ii) Estimate the time needed for the temperature to decrease by 50%. Does your answer depend on the temperature with which you start?

  iii) Explain the statement: "The temperature falls exponentially with time."

c) In parts a and b, you described two different models of how the temperature changes with time.

  i) How closely do the two models agree for the first 5 min? Explain.

  ii) According to each model, when does the syrup cool to 36°C? Which model gives the earlier time? Use the graphs to explain why.

  iii) Describe a practical situation when it would be appropriate to use the model of part a.

1. Determine the measure of each angle to the nearest degree.

   a) $\sin A = 0.423$　　b) $\cos B = 0.934$　　c) $\tan C = 4.705$

2. Solve each triangle. Round each unit to one decimal place.

   a) $\triangle ABC$　$\angle A = 52°$, $\angle B = 90°$, $b = 3.2$ cm

   b) $\triangle DEF$　$\angle E = 45°$, $\angle F = 36°$, $d = 7.8$ m

   c) $\triangle XYZ$　$\angle Z = 53°$, $x = 20.2$ mm, $y = 16.8$ mm

3. Two buildings are 50 m apart. One building is 76 m taller than the other.

   a) Draw a sketch of the buildings.

   b) What is the angle of depression from the taller building to the lower one?

4. Three ships, A, B, and C, can see one another. Ships A and B are 11.7 km apart. The angle between the line of sight from ship C to ship A and the line of sight from ship C to ship B is 36°. Ships A and C are 16.5 km apart. How far apart are ships B and C?

5. Simplify.

   a) $(5x^2 + 3x - 2) + (3x - 2x + 5)$　　b) $(2y^2 - 4y + 5) - (y - 6y - 7)$

   c) $(x + 3)^2$　　　　　　　　　　　d) $(2x + 3)(3x^2 + 4x - 5)$

6. Solve each system.

   a) $3x + y = 4$　　　　　　　b) $y = \frac{4}{3}x + 5$
   $x - 2y = 12$　　　　　　　　$3x - 5y = -28$

7. The sum of an arithmetic series S_n, with n terms is $S_n = \frac{n}{2}[2a + (n - 1)d]$, where a is the first term and d the common difference.

   a) Solve the formula for a.

   b) Determine the value of the first term in a series of 8 terms with a common difference of 5 and a sum of 196.

8. A banquet hall charges $200 for the rental of the hall and $45 per person.

   a) Write an equation to represent the total charges.

   b) Draw a graph to represent the amount the banquet hall would charge for any banquet with up to 100 people.

9. Factor.

a) $x^2 - x - 12$ **b)** $81 - 25x^2$ **c)** $a^2 - 12a + 35$

d) $3x^2 + 9x + 6$ **e)** $6b^2 + 7b + 2$ **f)** $6t^2 + 11t - 2$

10. Solve.

a) $x(x + 1) = 0$ **b)** $x^2 - 9 = 0$ **c)** $20x^2 + 3x - 2 = 0$

11. Convert each measure.

a) 7 pounds to ounces   **b)** 324 mm to inches

c) 42 L to gallons   **d)** 184 pounds to kilograms

12. Calculate the surface area and volume of a cylinder with radius 4 feet and height 15 feet.

13. The walls and ceiling of a room require one coat of primer and two coats of paint. The room is 25 feet by 18 feet and is 9 feet high. There is one window in the room that is 3 feet by 5 feet and a door 4 feet by $7\frac{1}{2}$ feet. Suppose a one-gallon can covers 250 square feet. How many cans of primer and paint must be purchased?

14. Copy the figure below left.

a) Draw all possible lines of reflection symmetry.

b) Determine all the possible angles of rotation symmetry other than 0° and 360°.

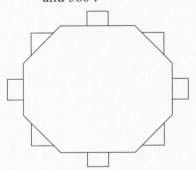 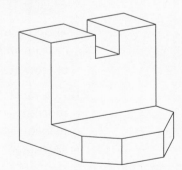

15. Provide a top, front, and side view of the isometric drawing, above right.

16. Create a net for a can of soup that is 10 cm high with radius 3 cm.

17. i) Identify the population you would survey for each topic.

  ii) Would you use a primary or secondary source of data for each?
  - **a)** The average age of first-year college students in Canada
  - **b)** The average mass of a Canadian dime
  - **c)** The number of teens who have at least one Barenaked Ladies CD

18. Health and Welfare Canada wishes to conduct a survey regarding mandatory flu vaccinations. Describe how the ministry could select a sample of each type.

  a) cluster sample   **b)** simple random sample

  c) systematic sample   **d)** stratified random sample

19. A survey was conducted to determine how many teenagers smoke. The question was: "At what age did you start smoking?" The survey was conducted during lunch break on the sidewalk in front of the school.

  a) Is the question valid?

  b) Is the sample of students representative of the population?

20. A price index was established by Brandon for a local convenience store. He established 1999 as the base year. Below is Brandon's index from 1995 to 2001.

YEAR	1995	1996	1997	1998	1999	2000	2001
BPI	99.2	100.2	99.4	99.6	100.0	101.7	104.6

  a) According to Brandon's index, what happened to the store prices from 1995 to 1997?

  b) How are prices in 2001 related to prices in 1999?

21. At a candy factory, 30 packages of candy were weighed during the morning, afternoon, and night shifts for quality control purposes. The mass of each package is given below.

Morning: 52, 56, 49, 57, 61, 53, 37, 65, 45, 62, 57, 49, 65, 60, 51
(g) 50, 64, 64, 45, 47, 59, 65, 58, 51, 46, 65, 49, 53, 47, 50

Afternoon: 60, 63, 67, 55, 64, 53, 57, 52, 55, 51, 48, 54, 65, 63, 50
(g) 64, 57, 60, 57, 65, 62, 58, 50, 61, 61, 60, 48, 53, 53, 63

Night: 68, 43, 59, 64, 41, 51, 46, 64, 50, 68, 44, 57, 50, 48, 46
(g) 55, 52, 51, 62, 52, 47, 47, 54, 62, 62, 51, 58, 47, 67, 56

a) Calculate the mean, median, mode, range, variance, and standard deviation for each shift.

b) Each package is supposed to be 55 g. Which shift had the best performance? Explain.

22. An inspector measures the mass of 13-g cookies. The mass is distributed normally with a mean of 13 g and standard deviation of 0.5 g.

a) Sketch the normal distribution of mass. Label the mean and points that are 1, 2, and 3 standard deviations from the mean.

b) Determine the percent of cookies for each mass.

   i) less than 12.5 g   **ii)** more than 13.5 g

   iii) between 12.0 g and 14.0 g

23. The graph shows the path of a basketball when a player makes an attempt at a shot.

a) What is the maximum height of the basketball?

b) Approximately how tall is the player?

c) How long does the ball travel in the air?

d) How would the graph change for a taller player?

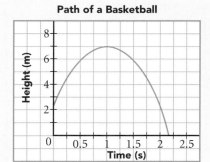

Path of a Basketball

24. Nick is starting a new job and can be paid using Plan A or Plan B as shown below.

a) Describe the trend in each of the plans.

b) Under what circumstances should Nick choose Plan A? Explain.

c) Under what circumstances should Nick choose Plan B? Explain.

d) What does the point of intersection illustrate?

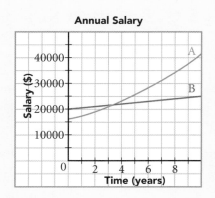

Annual Salary

Data Analysis

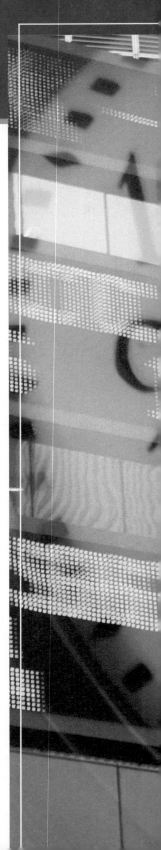

Background

Investing money in savings accounts, GICs (Guaranteed Investment Certificates), or Canada Savings Bonds, gives you a reliable, but limited return on your money. The stock market offers the investor an exciting opportunity to make larger profits. However, the stock market involves taking a risk; therefore, money can be lost.

In movies or television, you may have seen pictures of frantic stockbrokers buying and selling on a trading floor. This kind of trading is still done on many world stock exchanges, including the New York Stock Exchange. Since 1997, all trading on the Toronto Stock Exchange (TSE) is done through a computerized trading system. If you live in or near Toronto, you may want to visit the TSE. Although there is no trading floor to see, many multi-media and interactive activities and presentations are available. Information about such visits for individuals or classes is found on the TSE website: www.tse.com

When you buy stocks, you are buying a share in the ownership of a company. Shares in an established company, such as General Motors, may cost hundreds of dollars, while the price of shares in new or unsuccessful companies may be as low as $0.10.

Every stock on the TSE is represented by a symbol. For example, the symbol for Corel Corporation is COR. Refer to these symbols when getting stock information from the Internet.

Some companies that make a profit share it with their shareholders in the form of dividends. With these companies the stock price remains fairly stable. Growth stocks in newer, expanding companies don't

Suggested Group Size: work in pairs

Suggested Materials:

Daily national newspapers, computer spreadsheet, Internet access (optional).

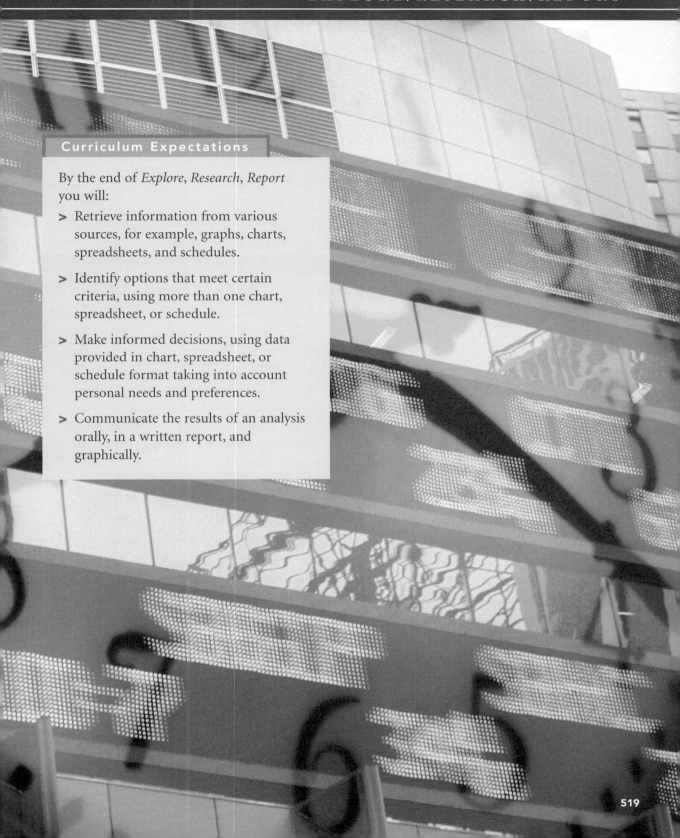

Curriculum Expectations

By the end of *Explore*, *Research*, *Report* you will:

> Retrieve information from various sources, for example, graphs, charts, spreadsheets, and schedules.

> Identify options that meet certain criteria, using more than one chart, spreadsheet, or schedule.

> Make informed decisions, using data provided in chart, spreadsheet, or schedule format taking into account personal needs and preferences.

> Communicate the results of an analysis orally, in a written report, and graphically.

pay dividends. Their stock prices may rise quickly, but they are also considered more risky.

This project will allow you to investigate the possibilities for buying stocks on the TSE.

- Where can you get information on stocks?
- Where and how can you buy and sell TSE stocks?
- What fees will you pay when buying or selling stocks?
- How do you obtain and read the daily TSE statistics?
- How can you use statistics to evaluate stocks for possible purchase?

Explore

1. Choosing a Broker

There are a variety of ways to buy stocks.

Full-service brokers are the most expensive, but they offer valuable investment information and individual attention. Companies such as Scotia McLeod, Merrill Lynch, and Wood Gundy provide this kind of service.

Discount brokers or *deep-discount brokers* charge less than full-service brokers, but they do not provide investment advice or offer the opportunity to work with the same broker each time you trade. All of the major Canadian banks have discount brokerage services.

On-line brokers provide the least expensive way to buy and sell stocks. This service is impersonal, but efficient. Most of the large Canadian banks have Internet sites for buying and selling stocks.

Information about brokers is available on the Internet, in the newspaper, or by telephone.

Contact two full-service brokers, two discount brokers, and two on-line brokerage services. List the brokers with information about their fees.

2. Buying and Selling a Stock

Suppose you decide to buy 100 shares of Corel Corporation, listed on the TSE at $4.60/share. You work through a discount broker whose commission rates are determined by the share price.

Share Price	Commission
$0–$2	$35 + $0.02/share
$2.01–$5	$35 + $0.03/share
$5.01 and over	$35 + $0.04/share

a) Calculate the cost of buying the shares. Note that you add the commission cost to the basic share cost.

$$\underline{\hspace{4cm}} \times \underline{\hspace{4cm}} = \underline{\hspace{4cm}}$$

number of shares   cost per share   basic cost

$$\underline{\hspace{4cm}} \times \underline{\hspace{4cm}} + \$35 = \underline{\hspace{4cm}}$$

number of shares   commission per share   total commission

$$\underline{\hspace{4cm}} + \underline{\hspace{4cm}} = \underline{\hspace{4cm}}$$

basic cost   total commission   TOTAL COST TO BUY

b) After a year, the stock has gone up in value to $5.25/share. Calculate the cost of selling the shares. Note that you now subtract the commission from the total revenue.

$$\underline{\hspace{4cm}} \times \underline{\hspace{4cm}} = \underline{\hspace{4cm}}$$

number of shares   cost per share   total revenue

$$\underline{\hspace{4cm}} \times \underline{\hspace{4cm}} + \$35 = \underline{\hspace{4cm}}$$

number of shares   commission per share   total commission

$$\underline{\hspace{4cm}} - \underline{\hspace{4cm}} = \underline{\hspace{4cm}}$$

total revenue   total commission   NET REVENUE

c) If you made money on this transaction it is called a capital gain. Otherwise, it is a capital loss. How much was your capital gain or loss on these transactions? Why?

d) An Internet broker charges a flat-charge commission of $29 for each order with less than 1000 shares. If you bought and sold your Corel stock through the Internet, what would your capital gain or loss have been?

3. **Reading a Stock Market Report**

Here are a few lines from a national newspaper stock market report for the TSE.

365-day High	Low	Stock	Symbol	Div	High	Low	Close	Chng	Vol (100s)	Yield	P/E Ratio
48.25	32.50	Shell Cda	SHC	0.80	41.89	39.26	40.81	−0.05	1504	2.0	10.9
10.00	6.00	Shermag	SMG		8.98	8.75	8.75	−0.20	99		6.7
28.25	19.00	Sobey's	SBY	0.24	24.50	24.00	24.35	+0.30	116	1.0	35.3

The *Div* column shows the yearly dividend, if dividends are paid.

The *High* and *Low* columns give the high and low prices paid for the stock that day.

The *Close* column gives the last price on the given day.

The *Chng* column shows the change from the close of the day before to the given day.

The *Yield* is the ratio of the dividend to the closing price, expressed as a percent.

The *P/E ratio* is the ratio of the stock price to the reported annual earnings of the company.

A P/E ratio of 25 means that the company earns $0.04 for every dollar invested.

A P/E ratio of 10 means that the company earns $0.10 for every dollar invested.

Generally, the lower the P/E ratio, the more profitable the company. A stock with a P/E ratio less than 10 is usually reliable, although it may not have much growth potential. Stocks with a P/E greater than 20 usually have greater risk, but may make larger profits. Many brokers recommend stocks with a P/E between 10 and 20. However, the P/E is not an exact number and should be used only as a guideline.

a) For each stock shown above, what is the range in price for the last 365 days and on the day of the report?

b) Use the Close price and Chng to find the previous day's closing price for each stock.

c) Check that the yield shown for Shell Cda and Sobey's is correct, then calculate the yield for stocks (i) to (iii).

   i) Brascan with a dividend of $1.00 and closing price of $27.68

   ii) BCE with a dividend of $0.72 and closing price of $47.50

   iii) If you want a stock that gives a good dividend for your investment dollar, which of these two stocks would you choose and why?

d) You can use a newspaper or the Internet to find the P/E of stocks.

   i) Which of the stocks listed above may be the best buy. Explain why.

   ii) Find three stocks with a P/E ratio less than 10.

   iii) Find three stocks with a P/E ratio between 10 and 20.

   iv) Find three stocks with a P/E ratio greater than 20.

4. **Using TSE Statistics to Choose Stocks**

There are many factors to consider when choosing stocks to buy. You can use a national newspaper or the Internet to find the TSE statistics which help investors make decisions. Some useful statistical terms to look for include:

- *Biggest % Gainers.* These are the stocks with the largest *percentage increase* in value in the last day.
- *Top Net Gainers.* These are the stocks with the largest *actual increase* in value in the last day.
- *Most Active Issues.* These are the stocks that have a high volume of trades.
- *The S&P/TSX Composite Index.* This index comprises approximately 71% of market capitalization for Canadian-based companies listed on the Toronto Stock Exchange. Since its launch on January 1, 1977, the S&P/TSX Composite Index is the premier indicator of market activity for Canadian equity markets. Refer to exercise 3b. You can calculate the percent change in an individual stock by finding the closing price for the day and the closing price for the previous day, then find the percent change. For example, if the stock closed at $2.50 yesterday and $2.55 today, the increase is $0.05 and the percent increase is $\frac{0.05}{2.50} = 2\%$.

a) Find the top five Biggest Percent Gainers for one day.

b) Find the top five Top Net Gainers for one day.

c) Find the five stocks on the Most Active Issues list which have the largest percent increase in value.

d) Choose three stocks from the TSE. Compare their percent change with the percent change in the S&P/TSX Composite Index.

5. **Using Other Information to Choose Stocks**

National newspapers, such as the *Globe and Mail*, or Canadian magazines, such as *Canadian Business* or *Money Digest*, provide in-depth information on TSE stocks.

The Internet provides a great deal of information about interesting companies. The TSE website has articles and tips for buying stocks. Other relevant websites are listed on MATHLINKS: www.awl.com/canada/school/connections/

A *mutual fund* is usually a collection of carefully chosen stocks and bonds. Since it is managed by a professional investor, you can get ideas about good stocks to buy by finding out what stocks the fund includes. Information about mutual funds is available on the Internet or by telephoning a fund's toll-free number. A complete list of Canadian mutual funds is in the business section of national newspapers. All of the major banks have mutual funds. Some other large fund companies are Trimark, Manulife, and Templeton.

Data Analysis

Your own experience and observations can be a guide to buying stocks. Products and stores which are popular, unusual, or of high quality may be good companies in which to invest. Companies that advertise frequently may also be worthwhile.

a) Using articles found in recent newspapers or magazines, select three stocks which seem to be worth buying. Explain your choices.

b) Investigate one of the websites that has information about the stock market. From the information found, select three stocks which appear to be good values. Explain your choices.

c) Choose a mutual fund. Get information on the fund from the Internet, by calling the fund, or by writing to the company. Select three stocks that the fund holds.

d) Make a list of products or stores which appeal to you, or which you think have a good future. Consider food chains, clothing companies or stores, auto makers, entertainment companies, and travel companies. You may have other ideas. Find stocks on the TSE listings for at least three of the products or stores.

Research

Together you and your partner will make some decisions about creating a stock portfolio and will decide which stocks to buy. You may decide to divide the responsibilities into a statistician and stock trader.

Statistician-Your job includes:

- finding information on the Internet or in printed material about the performance of each stock you are buying
- entering the stock information into a spreadsheet
- finding and recording the changes in stock prices each week
- creating graphs to show the overall trend of each stock

Stock Trader-Your job includes:

- deciding how many shares of each stock to buy
- calculating the commissions for the stock purchases
- selling the stock at the end of the project
- calculating the capital gains and losses for the stocks

1. Choosing Ten Stocks

In the Explore section of this project, you listed many stocks which might be good investments. From your lists, choose ten stocks to buy. Check their current prices on a TSE listing in the newspaper or on the

Internet. You should include some expensive, moderately priced, and inexpensive stocks. Try to choose stocks from a variety of areas such as consumer products, natural resources, industrial products, banking, transportation, or media.

2. **Buying the Stocks**

   a) Use the information from exercise 1. Choose the broker you want to use. You do not need to use the cheapest service. Record the broker's name and fees.

   b) Suppose that you have $10 000 to invest. Use current stock prices. Decide how much of each stock to buy. You should calculate the total cost of buying these stocks, referring to exercise 2a. Be sure to include a commission for each stock you buy. Keep your total cost close to $10 000.

3. **Getting More Information about Your Stocks**

   Though you have some information about your stocks, additional information on the company is useful. This may be found from the company's annual report and financial statement. This information is easily available on the Internet. However, you can request information through the company. Company names, addresses, and telephone numbers should be available through a broker, bank, or the library.

4. **Entering Your Stock Information into a Spreadsheet**

   You will be following the value of your stocks in the coming weeks using a computer spreadsheet program or graphing calculator. For information about setting up a spreadsheet, refer to Utility 6. Set up the spreadsheet to show the following information:

   Stock
   Symbol
   Number of Shares Purchased
   Purchase Price Per Share
   Total Value at Purchase
   WEEK 1: Price Per Share
   WEEK 1: Total Value
   WEEK 2: Price Per Share
   WEEK 2: Total Value
   WEEK 3: Price Per Share
   WEEK 3: Total Value

Include as many weeks as your teacher allows for this project. The longer the time, the more informative the data will be. Each week you should

update your spreadsheet with current prices. At the end of your project, total all the Value columns. A sample spreadsheet is shown below.

	A	B	C	D	E	F	G	H	I	J	W
1	Stock	Symbol	Number of	Purchase	Total Value	WEEK 1	WEEK 1	WEEK 2	WEEK 2	WEEK 3	W
2			Shares	Price Per	at Purchase	Price Per	Total Value	Price Per	Total Value	Price Per	To
3			Purchased	Share		Share		Share		Share	
4											
5	Imperial Oil	IMO	100	$37.60	$3,760.00	$38.00	$3,800.00	$38.04	$3,804.00	$37.58	$:
6	CIBC	CM	25	$53.20	$1,330.00	$54.00	$1,350.00	$54.33	$1,358.25	$54.58	$

5. Selling the Stocks and Calculating Capital Gains or Losses

a) Add columns for Commission and Capital Gains/Loss to your spreadsheet. For each stock, take the Total Value for the final week (minus the commission), and subtract the Total Value at Purchase (plus the commission). If the number is positive, you have made a profit or *capital gain*. A negative number, or loss, is a *capital loss*.

b) Total the gains/loss column to find your overall capital gain or loss.

6. Graphing Your Results

Create graphs to show the changing value of each stock and the total value of your portfolio. You can use your spreadsheet software to do this. If you have access to computer software, such as *Fathom* or *TI Interactive*, you will be able to import information about stocks from the Internet to create these graphs.

Report

Prepare a bulletin board or display to show the work you have done on the stock market. Include:

- a brief explanation of why you bought each stock
- information about the broker you used
- a printout of the spreadsheets and graphs you have created
- information about the companies in which you invested
- calculations showing your capital gain or loss

Present your display to the class. Explain briefly what you have learned in completing this project.

Contents

Resetting the TI-83 Default Settings

Have you ever picked up a calculator to solve a problem, only to find that the settings have been changed? This Utility will explain how to restore a calculator to its default settings. Default settings are set at the factory when the calculator is manufactured. The calculator will always revert to its default settings in the absence of other instructions.

The TI-83 has an easy way of returning the MODE, WINDOW, FORMAT, and STAT PLOT menus to their default settings. The default settings for these menus are shown below.

MODE MENU   WINDOW MENU

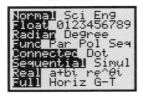

FORMAT MENU   STAT PLOT MENU

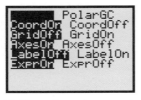

Follow these instructions carefully. If you press the wrong buttons you may erase your programs.

1. Display the Memory menu. Press [2nd] [+]. The screen should look like the one shown.

2. Press 5 to select Reset. The screen should look like the one shown.

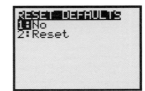

3. Press 2 to select Defaults. The screen should look like the one shown.

4. Press 2 to select Reset. The screen should look like the one shown.

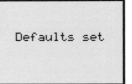

5. Press [ENTER] and you are done! The default settings are once again in use.

Most programmers assume that the calculator is using its default settings. Before running any program, you should always reset your calculator. An alternative is to include steps at the beginning of every program that direct the calculator to reset the defaults. Although this second choice is not difficult, it is a little more time consuming than resetting using the above steps.

ZOOM Features on a TI-83

There are ZOOM features on the TI-83 that allow you to zoom in or out on a graph, and draw a box around a section of a graph and enlarge this section. Another use of the ZOOM feature is to set the viewing window. This utility will explain how to use the ZOOM feature to determine the coordinates of the point of intersection of the lines $y = 2x - 1$ and $y = -2x + 7$. The WINDOW should be standard and have values for both x and y from -10 to 10 with increments of 1. (If you are not sure how to return to the standard settings, refer to Utility 1.)

1. Turn off any plots currently turned on by pressing [2nd] [Y=]. Select any plots that are On using the arrow keys, then press [ENTER]. Use the arrow key to highlight Off and press [ENTER].

2. Press [Y=]. If any equations are listed in the equation editor, clear them by using the arrow keys and [CLEAR]. Enter the equation $y = 2x - 1$ as Y1 and $y = -2x + 7$ as Y2 of the list.

3. Set the viewing window. To choose the standard window, press [ZOOM] 6.

4. Press [TRACE]. Use the arrow keys to move the cursor close to the point of intersection. The approximate x- and y-coordinates are displayed at the bottom of the screen.

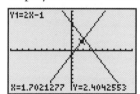

5. To determine the coordinates of the point of intersection more accurately, you may draw a box around the particular section of the graph you want to enlarge, or zoom in on the area around the cursor.

a) Use the ZBox:

1) Press `ZOOM` **1** to select Zbox. The screen above right will appear with the position of the zoom cursor indicated.

2) Define the box around the point of intersection. Move the cursor up and to the left of the point of intersection, then press `ENTER` to obtain a screen similar to the one above right. Notice that the cursor has been replaced by a small box.

3) Use the right arrow key to enlarge the box to the desired length (below left) and the down key to enlarge the box to the desired width (below right). The box should enclose the point of intersection.

 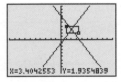

4) Press `ENTER` and the graphs are replotted within the new viewing window. Notice that the zoom cursor in the screen below appears in the centre.

 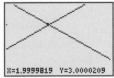

5) Move the cursor closer to the point of intersection, then repeat steps 1 to 4 until the point of intersection is determined to the desired accuracy (above right).

b) Use the Zoom In:

1) Press `ZOOM` and then right arrow to view the zoom memory. This shows the zoom factors. Select **4:** Set Factors. The zoom factors are positive numbers (not necessarily integers) that give the magnification or reduction factor used to **Zoom In** (or **Zoom Out**). Enter 10 for both settings, XFact and YFact, as shown below right. With these settings the x-scale and y-scale are multiplied (or divided) by 10 each time you zoom in (or out).

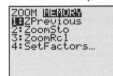 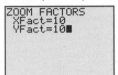

2) Press `ZOOM` **2**. A screen similar to the one below appears.

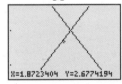

3) Move the cursor close to the point of intersection. Repeat steps 1 and 2 until the coordinates of the point of intersection are obtained to the degree of accuracy required.

When you use the ZOOM menu, remember:

- The viewing window settings change. Therefore, you will need to restore them later.
- Once you change the zoom factors, they will remain in memory even when you turn off the calculator.
- To cancel the **Zoom In** (or **Zoom Out**) command before you execute the command by pressing `ENTER`, press `CLEAR`.

Linking TI-83 Calculators

Using the LINK feature and the cable that is provided with each calculator, programs, lists, defined matrices, window settings, and basically anything that has been saved in the memory of one calculator can be transferred to the memory of another. Although this Utility will concentrate on transferring programs between calculators, other types of data can be transferred using the same process.

To begin, connect the two calculators using the cable provided. Ensure that the cable is pushed firmly into each calculator. In this process, one calculator will send the data and the other will receive it.

To Receive Data

- Press [2nd] [x,T,θ,n] to select the LINK function.
- Use your arrow key to move the cursor over to RECEIVE.
- Press [ENTER] and the receiving calculator is now ready to receive data (the message "Waiting" will be in the display). The sending calculator should then transmit the data. If the transmission is successful, the program name and the word "Done" will be in your display.

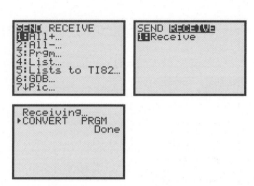

If the data being received already exist in your calculator, the screen below will appear. You can choose to Rename the program, Overwrite the program that is currently in your calculator (this means the current program in the receiving calculator will be lost), Omit the program, or Quit the transmission.

To Send Data

- Press [2nd] [X,T,θ,n] to select the LINK function.

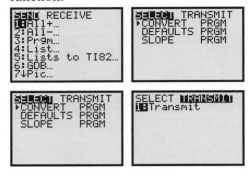

- In this case, since we wish to send a program, select 3:Prgm.... This allows us to choose from any of the programs in the memory we wish to transfer.

Note: These are examples only. These programs may not be in your calculator.

- Select the items you wish to transmit to another calculator using the arrow and [ENTER] keys. When an item has been selected, it is marked with a black box in front of it. To deselect a program, press [ENTER] again.

- To transmit the selected items, use your arrow key and move over to TRANSMIT. Once the second calculator is prepared to receive the data, press [ENTER] and the data will be transferred. Remember: the second calculator must be prepared to receive the data before the first calculator begins transmitting it.

If the cable is not making a good connection with one of the calculators, an error message will appear. Ensure that the cable is properly connected to both calculators and try to send the program again. Once all the data have

been sent, the screen should indicate what data have been transmitted and that the transfer is done.

Here is a list of the other functions on the LINK screen.

1: All+... allows you to select individual items, with all items selected initially.

2: All−... allows you to select individual items, with all items deselected initially.

3: Prgm... displays programs only, with no programs selected initially.

4: List... displays list names only, with no lists selected initially.

5: Lists to TI82... displays lists L1 to L6, with no lists selected initially.

6: GDB... displays graph databases only, with no databases selected initially.

7: Pic... displays all picture data types only, with none selected initially.

8: Matrix... displays matrices only, with no matrices selected initially.

9: Real... displays all real variables only, with no variables selected initially.

0: Complex... displays all complex variables only, with no variables selected initially.

A: Y-Vars... displays all Y= variables only, with no variables selected initially.

B: String... displays all string variables only, with no variables selected initially.

C: Backup... selects everything for backup to the TI-83.

Running a Program on a TI-83

Using the TI-83, three things can be done to a program. First, you can EXECute or run a program. Second, if a program that has been entered into the calculator is not protected, you can EDIT or make changes to it. Third, you can create a NEW program for the TI-83. Refer to the manual for instructions on programming.

To Run a Program

- Press PRGM.
- Select the program to be run using either the arrow keys and ENTER, or by pressing the appropriate number or letter.
- The program name should appear on the home screen. To run the program press ENTER.

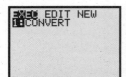 

Note: This is an example only. The program may not be in your calculator.

If a command (or partial command) that was on the home screen has not been executed, you might receive the Error message shown below right. In this case you would choose **2** and delete all of the characters that appear prior to the program name, and then press ENTER to begin the program.

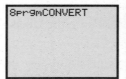 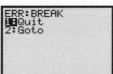

To Interrupt a Program

- ON will break the program. Select 1:Quit or ENTER to return to the home screen.

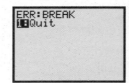 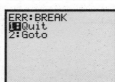

Note: If the program being executed is not protected, a second option, 2:Goto, will appear on the screen. If this option is selected, the calculator will return to the place within the program where the program was interrupted. To leave the program, press 2nd MODE. If any other keystroke is selected, the program will be altered.

Using *The Geometer's Sketchpad*

1. To construct △ABC using points:

Click on this tool … and do this:

a) Draw 3 points.

b) Click on each point to display its label. To change a label, double-click and type a new letter. Make sure the labels are A, B, and C.

c) Hold down the Shift key and click on each point. This selects the points. When a point is outlined in black, it is selected.

d) From the Construct menu, choose Segment.

e) Click anywhere on the screen to deselect segments and points.

2. To construct the midpoint of AB:

Click on this tool … and do this:

a) Click on the side AB to select it. The two black squares on the line segment show that it has been selected.

b) From the Construct menu, choose Point at Midpoint.

c) Click on the midpoint to display its label, D. Double-click on D, then change it to M.

3. To construct △PQR using segments:

Click on this tool … and do this:

a) Draw a horizontal line segment by clicking on the screen, then drag. The segment is selected.

b) Click anywhere on the screen to deselect the segment.

c) Construct a point on one side of the segment.

d) Click on the point on one side of the segment. Double-click on the label and change it to R.

e) Repeat this procedure to label the points you have constructed on the segment R and Q.

f) Click on P and R. From the Construct menu, choose segment.

g) Click anywhere on the screen to deselect the points and segments.

h) Click on Q and R, then construct segment QR.

i) Drag a vertex of △PQR until all the angles are acute.

4. To construct a circle:

Click on this tool ... and do this:

a) Hold down the mouse button anywhere on the screen. Move the mouse. Click anywhere to deselect.

b) Drag the control point to make the circle larger or smaller.

5. To measure the length of a segment AB:

Click on this tool ... and do this:

a) Select points A and B.

b) From the Measure menu, choose Distance. The length of AB is displayed on screen.

6. To measure ∠ABC:

Click on this tool ... and do this:

a) Select points A, B, and C in that order.

b) From the Measure menu, choose Angle. The measure of ∠ABC is displayed on screen.

7. To label a point:

Click on this tool ... and do this:

a) Use the mouse to move the hand to the point. The hand turns black. Click, and the point is labelled.

b) To change the label, double-click on the label. A dialog box appears. Type the new label, then click O.K.

8. To construct the perpendicular bisector of segment AB:

Click on this tool ... and do this:

a) Click anywhere on the screen, hold down the mouse button, drag to form a segment, and then release the mouse button.

b) Move the hand to one endpoint and click to label it A. Move the hand to the other endpoint and click to label it B.

c) Select segment AB.

d) From the Construct menu, choose Point at Midpoint.

e) Select the midpoint and the segment AB.

f) From the Construct menu, choose Perpendicular Line. This line is the perpendicular bisector of AB.

Spreadsheet Basics Using Microsoft Excel

When Excel is opened, a *workbook* that holds multiple worksheets appears. By default each workbook in Excel starts with three blank worksheets. Each tab at the bottom of the sheet identifies each worksheet.

Cell Name
(the selected cell) **Formula**   **Formula Bar**

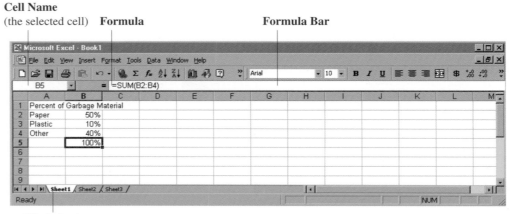

Worksheet

The Worksheet

The worksheet consists of 256 vertical *columns* and 65 535 horizontal *rows*. Letters, A, B, C, and the like, denote columns. Numbers, 1, 2, 3, and the like, denote rows.

Cells

A *Cell* is the "box" at the junction of each row and column. For example, the cell A1 in the top left-hand corner denotes column A, row 1. Data are entered in cells.

Formulas

We enter *formulas* to facilitate calculations.

We will use *Example 2*, page 315, to demonstrate how to format an Excel worksheet.

Creating a title

Always give a spreadsheet a title. Provide any instructions in the first few rows of the spreadsheet. For this example, enter "Percent of Garbage Material" in cell A1.

Highlighting/Selecting cells

Highlighting cells allows us to perform many functions within a worksheet. Cells are highlighted by clicking and dragging. For example, to bold face the title, highlight the cells, then press the bold button.

To select an entire column or row, click on the column heading or row number. By clicking and dragging on column headings or row headings, we can select multiple adjacent columns or rows.

To select non-adjacent cells, click and drag the first group of cells. Click and drag the second group of cells while holding the CTRL button.

Changing the width of a column

Adjust column widths to accommodate the data they contain. Excel's default worksheet presents all columns with equal widths. A column can be made wider or narrower. You can use a short cut to change the width of a column. Place the cursor between two column headings you want to alter. The cursor should appear as a double-headed arrow. Click and drag to adjust the column width; release when the desired width is achieved.

Changing the height of a row

Excel's default worksheet presents all rows with equal heights. You can use a short cut to change a row height. Place the cursor between two row headings that you want to alter. The cursor should appear as a double-headed arrow. Click and drag to adjust the row height, releasing when the desired height is achieved.

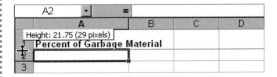

You can also change the width of a column by choosing Format, then Column, then Width from the menu.

You can also change the height of a row by choosing Format, then Row, then Height from the menu.

The Toolbar

Many buttons on the toolbar are identical to those found and used on other Microsoft Office applications, such as Word.

We will review some buttons that are unique to Excel and are very useful.

AutoSum:
Takes the sum of values in a column.

Paste Function:
Adds a built-in math function into a cell.

Sort Ascending:
Arranges values in a column from lowest, displayed at the top, to highest, or in alphabetical order.

Sort Descending:
Arranges values in a column from highest, displayed at the top, to lowest, or in alphabetical order.

Chart Wizard:
Launches a wizard to help create a graph from a data set.

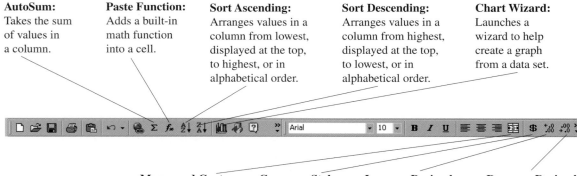

Merge and Centre:
Centres data within a cell or between two cells.

Currency Style:
Displays numbers with a currency symbol.

Increase Decimal:
Increases the number of decimal places displayed.

Decrease Decimal:
Decreases the number of decimal places displayed.

There are other tools and toolbars that Excel offers. We have reviewed the most common commands. If you would like to explore more tools, select View, then Toolbars from the menu.

From here, you can choose which toolbars you want displayed.

Creating cell borders

It is possible to highlight cells in a table by using borders around the top, bottom, or entire cell. To create borders, highlight the cell or cells around which you want a border, then press Ctrl + 1. A Format Cell dialog box will appear. Click the Border tab, as shown.

Select from the Presets or customize the position of the border by selecting from the Border buttons. Select a Line Style and Color, then click OK.

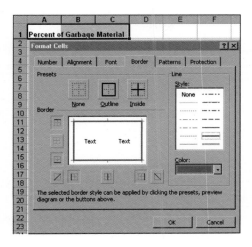

Formulas

Excel can be a powerful calculator. When a formula is entered, Excel can perform calculations. The table below shows symbols commonly used in formulas.

Symbol	Significance
=	Precedes a formula
+	Addition
−	Subtraction
*	Multiplication
/	Division
%	Percent
^	Exponent
:	Range of cells

When typing formulas, always start with an equal sign. Cells in the formula are referenced by their cell names, that is their row and column assignment. For example, to add cells B2, B3, and B4, place the cursor in the cell in which you would like the result to appear. Type: =B2+B3+B4 then press Enter.

Because the cells we want to add are contiguous, there are several alternatives to achieve the same result. One alternative is to type: =SUM(B2:B4) This formula tells Excel to take the sum of the cells from B2 down to B4.

A second alternative is to highlight cells B2 to B4 and the cell in which you would like the result, then press the AutoSum button. This is a shortcut to the first alternative above. If you click on cell B5, you will see the formula: =SUM(B2:B4)

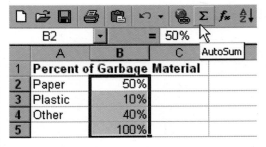

When the values in cells B2 to B4 are changed, the value in B5 will be automatically updated with the new result. To edit a formula, click on the cell in which its result appears, then edit the formula in the formula bar.

Functions

Excel is preprogrammed with a variety of formulas called *functions*. To input a function into your worksheet, ensure the cursor is in the cell you want the function to appear. Then press the Paste Function button on the toolbar (or choose Insert then Function from the menu). The Paste Function dialog box appears. In the Function Category list box, click the function category you would like to use. In the Function Name list box, click the function you would like to use. Excel gives a brief explanation of each function at the bottom of the dialog box when you click a function.

There are several hundred Excel functions. The table below lists those commonly used.

Function Name	Significance
AVERAGE	Calculates the average value of a set of data.
COUNT	Counts the number of cells containing numbers instead of text in a set of data.
MAX	Determines the greatest value in a set of data.
MIN	Determines the least value in a set of data.
PI	Returns the value of π to 15 decimal places.
POWER	Calculates the result of a number raised to a power
ROUND	Rounds a decimal to a particular number of digits
SQRT	Calculates the square root of a number.
SUM	Adds the values in a set of data.

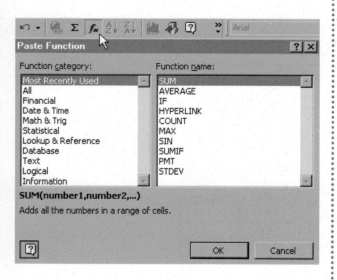

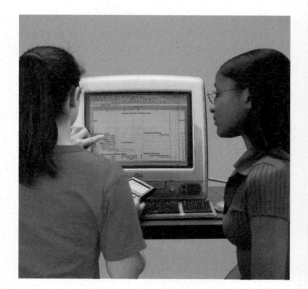

Creating Graphs with Microsoft Excel

The easiest way to create a graph from a set of data is to use the Chart Wizard.

1. Select the cells that contain the data you want in your graph.

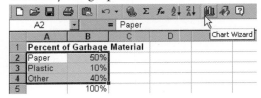

2. Press the Chart Wizard button on the toolbar (or choose Insert then Chart from the menu). The Chart Wizard dialog box appears.

3. Select the Chart Type and Subtype you want, then click Next.

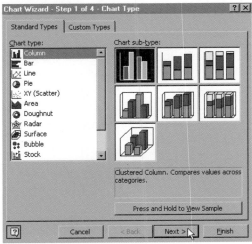

4. The next Chart Wizard dialog box appears, which gives you an idea of your chart's appearance.

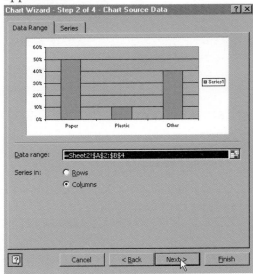

You may choose Rows or Columns to select the way Excel uses your data to create the graph. When you choose Rows, Excel will use your row labels (if any) to appear on the x-axis. When you choose Columns, Excel uses your column labels (if any) to appear on the x-axis of your graph. Once you have chosen Rows or Columns, click the Next button.

5. The next chart wizard dialog box appears, and asks you for chart and axis titles. Enter the chart titles you would like, then press Next.

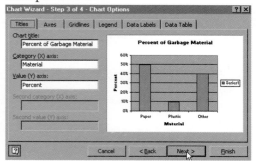

6. The next Chart Wizard dialogue box appears, asking whether you would like the graph to appear on a separate worksheet, or on the same worksheet as the data set. Click either As new sheet or As object in option, then click Finish.

7. Excel draws your chart and places it on your chosen worksheet. You may choose to re-size the graph by clicking and dragging a corner of the selected graph, as shown. For this particular graph, the Series 1 label on the right is distracting and unnecessary. To delete it, right click the Series 1 box, then click Clear.

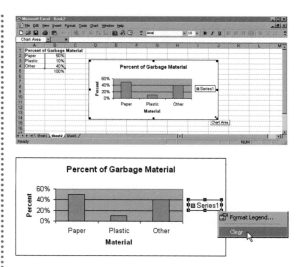

Editing

By right-clicking the grey area of the graph, you can format various aspects of the graph. If you want to change the graph type to a pie chart, click on Chart Type, Pie, then OK.

To re-insert the series labels into the graph, right-click the graph, then choose Format Data Series.

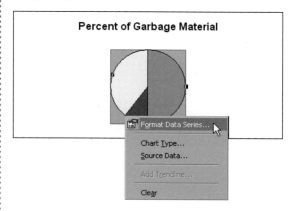

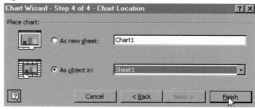

Select Show label and percent, then press OK.

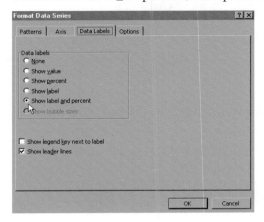

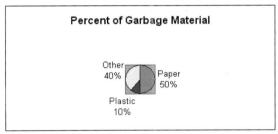

Spreadsheet Basics and Graphs with Corel Quattro Pro

When you open Corel Quattro Pro, a *notebook* that holds multiple sheets appears. Each letter tab at the bottom, denoted by letters, identifies each sheet.

The Notebook sheets, cells, and formulas are similar to that of Excel. To format the notebook, use the same methods for the Excel workbook. Refer to Utility 6 for these terms and procedures.

Cell Name   Formula   Text and Formula Bar

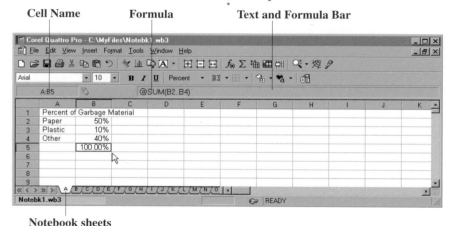

Notebook sheets

The Toolbar

Buttons on the toolbar are similar to those in other word-processing applications. We will review some buttons unique to Quattro Pro.

Paste the format from the current selection to all subsequent sections until Quick Format is turned off.

Create a floating chart on the notebook sheet.

Insert cells, rows, columns, or sheets.

Delete cells, rows, columns, or sheets.

Adjust a column width to its widest entry.

Build complex formulas with @function.

Totals the values in a selection.

Fill blank cells in a selection.

Apply a predefined format to the selection.

Join and centre cells.

Per exp

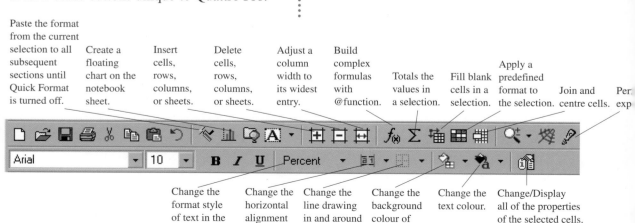

Change the format style of text in the selected cells.

Change the horizontal alignment of text.

Change the line drawing in and around selected text.

Change the background colour of selected text.

Change the text colour.

Change/Display all of the properties of the selected cells.

There are other tools and toolbars that Quattro Pro offers. If you would like to explore more tools, from the menu select View, then Toolbars.

Formulas

Some of the symbols used in formulas are:

Symbol	Significance
@	Precedes a formula
+	Addition
−	Subtraction
*	Multiplication
/	Division
%	Percent
^	Exponent
..	Range of cells

@Function

These are built-in formulas. They are called @functions because they are all preceded by an @ symbol. Quattro Pro comes with more than 450 built-in functions.

@Functions have these parts:

- the name of the @function (such as @SUM, or @AVG)
- the arguments (the values, cells, or text strings to be operated on)
- the commas that separate multiple arguments
- the parentheses around the arguments

For example:

@SUM(A1..A4,B1) is equivalent to +A1+A2+A3+A4+B1.

@AVG(A5..A8) finds the average of the values in A5 through A8.

Graphs

The easiest way to create a graph from a set of data is to use the PerfectExpert. By clicking on the toolbar icon the expert menu will appear on the left on the screen. Click Add Graphics. Highlight the data you want to graph, then click Create Chart.

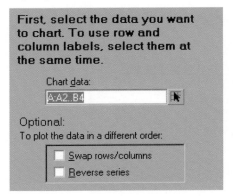

You will be led through a 5-step chart expert.

Step 1: Ensure the data you previously highlighted are correct, then press Next.

First, select the data you want to chart. To use row and column labels, select them at the same time.

Chart data:
A:A2..B4

Optional:
To plot the data in a different order:
- Swap rows/columns
- Reverse series

Step 2: Choose the chart type, then press Next.

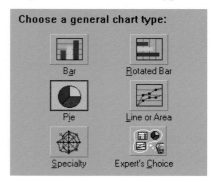

Step 3: Choose the specific chart type, then press Next.

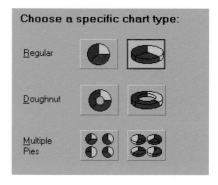

Step 4: Choose a colour scheme, then press Next.

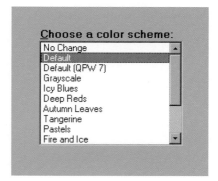

Step 5: Enter the Titles. If you would like the chart to appear on the notebook sheet, click Current Sheet. If you would like the chart to appear as a separate sheet, press Chart Window. Click Finish.

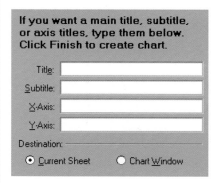

The cursor will change to a chart icon. Click and drag the icon on the worksheet to the desired size for your chart. By right-clicking the chart, you can change the graph type or attributes.

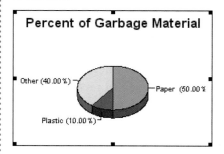

Using a Spreadsheet to Calculate Measures of Central Tendency and Spread

We can use a spreadsheet to calculate the mean, median, mode, range, standard deviation, and variance of a data set. These instructions are for Microsoft Excel. If you use a different spreadsheet program, consult the manual.

We will calculate the measures of central tendency and spread for Anne's pledge data from Section 6.1.

Anne's Pledge Data

Amount of Pledge ($)	Frequency
2	1
3	1
4	2
5	2
6	2
7	1
8	1

1. At the computer, open the spreadsheet program and start a new spreadsheet.

2. Enter the data. Excel has built-in functions to calculate the mean, median, mode, variance, and standard deviation. To use these functions, data must be entered as a list. If the data are displayed in a frequency table, they must be converted to raw data.

   a) Enter the heading "Anne's Pledges ($)" in cell A1.

   b) Enter the pledge amounts in cells A2 to A11.

   c) If the data are not arranged in order, sort them. To do this, highlight cells A2 to A11, then press the sort button, as shown.

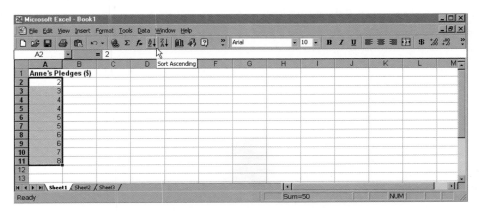

3. Calculate the measures of central tendency.

a) Enter the heading "Measures of Central Tendency" in cell D3.

b) Enter the headings "Mean," "Median," and "Mode" in cells D4 to D6.

c) To determine the mean of the data set, type: =AVERAGE(A2:A11) in cell E4.

d) To determine the median of the data set, type: =MEDIAN(A2:A11) in cell E5.

e) Determine the value(s) that occur(s) most frequently. Enter this value, the mode, in cell E6. If you type:=MODE(A2:A11) and there is more than one mode, Excel displays the lowest value only, in this case 4. If you would like the mode values justified to the right, place the cursor in that cell, then press the align right button, as shown.

The mean and median pledges are both $5. There are three modes, $4, $5, and $6.

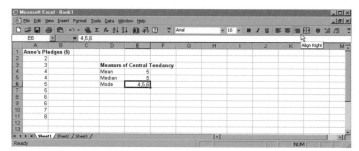

4. Calculate the measures of spread.

a) Enter the heading "Measures of Spread" in cell D8.

b) Enter the headings "Range," "Variance," and "Standard Deviation" in cells D9 to D11. You may need to change the column width to accommodate the headings.

c) Though Excel does not have a function to calculate the range, we can utilize the maximum and minimum functions for the data set.

Type:=MAX(A2:A11)-MIN(A2:A11) in cell E9.

d) To determine the variance, type: =VAR(A2:A11) in cell E10.

e) To determine the standard deviation, type: =STDEV(A2:A11) in cell E11

The range is 6, the variance is approximately 3.33 and the standard deviation is approximately 1.83.

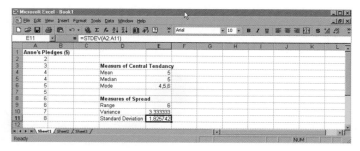

ANSWERS

Chapter 1 Trigonometry

Necessary Skills

1 Pre-Test, page 4

1. a) $\sin 47° \doteq 0.7314$; $\cos 47° \doteq 0.6820$; $\tan 47° \doteq 1.0724$
b) $\sin 23° \doteq 0.3907$; $\cos 23° \doteq 0.9205$; $\tan 23° \doteq 0.4245$
c) $\sin 65° \doteq 0.9063$; $\cos 65° \doteq 0.4226$; $\tan 65° \doteq 2.1445$
d) $\sin 88° \doteq 0.9994$; $\cos 88° \doteq 0.0349$; $\tan 88° \doteq 28.6363$

2. a) 45°   **b)** 64°   **c)** 58°
d) 3°   **e)** 6°   **f)** 13°

3. a)

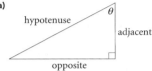

b) $\sin\theta = \dfrac{\text{opp}}{\text{hypot}}$; $\cos\theta = \dfrac{\text{adj}}{\text{hypot}}$; $\tan\theta = \dfrac{\text{opp}}{\text{adj}}$

4. a) 10.7 cm   **b)** 2.3 cm

5. a) 33°   **b)** 51°

6. a) 18.5°   **b)** 4.6 cm   **c)** 4.4 cm   **d)** 38.7°

7. 5.0 m

8. 54°

2 Review: Ratio and Proportion

Exercises, page 7

1. $\dfrac{3}{2}$

2. a) 3.3   **b)** 8.6   **c)** 15   **d)** 15.4

3. a) 4.5   **b)** 1.9   **c)** 88.4   **d)** 11.1

4. a) 13.5   **b)** 20.5   **c)** 88.4   **d)** 17.5

3 Review: The Pythagorean Theorem

Exercises, page 9

1. a) 5 cm   **b)** 40.8 cm

2. a) 10 cm   **b)** 16.2 cm   **c)** 17.7 cm   **d)** 3.9 cm

3. 4.8 m

4 New: Approximate Numbers and Significant Digits

Exercises, page 12

1. a) exact   **b)** approximate
c) exact   **d)** exact; approximate

2. a) 3   **b)** 4   **c)** 3   **d)** 3   **e)** 1
f) 4   **g)** 1   **h)** 3   **i)** 4   **j)** 5
k) 4   **l)** 3   **m)** 1   **n)** 6   **o)** 3

1.1 Exercises, page 17

1. a) $\dfrac{4}{5}$ **b)** $\dfrac{3}{5}$ **c)** $\dfrac{3}{4}$ **d)** $\dfrac{4}{5}$

2. a) $\tan X$ **b)** $\sin X$ **c)** $\cos X$

3. a) 0.6561   **b)** 6.3138   **c)** 0.7880   **d)** 0.4040
e) 0.2924   **f)** 0.4540   **g)** 0.1584   **h)** 0.9135

4. a) 3.4 cm   **b)** 5.5 mm   **c)** 9.7 mm

5. a) 4 cm   **b)** 40 mm   **c)** 27 m

6. a) 7.2 mm   **b)** 8.9 cm   **c)** 14.4 mm

7. a) 26 m   **b)** 202 m

8. a) 9 cm   **b)** 13 m   **c)** 11 mm

9. a) 17.2 m   **b)** 7.3 cm   **c)** 9.9 m

10. 75 m

11. a) 8.0 cm   **b)** 6.4 cm

12. 2.9 m

13. a) approx. 156 m   **b)** approx. 157 m

14. a)

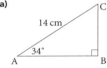

b) Leg c is longer because it is opposite a larger angle.
c) $a \doteq 7.8$ cm; $c \doteq 12$ cm

15. a) The lengths of the two legs should be the same since $\angle X$ equals $\angle Z$.
b) $x \doteq 6.1$ cm; $z \doteq 6.1$ cm
c) Sin 45° equals cos 45° since the opposite and adjacent legs of the triangle are equal.

16. Assuming that they continue to walk at 3 km/h, it will take them 1.98 h to walk the 5953 m to the tower. Since it will be dark in 1.5 h, they should stop for the night.

1.2 Exercises, page 24

1. a) $\dfrac{3}{5}$ **b)** $\dfrac{4}{5}$ **c)** $\dfrac{3}{4}$

2. a) 42°   **b)** 59°   **c)** 71°
d) 48°   **e)** 57°   **f)** 32°

3. a) 39°   **b)** 43°   **c)** 51°
d) 26°   **e)** 73°   **f)** 56°

4. a) 51°   **b)** 66°   **c)** 48°

5. a) $\angle A \doteq 43.4°$; $\angle C \doteq 46.6°$ **b)** $\angle X \doteq 37.6°$; $\angle Y \doteq 52.4°$
c) $\angle L \doteq 11.4°$; $\angle M \doteq 78.6°$

6. a) 7.7 cm   **b)** 34°   **c)** 10.7 cm   **d)** 36°

7. a) $b \doteq 9$ cm; $\angle A \doteq 53°$; $\angle C \doteq 37°$
b) $k \doteq 7$ cm; $m \doteq 6$ cm; $\angle M \doteq 42°$
c) $y \doteq 11$ mm; $z \doteq 10$ mm; $\angle X \doteq 22°$
d) $s \doteq 26$ m; $\angle S \doteq 71°$; $\angle T \doteq 19°$

8. a) 37°   **b)** 59°   **c)** 8.2 cm   **d)** 63°

9. a) $c \doteq 20.7$ cm; $\angle A \doteq 53°$; $\angle C \doteq 37°$
    b) $l \doteq 17.1$ m; $\angle J \doteq 66°$; $\angle L \doteq 24°$
    c) $p \doteq 3.0$ cm; $\angle P \doteq 37°$; $\angle R \doteq 53°$
    d) $y \doteq 8.9$ cm; $\angle X \doteq 27°$; $\angle Z \doteq 63°$

10. a) $\angle R \doteq 36°$; $s \doteq 12.5$ mm; $t \doteq 15.5$ mm
    b) $\angle N \doteq 53°$; $l \doteq 9.4$ cm; $n \doteq 12.5$ cm
    c) $\angle A \doteq 12°$; $a \doteq 1.0$ m; $c \doteq 5.0$ m
    d) $\angle D \doteq 49°$; $e \doteq 5.3$ cm; $f \doteq 3.5$ cm

11. 73°

12. 56.3°

13. 6°

14. 32.6°

15. a) 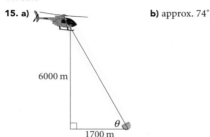   **b)** approx. 74°

16. approx. 72°

17. a) Triangles may vary.

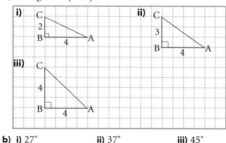

b) i) 27°   **ii)** 37°   **iii)** 45°

    c) As tan A increases, $\angle A$ also increases. The legs of the triangle become the same length, forming an isosceles triangle.
    d) The opposite leg of the triangle will be longer than the adjacent leg, and $\angle A$ will be larger than 45°. $\angle A \doteq 53°$

    e) As $\angle A$ approaches 90°, the value of tan A approaches infinity.

18. Using previously calculated measures introduces more error because they are approximate (rounded) values; so, it is better to use the given measures.

19. a) 13.7 cm   **b)** 6.1 cm   **c)** 37°

1.3 Exercises, page 35

1. a) 42.6   **b)** 3.3   **c)** 14.8

2. a) 52°   **b)** 41°   **c)** 49°

3. a) 27°   **b)** 53°   **c)** 5°

4. a) 5.1 cm   **b)** 10.6 cm   **c)** 14.2 cm

5. a) 61°   **b)** 70°   **c)** 64°

6. a) 8.1 cm   **b)** 7.4 cm   **c)** 6.0 cm

7. a) 37°   **b)** 10.8 cm   **c)** 12.3 cm
    d) 55°   **e)** 10.5 cm   **f)** 11.9 cm

8. a) $\angle P \doteq 47°$; $m \doteq 9.0$ cm; $p \doteq 6.9$ cm
    b) $\angle B \doteq 76°$; $\angle C \doteq 41°$; $c \doteq 4.8$ cm

9. a) $\angle A \doteq 70°$; $a \doteq 9.7$ cm; $c \doteq 7.6$ cm
    b) $\angle R \doteq 85°$; $p \doteq 5.2$ cm; $q \doteq 6.2$ cm
    c) $\angle M \doteq 70°$; $m \doteq 7.1$ cm; $n \doteq 6.2$ cm

10. 9 m

11. ship A: 19.4 km; ship B: 17.3 km

12. approx. $71

13. 11 km

14. 73 km

15. To calculate the length of a side using the Sine Law, you must know the measure of 2 angles and the length of 1 side.
To calculate the measure of an angle using the Sine Law, you must know the length of 2 sides and the measure of 1 angle opposite one of those sides.

Self-Check 1.1–1.3, page 38

1. a) 7.8 cm   **b)** 65°

2. 490 m

3. a) 8.4 cm   **b)** 9.4 cm

4. a) 50°   **b)** 50°

5. approx. 2600 m high; Explanations may vary.

1.4 Exercises, page 42

1. a) $\sin 6° \doteq 0.1045$; $\cos 6° \doteq 0.9945$; $\tan 6° \doteq 0.1051$
    b) $\sin 9° \doteq 0.1564$; $\cos 9° \doteq 0.9877$; $\tan 9° \doteq 0.1584$
    c) $\sin 81° \doteq 0.9877$; $\cos 81° \doteq 0.1564$; $\tan 81° \doteq 6.3138$
    d) $\sin 24° \doteq 0.4067$; $\cos 24° \doteq 0.9135$; $\tan 24° \doteq 0.4452$
    e) $\sin 53° \doteq 0.7986$; $\cos 53° \doteq 0.6018$; $\tan 53° \doteq 1.3270$
    f) $\sin 47° \doteq 0.7314$; $\cos 47° \doteq 0.6820$; $\tan 47° \doteq 1.0724$
    g) $\sin 174° \doteq 0.1045$; $\cos 174° \doteq -0.9945$; $\tan 174° \doteq -0.1051$
    h) $\sin 151° \doteq 0.4848$; $\cos 151° \doteq -0.8746$; $\tan 151° \doteq -0.5543$
    i) $\sin 99° \doteq 0.9877$; $\cos 99° \doteq -0.1564$; $\tan 99° \doteq -6.3138$
    j) $\sin 156° \doteq 0.4067$; $\cos 156° \doteq -0.9135$; $\tan 156° \doteq -0.4452$
    k) $\sin 127° \doteq 0.7986$; $\cos 127° \doteq -0.6018$; $\tan 127° \doteq -1.3270$
    l) $\sin 133° \doteq 0.7314$; $\cos 133° \doteq -0.6820$; $\tan 133° \doteq -1.0724$

2. a) positive   **b)** negative   **c)** positive
    d) positive   **e)** positive   **f)** negative
    g) positive   **h)** negative   **i)** negative

3. Cos A and tan A will be negative if ∠A is obtuse.

4. a) i) 0.7547   **ii)** 0.4540   **iii)** 0.7986
    iv) 0.9994   **v)** 0.5878   **vi)** 0.9903
  b) i) 131°   **ii)** 153°   **iii)** 127°
    iv) 92°   **v)** 36°   **vi)** 82°

5. a) one
  b) obtuse; Cos B is negative for obtuse angles.
  c) 112°

6. a) one
  b) acute; Cos Z is positive for acute angles.
  c) 55°

7. a) two   **b)** 26° or 154°

8. a) 30° or 150°   **b)** 37°
  c) 132°   **d)** 28° or 152°
  e) 126°   **f)** 0.1° or 179.9°

9. The sine of an acute angle and its supplementary obtuse
angle are the same, so there are two measures of ∠A for
every value of sin A. Cos A and tan A will be positive when
∠A is acute and negative when ∠A is obtuse.

10. a) 18°   **b)** 120°   **c)** 42° or 138°

11. a) −0.923   **b)** 0.565

12. a) i) $\sin 40° \doteq 0.6428$; $\cos 40° \doteq 0.7660$
    ii) $\sin 22° \doteq 0.3746$; $\cos 22° \doteq 0.9272$
    iii) $\sin 39° \doteq 0.6293$; $\cos 39° \doteq 0.7771$
    iv) $\sin 68° \doteq 0.9272$; $\cos 68° \doteq 0.3746$
    v) $\sin 50° \doteq 0.7660$; $\cos 50° \doteq 0.6428$
    vi) $\sin 1° \doteq 0.0175$; $\cos 1° \doteq 0.9998$
    vii) $\sin 51° \doteq 0.7771$; $\cos 51° \doteq 0.6293$
    viii) $\sin 89° \doteq 0.9998$; $\cos 89° \doteq 0.0175$
  b) $\sin 40° = \cos 50°$, $\sin 50° = \cos 40°$; $\sin 22° = \cos 68°$,
    $\sin 68° = \cos 22°$; $\sin 39° = \cos 51°$, $\sin 51° = \cos 39°$;
    $\sin 1° = \cos 89°$, $\sin 89° = \cos 1°$
    The sum of the angles is 90°.
  c) If the two angles are complementary, $\sin A = \cos B$ and
    $\cos A = \sin B$; that is, $\sin A = \cos(90 - A)$.

1.5 Exercises, page 47

1. a) 6   **b)** 38   **c)** 13.6   **d)** 10.7

2. a) 37°   **b)** 55°   **c)** 112°
  d) 116°   **e)** 83°   **f)** 172°

3. a) 38°   **b)** 79°   **c)** 120°   **d)** 108°

4. a) 5 cm   **b)** 32.5 cm   **c)** 9.7 cm

5. a) 46°   **b)** 39°   **c)** 128°

6. a) $a \doteq 10$ cm; $\angle B = 62.5°$; $\angle C = 62.5°$
  b) $\angle A \doteq 97.18°$; $\angle B \doteq 41.41°$; $\angle C \doteq 41.41°$
  c) $c \doteq 10.5$ cm; $\angle A \doteq 30°$; $\angle B \doteq 22°$
  d) $\angle A \doteq 51.5°$; $\angle B \doteq 108.8°$; $\angle C \doteq 19.7°$

7. a) $b \doteq 19.2$ cm; $\angle A \doteq 63°$; $\angle C \doteq 49°$
  b) $d \doteq 17.4$ cm; $\angle E \doteq 26°$; $\angle F \doteq 24°$
  c) $s \doteq 12.0$ cm; $\angle R \doteq 39°$; $\angle T \doteq 23°$

8. a) $\angle K \doteq 50°$; $\angle M \doteq 23°$; $\angle N \doteq 107°$
  b) $\angle P \doteq 139°$; $\angle Q \doteq 26°$; $\angle R \doteq 15°$
  c) $\angle X \doteq 91°$; $\angle Y \doteq 59°$; $\angle Z \doteq 30°$

9. 6.1 km

10. 50 km

11. 1320 m

12. 15°

13. 7.9 km

14. Yes. Explanations may vary.

15. 8.5°

16. 126.6°

1.6 Exercises, page 53

1. a) 3.7 cm   **b)** 2.8 cm   **c)** 5.9 cm

2. a) 84°   **b)** 15°   **c)** 71°

3. a) $\angle B \doteq 104°$; $a \doteq 14.4$ cm; $b \doteq 20.8$ cm
  b) $\angle P \doteq 40°$; $\angle Q \doteq 28°$; $q \doteq 22.8$ cm
  c) $\angle C \doteq 12°$; $b \doteq 6.0$ cm; $c \doteq 1.3$ cm

5. 14 km

6. a) 88.1°   **b)** approx. 147 m

7. 27 m

8. a) 138°   **b)** BC ≐ 2.9 m; AC ≐ 4.1 m

9. a) towns A and B   **b)** AB ≐ 58 km; CB ≐ 94 km

10. a) 70.5 m   **b)** 64°   **c)** 6.7 m

11. 9 km

12. a) cabin A: 1.1 km   **b)** 0.34 km
    cabin B: 0.37 km

1.7 Exercises, page 59

1. 12 m and 15 m

2. 27 m and 46 m

3. a) approx. 35 cm^2 **b)** approx. 54 cm^2

4. approx. 68 m

5. approx. 10 m

6. approx. 140 m

7. approx. 820 m

8. approx. 270 m

9. approx. 32°

10. a)

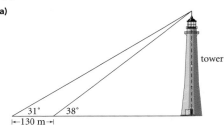

11. approx. 188 m

12. approx. 25 000 m^2

13. 19.4 m

15. Area $= \frac{1}{2} bc \sin A$

Self-Check 1.4–1.7, page 63

1. 72.63° or 107.37°

2. a) 15 cm   **b)** 4.4 cm

3. a) 101°   **b)** 50°

4. 9.4 m

5. 0.13 km

1.8 The Ambiguous Case and the Sine Law, page 69

1. 50° or 130°

2. $\angle C \doteq 49°$ or $131°$; $b \doteq 10.4$ cm or 1.9 cm

3. $\angle M \doteq 113°$; $\angle N \doteq 39°$; $m \doteq 4.7$ cm or $\angle M \doteq 11°$; $\angle N \doteq 141°$; $m \doteq 0.9$ cm

Chapter 1 Review Exercises, page 72

1. a) 5.8 cm   **b)** 9.7 cm   **c)** 11.0 cm

2. 52 m

3. a) 66°   **b)** 35°   **c)** 43°

4. 8.5°

5. a) 9.2 cm   **b)** 14.4 cm   **c)** 7.8 cm

6. a) 44°   **b)** 33°   **c)** 34°

7. 4.3 km

8. a) i) $\sin 55° \doteq 0.8192$; $\cos 55° \doteq 0.5736$; $\tan 55° \doteq 1.4281$
    ii) $\sin 133° \doteq 0.7314$; $\cos 133° \doteq -0.6820$;
       $\tan 133° \doteq -1.0724$
    iii) $\sin 79° \doteq 0.9816$; $\cos 79° \doteq 0.1908$; $\tan 79° \doteq 5.1446$
b) i) 55° or 125°   **ii)** 57° or 133°   **iii)** 79° or 101°

9. 26.31° or 153.69°

10. a) 5.8 cm   **b)** 10.0 cm   **c)** 61°

11. a) $\angle A \doteq 72°$; $a \doteq 7.8$ cm; $c \doteq 6.0$ cm
    b) $\angle P \doteq 29°$; $\angle R \doteq 43°$; $q \doteq 9.4$ cm
    c) $\angle X \doteq 50°$; $\angle Y \doteq 97°$; $\angle Z \doteq 33°$
    d) $\angle R \doteq 39°$; $\angle S \doteq 112°$; $s \doteq 9.2$ cm

12. 7.0 km

13. a) 9.4 cm   **b)** 8.3 cm   **c)** 2.9 cm

14. 1586 m

15. 137 m

16. 1.1 km

17. 1792 m

18. approx. 44 cm²

19. 19 m

20. 6 m and 9 m

Chapter 1 Self-Test, page 76

1. a) 29.8 cm   **b)** 73.2°   **c)** 22.7 cm

3. a) $\angle K \doteq 33°$; $\angle N \doteq 57°$; $m \doteq 8.9$ cm
    b) $\angle A \doteq 86°$; $a \doteq 8.4$ cm; $c \doteq 4.3$ cm
    c) $\angle X \doteq 83°$; $\angle Z \doteq 43°$; $y \doteq 5.8$ cm

4. approx. 130 m

5. 83 m

6. approx. 250 m

7. 20 cm²

8. a) Descriptions may vary. Angles are 26° and 64°.
    b) Descriptions may vary. The distance is approximately 74 cm.

Chapter 2 Algebra
Necessary Skills
1 Review: Assessing Your Mastery, page 80

1. a) $x = -1$ **b)** $x = -\frac{1}{2}$

2. a) $m = -2$, $b = 6$ **b)** $m = 3$, $b = 10$
    c) $m = \frac{1}{2}$, $b = 4$

3. a) 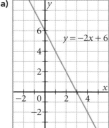   **b)**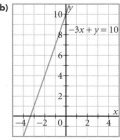

    c)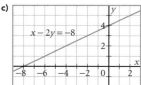

4. a) $(-1,\ 6)$ **b)** $(-3,\ -5)$ **c)** $(3,\ 1)$

5. a) $(-3,\ 0)$ **b)** $(5,\ 3)$ **c)** $(-4,\ 2)$

6. a) $(8,\ 2)$ **b)** $(-1,\ 5)$ **c)** $(3,\ 4)$

7. a) $2x^2 - 4x - 7$ **b)** $18x + 2$ **c)** $-4a - 7$

8. a) $x^2 + 7x + 12$ **b)** $a^2 - 2a - 24$
    c) $2y^2 - 6y + 4$ **d)** $-6m^2 + 6m + 36$

9. a) $(x + 1)(x + 2)$ **b)** $(a - 2)(a - 3)$
    c) $(m - 5)(m + 2)$

10. a) $(2x + 3)(x + 4)$ **b)** $(3w + 1)(2w - 3)$
    c) $(4x - 3)(2x - 1)$

11. a) $x = -3$ or $x = -4$ **b)** $y = 6$ or $y = -2$
    c) $x = \frac{4}{3}$ or $x = 2$ **d)** $y = -\frac{5}{2}$ or $y = \frac{1}{4}$

2 Review: Exponent Laws
Exercises, page 82

1. a) 3   **b)** 5^3 **c)** 7^7
    d) 8^8 **e)** 2^{10} **f)** 4^{10}

2. a) $\frac{1}{x^3}$ **b)** $\frac{1}{b^2}$ **c)** $\frac{1}{x^6}$

3. a) $3^2 = 9$ **b)** $6^2 = 36$ **c)** $\left(\frac{2}{5}\right)^2 = \frac{4}{25}$

4. a) 1 **b)** $\frac{1}{x^3}$ **c)** 1

3 Review: Collecting Like Terms
Exercises, page 83

1. a) $10x + 2$ **b)** $-3y + 8$ **c)** $5m - 9$
d) $7x^2 - 3x$ **e)** $-2ab + 4a$ **f)** $-3y^3 - 10y$

2. a) $x + 7y$ **b)** $-11y + 14x$ **c)** $-2x^2 - 10x$
d) $14a - 11b$ **e)** $-13a + 7b$ **f)** $x - 7y$

4 Review: The Distributive Law
Exercises, page 84

1. a) $8x + 10$ **b)** $9a - 21$ **c)** $-10x + 40$
d) $3y^2 - 6y$ **e)** $8x^2 + 20x$ **f)** $-21m^2 + 28m$
g) $27x - 72$ **h)** $-30x + 24x^2$

2. a) $12x^2 + 6x + 21$ **b)** $-6a^2 + 10a - 4$
c) $6x^3 + 9x^2 - 21x$ **d)** $20y^3 + 24y^2 - 12y$
e) $-12x^3 + 8x^2 - 20x$ **f)** $25m^3 + 20m^2 - 5m$
g) $-6x - 10x^2 + 16x^3$ **h)** $-9z^3 + 2z^2 + 4z$
i) $35x^3 - 28x^2 + 63x$

5 Review: Common Factoring
Exercises, page 85

1. a) $5(x - 2)$ **b)** $2(3y + 4)$ **c)** $7(a - 2b)$
d) $12(a + 3)$ **e)** $3(3j - 2k)$ **f)** $2(h - 1)$
g) $4(x^2 - 2)$ **h)** $3(2x + 3)$ **i)** $5(2w^2 - 3)$

2. a) $3(1 + 6x)$ **b)** $x(5y - 7)$ **c)** $m(12 + 5m)$
d) $y(5y - 1)$ **e)** $x(4 + 6x - 9x^2)$ **f)** $x(2y + 5z)$
g) $a(12 - 5c - 2b)$ **h)** $n(m + 2 - 5p)$ **i)** $a(1 - 4c - 7d)$

3. a) $9x(x + 2)$ **b)** $3a(2a - 5)$ **c)** $9x(2 + 3y)$
d) $4x(2x^2 - 1)$ **e)** $3n(2m + 3)$ **f)** $8x(3x + 2)$
g) $7a(2b - 3)$ **h)** $3x(x + 4)$ **i)** $5y(y^2 - 3)$

6 Review: Slope of a Line
Exercises, page 88

1. a) $-\frac{3}{5}$ **b)** 1 **c)** 0
d) undefined **e)** $-\frac{7}{3}$ **f)** $\frac{2}{7}$

2. a) line segment falls to the right, so slope is negative
b) line segment rises to the right, so slope is positive
c) line segment is horizontal, so slope is zero
d) line segment is vertical, so slope is undefined
e) line segment falls to the right, so slope is negative
f) line segment rises to the right, so slope is positive

3. a) 2 **b)** $\frac{1}{9}$ **c)** $-\frac{1}{3}$
d) undefined **e)** $\frac{7}{3}$ **f)** $-\frac{7}{5}$
g) 0 **h)** 2

2.1 Exercises, page 92

1. a) $x = 4$ **b)** $x = 3$ **c)** $x = 6$
d) $n = -8$ **e)** $x = -3$ **f)** $x = 8$
g) $y = 5$ **h)** $x = 5$ **i)** $z = -5$

2. a) $y = -12$ **b)** $x = 12$ **c)** $y = 6$
d) $m = 10$ **e)** $w = -2$ **f)** $w = 22$

3. a) $x = 5$ **b)** $b = 3$ **c)** $y = -4$
d) $a = 2$ **e)** $x = 3$ **f)** $y = 9$

4. a) $x = \frac{14}{3}$ **b)** $b = \frac{5}{4}$ **c)** $y = \frac{8}{3}$
d) $a = \frac{7}{2}$ **e)** $x = \frac{5}{2}$ **f)** $y = \frac{19}{5}$
g) $b = 5$ **h)** $x = -\frac{1}{2}$ **i)** $x = \frac{1}{3}$

5. a) $m = \frac{15}{4}$ **b)** $n = -10$ **c)** $x = 16$
d) $y = 16$ **e)** $x = -4$ **f)** $y = 8$

6. a) $x = 3$ **b)** $x = 3$ **c)** $y = -1$
d) $a = -2$ **e)** $x = 2$ **f)** $y = -1$
g) $b = -1$ **h)** $x = -3$ **i)** $x = 3$

7. a) $x = \frac{7}{6}$ **b)** $x = 3$ **c)** $y = 1$
d) $a = -\frac{2}{3}$ **e)** $x = \frac{4}{5}$ **f)** $y = -\frac{5}{2}$
g) $b = -\frac{1}{2}$ **h)** $x = \frac{3}{7}$ **i)** $x = \frac{13}{2}$

8. a) $x = 1$ **b)** $a = 2$ **c)** $x = 0$ **d)** $x = -1$
9. a) $x = 9$ **b)** $y = 9$ **c)** $x = -3$ **d)** $y = \frac{5}{3}$
10. a) $x = \frac{13}{6}$ **b)** $x = -\frac{1}{12}$ **c)** $y = \frac{19}{11}$ **d)** $x = -\frac{4}{5}$
11. a) $x = \frac{8}{5}$ **b)** $x = -\frac{3}{2}$ **c)** $y = \frac{4}{3}$ **d)** $x = -42$
12. a) $x = -3$ **b)** $x = -5$ **c)** $x = 0$ **d)** $y = 3$
13. a) $x = -1$ **b)** $x = 13$ **c)** $x = -\frac{5}{2}$ **d)** $y = \frac{5}{3}$

14. Multiplying by 18 instead of 54 simplifies the solution.

15. a) $x = 0$ **b)** $x = \frac{7}{5}$ **c)** $x = 2$ **d)** $x = -6$
16. a) $x = -\frac{39}{8}$ **b)** $y = \frac{20}{13}$ **c)** $x = -\frac{7}{17}$ **d)** $x = -\frac{20}{17}$
17. a) $x = \frac{3}{2}$ **b)** $x = \frac{3}{2}$ **c)** $x = -\frac{29}{15}$
d) $x = \frac{1}{10}$ **e)** $x = -\frac{129}{28}$ **f)** $y = -\frac{115}{41}$

2.2 Exercises, page 97

1. a) $A = 26.04\,\text{m}^2$ **b)** $A \doteq 380.13\,\text{cm}^2$ **c)** $P = 4.2\,\text{km}$
2. a) $D = 2.5\,\text{kg/L}$ **b)** $A = 5.5\,\text{cm}^2$ **c)** $S \doteq \$711.12$
3. a) $w = \frac{A}{l}$ **b)** $1.6\,\text{m}$
4. a) $d = St$ **b)** $85\,\text{m}$
5. a) $b = \frac{2A}{h}$ **b)** $8\,\text{cm}$
6. $7.64\,\text{cm}$
7. a) $r = \frac{I}{Pt}$ **b)** 0.01 or 1%
8. a) $P = \frac{A}{(1 + i)^n}$ **b)** $\$1350.29$
9. a) $m = \frac{y - b}{x}$ **b)** 1
10. $5.0\,\text{cm}$
11. a) $C = \frac{5(F - 32)}{9}$ **b)** $56.7°\text{C}$ **c)** $32°\text{F}$
12. a) $\cos A = \frac{a^2 - b^2 - c^2}{-2bc}$ **c)** $\angle A \doteq 9.3°$
13. a) $b = \frac{2A}{h} - a$ **b)** $4\,\text{mm}$
14. a) $a = \frac{S_n(r - 1)}{r^n - 1}$ **b)** 1

2.3 Exercises, page 105

1. a) $m = 2$, $b = 3$ **b)** $m = \frac{1}{2}$, $b = -2$ **c)** $m = -4$, $b = 1$

2. a) $m = -0.5$, $b = 23$ **b)** $m = 2.50$, $b = 24$
c) $m = -90$, $b = 450$

3. a) 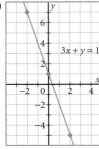 **b)**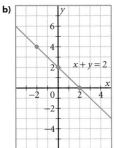

c)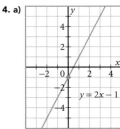

4. a) 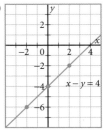 **b)**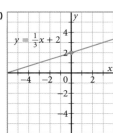

c)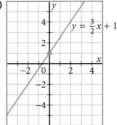

5. a) 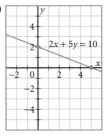 **b)**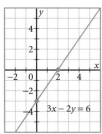

c)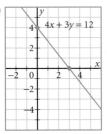

6. a) 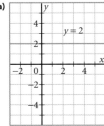 **b)**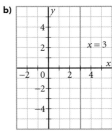

c) 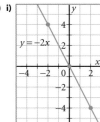 **d)**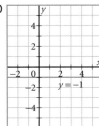

7. a) $m = -\frac{2}{3}$, $b = 3$ **b)** $m = 3, b = -1$ **c)** $m = \frac{2}{5}$, $b = 2$
d) $m = -\frac{1}{2}$, $b = 3$ **e)** $m = \frac{1}{3}$, $b = -1$ **f)** $m = \frac{4}{5}$, $b = 3$

8. a) i) 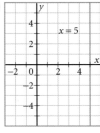 **ii)**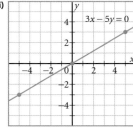

b) The x-intercept and y-intercept are both 0.

9. a) $m = 1$, $b = -3$ **b)** $m = \frac{7}{4}$, $b = -\frac{5}{4}$ **c)** $m = \frac{3}{2}$, $b = 2$
d) $m = \frac{1}{5}$, $b = -\frac{8}{5}$ **e)** $m = 3$, $b = 4$ **f)** $m = -\frac{5}{4}$, $b = \frac{5}{2}$

10. a) $m = \pi$, $b = 0$
b) The slope represents the ratio of the circumference of a circle to its diameter.
No, the slope has no unit.
c) The y-intercept represents the circumference of a circle with diameter 0.

d)

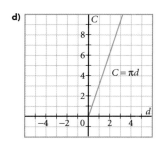

$C = \pi d$

e) *C* is doubled; *C* is tripled

11. a)

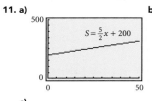

$S = \frac{5}{2}x + 200$

b)

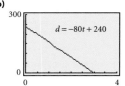

$d = -80t + 240$

c)

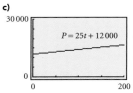

$P = 25t + 12\,000$

12. a)

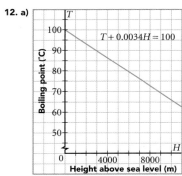

$T + 0.0034H = 100$

b)

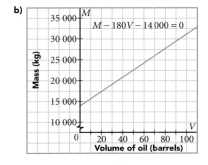

$M - 180V - 14\,000 = 0$

13. a)

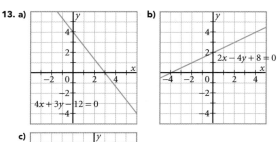

$4x + 3y - 12 = 0$

b)

$2x - 4y + 8 = 0$

c)

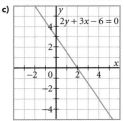

$-x + 5y - 5 = 0$

14. a)

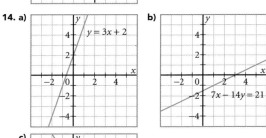

$y = 3x + 2$

b)

$7x - 14y = 21$

c)

$2y + 3x - 6 = 0$

15. a)   **b)**

c)   **d)**

e)   **f)**

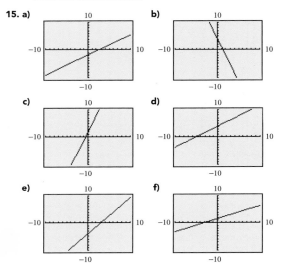
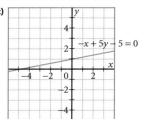

17.

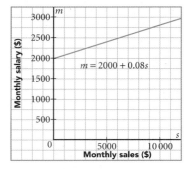

18. a) $C = 50 + 40h$

b)

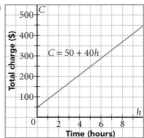

19. $1\frac{1}{2}$ h

2.4 Exercises, page 112

1. a) $(1,\ 2)$ **b)** $\left(\frac{5}{2},\ 4\right)$ **c)** $(-1,\ 1)$

2. a) $(-2,\ -3)$ **b)** $(4,\ 4)$ **c)** $(3,\ 0)$

3. a) $(1,\ 1)$ **b)** $(-1,\ 2)$ **c)** $(4,\ 5)$

4. a) $(3,\ 1)$ **b)** $(-1,\ -3)$ **c)** $(-2,\ 3)$

5. a) $(4,\ 3)$ **b)** $(4,\ 0)$ **c)** $(-3,\ 4)$

6. 5000

7. The two lines are parallel and do not intersect.

8. 80 months

9. a)

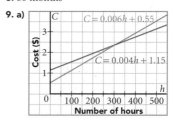

b) 300 h, $2.35 **c)** $1.40

10. a) $(4,\ -2)$ **b)** $(0,\ 3)$ **c)** $(-3,\ -3)$

11. 500 km

12. 15

13. 35 000 km

14. 432 units; Cost and revenue both equal $21 600.

15. b) No. There are an infinite number of lines passing through $(2,\ -5)$.

2.5 Exercises, page 119

1. a) $\left(\frac{5}{2},\ \frac{7}{2}\right)$ **b)** $(-1,\ 2)$ **c)** $(0,\ 4)$
d) $(-2,\ 1)$ **e)** $(-3,\ 4)$ **f)** $(2,\ -3)$

2. a) $(1,\ 1)$ **b)** $(2,\ -1)$ **c)** $(2,\ 3)$
d) $(1,\ 2)$ **e)** $(3,\ 1)$ **f)** $(-1,\ 2)$

3. a) $(1,\ 3)$ **b)** $(3,\ -2)$ **c)** $(1,\ 1)$
d) $(-3,\ 1)$ **e)** $(1,\ -1)$ **f)** $(2,\ -1)$

4. a) $(-3,\ 1)$ **b)** $(3,\ 5)$ **c)** $(1,\ 1)$
d) $\left(-3, -\frac{1}{4}\right)$ **e)** $\left(-\frac{3}{5},\ 1\right)$ **f)** $(1,\ 4)$

5. approx. 6.4 h

6. a) 3 h
b) Pyramid stables; It costs $4 less for 2 h of riding.

7. 100 wheelbarrows; 200 carts

8. approx. 466.7 km in the city; approx. 133.3 km on the highway

9. a) $(2,\ -5)$ **b)** $(-4,\ 3)$
c) $\left(-\frac{19}{7},\ -\frac{15}{7}\right)$ **d)** $(-2,\ 4)$
e) $(-1,\ 5)$ **f)** $(3,\ -2)$

11. 35 km/h wind speed; 765 km/h in still air

12. a) Let f represent the amount of dark French roast, in pounds. Let k represent the amount of Kenyan roast, in pounds.
b) $f + k = 50$; $4.95f + 3.75k = 217.50$
c) 25 pounds of each

13. 7 bundles of pine; 3 bundles of cedar

14. a) 7 h
b) the second company; The cost would be $40 less than that of the first company.

15. 150 deluxe shirts; 100 standard shirts

16. $300 000 in stocks; $700 000 in corporate bonds

17. $100/week

18. a) $(2,\ 3)$ **b)** $(3,\ 2)$ **c)** $(2,\ 1)$
d) $(5,\ 1)$ **e)** $\left(-\frac{29}{17},\ -\frac{25}{17}\right)$ **f)** $(6,\ 1)$

Self-Check 2.1–2.5, page 122

1. a) $x = 5$ **b)** $y = -\frac{3}{2}$ **c)** $x = 2$

2. a) $x = \frac{17}{9}$ **b)** $y = 11$ **c)** $x = -4$ **d)** $x = -\frac{27}{7}$

3. a) $h = \frac{2A}{b}$ **b)** $x = \frac{y - b}{m}$
c) $b = \frac{2A}{h} - a$ **d)** $n = \frac{t_n - a}{d} + 1$

4. a) $m = 3,\ b = -7$ **b)** $m = 4,\ b = 9$
c) $m = -1,\ b = -\frac{1}{2}$ **d)** $m = 2,\ b = -1$

5. a) 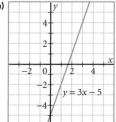 **b)**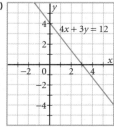

c)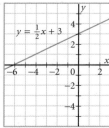

6. a) $(3, 2)$ **b)** $\left(\frac{2}{3}, -7\right)$ **c)** $(-1, 6)$

7. a) $(2, -3)$ **b)** $(-8, 9)$ **c)** $(3, 1)$

8. a) $(2, 3)$ **b)** $(3, -2)$ **c)** $\left(\frac{4}{5}, -\frac{3}{5}\right)$

9. If Nadia sells more than \$6250 per month, she should choose plan A because she would earn more money. If she sells less than \$6250 per month, she should choose plan B.

2.6 Exercises, page 125

1. a) $11x + 5$ **b)** $x - 7$ **c)** $8x - 6$
d) $2x$ **e)** $3x - 4$ **f)** $5x - 10$

2. a) $-2x - 2$ **b)** $-9z - 4$ **c)** $x + 3$
d) $a - 7$ **e)** $-2x$ **f)** $4w - 1$

3. a) $x^2 + 5x + 6$ **b)** $x^2 + x - 12$ **c)** $x^2 + 4x - 5$
d) $x^2 - 6x + 8$ **e)** $y^2 - 2y - 24$ **f)** $a^2 + 6a - 7$
g) $z^2 - 9z + 20$ **h)** $x^2 + 5x - 24$ **i)** $x^2 + x - 20$

4. a) $4x^2 + 5x + 6$ **b)** $5x^2 - 8x + 2$ **c)** $-9x^2 + 2x - 2$
d) $5y^2 - 2y - 4$ **e)** $11x^2 - 5x - 1$ **f)** $-2y - 11$

5. a) $x^2 + 9x - 2$ **b)** $5x^2 - 5x + 1$
c) $-10x^2 + 2x + 8$ **d)** $5y^2 + y + 2$
e) $-4x^2 - 2x$ **f)** $-14y^2 + 10y - 11$

6. a) $6x^2 + 11x + 4$ **b)** $-3x^2 + x + 2$ **c)** $8x^2 + 2x - 1$
d) $6x^2 - 13x + 6$ **e)** $12y^2 + y - 20$ **f)** $-6a^2 - 13a + 28$
g) $-15z^2 + 26z - 8$ **h)** $8x^2 + 10x - 25$ **i)** $18x^2 - 9x - 20$

7. a) i) $x^2 - 1$ **ii)** $x^2 - 4$ **iii)** $x^2 - 9$
iv) $x^2 - 16$ **v)** $4y^2 - 25$ **vi)** $a^2 - 49$
vii) $9z^2 - 4$ **viii)** $4x^2 - 81$ **ix)** $25x^2 - 64$
b) Each answer is the product of the two variable terms plus the product of the two numerical terms; $16a^2 - 9$

8. a) i) $x^2 + 4x + 4$ **ii)** $y^2 + 10y + 25$ **iii)** $x^2 + 14x + 49$
iv) $x^2 - 6x + 9$ **v)** $y^2 - 8y + 16$ **vi)** $x^2 - 16x + 64$
vii) $4x^2 + 20x + 25$ **viii)** $9y^2 - 6y + 1$ **ix)** $16x^2 + 24x + 9$
b) $(a + b)^2 = a^2 + 2ab + b^2$

9. a) $x^3 + 5x^2 + 7x + 2$ **b)** $-x^3 - x^2 + 7x + 15$
c) $x^3 - 6x^2 + 2x + 3$ **d)** $6x^3 + 13x^2 + 18x + 8$
e) $6y^3 + 13y^2 + 7y - 4$ **f)** $-6a^3 + 19a^2 - 4a - 15$

g) $15z^3 + 11z^2 - 18z - 8$ **h)** $-6x^3 + 25x^2 - 4x - 35$
i) $20x^3 + 11x^2 + 17x + 15$

10. a) $3x^2 + 18x + 15$ **b)** $2x^2 - 2x - 12$
c) $4x^2 - 28x + 40$ **d)** $10x^2 - 15x - 10$
e) $-16y^2 + 28y + 30$ **f)** $-18a^2 + 51a - 36$
g) $90z^2 - 66z - 72$ **h)** $12x^2 - 75$
i) $4x^2 - 24x + 36$

11. a) $3a$ **b)** $9m$ **c)** $-8x$
d) 4 **e)** $-3b$ **f)** $3z^2$

12. $3x^2 + 8x + 5$

13. a) $x^2 - 2x - 8$ **b)** $-2y^2 + 2y + 9$
c) $2x^2 + 10x + 10$ **d)** $-5x - 1$

14. a) $-2x^2 - 10x - 10$ **b)** $5x + 1$
c) $-2a^2 - 16a + 17$ **d)** $20x$

15. a) $5x^2 + 21x + 22$ **b)** $2x^2 - 8x - 54$
c) $-2x^2 - 10x - 4$ **d)** $-7x^2 + 14x + 85$

16. a) $-8a^2 - 44a + 69$ **b)** $-42x^2 - 10x + 28$
c) $24x^2 + 26x - 3$ **d)** $-13x^2 - 8x - 5$

17. a) $x^2 + 11x + 10$ **b)** $-13x^2 + 5$
c) $98y^2 + 112y + 35$ **d)** $-134z^2 + 132z - 34$

18. a) $x^3 + 3x^2 + 3x + 1$ **b)** $x^3 + 3x^2y + 3xy^2 + y^3$
c) $8x^3 + 12x^2y + 6xy^2 + y^3$ **d)** $27x^3 - 54x^2y + 36xy^2 - 8y^3$

19. a) $x^4 + 3x^3 + 6x^2 + 5x + 3$ **b)** $y^4 - 3y^3 - 2y^2 + 5y + 3$
c) $6a^4 + 5a^3 - 27a^2 + a + 15$ **d)** $-20z^4 - 7z^3 - 20z^2 - 7z - 6$
e) $x^4 + 2x^3 + 3x^2 + 2x + 1$ **f)** $-y^4 + 2y^3 + y^2 - 2y - 1$

20. a) $3x^3 - 3x^2 + x - 3$ **b)** $2w^4 + 3w^3 - 4w^2 + w + 16$
c) $-v^4 - 4v^3 + 26v^2 + 38v + 108$
d) $-24z^4 - 17z^3 - 12z^2 + 5z - 73$

2.7 Exercises, page 132

1. a) $2, 3$ **b)** $-2, -3$ **c)** $4, 4$ **d)** $-4, -4$
e) $-8, -2$ **f)** $8, 2$ **g)** $-4, 3$ **h)** $6, -2$

2. a) $(x + 1)(x + 2)$ **b)** $(x + 1)(x + 11)$ **c)** $(x + 1)(x + 3)$
d) $(x + 1)(x + 13)$ **e)** $(x + 1)(x + 7)$ **f)** $(x + 1)(x + 5)$
g) $(x + 1)(x + 17)$ **h)** $(x + 1)(x + 19)$ **i)** $(x + 1)(x + 23)$

3. $ax^2 + bx + c$; pattern is $b = c + 1$; binomial factors are $(x + 1)(x + c)$

4. a, d, e; The terms of the binomials are perfect squares.

5. a) $(x - 2)(x + 2)$ **b)** $(x - 3)(x + 3)$ **c)** $(a - 1)(a + 1)$
d) $(y - 5)(y + 5)$ **e)** $(x - 4)(x + 4)$ **f)** $(x - 9)(x + 9)$
g) $(x - 6)(x + 6)$ **h)** $(z - 7)(z + 7)$ **i)** $(x - 8)(x + 8)$

6. a) $(x + 2)(x + 6)$ **b)** $(x + 2)(x + 9)$ **c)** $(a + 3)(a + 5)$
d) $(y + 3)(y + 9)$ **e)** $(x + 2)(x + 7)$ **f)** $(x + 2)(x + 8)$
g) $(x + 7)(x + 5)$ **h)** $(z + 3)(z + 6)$ **i)** $(x + 7)(x + 3)$

7. a) $(x - 5)(x + 4)$ **b)** $(x - 8)(x + 3)$ **c)** $(a - 5)(a + 3)$
d) $(y - 4)(y + 2)$ **e)** $(x - 7)(x + 4)$ **f)** $(x - 6)(x + 3)$
g) $(x - 7)(x + 2)$ **h)** $(z - 6)(z + 5)$ **i)** $(x - 9)(x + 4)$

8. a) $(x + 5)(x - 3)$ **b)** $(x + 6)(x - 3)$ **c)** $(a + 9)(a - 7)$
d) $(y + 8)(y - 3)$ **e)** $(x + 8)(x - 6)$ **f)** $(x + 12)(x - 3)$
g) $(x + 10)(x - 2)$ **h)** $(z + 4)(z - 3)$ **i)** $(x + 8)(x - 2)$

9. a) $(x - 1)(x - 3)$ **b)** $(x - 2)(x - 3)$ **c)** $(a - 2)(a - 5)$
d) $(y - 3)(y - 6)$ **e)** $(x - 6)(x - 5)$ **f)** $(x - 3)(x - 5)$
g) $(x - 8)(x - 3)$ **h)** $(z - 7)(z - 8)$ **i)** $(x - 12)(x - 4)$

10. a) $(3x - 5)(3x + 5)$
b) $4(x - 2y)(x + 2y)$
c) $(6a - 1)(6a + 1)$
d) $(8y - 5a)(8y + 5a)$
e) $(2x - 9)(2x + 9)$
f) $(7x - 9z)(7x + 9z)$
g) $(5x - 6)(5x + 6)$
h) $(8z - 11)(8z + 11)$
i) $(12x - 7)(12x + 7)$

11. a) $(x - 12)(x + 5)$
b) $(9x - 5)(9x + 5)$
c) $(a + 2)(a + 5)$
d) $(y + 11)(y - 7)$
e) $(x - 7)(x + 3)$
f) $(3x^2 - 5y)(3x^2 + 5y)$
g) $(x - 10)(x - 6)$
h) $(z - 7)(z - 12)$
i) $(x + 5)(x + 9)$

12. a) $(x + 1)^2$
b) $(x + 3)^2$
c) $(a + 5)^2$
d) $(y - 2)^2$
e) $(x - 6)^2$
f) $(x - 7)^2$
g) $(x + 4)^2$
h) $(z - 8)^2$
i) $(x - 3)^2$

14. b) The method is $2\sqrt{c} = b$.
c) $2\sqrt{c} = b$ or $-2\sqrt{c} = b$

15. a) $2(x + 2)(x + 4)$
b) $5(x - 3)(x + 3)$
c) $3(a + 4)(a - 3)$
d) $5(y - 1)(y - 2)$
e) $x(x - 8)(x + 3)$
f) $(x - 2)(x + 2)(x^2 + 4)$

16. a) $2x^2(x - 5)(x + 2)$
b) $-3(z - 8)(z + 3)$
c) $x(x + 3)^2$
d) $2x(x - 3)(x + 3)$
e) $4z(z + 7)(z - 2)$
f) $2x(5x - 6)(5x + 6)$

18. a) i) 2
ii) 3
iii) 7
iv) 5
v) 3
vi) 6
b) Parts i and ii have only 1 answer. The rest have more than 1 possible answer.
19. Two factors of c must add to b.

20. a) $\frac{1}{2}$
b) 1
c) $\left(x + \frac{1}{2}\right)^2$
d) $\left(x - \frac{1}{2}\right)^2$
e) The factors in parts c and d $\left(\pm\frac{1}{2}\right)$ have the same absolute value as part a, and their sum is the absolute value of part b (± 1).

2.8 Exercises, page 137

1. a) $(2x + 1)(x + 3)$
b) $(2x + 1)(x + 2)$
c) $(2a + 1)(a + 5)$
d) $(2y + 1)(y + 7)$
e) $(3x + 1)(x + 2)$
f) $(5x + 1)(x + 1)$

2. a) $(2x - 1)(x + 2)$
b) $2(x - 3)(x + 1)$
c) $(2a - 1)(a + 3)$
d) $(y - 5)(2y - 1)$
e) $(2x - 5)(x - 1)$
f) $(2m + 1)(m - 5)$

3. a) $(3y + 2)(y - 1)$
b) $(3w + 5)(w - 1)$
c) $(3a - 1)(a - 2)$
d) $(3x - 2)(x + 1)$
e) $(3x - 1)(x - 2)$
f) $(3z - 1)(z + 2)$

4. a) $(2n + 1)(3n + 2)$
b) $(3x + 1)(2x + 3)$
c) $(3a + 1)(2a + 5)$
d) $(6y + 7)(y + 1)$
e) $(3x + 7)(2x + 1)$
f) $(2x + 7)(3x + 1)$

5. a) $(2b - 1)(3b - 2)$
b) $(2x - 3)(3x - 1)$
c) $(2a - 5)(3a - 1)$
d) $(6y - 7)(y - 1)$
e) $(3x - 7)(2x - 1)$
f) $(2m - 7)(3m - 1)$

6. a) 4a, 5a; 4b, 5b; 4c, 5c; 4d, 5d; 4e, 5e; 4f, 5f
b) Change the $+$ signs to $-$ signs or vice versa.

7. a) $(2x - 1)(3x + 2)$
b) $(2x + 1)(3x - 2)$
c) $(3a - 1)(2a + 3)$
d) $(3a + 1)(2a - 3)$

e) $(3x + 5)(2x - 1)$
f) $(3x - 5)(2x + 1)$

8. a) $(2x + 3)(4x + 5)$
b) $(2x - 3)(4x - 5)$
c) $(4x + 3)(2x - 5)$
d) $(4x - 3)(2x + 5)$
e) $(2x + 3)(4x - 5)$
f) $(2x - 3)(4x + 5)$

9. a) $2(2y + 1)(3y + 5)$
b) $(3a - 2)(4a + 5)$
c) $(3a + 2)(4a - 5)$
d) $(4y - 3)(3y + 5)$
e) $(4y + 3)(3y - 5)$
f) $2(2x - 1)(3x - 5)$

10. a) $(5x + 2)(3x - 4)$
b) $(5x - 4)(3x - 2)$
c) $(5x + 4)(3x + 2)$
d) $(3m - 2)(5m + 4)$
e) $(5x - 2)(3x + 4)$
f) $(3m + 2)(5m - 4)$

11. a) $(2x + 1)(x + 2)$
b) $(5x - 1)(2x - 3)$
c) $(7a + 2)(a + 1)$
d) $(5y + 4)(y + 1)$
e) $2(3x - 4)(x + 1)$
f) $(2m + 1)(2m - 3)$

12. a) $(5t - 3)(2t + 5)$
b) $2(2x - 3)(x - 2)$
c) $(5c + 3)(c - 2)$
d) $(4y - 1)(y - 4)$
e) $(7x - 3)(x + 2)$
f) $(9x - 1)(x - 3)$

13. a) $(2x + 1)^2$
b) $(2x + 3)^2$
c) $(2a + 5)^2$
d) $(2y + 7)^2$
e) $(2x + 9)^2$
f) $(2x + 11)^2$

14. a) $(3x - 1)^2$
b) $(3x - 2)^2$
c) $(3x - 4)^2$
d) $(3x - 5)^2$
e) $(3x - 7)^2$
f) $(3x - 8)^2$

15. a) They are all perfect squares.

16. a) i) $(3x + 1)(x + 1)$; $(3x + 1)(x + 2)$; $(3x + 1)(x + 3)$
ii) $(3x + 1)(x + 1)$; $(3x + 2)(x + 1)$; $(3x + 3)(x + 1)$
iii) $(3x + 1)(x + 1)$; $(4x + 1)(x + 1)$; $(5x + 1)(x + 1)$
c) i) $3x^2 + 13x + 4$; $3x^2 + 16x + 5$; $3x^2 + 19x + 6$
ii) $3x^2 + 7x + 4$; $3x^2 + 8x + 5$; $3x^2 + 9x + 6$
iii) $6x^2 + 7x + 1$; $7x^2 + 8x + 1$; $8x^2 + 9x + 1$

17. a) 20
b) 16
c) 30
d) 84
e) 60
f) 24

18. a) i) $(3x + 4)(x + 2)$; $(3x + 8)(x + 1)$; $(3x + 2)(x + 4)$
ii) $(3x - 4)(x - 2)$; $(3x - 8)(x - 1)$; $(3x - 2)(x - 4)$
b) Yes. Explanations may vary.

19. a) $2(3x + 2)(2x + 1)$
b) $3(3x - 1)(2x - 3)$
c) $3(2a + 3)^2$
d) $5(2y + 1)(4y - 3)$
e) $4(2x + 3)(3x - 5)$
f) $5(3x - 4)^2$

2.9 Exercises, page 144

1. a) $y = 0$ or $y = 3$
b) $x = 0$ or $x = -4$
c) $a = 0$ or $a = \frac{2}{3}$
d) $x = 0$ or $x = -5$
e) $n = 0$ or $n = -\frac{2}{3}$
f) $q = 0$ or $q = \frac{2}{3}$

2. a) $y = -2$ or $y = -5$
b) $x = \pm 4$
c) $a = \frac{3}{2}$ or $a = \frac{2}{3}$
d) $x = -5$ or $x = 1$
e) $x = -\frac{7}{2}$ or $x = -2$
f) $m = \frac{3}{5}$ or $m = -\frac{3}{2}$

3. a) $x = 0$ or $x = -2$
b) $y = 0$ or $y = \frac{3}{2}$
c) $a = 0$ or $a = 5$
d) $x = 0$ or $x = -18$
e) $x = 0$ or $x = \frac{7}{5}$
f) $m = 0$ or $m = -2$

4. a) $x = -1$ or $x = -2$
b) $n = -3$ or $n = -4$
c) $y = -7$ or $y = 3$
d) $x = 5$ or $x = -3$
e) $a = 7$ or $a = 1$
f) $x = -3$

5. a) $x = \pm 2$
b) $y = \pm 3$
c) $a = 1$
d) $p = 2$ or $p = 8$

e) $x = \pm 6$ **f)** $x = 0$ or $x = 27$

6. a) $x = 7$ or $x = -5$ **b)** $n = 3$ or $n = -10$
   c) $y = 6$ **d)** $x = -8$ or $x = 5$
   e) $a = 12$ or $a = -5$ **f)** $x = -9$ or $x = 2$

7. a) $x = 0$ or $x = 6$ **b)** $n = -5$ or $n = 1$
   c) $y = 2$ or $y = 4$ **d)** $x = -8$ or $x = -3$
   e) $a = -8$ or $a = 6$ **f)** $x = -8$ or $x = 4$

8. a) $y = 0$ or $y = \frac{5}{3}$ **b)** $n = \pm 5$
   c) $y = \pm 6$ **d)** $x = 0$ or $x = -\frac{11}{7}$
   e) $a = \pm 7$ **f)** $x = -7$ or $x = -4$

9. a) $x = \pm \frac{3}{5}$ **b)** $x = \pm \frac{7}{2}$
   c) $a = \pm \frac{5}{6}$ **d)** $c = \pm \frac{8}{5}$
   e) $b = \pm \frac{3}{2}$ **f)** $x = \pm \frac{9}{7}$

10. a) $x = \pm \frac{6}{5}$ **b)** $z = \pm \frac{11}{8}$
   c) $m = \pm \frac{7}{12}$ **d)** $x = 3$ or $x = -4$
   e) $a = 4$ or $a = -2$ **f)** $n = \pm 3$

11. a) $y = \pm 7$ **b)** $x = -3$
   c) $y = 6$ or $y = 5$ **d)** $z = \pm \frac{3}{2}$
   e) $t = \pm \frac{5}{3}$ **f)** $n = 8$ or $n = -6$

12. a) $x = \frac{1}{5}$ or $x = -3$ **b)** $a = -1$ or $a = -\frac{3}{2}$
   c) $n = \frac{2}{3}$ or $n = -2$ **d)** $a = -\frac{5}{2}$ or $a = 3$
   e) $x = 1$ or $x = -\frac{7}{3}$ **f)** $m = -\frac{5}{4}$ or $m = 3$

13. a) $z = -\frac{2}{7}$ or $z = -3$ **b)** $x = \frac{7}{2}$ or $x = -5$
   c) $n = \frac{5}{3}$ or $n = -2$ **d)** $x = \frac{3}{4}$ or $x = 8$
   e) $a = \frac{3}{8}$ or $a = -4$ **f)** $n = -\frac{7}{3}$ or $n = -\frac{1}{4}$

14. a) $a = -\frac{8}{5}$ or $a = \frac{1}{3}$ **b)** $x = \frac{4}{9}$ or $x = 5$
   c) $m = -\frac{3}{7}$ or $m = 6$ **d)** $z = -\frac{9}{2}$ or $z = \frac{1}{7}$
   e) $x = \frac{8}{3}$ or $x = -\frac{4}{3}$ **f)** $n = \frac{3}{5}$ or $n = -\frac{5}{4}$

15. Yes. Explanations may vary.

16. a) $x = \frac{1}{2}$ or $x = -\frac{2}{3}$ **b)** $y = \frac{5}{4}$ or $y = -\frac{3}{2}$
   c) $a = -\frac{2}{3}$ or $a = -\frac{5}{4}$ **d)** $x = -\frac{2}{5}$ or $x = -\frac{4}{3}$
   e) $m = -5$ or $m = 4$ **f)** $x = \frac{1}{3}$ or $x = -\frac{5}{2}$

17. a) $x = -\frac{7}{2}$ or $x = \frac{1}{2}$ **b)** $m = \frac{4}{5}$ or $m = 1$
   c) $y = \frac{7}{5}$ or $y = \frac{3}{2}$ **d)** $x = \frac{5}{6}$ or $x = 2$
   e) $x = 3$ or $x = -1$ **f)** $a = -1$ or $a = -\frac{3}{2}$

18. 4 s

19. 5 s

20. a) i) $x = 5$ or $x = 1$ **ii)** $x = 2$ or $x = 4$
   b) i) yes   **ii)** $x^2 - 6x + 9 = 0$, $x = 3$

Self-Check 2.6–2.9, page 146

1. a) $5x^2 - x + 3$ **b)** $-2x^2 - 4x + 7$

2. a) $3m^3 - 12m^2 - 6m + 24$ **b)** $3m^2 + 6m + 3$
   c) $3w^2 + 14w + 13$ **d)** $2x^2 - 3x + 1$

3. a) $2x$ **b)** $12w$ **c)** $4mn$

4. a) $4(x - 3)$ **b)** $(a - 3)(a + 3)$
   c) $w(5 - 10y + yz)$ **d)** $(x - 2)(x + 2)$

5. a) $(a + 2)(a + 6)$ **b)** $(x - 7)(x + 3)$
   c) $2(x + 2)(x + 1)$ **d)** $3(x - 5)(x + 5)$

6. a) $(2x - 3)(x + 1)$ **b)** $(5x + 1)(x + 3)$
   c) $(3x - 1)(x + 2)$ **d)** $(5x + 1)^2$

7. a) $x = 0$ or $x = 3$ **b)** $x = \pm 1$
   c) $x = \frac{4}{7}$ or $x = \frac{1}{2}$ **d)** $x = \frac{4}{3}$

8. b) $x = -5$ or $x = 4$

Chapter 2 Review Exercises, page 148

1. a) $x = 6$ **b)** $y = 1$ **c)** $x = -2$

2. a) $x = \frac{12}{13}$ **b)** $y = -5$ **c)** $x = -\frac{2}{13}$ **d)** $x = -\frac{8}{5}$

3. a) $x = -1$ **b)** $x = 2$ **c)** $x = 7$

4. a) $r = \frac{A}{2\pi h}$ **b)** 1.9 cm

5. a) $m = 3$, $b = 4$ **b)** $m = \frac{2}{5}$, $b = 1$
   c) $m = -\frac{3}{2}$, $b = -3$ **d)** $m = 0$, $b = -2$
   e) $m = -\frac{2}{3}$, $b = 2$ **f)** $m = \frac{5}{2}$, $b = -\frac{7}{2}$

6. a)
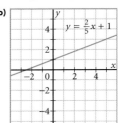

b)

c)
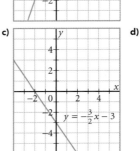

d)
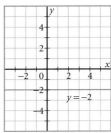

e)
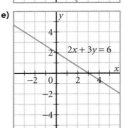

f)
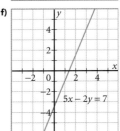

7. a)

$x + 2y - 4 = 0$

b)

$5x - 10y = 20$

c) $3y + 2x - 6 = 0$

d) $4x - 5y = 20$

e) $4y + 3x = 12$

f) $2x - y = 2$

e) $2x^3(x - 6)(x + 3)$ **f)** $(x - 3)(x + 3)(x^2 + 9)$

20. a) $(2y + 1)(y + 2)$ **b)** $(3x + 1)(x - 5)$
c) $(4m - 1)(m - 3)$

21. a) $(3y + 2)(2y + 1)$ **b)** $(2x - 1)(3x + 5)$
c) $(2m - 7)(5m - 1)$

22. a) $(2x + 3)(3x + 4)$ **b)** $(5a - 2)(3a + 4)$
c) $(4n - 7)(3n - 5)$

23. a) $2(2y + 1)(y - 3)$ **b)** $3(2x + 3)(3x - 5)$
c) $5(4m - 5)(2m - 3)$

24. a) $x = 0$ or $x = \frac{1}{2}$ **b)** $y = 3$ or $y = -5$
c) $x = 0$ or $x = -\frac{7}{2}$

25. a) $m = -4$ or $m = 2$ **b)** $x = -8$ or $x = -3$
c) $y = 3$ or $y = -2$ **d)** $x = -5$
e) $x = \pm 5$ **f)** $y = 3$ or $y = 4$

26. a) $x = 0$ or $x = \frac{5}{2}$ **b)** $x = 1$ or $x = 6$
c) $n = \pm \frac{8}{5}$ **d)** $x = 5$ or $x = -3$
e) $y = -2$ or $y = -3$ **f)** $w = \pm \frac{7}{3}$

27. a) $m = -\frac{1}{2}$ or $m = \frac{2}{3}$ **b)** $x = \frac{3}{4}$ or $x = 8$
c) $y = -\frac{2}{7}$ or $y = -3$ **d)** $x = -7$
e) $x = -\frac{7}{6}$ or $x = \frac{1}{3}$ **f)** $y = 9$ or $y = \frac{3}{2}$

28. 3 s

Chapter 2 Self-Test, page 152

1. a) $x = \frac{7}{2}$ **b)** $y = \frac{27}{7}$

2. a) $n = \frac{2S_n}{a + t_n}$ **b)** $n = 30$

3. a)

$y = -2x - 1$

b)

$2x + 5y = 10$

c)

$3x - 4y - 6 = 0$

4. a) $(3, 3)$ **b)** $(2, 3)$ **c)** $(2, -1)$

6. a) $2y^2 + 3y - 20$ **b)** $8x^3 - 10x^2 + 11x - 4$
c) $12x^2 - 26x + 12$ **d)** $-4a^2 - 16a + 18$

8. a) $(-1, 3)$ **b)** $(-1, 1)$ **c)** $(0, 2)$

9. a) $\left(\frac{8}{5}, -\frac{31}{5}\right)$ **b)** $(1, 4)$ **c)** $(-3, 2)$

10. a) $(4, 7)$ **b)** $(2, -3)$ **c)** $(-1, 6)$

11. a) $(-1, 3)$ **b)** $(-2, 0)$ **c)** $(-2, 2)$
d) $(5, -3)$ **e)** $(-1, -2)$ **f)** $(3, 0)$

12. a) $9x + 8$ **b)** $6x^2 - 7x + 12$
c) $x^2 - x - 20$ **d)** $12x^2 - 7x - 10$
e) $4y^2 - 49$ **f)** $6a^3 + 5a^2 - 8a - 3$

13. a) $2x^2 + 2x - 24$ **b)** $-12m^2 - 40m - 12$
c) $4y^2 - 20y + 25$

14. a) $-x^2 - 4x - 4$ **b)** $-2y^2 - 2y + 13$
c) $2x^2 + 13x + 19$ **d)** $4n + 2$

15. a) $7y^2 + 37y + 42$ **b)** $-x^2 + 9x + 6$
c) $-2x^2 - 14$ **d)** $2x^2 - 28x - 27$

16. a) $(x + 2)(x + 4)$ **b)** $(x - 6)(x + 3)$ **c)** $(a - 8)(a + 8)$
d) $(y + 7)(y - 2)$ **e)** $(5 - x)(5 + x)$ **f)** $(x - 4)(x - 5)$

17. a) $(4x - 3)(4x + 3)$ **b)** $(5x - 7y)(5x + 7y)$
c) $(a - 3)^2$ **d)** $(y + 8)^2$
e) $(n - 7)(n - 4)$ **f)** $9(3x - 4)(3x + 4)$

18. a) $2(x + 3)(x + 5)$ **b)** $3(x - 3)(x + 3)$
c) $3(a - 4)(a + 3)$ **d)** $5(y - 3)^2$
e) $-4(x + 5)(x - 3)$ **f)** $2(7 - x)(7 + x)$

19. a) $2x(x + 4)(x + 1)$ **b)** $3n(2n - 5)(2n + 5)$
c) $4a(a - 4)(a + 3)$ **d)** $-3y(y + 9)(y - 2)$

7. a) $2(2x + 4xy - 3y)$ **b)** $(y - 6)(y + 5)$
c) $(a - 7)(a + 7)$ **d)** $(3y - 2)(y + 1)$
e) $(x - 6)(x - 4)$ **f)** $(5x - 8)(5x + 8)$

8. a) $2(x + 6)(x - 3)$ **b)** $3(3m - 5n)(3m + 5n)$
c) $3(3a + 5)(2a - 1)$

9. a) $y = 0$ or $y = -\frac{7}{3}$ **b)** $x = -6$
c) $x = \frac{5}{2}$ or $x = -\frac{2}{3}$

10. a) $2x^2 - 15x - 8$; $2x^2 + 15x - 8$; $2x^2 + 6x - 8$; $2x^2 - 6x - 8$
b) 4

11. no

Cumulative Review, page 154

1. 7.4 m

2. 19.5 m

3. a) $34°, 146°$ **b)** $54°$ **c)** $37°$ **d)** $69°$

4. a) $\angle B = 72°$; $c \doteq 48.5$ cm; $b \doteq 46.2$ cm
b) $\angle D = 90°$; $e \doteq 2.1$ mm; $f \doteq 2.9$ mm
c) $\angle X = 90°$; $\angle Y \doteq 53°$; $\angle Z \doteq 37°$
d) $\angle P \doteq 61°$; $\angle R \doteq 9°$; $r \doteq 22.1$ mm

5. a)

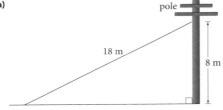

pole

18 m

8 m

b) $26°$

6. a)

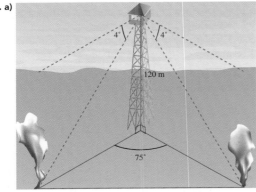

4° 4°

120 m

75°

b) 1716 m

7. a) $\angle A \doteq 42°$ or $138°$ **b)** $\angle B \doteq 53°$
c) $\angle E \doteq 74°$ **d)** $\angle F \doteq 81°$ or $99°$

8. $39°$

9. 3.6 km

10. a) $a = 3$ **b)** $b = -5$ **c)** $x = -\frac{20}{9}$ **d)** $x = -\frac{40}{13}$

11. a) $v = \frac{d}{t} - \frac{1}{2}at$ **b)** 50 m/s

12. a) $m = 3$, $b = -2$ **b)** $m = -\frac{4}{3}$, $b = -5$ **c)** $m = \frac{2}{7}$, $b = 3$

13. a) $(2, -5)$ **b)** $(1, 4)$

14. a) $C = 100 + 5d$; $C = 15d$
b) Kadeisha; It would cost $30 less.

15. a) $7x^2 + 4$ **b)** $x^2 + x - 6$
c) $2x^2 - 16x - 10$ **d)** $38x^2 + 108x + 82$

16. a) $(y + 7)(y - 3)$ **b)** $(a - 4)(a - 5)$
c) $(b - 8)(b + 2)$ **d)** $(11 - x)(11 + x)$
e) $(6x - 5y)(6x + 5y)$ **f)** $5g(g + 5)(g - 2)$

17. a) $(3x + 1)(x - 2)$ **b)** $(2y + 7)(3y + 4)$
c) $(5a + 2)(2a + 1)$ **d)** $2(2g - 5)(g - 2)$
e) $2(3x + 2)(2x + 1)$ **f)** $6(3d - 2)(4d + 3)$

18. a) $a = 0$ or $a = 2$ **b)** $x = 5$ or $x = 1$ **c)** $y = 6$ or $y = -3$

Mathematics Placement Test, page 162

1. a) i) $\frac{1}{4}$ **ii)** $\frac{1}{3}$
b) i) 0.25 **ii)** 0.33

2. a) 33 **b)** 16 **c)** 6 **d)** $\frac{2}{3}$

3. a) 5.261 **b)** -10.9 **c)** -5.85 **d)** 8.1
e) 0.0012 **f)** 0.298 **g)** 4 **h)** 53.96

4. a) 35% **b)** 500% **c)** 5.6%

5. a) i) 0.15 **ii)** 1.4 **iii)** 0.002
b) i) $\frac{3}{20}$ **ii)** $\frac{7}{5}$ **iii)** $\frac{1}{500}$

6. a) 60 **b)** 22% **c)** 500

7. a) $33.00 **b)** $39.75

8. a) $x = 6$ **b)** $x = 2$ **c)** $x = -4$

9. a) $(6, 2)$ **b)** $(4, 1)$

10. a) $A = 14.2$ cm **b)** $M = 35$ **c)** $K = 2.8$ kg

11. a) $A = 84$ cm^2; $P = 38$ cm
b) $A = 314$ m^2; $C = 62.8$ m
c) $A = 1.7$ mm^2; $P = 6$ mm

12. a) $\angle A = 55°$ **b)** $a = 9.84$ **c)** $b = 6.84$

13. a) 9 feet, 10 inches **b)** 44.793 m **c)** 38 L

Chapter 3 Measurement in Design

Necessary Skills

1 Review: Operations with Fractions

Exercises, page 169

1. a) $\frac{4}{5}$ **b)** $\frac{9}{4}$ **c)** $2\frac{3}{4}$ **d)** $-\frac{3}{2}$

2. a) 0.8 **b)** 2.25 **c)** 2.75 **d)** -1.5

3. a) $\frac{1}{14}$ **b)** $\frac{44}{15}$ **c)** $\frac{11}{24}$ **d)** $\frac{17}{10}$

4. a) $\frac{4}{3}$ **b)** $-\frac{49}{60}$ **c)** -2 **d)** $-\frac{3}{10}$

1. a) 0 g **b)** 500 mm

  000 mL **d)** 8000 mg

2. a) 0.4 L **b)** 0.002 kg **c)** 10 km **d)** 0.05 m

3 New: Precision and Rounding
Exercises, page 173

1. a) 7.2 **b)** 2.97 **c)** 9
  d) 890 **e)** 2.2952 **f)** 62

2. a) 11.27 **b)** 900 **c)** 7 000 000
  d) 1.4 **e)** 40.00 **f)** 8

3.1 Exercises, page 179

1. a) 160 cm **b)** 18 inches
  c) 3400 m **d)** 3520 yards

2. a) 7 feet **b)** 5.959 km **c)** 7.07 m **d)** 5 yards

3. a) pounds **b)** inches **c)** yards **d)** gallons
  e) inches **f)** miles **g)** tons

4. a) i) 5.1 cm **ii)** 7.2 cm **iii)** 3.5 cm
  b) i) 2 inches **ii)** $2\frac{13}{16}$ inches **iii)** $1\frac{3}{8}$ inches

5. a) 76.2 mm **b)** 182.9 cm **c)** 12.9 km **d)** 18.3 m

6. a) $\frac{7}{10}$ ounces **b)** 11 pounds
  c) $2\frac{1}{5}$ pounds **d)** $2\frac{1}{5}$ tons

7. a) 3.3 L **b)** 15.1 L **c)** 177.4 mL **d)** 1892.5 mL

8. Yes. The saw can cut wood up to $4\frac{1}{8}$" thick, and the wood is approximately $3\frac{15}{16}$" thick.

11. a) 42 inches **b)** 3960 yards **c)** 90 inches
  d) $2\frac{1}{2}$ miles **e)** $4\frac{2}{3}$ feet **f)** $1\frac{1}{4}$ miles

12. a) $\frac{17}{20}$ ounces **b)** $6607\frac{9}{10}$ lbs
  c) $1\frac{1}{3}$ gallons **d)** 11 tons

13. a) 1310.6 cm **b)** 0.9 L **c)** 1.6 km
  d) 6.4 m **e)** 113.6 L **f)** 2.3 kg

14. $1\frac{3}{4}$"

15. $1\frac{7}{32}$"

16. 105 km/h

17. $14\frac{1}{2}$ gallons

18. $1\frac{1}{4}$" screws will go completely through one board and most of the way through the second board to be secure. Explanations may vary.

19. 50 mi/h = 80.45 km/h; The speed limit is essentially the same.

20. 42.2 km

21. 3

22. Yes. The truck is approximately 1.93 tons, which is below the load restriction of 2 tons.

23. 99

3.2 Exercises, page 187

1. a) 14.6 cm **b)** 15.0 cm **c)** 25.2 cm **d)** 7 inches

3. a) 38 feet **b)** 72.5 m **c)** 39 inches **d)** 21.8 cm

4. a) 3.8 m **b)** 11 inches **c)** 28 mm

5. a) 157 mm **b)** 22" **c)** 94 cm
  d) 11 m **e)** $20\frac{2}{5}$' **f)** $75\frac{2}{5}$ yards

6. Agree. Since $d = 2r$, the equations are the same.

7. 144 feet

8. a) 3200 m **b)** 3.2 km **c)** 2 miles

9. a) 2.7 m/s **b)** 9.6 km/h
  c) 6 miles per hour

10. 3

11. a) i) 5400 m **ii)** 5.4 km **iii)** $3\frac{2}{5}$ miles
  b) 1921 m

12. a) 39.6 cm **b)** 40 inches

13. No. A 50' hose will not reach all areas of the yard, as the diagonal is $52\frac{1}{5}$'.

14. $31\frac{2}{5}$ feet

15. 23.1 m

16. 28 inches

17. 6

18. a) 88 feet **b)** $31\frac{1}{2}$ feet

19. 16 m

20. 24.4 cm

21. $P = ns$; the number of sides multiplied by the length of each side

3.3 Exercises, page 194

1. a) 12 square inches **b)** 39.3 cm^2
  c) 21.8 m^2 **d)** $19\frac{3}{5}$ square feet

2. a) 1768 mm^2 **b)** 28.4 cm^2
  c) $12\frac{1}{4}$ square yards **d)** 130.7 m^2

3. a) $113\frac{1}{10}$ square feet **b)** $73\frac{1}{2}$ square feet
  c) 152 m^2 **d)** $32\frac{1}{2}$ square feet
  e) 227.0 cm^2

4. 27.2 cm^2

5. a) 29 cm^2 **b)** 25 square inches
  c) 18 574.0 mm^2 **d)** 62.9 m^2
  e) 169.3 cm^2 **f)** 7627.4 square feet

6. property A

7. 3

8. $1238.53

9. a) 196.4 m^2 **b)** 641 square feet

10. No. The area of one rectangle is 21 cm^2; the area of the other rectangle is 24 cm^2.

11. The rectangular-faced sander covers 54 square inches; the circular-faced sander covers $50\frac{1}{3}$ square inches.

12. $70\frac{7}{10}$ square feet

13. Yes. The total area is $55\frac{2}{5}$ square yards.

14. a) 8.5 m   **b)** 144 inches

15. 969 square feet

16. 517 square feet

17. 274

18. 120

19. You must square both sides of the equation.
$$(1\,\text{foot})^2 \doteq (0.3048\,\text{m})^2$$
$$1\,\text{square foot} \doteq 0.0929\,\text{m}^2$$

Self-Check 3.1–3.3, page 198

1. a) 60 inches   **b)** 6000 mL   **c)** 12.8 m   **d)** 45.4 L
   e) 15 pounds, 6 ounces   **f)** 3 feet 11 inches

2. a) 74.3 m   **b)** 34 inches
   c) $28\frac{5}{16}$ inches   **d)** $19\frac{1}{2}$ inches

3. 8.6 cm

4. a) $120.8\,\text{m}^2$ **b)** $40\frac{1}{2}$ square feet
   c) $14\frac{1}{4}$ square inches   **d)** $56.8\,\text{cm}^2$

5. a) 80
   b) The $8\frac{1}{4}$" saw is the most economical.
   c) Answer depends on how much urethane is required for
     1 coat.

3.4 Exercises, page 202

1. a) $63.4\,\text{cm}^3$ **b)** $650.3\,\text{cm}^3$ **c)** $178\frac{1}{2}$ cubic feet

2. a) $V = 84\,000\,\text{mm}^3$; $SA = 11\,800\,\text{mm}^2$
   b) $V \doteq 503$ cubic inches; $SA \doteq 352$ square inches
   c) $V = 6.8$ cubic feet; $SA = 27.2$ square feet

3. a) 96 cubic feet   **b)** $475.2\,\text{cm}^3$ **c)** $3.2\,\text{m}^3$

4. 3299 square feet

5. 2016 cubic feet

6. The sandbox does not have a lid, so the sand can pile up
   above ground level.

7. $58.7\,\text{m}^2$

8. 1178 L

9. 24 square yards

10. a) 17 cm   **b)** 2.2 m

11. 45 mm

12. 44 cubic feet

13. $28.8\,\text{m}^3$

14. $8910

15. 60 cubic yards

16. 98 L

18. approx. $1800\,\text{cm}^3$

3.5 Exercises, page 208

1. a) $82\,\text{cm}^3$ **b)** $132\frac{1}{2}$ cubic inches
   c) $9533\,\text{mm}^3$ **d)** 600 cubic feet
   e) $1240\,\text{m}^3$ **f)** $2392\,\text{cm}^3$

2. 264 square inches

3. a) $67.3\,\text{cm}^2$ **b)** $32.3\,\text{m}^2$

4. a) $141.1\,\text{cm}^2$ **b)** $150\frac{4}{5}$ square inches
   c) $14.1\,\text{m}^2$

5. a) $169.6\,\text{cm}^2$ **b)** $201\frac{1}{10}$ square inches
   c) $21.2\,\text{m}^2$

6. a) $314.2\,\text{m}^2$ **b)** $201.1\,\text{cm}^2$
   c) $452\frac{2}{5}$ square inches

7. a) $904.8\,\text{m}^3$ **b)** $904.8\,\text{cm}^3$
   c) $268\frac{1}{10}$ cubic feet

8. a) $V \doteq 21.3\,\text{cm}^3$; $SA \doteq 35.8\,\text{cm}^2$
   b) $V \doteq 39.3\,\text{m}^3$; $SA \doteq 51.1\,\text{m}^2$
   c) $V = 32\,000\,\text{mm}^3$; $SA \doteq 5059.6\,\text{mm}^2$
   d) $V \doteq 142.5\,\text{cm}^3$; $SA \doteq 125.5\,\text{cm}^2$

9. 0.5 g

10. $V = 382$ cubic inches; $SA \doteq 255$ square inches

11. $855\,\text{cm}^2$

12. a) 155   **b)** $17\,255\,\text{cm}^2$

13. a) $152\,731\,260\,\text{km}^2$ **b)** 6%

14. $1267\,\text{m}^3$

15. $38.6\,\text{m}^2$

16. 12 828 cubic feet

17. 12 cm

18. 14.5 mm

19. $V \doteq 203.7\,\text{cm}^3$; $SA \doteq 249.4\,\text{cm}^2$

3.6 Exercises, page 216

1. a) 132 square inches   **b)** $144\,\text{m}^2$

2. a) 3240 cubic feet   **b)** $1009\frac{1}{2}$ square feet

3. $V \doteq 754\,\text{cm}^3$; $SA \doteq 414.7\,\text{cm}^2$

4. $SA = \pi r(r + 2h + s)$

5. $1455

6. 20

7. 3

8. 9871 cubic feet

9. 31 252.3 L

10. 21.6 L

11. 6 107 256 square feet

12. $3141.59

13. $4863.15

14. No. The room dimensions of 18' by 14' do not divide
   evenly by the drywall dimensions of 4' by 8'.

15. 72.7 cubic feet

16. $2293.44

17. $573.35

18. 9 batches

19. a) 381.2 cm^3 **b)** 4.5 cm

21. 10 412 square feet

Self-Check 3.4–3.6, page 220

1. a) 2 144 660.6 L   **b)** 22

2. 8668.8 g

3. a) $42\frac{2}{5}$ cubic inches   **b)** 0.39 cm^3
   c) $\frac{5}{6}$ cubic feet

4. 104 000 cm^3

5. a) $98.00
   b) after calculating surface area, to avoid too many rounding errors

Chapter 3 Review Exercises, page 226

1. a) inches   **b)** ounces   **c)** miles   **d)** gallons

2. a) 96 inches   **b)** 2000 g   **c)** 5720 yards   **d)** 3750 mL

3. a) 11.0 m   **b)** 7.6 L   **c)** 579.1 cm   **d)** 0.9 kg

4. a) $2\frac{3}{4}$ inches   **b)** 11 pounds
   c) $101\frac{2}{5}$ fluid ounces   **d)** 71 yards, 3 inches

5. a) 46 feet   **b)** 50.5 m   **c)** $26\frac{1}{4}$ feet   **d)** 24 inches

6. a) 163.4 cm   **b)** $28\frac{1}{4}$ feet   **c)** 22 yards

7. 49.8 cm

8. 45.5 cm

9. a) 745.1 m^2 **b)** $40\frac{1}{2}$ square feet
   c) 144 square inches   **d)** 93.8 cm^2

10. 52.3 cm^2

11. a) 108 square inches   **b)** 225 cm^2
   c) 11 426.5 m^2

12. No. The area of the two bathroom floors is 183 square feet.

13. a) V = 160 cubic feet; SA = 184 square feet
   b) $V \doteq 302$ m^3; $SA \doteq 251$ m^2
   c) $V \doteq 32.8$ cm^3; $SA \doteq 61.4$ cm^2
   d) V = 836 cubic inches; $SA \doteq 457$ square inches

14. 2.7 cubic yards

15. 3

16. a) 162 cubic inches   **b)** 183.5 cm^3
   c) 17 360 mm^3 **d)** 1475 m^3

17. 302 square inches

18. $SA \doteq 1017.9$ cm^2; $V \doteq 3053.6$ cm^3

19. SA = 85 square inches; $V \doteq 45\frac{1}{2}$ cubic inches

20. V = 13.5 m^3; SA = 27 m^2

21. the super kit; The pool is 21 136 gallons.

22. $V = s^3\left(\frac{\pi}{6} + 1\right)$

23. vinyl flooring cut from a roll

Maintaining Your Mastery, page 231

1. a) $4x + 8$ **b)** $-7w^2 + 21w - 7$
   c) $5y^2 + 40y + 80$

2. a) $2x(3w + 4y - 2z)$ **b)** $3(b^2 - 3)$
   c) $(m + 4)(m + 7)$ **d)** $(x - 2)(x + 2)$
   e) $(x - 5)(x + 4)$ **f)** $(4w - 5z)(4w + 5z)$

3. a) $(2x + 3)(x + 1)$ **b)** $(2x + 1)(3x - 4)$
   c) $(3x - 5)(4x - 3)$

4. a) $x = 4$ **b)** $b = 8$
   c) $y = -16$ **d)** $x = -1$ or $x = -2$
   e) $m = 6$ or $m = -4$ **f)** $x = -\frac{1}{2}$ or $x = \frac{3}{2}$

Chapter 3 Self-Test, page 232

1. a) 108 inches   **b)** 400 ounces
   c) 6 gallons, 32 fluid ounces   **d)** 12 feet, 0 inches
   e) 41.6 L   **f)** 160.9 km
   g) 33 pounds, 1 ounce

2. a) 16"   **b)** 30"   **c)** 22.6 cm   **d)** 37.6 cm

3. a) 139 cm^2 **b)** 95.4 cm^2

4. 16 m^3

5. dome tent

6. 197 cubic yards of top soil; 2300 rolls of sod

Chapter 4   Geometry in Design

Necessary Skills

1 Review: Translations
Exercises, page 237

1. a) 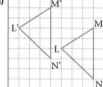   **b)**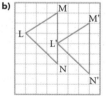

2 Review: Reflections
Exercises, page 238

1. a) yes   **b)** no
2. a) yes   **b)** no

3 Review: Rotations
Exercises, page 240

1. 60°

4.1 Exercises, page 246

2. a) i) parallelograms, hexagons **ii)** octagons, squares
   iii) hexagons, squares **iv)** triangles, squares
   v) triangles, squares, rectangles
   vi) squares, pentagons
b) i) yes   **ii)** no   **iii)** no
   iv) yes   **v)** no   **vi)** no

3. no

4. b) no

5. a) It depends on the type/size of the triangle.
   b) yes

6.

	a)	**b)**
i)	parallelograms squares triangles	4 green and 4 grey 4 orange 8 white
ii)	large triangles small triangles	4 red and 4 grey 16 white
iii)	squares triangles	4 white and 4 yellow 8 purple and 8 white
iv)	large squares small squares parallelograms triangles	4 white 8 white 8 green 12 green and 12 white

4.2 Exercises, page 252

1.

Rotation Symmetry	Reflection Symmetry	No Symmetry
H, I, N, O, S, X, Z	A, B, C, D, E, H, I, K, M, O, T, U, V, W, X, Y	F, G, J, L, P, Q, R

2. a) rotation, translation   **b)** reflection
   c) translation, reflection   **d)** translation
   e) rotation   **f)** rotation

4. a) 51.4°, 72°, 360°   **b)** yes

8. a) i) rotation   **ii)** translation
   iii) reflection, rotation   **iv)** rotation, reflection
   v) rotation, reflection   **vi)** translation
   vii) translation, reflection   **viii)** rotation, reflection
   ix) reflection   **x)** reflection

4.3 Exercises, page 261

4. a) The top face becomes less circular as the can is raised.
   b) The top of the cylinder is almost at the eye level of
   the observer.
   The top of the cylinder is way below the eye level of
   the observer.

5. b)

c) VW lies below the height of IJ.
The back of the building is not as tall as the front.
d) W = L and V = N

7. a)

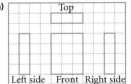

b)

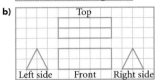

c)

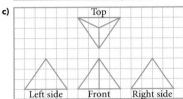

Self-Check 4.1–4.4, page 269

1.

	a)	**b)** 30 blocks are needed
i)	large triangle medium triangle small triangle	60 orange and 60 white 180 orange and 180 white 120 orange and 120 white
ii)	large triangle small triangle large square small square	240 white, 240 blue, 120 green 240 orange 120 green 120 blue

2. a) reflection—line of symmetry is the horizontal line
   through the centre of the middle arrow
   b) rotation—180° angle of rotation

3.

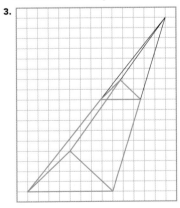

5. a)

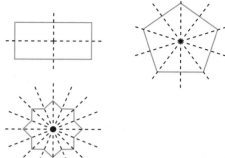

b) 3; An equilateral triangle has the least number of mirror lines.

4.5 Exercises, page 273

1. a) cube   **c)** rectangular prism

4.7 Exercises, page 288

4. 646
5. a) 1304   **b)** 50 mm

Chapter 4 Review Exercises, page 295

1. 60° and 120°
2. ii), iv), v), vi)
5.

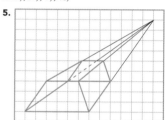

9. a) cube   **b)** triangular prism
14. a) 798
    b) The height of the bricks, cap, and mortar joints does not divide evenly into the height of the wall. The wall will be slightly higher than 1.5 m.
16. $r = 0.44$ m; $h = 10.1$ m

Maintaining Your Mastery, page 299

1. a) $x = 3$ **b)** $y = -4$ **c)** $v = \frac{11}{4}$
  d) $x = -2$ **e)** $p = -5$ **f)** $m = \frac{4}{5}$
2. a) $3b + 3$ **b)** $4x^2 - 8x$ **c)** $-6q^2 + 9q$
  d) $4w^3 + 12w^2 - 4w$ **e)** $-11k + 40$
3. a) $5(x - 3)$ **b)** $-3(z - 4)$
  c) $xy(7xy + 14x - 4)$ **d)** $(w + 4)(w + 2)$
  e) $(m - 3)^2$ **f)** $(h - 7)(h + 3)$

4. a) $x = -2$ or $x = -\frac{1}{3}$ **b)** $x = -\frac{1}{2}$ or $x = 5$
  c) $x = \frac{3}{5}$ or $x = 2$

Chapter 4 Self-Test, page 300

1. a) Interior angles are 135°. 360° is not evenly divisible by 135°, therefore they will not tessellate.
  b) Interior angles of any triangle must have a sum of 180°, and therefore are factors of 360°.

2. a)

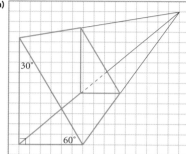

b) The triangles are similar. The corresponding sides are proportional and the corresponding angles are equal.

6.

Cumulative Review, page 302

1. a) $\angle A = 60°$, $b \doteq 4.3$ cm, $c = 2.1$ cm
  b) $\angle D \doteq 58.7°$, $\angle E \doteq 85.3°$, $f \doteq 4.1$ mm
  c) $\angle N = 72.0°$, $k \doteq 7.6$ m, $m \doteq 9.3$ m
2. a) $x^2 - x - 12$ **b)** $6y^3 - 13y^2 - 2y + 1$
  c) $6x^2 + 5x - 4$ **d)** $8y^2 + 12y$
3. a) $(x - 4)(x - 3)$ **b)** $(2y - 9)(2y + 9)$
  c) $2(2x - 5)(x + 3)$
4. a) $x = -4$ or $x = 3$ **b)** $y = \frac{3}{2}$ or $y = -\frac{2}{5}$
5. a) $96"$ **b)** 640 oz.   **c)** $10\frac{1}{10}"$
  d) $3\frac{1}{5}$ gal.   **e)** 68.1 kg   **f)** 128.7 km
6. a) $72'$ **b)** 12 km
7. a) $SA = 28\,200$ mm^2; $V = 252\,000$ mm^3
  b) $SA = 233.4$ cm^2, $V = 222.5$ cm^3
8. $SA = 187.7$ m^2, $V = 63$ m^3
9. a) 150 square feet   **b)** 19 pieces
  c) 25 square feet
10. approx. $4\frac{2}{5}$ gallons
11.

Rotation Symmetry	Reflection Symmetry	No Symmetry
1, 8, 11	1, 3, 8, 10, 11, 13, 18	2, 4, 5, 6, 7, 9, 12, 14, 15, 16, 17, 19, 20

12. a)

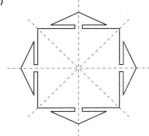

b) 90°, 180°, 270°

13.

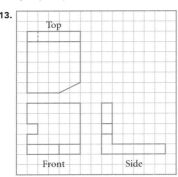

14. a) b)

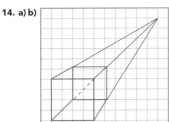

Chapter 5 Sampling

Necessary Skills

1 Review: Frequency Tables

Exercises, page 313

1. a) 5   **b)** 10   **c)** 0.5

2.

Interval	Tally	Frequency
0–2	II	2
2–4	IIII	4
4–6	IIII I	6
6–8	IIII II	7
8–10	IIII	4
10–12	III	3

2 Review: Graphing Data

Exercises, page 316

1.

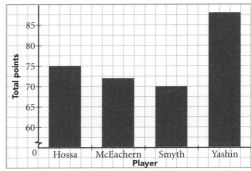

Total Points in the 2000–2001 NHL Hockey Season for 4 Ottawa Senators

2. a)

Interval	Frequency
155–160	3
160–165	3
165–170	4
170–175	3
175–180	2
180–185	7
185–190	4
190–195	1
195–200	1
200–205	2

b) Height of Students in a Grade 11 Class

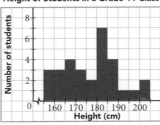

c) 180–185 cm

3 Review: Drawing Scatter Plots and Lines of Best Fit

Exercises, page 318

1. a) c) Height versus Age for 10 Students

b) Yes. Most of the points lie close to a straight line.

2. a) c)

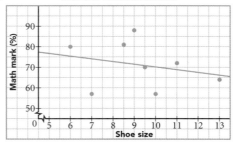

Shoe Size versus Math Mark

b) No. The size of your feet is not related to your mathematical ability.

d) No. The data do not fit a straight line.

5.1 Exercises, page 322

1. a) all people who travel by VIA rail
   b) all provincial taxpayers
   c) all Ontario parents with children in daycare

2. a) all urban high school students who drive to school
   b) all students who eat in the school cafeteria
   c) all students who participate in school athletic teams

3. a) primary **b)** secondary
   c) primary **d)** secondary

4. a) secondary **b)** secondary
   c) primary **d)** secondary

5. a) The number of drivers is too large to poll.
   b) If you tested all batteries, you would not have any to sell.
   c) You do not want to spoil every 2-L carton.
   d) It would be difficult to collect data on such a large population.

6. a) secondary **b)** primary
   c) primary **d)** secondary

7. A valid survey sample means that the results of the survey represent the entire population.

8. a) No. The survey is not valid as it only surveys the readers of the magazine.
   b) No. The survey is not reliable because it is a biased sample. Only magazine readers interested in the topic will respond.

10. A population is an entire group of items or individuals. A sample is a small group representative of the population.
   a) faster, easier; results may not be valid
   b) results are always valid; difficult, expensive, time-consuming

12. a) No. The two grade 12 classes are not representative of the entire school population.
   b) No. The results are biased because students in the other grades were not surveyed.

5.2 Exercises, page 329

1. a) all students at the school **b)** self-selected

c) Yes. It only surveys the students, and only those who feel strongly will make a suggestion.

2. a) all patient records at the hospital
   b) systematic
   c) Yes. Since each patient record was selected systematically by number, the sample should represent the entire population.

3. Friends and family members do not represent the entire population.

4. No. Only those people who watch that channel, who want to see the movie, and who are willing to pay $0.75 will be included in the sample.

5. a) people who make fur coats; animal rights activists
   b) exotic pet store owners; biologists and animal rights activists

6. No. Only the first hour's production is in the sample. The entire day's production should be sampled.

7. a) It depends on the population that the sample is taken from.
   b) the size of the overall population, and what percentage of the population will provide valid results

8. a) women may be pregnant; children are still developing; seniors may have complicating illnesses
   b) Yes, but only for young and middle-aged men.

11. a) Give each student a number and randomly pick the numbers.
   b) Every nth parking spot is selected.
   c) Select a specific geographic area of the city. All residents in the area are in the sample.
   d) A field is divided into sections. A random sample is selected from each section of the field proportional to the size of the section.

12. systematic sample; Survey every nth student going through the cafeteria line.

13. a) Divide the city into geographic areas, then randomly select one section as the cluster sample.
   b) Divide the city into sections, then randomly select a sample from each section that is proportional to the size of the section.

14. Yes. All the wine in the bottle will be the same.

15. simple random or systematic sample

16. selecting calculators randomly throughout the day from the production line

17. a) It biased the sample to only those who subscribed to the magazine, and to only those who wished to respond.
   b) The sample may not have been large enough and was probably biased.
   c) All American voters had an equal chance of being selected, and the sample was a true random sample.

18. a) The poll was biased because it was a self-selected sample of Europeans who read Time magazine on the web.
   c) Yes. Explanations may vary.

19. Yes. Explanations may vary.

20. a) Use a stratified random sample and select 100 students: 27 from grade 9, 30 from grade 10, 23 from grade 11, and 20 from grade 12.
  b) This best represents the school population by grade level.

5.3 Exercises, page 335

1. a) The question asks if students like mathematics, not whether they will take an optional math course.
    "Would you take an optional math course? Yes   No"
  b) Only 2 choices are given, which leaves out many students.
    "What language is your mother tongue?"

3. a) The question is leading.
    "Would you support an increase in municipal taxes?"
  b) The question asks about past donation, not about future donation.
    "Would you be willing to donate blood? Yes   No"

4. a) No. They are both leading questions.
  b) first question: more responses for
    second question: more responses against
  c) "Should stores be open on Sunday?"

5. a) No. The last purchase may not be typical.
  b) "What is your favourite food or drink sold in the school cafeteria?"

6. a) The owner wishes to find out about customer satisfaction regarding food and service.
  b) No. Some customers may wish to answer yes to one part of the question and no to the other.
  c) "Are you happy with the quality of food served in the restaurant? If not, explain why."
    "Are you happy with the quality of service in the restaurant? If not, explain why."

7. a) No. The question does not address the issue of quantity or quality of resources.
  b) "For your last project or assignment, were you able to find all the resources you needed in the school library?"

8. a) The first question is from the Ontario Secondary School Teachers' Federation. The second question is from the *National Post*.
  b) "The Ontario government is proposing to give tax credits to parents whose children attend private schools. Do you agree or disagree with this idea?"

9. b) No. Both questions are leading.

10. the sample size, the population that represents the sample, the types of quesitons asked, a copy of the survey if possible

Self-Check 5.1–5.3, page 339

1. a) all people who drive in and around Metro Toronto and the bypass area
  b) all people in the workforce
  c) all property taxpayers in Burlington, Ontario

3. a) secondary   **b)** secondary   **c)** primary

4. No. The tasters only tried the chilis that they wanted to try, not every one. A different sample of tasters would try

different chilis, and would probably choose a different winner.

5. a) The question is vague.
  b) "When you leave high school, do you plan to go to
    A. University   B. The Workplace   C. College?"

5.4 Exercises, page 345

1. a)

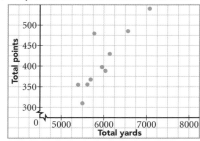

  b) Yes. As the total yards increase, the total points also increase.

2. a)

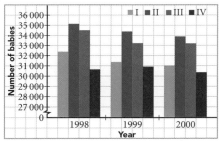

  b) In each year, more babies are born in quarters II and III than in I and IV. The number of babies in each quarter decreases each year except for the fourth quarter.

3. a) Enter them as decimals. The first quarter would be halfway between 1998 and 1998.25, the second would be halfway between 1998.25 and 1998.5, and so on.
  b)

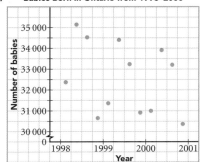

  c) The scatter plot is harder to interpret, but the same conclusions can be drawn.

4. a) Enrolment in 5 Toronto Colleges on Sept. 18, 2000 for Ministry-Funded Programs

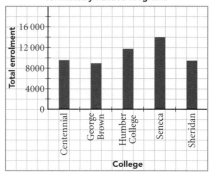

5. a) histogram: used for continuous data
b) bar graph: used for discrete data
c) scatter plot: used for data in sets of ordered pairs when we want to examine the relationship between the data

6. a) Percent of Games Won versus Average Points Scored per Game for the WNBA 2000 Season

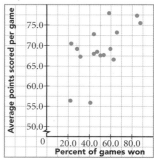

b) No. A line of best fit does not represent the data.

7. a) bar graph; The data are discrete, or counted.
b) Average Number of People in Canadian Families

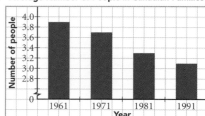

c) Yes. You could use a scatterplot to look for a linear relationship.

8. a) 2000–2001 NHL Season

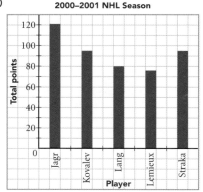

b) the graph; It clearly shows the differences between the players.

10. b)

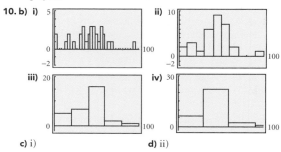

c) i)   **d)** ii)

e) If the horizontal scale interval is too small, there are too many bars and the graph is hard to interpret. If the interval is too large, the data are grouped together and the graph is not informative.
f) Changing the Yscl value changes the vertical scale. The differences in the heights of the bars can be made more or less obvious by changing this scale.

11. b) because the intervals should be on the horizontal axis and the frequency on the vertical axis
c) Xmin = 30   the lowest mark on the test
Xmax = 100   the highest mark
Xscl = 10   the difference between midpoints is 10
Ymin = 0   to ensure that the lowest frequency will show on the graph
Ymax = 12   to ensure that the highest frequency will show on the graph
Yscl = 1   some of the frequencies differ by only 1

d)

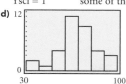

5.5 Exercises, page 353

1. The sizes of the sections are not proportional to the percentages shown.

2. The $5m bag should only be $\frac{5}{3}$ bigger than the $3m bag, but it appears much larger.

3. a) If the poll was taken 20 times, 19 times it would show that 47% to 55% of Canadians think the Prime Minister is doing a good job.

   b) No. The range is 47% to 55%, so the results could be below a majority.

4. a)

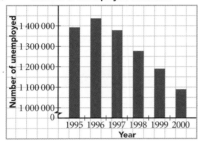

Number of Unemployed Canadians

5. a) The differences in the value of the CDN$ are exaggerated by the vertical scale. Also, the values shown do not represent the entire year, but only the value on one day.

   b)

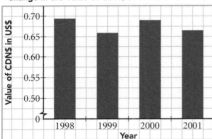

Change in the Value of CDN$ in Terms of the US$

7. No. The percents total only 94%. Six percent of the sample is missing.

8. a) driving long distances is safer
   b) We need to know the margin of error.

9. a) The prices have increased by 18.5%.
   b) Ontario; Ontario's increase is 18.5%, Canada's is 17.5%.

10. a) They increased by 33.4%.
   b) The demand for energy is greater that for other products.

13. a) all large technology stocks traded on the TSE
   b) Divide the total number of stocks by 20 to get n, then go down the alphabetical list and choose every nth stock.

Self-Check 5.4, 5.5, page 357

1. a)

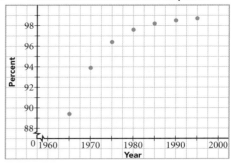

Percent of Canadian Homes with Telephones

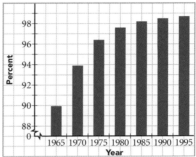

Percent of Canadian Homes with Telephones

   b) Yes. They both show that the percent of homes with telephones is levelling off.

2. a) The price for clothing and footwear increased by 6.6%, the cost for transportation by 30.9%.
   b) increased energy prices

3.

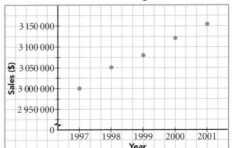

Annual Sales for Magic Inc.

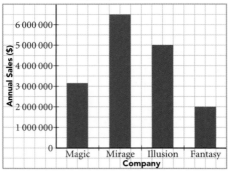

2001 Annual Sales

More consumers prefer Magic Inc. over all of its competitors.

Chapter 5 Review Exercises, page 361

1. a) all people aged 15 to 25 years who have committed a crime
   b) all schools with children aged 5 to 19 years
   c) all new immigrants to Canada in 2001

2. a) Only those people who use the library were surveyed.
   b) Her classmates are the same age and from the same community. They are not representative of all teenage girls.

3. a) secondary   b) primary   c) secondary

4. a) sample   b) sample

6. No. Coaches and managers may be biased towards their own team members.

7. a) systematic sample of a self-selected sample
   b) No. The results represent only those listeners who wished to call in, not the entire listener population.

8. The survey costs money, and people may not admit to having stolen, especially when their phone numbers are recorded.

9. A small selected sample that is unbiased can represent the entire population. A biased sample, no matter what size, will not represent the population.

10. a) The question is leading and confusing because it's phrased in the negative.
    b) No. The results will be biased because the supporters of the team are conducting the survey.
    c) "Should there be a rugby team at the school?"

11. a) if there would be support for increasing the length of the school year
    b) "If it meant improving your education and getting you a better-paying job, would you support a longer school year?"

12. People have to record their names. An anonymous survey would be better. Also, the question does not determine the type of heart problem.

13. a) No.
    b) "Which sport do you most like to participate in?"

15. a)
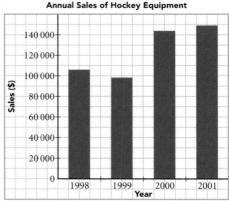
Annual Sales of Hockey Equipment

b) The graph shows the trend more clearly.

16. a)

Interval	Frequency
40–50	1
50–60	4
60–70	7
70–80	10
80–90	7
90–100	1

b)
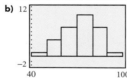

c) 70–80; Yes. Only 1 person failed and only 5 people out of 30 scored below 60%.

17. a)
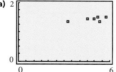

b) Yes. As the bank rate increases, so does the exchange rate.

18. a) A scatter plot will allow for comparison between the mass of players and their total points.

b)
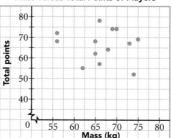
Mass versus Total Points of Players

19. $1072.50–$1127.50

20. There are many fewer motorcycles on the road than cars; therefore, fewer people are killed in motorcycle accidents.

21. a) They decreased by 0.9%.   **b)** They increased by 4.7%.

Maintaining Your Mastery, page 365

1. a) $5x^2 + 15x - 140$ **b)** $6x^2 - 36x + 54$
c) $2x^2 + 27x + 1$

2. a) $(x + 7)(x + 1)$ **b)** $4(x - 5)(x - 2)$
c) $3(x + 3)(x - 3)$

3. a) $(4x + 7)(x + 1)$ **b)** $(5x + 3)^2$
c) $5(x + 1)(3x - 1)$

4. a) $x = 10$ **b)** $x = -\frac{1}{3}$ or $x = \frac{1}{2}$

Chapter 5 Self-Test, page 366

1. a) all students and staff who buy food in the cafeteria
b) all people applying for driver's licences

3. a)

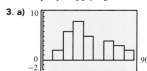

b) If the interval width was smaller, there would be more bars, and their heights would be smaller. If the interval width was greater, there would be fewer bars with more data in each interval.

4. a) The vertical scale exaggerates the differences in the bank rate.

b)

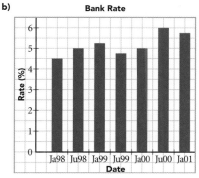

5. Yes. The company survey shows that 44% to 54% prefer liquid and 46% to 56% prefer powder. Sandra's results are within these ranges.

6. b) When the sample size increases, the margin of error decreases. No.

Chapter 6 Data Analysis

Necessary Skills

Review: Measures of Central Tendency

Exercises, page 372

1. mean = 17.44 years; median = 18 years; mode = 18 years the mean; There are 17 ages below and 19 above this value. For the median and mode there would be 17 below and 8 above.

2. mean = 4.53 km; median = 5 km; mode = 5 km
The mean and mode best represent the average distance since the distance was given as a range, and 5 km is the midpoint of the range.

6.1 Exercises, page 378

1. a) mean = 30; range = 20; $s^2 = 66.67$; $s = 8.16$
b) mean = 24; range = 12; $s^2 = 22.50$; $s = 4.74$
c) mean = 21.67; range = 10; $s^2 = 10.75$; $s = 3.28$
d) mean = 26.50; range = 33; $s^2 = 151.10$; $s = 12.29$

2. a) mean = 28.88; range = 4.0; $s = 1.08$
b) mean = 70.75; range = 30; $s = 8.39$

3. a) mean = \$15.77; median = \$14.99; $s = 2.90$
b) There was a wide range of prices.

4. a) mean = 6.08 mm; median = 6.50 mm; $s = 1.39$
b) quite well; The standard deviation is small.

6. a) $s = 0.95$ **b)** $s = 1.44$ **c)** $s = 0.64$

8. a) $s = 6.87$ **b)** $s = 5.90$ **c)** $s = 9.87$

9. the 40 randomly selected people; The soccer players would have less variation between them because they all have been training to play soccer.

10. a) \$10.06   **b)** 0.69

11. The mode is determined by finding the tallest bar(s).

12. a) mean = 35.50 cm; median = 30.00 cm; mode = 25.00 cm; $s = 17.07$
b) mean would be larger; median would be the same; mode would be the same; standard deviation would be larger
c) mean = 42.50 cm; median = 30.00 cm; mode = 25.00 cm; $s = 38.89$
d) mean; It will greatly affect the sum of the data.

13. a) class A: $\bar{x} = 65.29$; median = 65.00; mode = 45, 54, 55, 65, 75, 80; range = 36; $s^2 = 146.01$; $s = 12.08$
class B: $\bar{x} = 67.57$; median = 58.00; mode = 55; range = 58; $s^2 = 382.96$; $s = 19.57$
b) class A; The mean is slightly lower, but the range and standard deviations are much smaller. The median mark for class A is also much higher.

14. a) The mean and median also increase by \$5.00. The standard deviation stays the same.
b) The mean, median, and standard deviation all double.
c) The mean and median stay the same. The standard deviation decreases.

15. data set A: The mean is not a good representation of the population because the standard deviation is large in comparison to the mean.

data set B: The mean is a good representation of the population because the standard deviation is small in comparison to the mean.

17. mean daytime temperature; This measure is more indicative of the temperature during the day.

18. a) brand A: $\bar{x} = 1014.38$ h; $s = 104.94$
brand B: $\bar{x} = 1024.33$ h; $s = 69.25$
b) brand B; The mean is higher and standard deviation is smaller. Brand B will last longer.

6.2 Exercises, page 387

1. a) skewed right   **b)** bimodal
c) normal   **d)** skewed left

2. a) skewed right   **b)** bimodal

c) normal   **d)** skewed left

3. a)

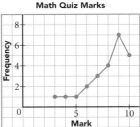

b) skewed left
d) $\bar{x} = 7.85$, median $= 8.5$, mode $= 9$
e) median; The mean is affected by the extreme values in the tail of the curve.

4. a) skewed right

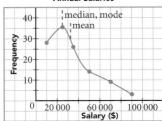

b) $\bar{x} = \$32\,695.65$; median $= \$25\,000$; mode $= \$25\,000$

c) the mean; For this value, the number of employees making a higher or lower salary is most even.

5. a)

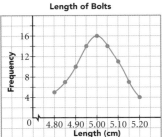

b) normal; It appears symmetrical, and the mean, median, and mode are all 5.00 cm.
c) Yes.
d) No. The distribution of lengths is symmetrical about the mean.

6. a) normal; The mean, median, and mode are almost equal.
b) skewed left; The median is lower than the mode, and the mean is lower than the median.
c) bimodal; The mean and median are in between the two modal values.
d) skewed right; The mean is greater than the median, which is greater than the mode.

8. a) There are two main subgroups in the population—one with students 8 years old, and one with students 12 years old.
b) to decide how many classes are needed at each grade level and how many teachers are needed
c) The mean and median will be between 8 and 12, the two peaks of the distribution.

9. a) Most houses are priced around $150\,000.
b) the mode; It is the lowest dollar value.
c) the mean; It is the highest dollar value.

10. a) skewed left   **b)** skewed right
c) normal

12. bimodal–one peak for girls and one peak for boys

6.3 Exercises, page 397

1. Curve c has the highest because it is the most spread out. Curve b has the lowest because it is the narrowest.

2. a) i) 66 and 78   **ii)** 60 and 84   **iii)** 54 and 90
b)

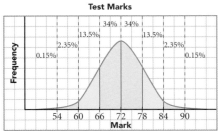

3. a) ii) All bottles should be very close to 1 L, so the standard deviation will be small.

b)iii) The standard deviation will be high because the range of salaries is large.

c) i) The standard deviation will be moderate. Some students will do worse and some will do better than average.

4. a) within 1 standard deviation: 23 h to 27 h
within 2 standard deviations: 21 h to 29 h
within 3 standard deviations: 19 h to 31 h
b) i) 68%   **ii)** 2.35%   **iii)** 83.85%

5. a)

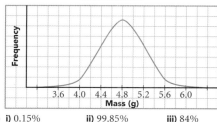

Mass of Stones

b) i) 0.15%   **ii)** 99.85%   **iii)** 84%
iv) 34%   **v)** 99.7%
c) 2.4 g

6. a)

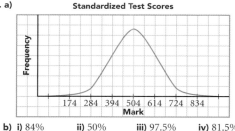

Standardized Test Scores

b) i) 84%   **ii)** 50%   **iii)** 97.5%   **iv)** 81.5%
c) 660

7. a) Both will have the same mean. The one with a standard deviation of 20 will be broader.

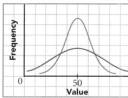

b) Both curves will be the same shape and size because they have the same standard deviation, but the one with a mean of 50 will be translated right.

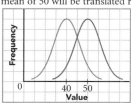

8. a) 2.5%   **b)** 135.4

9. a) The peak will be lower and the curve will be broader.

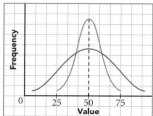

b) The curve will translate 25 units to the right.

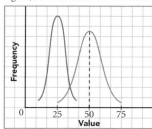

c) The curve will translate 25 units left, the peak will be higher, and the curve will be narrower.

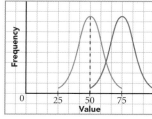

10. Yes. 2000 h is about 0.8 standard deviations below the mean, which means approximately 77% of light bulbs will work for 2000 h or more.

11. a) district A; The mean score is higher with a lower standard deviation.
b) district A; The standard deviation is lower.

12. Both curves would be normal distributions, but the curve after taking cold medication will be shifted left due to slower reaction times.

13. a) 95% of the data values are within 2 standard deviations. The range is 65.6 kg − 56.4 kg = 9.2 kg. Divide this value by 4 since there are 2 standard deviations to the left and 2 to the right.
c) 2.3

14. a)

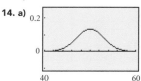

b)
```
WINDOW
Xmin=40
Xmax=60
Xscl=2
Ymin=-.1
Ymax=.25
Yscl=.1
Xres=1
```

c)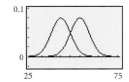

15. a) 81.8% **b)** 4.8%

16. a)

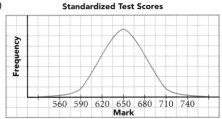

Standardized Test Scores

b) 15.9%
c) 680; 84% of the data (test scores) are below 680.

Self-Check 6.1–6.3, page 402

1. a)

Number of children	Frequency
0	3
1	5
2	8
3	6
4	2

b) 2
c) $\bar{x} = 1.96$; median = 2; $s = 1.16$
d) range = 4; $s^2 = 1.35$
e) The mean, median, and mode all indicate that the typical number of children is 2, but the standard deviation is high, so 2 is not really representative of the population.

2. a) skewed right; The mean is greater than the median, which is greater than the mode.
b) skewed left; The mean is less than the median, which is less than the mode.
c) bimodal; The mean and median are between the two modes.

3. a) skewed left

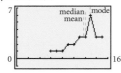

b) mean = 11.8; median = 12; mode = 13
c) the mode; The distribution is skewed left, so the mean and the median are affected by the extreme values.
d) Yes.

4. a) i) 97.5% **ii)** 49.85%
b) less than 1 out of 100 **c)** 11.4 cm

6.4 Exercises, page 409

1. a) single-variable; There is only one variable—length.
b) two-variable; Length and width are two different variables.

2. a) negatively correlated; The data points show a downward trend from left to right.
b) not correlated; There does not seem to be a pattern.
c) positively correlated; The data points show an upward trend from left to right.

3. a) positively correlated; Taller people tend to have larger feet.
b) negatively correlated; As time increases, the height of the ball decreases.
c) no correlation; The number of shirts you own is not related to your height.

4. a) Yes. The more you study, the higher your mark will be.
b) Yes. Since tutors are usually paid by the hour, the more money spent means the more time spent working on mathematics.
c) No. There is no relationship.
d) Yes. The longer the ice cube sits at room temperature, the smaller its surface area.

5. a) d)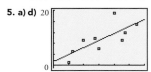

b) As the age increases so does the diameter. Yes.
c) $y = 0.64x + 1.39$
e) 37 years **f)** 8 cm

6. a) c)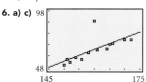

b) $y = 1.05x - 103.24$
c) Yes. Most data are close to the line. There is one outlier.
d) 174 cm **e)** 106.76 kg

8. a)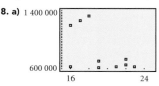

b) no trends; no correlation
c) No.

9. a) $y \doteq -0.0063x + 22.4814$ **b)** 9.84 s
10. a) $y \doteq 0.991x - 3.018$ **b)** 26.7 cm
c) 24 weeks

11. No. The fetal head circumference of 28.3 cm occurs at week 31.6, which is within the 2-week range.

12. a) $y = 10.217x - 0.528$

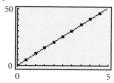

b) 51 V
c) -0.528; No, it cannot be negative.

6.5 Exercises, page 420

1. a) -0.9 **b)** 0.8   **c)** 0

2. a) The data are negatively correlated and very close to linear.
b) The data are positively correlated and exactly linear.
c) The data are scattered with no real trend.
d) The data are positively correlated. There may be an outlier present, or some data is spread out from the line of best fit.

3. a) The taller the player, the more likely she is to get rebounds.

4. a) $r = -0.5$

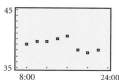

b) $y = -0.125x + 40.875$; $r = -0.573$
c) because the correlation coefficient tells us that the equation is not a good fit for the data

5. a) $y = 1.375x + 3.375$
b) The line fits the data exactly.

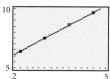

c) 6.8 L/100 km; 10.24 L/100 km

6. a) $r = 1$
b) With a correlation coefficient of 1, the equation is an excellent model of the data.

7. When $r = 1$ or -1, the points in a scatter plot will fall in a straight line. The smaller r becomes, the more scattered the points.

8. a) $y = 0.57x + 32.66$
b) not very well; $r = 0.65$
c) No. Because the line doesn't fit the data very well, it is not a good predictor of the relationship between entrance test and first term marks.

9. A line can always be drawn between two points. If the two points form a vertical line, then r is undefined.

10. a) Yes, but with one outlier.

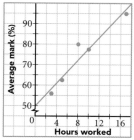

b) No. Although the data suggest this, the sample is too small.
c) 17.7 hours   **d)** 50%
e) The sample is too small, and the context of the data needs to be kept in mind.

11. a) No. Not enough data points are available.
b) 18.2 hours   **c)** 48%
d) There was no legitimate reason to reject the point (8, 80) as an outlier.

12. a) 4 cm
b)

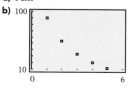

c) negative correlation
d) $y = -19.2x + 99.2$; $r = -0.96$
e) Yes. The correlation coefficient is high.
f) -35.2 cm; This is different from the prediction. The context of the data must be considered, since a ball can bounce no less than 0 cm.

13. a) $y = -0.177x + 0.769$ **b)** $y = 0.000\,55x + 1.221$

Self-Check 6.4, 6.5, page 424

1. a) negatively correlated; As the distance travelled increases, the amount of fuel remaining decreases.
b) no correlation; The amount of education you have has no bearing on how many children you have.
c) positive correlation; The further you drive your car, the more oil changes required.

2. a) $y = -1.2x + 230$
b) exactly; The correlation coefficient is -1.
c) i) 206 beats/min   **ii)** 146 beats/min   **iii)** 188 beats/min
d) $r = -1$
e) No. The data seems reasonable, and the correlation coefficient is -1. However, the sample size is very small.

3. a) i) positive correlation   **ii)** no correlation
b) i) $y = 1.16x - 37.98$; $r = 0.81$
ii) $y = 0.50x + 87.54$; $r = 0.51$
Daughter's height versus father's height has the stronger correlation because the r-value is closest to 1.
c) Yes. The correlation coefficient is 0.78. However, the father's height alone is a better predictor.

Chapter 6 Review Exercises, page 430

1. students; Professional golfers' scores will be closer together because students may or may not have played golf before, so their range of scores will be greater.

2. mode

3. a)

	Team A	Team B	Team C
mean, $\bar{x}$	36.4	40	37.2
median	32	42	32
mode	21, 25, 32, 42, 65	12, 32, 42, 52, 62	16, 24, 32, 52, 62
range	41	50	46
variance, s^2	268.3	370	371.2
standard deviation, s	16.4	19.2	19.3

b) team B; They had the highest mean and median.
c) team A; The standard deviation is lowest.

5. a)

	Day Shift	Afternoon Shift
mean, $\bar{x}$	149.3 g	154.3 g
standard deviation, s	5.6	7.8

b) day shift
c) day shift; The mean is only 0.7 g off, with a smaller standard deviation.

7. a) skewed left; The median is less than the mode, and the mean is less than the median.
b) normal; All three measures are the same.
c) bimodal; The mean and median are in between the two modes.

8. a) skewed left   **b)** skewed right
c) bimodal

9. a) The normal curve will be the same but will shift horizontally to the right.
b) The peak will increase, and the curve will be narrower.

10. a)

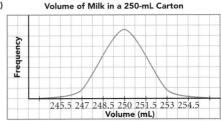

Volume of Milk in a 250-mL Carton

b) i) 2.5%   **ii)** 97.5%
c) 250

11. 2.5%

12. $s = 35$

13. a) two-variable; The two variables are annual income and years of service.
b) single-variable; Annual income is the only variable.

14. a) i) positively correlated   **ii)** not correlated

iii) negatively correlated
b) i) yes   **ii)** no   **iii)** yes

15. a) negatively correlated; Newer cars cost more money.
b)

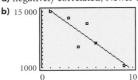

c) negatively correlated
d) $y = -1656.25x + 16\,912.5$; $r = -0.879$
e) quite well; It is fairly close to -1.
f) It fits quite well; 3 points are very near the line, and the other 3 are close.
g) $13\,600

16. If $r = -1$ or 1, the data are perfectly correlated. If r is positive, the data are positively correlated. If r is negative, the data are negatively correlated.

17. Consider excluding a data point when an error was made collecting or reporting the data, or when outside factors have affected the data.

18. a) $y = -1745.11x + 18\,156.52$; $r = -0.960$ which is much closer to -1
b) The new line is a better predictor.

19. a) $y = -0.530x + 8.166$; $r = -1.0$
b) very reliable; The correlation coefficient is essentially -1.

Maintaining Your Mastery, page 435

1. a) $17x^2 - 7x + 18$ **b)** $5x + 33$
2. a) $3(x - 3)(x + 4)$ **b)** $(2x - 3)(2x + 5)$
3. a) $H = \frac{100 - T}{0.0034}$ **b)** $h = \frac{S}{2\pi r} - r$
4. a) $(3, 1)$ **b)** $(-0.5, 1)$

Chapter 6 Self-Test, page 436

1. a) $\bar{x} = 354.2\overline{3}$ mL; median = 354 mL; $s = 2.37$
On average, the machine is doing a good job, but the standard deviation may be a little high.
b) The range of volume will be greater and more cans will be underfilled and overfilled.

2. There are two peaks, or modes. The class is divided into 2 subgroups, one performing better than the other.

3. a)

Heights of Tomato Plants

b) 84%   **c)** 36 cm

4. a) negative correlation

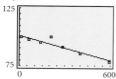

b) $y = -0.0036x + 101.47$; $r = -0.936$
The line is very close to a perfect fit with 1 outlier.
c) 102.6°C; This estimate is fairly reliable.
d) (2100, 100.4); $y = -0.0036x + 100.155$; $r = -0.997$;
101.6°C
These results are more reliable because the equation is almost an exact fit of the data.

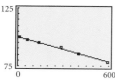

5. a) Find the equation of the line of best fit and plug in 2 and then 45 for the value of x.
b) 19%; −12%   **c)** They are very different.
d) No. The data appear to form a curve.

Chapter 7 Analysis of Graphical Models

Necessary Skills

1 Review: Arithmetic and Geometric Sequences
Exercises, page 442

1. a) geometric; $r = 1.1$ **b)** arithmetic; $d = 4$
   c) arithmetic; $d = -2$ **d)** geometric; $r = 0.1$
2. a) 100, 50, 25, 12.5, 6.25   **b)** 7, 9, 11, 13, 15

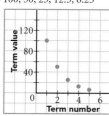
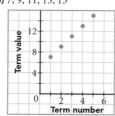

2 Review: Characteristics of Linear, Quadratic, and Exponential Graphs
Exercises, page 447

1. a) exponential; The differences between successive
y-values increase by increasing amounts. The ratio of
successive y-values is constant (2).
b) linear; The graph is a straight line. The differences
between successive y-values are constant (1).
c) quadratic; The graph is a curve. The differences between
successive y-values increase by a constant amount (1).

2. a) i)

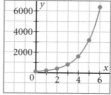

ii) The graph curves up. For large values of x, the graph
grows faster and faster.
iii) exponential
b) i)

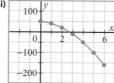

ii) The graph curves down in the shape of a parabola.
iii) quadratic
c) i)

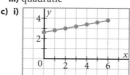

ii) The graph is a straight line.   **iii)** linear
d) i)

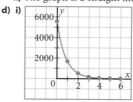

ii) The graph decreases faster and faster for small values
of x, then levels off.
iii) exponential
e) i)

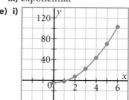

ii) The graph curves up in the shape of a parabola.
iii) quadratic

7.1 Exercises, page 453
1. a) $m = -1$, $b = 2$ **b)** $m = \frac{1}{2}$, $b = 1$ **c)** $m = 2$, $b = 0$
2. a) i) $m = 4$ **ii)** °C/h
   iii) the change in temperature per hour
   b) i) $m = 25$ **ii)** $/m^2$
   iii) the cost per square metre
   c) i) $m = 3$ **ii)** m/s
   iii) the distance travelled per second
3. a) $y = x + 1$ **b)** $y = -2x + 5$ **c)** $y = -x + 4$

4. a) Landscaping Rates of Pay

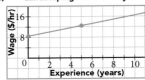

b) $m = 0.8$ \$/year; the hourly wage increase for every year of experience

c) \$10.90

5. a) Temperature in a Wall

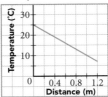

b) 25°C; 7°C   **c)** $m = -15$°C/m

d) the change in temperature for every metre into the wall

6. a) time   **b)** temperature   **c)** 8°C/h

d) For every hour the yogurt sits on the counter, its temperature increases by 8°C.

7. a) \$500   **b)** \$350

c) $m = -50$ \$/month; October = month 0

d) $y = -50x + 500$ **e)** March

8. a) 32°F   **b)** -17.8°C   **c)** $T_F = 1.8T_C + 32$

d) 392°F   **e)** -73.3°C

9. a) 20 m   **b)** -0.3 m/week

c) $H = -0.3t + 20$

d) No; It will fall more rapidly during dry spells.

10. a) approx. 365 km   **b)** approx. 24.5 L   **c)** 0.055 L/km

d) 18.2 km   **e)** 5.5 L/100 km

11. a) \$600   **b)** \$100   **c)** at 14 months

12. a) 50m/min; Marla can walk 50 m each minute.

b) c) Marla's Distance from Home

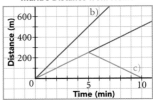

13. a) b) Number of Cookies Remaining

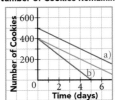

c) d) Number of Cookies Remaining

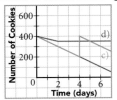

14. a) 6 m   **b)** 1.33 m/s   **c)** $d = 1.33t + 1$ **d)** 1.65 s

15. Since Tim runs faster, the slope of the graph representing his motion is greater than that of Zack's. Tim's line starts some time after Zack's since he gave Zack a head-start.

Tim and Zack's Race

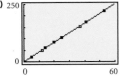

16. a) The values for volume do not increase by a constant amount either.

b) e)

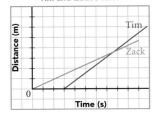

c) It appears linear.   **d)** $y = 4.20x - 0.14$

e) very good fit

f) 4.20 g/mL; Every 1 mL of sand has a mass of 4.2 g.

g) approx. 0 g; This is the mass (g) of no sand (0 mL).

h) 4.20 g/cm^3

7.2 Exercises, page 463

1. a) opens up   **b)** opens down   **c)** opens down

2. a) i) minimum   **ii)** (3, 1)

b) i) maximum   **ii)** (1, 80)

c) i) minimum   **ii)** (10, 2000)

3. a) B; The differences between successive y-values increase by an almost constant amount and form an arithmetic sequence.

b) B; The differences between successive y-values decrease by a constant amount and form an arithmetic sequence.

4. a) Cost of a Television Set

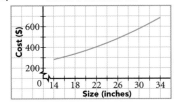

b) The differences in cost increase by a constant amount and form an arithmetic sequence.

c) $200 is the base cost to manufacture any size television.

d) $0.42D^2$ is the additional cost of a television based on the size in inches.

5. a)

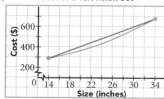

Cost of a Television Set

b) $y = 20.16x + 0.08$

c) i) $441.92   **ii)** $483.92

6. a) 1 L   **b)** approx. 6.3 cm

c)

Radius (cm)	Volume (L)	Difference
0	0	
		1.6
5	1.6	
		4.7
10	6.3	
		7.8
15	14.1	

d) yes   **e)** 25 L

7. a) 5 m, 10 m, 5 m   **b)** 75 m, 93 m, 18 m

c) The faster your speed, the longer it takes to reach 0 m/s when you brake, so more distance is required.

d) 5 m

8. a) i) approx. 1.3 kN   **ii)** approx. 5 kN

iii) approx. 11.5 kN   **iv)** approx. 20 kN

b) Maybe; It's hard to tell because the values are difficult to read from the graph; The differences between consecutive drag values increase by an almost constant amount.

9. a) The differences in successive costs increase by a constant amount.

b) The pizza surface area increases at a faster rate than the diameter; therefore, the cost would not be linear.

c) (8, 7); the cost of the smallest pizza available

d) There is no pizza with diameter 0.

10. a)

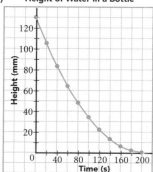

Height of Water in a Bottle

b) The differences in successive heights decrease by an almost constant amount.

c) from 0 to 20 s; The differences in height are the greatest over this time period.

d) (200, 0)

11. i)

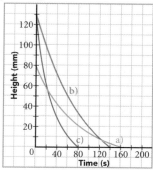

Height of Water in a Bottle

ii) a) The height of the water is lower at the start, and less time is required for the bottle to empty.

b) The graph starts at the same height but is steeper because the larger hole allows the bottle to empty faster.

c) Assuming the height of the water is the same at the start, the bottle will empty faster because it holds less volume.

12. a) At the start, as the skateboarder starts to roll down the slope, he or she is moving slowly. Then, the skateboarder gains speed and the slope of the graph increases. As the skateboarder approaches maximum speed, the graph approximates a straight line.

b)

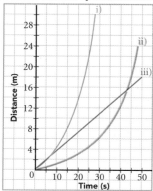

Distance Travelled by a Skateboarder

13. a) The graph curves up. The cyclist starts from a stop and slowly gains speed.

b) The graph is a straight line. The cyclist is moving at a constant speed.

c) The graph curves down. The cyclist is braking and slowing down until he or she stops.

14. a) The graph is a straight line and the slope is constant.

b) 2 m/s

c) Car B starts from a stop and gradually increases speed until the graph approximates a straight line, during which time the car travels at an almost constant speed.

d) after 30 s or 80 m

e) after 15 s; From 10 to 15 s, car B has a speed of approximately 2 m/s.

15. a)

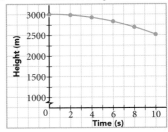

Motion of a Skydiver

b) 20 s

c) e)

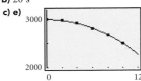

d) $y = -5x^2 + 3000$
e) exactly; All the data points satisfy the equation.
f) 20 s

7.3 Exercises, page 476

1. a) i) 5   **ii)** 1
  b) i) 100   **ii)** 4
  c) i) 1   **ii)** 15

2. a) i) 60   **ii)** 1
  b) i) 5000   **ii)** 30
  c) i) 12   **ii)** 8

3. a) This represents the number of active bacteria present on a surface, expressed as a percent.
  b) 0.5 min   **c)** 0.75   **d)** approx. 2 min 10 s

4. a) $1000   **b)** approx. 17.5 years
  c) 8 years   **d)** 9.05%

5. a) the population of fruit flies over time
  b) 2 weeks   **c)** 5.1%   **d)** approx. 18.5 days

6. a) approx. 3000
  b) i) approx. 14 years   **ii)** approx. 18 years
    ii) approx. 17 years
  c) 17 years
  d) 1100; It was assumed that the graph continues to decrease exponentially.

7. a) i) $40 billion   **ii)** $600 billion
  b) approx. 7 years   **c)** 10.4%
  d) approx. $2600 billion
  e) It was assumed that the debt doubles in 7 years, that the debt in 1995 was $600 billion, and that the graph continues exponentially.

8. a) $\frac{3}{4}$ h   **b)** 40 mg
  c) The isotope used to treat patients has a short half-life, so it would decay too much if it had to travel far.

9. a) 5 s
  b) i) 7.8 V   **ii)** 4.5 V   **iii)** 2.3 V
  c) 8.9 V

10. a) 100 kPa   **b)** 8 km   **c)** approx. 26 km
  d) i) approx. 91.0 kPa   **ii)** approx. 59.2 kPa
    iii) approx. 46.5 kPa
  e) 0.017 kPa; 0.017 %

11. a)

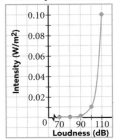

Intensity vs. Loudness

  b) It curves up exponentially.
  c) It increases by a factor of 10.
  d) 3 dB
  e) i) 100 W/m^2 **ii)** 10 W/m^2 **iii)** 10 000 W/m^2
  f) i) 130 dB   **ii)** 160 dB

12. a) i) approx. 15   **ii)** approx. 40   **ii)** approx. 100
  b) approx. 1.5 weeks   **c)** approx. 59%

13. a) The interest earned every year is the same.
  b) 5%   **c)** $y = 125x + 2500$
  d) f)

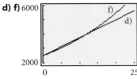

  e) Each year the interest earned is added to the total. The interest for the next year is then calculated on a greater amount of money.
  g) after 12 years   **h)** 4.3%
  i) increase; The rate must increase for the curves to intersect at 8 years instead of 12.
  j) 7.2%

Self-Check 7.1–7.3, page 481

1. a) 500 s   **b)** 5 m/s
  c) The jogger runs at a constant rate of 5 m/s.
  d) $D = 5t$

2. a) plan A; plan B
  b) The differences in successive vacation days form an arithmetic sequence.
  c) The successive number of vacation days form a geometric sequence with a common ratio.
  d) 3 years

3. a) i) coral B   **ii)** coral A
  b) coral B; The successive values of mass form a geometric sequence with a common ratio.
  c) i) 20 years   **ii)** 3.5%
  d) quadratic; The differences in successive values of mass form an arithmetic sequence with a common difference.

7.4 Exercises, page 486

1. a) i) c   **ii)** a   **ii)** b

2. a) 20   **b)** 18   **c)** 0.7

4. a) The value is decreasing but levelling off.
  b) The value is increasing at a constant rate.
  c) The value is increasing faster and faster.

5. a) The object moves at a constant speed, then slows down to a very slow speed as the graph levels off.
  b) The object is stationary for some time, then increases speed quickly and maintains it.
  c) The object is moving at a constant speed in the opposite direction.

6. a) Ola's height increased rapidly when he was young, but started to level off as he got older.
  b) 72 inches

7. a) Continue the trend of the curve and read the value from the graph.
  b) The graph would be exponential, and the curve would get steeper.

8. a) The graphs show the same straight line. The difference is the size of the graphs due to the different scale of the axes.
  b) The accuracy would be greater from the larger graph because the scale allows for a more accurate value to be read from the graph.

9. a) The curve decreases rapidly at first, then decreases more gradually and levels off.
  b) 0.2 W/m^2 **c)** 16 W/m^2
  d) estimate in part b; The graph has levelled off at 6 m, and the intensity at 6.5 m will not be very different. To estimate the intensity at 0.5 m, it is difficult to know how steep to draw the curve.

10. a) 93 000   **b)** by approx. 10 000   **c)** 95 000

11. a) The temperature decreases rapidly from 21°C and levels off at 12°C.
  b) The temperature rises rapidly from 12°C and levels off at 22°C.
  c) The temperature gradually decreases to 18°C and stays there.

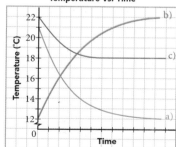

Temperature vs. Time

12. a) The graph increases at an almost constant rate at the beginning.
  b) $265 000   **b)** approx. $27 000

13. a) The speed of the skydiver increases rapidly.
  b) The speed decreases rapidly.
  c) approx. 124 m/s
  d) The speed decreases more slowly and then levels off.
  e) approx. 5 m/s

14. a) A: increases faster and faster with years of service
    B: increases at a constant rate
    C: increases quickly at first but then levels off
  b) for the first 2.75 years   **c)** for the first 3.5 years
  d) curve C

15. a)

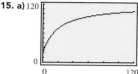

  b) 20°C   **c)** 100°C
  d) at the beginning, from 0 to 20 s
  e) The temperature increases rapidly at first, then increases more slowly and levels off.

7.5 Exercises, page 493

1. a) same starting point; different rate of increase
  b) different starting point; same rate of increase
  c) same starting point; one curve increases faster and faster, the other decreases faster and faster

2. a)   **b)**  **c)**

3. a) culture A; The curve rises more quickly.
  b) temperature; available nutrients

4. a) Shopper A started at 20 m. Shopper B started at 0 m. They both moved at 2 m/s.
  b) Shopper A didn't move for the first 10 s. Shopper B stopped moving after the first 10 s.

5. a) town E: 10 000; town F: 30 000
  b) 5 years   **c)** 5 years   **d)** 20 000   **e)** 60 000
  f) The starting points are different, so the curves appear different.

6.

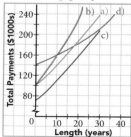

Total Mortgage Payments

8. a) The graph increases rapidly at first when the potato is placed in the oven. It then starts to level off as the outside of the potato heats up and reaches the same temperature as the oven.

b) The temperature of the centre of the potato rises slowly at first and then more quickly. It levels off at 100°C.

Temperature of the Centre of a Potato

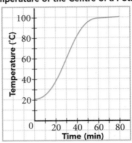

c) The temperature would increase slower and would level off at a lower temperature.

Temperature of a Potato

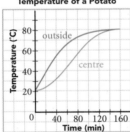

9. In the first month, the plant needs time to get established and the height increases slowly. The plant then grows quickly and the slope increases. As the plant reaches maturity, the growth rate decreases and the graph starts to level off.

10.

Voltage on a Capacitor

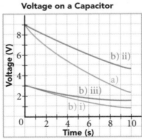

11.

Height of a Tomato Plant

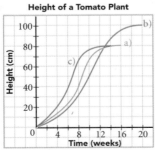

12.

Growth Record

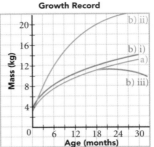

13.

Dipping of the Centre of a Trampoline

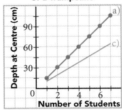

a) The graph is linear.
b) approx. 150 cm
c) It would not be as steep, and the starting value would be smaller.

Self-Check 7.4, 7.5, page 497

1. a) Both curves start at the same price, but the prices for curve A increase at a faster rate than for curve B.
b) curve A; The reflective signs would be more expensive.

2. a) Short-term trend: Each year, the number of American cars entering Ontario increases rapidly in the summer. Long-term trend: The total number of American cars entering Ontario each year has increased.
b) i) no change
ii) More Americans will enter Ontario, so the short-term trend of the graph will continue, but the number of cars will increase.
iii) Fewer Americans will cross into Ontario, so the short-term trend will continue, but the number of cars will decrease.
c)

Cars with American Licence Plates Entering Ontario

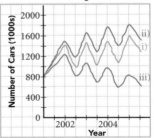

7.6 Exercises
Canada's Population, page 498

1. a)

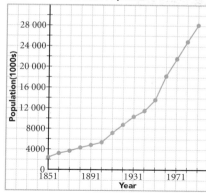

b) i) a bit low: 1881–1901, 1931–1941
a bit high: 1901–1911, 1951–1961

2. a) i) 2 437 000 people   ii) approx. 1891
iii) approx. 40 years
b) approx. 1929, 38 years later
i) 3 times
ii) 1851–1891, approx. 40 years
1891–1929, approx. 38 years
1929–1969, approx. 40 years
Yes.
iii) The graph is very close to being exponential.
iv) approx. 39.3 years

3. a) $2437(1 + r)^{140} = 28\ 111$
2437 is the population in 1851.
28 111 is the population in 1991.
140 is the total number of years; 1991–1851 = 140.
r is the rate of population growth.
b) $r \doteq 0.017\ 62$
c) approx. 1.76%

4. a) $2437(1 + r)^{50} = 5371$; approx. 1.59%
b) $5371(1 + r)^{50} = 13\ 648$; approx. 1.88%
c) $13\ 648(1 + r)^{40} = 28\ 111$; approx. 1.82%

5. a)
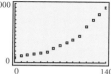
b) 2437 is the initial population.
1.0173 is the rate of population growth plus 1
(the original population).
x is the number of years since 1851.
y is the final population.

c) The curve fits the data quite well except for the
years 1961–1991.
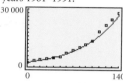
d) $y = 2509(1.0176)^x$
e) The curve fits the data better than in part b because it
fits the years 1961–1991 more closely.
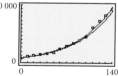

Provincial Populations, page 500

1. a) i) Canadian and Provincial Populations
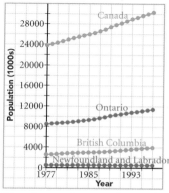

ii) It is easier to make comparisons and see similarities
and differences between the 4 data sets.
iii) The graph may be harder to read (crowded) and it
may be difficult to choose a vertical scale that will suit
all 4 data sets.
b) The populations of British Columbia, Canada, and
Ontario are increasing at a fairly constant rate. The
population of Canada is increasing the fastest. The
population of Newfoundland and Labrador is fairly
stable.

2. a) Canada:
i) $23\ 796.4(1 + r)^5 = 25\ 201.9$; $r \doteq 0.012$
ii) $25\ 201.9(1 + r)^5 = 26\ 549.7$; $r \doteq 0.010$
iii) $26\ 549.7(1 + r)^5 = 28\ 542.2$; $r \doteq 0.015$
iv) $28\ 542.2(1 + r)^5 = 30\ 286.6$; $r \doteq 0.012$
Newfoundland and Labrador:
i) $566.6(1 + r)^5 = 576.3$; $r \doteq 0.003$
ii) $576.3(1 + r)^5 = 576.5$; $r \doteq 0.000\ 07$
iii) $576.5(1 + r)^5 = 583.6$; $r \doteq 0.002$
iv) $583.6(1 + r)^5 = 563.6$; $r \doteq -0.007$
Ontario:
i) $8525.6(1 + r)^5 = 8951.4$; $r \doteq 0.010$
ii) $8951.4(1 + r)^5 = 9684.9$; $r \doteq 0.016$
iii) $9684.9(1 + r)^5 = 10\ 646.8$; $r \doteq 0.019$

iv) $10\,646.8(1 + r)^5 = 11\,407.7;\ r \doteq 0.014$

British Columbia:
  i) $2581.2(1 + r)^5 = 2886.3;\ r \doteq 0.023$
  ii) $2886.3(1 + r)^5 = 3064.6;\ r \doteq 0.012$
  iii) $3064.6(1 + r)^5 = 3476.6;\ r \doteq 0.026$
  iv) $3476.6(1 + r)^5 = 3933.3;\ r \doteq 0.025$

Regional Populations, page 502

1. a) Population of Metropolitan Areas

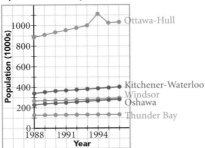

2. a) Kitchener-Waterloo: $341.4(1 + r)^8 = 403.3;\ r \doteq 0.021$
Oshawa: $228.6(1 + r)^8 = 280.9;\ r \doteq 0.026$
Ottawa-Hull: $884.0(1 + r)^8 = 1030.5;\ r \doteq 0.019$
Thunder Bay: $127.1(1 + r)^8 = 131.3;\ r \doteq 0.004$
Windsor: $266.1(1 + r)^8 = 291.7;\ r \doteq 0.012$

Chapter 7 Review Exercises, page 504

1. a) i) 16 $/m **ii)** $C = 16d$
  b) i) 25 km/h **ii)** $d = 25t + 50$
  c) i) 20°C/min **ii)** $T = 20t + 20$

2. a) area of the pathway
  b) the price of the flagstone pathway
  c) 13.33 $/m^2
  d) the cost of 1 m^2 of flagstone pathway
  e) the base cost of installation
  f) $766.50 **g)** 30 m^2

3. a) −285.71 $/°C
  b) The sales drop by $285.71 with every 1°C increase in temperature.
  d) $S = -285.71T + 15\,142.86$
  e) i) $5143.01 **ii)** $12\,285.76

4. a) 60 kg **b)** approx. 270 **c)** 0.15
  d) the mass of 1 apple
  e) 30 kg; This is the mass of an empty crate.

5. a) between 2 and 3 s **b)** at 6.5 s
  c) 30 m
  d) The bungee cord retracts and pulls the jumper back up.

6. a) up **b)** approx. $22 **c)** approx. $46
  d) at the end; the more overtime, the greater the bonus

7. a) 484 mL **b)** 3.87 m
  c) The surface area of each face is the side length squared; therefore, as you increase the side length, the surface area increases at a faster and faster rate.

8. a) 10 rabbits **b)** 3 months **c)** 26%

9. a) 14 m **b)** 27.5 m
  c) As the depth doubles, the percent of light transmitted decreases by about 50%.
  d) 0.73%

10. a) i) 4000 **ii)** 2500 **iii)** 450
  b) 3 years **c)** 20.6%

11. a) $50\,000 **b)** 5 years **c)** approx. 15%

12. a) The house prices increase almost at a constant rate for the first 6 months, then increase faster towards the end of the 12-month period.
  b) during the last month
  c) i) approx. $160\,000 **ii)** approx. $175\,000
  d) that the general trend of the graph continued

13. a) i **b)** ii **c)** iii

14. a) The temperature increases at a constant rate.

15. account B; Simple interest pays interest on the same amount of money each year, so the increase is constant.

16. a) The curve decreases fairly fast at first, then starts to level off.
  b) approx. 2.5% **c)** approx. 2%
  d) not very reliable; The graph could start to increase at any time.

17. a) Both graphs fluctuate during July and August, decrease sharply in September, and then start to rise again.
  b) They both show the same trend, but they start at different values and the second graph has a greater decrease in September.

18. a)

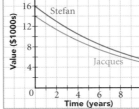

Car Values

  b) same trend and shape; different initial values

19. a) The slope would be greater.
  b) The curve would increase faster and faster.
  c) The curve would increase slower and slower and then level off as the cyclist stops.

Distance of a Cyclist from Start of Trail

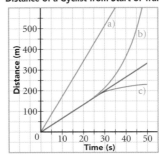

Maintaining Your Mastery, page 511

1. a) $-x + 29$ **b)** $6x^2 - 13x$ **c)** $-2x^2y^2 + 6xy^3$

2. a) $x^2 + 3xy - 4y^2$
  b) $4x^2 + 3xy + 4x - 5y - 10y^2$
  c) $4x^2 - 8x - 60$

3. a) $3x(2x - 3y)$ **b)** $(n + 3)(n + 4)$
  c) $(10 + 3z)(10 - 3z)$ **d)** $4(t - 8)(t - 1)$
  e) $3(x + 4)(x - 4)$ **f)** $y(y + 5)(y + 8)$

4. a) $c = 2$ **b)** $s = 0$ or $s = 4$ **c)** $k = 2$ or $k = -13$

5. a) $(-3, -2)$ **b)** $(10, 3)$ **c)** $(6, 0)$

Chapter 7 Self-Test, page 512

1. a)

Time	Temperature (°C)	Difference
1:00	16	
		6
2:00	22	
		2
3:00	24	
		-2
4:00	22	
		-6
5:00	16	

The graph is quadratic because the differences between successive temperatures form an arithmetic sequence.
  b) 3:00   **c)** between 1:00 and 1:30

2. a) approx. 2 years
  b) i) approx. 168 million   **ii)** approx. 1300 million
  c) Yes; Following the trend backwards gives a value fairly close to 2300.

3. a) The graph is almost a straight line since the mass increases at a reasonably constant rate. As the dog reaches maturity, the graph levels off.
  b) The rate of growth for Ottis is slower, so the slope of the curve will not be as steep. The graph for Ottis will level off earlier at a lower weight.

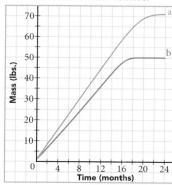

Mass of a Labrador Retriever

4. a) i) The graph is linear. The temperature decreases at a constant rate.

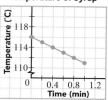

Temperature of Syrup

ii) $T = -5t + 116$, where T is the temperature in °C and t is the time in minutes.
  iii) 16 min
  b) i) The temperature decreases quickly at first, and then starts to level off.

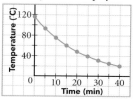

Temperature of Syrup

ii) 16 min; no
  iii) The ratio of successive temperature values is constant.
  c) i) quite closely; Both graphs decrease similarly over the first 5 min.
  ii) linear model: 16 min
      exponential model: approx. 27 min

Cumulative Review, page 514

1. a) 25°   **b)** 21°   **c)** 78°

2. a) $\angle C = 38.0°$, $a \doteq 2.5$ cm, $c \doteq 2.0$ cm
  b) $\angle D = 99.0°$, $e \doteq 5.6$ m, $f \doteq 4.6$ m
  c) $\angle X = 74.0°$, $\angle Y \doteq 53.0°$, $z \doteq 16.8$ mm

3. 56.7°

4. 19.9 km

5. a) $5x^2 + 4x + 3$ **b)** $2y^2 + y + 12$
  c) $x^2 + 6x + 9$ **d)** $6x^3 + 17x^2 + 2x - 15$

6. a) $\left(\frac{20}{7}, -\frac{32}{7}\right)$ **b)** $\left(\frac{9}{11}, \frac{67}{11}\right)$

7. a) $a = \frac{S_n}{n} - \frac{d(n - 1)}{2}$ **b)** 7

8. a) $C = 45p + 200$
  b)

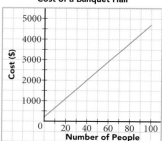

Cost of a Banquet Hall

9. a) $(x - 4)(x + 3)$ **b)** $(9 - 5x)(9 + 5x)$
c) $(a - 7)(a - 5)$ **d)** $3(x + 2)(x + 1)$
e) $(3b + 2)(2b + 1)$ **f)** $(6t - 1)(t + 2)$

10. a) $x = 0$ or $x = -1$ **b)** $x = \pm 3$
c) $x = -\frac{2}{5}$ or $x = \frac{1}{4}$

11. a) 112 ounces **b)** $12\frac{3}{4}$ inches
c) $11\frac{1}{10}$ gallons **d)** 83.5 kg

12. $SA \doteq 478$ square feet; $V \doteq 754$ cubic feet

13. 5 cans of primer and 10 cans of paint

14. a)

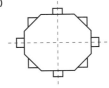

b) 90°, 180°, 270°

15.

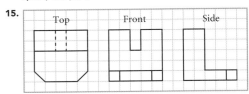

16.

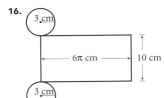

17. i) a) all first-year college students in Canada
b) all Canadian dimes
c) all teens
ii) a) secondary **b)** primary **c)** primary

19. a) no **b)** no

20. a) They increased 0.2%.
b) Prices in 2001 are 4.6% higher.

21. a)

	Morning	Afternoon	Night
Mean	54.4	57.6	54.1
Median	53	57.5	52
Mode	65	53, 57, 60, 63	47, 51, 62
Range	28	19	27
Variance	56.4	30.8	61.2
Standard Deviation	7.5	5.5	7.8

b) the morning shift

22. a)

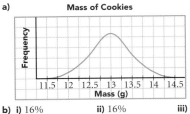

b) i) 16% **ii)** 16% **iii)** 95%

23. a) 7 m **b)** approx. 2.3 m **c)** 2.2 s
d) It would translate up by the increase in height.

24. a) Plan A starts lower but increases faster than plan B. Plan B starts higher but increases much slower than plan A.
b) If he plans on staying more than 3.25 years, plan A will earn him more money.
c) If he plans on staying 3.25 years or less, plan B will earn him more money.
d) the time at which both payment plans are equal

GLOSSARY

absolute cell reference: in a spreadsheet formula, a reference to one particular cell of the spreadsheet that will not change when the formula is moved to a different cell

B3 indicates that the value or expression contained in cell B3 is to be used in the formula.

accuracy: when referring to a measurement, it indicates how close the measurement comes to its true value

active cell: the cell of a spreadsheet into which an item of data is placed when you start to type

acute angle: an angle whose measure is less than 90°

adjacent side: in a right triangle, the side next to the named angle that is not the hypotenuse

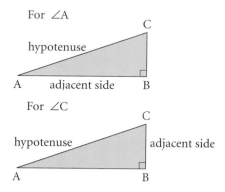

algebraic expression: a mathematical expression that contains at least one variable

6x + 4 is an algebraic expression.

altitude: the perpendicular distance from the base of a figure to the opposite side or vertex; the height of an aircraft above the ground

ambiguous case: see page 68

angle: the geometric figure formed by two rays that have the same endpoint

angle of depression: the angle between the horizontal and the oblique line joining the observer's eye to a point lower than eye level

angle of elevation: the angle between the horizontal and the oblique line from the observer's eye to some object above eye level

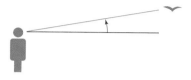

angle of inclination of a line segment: the acute angle, measured from the horizontal to the line segment

approximation: a number close to the exact value of a quantity or an expression; the symbols $\doteq$ and $\approx$ mean "is approximately equal to"

3.14 is an approximation for π.

area: the number of square units needed to cover a surface; common units used to express area include cm^2, m^2, and hectares

average: a single number that is used to represent a set of numbers; to find the average, all the numbers in the data set are added together and the sum is divided by the number of entries in the data set; see *mean*

The data set 1, 3, 4, 7, 7, 8 has 6 entries.

$$\text{Average} = \frac{1 + 3 + 4 + 7 + 7 + 8}{6}$$
$$= 5$$

axis of symmetry: a line about which a geometric figure is symmetrical

bar graph: a graph that displays data by using horizontal or vertical bars whose lengths are proportional to the number they represent

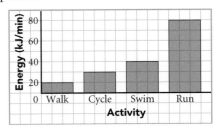

base: the side of a polygon, or the face of a solid, from which the height is measured; also, the factor repeated in a power

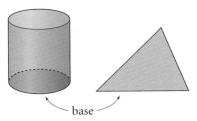

In the expression 5^3, 5 is the base.

bearing: the 3-digit angle, measured in a clockwise direction, between the north line and a given direction

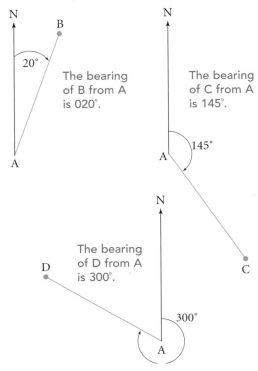

The bearing of B from A is 020°.

The bearing of C from A is 145°.

The bearing of D from A is 300°.

bias: an emphasis on characteristics that are not typical of the entire population

biased sample: a sample containing members of the population that are not representative

bimodal distribution: a distribution of data in which there may be more than one mode; the mean and median are between the modes

bisect: divide into two equal parts

blueprints: the initial drawings used in a construction project, originally on blue paper drawn in white lines; hence, the name "blueprints"

break-even point: the value at which a company's revenue from sales is equal to all costs of the production of its item(s)

broken-line graph: a graph that displays data by using points that are joined by line segments

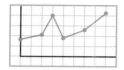

budget: a written plan to outline how money will be spent

calibrate: determine the scale of a measuring instrument by comparison to a standard

cell: a rectangle in a spreadsheet into which data may be entered

cell reference: the name of a cell in a spreadsheet, given by indicating the column and row to which it belongs
   Cell B3 is the cell in column B and row 3 of the spreadsheet document.

census: an official count of the people of a country or district

circle: the set of points in a plane that are a given distance from a fixed point (the centre)

circumference: the distance around a circle; the boundary of any region whose boundary is a simple closed curve

clinometer: a device used by surveyors to measure angles of elevation and depression; see *angle of depression,* and *angle of elevation*

cluster sample: a sample in which every member of a randomly chosen section of the population is selected

collecting like terms: putting together terms with exactly the same variable expressions, then simplifying by addition or subtraction

collinear points: points that lie on the same line

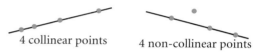

4 collinear points   4 non-collinear points

commission: a fee or payment given to a salesperson, usually a specified percent of the person's sales

common ratio: the ratio of one term in a geometric sequence to the preceding term

complementary angles: two angles whose measures add up to 90°
   $\angle ABC$ and $\angle CBD$ are complementary angles.

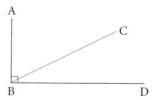

cone: a solid that is formed by a region (the base of the cone) and all the line segments joining points on the boundary of the region to a point not on the region

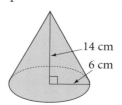

14 cm
6 cm

congruent: figures that have the same size and shape, but not necessarily the same orientation

conjecture: a conclusion based on examples

constant: a particular number

constraint: a condition that restricts the acceptable range of values of variables, usually written as an inequality; also limitations in construction such as joints and spans

convenience sample: a sample whose members are selected based on convenience

convex polygon: a polygon with all interior angles less than 180°

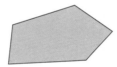

coordinate axes: the horizontal and vertical number lines on a grid that represents a plane

coordinate plane: a two-dimensional surface on which a coordinate system has been set up

coordinates: also called Cartesian coordinates; the numbers in an ordered pair that locate a point in the coordinate plane

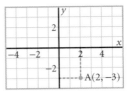

The coordinates of point A are (2, −3).

correlation coefficient: a measure of how closely data can be described by a certain type of function; the closer the value of the correlation coefficient to 1 or −1, the closer the data fit the function

corresponding angles in similar triangles: two angles, one in each triangle, that are equal

Cosine Law: a trigonometric law used to solve triangles that are not right triangles; see page 44

cube: a rectangular solid whose length, width, and height are all equal

cube root: a number that, when raised to the power 3, results in the given number
$\sqrt[3]{8} = 2$, since $2^3 = 8$

cubic units: units that measure volume; common cubic units include cm^3 and m^3

cylinder: a solid with two parallel, congruent, circular bases

data: numeric or non-numeric facts or information

debt: money owing

deficit: when expenses exceed revenues

A business owed $15 000 and had only $12 000 in funds. The deficit is $3000.

density: the mass of a unit volume of a substance; common units for measuring the density of a substance include g/cm^3, kg/m^3, g/mL, or kg/L

Find the density of an object that has a mass of 577.8 g and a volume of 214 cm^3.

$$\text{Density} = \frac{\text{Mass}}{\text{Volume}}$$

$$= \frac{577.8 \text{ g}}{214 \text{ cm}^3}$$

$$= 2.7 g/cm^3$$

dependent variable: the output of a relation, often denoted y; also called the responding variable

diagonal: a line that joins two vertices of a figure, but is not a side

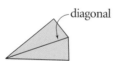
diagonal

diameter: a line segment that joins two points on a circle (or sphere) and passes through its centre; the diameter of a circle is twice the length of the radius; see *circle*

diameter
O

dilatation or **dilation:** a transformation that changes the size of an object but not the shape

direct variation: when the ratio of two variable quantities remains constant

If y varies directly as x, the equation that relates y to x is $y = mx$, where m is a constant; the graph of a direct variation is a straight line that passes through the origin

distance: the space between two points; also, the distance travelled by an object that is moving at a constant speed for a time is determined from the relation Distance = Speed × Time, where a consistent set of units must be used

distance formula: a formula used to determine the distance between two points whose coordinates are known

If $A(x_A, y_A)$ and $B(x_B, y_B)$, then $AB = \sqrt{(x_B - x_A)^2 + (y_B - y_A)^2}$

distributive law: the property stating that a product can be written as a sum or difference of two products; for example, for all real numbers a, b, and c: $a(b + c) = ab + ac$ and $a(b - c) = ab - ac$

domain of a relation or function: the set of all possible x-values (or valid input values) represented by the graph or equation

double-bar graph: a bar graph that shows two sets of data

elimination method: to solve a linear system of equations by eliminating one variable by addition or subtraction of multiples of the equations

equation: a mathematical statement indicating that two expressions are equal

$2x + 5y = -4$

equation of a line: an equation that gives the relationship between the coordinates of every point on the line

The common forms for the equation of a line are:

The slope-intercept form: $y = mx + b$, where m is the slope of the line and b is the y-intercept of the line

The standard form: $Ax + By + C = 0$, where A, B, and C are numbers

equidistant: the same distance apart

Points A and B are equidistant from the y-axis since they are both 3 units from the y-axis.

equilateral triangle: a triangle with three equal sides

error: the difference between the observed or approximate amount and the correct amount

evaluate an expression: substitute a value for each variable in the expression, then work out the resulting arithmetic expression applying the order of operations rules

Evaluate $2x^2 + 3y - 4$, if $x = -3$ and $y = 5$.

Replace the letters by their value, placing each number in a bracket to prevent errors with signs.

$$2x^2 + 3y - 4 = 2(-3)^2 + 3(5) - 4$$
$$= 2(9) + 3(5) - 4$$
$$= 18 + 15 - 4$$
$$= 29$$

exponent: a number, shown in a smaller size and raised, that tells us how many times the number before it is used as a factor

exponential function: a function in which the variable occurs in the exponent

$y = 2^x$ is an exponential function.

extrapolate: estimate a value beyond the known values

Using the graph to estimate the distance travelled after 10 h requires extrapolation; the last known value occurs when the time is 8 h.

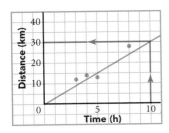

Fathom: dynamic statistical software used for data analysis, statistics, and mathematics

fixed cost: a cost, such as rent, that remains constant over a time period

force: a push or a pull on an object in a certain direction

A force of 1 Newton (N) will cause a 1-kg object to accelerate at a rate of 1 m/s.

formula: an equation that is used to describe the relationship between two or more quantities

The formula that describes how the volume, V, of a sphere is related to its radius, r, is $V = \frac{4}{3}\pi r^3$.

frequency: the number of times an event occurs in an experiment; the number of times that something occurs in a given time; a common unit is the Herz (Hz), which is the number of cycles that occur in 1 s

If you eat breakfast, lunch, and dinner every day, your meal frequency is 3 times a day. If a pendulum swings back and forth 10 times in 5 s, its frequency would be 10 cycles/5 s = 2 cycles/s = 2 Hz.

frequency distribution: a function often described using a table of values or a histogram, that provides the frequency for every outcome of an experiment

frequency table: a table for organizing a set of data that shows the number of times each item or number appears

function: a rule that gives a single output number for each input number

function notation: the use of the function name, such as *f*, to indicate the output value for a particular input

glide reflection symmetry: symmetry that is the result of a translation and reflection

graph: a drawing that shows the relationship between certain sets of quantities by means of lines, points, or bars

grid method: the process of using a grid to change the size of an object but not the shape

hectare: a metric unit used for land area; the area of a square of side 100 m, so 1 ha = 10 000 m^2

histogram: a graph that uses bars, where each bar represents a range of values and the data are continuous

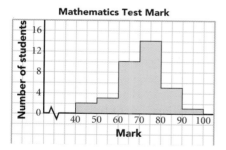

Mathematics Test Mark

hypotenuse: the side opposite the right angle in a right triangle

imperial system: a system of measures that was used in Canada prior to 1971 and a variant is still used in the U.S.A.; measuring devices using this system often have each unit subdivided by halving, then halving the subdivisions

independent variable: the input variable in a relation, often called *x*; also called the manipulated variable

integers: the set of numbers that contains all positive and negative whole numbers, together with zero; see *number systems*

... −3, −2, −1, 0, 1, 2, 3 ... is the set of integers.

intercepts: the horizontal and vertical coordinates of the points at which a graph crosses the horizontal and vertical axes

interpolate: estimate a value that lies between known values

irrational numbers: the set of numbers that cannot be written in the form $\frac{m}{n}$, where *m* and *n* are integers and $n \neq 0$; see *real numbers*

π and $\sqrt{2}$ are irrational numbers.

joint: the place or method in which two things or parts are joined; butt, mitre, dovetail are some examples of wood-working joints

layout: a plan or scale diagram that shows placement of objects, walls, stairs, and the like, as shown from above

least squares method: for a set of data, a method of determining a line of best fit that is used by many calculators and computers

line of best fit: a line that passes as close as possible to a set of plotted points; it can be estimated by eye, or determined using the median-median method, or the least squares method

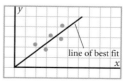

line segment: the part of a line between two points on the line, including the two points

linear equation and its graph: an equation that represents a straight line; can be written in the form $y = mx + b$, where m is the slope and b is the y-intercept, or $Ax + By + C = 0$, where A, B, and C are numbers

Slope–Intercept method of graphing: Graph the line $y = 3x + 2$.

This line has a slope of 3 and a y-intercept of 2. Mark the point (0, 2) on the y-axis. From that point, move up 3 for every 1 to the right. Mark this point, and then draw the line joining these points.

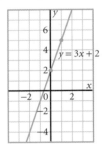

Intercept method of graphing: Calculate the points at which the line intersects the axes.

y-intercept: when $x = 0$, $y = 3(0) + 2 = 2$

x-intercept: when $y = 0$, $0 = 3x + 2$
$$-2 = 3x$$
$$-\frac{2}{3} = x$$

Plot, then join the intercepts $(-\frac{2}{3}, 0)$ and (0, 2).

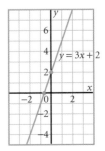

linear function: a function whose equation can be written in the form $y = mx + b$, and whose graph is a non-vertical line

mass: a measure of the amount of material in an object; common units are grams or kilograms

mean: the average of a set of numbers; see *average*

measurement error: see *uncertainty of measurement*

measurement standards: the standard set by the General Conference on Weights and Measures, in 1889, so that all persons would be dealing with the same measurements

median: the middle number of a set of numbers arranged in numerical order; if there are two middle numbers, their average is the median of the data set

For the data 2, 4, 8, 9, and 11 the median is 8.

For the data 2, 4, 6, 8, 9, and 11 the median is 7, since $\frac{6+8}{2} = 7$.

median-median line of best fit: the line of best fit for a set of data points determined using the median-median method

metric system: also called the *SI system*; based on a decimal system, with each unit subdivided into tenths and prefixes showing the relation of a unit to the base unit

micrometer: a measuring device that can be used to measure small objects to the nearest 0.01 mm

midpoint: the point that divides a line segment into two equal parts

On a coordinate grid, if the endpoints are $A(x_A, y_A)$ and $B(x_B, y_B)$, the coordinates of M are:

$$x_M = \frac{x_A + x_B}{2} \qquad y_M = \frac{y_A + y_B}{2}$$

mode: the most frequently occurring value in a set of data

> In the data set {5, 12, 8, 7, 3, 5, 3, 10, 5}, the mode is 5.

model: a small-scale copy of an object

natural numbers: the set of counting numbers 1, 2, 3, 4, …; see *number systems*

net: a diagram of the faces of a hollow three-dimensional object arranged so that the faces could be folded to form the three-dimensional object

net profit: the difference between revenue and total cost when the result is positive

95% confidence interval: the range of values that lie within 1.96 standard deviations of the mean; the probability a particular data value lies in that range is 0.95

non-linear system: two or more equations in which at least one is not a linear equation

normal distribution: a probability distribution with mean μ and standard deviation σ; the bell-shaped graph is symmetrical about the mean; obeys the 68-95-99 rule

number systems: N = natural numbers, W = whole numbers, I = integers, Q = rational numbers and R = real numbers

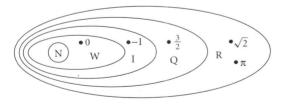

oblique triangle: a triangle that does not contain a 90° angle

obtuse angle: an angle greater than 90° but less than 180°

obtuse triangle: a triangle with one obtuse angle

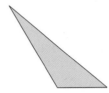

open survey question: in survey design, a question answered by the respondent in her/his own words

opposite side: the side opposite a given angle in a right triangle

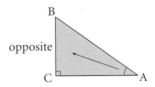

optimization problem: a problem in which the object is to find the maximum or minimum value of a quantity, subject to given conditions

order of operations: the rules that are followed when simplifying or evaluating an expression:

   Complete all operations within brackets following the order of operations.

   Evaluate all exponents.

   Complete all multiplication and division in the order they appear from left to right.

   Complete all addition and subtraction in the order they appear from left to right.

ordered pair: a pair of numbers, written as (x, y), that represents a point on the coordinate plane; see *coordinates*

orthographic diagram: a diagram used in industry that shows up to six views and internal features of an object. It usually shows the top, front, and side views.

outcome: a possible result of an experiment; a possible answer to a survey question

outlier: an observed value that differs markedly from the pattern established by most of the data

parabola: the name given to the shape of the graph of a quadratic function

parallel lines: lines in the same plane that do not intersect

parallelogram: a quadrilateral with opposite sides parallel

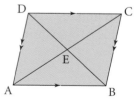

A parallelogram has the following properties:

The opposite sides have equal lengths.
AB = CD and AD = BC

The opposite angles have equal measures (congruent). ∠A = ∠C and ∠B = ∠D

The diagonals bisect each other (cut each other into equal lengths).
AE = EC and DE = EB

parquetry: woodwork of small pieces of wood often in different types and sizes arranged in a geometric pattern

pattern: a model or guide for making something

perimeter: the distance around a closed figure

perpendicular: intersecting at right angles

Two lines are perpendicular if their slopes are negative reciprocals of one another

perpendicular bisector: the line that is perpendicular to a line segment and divides it into two equal parts

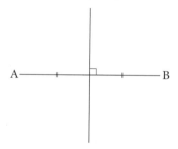

pi (π): the ratio of the circumference of a circle and its diameter; $\pi \doteq 3.1416$

pictorial diagram: a two-dimensional representation of a three-dimensional object drawn from one perspective

piecework: payment based on the number of items produced

plan: a drawing or diagram that shows the arrangement of, for example, a floor of a building and the relative sizes of its rooms

point at infinity: a point at which parallel lines moving away from us appear to meet

point of intersection: the point that is common to two or more figures

polygon: a closed figure that consists of line segments that only intersect at their endpoints

The above figures are polygons.

These figures are not polygons.

polynomial: a mathematical expression with one or more terms, in which the exponents are whole numbers and the coefficients are real numbers

population: the entire set of objects, people, or processes being studied

power: see *exponent*

precision: an indication of how close a set of measurements are to one another; the smallest scale division of a measuring instrument

primary source data: data collected directly by the person or group requiring the information

prism: a solid with two congruent and parallel faces (bases), all other faces are parallelograms

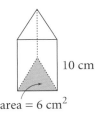

10 cm

area = 6 cm^2

probability: an indication of the likelihood of an event occurring; if the outcomes of an experiment are equally likely, it is the ratio of the number of favourable outcomes to the total number of outcomes

pyramid: a solid with one face that is a polygon (base) and other faces that are triangles with a common vertex

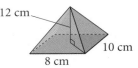

12 cm

10 cm

8 cm

Pythagorean Theorem: for any right triangle, the area of the square of the hypotenuse is equal to the sum of the areas of the squares of the other two sides

In right triangle ABC: $a^2 + b^2 = c^2$

quadrant: one of the four regions into which the coordinate axes divide the plane, usually numbered as shown in the diagram

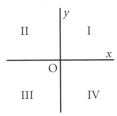

quadratic equation and its graph: an equation of the form $y = ax^2 + bx + c$ and its graph, $a \neq 0$; the graph is a parabola

quadrilateral: a four-sided polygon; see *polygon*

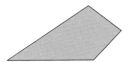

radical: the root of a number

$\sqrt{5}, \quad \sqrt[3]{5}, \quad \sqrt{2.6}$

radius: the distance from the centre of a circle to any point on the circumference; also, a line segment joining the centre of a circle to any point on the circumference

> The radius of a circle is half the length of its diameter.

random sample: a sampling in which all members of the population have an equal chance of being selected

range: the difference between the highest and lowest values in a set of data

rate: a certain quantity of one thing considered in relation to one unit of another

rational numbers: the set of numbers that can be written in the form $\frac{m}{n}$, where m and n are integers and $n \neq 0$; see *number systems*

real numbers: the set of numbers that includes both rational and irrational numbers; that is, all numbers that can be expressed as decimals; see *number systems*

reflection: a transformation that flips a figure over a mirror or reflection line

reflectional symmetry: after reflecting the figure over a line, the figure lines back up with itself

regression: a process by which a curve or line of best fit is fitted to a set of data using a least squares process

regular polygon: a polygon with all sides and all angles equal

reliability: for a sample statistic, if nearly the same result is obtained in subsequent studies

revenue: money brought in from the sale of goods or services

> The sale of 158 tickets costing $20 each produces a revenue of $3160.

rhombus: a parallelogram with four equal sides

right angle: a 90° angle

right triangle: a triangle with one right angle

rise: the vertical distance between two points; see *slope*

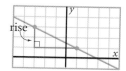

root of an equation: value of the variable that satisfies the equation

rotation: a transformation that turns a figure about a fixed point through a given angle in a given direction

rotational symmetry: after rotating a figure by an angle other than 360° about its centre, the figure lines back up with itself

run: the horizontal distance between two points; see *slope*

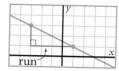

sample: part of a population chosen to represent the total population in a study

sample statistic: a numerical value that is used to describe a sample, such as the *mean*

sampling: the process used to choose part of a population to represent the total population in a study

scale: for a map, model, or diagram, the ratio of the distance between two points to the distance between the actual locations; also the numbers on the coordinate axes

scale break: a small zig-zag mark on a graph's axis to indicate a break in the scale

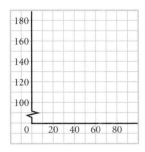

scatter plot: a graph of data that are a series of points

Height (cm)	154	162	172	178
Mass (kg)	56.3	60.1	72.2	64.3

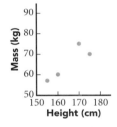

scientific notation: a way of expressing a number as the product of a number greater than -10 and less than -1, or greater than 1 and less than 10, and a power of 10; used to express very large and very small numbers
$47\ 000 = 4.7 \times 10^4$, and $-26 = -2.6 \times 10^1$

secondary source data: data already collected and made available to the public

self-selected sample: a sample in which only interested members of the population will participate

SI system: SI stands for Système Internationale des unités; also known as the metric system

significant digits: the meaningful digits of a number that represent a measurement

similar objects: objects that have the same shape but not necessarily the same size
All the corresponding angles will have equal measures and all dimensions will be proportional.

simple random sample: see *random sample*

sine bar: a highly accurate device used for measuring angles and precision layout work on angle plates

Sine Law: a trigonometric law used to solve triangles; see page 31

68-95-99 rule: about 68% of the population are within 1 standard deviation of the mean; about 95% of the population are within 2 standard deviations of the mean; about 99.7% of the population are within 3 standard deviations of the mean

skewed distribution: a non-symmetrical distribution of data

slope: a measure of the steepness of a line
The slope of a line segment joining $A(x_A, y_A)$ and $B(x_B, y_B)$ is:
$$\text{Slope} = \frac{\text{rise}}{\text{run}} = \frac{y_A - y_B}{x_A - x_B}$$

slope y-intercept form: the equation of a line in the form $y = mx + b$, where m is the slope of the line and b is the y-intercept of the line

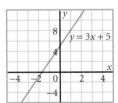

The equation $y = 3x + 5$ is that of a line with a slope of 3 and a y-intercept of 5.

span: the distance between two supports

sphere: the set of points in space that are a given distance (radius) from a fixed point (centre)

spreadsheet: a computer-generated arrangement of data in rows and columns, where a change in one value can result in appropriate calculated changes in the other values

square root: a number which, when multiplied by itself, results in the given number

standard deviation: a measure of the extent to which data cluster around the mean

standard form: for the equation of a line, the standard form is $Ax + By + C = 0$, where A, B, and C are integers; see *equation of a line*

statistics: the branch of mathematics that deals with the collection, organization, and interpretation of data

stratified random sample: a sample in which all members of different segments of the population have an equal chance of being selected

substitution method to solve linear systems: to solve a linear system by first isolating one variable in one equation and substituting it into the second equation

supplementary angles: two angles whose sum is 180°

∠1 and ∠2 are supplementary.

surface area: a measure of the area on the surface of a three-dimensional object

survey: an investigation of a topic to find out people's views

symmetry: a regular balanced arrangement on opposite sides of a line or plane or around a centre or axis

systematic sample: a sample in which every *nth* member of a population is selected

tangent: for an acute ∠A in a right triangle, the ratio of the length of the opposite side to the length of the adjacent side

tessellation: a tiling pattern that covers the plane with no gaps or overlaps

three-dimensional: having length, width, and depth, or height

trajectory: the path of an object as it moves through the air

transit: a device used by surveyors to measure horizontal angles and distances

translation: a transformation that moves a point or a figure in a straight line to another position in the same plane

translational symmetry: after sliding all points by a constant, the figure lines back up with itself

trapezoid: a quadrilateral that has only one pair of parallel sides

trend: general pattern of a relationship; general direction, or tendency of the data

triangle: a three-sided polygon

trigonometric ratios: $\sin \theta = \dfrac{\text{opposite}}{\text{hypotenuse}}$, $\cos \theta = \dfrac{\text{adjacent}}{\text{hypotenuse}}$, $\tan \theta = \dfrac{\text{opposite}}{\text{adjacent}}$

trigonometry: the branch of mathematics concerned with the properties of trigonometric functions and their application to the determination of the sides and angles of triangles

uncertainty of measurement: for any measurement, the uncertainty is equal to the smallest scale division of the instrument

validity: an indicator of how well a test really measures what it is supposed to measure; a sample statistic is valid if it closely approximates the quantity for the population

variable: a letter or symbol used to represent a quantity that can vary

variance: a measure of the distribution of a variable obtained by taking the expected value of the square of the difference between the variable and its mean

vertex: the corner of a figure or solid

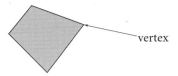

volume: the amount of space occupied by an object

whole numbers: the set of numbers 0, 1, 2, 3, ...; see *number systems*

x-**axis:** the horizontal number line on a coordinate grid

x-**intercept:** the *x*-coordinate where the graph of a line or function intersects the *x*-axis

y-**axis:** the vertical number line on a coordinate grid

y-**intercept:** the *y*-coordinate where the graph of a line or function intersects the *y*-axis

zeros of a function: the values of x for which a function $y = f(x)$ has the value 0

PHOTO CREDITS AND ACKNOWLEDGMENTS

The publisher wishes to thank the following sources for photographs, illustrations, articles, and other materials used in this book. Care has been taken to determine and locate ownership of copyright material used in the text. We will gladly receive information enabling us to rectify any errors or omissions in credits.

PHOTOS

Cover, © Trevor Bonderud/Firstlight.ca; **Inside Front Page** (centre right), © Trevor Bonderud/Firstlight.ca; **p. 1** (centre), Artbase Inc.; **p. 27** (centre), © Dave McKay; **p. 29** (top), © CORBIS/Adamsmith Production/Firstlight.ca; **p. 34** (top right), Artbase Inc.; **p. 44** (centre right), © Dave McKay; **p. 62** (centre), © Dean Conger/CORBIS/MAGMA; **p. 71** (top right), © Michael Keller/Index Stock Imagery/Picture Quest; **p. 79** (centre), Artbase Inc.; **p. 107** (centre), Artbase Inc.; **p. 118** (top right), Artbase Inc.; **p. 147** (top right), Artbase Inc.; **p. 156** (top left), © Jose L. Pelaez/The Stock Market/Firstlight.ca; **p. 157** (background), © Jose L. Pelaez/The Stock Market/Firstlight.ca; **p. 158** (top left), © Jose L. Pelaez/The Stock Market/ Firstlight.ca; **p. 160** (top left), © Jose L. Pelaez/The Stock Market/Firstlight.ca; **p. 162** (top left), © Jose L. Pelaez/The Stock Market/Firstlight.ca; **p. 165** (centre), © Greg Scott/ Masterfile; **p. 225** (top right), Artbase Inc.; **p. 234** (centre), Mimmo Jodico/CORBIS/ MAGMA; **p. 241** (centre left), © Mike Mazzaschi/Stock Boston Inc./PictureQuest; **p. 241** (centre right), © Steve Raymer/ MAGMA/CORBIS; **p. 241** (centre left), Artbase Inc.; **p. 241** (centre right), Artbase Inc.; **p. 252** (top left), Artbase Inc.; **p. 252** (top right), Artbase Inc.; **p. 252** (top right), Dave Starrett; **p. 252** (centre left), © Sandy Felsenthal/CORBIS/ MAGMA; **p. 253** (top right), Dave Starrett; **p. 253** (top right), Dave Starrett; **p. 253** (centre left), Dave Starrett; **p. 253** (centre right), Dave Starrett; **p. 253** (bottom centre), © Christian Sarramon/CORBIS/MAGMA; **p. 253** (bottom right), Premium Stock/Firstlight.ca; **p. 254** (top centre), Dave Starrett; **p. 254** (top centre), Dave Starrett; **p. 254** (top centre), Dave Starrett; **p. 254** (centre right), © Reinhard Eisele-ze/Masterfile; **p. 254** (bottom right), © Adam Woolfit/CORBIS/MAGMA; **p. 255** (top centre), Ivy Images; **p. 255** (top right), COMSTOCK IMAGES; **p. 255** (centre), © Jim Cochrane/Firstlight.ca; **p. 255** (centre right), © Jim Cochrane/Firstlight.ca; **p. 255** (bottom centre), © Ken Straiten/Firstlight.ca; **p. 255** (bottom right), COMSTOCK IMAGES/W. Griebeling; **p. 256** (top centre), © Larry Fisher/Masterfile; **p. 256** (top right), © Mike Dobel/Masterfile; **p. 256** (centre right), Courtesy of "African Textiles" by Christopher Spring/Bracken Books; **p. 256** (bottom left), Dave Starrett; **p. 256** (bottom right), Dave Starrett; **p. 256** (centre), Artbase Inc.; **p. 257** (centre), © Lawrence Migdale/Stock Boston; **p. 257** (top centre), Artbase Inc.; **p. 257** (top right), © Damir Frkovic/Masterfile; **p. 257** (centre right), Dave Starrett; **p. 257** (centre left), Dave Starrett; **p. 257** (centre right), Dave Starrett; **p. 258** (centre right), © Guy Grenier/Masterfile; **p. 277** (top right), © Tom Stewart/Firstlight.ca; **p. 292** (centre left), Artbase Inc.; **p. 292** (centre), Artbase Inc.; **p. 292** (centre right), Artbase Inc.; **p. 292** (centre right), Robert Estall/CORBIS/MAGMA; **p. 294** (top right), © MTPA Stock/Masterfile; **p. 304** (top left), Artbase Inc.; **p. 304** (top left), Artbase Inc.; **p. 305** (centre), Artbase Inc.; **p. 306** (top left), Artbase Inc.; **p. 308** (top left), Artbase Inc.; **p. 311** (centre), Photo Disk, Inc.; **p. 332** (bottom centre), © Antoni Mo/Getty Images/FPG; **p. 334** (centre left), Artbase Inc.; **p. 334** (centre), Artbase Inc.; **p. 334** (centre right), Artbase Inc.; **p. 334** (centre right), Artbase Inc.; **p. 344** (top centre), Dave Starrett; **p. 344** (top centre), Artbase Inc.; **p. 346** (centre right), © Dave Starrett; **p. 356** (top centre), © Tim Flach/Tony Stone Images; **p. 359** (bottom centre), © Spencer/Stock Boston; **p. 360** (top right), Masterfile; **p. 369** (centre), Artbase Inc.; **p. 369** (centre), Artbase Inc.; **p. 369** (centre), Artbase Inc.; **p. 369** (centre), Artbase Inc.; **p. 369** (centre), Artbase Inc.; **p. 389** (top centre), © Ed Bock/Firstlight.ca; **p. 429** (top right), Premium Stock/Firstlight.ca; **p. 437** (centre right), Artbase Inc.; **p. 438** (centre left), © Duomo/CORBIS/MAGMA; **p. 439** (background), Artbase Inc.; **p. 459** (top right), © Lester Leftkowitz/Firstlight.ca; **p. 459** (top centre), © Peter Christopher/Masterfile; **p. 503** (top right), © Kit Kittle/CORBIS/MAGMA; **p. 510** (centre), © Reprinted with permission–The Toronto Star Syndicate; **p. 518** (top left), © Bert Klassen/Firstlight.ca;

p. 518 (centre), © Alan Schein/The Stock Market/Firstlight.ca; **p. 520** (top left), © Bert Klassen/Firstlight.ca; **p. 522** (top left), © Bert Klassen/Firstlight.ca; **p. 524** (top left), © Bert Klassen/Firstlight.ca; **p. 526** (top left), © Bert Klassen/Firstlight.ca; **p. 529** (bottom left), © Detlef Schnepel; **p. 531** (bottom right), © Dave Starrett; **p. 535** (bottom right), © Detlef Schnepel; **p. 540** (centre right), © Dave Starrett.

ILLUSTRATIONS

Michael Herman **p. 153** (centre)

Dave McKay **p. 44** (top right)

Jun Park **p. 16** (centre right), **p. 16** (bottom right), **p. 20** (top right), **p. 21** (top right), **p. 49** (top centre), **p. 55** (bottom centre), **p. 58** (bottom centre), **p. 59** (centre), **p. 59** (bottom centre), **p. 60** (centre), **p. 75** (centre right), **p. 75** (bottom centre), **p. 170** (centre right), **p. 170** (bottom right), **p. 246** (centre), **p. 246** (centre right), **p. 246** (bottom centre), **p. 246** (bottom right), **p. 247** (top centre), **p. 247** (top right), **p. 250** (centre), **p. 264** (bottom centre), **p. 268** (centre), **p. 275** (centre), **p. 283** (bottom centre), **p. 286** (top centre), **p. 288** (centre), **p. 290** (top centre), **p. 290** (bottom centre), **p. 297** (top right), **p. 298** (bottom right)

Pronk&Associates Inc. **p. 19** (centre left), **p. 26** (bottom right), **p. 36** (bottom right), **p. 37** (top right), **p. 38** (centre right), **p. 57** (top right), **p. 170** (top right), **p. 174** (centre), **p. 174** (bottom centre), **p. 210** (bottom centre), **p. 212** (centre), **p. 218** (top centre), **p. 218** (centre), **p. 220** (centre left), **p. 220** (centre), **p. 220** (centre right), **p. 221** (bottom centre), **p. 222** (bottom centre), **p. 223** (top centre), **p. 223** (centre), **p. 223** (bottom centre), **p. 224** (centre), **p. 233** (bottom centre), **p. 247** (centre), **p. 249** (bottom centre), **p. 251** (top centre), **p. 251** (bottom centre), **p. 281** (centre right), **p. 281** (bottom centre), **p. 282** (centre), **p. 306** (bottom right), **p. 307** (top right), **p. 461** (centre right), **p. 482** (top right), **p. 501** (top centre), **p. 510** (centre left), **p. 510** (centre right)

Greg Stevenson **p. 369** (full page)

p. 477 (bottom right), Adapted from data published on the Statistics Canada E-Stat site http://www.estat.statcan.ca; **p. 482** (top right), Data based on the Statistics Canada "Labour Force Survey"

Statistics Canada information is used with the permission of the Minister of Industry, as Minister responsible for Statistics Canada. Information on the availability of the wide range of data from Statistics Canada can be obtained from Statistics Canada's Regional Offices, its World Wide Web site at http://www.statcan.ca, and its toll-free access number 1-800-263-1136.